I0800659

MODERN MARINE SALVAGE

MODERN MARINE SALVAGE

William I. Milwee, Jr.

CORNELL MARITIME PRESS
CENTREVILLE, MARYLAND

Copyright © 1996 by Cornell Maritime Press, Inc.

All rights reserved. No part of this book may be used or reproduced in any manner whatsoever except in the case of brief quotations embodied in critical articles or reviews. For information, contact Cornell Maritime Press, Inc., Centreville, Maryland 21617.

Library of Congress Cataloging-in-Publication Data

Milwee, William I.
Modern marine salvage / William I. Milwee, Jr. — 1st ed.
p. cm.
Includes bibliographical references (p.) and index.
ISBN 0-87033-471-9 (hardcover)
1. Salvage. I. Title
VK1491.M53 1995
627'.703—dc20 95-30816

Manufactured in the United States of America

First edition

To my wife, Wanda, who
increases my aspirations,
broadens my horizons,
decreases my frustrations, and
multiplies my joys.

CONTENTS

PREFACE

The sea is a wonder. It is whimsical and difficult; it has myriad moods with faces to match, some beautiful, some beguiling, some frightening—all interesting. The sea is the most vital and difficult environment in which man works. The types of work vary widely; all have challenges. Salvage of ships and the art and science of dealing with marine casualties are in, or very near, first place among the challenges undertaken at sea. Each salvage case requires application of a balanced mixture of engineering and seamanship matched first to the type of casualty, then to the particular casualty. Each operation requires a balance of planning, logistics, and operations. Each is difficult; each is dangerous. There is nothing routine or ordinary in salvage. Casualties carry unique sets of problems and difficulties, all apparently designed by malevolent spirits to frustrate and annoy salvors. Meeting and beating them makes salvage damned satisfying.

Early in the writing of this book, a friend—an experienced salvor, naval architect, and brilliant man—told me that he had often thought about writing a book on salvage, but had decided the subject was too broad. The further I progressed in writing this book the more I realized that he was right. The subject is tremendously broad. Salvage includes almost all maritime activities and disciplines. No person in a single lifetime can know all there is to know about salvage and the management of marine casualties. Any salvor who thinks he does is setting himself up for an eye-opening experience accompanied by a hard bite on the backside. This book is not a definitive book on salvage. It is a collection of education, study, and experience that addresses some aspects of a broad and fascinating field. I have not attempted to cover those types of salvage operations with which I have limited experience because I feel it is better to provide no information than to speak authoritatively on subjects where my ignorance overwhelms my knowledge.

There are as many ways to approach salvage work as there are to skin cats—perhaps more. The methods and techniques described in the following pages are not the only approaches to salvage work. They are both basic principles and methods that have worked under particular sets of conditions. Other approaches may have worked as well or better. Readers will notice that discussions in the book are not presented as dogma. The word "should" is far more prevalent than "must." In salvage work, there is no substitute for thinking about the job and the conditions before doing anything, after doing something, and after what was done has worked or failed. There are few salvors who would approach a job the same way if they could do it again.

In structuring the book I have avoided detailed references to specific casualties and the case study approach, preferring to present general approaches and principles. The choice is purely one of personal preference boosted by understanding that the choice of techniques and methods for any casualty is always a compromise to fit the particular conditions. Salvors who understand the principles of the profession and know what to do in the ideal case can make sound choices and compromises and can evaluate what limitations the compromises inflict. Effective case studies must not only describe what was done but the salvor's reasons for doing so and how the balance sheet leading to the decision was drawn. The latter are often hard to deduce from salvage reports.

I have not followed the modern trend in writing by trying to avoid gender-specific words through convoluted sentences or clumsy and silly-sounding "he or she," "his or her" constructions. I do not intend any offense to the capable women at sea or in the many professions associated with marine casualties.

There is a traditional symbiotic relationship in salvage between the technical and commercial aspects of the work. To this has been added a second equally symbiotic relationship between salvage work and the prevention or minimization of environmental damage. The former is well established. The latter, formalized by the 1989 International Convention on Salvage, is in a state of flux and development. The influence of prevention of environmental damage during salvage operations and the award of special compensation makes the relationship three-sided. Throughout, this book emphasizes these relationships that make up the whole of salvage.

No one ever does a salvage job single-handed, a fact anyone listening to sea stories after the job (particularly long after and far away) would never know. In like manner, a book like this is not the effort of one man. The efforts of many have gone into it, some knowingly, most not. I would like to be able to acknowledge each individual from whom I have learned, both positive and negative things, over the years. Unfortunately, such acknowledgment is both impossible and impractical as names and places are lost in the depths of memory and the list would make the most boring of reading, of real interest only to those who enjoy seeing their name in print. The list would include not only the salvors, surveyors, shipowners, insurers, members of the Admiralty bar, and others I have worked directly with, but those who have written salvage reports, and especially those who have produced the many objective technical papers, articles, and books listed in the Bibliography, as well as many others who were not appropriate for direct reference in this book.

There are some whose contribution deserves special note. Among these is Captain Eugene B. Mitchell, U.S. Navy (Ret), who as Supervisor of Salvage, U.S. Navy, had the leadership and fortitude to give a young salvage officer his head and the opportunity to make and learn from mistakes. His technical and operational guidance, "Do what's right, Bill," is memorable and about as good as you can get. Captain David Hancox, himself a salvor and the author of a fine book on salvage, read every word of the draft text and provided not only invaluable comments but a number of photographs. David also provided a good sounding board for a frustrated author. His most appreciated comment was that one chapter was "like baby bear's porridge, just right."

Two people deserve sainthood for their contribution. An onerous but very important task that makes a great difference in the usefulness of a book is preparation of the index. There are few tasks for which any author, especially this one, is less qualified. The index for this book was prepared by Jennifer Deaton and Kirk Howard, both documentation professionals. I admire their work.

Captain Richard P. Fiske, USN, as Supervisor of Salvage, U.S. Navy, gave permission to use many of the drawings and sketches which we developed during the writing of the U.S. Navy *Ship Salvage Manual.* The Committee of Lloyd's, the Japanese Shipping Exchange, Inc., the International Salvage Union, and the Baltic and International Maritime Council gave permission to reproduce the contracts and other copyrighted material in Appendix B and elsewhere in the book. Bev Morgan of Diving Systems International provided many of the photographs of diving equipment and working divers. J.H. "Mick" Leitz of Fred Devine Diving and Salvage Co. also provided a number of photographs and, like many others, was a participant in many conversations which resulted in input to this book.

There are many who fit in the last category who have been part of conversations on the bridge, on deck, or in the mess late at night or early in the morning, on an airplane, or over a beer or cup of coffee. The few who stand out (in no particular order): Jim Bladh, Fred Aichele, Doug Davis, Chuck Maclin, Billie Delanoy, Graham Daines, Alan Colquhoun, Bill Gibbs, Bill Searle, Bob Kutzleb, Reino Matilla, Bob Belsher, Bill Tageson. There are many, many others.

Finally, there is Downeast Stormy Weather, the Portuguese water dog that came to live with me about the time I started writing this book. Storm's a boon companion and has better sense than I about when it's time to put away the book and do something else.

SYMBOLS, ACRONYMS, AND ABBREVIATIONS

The following are the symbols, acronyms, and abbreviations used throughout this book. Some symbols have multiple meanings; the choice should be clear from the context. Letter subscripts are used to make the symbols specific. Only major subscripted symbols are listed below. Numerical subscripts indicate sequential values of the same quantity.

A	Area
a	Area
A_M	Midships section area
ABS	American Bureau of Shipping
acf	Actual cubic feet
AHTSV	Anchor-handling tug supply vessel
AMA	Actual mechanical advantage
AP	After perpendicular
API	American Petroleum Institute
B	Beam, center of buoyancy
b	Transverse dimension
BC	Between centers
BHP (bhp)	Brake horsepower
BM	Metacentric radius, distance between the center of buoyancy and the metacenter
BM_L	Longitudinal metacentric radius
BM_T	Transverse metacentric radius
BP	Bollard pull
BS	Breaking strength
C	Centigrade, Celsius (temperature), coefficient
cm	Centimeters
C_B	Block coefficient
C_M	Midships section coefficient
C_p	Prismatic coefficient
C_{WP}	Waterplane coefficient
CFC	Chlorofluorocarbon
CFR	Code of Federal Regulations

CHRIS	Chemical Hazards Response Information Service
CHEMTREC	Chemical Transportation Emergency Center
D	Depth, diameter, distance
d	Distance
DFA	Arctic diesel fuel
DFM	Marine diesel fuel
DNV	Det Norske Veritas
dwt	Deadweight tons
E	Modulus of elasticity, percentage elongation
F	Fahrenheit (temperature), freeboard
FP	Forward perpendicular
ft, ft^2, ft^3	Feet, square feet, cubic feet
G	Center of gravity
GM	Metacentric height, distance between the center of gravity and the metacenter
GM_L	Longitudinal metacentric height
GM_T	Transverse metacentric height
gpm	Gallons per minute
grt	Gross registered tons
GZ	Righting arm
H	Height
HMPE	High molecular weight polyethelene
I, i	Moment of inertia
ihp	Indicated horsepower
IMDG	International Maritime Dangerous Goods (Code)
IMO	International Maritime Organization
ISO	International Standards Organization
K, k	Constant, coefficient
KB	Height of the center of buoyancy above the keel
KG	Height of the center of gravity above the keel
kg	Kilograms
KM	Height of the metacenter above the keel
kw	Kilowatts
L	Length, lift force
l	Longitudinal dimension
LBP	Length between perpendiculars
LCB	Longitudinal position of the center of buoyancy
LCG	Longitudinal position of the center of gravity
LEL	Lower explosive limit
LOA	Length overall
LOF	Lloyd's Open Form
LNG	Liquefied natural gas
LPG	Liquefied petroleum gas
LR	Lloyd's Register of Shipping
LWL	Length on the waterline

M	Metacenter, moment, bending moment
m, m^2, m^3	Meters, square meters, cubic meters
min	Minutes
mm	Millimeters
MTC	Moment to change trim one centimeter
MT1	Moment to change trim one inch
MODU	Mobile Offshore Drilling Unit
n	Number
OBO	Ore/bulk/oil
OSV	Offshore supply vessel
P	Pressure load
PL	Proof load
p-v	Pressure-vacuum
Q	Flow rate, pump discharge
R	Ground reaction, tide range, range
r	Radius
RO/RO	Roll-on/Roll-off
ROV	Remotely operated vehicle
S	Stress factor
s	Scope (of chain or rope)
scf	Standard cubic feet
sec	Seconds
SG	Specific gravity
shp	Shaft horsepower
SM	Section modulus
SWL	Safe working load
T	Draft, tension, temperature
t	Total trim, thickness, time
TMA	Theoretical mechanical advantage
TPC	Tons per centimeter immersion
TPI	Tons per inch immersion
UEL	Upper explosive limit
ULCC	Ultra large crude carrier
USC	United States Code
V	Displacement volume, volume
v	Service speed, velocity, volume
VLCC	Very large crude carrier
W	Displacement
w	Weight
WDP	Water damage protection
Δ, δ	Change in
μ	Coefficient of friction
σ	Bending stress
τ	Shear stress

MODERN MARINE SALVAGE

1

MARINE SALVAGE—WHAT IT'S ABOUT

A simple, comprehensive definition of marine salvage is elusive. Simplistic ones appear in general dictionaries; long and complex ones appear in specialized works. Salvage means something different to each participant and interest. The definition important to the lawyer putting forward a salvage claim in arbitration or in court may have no value to the salvor in the field. This book is for the latter.

Even among salvors unanimity prevails in only two matters: that salvage centers upon saving property at risk at sea and reducing environmental damage, and that salvage is all the actions taken aboard and ashore to resolve a marine casualty and to save property at risk at sea. Seamen define salvage as specialized seamanship; engineers define it as a branch of engineering. Both are correct, neither totally. In any salvage case both seamanship and engineering must be present in a balance that suits the casualty.

In fires, pollution hazards, or strandings, for instance, salvage is time critical. These cases always involve immediate danger to the casualty or to the environment and require salvors to act promptly. Wreck removals, closely related in their technology and techniques to time-critical salvage, may be planned and carried out in a comparatively leisurely manner. Time critical or not, all the actions to resolve the casualty or correct the conditions it causes make up salvage.

Marine salvage is hard, dirty, sometimes dangerous work. It requires large portions of single-mindedness, imagination, and technical knowledge. It is not as lucrative as the sea stories suggest.

Salvors work for a reward, gloriously lucrative or something less. The principle of salvage of property at risk at sea for reward is very old and is well established in law. It is different from the principle that governs aid on land. Landsmen do not expect and normally have no entitlement to rewards for Good Samaritan acts in saving life and property ashore. Salvors of property at sea expect and are entitled to a reward. Salvage and the resulting award do not apply to saving human lives. However, the term *life salvage* is heard, and awards for saving life accompany awards for saving property. A new principle has appeared in recent years: *liability salvage*. Under liability salvage salvors receive awards for saving the owner from the liability that would have existed if the salvor had not acted. At this writing, neither the meaning of liability salvage nor how it could work in practice is clear.

While the principle of salvage is ancient, salvage as a commercial enterprise is much newer. When ships were wind driven, kedging an anchor out and hauling the ship off with muscle power could often free a stranded ship. More often ships were abandoned; little was possible except taking off cargo and fittings. The wreck was usually a boon to the local community. Powered tugs with the ability to maneuver independently of the wind were the basis of the early commercial salvage industry that began forming about the middle of the nineteenth century. Basic techniques, developed early in the game, have changed and grown to meet the needs of changing and growing ships. They must continue to change and grow as ships and their cargoes change.

There have long been two distinct, symbiotic, and equally important elements in any salvage operation: the technical and the commercial. Ships are very complex structures, designed and built to exacting standards. Salvors must understand not only the technical aspects of the salvage trade, but also the behavior of ships under normal and abnormal circumstances. Simultaneously, they must approach salvage as a commercial enterprise with the purpose of making money and must manage it accordingly. A technically precise and elegant salvage operation that is not a commercial success is a failure. Salvage is a high-risk business. Far more difficult than any technical or seamanship decision for a salvor is deciding, with scant information, if a potential operation has sufficient opportunity for commercial success and on what terms he should undertake it. Many salvage contracts are no cure–no pay agreements. Salvors must consider carefully the commercial feasibility of these contracts and their high degree of risk and propose other terms when no cure–no pay is not commercially acceptable. Failure to weigh correctly the values of ship, cargo, risk, and complexity of salvage has brought salvors some nasty surprises.

A third element has joined the two traditional governing elements of salvage. Environmental factors now have equal billing with technical and commercial matters. In many ways eliminating or reducing environmental damage has become the driving force behind and during salvage operations. Emphasis on protecting the environment and the huge liabilities that can result from environmental damage has affected the salvor's approach to both the technical and commercial aspects of his work. It has had a major effect on the organization of marine emergency response operations and has, with polluting or hazardous cargo, redefined the traditional roles of the parties to salvage operations. In the decision to undertake an operation, salvors must evaluate the environmental risk and the effect of environmental matters on operational complexity, potential liability, and contractual arrangements. Because environmental laws differ among nations the salvor must ensure that he can carry out the operation while meeting local regulations.

Ideally, salvaged ships quickly return to service, salvaged cargo reaches its consignee intact, and no environmental damage occurs. But, like most ideals, this one cannot always be reached and the value of the ship and cargo may decline during salvage operations. Some cargo may be lost or made valueless. Saving property is basic to salvage; salvors have a duty to consider the value of property in every salvage action and to use their best efforts to retain that value whenever possible. The best salvage decisions are normally those that retain the greatest value of ship and cargo.

To that general rule there are major exceptions, primarily because reasons other than saving property often motivate salvage operations. The major "other" reason is prevention of environmental damage. Salvage operations may remove an environmental hazard, or remove a hazard or impediment to navigation or other maritime commerce. A government agency may direct salvage in carrying out its legislated responsibilities.

Marine casualty management is more complex than salvage in that it concerns itself with all aspects of the casualty, not only salvage. The key in casualty management is balancing all the elements and ordering the possible actions so that total losses from the casualty are minimal under the circumstances.

The purpose of the salvage affects the terms for the work. Fixed price, daily rate, or time and materials may be suitable terms for an operation and may carry a balanced risk to both the salvor and the organization contracting the salvage. Government agencies usually contract for salvage on a daily-rate basis. The salvor must be attuned to the underlying reasons for the work, and balance risk and potential return in fixing the terms under which he works and makes operational decisions. While value may not be the *primary* consideration, it is always a consideration; the salvor who wantonly destroys the value of ship or cargo is derelict.

Some marine operators dealing with owners of property at risk have demanded terms disproportionate to the value of the services. This practice is unscrupulous and unprofessional and gives all salvors a bad name. Salvage awards are fair compensation for prompt, skillful services, provided at some risk to the provider; they are not a means to rob people in distress. Giving gratuities or payment of kickbacks by salvors for the contract is equally unscrupulous and unprofessional.

The nature of the business of salvage changes constantly in response to changes in the maritime world. Accurate, user-friendly navigation systems, vessel traffic systems, optimum track routing, well-trained mariners, and fewer ships at sea translate into fewer casualties and fewer requirements for salvors. On the other hand, casualties to large complex ships can be very serious and require a rapid response with specialized knowledge and equipment. Emphasis on the prevention of environmental damage and cleanup of pollutants has changed priorities for salvors on site. Rapid communications, large-volume air transportation, the economics of keeping salvage ships on station along major trade routes, and environmental awareness have changed the basic ways salvors operate.

Public policy sometimes addresses salvage as a part of the general topic of marine safety. Following the casualty to the *Amoco Cadiz* on the coast of Brittany in 1978, the French government established a joint venture with industry. Tugs chartered through the French navy provide salvage services to vessels threatening environmental damage on the Atlantic and Corsican coasts. Similar joint venture arrangements exist between the government and salvage operators in Spain and South Africa. Large government-owned salvage fleets support Russian and Chinese maritime interests and do some work in the open market.

U. S. law authorizes the secretary of the navy to provide salvage services to public and private vessels of the United States "by contract or otherwise."[1] The law is permissive in that it allows but does not require the navy to provide these services. The navy has chosen to maintain only sufficient forces for its own needs. It does so by maintaining commissioned salvage ships, a salvage school, and uniformed salvage forces supplemented by a series of contracts administered by its supervisor of salvage. These contracts amount to a de facto subsidy to a few American salvors.

Although authorized to provide services to private vessels, the navy holds to a strict policy of noncompetition with industry. The navy salvages private vessels only with certification that no commercial salvor is available. The services are charged for at a daily rate higher than that for equivalent commercial services. Other government agencies with responsibilities in casualty management, such as the Coast Guard and Corps of Engineers, frequently call upon the navy for salvage advice, especially in view of the expanded role the Coast Guard plays in casualty operations following the Oil Pollution Act of 1990 (OPA-90).

The United States and some other nations have cabotage laws that, following a protectionist philosophy, restrict salvage work to national salvors.[2] Foreign salvors can work in U.S. waters only when no American salvor can do the work and, then, with a ruling from the commissioner of customs. Some nations do not restrict foreign salvors. Many allow foreign salvors to work in their waters only in joint ventures with local companies and a local license. Cabotage restrictions on salvage inhibit provision of efficient salvage services because severe casualties are too infrequent to justify many national salvage fleets.

Far more inhibiting to salvors than restrictive cabotage regulations is the possibility of intervention in salvage by the coastal state's government acting under its right and obligation to protect its coastline. Intervention may take the form of taking charge of the operation, ordering the casualty destroyed, or not allowing the casualty into the nation's waters. Difficulty arises when the government moves precipitously and does not have the experience, expertise, or resources to deal effectively with the casualty. The potential commercial threat to salvors from government intervention is so serious that open form, no cure–no pay contracts now provide means, known as safety nets, for salvors to recover their costs plus special compensation of a percentage of their costs when governments intervene.

The threat of environmental damage, particularly by oil and chemical cargoes, overrides the other threats from casualties. Public policy addresses environmental damage liability more often than salvage. As an example, in the United States, the Oil Pollution Act of 1990 failed to address salvage as a means of preventing environmental damage from marine casualties. Salvors must be aware of the entire spectrum of maritime law governing their operations in any specific nation's waters. As a practical matter, salvors must have representation by attorneys experienced in salvage-related law both in their home country and where they intend to work.

PARTIES TO SALVAGE

There are many parties involved in any salvage case. Each has a specific role and specific interests. The interests may not always be compatible. For example, cargo owners, underwriters, and salvors have a legitimate interest in retaining the value of the cargo while regulators may see the cargo only as a source of environmental damage and care little for its value. Understanding salvage requires not only understanding who the parties are but also what their interests are. The paragraphs that follow discuss the parties to a major salvage operation and how each fits into the whole, as well as their traditional roles as they grew with the industry. In the United States the Oil Pollution Act of 1990 changed the traditional roles in a number of ways that are not yet fully defined. Following the description of the traditional roles of the parties, a few paragraphs attempt to describe the changes in the United States. It is not unusual for people who work with casualties to find themselves in different roles on different casualties. These people must understand the roles and play each within its limits.

The Salvors

Probably the most important party in any salvage operation are the salvors, for without the salvors there could be no salvage operations. Two basic types of mariners perform salvage: casual salvors and professionals.

Casual salvors are those who happen upon a marine casualty or respond to a distress call. They do not make a business of salvage and maintain neither ships nor other plant for the work. They often work without a contract and pursue their claims for compensation through the courts. To put forward a salvage claim only three conditions must exist: (1) property must be at risk, (2) the service must be voluntary—not required by a contract or by law—and (3) the services must be successful in saving the property. Casual salvors have done some excellent work. Federal courts in the United States encourage casual salvors by awards that are generous but proportional to the effort made and risk taken.

Professional salvors are in the salvage business full-time and maintain organizations, ships, and specialized equipment for salvage. This class of salvor ranges from large businesses with considerable investments in salvage equipment and vessels, sophisticated operations centers, and a trained staff operating over a large geographical area to small organizations with limited resources serving restricted geographical areas. Because salvage work is neither regular nor predictable, a professional salvage organization usually is a part of a large, multifaceted maritime corporation where the core business yields the regular cash flow and puts the meat and potatoes on the corporate table. The salvage company provides the gravy or, more likely, the hot sauce. Arbitrators of open form salvage agreements enhance professional salvors' awards in recognition of their substantial investment in salvage. In the past, the mark of the professional salvor was salvage ships or tugs on salvage station. This is no longer true. In modern salvage, with the emphasis on protection of the environment, tugs are of minor importance. People make things happen. Professional salvors have trained people who know how to go about the work and have equipment on hand. They are willing to risk their money and take charge of the operation.

Somewhere between the casual salvor and the true professional are the salvage consultants or "yellow pages salvors." These people have widely varying degrees of salvage knowledge and experience. They seek opportunities for salvage, but maintain no salvage equipment, preferring to hire it for the job, often literally from the yellow pages, and to put together an ad hoc organization. True yellow pages salvors usually operate in a limited geographical area.

To confuse the situation even more, the phrase "alternative arrangements" is often heard in salvage cases. This usually means that some alternative to hiring professional salvors on conventional salvage contracts is employed. The alternative arrangement may be a yellow pages salvor or a reputable consulting or surveying firm hired to put the operation together and run it. The usual motivation for alternative arrangements is to reduce the cost of the salvage effort. For serious casualties where very valuable property is at risk and/or there is the potential for great pollution liability, shopping for alternative arrangements is analogous to shopping for a cheap brain surgeon. The long-term overall cost of going cheap can be much greater than going first class from the outset.

Casual salvors, professional salvors, and alternative arrangements do not provide adequate confusion. Subsidized or quasi-governmental salvors, operating under the control of local administrations, provide salvage protection in certain waters. Use of these salvors by casualties in the area may be directed by local administrations and backed with armed force, especially when the casualty presents a pollution threat. Subsidized salvors, since they operate under government direction, and are not profit- and income-motivated, may not be as technically sharp as commercial operators to whom good performance equates to good profits and good income. Subsidized salvors simply may not have enough work to be practiced and proficient when called out in an emergency.

Salvage uses almost every discipline in the marine field, from naval architecture to dredging and more. Salvors must have a broad general knowledge of a variety of marine operations. They cannot be expected to be expert in every situation they may encounter, but they must have some knowledge of where to start looking for the particular knowledge and expertise they need. Salvors commonly develop great expertise in limited areas, such as a particular type of ship or cargo. All expertise must stay current or it becomes no more than fodder for sea stories. Keeping current requires a considerable investment of time and effort. Time and effort spent staying current contributes to technically successful and profitable operations. Currency is equally mandatory in the reference materials salvors maintain in their library. The library should contain not only general works on maritime matters, but specialty works on all the areas the salvors may need. Beyond general and specialty maritime titles a good salvage library should contain an ample supply of technical manuals, manufacturers' technical data, and catalogs. Books, manuals, and catalogs do not salvage ships, but they contain information and data whose application can make the difference between success and failure.

The organization for a particular salvage operation is tailored to the particular job and includes the skills called for by the case. The following paragraphs describe the general components of the salvor's organization, all or a few of which are present every time a salvor undertakes a job.

The Salvage Master

The salvage master, also known as the salvage officer, salvage inspector, salvage team leader, or project manger, is in overall charge of the salvage operation at the site. The job calls for a combination of management, technical, and public relations skills. There are no formal qualifications or license requirements for salvage master. Salvage masters may come from the ranks of tug masters, salvage mechanics, engineers, or naval architects. The primary requirements are a thorough knowledge of salvage techniques, experience in a variety of salvage situations, knowledge of the commercial aspects of salvage, leadership and management skills, and, perhaps most important, the ability to think imaginatively. However, good salvage technical skills are by no means enough. As project managers, salvage masters must have considerable skill in the commercial aspects of cost tracking and in generating and collecting documentation. As the principal representative of the salvage organization, the salvage master must deal directly with the other parties having an interest in the work. Salvage masters must work constructively with and be skillful in accommodating the often competing interests of ship, cargo, insurers, regulators, and all others with an interest in the work. It is said that the competence of a salvage master is directly proportional to the percentage of his hair that is grey (or missing) and his girth. This, like most generalizations, mixes fact and fallacy, but emphasizes the value of experience and maturity across the entire technical, commercial, and management spectrum to senior salvors.

The On-Board Salvage Team

The skills and size of the salvage team working on board the casualty fit the job. The team should be small and tight—no larger than necessary to do the work effectively. Too many people simply get in one another's way without a proportionate increase in effectiveness. Living conditions aboard the casualty are often hard, without adequate berthing, messing, and sanitary facilities. Extra hands impose heavy loads on available facilities.

There are sound commercial reasons for limiting the size of a salvage team. Where arbitrators or courts decide salvage awards, excessive salvage crew does not increase and may decrease award. Salvage crews that do not share in the award, as is normal for professional salvors, must still be paid, decreasing the net to the salvor. On day rate or time and materials contracts, the salvor is under an ethical obligation not to load the job with excessive people.

The salvage master leads the salvage team on board. Principal assistants to the salvage master aboard the casualty are the salvage foreman or foremen and the salvage engineer. Salvage foremen directly supervise the salvage crew. Two traits additional to those found in any good supervisor are essential in a salvage foreman. Salvage can be dangerous; risk is inherent. A good salvage foreman differentiates between necessary and unnecessary risk and avoids the latter. Similarly, he never directs his crew to do anything too risky for him to do himself. A good salvage foreman fears neither dirt nor sweat. He works alongside his people and gets his hands dirty when necessary. While always willing to jump in and lend a hand, he must never forget that his first job is supervision and that it is very difficult to supervise properly with his head down and his backside up.

The complexity of ships and of salvage operations usually requires a salvage engineer on scene. The salvage engineer's job is the engineering associated with the casualty. This work may include defining the casualty and the effects of the damage, determining from an engineering viewpoint the feasibility of the salvage plan, and designing and overseeing the fabrication and installation of special structures and systems for the operation. More than that, the salvage engineer may be the only member of the salvage team trained in logic and problem solving. Good salvage engineers have characteristics very different from those of engineers who excel in design offices. Salvage engineering may be the last bastion of the dirty-booted, seat-of-the-pants engineer who can feel his work as well as calculate it.

Salvage calculations are seldom as accurate as is normally possible in design. Basic technical information about the ship may not be available for any of several reasons. In salvage, engineers must make broad assumptions based on their knowledge of ships and their expertise and experience. They may be unable to reach some portions of the ship to observe and measure. They must feel the ship and read her signs—distorted structure remote from apparent damage, an oil odor in the wrong place—the way a tracker reads a trail. Perhaps the most important trait of a good salvage engineer is the ability to sort out what factors are important to the salvage at hand. An over-engineered job is a waste of time, effort, and money; an under-engineered one has a high risk of failure. A salvage engineer sitting in air-conditioned accommodation with his computer is doing only part of his job. The engineer should spend time on deck seeing what is happening and why, pitching in to help the crew, and always asking himself, "What is really going on here?" He should try to foresee the salvage master's requirements and keep him well advised. Like the salvage foreman, the salvage engineer should fear neither dirt nor sweat.

Some salvage organizations prefer to keep the engineers at a base where they have full access to their computer and other facilities. This system works well enough for relatively simple casualties, with excellent telephone and facsimile communications between the base and the casualty. The power available in laptop computers and the flexibility and capability of salvage engineering programs now allow engineers to carry powerful computing tools to the site where the engineer belongs. Only at the site can he get a feel for the casualty, respond to changing conditions, and brainstorm with the salvage master. As good as modern communications are, they do not fully substitute for being on site.

The salvage mechanics and divers who make up the balance of the salvage team are multiskilled people willing to work outside their primary trade. Good leadership takes advantage of people's primary skills and recognizes both the existence and the absence of others. Teams that work together on several jobs develop mutual understandings and their own way of working.

Properly motivated salvage crews work hard willingly, enduring the discomforts and risking the very real dangers of salvage. Their incentive: the prospect of success in a worthwhile effort and reward connected with the salvage of a "live" casualty. The same crews are quick to recognize when they are at risk unnecessarily or for purposes for which they do not consider the risk warranted. They do not work well under these conditions and seldom achieve the best results.

Logistics

In years past, fully found salvage ships, waiting on station where casualties were likely, conducted most salvage. These ships carried salvage crew and a varied outfit of equipment. The economics of the maritime world have changed so that this method of operation is no longer common. Salvors now maintain their salvage teams and equipment at central bases and deploy them by air to the casualty. The salvor's ships that happen to be in the area on other work or ships chartered for the job support the salvage team. Logistics, moving the resources to the job site and supporting them there, play a major role in modern salvage. Preparation for a salvage operation cannot begin after the casualty happens. As part of their logistics effort, salvors should have standing agreements with air cargo carriers; established access to providers of specialized equipment and services; packing for air shipments; knowledge of customs, immigration, and conduct of business requirements in countries in their operating area; arrangements with agents in ports where they expect to operate; and myriad other details. Good logistics are particularly important in remote areas with limited local resources. Normally, the salvage master coordinates logistics at the scene through an agent who has detailed knowledge of how things work locally. On major operations with large quantities of equipment or in remote areas, a separate logistics coordinator may be necessary at the site, in major logistics ports, or both, to handle the volume of work and reduce the load on the salvage master, and to insure that the salvage master's requirements are correctly interpreted and met by local agents.

Backup

A team at the home office supports the salvors in the field. The job of the backup in the home office is to provide the salvors in the field with whatever they may need, anticipate requirements, divert distractions, and track costs in detail. During an operation, the support of the backup team is primarily administrative—dealing with the owners on the contract, administrative support for the crew, etc.—and logistical—arranging for and delivering additional or specialized salvage equipment and other supplies and assistance. Regular communication between the home office and the salvors in the field helps both parties' work.

Specialists

Salvors cannot have detailed, practical knowledge of the entire variety of ship's cargoes and the potential hazards of some. Specialists are often necessary to define the hazards of the cargo and methods for handling it to retain the maximum value, to operate special equipment, and to provide other assistance uneconomical for the salvor to have on hand full-time. Marine chemists are often invaluable to salvors dealing with chemical or liquid cargoes and in defining the requirements for entering confined spaces. Structural or stability specialists with access to mainframe computers sometimes back up the salvage engineer on-site in complex casualties.

Money to hire specialists is usually well spent. Specialists increase the efficiency of the operation and prevent the development of hazardous situations that can be costly in both time and money.

Salvors who concentrate their business in a limited geographical area or along particular sea routes should be aware of the dominant cargoes on these routes and have ready access to specialists they may need. For example, a salvor serving a route where a major cargo is grain in bulk should have standing agreements with companies that can provide vacuum unloading equipment and operators and with others that have grain barges.

Owners

The owner of the casualty has a primary interest in the salvage because it is his income-producing property that is at risk. The owner normally contracts for salvage services. Historically, the master of the casualty has engaged salvors. Modern communications have altered this situation somewhat, as many owners prefer to reserve the authority for themselves. Most salvage contracts are now executed between the offices of the salvage company and the owner. In time-critical casualties, delay in beginning services may imperil the success of the operation. However, the salvor should not begin services without a contract in place. Doing so places him more at risk than is warranted. An owner normally benefits by agreeing to a contract as soon as possible after the casualty and by informing his underwriters immediately. The standard open form salvage contracts—Lloyd's Open Form (LOF) and a variety of others—provide a set of terms for the work and an agreement to the method of settling the costs. They are quick and eminently fair to both the salvor and the shipowner. Several such contracts appear in Appendix B.

Open form contracts are most familiar to salvors. Accordingly, the contracts and the settlement processes are frequently criticized as favoring salvors. This is simply not true. Open form contracts are high-risk contracts for salvors who receive no award for unsuccessful services, cannot predict their award with any accuracy, are subject to government interference, and who may have undue difficulty in collecting. If the job goes badly, a salvor cannot simply declare "no cure" and walk away. They must get permission to end services from the authority overseeing the contract. Costs—losses—mount until permission is forthcoming. Lastly, the authority exercised by regulatory agencies in some administrations and the likelihood of takeover of well-intentioned but ill-conceived or ignorant direction by regulatory bodies have decreased the chance of success with open form salvage contracts.

Usually, a member of the shore staff represents owners at the scene. The owners' technical staff may help the salvor with particular unusual aspects of the ship's design and operation. Occasionally—*Exxon Valdez* is a notable example—owners may take on the management of all aspects of the casualty response.

Most owners want their ships salvaged and help in every way they can. Occasionally, declaration of a constructive total loss and payoff of the insured value is advantageous to the owner. In these cases, the salvor and owner may find themselves working at cross purposes. The salvor must maintain his integrity and make his best efforts to fulfill his contract. He also must watch his back.

Delivery

Salvors are obligated to deliver the salved vessel safely afloat to the owners. The salvor has no duty to deliver the vessel to the nearest port if that port does not offer facilities for handling the vessel and its cargo. In addition, a salvor does not have any obligation to deliver the vessel until security has been posted under the terms of the contract, or other arrangements to protect his compensation are in place. Owners are obligated to accept the vessel when it is safely afloat and presented for delivery. It is at delivery that the greatest difficulty between salvors and owners often occurs and when the salvor must be most alert to protect himself and his award.

Insurers

Marine insurance follows a fairly complicated pattern that has evolved over time and is generally standard throughout the industry. Salvors are not expected to be experts in marine insurance, but a basic knowledge of the structure of insurance is important to them, as insurers are normally the source of their payment. Insured value—the dollar amount of the coverage—is important to salvors, only in giving an idea of the vessel's worth and an upper limit of the salvage operation's value. The insured value is not the amount of money the salvor receives for his efforts. The salvor's remuneration depends upon the *salved* value in a salvage done without a contract or on an open form contract. In a daily rate, time and materials, or fixed-price contract, remuneration depends on the contract terms.

Hull and Machinery

Hull and machinery underwriters—commonly called simply *hull*—insure the basic value of the ship, its equipment, and outfit. Hull insurance is vitally important in casualties, for if the expected cost of the salvage, the transit to a repair port, and repairs exceed the value of the hull and machinery coverage there is little economic sense in conducting the salvage. When the costs of returning the ship to service exceed the value of the hull and machinery coverage, the vessel usually is a constructive total loss.

Often, independent surveyors and salvage associations represent hull on the casualty. Historically, most hull insurance worldwide was written in the London market, primarily at Lloyd's. The largest and best-known organization providing salvage advice to underwriters is The Salvage Association (often called London Salvage), an independent, nonprofit, London-based organization with offices throughout the world. The Salvage Association does not operate ships nor does it own salvage plants; it acts purely as an adviser or consultant to underwriters, owners, banks, and other interests and charges fees for its services. Although closely identified with the London insurance market, The Salvage Association accepts instruction from underwriters worldwide, particularly since marine insurance increasingly is written in several markets.

The Salvage Association's or other hull surveyor's roles of most interest to salvors are those in which the surveyors make recommendations for salvage or declaration of a constructive total loss, negotiate the salvage contract for the owners and underwriters, and represent the underwriter during the salvage operation. The salvor should keep the surveyor representing hull thoroughly advised of the progress of and intentions for the operation.

Cargo and Other Underwriters

Just as hull and machinery underwriters insure hull and machinery, so, too, specialized cargo underwriters insure cargo. A single homogenous cargo may have a single underwriter, while many underwriters normally insure mixed cargoes belonging to several owners. Separate underwriters may cover freight and the bunkers carried by the ship. Surveyors representing cargo and other underwriters may be present at a casualty site. In some cases, the same surveyor, often The Salvage Association, may represent hull, cargo, and other interests.

In a practice unique to the marine industry, shipowners and cargo owners share the risk of the voyage in proportion to the value of their participation. This sharing of risk is known as *general average*. Under general average, cargo owners and their underwriters each bear some of the cost of a casualty to the ship. Each underwriter's portion is related to the proportion of the salved value of the cargo they insure as a fraction of the total value of the ship and cargo. Salvors look to the owners and their underwriters for security. The owners are responsible for working with average adjusters to get security from the cargo interests.

Recent years have seen situations where the cargo has far greater value than the hull, particularly with oil cargoes or inherently high-value equipment. In such cases cargo interests may step in and participate actively in and even dominate the salvage arrangements and commercial decisions. Particularly in these cases, salvors must take care to preserve the value of the cargo and in doing so preserve the salvage award.

Protection and Indemnification (P&I)

A variety of risks not covered by normal hull and machinery or cargo insurance require insurance coverage. To provide this coverage shipowners have formed nonprofit mutual assurance societies known as Protection and Indemnification (P&I) Clubs. Basically, the clubs cover all third-party risks and other risks not covered by hull and machinery or cargo underwriters. The clubs provide the certificates of financial responsibility required for ships operating in the United States.

The principle of these nonprofit clubs is simple. Shipowners contribute to a pool in proportion to their ships' values, the coverage they require, and their claims history. The managers of the club use this money, known as *calls,* to pay claims for all the members and manage the club. All P&I clubs are represented worldwide by correspondents who act for them. In the United States, P&I correspondents are normally attorneys; in other countries they may be legal (attorneys) or commercial correspondents. Correspondents appoint consultants experienced in the particular type of casualty to advise them and represent them on the site.

P&I is of interest to the salvor primarily because it provides coverage for environmental damage, special compensation under safety net clauses in no cure–no pay contracts and Article 14 of the 1989 International Salvage Convention, and wreck removal. Environmental damage prevention, control, and cleanup are critical in casualty operations because of the huge liabilities that can result from environmental damage. P&I clubs have interests in every casualty. Surveyors and consultants usually represent P&I clubs at the casualty site. P&I representatives normally set up, operate, and control the pollution prevention and cleanup operation at the casualty and monitor both the salvor and the regulatory bodies. The club also may provide environmental and other specialists.

Pollution carries not only extremely large liabilities, but also the possibility of both civil and criminal penalties. Accordingly, while P&I clubs are not usually a party to the salvage contract, P&I representatives at the scene bear a great responsibility and carry a very big stick. The salvor must keep them informed and should seek their opinion and concurrence on salvage actions, particularly those involving bunkers, oil cargoes, and other potential pollutants or hazardous substances.

If the vessel is an actual or constructive total loss, salvage work stops and the job may become a wreck removal under the auspices of a P&I club.

Regulatory Agencies

With heavy emphasis on the environment and the environmental hazard presented by casualties, regulatory bodies at all levels have intense interest in every casualty. In the United States, the Coast Guard is the agency with the most clout. Other federal agencies and many state and local agencies may take an interest and have representatives at the scene to assure all their regulations are followed to the letter. In other countries, local agencies are equally enthusiastic.

The regulatory agencies levy fines, impose criminal and civil penalties, stop operations, and form public opinion through their relationships with the press. Environmental agency representatives at the casualty site are devoted to the protection of the environment, knowledgeable in their specialty, and usually ignorant of the realities of marine salvage. Most regulators are reasonable people with whom a satisfactory working relationship can develop. Some are quite impressed with themselves and their authority. The salvor can always appeal decisions by regulators to the regulators' bosses. Unfortunately, making such appeals can consume valuable time in a time-critical operation.

The U.S. Coast Guard is present at every casualty in American waters. Their legislated authority is broad and undenied. They can be expected to be present in large numbers and to involve themselves in the details of every phase of the operation. Salvors and the surveyors representing the various insurers should keep records of the numbers of Coast Guard personnel aboard, floating plant, aircraft committed to the operation, and equipment brought aboard. Detailed notes should be kept of all instructions or requirements issued by the Coast Guard and other regulators that delay or disrupt the operation or cause increased costs for any party. These same surveyors should object to any action by a regulatory authority they find unnecessary or objectionable. In all cases, they should keep in mind that regulators have great authority and should not allow their objections to reach the point of obstructing work.

In major salvage operations the demands of regulatory matters on the salvage master's time may be so great that it becomes necessary to appoint a person with no duties other than dealing with the regulators. This person should have knowledge of regulators' authority, considerable authority of his own in the operation, and direct and frequent access to the salvage master. Tact is required so that regulators do not feel they are getting short shrift and bumped down the line. Patience and tolerance are always necessary in dealing with regulators; animosity is counterproductive.

The Media

Strictly speaking, the media are not a party to the salvage, but a casualty is a news event and media reports can make a difference in the public perception of the casualty and its handling. While no one can control media reporting, all parties can only benefit from the media having the best information available. A frank, open approach to the media is best in developing a satisfactory working relationship. If the media believe information is being withheld or that they are being misled, they can quickly become a major problem.

The shipowner should control all communications with the media. Any communication with the media should come from a single knowledgeable source. Ship and salvage crew members should refer media members to the spokesperson. In major operations where media interest is great and the media presence nearly constant, it may become necessary for the shipowner to appoint someone with no duties other than working with the media, to prepare press releases, and to hold regular press conferences. All information provided should be in simple, nontechnical terms that are understandable to people without much knowledge of the maritime world and with no knowledge of salvage. Even with the most meticulous care in giving information to the press, accurate reporting is very rare.

The media can be expected to attempt to board any accessible casualty. Boarding of the media is solely at the discretion of the owner. The salvor, a contractor to the owner, should never allow the media to board without the owner's concurrence. While aboard, media representatives must not delay or disrupt the work, put themselves in hazardous situations, or present liabilities to any party to the salvage.

Enthusiastic reporting giving widespread publicity for salvage work in progress frequently brings on one of the plagues that beset salvors. It often appears that everyone is a would-be salvor and knows how to do the job easier and quicker than the professionals with the responsibility. Most of the ideas put forward by the would-be salvors require the repeal of the laws of physics or another unlikely event. Salvors do well, though, not to ignore altogether even the most farfetched idea; sometimes there is a jewel in the muck.

In the United States

Increasing worldwide concern for the environment has affected the relationships among the parties in casualty operations. Regulators have taken a more active part and P&I has become more involved early in the game because of their coverage for environmental cleanup and environmental damage liabilities. Nowhere are the changes greater than in the United States. The Oil Pollution Act of 1990 (OPA-90), legislation that followed the *Exxon Valdez* casualty in Prince William Sound, has caused major changes to tanker casualty operations in particular and to a lesser but growing degree to all casualty operations.

OPA-90 has shifted the emphasis from the ship and property at risk to actual or potential pollution from the casualty. Furthermore it established such huge liabilities for pollution and natural resource damage that the major focus of casualty has become pollution centered.

Coast Guard policy is to take an active interest in any casualty where a potential for pollution exists. Because oil is present in every ship and the policy is interpreted broadly, a heavy Coast Guard response can be expected to any casualty.

Under OPA-90, response to casualties threatening pollution imposes a system known as the Incident Command System or Unified Command System (UCS). This system, originally developed for fire-fighting groups, has expanded to include all types of emergency response in potentially cross-jurisdictional situations. The system is a partnership of the responsible party, the Federal On-Scene Coordinator (FOSC), and affected state and federal jurisdictions, based on the premise that all parties must contribute to the planning, strategy, and employment of resources. The system provides a consistent organization familiar to participants and easily expanded as the operation grows.

Under the Unified Command System, the responsible party—the owner or his designated qualified individual—the Federal On-Scene Coordinator (Coast Guard), and the state, as trustee for the natural resources, share command. To predict the success of such a system, one has only to remember that a camel is a horse designed by a committee. Its salvation may lie in the designation of the FOSC as the party to resolve disputes and ensure timely decisions—if the FOSC is sufficiently experienced and knowledgeable to make the correct decision, or wise enough to listen to those who are.

The greatest danger in the system lies in force-fitting a system designed for cross-jurisdictional situations to situations that call for single line military-type command systems. Another grave danger lies in submergence of the salvage organization in the casualty response organization and emphasis on the oil spill, a by-product of the casualty to the ship. A third danger lies in inappropriate or incorrect salvage actions directed by the command group, because the salvage organization is submerged in the preoccupation with environmental damage, and the command group does not have sufficient technical knowledge to make sound salvage decisions.

At the time this is being written there have been insufficient operations for the applicability and effectiveness of the Unified Command System in marine casualties to be analyzed critically with good twenty-twenty hindsight. Application of the system to marine casualties was not a natural evolution and is therefore suspect. The concept and structure of casualty management under OPA-90 should be evolutionary and approached with an open mind by all parties.

The net result is that management of marine casualties in the United States is very different from that of the rest of the world and is not totally defined. Anyone participating in casualty management or salvage operations in the United States must be prepared to tread carefully and to be ready for surprises and frustrations.

Relationships among the Parties

A salvage operation is, in effect, a short-lived closed community that brings together a diverse group of people who nominally are working toward a common goal with a variety of differing interests. Most are highly professional and function efficiently to see that the work is accomplished quickly and effectively. Most people who work in salvage have strong personalities and very different ideas. In particular, surveyors representing the various insurance interests are usually very knowledgeable and experienced. Their knowledge and experience can often be of considerable use to the salvor. Prudent salvors work closely with the surveyors and other parties, keep them informed, and consider their ideas in the context of the entire operation and the terms of the salvage contract. On occasion, surveyors may become overzealous in their emphasis on their particular interest, to the detriment of other interests, or may make demands at odds with the salvor's contractual obligation. These situations are best handled tactfully on a case-by-case basis.

As casualties become more complex, with oil spill response operations and other environmental concerns becoming a part of every casualty, effective and complete communication among the parties takes on greater importance. The principles of effective communication and information exchange that have proved effective in the cockpit and the bridge management team concept apply equally to casualty management. While each party to a casualty has specific roles and interests, there should never be any "us guys and them guys." There is no room for it; contentiousness and secrecy are in no one's interest; openness and cooperation are in everyone's.

Because the parties have strong personalities and definite ideas and the situation is stressful and fatiguing, conflicts occur. While all parties usually keep a cap on the conflicts and work to see the operation go forward, it is not unusual for the conflict to reach the point where the principals eat at separate tables or at different times in the common mess. It is even less unusual to find the same principals standing together at the bar celebrating success following an operation.

The remainder of this volume discusses the specifics of salvage operations and the business of salvage. Safety is a subject so important to salvage that it deserves more than a passing mention before beginning discussion of the specifics of salvage.

Salvage is inherently dangerous. Safety in salvage is attention to detail and preparation to deal sensibly with the risky situations inevitable in salvage operations. Personnel must accept considerable risks, but there is no room for macho, stupid, or unnecessary risks or for the people who take them. People taking such risks endanger not only themselves, but other members of the salvage crew and the operation itself. Safety is thought of as expensive in time and effort. It is not; it is dirt cheap. Accidents are expensive, not only in injury or death to humans but in hazard to the operation's commercial purposes.

Safety is a combination of equipment, personnel, and attitude. Equipment failure is far less significant in accidents than human error or ignored safety precautions. The heavy and unpredictable use of equipment makes it sensible to use only first-class equipment with generous safety factors in salvage. Any accident results from a combination of circumstances; only a single factor need be out of line to produce the accident. Salvors who wish to remain alive and uninjured must consciously take precautions throughout the operation. Supervisors concerned with both personnel safety and commercial success must be aware of safety and take positive steps to abort the development of unsafe situations. A particular safety practice should be suspended for any part of an operation only after a conscious decision accompanied by thorough review of circumstances and potential consequences.

Personal and workplace cleanliness is an important part of salvage safety. It is seldom easy to maintain either type of cleanliness in salvage situations—facilities to maintain personal cleanliness may be limited, casualty crews may become lax in their housekeeping duties in the unusual situation, or the ship may be dirty from the outset. Accidents are more likely to happen in dirty places. Salvors are not expected to shine the brightwork, but time should be set aside to keep trash and fire hazards from accumulating and to clean up spilled materials and work-generated debris. Personal cleanliness and the best possible personal hygiene prevent disease and maintain a positive attitude. Oil-soaked coveralls and personal clothing are particularly dangerous and should not be allowed.

When the crew is mobilizing for a job, it is already too late to start thinking about salvage safety and installing an attitude that emphasizes working safely. Ideally, all salvage personnel should attend marine fire-fighting courses and first-aid courses, and all should be qualified in CPR. Supervisors should attend ship's officers' courses dealing with safety in specialized ships and cargoes and in diving safety. Salvage masters should have training in disaster management, incident command, and the reaction of people to disaster. Regular, realistic drills should supplement course training directly and indirectly related to safety.

Safety so permeates salvage operations that no single guide can cover the subject fully. Safety is addressed throughout this book with specific salvage subjects. Not every potential situation and discussion can possibly be discussed. Safety depends upon thinking out every situation and doing what is right without equivocation. Three subjects have such across-the-board application that they are worthy of mention in this initial general discussion. These are workboat safety, breathing apparatus, and electrical safety.

Workboats—aluminum skiffs, rigid inflatable boats, and the like—are a part of most salvage operations. These boats are for work; they are not hot rods on the job for amusement. A boat operator should be designated and made solely responsibly for each boat, her operation, equipment, and safety. Every boat should have a set of basic tools for the motor, some pyrotechnics, a flashlight, radio, fire extinguisher, and oars. It is too much to expect all hands in a salvage operation to wear immersion suits in boats, but no one should ever be in a boat without the correct type of personal flotation device. In cold weather passengers and crew should wear buoyant work suits.

A great danger in salvage involves entry into spaces that are not properly ventilated, contain toxic or hazardous fumes, or are anoxic. The safety precautions for normal entry into potentially dangerous spaces are well known in general marine safety. They must be followed meticulously in salvage. Salvors should have a liberal allowance of breathing apparatus for fire fighting and for working in spaces that may contain hazardous fumes or inadequate oxygen. Breathing apparatus should be used whenever there is the slightest sign that they may be necessary. Salvors should be trained and practiced with any device they use and should not attempt to use apparatus they do not know. Breathing apparatus should be controlled by an individual in compliance with a strict system based on those developed by fire departments.

Ships are easy places to get electrocuted. Even very low voltages that give no more than an unpleasant tingle ashore can result in death in the all-metal, all-conductor environments of ships. The most severe electrical danger in salvage comes from temporary circuits rigged for the job. Temporary power panels can be very dangerous. Making up the panels ashore and conforming to accepted maritime standards rather than jury-rigging them aboard the casualty can decrease the danger. Ship's power panels and distribution systems may often be used.

Temporary circuits should be rigged properly with wiring laid out properly in protected cable runs, circuits labeled, and all connections made correctly. Power to temporary circuits should be secured whenever circuits are not in use. An electrician should walk all circuits through daily and should correct any improper or below-average conditions. In particular, broken light bulbs should be replaced as they occur so live conductors are not exposed.

Power cables run aboard the casualty from a vessel alongside must have chafing gear and be checked frequently for chafing. In heavy weather power should be secured or extra attention paid to chafing. Action to prevent exposure of conductors should be taken at the first signs of wear on the cables.

The personal equipment of every member of the salvage crew must include a flashlight suitable for the type of casualty and fitted with a lanyard. All hands working at night or entering a dark or poorly lighted space should carry a flashlight.

Site security is an aspect of safety in its broadest sense. It is unwise from a standpoint of potential theft, liability, sabotage, arson, terrorism, or malicious mischief to allow unauthorized people access to a salvage site or to areas ashore being used as staging areas or for temporary storage of cargo. Marine casualties are usually accompanied by oil spills or other damage that when reported by a poorly informed or activist press inflames environmental extremists. The latter may inappropriately serve their cause by attacks or vandalism directed at salvage and environmental response organizations. Sensitive operational and storage areas may have to be protected against intrusions. The security of the vessel is the responsibility of the owner but the salvor may have to make arrangements for security of shore sites and vessels he is using. The salvor's local agent can usually advise on the need for security and for the hire of security guards.

TWO MOST UNPLEASANT SUBJECTS

Before concluding this introductory chapter, two most unpleasant subjects—stealing from casualties by salvors and drug and alcohol abuse—must be addressed.

Any pilferage or stealing of the ship's stores, cargo, equipment, fittings, provisions, or of the crew's effects is strictly prohibited and can result in legal penalties for the individual and in reduction of the salvage company's award. Salvors can use the ship's stores and equipment in the salvage operation, but must restrict their general use within specific permission in writing signed by a responsible party.

When no crew is aboard the casualty, the salvor may protect himself by photographing all crew's rooms, storerooms, and repositories for pilferable material, then locking them. Locking up is seldom possible with crew aboard. Salvors can protect themselves against theft by third parties by hiring guards and discussing the possibility with the casualty's master at the outset of operations.

Accusations of theft by salvage crew should be taken most seriously. The salvor should insist that local police be called and that the incident and all accusations and events be investigated thoroughly. All parties should realize that the salvor takes the matter very seriously and, if the charge is unfounded or malicious, civil action by the salvor can follow.

Drug introduction or use by salvors aboard casualties or at a salvage site is intolerable and is cause for instant dismissal. Drug users incapacitate themselves for duty and present a danger to themselves, other salvage crew, the casualty's crew, and others at the scene. Any salvor using drugs should not be permitted aboard the casualty.

Restrictions on alcohol need not be quite so severe. In general, it is good practice for salvors to follow the alcohol policy of the casualty and local law about alcohol and work. If the ship is dry, the salvors should be dry. If alcohol is permitted the casualty crew, the salvage master may permit a limited amount of alcohol to salvage crew subsisting aboard the casualty for long periods. Courtesy requires that the salvage master discuss the matter with the casualty's master and establish his policy based on that discussion and his evaluation of the job conditions and his crew. Excessive and frequent use of alcohol by salvors aboard a casualty puts forth a negative and unprofessional image to the casualty's crew and others involved in the casualty response. Drunkenness by salvors, like drug use, is absolutely unacceptable for much the same reasons. Drunkenness aboard a casualty or that causes incapacity for work is grounds for instant dismissal.

SUMMARY

Salvage is many things. Most of all it is a technical and commercial evolution undertaken at sea under adverse circumstances. The entire subject cannot be covered in a single volume. Probably many volumes would never give complete coverage, for the fascination and challenge of salvage is the variety of problems it creates and the imagination, technical ability, and common sense that salvors must have to solve them. The chapters that follow describe many, but hardly all, of the aspects of salvage. Complete knowledge of every word does not make anyone a salvor. That requires experience, judgment, and the ability and willingness to think beyond rules and accepted practice.

2

SHIPS AND THEIR STRUCTURE

Ships are complex structures that carry passengers and goods and perform services at sea. They resist the loads of the sea, float upright, and do their particular job. A casualty is in a position its designer never intended. It faces forces and loads that are far from normal and that can damage it seriously. Salvage—removal of a casualty from its position of peril—requires a thorough knowledge of ships, their structure, and their stability. The characteristics of the ship, her cargo, her arrangement, and her structural design all influence the planning and execution of the salvage operation. Only well-conceived, carefully planned salvage actions undertaken with knowledge of their effect lead to successful salvage operations.

Ships carry goods or equipment at sea. The type and quantity of goods and equipment define the size and characteristics of a particular ship. They also determine the arrangement of the ship and, to some extent, the structural design of the ship. A complete discussion of ship types would occupy a volume far larger than this. A general and limited discussion is warranted here because salvors must have general knowledge of the arrangements and characteristics of ships they can expect to encounter.

Ships fall into four broad classifications: commercial vessels, industrial vessels, service vessels, and warships. Commercial vessels are ships and barges in traditional maritime commerce. They include various types of dry and wet cargo carriers, passenger ships, ferries, cruise ships, and any other vessel that carries goods or passengers for freight. The diversity of cargoes carried, the requirements and facilities for particular trades, and economic pressures on shipowners to produce return on investment have resulted in a wide range of types of commercial vessels. These vessels make up the bulk of the ships at sea and include the largest vessels afloat. Industrial vessels include fish catchers, processors, catcher/processors, ocean construction platforms, mobile offshore drilling units (MODUs), mining support vessels, incinerator vessels, research vessels, survey vessels, dredges, and others that perform an industrial function afloat. Service vessels—tugs, salvage ships, offshore service vessels, crane vessels, diving support ships, and others—provide services and support to ships, platforms, structures, and other facilities. Navies and other government agencies own and operate warships, naval auxiliaries, and other vessels in support of national policies. The classifications are convenient, but lines of demarcation are neither always clear nor of great significance to salvors.

A ship is an elongated and shaped box made of steel plate stiffened by a grill-like structure of internal longitudinal and transverse frames. Decks and bulkheads divide her into watertight compartments. The arrangement of the spaces within the ship, their shape, and their structure vary with the mission of the ship and the purpose of the particular space.

Welded construction is almost universal in steel ships. Some riveted ships are still sailing, but their numbers have declined to the point that riveted ships are a curiosity. Occasionally, riveted seams are found in some ships, particularly warships, constructed of high-strength or ballistic steels that are subject to cracking.

COMMERCIAL SHIPS

As economic units in trade, commercial ships carrying any of a variety of dry and wet cargoes are characterized by (1) large cargo holds or tanks that occupy most of the hull volume and (2) means for loading and discharging their cargoes. The size and arrangement of the cargo spaces and the handling arrangements vary with the type of cargo.

General Cargo Ships

General cargo ships, such as illustrated in figure 2-1, carry bagged, boxed, palletized, break-bulk, unitized, or bulk cargoes in their holds, containers, or other weather-resistant cargo on deck; refrigerated cargo in insulated holds; and some liquid cargoes in deep tanks. Some carry a single principal product—livestock, newsprint, logs, lumber—in a specific trade; others trade as tramps. Break-bulk ships were once the dominant type of ship at sea, but because of the economics of shipping their numbers have declined in favor of specialized cargo carriers. Formerly, in this type of ship, the machinery was amidships with cargo holds located forward and aft of the machinery space. Now it is more common to locate the machinery aft. The holds usually have a 'tween deck or shelter deck located in the upper one-third of the hold. Access to the holds is through large hatches with removable covers. Cranes or derricks and kingposts with electric winches serve the hatches. Some ships have heavy lift booms and may have an extra long hold.

These ships carry cargo in small packages and have cargo and cranes or derricks that can be jury-rigged easily. This equipment can handle cargo during salvage operations as well as during normal loading and discharge.

These ships usually are framed transversely. Deep tanks, often used to control excessive trim in lightly loaded, machinery-aft ships, may be anywhere along the length of the ship. Double-bottom tanks carry bunkers.

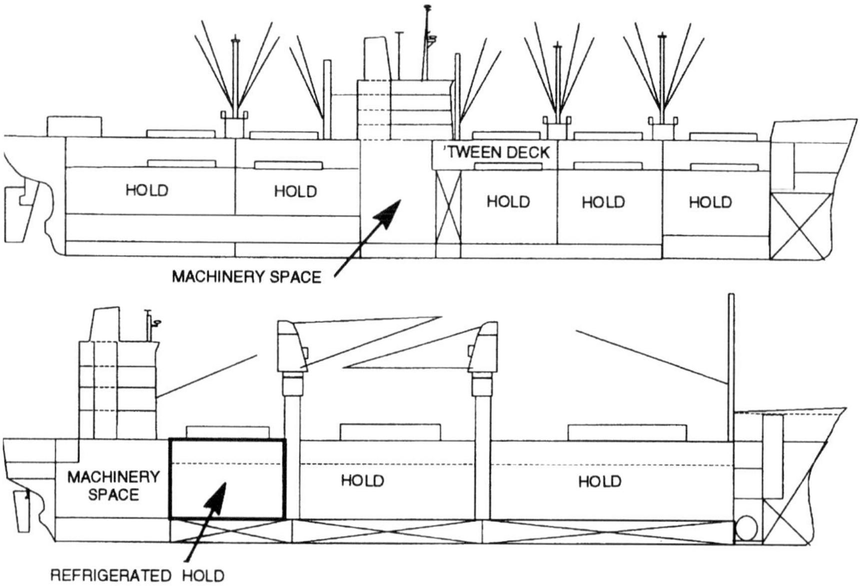

Fig. 2-1. General cargo ships

Containerships

Containers, interchangeable to different modes of transportation, have replaced break-bulk for carriage of general cargo, primarily because containerships can load and discharge up to ten times as fast as break-bulk ships. Containerships generally carry standard 20- and 40-foot containers stacked vertically in cells below deck and lashed on deck. There are two basic types of containerships: shallow-depth ships with several tiers of containers on deck and an unusually high forecastle to protect cargo from boarding seas, and deep ships with most of their containers below deck and a high freeboard. Sectional holds containing cells into which the containers fit take up the entire cargo space. Because the cargo units are standardized and movement is only vertical, loading and discharging operations in regular service are fully mechanized. Large hatches are necessary to use the holds most efficiently. Depending upon their trade and the ports in which they call, the ships may rely upon shore-based cargo-handling cranes or may have their own container cranes. Containerships that rely on shore installations for container handling can be particularly difficult salvage cases when significant amounts of cargo must be removed or redistributed.

Recent years have seen the development of hatchless containerships in which the container cells extend from the inner bottom through the deck to the full height of the container stack, usually about ten containers. The containers throughout the stack lock in their cells in the normal manner, eliminating the need for lashings. An advantage of the system in normal operations is that any container can be reached by removing only those containers in the stack above it rather than a full hatch load. This arrangement can be useful in salvage where it is necessary to remove containers containing hazardous or polluting materials that are stowed low in the stack. High-capacity pumps that could be useful in salvage control flooding in the holds.

Containerships are normally framed longitudinally with deep web frames separating and supporting the cells and adding rigidity to the hull structure. Double bottoms, wing tanks, or a combination carry bunkers and ballast.

Refrigerated Cargo Ships

Refrigerated holds in general cargo ships, refrigerated containers, or ships with all holds refrigerated carry refrigerated cargo. All-refrigerated ships primarily transport food—meat, fruit, and fish. The configuration of storage and temperature depend upon the cargo. While refrigerated containers have replaced refrigerated cargo ships in many trades, refrigerated fish carriers of Korean and Japanese registry serve these nations' far-flung fishing industries. These ships are usually around 300 feet (92 meters) long, have three refrigerated holds, machinery aft, and carry fuel in double-bottom tanks or foredeeps. They present no particular difficulties in salvage other than those associated with preservation of cargo, decay of organic cargo, and release of refrigerant gases. The heavy insulation in the holds may be a problem during wreck removals or cleanups.

Roll-On/Roll-Off Ships

Car carriers and other ships carrying wheeled cargo—cars, trucks, tractors, trailers, military vehicles, etc.—are roll-on/roll-off (RO/RO) ships. In these ships the cargo is loaded under its own power or by mobile equipment by bow, stern, and side-ramps and an internal ramp system between the decks. As cargo, vehicles are small, low-density units. Car carriers and other RO/RO ships are high-freeboard (high windage area) shallow-draft ships. Characteristically, cargo spaces in these ships have several decks. Transverse subdivision may be limited. Many RO/RO ferries and some naval vessels may carry their vehicular cargo on one or more large vehicle decks. RO/RO ships may carry a variety of cargo including containers and break-bulk. Double-bottom or in-wing tanks carry bunkers and ballast.

A number of RO/RO ships have capsized because of improper loading. In any operation involving RO/RO ships, particularly salvage operations, careful attention to loading is necessary to insure that the ship does not become unstable.

Bulk Carriers

Bulk carriers are normally single-deck ships with machinery aft designed primarily for grain, ore, or coal cargoes. Dry bulk cargoes vary in specific gravity and nature from iron ore at 3.49 (10 ft^3/ton)(0.28 cubic meters/ton) to light grains at 0.36 (100 ft^3/ton)(2.83 cubic meters/ton). The wide variation of specific gravities of cargoes has a significant effect on ship design and on salvage operations.The effect of cargo on design is shown by the transverse sections of three types of bulk carriers, illustrated in figure 2-2. Cargo can be loaded into the ships' holds by gravity and discharged by grabs, a conveyor system, or with grain by vacuum. Some ships carry cranes and grabs for discharging; others rely on shore facilities. Bulkers approach very large crude carriers in size, some exceeding 200,000 tons deadweight. Even the largest bulkers must load and discharge inside a port rather than at an offshore terminal as large tankers do. The physical characteristics of the ports limit the size of the ships. During navigation of restricted channels the larger ships are at risk of stranding and becoming a severe casualty. This risk has prompted some ports where large bulkers are a major part of the traffic to prepare contingency plans for such an event.

Bulk carriers fall into several subtypes classified by the types and densities of their cargo. Ships designed for lower-density cargoes have simple, large-volume holds fitted with double bottoms sloped up at the sides to form wing tanks and tanks fitted at the upper corners to provide for self-trimming and to prevent the cargo from shifting. Piping that serves as vents and drains usually connects the upper and lower wing tanks. The holds have a minimum of obstructions. Broad corrugations rather than conventional tees stiffen bulkheads between holds. Large hatches are fitted with mechanically operated covers. Because large hatches and their gear take up almost the entire main deck, there are often underdeck passages for personnel, piping, and electrical cabling.

Ships designed for iron ore and other heavy cargoes customarily have two longitudinal bulkheads with the cargo carried on top of a deep double bottom. The deep double bottom keeps the center of gravity of the cargo high to prevent the ship from becoming excessively stiff when loaded. Some ore carriers have a combination of conventional bulk carrier holds and the shallow holds described above.

The ore/oil carrier is configured much like the ore carrier, but is virtually a tanker with a hatch in the center tank for loading and discharging high-density ore.

Ore/bulk/oil (OBO) ships are similar in configuration to conventional bulk carriers. These ships combine the features of a bulk carrier—open, self-trimming holds—with the oil-tight structure and piping systems of a tanker. Holds are rein-

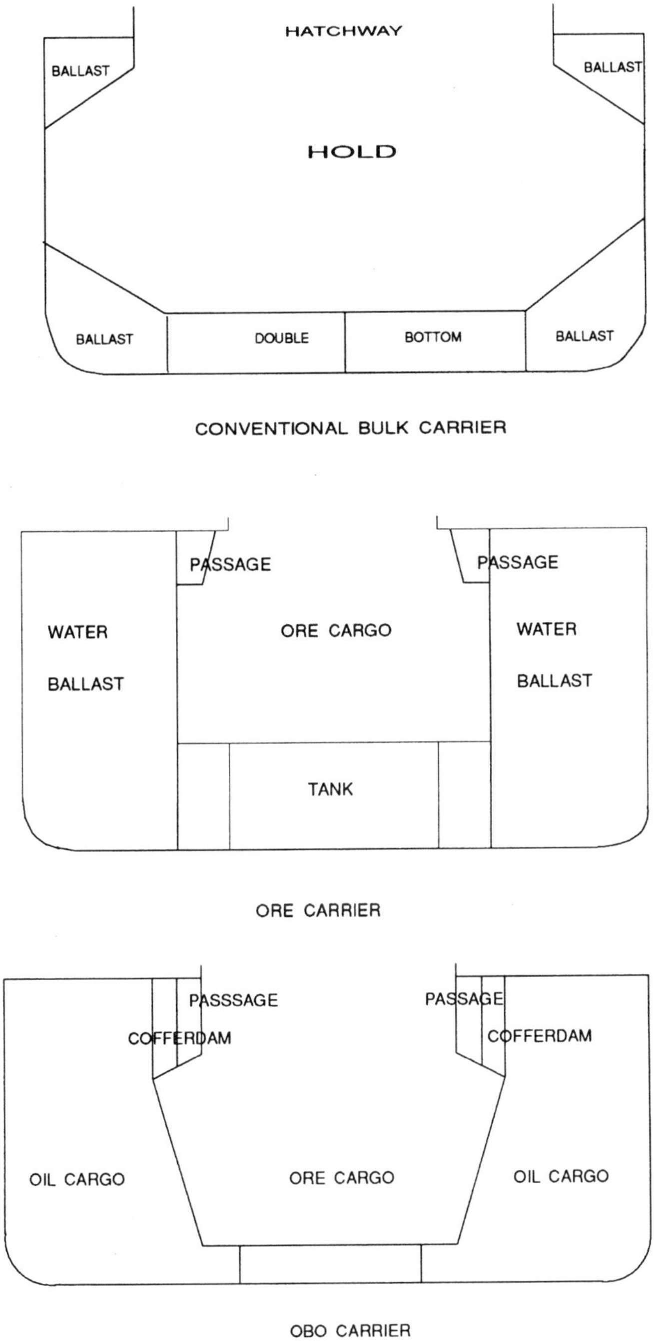

Fig. 2-2. Bulk carrier transverse sections

forced to carry high-density ore cargoes. In some ships, only smaller alternate holds are loaded for ore transport. Ore and oil are not carried simultaneously.

Bulk carriers have suffered several serious structural failures and mysterious disappearances. The cause of these failures may be design, operation, maintenance, or a combination of these. The cause is not of concern here, however; there are ramifications for salvors in bulk carrier casualties. Chapter 6 provides some information on checks on hull structure in bulk carriers that should be made during salvage surveys. Cargo blocking access to hull structure in a casualty is highly probable; even so, salvors should be aware that bulk carriers can be prime candidates for structural failure and allow wide margins for unknowns.

Crude Oil Carriers

Crude oil tankers carry a single type of petroleum cargo. They range from about 35,000 deadweight tons (dwt) to the largest ships afloat at over 500,000 deadweight tons. Arbitrary classifications have been assigned for the very large ships. Ships from 160,000 to 300,000 deadweight tons are Very Large Crude Carriers (VLCCs) and those over 300,000 tons are Ultra Large Crude Carriers (ULCCs).

Traditionally, tankers have been one of the few ship types in which the cargo rested directly against the skin of the ship. Regulation, legislation, and concern about pollution from hull ruptures are changing this. Tankers of all types are being constructed with double hulls to meet legislated requirements intended to limit cargo release in a casualty.

Crude oil carriers are in many ways the simplest of tankers, for they carry only one grade of cargo on any voyage. Their arrangement is relatively simple, consisting of a series of tanks, usually three across, with machinery and accommodation located aft. Cargo is handled through a filling and discharge piping system by pumps located in a separate well-ventilated pump room or pump rooms. A gas-tight bulkhead separates pump ends from their prime movers. The pump room is usually between the cargo tanks and the machinery space.

Tankers are longitudinally framed to take advantage of the strength of this system of framing. Large crude carriers have inert gas systems that significantly reduce the danger of fire or explosion. Single-skin tankers normally carry bunkers in wing or double-bottom tanks in the machinery space or in foredeeps.

While a stranded tanker with no hull ruptures can be a very straightforward salvage case, tanker casualties generally are very difficult and dangerous for salvors. Breakdowns at sea are difficult because of the size of the ship and the high bollard pulls (130 tons or more) required for tugs to control a casualty of VLCC size. The difficulties in fires and other types of salvage derive from the massive size of the vessels, their huge cargoes, and handling the flammable or explosive cargoes.

Crude carriers and their loads are so large that very high stresses can result from loading or discharging them improperly in routine operations. On-board computer systems are provided for sequencing loading and maintaining checks on stability and hull loads. Chapter 13 discusses tanker salvage in detail.

Product Carriers

Product carriers, tankers that carry refined cargoes, are both smaller and more sophisticated than crude carriers. These ships may carry a variety of carefully segregated products on a single voyage. The products carried have specific gravities that range from 0.70 to 1.05. The cargo-handling systems must maintain the segregation while allowing for simultaneous handling. Segregation must be maintained in salvage operations to prevent mixing of incompatible cargoes and contamination of cargoes, adding a complication to an already difficult type of salvage.

While product carriers are simultaneously smaller and more complex than crude carriers, the comments about crude carriers also apply to the carriers of petroleum products. The exception lies in those comments pertinent to the size of the crude carriers.

Chemical Tankers

Tankships transport many liquid cargoes other than petroleum. More than three hundred different chemicals can be carried as bulk liquids at sea. Chemical tankers transport many chemical products simultaneously, carrying as many as fifty small parcels of different products in many tanks. Strict segregation of the products in intact ships and in casualties is absolutely mandatory for cargo safety and cargo quality control. Because of the nature and variety of the cargoes, tanks in chemical tankers have special coatings or are clad with stainless steel.

Chemical tankers carry bulk liquid products that are not usually thought of as "chemical" in nature. These products—molasses, orange juice, wine, vegetable oils, animal fats, and many others—have special requirements and problems that must be allowed for to preserve the value of the cargo during normal cargo operations and especially during salvage operations. Extreme care is necessary in cargo handling in any chemical tanker casualty. It is usually wise to call in an expert in the particular chemicals carried. Based on a chemical hazard rating profile developed by the National Academy of Sciences in the United States, the International Maritime Organization (IMO) generated the Code for the Construction and Equipment of Ships Carrying Dangerous Materials in Bulk (BCH Code) and its successor, the International Code for the Construction and Equipment of Ships Carrying Dangerous Materials in Bulk (BIC Code). These codes apply to specific chemical cargoes:

With fire hazards greater than petroleum or similar flammable products.

That have significant hazards other than or in addition to flammability.

That may be hazardous if released to the environment.

The codes specify three ship types differing in the degree of protection offered and survivability of collision damage. Cargo hazard is the criterion for matching ship and cargo.

Type 1 ships give the highest level of protection. Release of Type 1 cargoes would have effects far beyond the immediate vicinity of the ship. These cargoes must be placed in tanks well inside the sides and bottom of the ship. The ship must survive serious damage described in the code.

Type 2 ships are the mid-standard of protection required for cargoes with serious hazards but unlikely to have far-reaching effects. Cargoes are located at prescribed distances from the sides and bottom and the ship must be able to survive the level of damage associated with vessels in port.

Type 3 ships have the lowest level of protection prescribed by the code. These ships are designed for cargoes that require a moderate degree of containment. The prescribed level of survivable damage is less than for Type 1 and 2 ships. Type 3 cargoes can be located at the sides and bottom of the ship.

The codes also contain standards for cargo transfer, construction materials, cargo temperature control, tank venting, environmental control, electrical installations, fire prevention and extinguishment, cargo area ventilation, instrumentation, and personnel protection. There are also many special requirements for particular cargoes that recognize their particular hazards.

All of the above items are important to salvors because of the close interface between the cargo and the ship in chemical tankers and the potential for disaster with these ships. The codes are subject to periodic review, change, and updating. Code users are advised to refer directly to the code and to make sure the one they have is the current edition. An out-of-date code is no more useful than an out-of-date chart. Salvors should be aware that the code is only a recommendation and that chemical tankers that become casualties may not comply with the code.

Liquefied Gas Carriers

Liquefied gases are substances that are normally gaseous, but have been liquefied by cooling, pressurization, or a combination for economical storage or transportation. These products are carried at or near their boiling temperature for the storage pressure. Ships that carry liquefied petroleum gas (LPG) and liquefied natural gas (LNG) are among the most complex and sophisticated vessels at sea because of their cargo systems. Liquefied gas carriers must be capable of loading, carrying, and discharging their cargoes and of gas-freeing the tanks for repairs or changing cargoes.

The pressure and temperature characteristics of the gases demand specially constructed cargo tanks. These tanks do not form an integral part of the hull strength structure as they do in liquid cargo tankers, but are located well inboard of the hull boundaries. Tank support systems allow some movement of the tanks to account for hogging and sagging of the hull and expansion and contraction. The IMO's Code for the Equipment and Construction of Ships Carrying Liquified Gases in Bulk (IGC Code) contains technical requirements for gas carriers.

Cargo-handling equipment is located in a well-ventilated deckhouse split by a gas-tight bulkhead that separates pumps from their prime movers. No joints or glands are permitted below decks to preclude the possibility of unnoticed gas leaks. Loading and discharge lines and other lines that enter the tank pass through domes that protrude through the main deck.

LPG is carried in one of three ways:

1. Fully pressurized with pressures of about 19 atmospheres (280 psia) and temperatures about 32 degrees Fahrenheit (0 degrees centigrade). These ships are small. Most have 2,500 cubic meters of cargo capacity or less, although some have capacities of up to 4,000 cubic meters. Tanks may be spherical, cylindrical, or lobed. Boil-off gas is wholly contained by the pressure vessel tanks. The strength of the pressure vessels, their location well inside the ship, and their protection by double-bottom ballast makes this type of ship very rugged with much reserve buoyancy.
2. Semipressurized/refrigerated with temperatures as low as –48 degrees centigrade (–54.5 degrees Fahrenheit) and pressures as high as 7 atmospheres (100 psi). The tanks are spherical or cylindrical, constructed of special grade steels, and insulated. Boil-off maintains the required cargo temperature. In turn, the cooling of evaporation of the boil-off gas maintains tank pressure in the design range. The boil-off gas is reliquefied and returned to the tank. The capacities of these ships are up to 15,000 cubic meters.
3. Fully refrigerated with temperatures about –50 degrees C. (–58 degrees F.) and pressures of about 0.7 atmospheres (10.5 psia). These ships, generally with capacities from 5,000 to 100,000 cubic meters, have large reliquefication plants. The cargo tanks do not have to withstand great pressure; they are generally internally stiffened prismatic tanks constructed of special steel and heavily insulated. All ships have double bottoms and many have side ballast systems. Tanks are located at a minimum of 30 inches (760 mm) from the ship's sides and bottom. Tanks are made of special grade steel to form a secondary barrier to cold cargo. Void spaces and spaces surrounding tanks in these ships are normally inerted. Figure 2-3 illustrates the three types of LPG carriers.

Commercially transported LNG—normally 95 percent methane, 5 percent ethane with traces of butane, propane, and pentane—is carried as a cryogenic liquid in a boiling state at temperatures of about –165 degrees C. (–265 degrees F.)

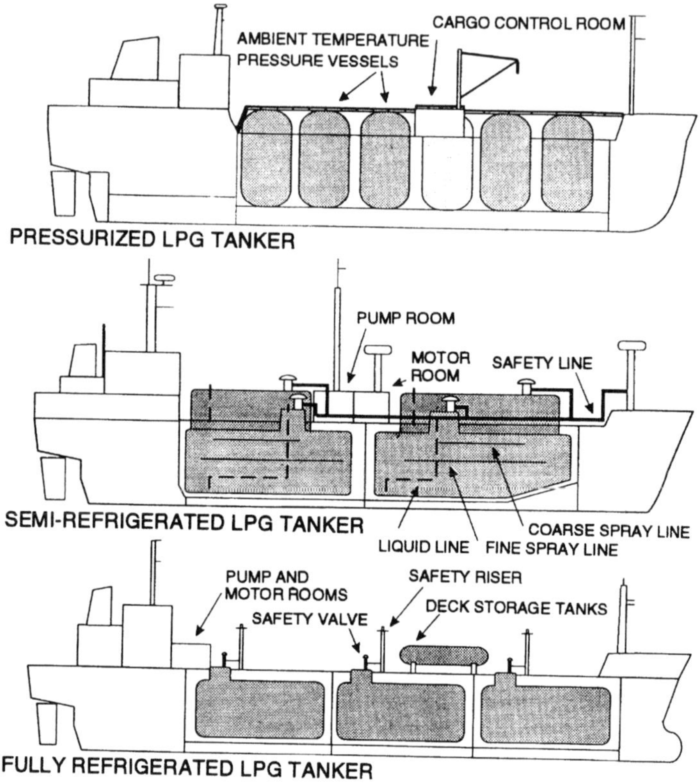

Fig. 2-3. LPG carrier types

and a pressure of 0.5 to 2.5 psia (0.034 to 0.17 atmospheres). Very large fully refrigerated ships with capacities greater than 133,000 cubic meters carry the cargo. These ships are constructed following any of several patented containment systems. A cargo with an extremely low specific gravity (0.45 to 0.50) results in large ships with shallow drafts and very high freeboard. The requirements of the cargo containment and handling system determine structure, arrangement, and subdivision. The ships have full double bottoms of about 6.5 feet (2 meters) depth and side or topside ballast systems. LNG carriers are very sophisticated and very expensive.

Cryogenic liquids present two dangers beyond fire or explosion—boil-off that exceeds the capacity of the relief valve system, and brittle fracture of metals contacting the cryogenic liquid. A casualty to an LNG ship is potentially very dangerous not only to the ship, but also to her environs. Because of the sophistication and potential hazards of these ships, many operators maintain emergency response teams to supplement salvors.

Cruise Ships and Ferries

With the virtual disappearance of scheduled passenger liner service from the seas, only cruise ships and ferries carry many passengers commercially. Cruise ships are multidecked vessels with long, high superstructures and extensive hotel facilities designed to carry passengers in comfort on pleasure cruises. Some older passenger liners have been adapted for cruise service. Some newer ships are of innovative design. Normally, machinery is located amidships, although a tendency in recent designs has been to place machinery aft. Usually, double bottoms carry bunkers. In cruise ship casualties the first concern is for the safety of the passengers. Fire is a major hazard aboard cruise ships because of large amounts of combustible materials. Extensive joiner type subdivision complicates fire fighting and salvage on cruise and other passenger ships.

Ferries come in many sizes ranging from quite small boats to those that carry vehicles and cargo on overnight or longer service. Vehicles, cargo, and passengers are strictly segregated on these ships. Local loads, rather than sea-induced longitudinal bending, determine the structural arrangement of ferries that normally operate in sheltered waters. Structure in ferries tends to be lighter than in seagoing ships.

INDUSTRIAL AND SERVICE VESSELS

Service and industrial vessels differ from commercial vessels in that the former carry equipment and goods with which to do work at sea while the latter carry goods between ports. Space in commercial vessels is devoted primarily to carriage of goods. Service and industrial vessels devote their space to equipment for a job and storage of the raw material or product. There are as many or more types of industrial or service vessels as there are commercial vessels. Their mission dictates the characteristics of these vessels. The following paragraphs discuss a few of the more common types of industrial and service vessels.

Fishing Vessels

Fishing vessels are ubiquitous; they are the most numerous vessels at sea. They are also the most varied in type and size. There are three basic methods of fishing: towed or encircling nets, lines, and traps. The method employed by a particular vessel, the type of catch, and the method of handling the catch dictate many of the features of the vessel.

Catcher boats do no processing on board; rather they deliver their catch to processors either afloat or ashore for processing. Catcher-processors, as their name indicates, both catch fish and process it on board. These boats are necessarily larger than catcher boats to hold processing machinery and crew. Processors, or factory ships, do no catching but process the catch of the catcher boats and store it. These ships may operate under way, but it is usual for them to lie at anchor to process. Processors may be large ships with large processing crews. U.S.-flag processors usually remain below 5,000 gross registered tons to operate as uninspected vessels. Many of these ships began their careers long ago as something very different. Accordingly, generalizations about their arrangement or structure are impossible.

Fishing vessels, particularly the larger catcher-processors and processors, can be very attractive to salvors. These vessels have a high value because of the fishing gear and processing equipment on board.

Tugs and Towboats

Tugs and towboats rival fishing vessels in their variety of sizes and shapes. They vary from small barge jockeys, to various size harbor tugs, to several sizes of oceangoing tugs, culminating with large vessels of more than 20,000 horsepower. Tugs are utilitarian craft. Their utility is their power and maneuverability and their ability to transfer their power to another vessel. The tug is a platform for its engines and towing gear.

Horsepower is often a parameter for discussing and comparing tugs. It is meaningless unless the type of horsepower—brake, shaft, etc.—is specified. Tug operators often exaggerate horsepower as a commercial expedient. Bollard pull, the maximum force the tug can exert against a towline at zero speed, is a more meaningful parameter. Bollard pull may be measured in bollard pull trials or estimated by designers. Owners seldom run bollard pull trials because of the cost. At the same horsepower, controllable pitch propellers and propeller shrouds significantly increase bollard pull. Chapter 7 discusses methods of estimating bollard pull.

Tugs have several functions in salvage operations. Salvors should have a good understanding of tugs and their capabilities and limitations. Some tugs, designated as salvage tugs, carry salvage equipment. These ships no longer wait for casualties on salvage stations astride sea lanes and at choke points. The economics of their operation requires them to pursue towing business and take salvage opportunities when they are able. The Bibliography lists several excellent books on tugs and towing.

Offshore Supply Vessels

Offshore supply vessels originated in the Gulf of Mexico to service offshore drilling rigs. A large, open, low-freeboard working deck aft, high forecastle, and house located right forward characterize these vessels. These vessels have grown in size and diversified in function, but the basic pattern remains.

Diversification has led to increase in power and the installation of specialized equipment such as winches and fittings for towing and cranes and deck rollers for anchor handling. Some ships have four-point mooring spreads and moon pools. Supply remains the principal function and most ships have the large open decks and tankage associated with rig supply.

Because of their diversity and the large, unencumbered deck available for loading and working equipment, offshore supply vessels make excellent platforms for salvage operations and other operations at sea. Vans placed on the afterdeck can augment limited accommodation and provide storage for specialized equipment.

MOBILE OFFSHORE DRILLING UNITS (MODUs)

There are four basic types of mobile offshore drilling units: jack-up, submersible, semisubmersible, and drillships. The sea floor supports the first two. Semisubmersibles and drillships work afloat.

Jack-up rigs consist of a barge with a number of legs attached at the bottom to a bargelike mat or to individual spud cans. The legs are jacked—together for mats, individually for spuds—until the mat or spud rests on the bottom. Jacking continues and the barge rises out of the water to reach its drilling position. To move the rig the procedure is reversed and the rig is either wet- or dry-towed to her new location. Most casualties to jack-up rigs occur during wet tows.

Submersible rigs have the drilling platform located on long columns that end in large cylindrical cans. The columns contain systems that allow ballasting the rig until she rests on the bottom. The column-supported submersible is like a jack-up with fixed rather than movable legs.

The leg lengths of both jack-up and submersible rigs limit the depth of water in which they can operate. In a logical extension of the submersible principle, pontoons were fitted to the columns of submersible rigs to create deep-draft, stable, semisubmersible rigs that can operate in deep water.

Drill ships are ship-shaped platforms with the drilling derrick extending above the main deck and drilling operations taking place through a moon pool. Drill ships have the advantage of being self-propelled and thus highly mobile, but have more motion and spend more time waiting on the weather than other MODUs.

Multipoint moors keep both semisubmersible rigs and drillships on station.

MODUs are subject to all the hazards of the sea as well as the fire and explosion hazards of petroleum drilling. They may become casualties in the same ways as other maritime vehicles. Salvors handling a MODU casualty may find themselves in a different world where "oil field" rather than "sailor" is the dominant and sometimes incomprehensible language, and where some unusual seamanship practices prevail.

WARSHIPS AND NAVAL AUXILIARIES

There are many types and classes of warships and naval auxiliaries. Some auxiliaries are similar to commercial and industrial vessels with special features that suit them for their particular service. For instance, naval oilers are tankers fitted with equipment and carrying crews for underway transfer of oil to warships. Underway replenishment ships are similar to conventional cargo ships but are outfitted to transfer their cargo at sea and to allow operation of helicopters. Naval tugs and salvage ships operate exactly as their commercial counterparts, but may work in combat.

Amphibious ships that carry large numbers of marines, vehicles, helicopters, boats, and other assault equipment and cargo are distinct types with no direct commercial counterparts.

Warships vary from small patrol boats to aircraft carriers that approach the length, but not the displacement, of VLCCs. Extensive subdivision and damage control features, weapons, aircraft, and sensors characterize warships. Warships are by their nature sophisticated and complex ships that defy generalizations. Salvors of warships find that a wealth of help—perhaps even more than is wanted or needed—is available from the government that owns the ship.

HULL STRUCTURE

When a ship becomes a casualty, her structure may be damaged and subject to different types of loads than those of normal service. Proper salvage action by salvors who understand the construction of ships may prevent structural failure that can result in loss of the ship.

The structure has two primary purposes. Weather decks, the bottom, and sides serve the first purpose, forming a watertight envelope that defines the ship and provides the buoyancy to keep her afloat. The second purpose is to resist the three types of load on the ship. These loads are:

Primary loads or bending loads that affect the entire ship.

Secondary loads spread over a limited area of the ship.

Tertiary or concentrated (point) loads.

The strength deck, bottom, and sides of the ship act as a box girder to resist the primary bending loads on ships. Other structures contribute directly to this function, keep the primary members in position for efficient performance, and provide local strength.

The bottom structure acts as the lower flange of the hull girder. Stiffness and strength built into the bottom to carry loads in docking and to resist slamming in a seaway enable the bottom structure to withstand grounding loads. The side plating acts as the web of the girder and resists the loads imposed by the hydrostatic pressure of the sea and the dynamic effects of the ship's motions. Additional plating thickness in way of the waterline is necessary for navigation in ice and to resist impact from the sea and from striking tugs, piers, and the like. One or more strength decks form the upper flange of the girder and are subject to local water, cargo, and equipment loadings.

All of the structural components described above are large plates whose thickness is very small compared to their length and width. These plates must be stiffened to do their job well. Structural shapes such as angles and tee-sections welded to the plating usually stiffen decks, bottom, and side plating. Bulkheads may be stiffened conventionally or by corrugations. Transverse bulkheads are corrugated either vertically or horizontally. Longitudinal bulkheads are always corrugated horizontally.

Ships are usually transversally or longitudinally framed. Transverse framing systems have closely spaced, continuous transverse frames or stiffeners that in turn are supported in decks and bulkheads by widely spaced, intercostal longitudinal girders. On the decks the transverse members are known as beams, in the double bottom as floors, and on the sides as frames. Longitudinal systems have closely spaced, continuous longitudinal members supported by widely spaced intercostal solid floors and deep web frames. In longitudinally framed ships, there is transverse framing at the bow and stern, where longitudinal framing has no advantage and transverse framing is simpler to build. Tankers have a longitudinal framing system that differs from that in dry-cargo ships. Longitudinal framing is more efficient and effective than transverse framing and is usual in containerships, tankers, bulk carriers, and warships. In general cargo ships and refrigerated ships, the deep web frames interfere with cargo storage and in passenger ships interfere with joiner work in passenger spaces and with runs of engineering service systems. A combination system, a practical solution adopted for many cargo ships, frames the bottom shell, inner bottom, and strength decks longitudinally and has transverse frames along the side shell. Plate floors and deep transverse beams are fitted at intervals, usually every third frame space. The cantilever system is a modification of the combination system appropriate for ships that have very wide hatchways with too little deck and beam structure to give enough strength. Figure 2-4 is a schematic of various framing systems.

The double bottom is a strong cellular structure of transverse floors and girders that provides space for tankage and a smooth inner bottom free of stiffening for cargo stowage or equipment installation. Double bottoms are usually 3 to 4.5 feet (1 to 1.5 meters) deep. In very large ships and in those in which the double bottom is primarily a pollution prevention measure, statutory requirements may dictate a deeper double bottom. The double bottom can withstand considerable grounding damage without flooding the holds or releasing liquid cargo from tanks above it.

Keels primarily transfer docking loads to drydock blocks and provide the center about which the structure is built. The usual keel is a flat plate along the centerline with a vertical member that extends the full depth of the double bottom and joins the inner bottom plating. Duct keels are hollow box structures that provide a convenient passage for piping and cabling. In addition to or instead of a center keel, some large ships have side keels (also known as docking keels or keelsons) to support docking loads on several rows of blocks. Some small ships have bar keels.

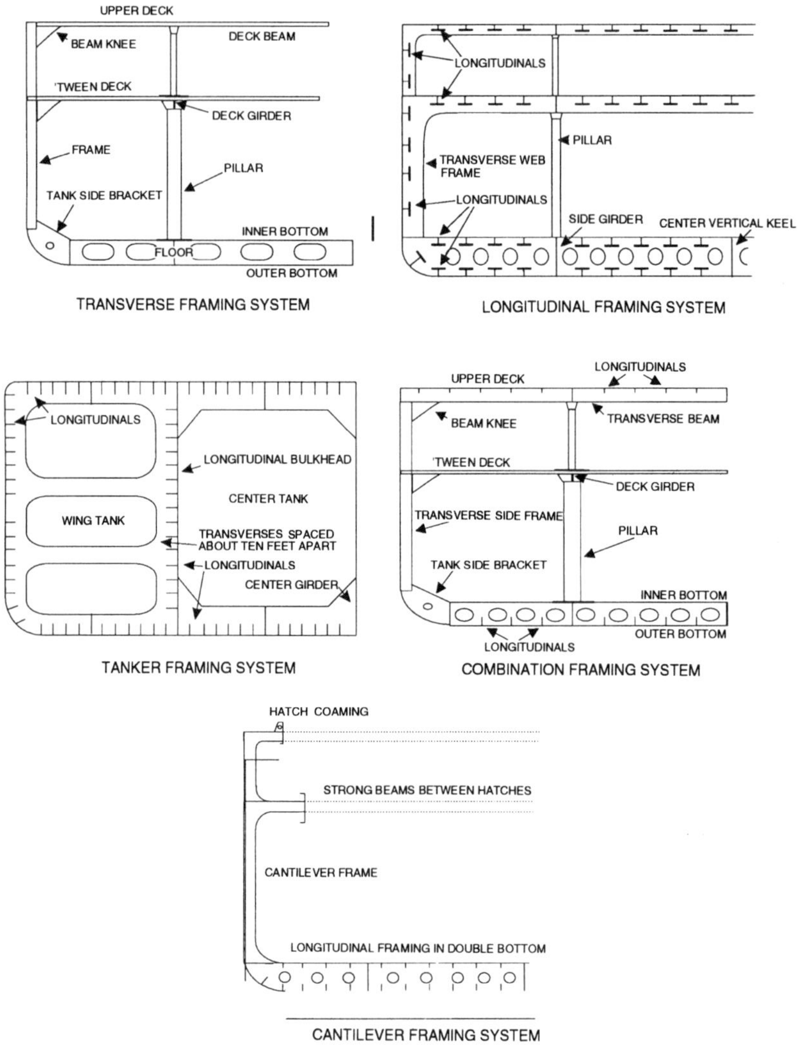

Fig. 2-4. Framing systems

Bow and stern structures are heavy and may be fabricated from forgings, castings, weldments, or a combination. Superstructures and deckhouses are not integral parts of the hull girder and contribute little or nothing to the overall strength of the ship.

Bulkheads are a major component of internal structure. Transverse bulkheads act as internal stiffening diaphragms for the hull girder and resist torsional (racking) loads. Longitudinal bulkheads more than one-tenth the length of the ship add to longitudinal strength. Bulkhead plating strakes may be laid either horizontally or vertically. Horizontal strakes with plates thinning toward the top are most common. Bulkhead stiffeners are usually about 30 inches (75 centimeters) apart except on collision bulkheads where the spacing reduces to about 24 inches (60 centimeters).

Pillars are vertical members that support the deck above them and tie the deck beams into the deck below. In multideck ships, pillars are aligned vertically.

Scantlings for hull structure usually are taken from the rules of the classification society under whose cognizance the ship is built. Some ships, particularly very large or innovative ships, may be based upon engineering calculations that the classification society reviewed and approved. Plans showing construction details usually are available on board or can be obtained from shipowners or the building yard. Midships sections and plating expansion plans provide a great deal of information on scantlings and structural arrangements. Where plans cannot be obtained, scantlings can be estimated from classification society rules or observed and measured.

Openings in hull structure, whether hatchways, accesses, or damage, interrupt the continuity of the hull structure and create stress concentrations. The stress concentrations can lead to fractures at corners. Round holes produce the least interruption; thus hatch corners and other deck and shell openings have rounded corners. Corner radii should be at least 1/24 of the breadth of the opening, but never less than 12 inches (300 millimeters). Corners and edges of damage openings in casualties should be rounded if they are to be patched or if an open sea passage is required. The 1/24 breadth rule for the radius is the minimum for rounding off hull damage. Damage should be inspected carefully for cracking. Any cracks found should be stop-drilled.

Doubler plates, heavy stiffeners in way of the opening, or ring stiffeners, reinforce structural discontinuities built into the ship. Serious unpatched damage should be reinforced for open sea passages. As a rule, the volume of steel in the reinforcement should equal the volume of the hole.

To avoid stress concentrations and especially high shear forces that can cause cracking, stiffeners and longitudinals should always be sniped. The minimum taper for stiffeners and longitudinals is four lengths to one height with six to one preferred for emergency repairs.

Much structural damage—holes, buckles, cracks, and torn plating—is obvious. Some is not, or may be inaccessible for inspection. During salvage operations, structure should be inspected frequently for signs of damage. Some of the signs are:

Inner bottom or other plating set up with lines of internals very obvious.

Buckled pillars.

Cracking at the corners of an opening, at the foot or head of pillars, in welds, or in deck coatings.

Tripped stiffeners.

Newly flaked scale or rust.

Long shallow indentations in plating.

Misalignments.

Changes in the ship that coincide with changes in tide, cargo removals, or other conditions that affect hull loading.

Ships' structures are not collections of components functioning independently; they are integrated systems in which the components work together and support one another. Stiffeners work with plating; web frames work with longitudinals. Pillars not only support decks, but also carry local loads from cargo and equipment, and keep the decks and bottom from moving together as the ship hogs and sags in longitudinal bending. In a ship, the elements of the structure act together to provide support and carry loads. When a casualty destroys the integrity of a ship's structure, the results may be far-reaching. When structure is not continuous or properly aligned, it cannot function properly. Structural interaction can be very complex. Complete analysis of the effects of damage may easily exceed the facilities available at a salvage site. In complicated situations, comprehensive finite-element, three-dimensional models analyzed by computers that exceed micro-computer capacity are often required. Salvors should be alert to structural discontinuities and aware that thorough analysis may be necessary.

Shipbuilding Materials

Notch-tough, plain carbon, mild steels such as American Bureau of Shipping (ABS) Grades A, B, D, CS, DS, and E or their equivalent specified by other classification societies are the most common in shipbuilding. These steels:

Are comparatively cheap to purchase and work.

Have good mechanical properties.

Can be cold worked easily.

Can be hot worked without losing their mechanical properties.

Are readily weldable.

The properties of these steels depend upon their chemical composition and microstructure. Besides carbon they contain manganese, phosphorus, sulfur, silicon, and small amounts of other elements.

Alloy steels known as higher-strength steels with tensile strengths some 20 percent or so greater than mild steels are used in large ships such as tankers, bulk carriers, and large cruise ships to reduce the mass of steel in the vessel. High-strength steels with even higher tensile strengths sometimes are used in ships such as containerships that have small deck areas to serve as the upper flange of the hull girder, and in the legs of jack-up MODUs where the strength-to-weight ratio is important.

Warships may be constructed of high-yield, very tough steels with characteristics that conform to military specifications. Such steels seldom are found in commercial vessels because the cost of materials and fabrication is very high and the extraordinary toughness is not required. These steels require pre- and post-weld heat treatment. Field welds in salvage are difficult and seldom attempted. Warships normally carry plans that show where such steels are located in the ship.

Special steels with enhanced properties are available for applications with requirements such as unusual temperatures, corrosion resistance, or special loading. Typical applications for low-temperature steels are next to refrigerated areas in refrigerated ships and in tanks and areas that may be exposed to the cargo in liquefied gas carriers. Corrosion-resistant steels may be used where clad products are not available or in cargo tanks that also carry ballast.

Their low density, high strength-to-weight ratio, and corrosion resistance make some aluminum alloys attractive for some marine service. Applications include superstructures of large ships and the hulls of ferries, crew boats, hydrofoils, and surface effect craft. Aluminum alloys are also suitable for containment of cryogenic materials. Most aluminum alloys in marine service are weldable; however, some lose large amounts of strength and ductility in the heat-affected zone. Aluminum in contact with steel in the marine environment sets up a galvanic cell. Faying surfaces and other places where aluminum and steel are in contact should be well insulated even for short exposures. A satisfactory joint for short-term service can be made by covering the adjacent surfaces of the aluminum and steel plates with ordinary electrical tape or by inserting a rubber or other nonconducting gasket. The shanks of bolts should be wrapped with tape and the outside of the aluminum plate taped to prevent direct contact with the steel bolt heads or nuts.

Boats, particularly fishing vessels up to 164 feet (50 meters) long, have been constructed of ferrocement—steel mesh in concrete. This construction technique is particularly applicable where sophisticated production facilities are not available. Ships including tankers of up to 7,500 tons deadweight have been built of reinforced concrete. These ships were built to a large degree as part of wartime emergency shipbuilding programs. With the coming of prestressed concrete, reinforced concrete is normally considered only for drydocks and small ships.

Because concrete has very poor tensile strength and cracks under tension, the type of reinforcement in concrete structure in a casualty should be determined before applying tensile loads.

Rules of the classification societies contain detailed specifications for steels and other shipbuilding materials. Normally, salvors' primary interests lie in the tensile strength and weldability of the steel in the casualty.

Welding

Ships are assembled with welds designed and made under the rules and procedures set down by the classification society. Repair welds are made to the same standard. Under salvage conditions, it is seldom possible to produce welds of the same quality as in a shipyard, but welded joints must be strong enough for their purpose. The primary concern of salvors is that welds are strong enough and do not introduce any undesirable hard spots.

The process of welding consists of three events:

1. Filler metal and base metal melt and resolidify to form a fused connection.
2. Heat affects the area near the weld to various degrees causing metallurgical changes in the base metal.
3. Residual stresses that may exceed the tensile strength of the base metal may result from the melting, solidification, and plastic flow.

The chemical composition of the material being welded determines the effect of the changes and the weldability of the material. Ordinary strength steels most common in ships are readily weldable with procedures suitable for salvage conditions. Higher-strength steels should be welded with low-hydrogen electrodes. It is good practice with these steels to dry the surfaces by heating them with an oxy-gas flame to reduce the possibility of hydrogen embrittlement from excess moisture. High-strength steels may require such extensive preheating and postheating that effective field welds are impractical.

Eight types of weld joints, illustrated in figure 2-5, are of interest in salvage:

1. Square butt joints are for thin plates. This joint requires complete fusion.
2. Single vee butt joints are for heavier, more heavily loaded plates.
3. Double vee butt joints are for heavier plates where the joint is accessible from both sides.
4. Square joints are for joints loaded in longitudinal shear.
5. Single bevel tee joints are for greater longitudinal shear loading where the work is accessible from one side only. This type of joint is inappropriate when the root of the weld is subject to tension bending.
6. Double bevel tee joints join heavy members in longitudinal and transverse shear when the joint is accessible from both sides.
7. Single fillet lap joints are for any thickness of plate where loading is not severe.
8. Double fillet lap joints are for any thickness of plate for high stresses and compression loading.

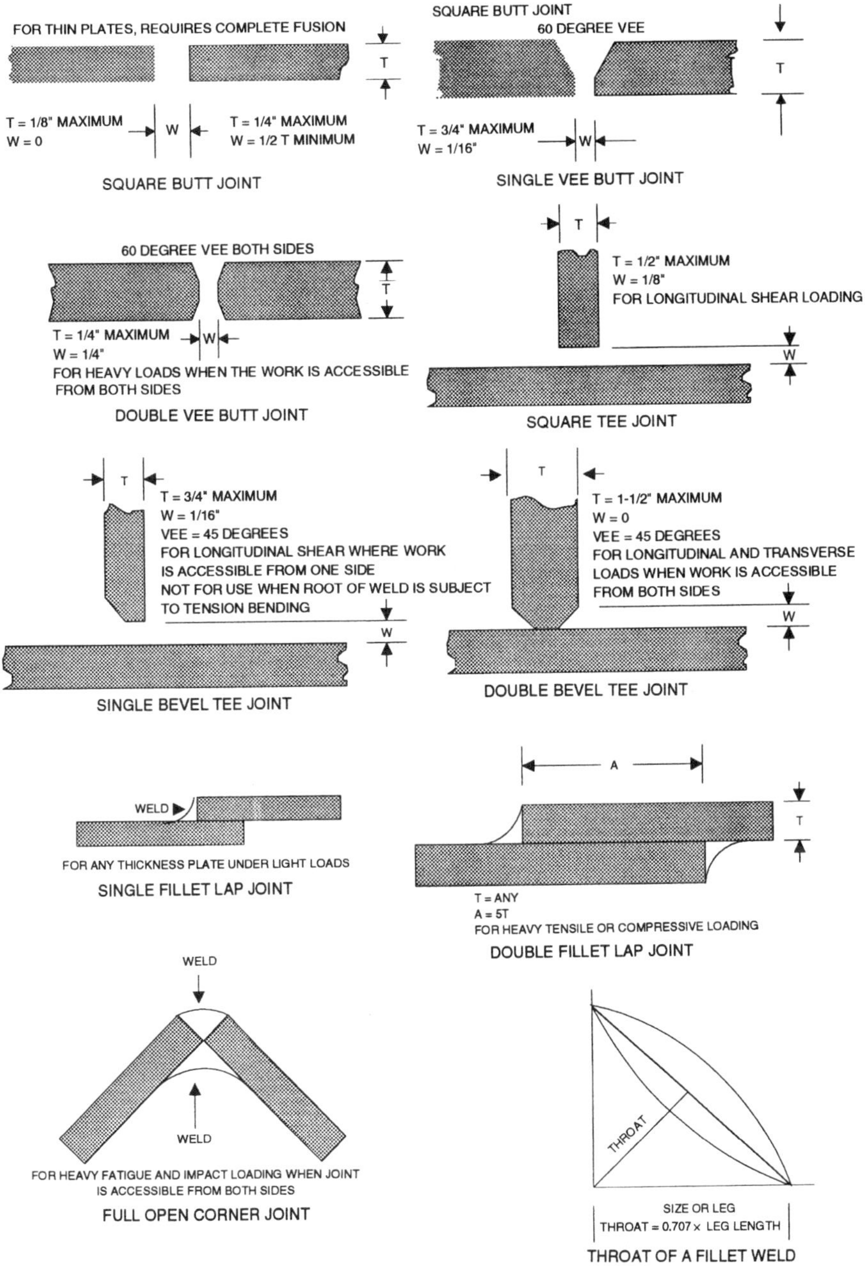

Fig. 2-5. Weld data

The strength of the weld depends upon the strength of the parent metal and the properties and geometry of the weld. Good welds have the full strength of the parent metals so axially loaded butt welds are as strong as the thinner of the plates joined.

The throat of the weld is the thinnest section through the weld. In a butt weld, the plating thickness defines the throat. The throat of a fillet weld is as shown in figure 2-5. Weld size is the length of one leg. The throat is the length of the leg multiplied by 0.707. The length of the weld is the length of the bead. Cross-sectional area is the product of the length and the area at the throat. The size of butt welds is the thickness of the thinner plate. The permissible load on a weld is the product of the allowable stress and the cross-sectional area. Reasonable allowable stresses for welds in mild steel in salvage work are 16,000 psi in tension and compression and 13,000 psi in shear.

Chained or staggered welds often found in ships are not appropriate in salvage operations where time does not usually permit complicated weld joint design. In salvage, the best practice in weld joint design is to follow the old oil patch adage and "make her hell for stout." Welds made on salvage operations are seldom subject to nondestructive or destructive testing. Exceptions occur on installations where large forces or moments are applied to structure fabricated and installed on site and where failures can be catastrophic.

3

NAVAL ARCHITECTURE FOR SALVORS

Anyone structuring responses to ship casualties must understand ship geometry, stability, and strength. All salvors are not expected to be naval architects and/or to have professional expert knowledge of the construction and economics of ships. They must, however, have a more thorough understanding of the technical aspects of naval architecture than most seamen. In particular, they must thoroughly understand the role of naval architecture in salvage operations.

Salvage naval architecture is not a precise science. Calculations cannot have the same precision as they do in a design office. Calculations must be based upon the information that is available or can be obtained at the scene or from owners or the building yard. More often than not, this information is sketchy or incomplete; sometimes estimates are the only choice. To make good estimates salvors must know what to look for, how to interpret what they see, and how to extrapolate logically from the information they can obtain.

Despite the best efforts of classification societies, flag states, and port states, only data availability can be mandated. Reliability cannot be, and realism precludes any expectation of either availability or reliability of ship's data in casualties—especially in the earliest stages when it is needed to draw a picture of the situation. Many ships simply do not have the needed data or cannot locate them. The expectation of finding such data aboard—or receiving them quickly—is so tenuous that salvors must assume they are not available and must be prepared to make logical and reasonable assumptions. Lack of data does not present an insurmountable obstacle to experienced salvors; it does challenge their abilities to improvise. In improvising data salvors must be expert in deducing, approximating, reasoning, and plain guessing to a degree that would send design office perfectionists away babbling and crossing themselves.

Most ships and, therefore, most casualties use the metric (SI) system of measurement. To be able to deal with these ships as well as ships built with the U.S. system the salvor must be able to work in both systems and to switch from one to another with some facility—as many mariners routinely do. Previous chapters give U.S. units as the primary units with the metric equivalent, or near equivalent, following in parentheses. This practice continues throughout the volume. Some naval architectural works develop coefficients and other factors specific to only one system. Equations, expressions, and formulas containing coefficients or constants developed empirically, through regression analyses, or by other means appear frequently in these pages. These work correctly only when the proper units are used. When incorrect units are used the results may appear very strange, or close enough to be right. In either case they are wrong. The only way to be sure is to pay strict attention to the units in each case.

GEOMETRY OF THE SHIP

A ship is a three-dimensional object that can be defined accurately by comparing it with two- and three-dimensional figures. Standard reference lines and planes provide the means of locating points in ships. The standard reference lines and planes are:

Forward Perpendicular (FP): A vertical line through the intersection of the design waterline with the stem. Points in the ship are measured fore and aft from the FP.

After Perpendicular (AP): A vertical line passing through the rudder post or through the intersection of the design waterline with the stern. The AP is an alternative to the FP for locating points fore and aft.

Midships Section: A vertical athwartships plane halfway between the forward and after perpendiculars.

Centerline: A vertical fore and aft plane passing down the center of the ship.

Baseline: A horizontal plane passing through the lowest point in the ship.

The position of any point in the ship is described by locating its height above the baseline, position to either side of the centerline, and distance fore and aft from one of the perpendiculars or the midships section.

The principal dimensions of a ship are:

Length Between Perpendiculars (LBP): The distance between the forward and after perpendiculars measured in feet or meters.

Beam (B): The maximum breadth of the ship measured in feet or meters.

Draft (T): The distance, measured in feet or meters, between the keel and waterline at any point along the length. When the point at which the draft is taken is not specified, it is assumed to be the midships or mean draft.

Depth (D): The distance between the keel and the uppermost watertight deck measured in feet or meters.

Other quantities used in describing ships include:

Length Overall (LOA): The extreme length of the ship measured along the centerline in feet or meters.

Displacement Volume (V): The underwater volume of the ship measured in cubic feet or meters.

Displacement (W): The weight of the ship and all the material on board measured in long tons (2,240 pounds) or metric tons (1,000 kgs or 2,204 lbs). Displacement is directly related to displacement volume. In salt water one ton of displacement equals 35 cubic feet of volume; in fresh water one ton equals 36 cubic feet. In SI units in salt water one ton is equivalent to one cubic meter, in fresh water 1.025 cubic meters.

Lightship: The weight of the structure, machinery, and permanent outfit of the ship.

Deadweight (dwt): The total weight of cargo, passengers, crew, stores, and water carried by the ship. A deadweight scale relating deadweight to draft, displacement, and other quantities normally appears on the ship's Capacity Plan. In the absence of a deadweight scale, maximum displacement can be estimated for ships of 100,000 tons dwt or less by multiplying maximum deadweight by 1.3. Above this point the multiplier decreases to 1.15 at 150,000 and 1.05 at and above 200,000 tons.

Gross Registered Tonnage (grt): A measure of the earning capacity or the cubic capacity of the ship and a basis for charges levied against the ship. One ton is equal to 100 cubic feet or 3 cubic meters. Gross registered tonnage is a volume, not a weight, and has no meaning in salvage calculations.

Net Tonnage: A figure derived from gross registered tonnage by deducting the volume of spaces not contributing to the earning capacity of the ship.

Load Line: The maximum draft to which a ship may be loaded and still maintain a statutory amount of reserve buoyancy.

Freeboard (F): The distance between the waterline and the uppermost watertight deck measured in feet or meters.

Reserve Buoyancy: The volume of the hull between the waterline and the uppermost watertight deck.

Trim: Fore and aft inclination measured as the difference between the drafts at the forward and after perpendiculars. Ships designed with drag have zero trim when floating at their design drafts. Excessive trim is defined as more than one percent of the ship's length.

List: Athwartships inclination, usually measured in degrees.

The ship's shape is related to the rectangles and blocks defined by its principal dimensions by a set of dimensionless coefficients of form. Three of these coefficients are meaningful in salvage:

1. *Block Coefficient (C_B):* The ratio of the underwater volume of the ship to the product of its length between perpendiculars, beam, and draft.

$$C_B = \frac{V}{L \times B \times T}$$

where: C_B = block coefficient
V = displacement volume
L = length between perpendiculars (LBP)
B = beam
T = mean draft

Block coefficient allows displacement to be determined directly from principal dimensions:

$$W = C_B \times \frac{L \times B \times T}{K}$$

where: W = displacement in tons (tonnes)
K = a coefficient from table 3-1

TABLE 3-1.

	U.S. Units	*SI Units*
Seawater	35	0.975
Fresh water	36	1.000

Values of block coefficients range from 0.50 to 1.00, the latter being a rectangular barge.

2. *Midships Section Coefficient (C_M)*: The ratio of the area of the midships section to the product of its beam and draft.

$$C_M = \frac{A_M}{B \times T}$$

where: C_M = the midships section coefficient
A_M = the area of the midships section
B and T are as defined before

Midships coefficients vary from about 0.80 for very fine ships to near 1.00. Most ships have a midships coefficient between 0.95 and 1.00 to give a full form that makes maximum use of the available space.

3. *Waterplane Coefficient (C_{WP})*: The ratio of the area of the plane of the waterline to the product of its length and beam.

$$C_{WP} = \frac{A_{WP}}{L \times B}$$

where: C_{WP} = the waterplane coefficient
A_{WP} = the area of the waterplane section
L and B are as defined before

The three relationships described above are illustrated in figure 3-1.

While important to salvage calculations, coefficients of form are designer's tools and not always easily available aboard casualties. Some methods of estimating coefficients based on the characteristics of the ship have been developed by regression analysis of existing vessels. These equations are available only in U.S. units. Metric units can be converted to U.S. units and the latter entered into the equations.

The block coefficient may be estimated by:

$$C_B = k \times \left(1.10736 - 0.550401 \times \frac{v}{\sqrt{L}}\right)$$

where: C_B = block coefficient
v = the service speed of the ship in knots
L = length between perpendiculars in feet
k = a constant that depends upon the ship type (see table 3-2)

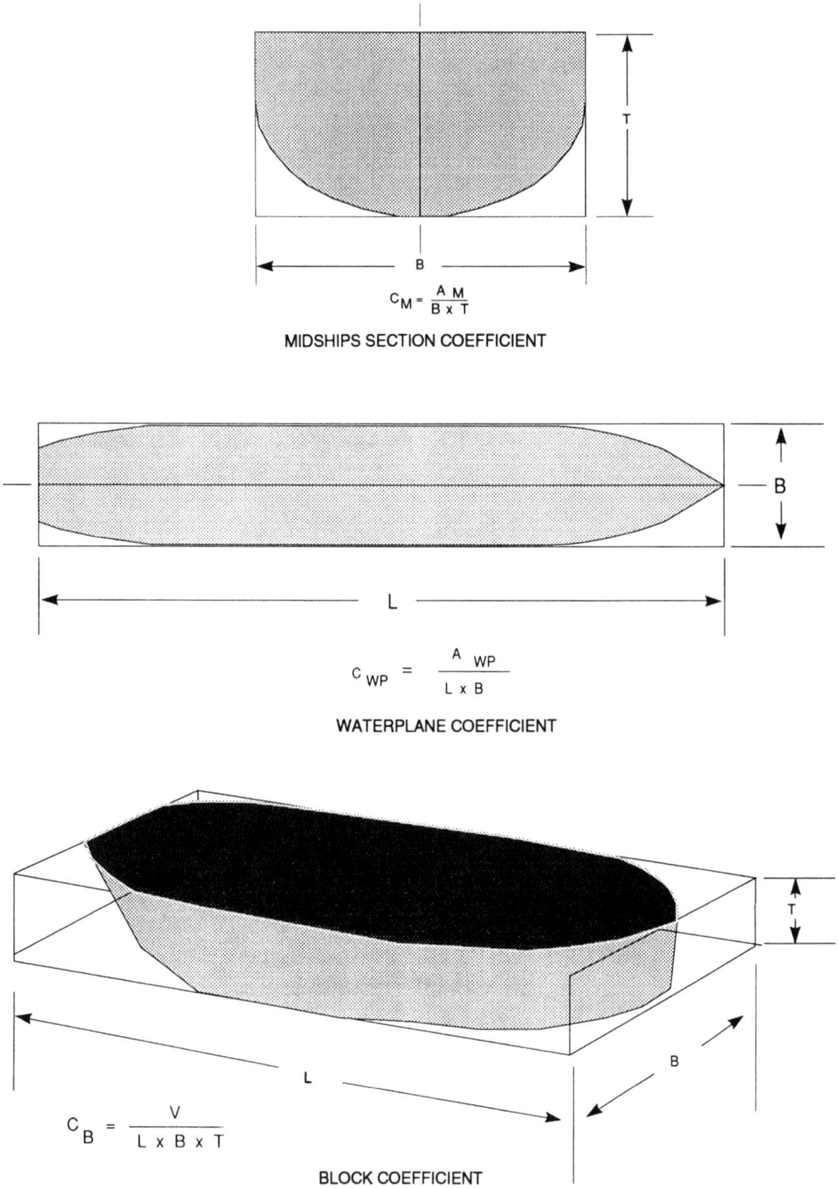

Fig. 3-1. Hull coefficient relationships

TABLE 3-2.

Ship Type	*k*
Bulk Carrier	1.08
LPG Carrier	1.06
LNG Carrier	1.04
OBO or Lumber Carrier	1.03
Product or Chemical Tanker	1.025
Crude Carrier	1.01
General Cargo Ship	1.00
Containership	0.97
RO/RO	0.95

The waterplane coefficient may be estimated by:

$$C_{WP} = K + 0.702 \times C_B$$

where: All quantities are as defined previously and K is:

0.325 for containerships
0.336 for RO/ROs
0.306 for all other types

Two additional naval architectural quantities are needed by salvors for most salvage operations.

1. *Tons (Tonnes) Per Inch (Centimeter) Immersion (TPI or TPC)*: The weight in tons (tonnes) added or removed that increases or decreases the draft one inch (centimeter). Tons per inch (centimeter) immersion is equivalent to the displacement of a one-inch (centimeter) thick slice of the waterplane.

$$TPI = \frac{A_{WP}}{420}$$

where: TPI = tons per inch immersion
A_{WP} = waterplane area in square feet

If the ship is in fresh water, the denominator in the above equation is 432 vice 420.

$$TPC = 0.01025 \times A_{WP}$$

where: TPC = tonnes per centimeter immersion
A_{WP} = waterplane area in square meters

If the ship is in fresh water the coefficient in the above equation is 0.01. TPI decreases approximately linearly as draft decreases at the rate of approximately 0.75 percent of full load TPI for each foot of decrease in draft, or:

$$TPI_2 = TPI_1 \times (1 - 0.0075 \times (T_1 - T_2))$$

where: $T_2 < T_1$

2. *Moment to Change Trim One Inch (Centimeter) (MT1 or MTC)*: The moment required to cause a one-inch (centimeter) change in trim. Calculation of MT1 is neither as simple nor as straightforward as that of TPI. Methods of calculating and estimating MT1 are discussed later in this chapter in connection with longitudinal stability.

MT1 decreases approximately linearly as draft decreases at the rate of 2.5 percent of full load TPI for each foot of decrease of draft, or:

$$MT1_2 = MT1_2 \times (MT1_1 \times (1 - 0.025 \times (T_1 - T_2)))$$

where: $T_2 < T_1$

Four physical centers illustrated in figure 3-2 are important in salvage calculations:

1. *The Center of Gravity (G)* is the center of mass of the vessel and the point through which the weight of the vessel and all cargo and other material on board acts vertically downward. The position of the center of gravity varies in three dimensions with the amount and placement of weights in the ship. The vertical position of the center of gravity is a critical factor in transverse stability. The height of the center of gravity above the keel (KG) for specific conditions of loading may be found in the Report of Inclining Experiment or the Trim and Stability Booklet. The depth of the hull multiplied by 0.60 gives an initial estimate of KG that is accurate enough in most ships for initial salvage calculations.
2. *The Center of Buoyancy (B)* is the center of mass of the underwater body of the ship and the point through which the force of buoyancy equal to the weight acts vertically upward. The longitudinal position of B (LCB) is important because, when the ship is afloat, B and G are in the same longitudinal position. If they are displaced from one another, the ship trims until the two centers are in the same longitudinal position. When the ship is aground it may be unable to trim, so there is a considerable longitudinal distance between B and G.

In most ships, the height of the center of buoyancy above the keel (KB) lies between 0.53 and 0.58 of the ship's mean draft, depending upon the shape of the ship's bottom. A reasonable quick first estimate of the height of KB is 0.55 times the mean draft. Two equations give a more accurate estimate of the height of the center of buoyancy:

$$KB = \frac{C_{WP}}{C_B + C_{WP}} \times T_M$$

where: KB = the height of the center of buoyancy above the keel
C_B, C_{WP}, V, A_{WP}, and T_M are as defined previously

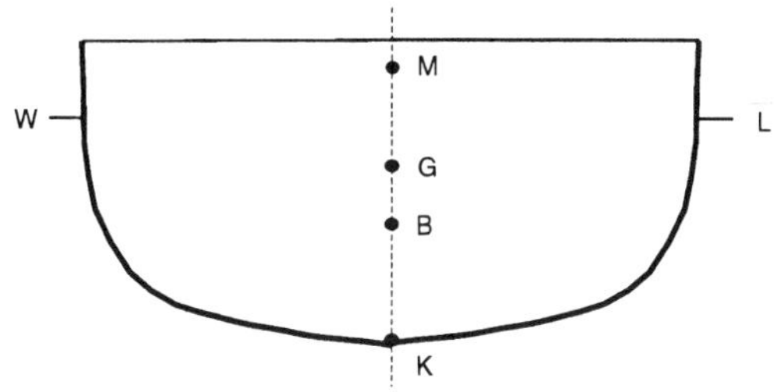

KEEL (K), CENTERS OF BUOYANCY (B) AND GRAVITY (G) AND METACENTER (M) IN A STABLE, UPRIGHT SHIP

Fig. 3-2. Physical centers

and Morrish's formula:

$$KB = T_M - \frac{1}{3}\left(\frac{T_M}{2} + \frac{V}{A_{WP}}\right)$$

In most ships of normal form, the center of buoyancy lies between 1 percent of the length forward of amidships in full ships and up to 2½ percent of length abaft amidships in fine ships. The longitudinal position of the center of buoyancy as a function of the block coefficient can be approximated as:

$$LCB = L \times (0.5 - (0.160 \times C_B - 0.112))$$

where: LCB is the longitudinal position of the center of buoyancy and
L and C_B are as defined previously.

3. *The Center of Flotation (F)* is the center of mass of the ship's waterplane and is the point about which the ship trims.

   Normally the center of flotation lies abaft amidships within 2 percent of the length. The longitudinal position of the center of flotation can be estimated as a function of length and speed for various ship types by the equations given in table 3-3:

TABLE 3-3.

Ship Type	*Location of LCF*
Tankers	$LCF = 0.50 \times L \times (\frac{V}{160} + 0.914)$
Bulk carriers	$LCF = 0.485 \times L \times (\frac{V}{100} + 0.90)$
Single-screw cargo	$LCF = 0.50 \times L \times (\frac{V}{135} + 0.924)$
Twin-screw cargo transom sterns	$LCF = 0.50 \times L \times (\frac{0.95}{V} + 1.03)$
Twin-screw cargo cruiser sterns	$LCF = (0.50 \times L \times (\frac{V}{135} + 0.23))$

where: LCF is the longitudinal position of the center of flotation
L and V are as defined previously

4. *The Metacenter (M)* (figure 3-3) is the intersection of a vertical through the center of buoyancy of an inclined ship and the vertical through the center of buoyancy when the inclination approaches zero as a limit. The same principle applies to both the transverse and longitudinal metacenters. The metacenter and the relative positions of the metacenter and the center of gravity are prime factors in establishing the initial stability of a ship.

These centers and their importance are discussed in greater detail in connection with specific applications.

Sources of Information

Basic information on ships—their principal dimensions, hold arrangement, machinery installation, etc.—can be obtained from *Lloyd's Register of Shipping, The Record of the American Bureau of Shipping*, and similar publications. More detailed information is available on board the vessel in its plans and certificates or may be obtained from the owner or builder. The plans of newer vessels may be on microfiche or a similar system. A printed plan that can be carried around and marked up is more useful to a salvor than a microfiche card. The amount of detail available depends to a large extent on the owner, shipbuilder, and classification society. It also depends upon the age of the vessel, how many times she has changed hands, and how faithfully alterations have been recorded.

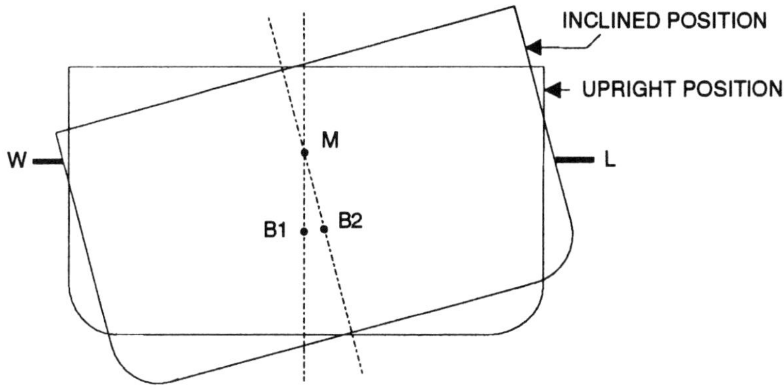

Fig. 3-3. The metacenter

Curves of Form or Displacement and Other Curves are prepared for a ship during design and construction and are normally available on board. These curves are graphical representations of various quantities as they change with draft. Information available in the Curves of Form includes:

Displacements in sea- and fresh water.

Vertical and longitudinal positions of the center of buoyancy.

Tons per inch immersion.

Moment to change trim one inch.

Area of wetted surface.

Trim correction to displacement.

Longitudinal position of the center of flotation.

The curves may contain more or less information depending upon the shipbuilder's practice.

The Trim and Stability Booklet (alternatively, Loading and Stability Information) contains information on the stability of the intact ship in several loading conditions. A typical booklet contains a general arrangement, capacities and centers, and calculations of metacentric heights for the full load departure condition, several partial load conditions, and the arrival and minimum operating conditions. The most complete booklets, some running to three or four hundred pages, contain free surface information for each tank, curves of center of gravity location, height of center of gravity above keel, moment of inertia for each tank, methods of calculating various effects of changed conditions for the particular vessel, and longitudinal bending and shear stress calculations. Salvors invariably find that none of the conditions in the booklet corresponds exactly to those at hand. Nonetheless, the booklet provides a convenient departure point for salvage calculations. The chief mate usually has custody of several copies.

The Capacity Plan is probably the single most useful plan for a salvage operation. This plan summarizes in convenient form the amount of cargo, fuel, fresh water, and stores that the ship may carry and designates spaces for their stowage. There is always an inboard profile on the plan along with principal dimensions, capacity tables, and a scale showing deadweight, TPI, and MT1. Additional information may be included on the plan at the option of the shipowner and builder. A copy of the capacity plan normally is posted in the accommodations, on the bridge, or in the cargo control room. The chief mate can be expected to have extra copies.

Structural Plans provide salvors with the information necessary to calculate residual strength and to plan temporary repairs and patch scantlings and arrangement. The midships section gives the scantlings at midships. These scantlings normally are carried through 60 percent of the ship's length centered on the midships section. The shell expansion shows plating thicknesses and arrangement of longitudinals, detailed drawings of major structural features, such as decks and bulkheads, and of structural details normally on board. The chief engineer has custody of structural plans.

Lines Plan and Offsets are graphical and numerical representations of the shape of the ship. The lines plan is the graphical representation of three mutually perpendicular planes with the ship's hull. Offsets are measurements from a reference plane, normally the centerline, to positions on the hull. As they are a building tool, lines plans and offsets seldom are found aboard ships. They may be obtained from owners or builders. In salvage, lines and offsets are most useful as input to computer programs that require an accurate definition of the ship. Data entry can be a long and tedious process. Many ships, especially tankers of all types, large bulk carriers, and containerships, may have the information loaded into a computer aboard ship or into a computer ashore.

SHIP STABILITY

A basic knowledge of stability on the part of seamen is inherent in all ship operations. Detailed discussions of stability—some directed toward naval architects, others toward ship's officers—are found in the Bibliography. This section contains a brief refresher on stability, with more detailed information about the particular problems of stability that affect salvage operations.

There are several national and international standards for stability that apply to ships of various types. These standards address both the initial stability of the vessel and its ability to survive damage. These standards are of great importance to shipowners and designers, but are of little practical significance to salvors. Salvors are dealing with existing ships that are usually no longer in their intact, as-designed condition. Damaged ships under salvage or en route to a repair facility cannot be expected to meet stability regulations. Salvors must take a common sense approach and deal with basic stability to assure the casualty has enough stability for any voyage or voyage-in-tow it may undertake as a salvaged casualty. There must be full realization on the part of all parties that the voyage involves extraordinary conditions and some risk.

Stability is the measure of a ship's ability to return to the upright position when she is disturbed and after the disturbing force is removed. A ship with positive stability returns to the upright, one with negative stability continues in the direction of the disturbance (capsizes), and one with neutral stability remains in the position she took as a result of the disturbance.

Both transverse and longitudinal stability interest salvors. These two types of stability are exactly alike in principle. Transverse stability and the prevention of capsizing are of the greatest concern, although ships sometimes become unstable and capsize longitudinally (plunge).

The position of the metacenter relative to the center of gravity (GM) is a measure of initial stability. If the metacenter is above the center of gravity (positive GM), the ship is stable. If M is below G (negative GM) the ship is unstable. In the rare cases where G and M are coincident, the ship is neutral.

When the ship is displaced from her initial position of equilibrium, the center of buoyancy shifts to the more deeply immersed side and end. In a stable ship, the couple formed by the weight acting downward through the center of gravity and the buoyancy acting upward through the center of buoyancy act to right the ship. The righting moment is the product of the displacement of the ship (W) and the distance through which the couple acts. The latter quantity is the *righting arm* (GZ) and is equal to GM sin θ for small angles where θ is the angle of inclination.

The height of the metacenter is a function of the form of the ship. The distance from the center of buoyancy to the metacenter, the *metacentric radius* (BM), is the quotient of the moment of inertia of the waterline plane (I) and the underwater volume of the ship (V), or:

$$BM = \frac{I}{V}$$

In transverse stability the moment of inertia is taken about the centerline or the longitudinal axis of the waterline plane and may either be calculated directly or estimated by:

$$I = C_{IT} \times L \times B^3$$

where:

$$C_{IT} = \frac{C_{WP}^2}{11.7}$$

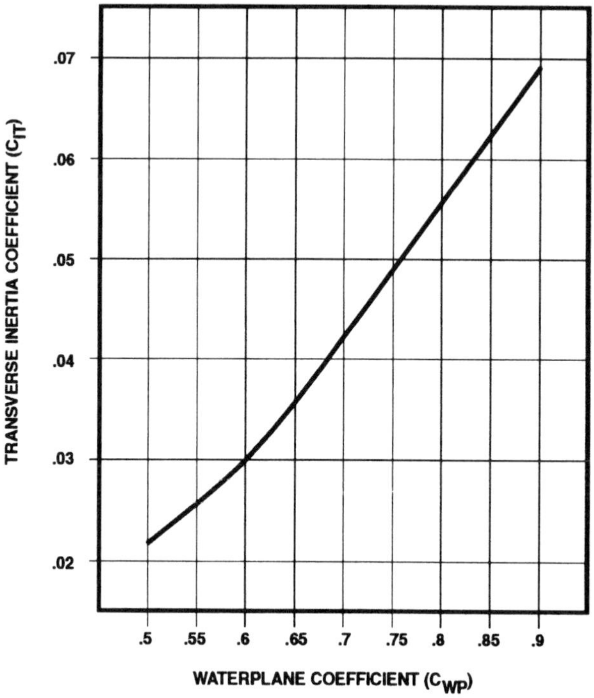

Fig. 3-4. Transverse inertia coefficient. Courtesy of U.S. Navy.

where: C_{IT} = a dimensionless coefficient (C_{IT} may also be taken from figure 3-4.)

Because:

$$V = C_B \times L \times B \times T$$

the transverse metacentric radius (BM_T) may be calculated directly as:

$$BM_T = \frac{C_{IT} \times B^2}{C_B \times T}$$

The heights of the centers of gravity and buoyancy above the keel (KG and KB) may be determined from the ship's data or estimated by the methods given previously. Then the metacentric height (GM) may be calculated:

$$GM = KB + BM - KG$$

Stability calculations are vitally important. Under no circumstances should the precaution of making calculations be omitted. The mathematics are not difficult.

Omission of simple calculations can result in treating an unstable ship as if she were stable. The capsizing of a supposedly stable vessel is an unpleasant surprise.

Weight and Its Effect

The amount of weight and its location in the ship determines the displacement and the position of the center of gravity and thus the stability, buoyancy, trim, and inclination of the vessel. Weight management is one of the most important tools for dealing with strandings and is a major part of other types of salvage operations.

Lightship weights and the location of the lightship center of gravity are provided with the ship's data in the Trim and Stability Booklet or in the inclining experiment report. With this information and detailed information on the amounts and locations of movable weights on board, the position of the center of gravity of the ship in any condition can be calculated.

There are only three things that may be done with weight aboard ship: It may be added, removed, or moved within the ship.

Adding or removing weight increases or decreases the displacement of the ship in proportion to the amount of weight added or removed and the tons per inch (tonnes per centimeter) immersion of the ship:

$$\delta T = \frac{w}{TPI}$$

where: w is the weight added or removed in tons

When weight is added or removed at a location that does not coincide exactly with the center of gravity, or when weight is moved, the center of gravity moves. The direction of the change in the center of gravity can be seen intuitively:

Weight additions move the center of gravity toward the weight.

Weight removals move the center of gravity away from the point from which the weight was removed.

The magnitude of the change—the distance the center of gravity moves—depends upon the size of the weight and its distance from a reference plane:

$$D_1 = \frac{(D \times W) + (d \times w)}{(W + w)}$$

where: D_1 = new distance of the center of gravity from the reference plane

D = original distance of the center of gravity from the reference plane

W = displacement before weight addition or removal

d = distance of the center of gravity of the weight added or removed from the reference plane
w = weight added or removed

The usual reference planes are shown in table 3-4.

TABLE 3-4.

Vertical changes	Keel
Athwartship changes	Centerline
Fore-and-aft changes	Midships section or forward perpendicular or after perpendicular

Often, knowing the distance the center of gravity moves is good enough.

$$D_l = \frac{d_G \times w}{W + w}$$

where: D_l = the distance between the old and new centers of gravity
d_G = the distance between the center of gravity of the ship and that of the weight being added or removed
w = the weight added
W = the displacement of the ship

Weight movements within the ship are equivalent to weight removal at the original location followed by weight addition at the new location.

Vertical weight changes affect stability because the center of gravity moves up or down, causing the metacentric height to decrease or increase.

If the center of gravity moves off the centerline, the ship assumes a list. The center of gravity moves toward the low side until it is vertically aligned with the center of buoyancy and equilibrium is established.

The list that occurs from a weight movement is:

$$\theta = \arctan \frac{w \times d_G}{W \times GM}$$

Center of gravity movements in the fore-and-aft direction and the consequent realignment of the centers of gravity and buoyancy and gravity causes trim. The section of this chapter on longitudinal stability discusses trim in more detail. A single weight movement can, and often does, affect displacement, stability, list, and trim. No weight should ever be moved on a casualty without detailed knowledge of the effect of the move.

Free Surface and Free Communication

Whenever the surface of a liquid or a dry bulk cargo is free to move within a ship, a free surface exists. Free surface in a ship always decreases both transverse and longitudinal stability. It is particularly critical in salvage where there is likely to be flooding in the ship and free surface in spaces that do not normally contain liquid.

The effect occurs because, as the ship inclines, the free surface remains level, causing a virtual rise in the center of gravity. The size of the rise is proportional to the dimensions of the free surface, specifically its moment of inertia, and the displacement volume of the ship. The rise in the center of gravity causes an equal decrease in the metacentric height.

For any inclination the virtual rise in the center of gravity is given by:

$$GG_1 = \frac{i}{V}$$

where: GG_1 = the virtual rise in the center of gravity
i = the moment of inertia of the free surface about the proper axis
V = the underwater volume of the ship

For a transverse inclination the moment of inertia of the free surface is:

$$i = \frac{b^3 \times l}{12}$$

where: b = the transverse dimension of the free surface
l = the longitudinal dimension of the free surface

Similarly, for a longitudinal inclination the moment of inertia of the free surface is:

$$i = \frac{b \times l^3}{12}$$

Each free surface must be calculated individually and summed to get the total virtual rise of the center of gravity.

Note that free surface depends only on the dimensions of the free surface and the underwater volume of the ship. The volume in the space matters not at all. Residual water from pumping or fire fighting is a dangerous source of free surface in salvage that should be eliminated as quickly as possible. Free surface may be removed by removing all the water or dry bulk material or by pressing the space.

Cargo, equipment, or stores penetrating the surface reduce free surface effect. Surface permeability is the moment of inertia of the actual free surface divided by the moment of inertia without penetration. Surface permeability is seldom calculated in salvage because it is difficult to estimate in a salvage situation and the error resulting from ignoring it is on the safe side for salvors.

Pocketing occurs when a transverse inclination causes the liquid to move so the deck is exposed or the overhead is wetted and some of the surface area is lost. When pocketing is certain because of the dimensions of the space and quantity of liquid, the free surface effect for that space may be reduced by 25 percent.

A loss of transverse stability occurs when water can flow freely in and out of the ship, such as through an unpatched hole. There are three effects:

1. Water is taken on board. The weight of the water is usually low and may lower the center of gravity.
2. There is free surface effect from the loose water that causes a virtual rise in the center of gravity.
3. If the flooding is off center, free communication effect causes an additional virtual rise in the center of gravity.

Free communication occurs only in off-center compartments that are open to the sea. It is caused by:

The ship taking a list from the off-center flooding.

As the list increases, additional water enters, the ship lists more, and more water enters until the ship reaches equilibrium.

The additional water is the free surface effect that always causes a loss of transverse stability.

Free communication effect can be quantified by:

$$GG_1 = \frac{a \times y^2}{V}$$

where: GG_1 = the virtual rise in the center of gravity from free communication effect

a = the surface area of the affected space

y = the distance from the ship's centerline to the center of gravity of the affected space

Free communication effect can be eliminated by patching the hole so that the compartment no longer communicates freely with the sea.

Transverse Stability

Knowledge of the principles of stability allows salvors to evaluate the stability of a casualty so they may take the action necessary to keep the casualty from capsizing. There are a few tools that are central to this process. Righting arm is of the first importance because of its widespread application. Righting arm (figure 3-5) is the perpendicular distance between the center of gravity and the vertical through the center of buoyancy. During the design of a ship the righting arm at various inclinations is developed and plotted as a function of displacement for an assumed height of the center of gravity (KG). These curves, the cross curves of stability (figure 3-6), are the basis for developing the curve of statical stability which may be corrected for various factors that affect the ship's stability.

The curve of statical stability (figure 3-7) or, more simply and more commonly, the stability curve, is constructed by entering the cross curves of stability for a particular displacement and plotting the righting arm as function of angle of inclination. The stability curve gives:

- The range through which the ship is stable.
- Righting arm at any inclination and by multiplying righting arm by displacement, righting moment.
- The angle at which the maximum righting angle occurs.
- Metacentric height.

Two corrections to the stability curve are common: a correction for the height of the center of gravity and a correction for an off-center weight. To correct for the height of the center of gravity:

1. Multiply the distance between the center of gravity for which the cross curves are plotted and the height of the center of gravity in the existing condition by the sine of the angle of inclination.
2. Subtract the results for higher centers of gravity from the values of righting arms from the cross curves, or add those for lower centers of gravity.

Correct for center weight by subtracting the product of the distance of the center of gravity off the centerline and the cosine of the angle of inclination from the values of righting arm derived from the cross curves of stability.

Application of a correction for off-center weight moves the point where the stability curve crosses the axis away from the origin. The angle at which the stability curve crosses the axis is the list from the off-center weight.

The number of degrees through which the righting arm is positive is the range of stability, or the number of degrees through which the ship is stable. The ordinate of the curve at any point is the righting arm for that number of degrees. The maximum ordinate lies at the angle of maximum righting arm. The curve normally drops sharply beyond the angle of maximum righting arm. The angle of maximum righting arm is closely associated with the angle of deck edge immersion. The moment of inertia of the waterline plane and the metacentric radius drops sharply when the deck edge goes under. Freeboard does not contribute to maximum stability but directly affects the angle of deck edge immersion and is important to the

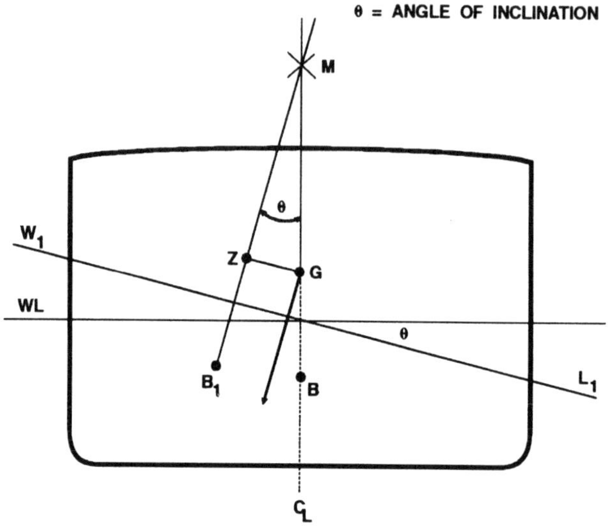

Fig. 3-5. Righting arm. Courtesy of U.S. Navy.

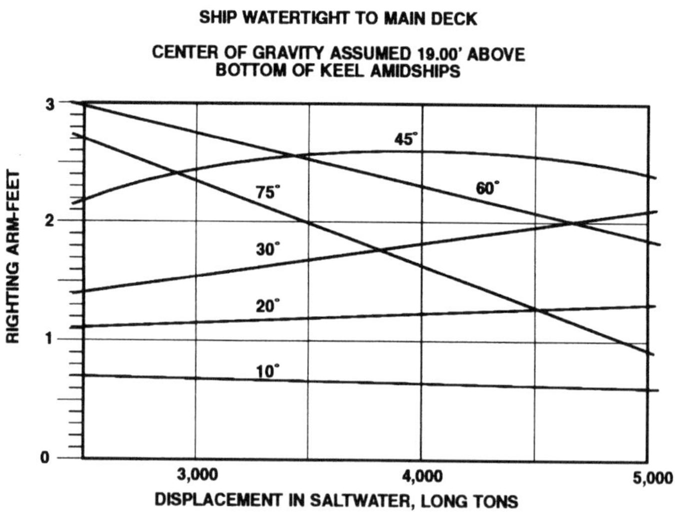

Fig. 3-6. Cross curves of stability. Courtesy of U.S. Navy.

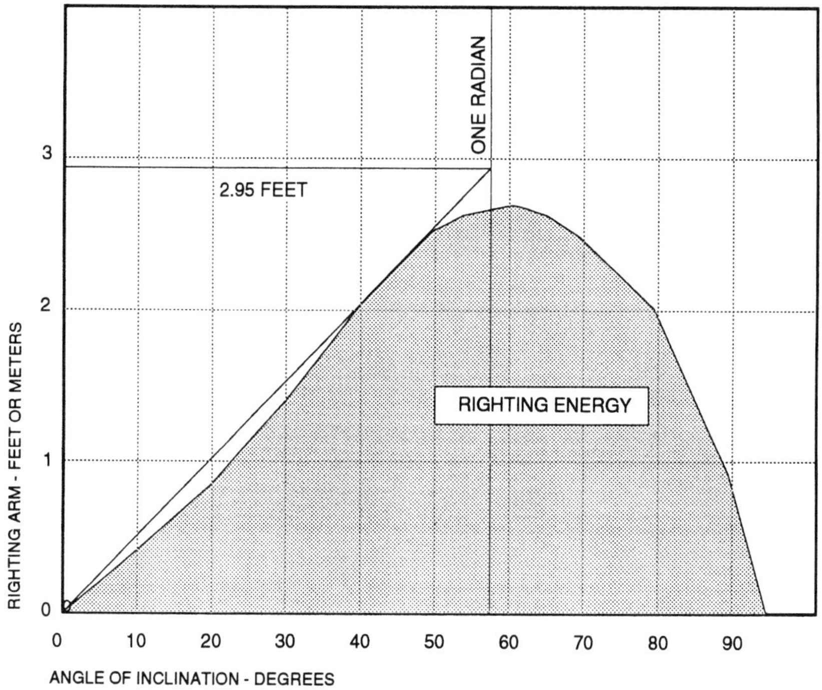

Fig. 3-7. Static stability curve

range of stability. Salvors dealing with a casualty with low stability should work to increase freeboard to increase the angle of deck edge immersion.

Because the righting arm drops sharply after passing the angle of maximum righting arm, a ship, especially a casualty, should not be allowed to approach this angle in roll and particularly not in list. A ship that puts her deck edge under in list is in danger of capsizing in a moderate seaway.

The metacentric height can be determined graphically from the stability curve. A perpendicular is erected at an angle of 57.3 degrees (1 radian) and a tangent to the stability curve drawn through the origin. The intersection of the two lines is at the metacentric height on the vertical scale.

The product of righting arm and displacement is of little interest to salvors. Righting arm alone provides all the information needed because inclination does not change the displacement. A positive righting arm equates to a positive righting moment whatever the displacement may be.

Righting energy, the energy necessary to heel a ship to a particular angle or return her from that angle, is equal to the area under the stability curve between the origin and the angle of interest. A ship with good initial stability has a good metacentric height, a steep stability curve for small angles, and high righting energy at small angles. Righting energy and righting energy distribution, particularly the amount that must exist at small angles of inclination, form important criteria in the various regulations addressing stability. Salvors, more interested in quantity than quality of stability, find it of little more than passing interest.

List may be caused by three conditions: off-center weight, negative metacentric height, or a combination of the two. Salvors must recognize the cause and take the proper corrective action. Table 3-5 specifies causes, methods of recognition, corrective action, and the purpose of the correction. The table must be used with care and not too much confidence must be placed in any diagnosis, for external factors may mask the real cause. As with all else in salvage, thinking out the conditions thoroughly and paying attention to the smallest details are of the first importance.

Longitudinal Stability and Trim

The principles of longitudinal stability are exactly the same as those of transverse stability. A superficial difference is that cubing the length in the equation for longitudinal metacentric radius (BM_L) makes this quantity and the longitudinal metacentric height (GM_L) much larger than their transverse counterparts. Another nominal difference is that inclination is measured as trim in feet (meters) rather than in degrees.

The longitudinal position of the center of gravity (LCG) normally is measured from the midships section or the forward perpendicular. Dividing the total of the moments of weights about the reference point by the displacement of the ship yields the position relative to the reference. The center of gravity usually lies within a short distance of the midships section.

TABLE 3-5.

NEGATIVE METACENTRIC HEIGHT			
Cause	*Recognition*	*Correction*	*Purpose*
1. Removal of low weight.	1. Vessel lists either to port or starboard.	1. Add low weight or remove high weight symmetrically about the centerline.	To move the center of gravity below the transverse metacenter.
2. Addition of high weight.	2. Vessel lolls from one side to the other at the same angle.	2. Move weights downward.	
3. Upward movement of weight.	3. Vessel has a long slow roll.		
4. Free surface.			

OFF-CENTER WEIGHT			
Cause	*Recognition*	*Correction*	*Purpose*
1. Weight distributed unevenly about the centerline.	1. Vessel lists to one side.	Eliminate off-center weight.	To return the center of gravity to the center-line.
2. Transverse weight moves.	2. Roll is normal about the angle of list.		Correct only when absolutely sure an off-center weight exists.
3. Addition or removal of weight to one side of center-line.	3. GM is known to be positive.		
	4. Off-center weights are known to exist.		

COMBINATION			
Cause	*Recognition*	*Correction*	*Purpose*
A combination of off-center weight and negative metacentric height.	1. A permanent list to one side without lolling.	1. Eliminate free surface.	
	2. Very slow rolling about this angle.	2. Eliminate off-center weight.	
	3. List is out of proportion to off-center weight.	3. Add low weight or remove high weight with due consideration for off-center weights.	To move the center of gravity onto the center-line and below the metacenter.

The center of buoyancy (LCB) lies in a vertical line with the center of gravity for ships in equilibrium. The longitudinal position of the center of buoyancy can be calculated by summing moments and dividing by the total buoyancy. It is usually more convenient to pick the position off the Curves of Form. Salvors should recognize grounded ships are probably not in equilibrium and that the centers of gravity and buoyancy are not likely to lie in the same vertical line.

In longitudinal stability the moment of inertia is about the transverse axis through the center of flotation. It can be calculated directly or estimated by:

$$I_L = C_{IL} \times B \times L^3$$

where:

$$C_{IL} = 0.143 \times C_{WP} - 0.0659$$

C_{IL} = a dimensionless coefficient (C_{IL} may be taken from figure 3-8.)

and the longitudinal metacentric radius (BM_L) may be calculated by:

$$BM_L = \frac{C_{IL} \times L^2}{C_B \times T}$$

The height of the longitudinal metacenter (KM_L) is the sum of the height of the center of buoyancy (KB) and the longitudinal metacentric radius (BM_L). The longitudinal metacentric height (GM_L) in turn is the difference between the height of the longitudinal metacenter and the height of the center of gravity.

$$KM_L = KB + BM_L$$

$$GM_L = KM_L - KG$$

In practice, particularly in rough calculations such as most salvage calculations, BM_L and GM_L are interchangeable because of the small difference in their values.

In salvage, the primary use of the longitudinal metacentric height is in calculating the moment to trim one inch (centimeter) by the expression:

$$MT1 = \frac{GM_L \times W}{12 \times L}$$

or in the approximation:

$$MT1 = \frac{BM_L \times W}{12 \times L}$$

Moment to trim one inch may also be approximated by:

$$MT1 = \frac{k \times TPI^2}{B}$$

where k, a function of C_B, is shown in table 3-6.

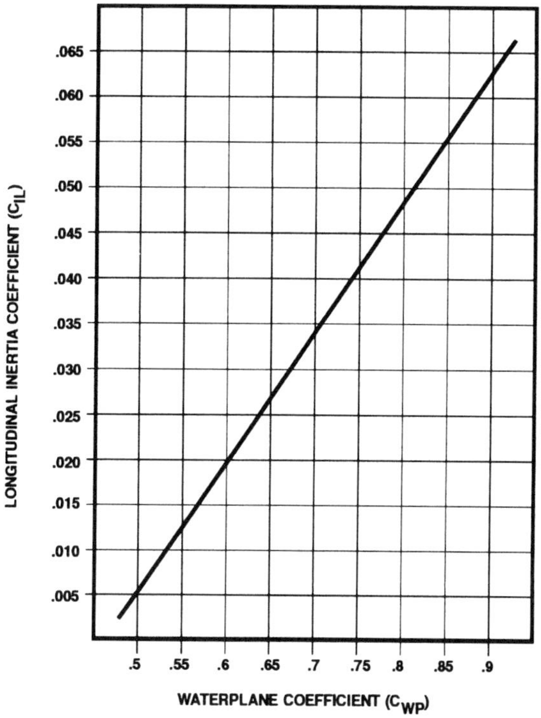

Fig. 3-8. Longitudinal inertia coefficient

TABLE 3-6.

Block Coefficient (C_B)	*k*
0.65	28
0.70	29
0.75	30
0.80	31
0.85	32

or

$$MT1 = \frac{L^2 \times B}{10{,}000}$$

Moment to change trim one centimeter may be approximated by:

$$MTC = \frac{W}{100}$$

Often, the moment to change trim one inch (centimeter) may be taken from the Curves of Form.

Ships trim about the longitudinal center of flotation (LCF), the center of gravity of the waterline plane. The exact location of the center of flotation depends upon the shape of the waterline plane, but it usually lies within 0.02L of amidships, normally aft. The position of the LCF can be read from the Curves of Form.

Weight removal, addition, and movement produce a trimming moment equal to the product of the weight and the distance from the LCF. The total change of trim is the quotient of the trimming moment and the moment to change trim one unit:

$$t = \frac{TM}{MT1}$$

where: t = total trim
TM = trimming moment

The total change of trim is the sum of the changes of trim at the forward and after perpendiculars. The change at either perpendicular is proportional to the distance of the perpendicular from the LCF.

For the change in trim forward:

$$\delta t_A = t \times \frac{d_{AP/LCF}}{LBP}$$

Similarly, the change in trim aft is:

$$\delta t_F = t \times \frac{d_{FP/LCF}}{LBP}$$

Draft at one perpendicular always increases with a change in trim while the draft at the other perpendicular decreases. A worksheet such as shown in Appendix C is convenient for trim calculations.

Control of trim is an important factor in weight management, particularly in refloating from a strand, for the most efficient method of refloating is to trim a ship parallel to the bottom and remove weight until she is just afloat, keeping her in that attitude.

Trim of more than 0.01L is considered excessive for properly ballasted ships of normal form. Ships with machinery aft may have more trim than this when not laden. Trim by the head adversely affects a ship's directional stability and may cause it to yaw unpredictably during tow. To control a casualty during emergency tows or after refloating, it is sometimes desirable to tow her stern first to reduce yawing if she is well-trimmed by the head.

Ship Strength

A ship must have enough strength to remain intact while carrying loads imposed by her own loading and the sea with a sufficient margin to allow for unknown or unexpected conditions including salvage. Strength analysis sequentially determines the effect of forces acting on the ship, the resulting stresses, and the ability of the hull to carry these stresses. In salvage, these analyses determine:

The strength of the ship as the salvors find her.
The effect of planned salvage actions.
The ability of a damaged hull to carry loads.

Ships' hulls are exposed to three different types of loading:

1. *Primary loads* are bending and shear that affect the ship as a whole. Excessive primary loads may cause massive, catastrophic failure of the hull and loss of the ship.
2. *Secondary loads* affect a definable portion of the ship, such as the tank top in a hold or a bulkhead.
3. *Tertiary loads* affect a very limited area of the ship, perhaps a single panel of plating or stiffener.

Primary loads, because of their size and the consequences of failure, determine the scantlings of the primary structure of the ship—the shell and deck structures. Other portions may be heavier than required by the primary loads to accept and carry local loads efficiently. Structures that are heavily built to carry secondary and tertiary loads may or may not contribute to longitudinal bending strength depending upon their length and location in the ship.

The basic strength of ships derives from considering the hull as a box beam or girder and applying beam theory. The remainder of this discussion assumes that the reader has a basic knowledge of beam theory. Readers without such knowledge are referred to any of the many excellent texts on strength of materials or beam theory.[1] The following discussion is general. It is supplemented by sample calculations in Appendix A.

Buoyant forces acting vertically upward support a floating ship along her length. As the shape of the ship's underwater body changes, buoyancy varies. The buoyancy of any section is proportional to the underwater volume of the section. Weight acting vertically downward opposes buoyant forces. The total weight of the ship is the sum of her structure and outfit, the lightship weight, and the deadweight. Weight usually is distributed with considerable unevenness along the length of the ship.

Although the total weight and the buoyancy of the ship are always equal, weight and buoyancy differ at any section. The difference at any section results in a local excess of either weight or buoyancy. The net algebraic difference is the *load* or net force on that particular section.

Grounded ships are supported in part by their buoyancy and in part by the ground. Chapter 4 discusses methods of quantifying ground reaction. The sum of the ground reaction (R) and the buoyancy (B) is always equal to the weight.

$$R + B = W$$

Weight, buoyancy, and load normally are represented by curves whose horizontal coordinate is length and whose vertical ordinates are force or weight-per-unit-length units. Weight curves are represented as a stepped curve or a series of blocks, each representing a weight distributed uniformly over a length. This method, with ten to twenty equally spaced stations, produces a reasonably close approximation and is suitable for hand calculation. The stations, equal segments of the length between perpendiculars, are numbered 1 through 10 or 20. They have no relationship to frames and frame numbers. Half and fractional stations are sometimes seen. Structure and weight beyond the perpendiculars are accounted for by stations numbered less than zero or greater than twenty. Depending purely upon local practice the stations are normally numbered fore to aft, but sometimes are numbered aft forward. As the interval is shortened the curve becomes more accurate. The calculation quickly becomes so lengthy and tedious that a computer becomes a practical necessity.

Weight curves are made up of two major parts. The lightship curve includes the weight of the hull, machinery, and outfit. The deadweight includes cargo and other variable weights. Deadweight can normally be distributed throughout the ship by putting known weights in their known locations. Unless the loading and stability data for the ship include a lightship weight distribution in either printed material or the load computer programming, the distribution must be estimated. Any estimated curve will be at best approximate. The rough shape of the curve can be developed by simply looking at the ship and noting where weight concentrations occur—in machinery spaces and where heavy items are concentrated. Likewise large portions of the ship—cargo areas—are likely to have the same weight distribution over their length.

A method of working out weight distributions from constants has been developed for a limited number of ship types. These constants are listed in table 3-7. A description of their use follows the table.

TABLE 3-7.

	SHIP TYPE		
	Tanker	*Cargo Machinery Space Three Quarters of Length from FP*	*Container Forward and Aft Accommodation*
Station	K_{LS}	K_{LS}	K_{LS}
–0.55-0	—	0.387	—
0-0.50	0.431	0.406	0.513
0.5-1	0.459	0.425	0.544
1-1.5	0.473	0.449	0.634
1.5-2	0.501	0.483	0.664
2-2.5	0.515	0.503	0.679
2.5-3	0.529	0.522	0.695
3-3.5	0.557	0.541	0.664
3.5-4	0.570	0.561	0.679
4-4.5	0.598	0.580	0.701
4.5-5	0.612	0.599	0.701
5-5.5	0.658	0.619	0.701
5.5-6	0.658	0.638	0.701
6-6.5	0.658	0.657	0.701
6.5-7	0.658	0.684	0.701
7-7.5	0.658	0.684	0.701
7.5-8	0.658	0.684	0.701
8-8.5	0.658	0.684	0.701
8.5-9	0.658	0.684	0.701
9-9.5	0.658	0.684	0.701
9.5-10	0.658	0.684	0.701
10-10.5	0.658	0.684	0.701
10.5-11	0.658	0.684	0.701
11-11.5	0.658	0.684	0.701
11.5-12	0.658	0.684	0.701
12-12.5	0.658	0.684	0.701
12.5-13	0.658	0.831	0.701
13-13.5	0.658	1.547	1.359
13.5-14	0.658	1.643	1.329
14-14.5	0.658	1.585	1.268

Table 3-7 continued on next page

Table 3-7 continued

	SHIP TYPE		
	Tanker	*Cargo Machinery Space Three Quarters of Length from FP*	*Container Forward and Aft Accommodation*
14.5-15	0.658	1.218	1.208
15-15.5	0.658	0.986	1.208
15.5-16	0.668	0.967	0.785
16-16.5	0.668	0.696	0.785
16.5-17	0.668	0.657	0.921
17-17.5	0.904	0.638	0.876
17.5-18	1.043	0.619	0.770
18-18.5	1.016	0.619	0.710
18.5-19	0.904	0.619	0.634
19-19.5	0.557	0.657	0.559
19.5-20	0.473	0.425	0.468
20-20.5	0.417	0.367	0.332
20.5-21	—	—	0.196
ΣK_{LS}	26.381	29.652	29.940

The tabulated constants are of little use on their own. They must be combined with the station length (length between perpendiculars divided by 40) and lightship displacement to give a weight per unit length for each station space. This quantity (w_S), is calculated by:

$$w_S = \frac{K_{LS}}{\Sigma K_{LS}} \times \frac{W_{LS}}{\frac{LBP}{40}}$$

where: K_{LS} = weight distribution constant for the station
ΣK_{LS} = the sum of the weight distribution constants for the particular ship type
W_{LS} = lightship displacement in tons or tonnes
LBP = length between perpendiculars in feet or meters

Deadweight is added to the lightship weights by dividing deadweight into increments that correspond with loading and spreading it over known lengths. The entire process is simple and straightforward enough for hand calculation, can be speeded up by a spreadsheet program in any PC, and can be carried out most accurately by a preprogrammed system. The important thing for any calculation system is inclusion of a means by which the input can be edited over a wide range to approach actual conditions in the casualty.

The area under the buoyancy curve for a floating ship, like the area under the displacement curve, is exactly equal to the displacement of the ship. The area under the buoyancy curve of a stranded ship equals the displacement less the ground reaction. For a floating ship the longitudinal positions of the centers of gravity of the buoyancy and weight curves correspond exactly. They do not correspond when the ship is stranded because the ship is not necessarily balanced as she is when floating.

Buoyancy curves are smooth curves most accurately derived from curves of sectional areas (Bonjean's curves) or directly from the lines drawing or offsets. Calculation from lines plans or offsets is difficult and tedious without a computer.

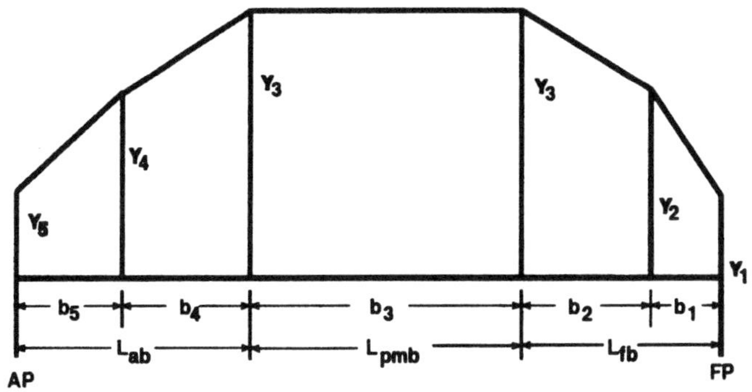

Fig. 3-9. Approximate buoyancy curve. Courtesy of U.S. Navy.

Approximation of buoyancy curves of floating ships by five trapezoids, essentially approximating buoyancy distribution as a function of block coefficient (C_B), is often accurate enough for salvage. Figure 3-9 illustrates the five trapezoids and their defining characteristics.

In this process the ship's length in feet or meters is first divided into three parts: the parallel midbody (L_{pmb}), the forebody (L_{fb}), and the afterbody (L_{ab}), where:

$$L_{pmb} = (1.74 \times C_B - 1.002) \times L$$

$$L_{fb} = (1.186 - 1.17 \times C_B) \times L$$

$$L_{ab} = L - L_{pmb} - L_{fb}$$

The buoyancy in tons or tonnes of the parallel midbody is:

$$B_{pmb} = \frac{L_{pmb} \times B \times T_M \times C_M}{35}$$

The distribution of buoyancy through the parallel midbody is constant and in tons/foot (tonnes/meter) is:

$$b_{pmb} = \frac{B_{pmb}}{L_{pmb}}$$

Buoyancy distribution in both the forebody and abaft the parallel midbody is approximated by two trapezoids in each portion. Table 3-8 gives baseline lengths and ordinates of these trapezoids.

TABLE 3-8.

	l	*b*
1	$(0.61 - 0.615\ C_B)\ L$	$0.04\ b_{pmb}$
2	$L_{fb} - l_1$	$C_B \times B_{pmb}$
4	$L_{ab} - l_5$	$C_B \times B_{pmb}$
5	$0.2L$	$0.08b_{pmb}$

In grounded ships the ground reaction can be calculated by methods given in the following chapter, a ground reaction distribution assumed or deduced, and ground reaction subtracted from the buoyancy curve to produce a grounded buoyancy curve.

Weight and buoyancy curves calculated by these methods are *approximations*. There is absolutely nothing holy about them; they can be jiggled and fiddled as much as necessary—within reason. Normal practice is to adjust the buoyancy curve so the areas are equal and the centers of gravity and buoyancy are in the same longitudinal location as those of the weight curve. It is equally practical to adjust the weight curve, but trying to adjust both curves at the same time leads to frustration.

Load curves are the algebraic sum of the weight and buoyancy curves. If the weight and buoyancy are everywhere equal, the load curve is a straight line equal to zero all along its length. Because the total weight and buoyancy are equal and act in opposition, the load curve is equal to zero at both ends with equal areas above and below the axis.

The shear force (τ) at any point along the ship's length is the sum of all forces (loads) to the left of the point. The shear force curve is developed by summing the area under the load curve from left to right. Shear force is zero at both ends of the curve. A residual value of shear may result from small errors in the weight and buoyancy measurements. A small value does not result in bending moment errors large enough to have significance in salvage. If the residual shear is large, weight, buoyancy, load, and shear curves should be checked and adjusted to reduce the error.

The bending moment at any point is equal to the area under the shear curve to the left of that point. The bending moment curve is developed by summing the area under the shear force curve.

There are some relationships between the curves that serve as checks:

When load is zero, except at the bow and stern, shear is a maximum or minimum, and there is a change in curvature of the bending moment curve.

When the load is maximum, the curvature of the shear curve changes.

When shear force is zero, the bending moment is a maximum or minimum.

Shear force and bending moment are significant because by applying the characteristics of the section, specifically the shear area and section modulus, the shear or bending stress in the section can be determined.

When two forces act in opposite directions along parallel lines, shear stresses develop. The size of these stresses depends upon the size of the shear force and the area resisting the shear:

$$t = \frac{F}{A}$$

Bending, because it produces tension in one flange of the hull girder and compression in the other, also sets up shear in the hull. The shear stress caused by bending is minimum at the deck and bottom and maximum at the neutral axis.

Wrinkles or cracks at a 45-degree angle to the lines of stress characterize shear failure. Usually the wrinkles appear first in the side plating near the neutral axis—the horizontal plane about which the effective ship's structure is evenly distributed. Shear failure is unlikely to carry through to catastrophic failure. It can usually be tolerated in all but very large ships.

Bending stress (σ), either tensile or compressive, in the deck or bottom is determined by dividing the bending moment (M_y) by the section modulus (SM) of the section:

$$\sigma = \frac{M_y}{SM}$$

The section modulus, a property of the particular section, is defined by the quantity and arrangement of material in the section. Section modulus is tedious and difficult to calculate unless the information for the particular ship is already entered into a computer and can be edited to allow for missing or ineffective structure.

Classification society rules define minimum section moduli for ships in terms of the ship's principal dimensions and hull coefficients. In the absence of definitive information for the specific ship, these minimum section moduli are a good starting point for salvage calculations.

Section modulus requirements vary among the societies. The equations and method given below are those appearing in the American Bureau of Shipping rules and may be applied in salvage work with the understanding that they provide only ballpark figures.

For a ship under 200 feet (61 meters) long:

$$SM_{min} = k \times B \times (C_B + 0.05)$$

where: SM_{min} = minimum section modulus amidships in inches-squared-feet or centimeters-squared-meters
k = a constant from table 3-9; intermediate values may be determined by interpolation
B = beam in feet or meters
C_B = block coefficient (always at least 0.60)

TABLE 3-9.

L (feet)	*k*	*L (meters)*	*k*
40	5.0	12	31.6
60	7.7	18	48.9
80	10.5	24	66.5
100	14.0	30	88.5
120	17.4	36	110.3
140	21.9	42	137.9
160	27.3	48	170.8
180	34.4	54	215.3
200	43.3	61	279.7

Ships between 200 and 295 feet (61 and 90 meters) long fall into a gray area where there is no easy and convenient formula. Instead, the total bending moment must be determined and the minimum section modulus calculated by:

$$SM_{min} = \frac{M_t}{K}$$

where: M_t = total bending moment of the ship as further defined below
k = a constant, a function of length, also defined below

M_t is the sum of still water and wave bending moment and is defined as:

$$M_t = 10^{-3} C_1 L^{2.5} B (C_B + 0.5) + C_2 (C_B + 0.088) L^2 B (0.0172L + 3.653) k_B$$

where:
In U.S. units:

$$C_1 = 0.312 + \frac{360 - L}{2090}$$

$$C_2 = 6.45 \times 10^{-4}$$

and in SI units:

$$C_1 = 60.6 + \frac{110 - L}{4.71}$$

$$C_2 = 22.7 \times 10^{-2}$$

$$k_B = 1.0 \text{ for } C_B \geq 0.80,\ 1.4 - C_B \text{ for } 0.64 \leq C_B < 0.80$$

These equations are not a joy to use. At lengths greater than 295 feet (90 meters) the sun breaks through and the equation for minimum section modulus is a little more workable:

$$SM_{min} = 0.01kL^2B\,(C_B + 0.70)$$

where: k is a function of L given by the expressions in table 3-10

TABLE 3-10.

U.S. UNITS	
Length	*k*
295 to 984 feet	$0.01441 \times (10.75 - (\frac{984 - L}{328})^{1.5})$
984 to 1148 feet	0.155
1148 to 1400 feet	$0.01441 \times (10.75 - (\frac{L - 1148}{492})^{1.5})$
SI UNITS	
Length	*k*
90 to 300 meters	$10.75 - (\frac{300 - L}{100})^{1.5}$
300 to 350 meters	10.75
350 to 427 meters	$10.75 - (\frac{L - 350}{150})^{1.5}$

In normal naval architectural practice the bending moment is made up of a still water bending moment and a wave-induced bending moment. The latter accounts for the uneven distribution of buoyancy in a seaway. In salvage, a different situation occurs. Salvors may have the option of avoiding heavy seas and the increases in bending moment that accompany them. They may be able to move the ship entirely within protected waters where they can allow a still water moment near the maximum with little or no allowance for wave-induced bending moment. Accordingly, their interest is in the maximum bending moment the ship can withstand in her existing condition, not the normal still water and wave-induced bending moments. An exception occurs when the damaged vessel must be steamed or towed large distances in the open sea. In these cases, allowance must be made for the seas and wave-induced bending moment that can be expected during the transit.

The maximum bending moment normally occurs at or near amidships. Midships section scantlings are designed to keep stresses in the section well below the yield point of the steel. Loss of effective structure through damage reduces the section modulus and raises the stress in the section. Loss of enough structure can lead to bending failure.

Bending loads simultaneously cause tensile and compressive stresses that can cause ships' hulls to fail. Tension and compression failures have very different characteristics and results. Steel fails in tension when it is loaded beyond its yield point—a characteristic of the particular steel. At stresses below the yield point, steel is elastic; that is, the deformation is proportional to the stress and the material returns to its original shape when the load is reduced. Above the yield point, the stress grows very little and deformation increases greatly as load increases. When the ultimate strength is reached the material fails catastrophically. Steel is considered to have failed at the yield point although it has not fractured and can carry some additional tensile load. If a section has passed the yield point and the load decreases, it returns to its normal elastic behavior, although with some permanent deformation. After catastrophic failure, the section is discontinuous and thus can carry no load. Steel fails in compression by buckling. In-and-out wrinkles perpendicular to the load, normally athwartships in a hull girder, characterize buckling. Buckled structure can carry considerable tensile loads, but cannot accept compressive loads without additional failure. Buckled plating and structural members should be cropped out and replaced, not straightened. Straightening, particularly under salvage conditions, is unlikely to produce useful results.

Ships' structures have safety factors specified by their classification societies. Safety factors may be specified indirectly. For example, the American Bureau of Shipping rules specify maximum permissible bending stresses as a function of length. The safety factor based on these stresses and the yield point averages about 1.5 for ordinary strength shipbuilding steels. In salvage, the safety factors are seldom as large as in normal service. A reduced safety factor is permissible, but each situation must be examined on its own merit to determine how much reduction and how much increased risk of failure is acceptable.

Many load calculators define acceptable loads as maximum allowable bending moment and shear force. These figures assume an intact ship. In a damaged ship part of the section modulus is ineffective, so the bending stress is higher for the same bending moment. The allowable bending moment must be calculated for the actual conditions.

Initial structural analysis for salvage includes development of the shear force and bending moment curves and the calculation of actual section moduli and shear areas. These calculations establish both the conditions that actually exist and a baseline for further calculations. Maximum allowable bending moment is calculated by multiplying the allowable bending stress by the section modulus:

$$M_a = \sigma_a \times SM$$

Similarly, the maximum allowable shear may be calculated by multiplying the allowable shear stress by the shear area. Allowable bending moment and shear force should be plotted with shear force and bending moment curves.

Flooding, grounding, or other unusual loading conditions may move the point of maximum bending moment well away from midships and the point of maximum shear force may be moved well away from the quarter points. When damage is not at the point of maximum bending moment, bending stresses may rise to dangerous levels by the local loss of section modulus. Stresses should be checked wherever there is significant structural damage. Normally, the midships scantlings carry through the midships 6/10 of the ship's length and decrease forward and abaft of these points where the bending moment normally is less. If a section outside the midships 6/10 length is a potential high stress point, the actual scantlings should be employed in the calculations. Where the actual scantlings are not available, an estimated reduction of intact section modulus of 10 to 20 percent is suitable for salvage work.

The initial salvage survey (Chapter 6) determines damage to structural members. Later surveys refine this knowledge. Holes, tears, cracks, and buckled structure are obvious. Some of the signs of structural damage are more subtle. These include:

Paint, coatings, rust, or scale newly cracked or flaked from structural members.

Plating, particularly inner bottom plating, upset, with the lines of internals showing plainly.

Misalignment of fixed structures and installed equipment.

Cracked welds.

Long shallow indentations in plating.

Changes in any of the above.

The severity of damage in any section depends upon its location. Damage far from the neutral axis in the deck or bottom causes a more serious loss of section modulus than *apparently* more serious damage near the neutral axis.

Usually strength analyses consider all damaged plating as missing. In fact damaged plating does have some residual strength that can carry loads and contribute to section modulus. The residual strength in tension and compression for the same damage may be very different. Engineers experienced in dealing with damaged structure should make estimates of residual strength. These estimates are apparently made by black magic or divine inspiration. Not even the most experienced engineer could lay out his procedure.

Salvors should be aware of the types of damage that are particularly dangerous. These include:

- Buckled structure that has no ability to carry compressive loads.
- Heavily indented or dished plating that cannot carry compressive loads as well as straight plating can, but can carry a full tensile load.
- Cracking. Cracks can grow under tensile load. Athwartships or vertical cracks are more likely to grow than fore and aft cracks. Diagonal cracks are also dangerous because of the fore and aft component.
- Fire-damaged plate that may have lost most of its strength from wastage and characteristics changes. It often has no effective residual strength in either tension or compression.

Salvors have two choices in dealing with strength problems. The first is to make temporary repairs to restore the lost strength. Such repairs should emulate as nearly as practical the original structure. They should tie into sound structure in a way that does not introduce problems worse than they solve and also should be the minimum repairs that the situation calls for. The second alternative is to manage weight and buoyancy in a way that reduces shear force and bending moments to acceptable levels. Management of weight and buoyancy for bending moment control must be compatible with management of the same quantities for stability, trim, and ground reaction control—not always an easy task.

4

TYPES OF CASUALTIES

Ship casualties may be grouped, generally in two categories. There are casualties that require immediate action to control and mitigate the damage, and there are those for which a somewhat leisurely approach is possible. Most casualties—hull and machinery damage, strandings and wreckings, collisions, and fires and explosions—belong to the first category. The second category consists entirely of sinkings and capsizings. In almost all casualties there is a threat of environmental damage. This factor complicates the situation far beyond the hazard to the casualty itself, and increases the need for prompt action in any case.

Seldom is a casualty either straightforward or simple. Analyses of casualty statistics show that the most common category is hull or machinery damage. This type of casualty makes up more than 30 percent of the total; the vast majority occur in the open sea.

Strandings and wreckings make up about 20 percent of the total casualties. Simplistically, strandings are groundings ending in salvage while wreckings result in constructive or actual total losses. The initial determination of whether a ship is to be salvaged or declared a constructive loss goes beyond the technical aspects and cost of refloating. The decision considers such factors as cost and probability of success in the transit to a repair yard and the cost of repairs. In a remote area distant from salvage services and repair yards, a simple stranding may turn into a constructive total loss.

Strandings or wreckings are the most likely type of casualty to cause a pollution incident. Tankers are not necessarily the most serious threat, primarily because there are many more dry cargo ships—all carrying bunkers—at risk. Some dry cargo ships, notably containerships, have bunker tanks with as much pollution potential as a cargo tank in a product carrier. Whatever the source, a minor casualty-related oil spill in an area of particular environmental sensitivity may turn into an operational and financial nightmare.

Ship collisions, the third most common type of casualty, make up about 15 percent of the total. The incidence of collisions depends upon the traffic density, the difficulty of navigation, and the effectiveness of vessel traffic systems. As expected, a large percentage of collisions occurs in ports and on approaches. The threat of a pollution incident resulting from a collision is high, particularly with the trend toward carrying bunkers in wing tanks.

The percentage of fires and explosions is almost the same as that of collisions. Almost equal numbers of fires and explosions occur in ports and at sea. A few more occur at sea.

About 7 percent of casualties are collisions with objects other than ships—piers, bridges, etc. Not surprisingly, most of these casualties occur in and near ports.

Even in these days of excellent and usually instantaneous communications, unexplained disappearances with the ship listed as missing make up 6 percent of ship casualties. These events, whatever they may be—founderings, structural failure, fires, sea monsters, or falling off the edge—require little in the way of salvage services. Only founderings in a port area with a known location require salvage services. There are several of these casualties annually, but they are not true "missing ship" events.

The remaining casualties are war losses, a type that varies widely in number and importance with geography and political climate.

Casualties also are classified by ship type, size, and age, but these characterizations are primarily of interest to academics and insurers. Some inferences may be drawn, particularly concerning age, but casualty occurrence has more to do with the nature of the population at risk than any other factors. The types and sizes of ships serving or transiting an area influence the types of casualties occurring there. For instance, a casualty other than a VLCC or a fishing vessel in Prince William Sound, Alaska, would be remarkable. The characteristics of the particular area and the dangers to navigation presented influence the types of casualty in or near shore—witness the history of collisions in the lower Mississippi River.

The types of casualty determine the salvage actions; thus, salvors have an intense interest in types of casualties and the distribution of the types in their operations area. On the other hand, they have no interest in the cause of the casualty. Their only interest lies in the "as is" condition of the ship and how it can be seen safely afloat or the wreck removed. Their understanding of the condition of casualties and their ability to evaluate the situation's advantages and dangers and to develop a plan to see the ship safely afloat set salvors apart from other seamen.

The remainder of this chapter discusses in general terms the types of casualties, the factors that set them apart from each other, and the general requirements for salvage. Later chapters give more detail on the specific problems and techniques of salvage.

Hull and Machinery Damage and Rescue Towing

The most common type of casualty is machinery breakdown at sea or hull damage from storms, cargo shifts, or another cause that leaves a ship unable to maneuver and places both the ship and cargo at risk (figure 4-1). Loss of maneuverability close inshore can lead to grounding. Breakdowns require taking the ship under tow at sea and towing it to a port.

Fig. 4-1. This ship, listing heavily and afire, is a classic candidate for a rescue tow.

Rescue towing, a classic type of salvage, is an exercise in towing seamanship. This book does not purport to be a treatise on towing. Several specialized works, some of which are listed in the Bibliography, address the subject expertly. A few general comments on the particular art and science of rescue towing are included. This book does not address the subject of shiphandling for rescue towing, as others better qualified than the author have done so well.

Two features of rescue tows set them apart from the point-to-point tows: picking up the tow at sea, and getting under way in the open sea with a short scope of towline. Rescue towing requires passing towline and getting under way slowly to reduce dynamic loads on towline while at short scope and handling a difficult tow at sea. Rescue towing is at the far seamanship end of the seamanship-engineering spectrum of salvage operations. The engineering for rescue towing must be complete in the design of the towing vessel and of the towing connection.

In the right conditions any ship or tug can take another ship in tow. The effectiveness of a ship or of most tugs is much less than that of a rescue tug properly sized and equipped for the work. A tug should be designed, crewed, and equipped specifically for taking a distressed ship in tow, controlling her, and towing in all sorts of weather. Unfortunately, optimization for particular tasks limits versatility, so there are few, if any, operating tugs purpose-designed and built for rescue towing. The economics of tug operation prohibit not only specialized design, but also operation that limits a large expensive tug to a particular task.

Rather than fruitlessly lamenting the scarcity of tugs for a very specialized service, let us examine some requirements for rescue tugs and the best way to fill these requirements. In doing so we can consider how some more prosaic multipurpose tugs may handle the task.

A rescue tug should be fast to reach the casualty before the situation deteriorates beyond recovery and before another tug gets there first. In rescue towing, as in war, early arrival with the most appropriate force (apologies to General Nathan Bedford Forrest, CSA) usually takes the day. The requirement for high speed must be balanced against high bollard pull, as the two are not normally compatible requirements for the same propeller. The weight given to each depends upon the geography of the area and the type of shipping expected. If it is more important to reach the casualty ahead of weather and the competition, high speed is the obvious choice. If the casualties are likely to be very large ships, the choice is weighted in favor of bollard pull. Controllable pitch propellers allow a broader spectrum of propeller performance, but require compromises with optimization for either purpose. Ideally, a rescue tug can (1) Arrest the leeward drift, (2) Turn the distressed vessel to reduce environmental effects, and (3) Make headway with the largest ship she is likely to see in her area of operations. The question of offering salvage services without enough bollard pull to control the casualty is not simple. Depending upon the geography and the weather, the tug may influence the drift of the casualty enough either to keep her in safe waters or to put her in greater danger. The decision requires expert evaluation of the conditions at the site and realistic appraisal of the tug's capability. In the worst case, the casualty may drag the tug about.

Excellent maneuvering systems are a feature of tugs. A rescue tug working close in to a casualty must maneuver with authority and hold position at or very near zero speed.

There are several other features desirable in rescue tugs:

A high degree of seaworthiness and sea kindliness will allow her to proceed at best speed in bad weather and ride well enough with dry enough decks that men can make the tow connection. A deep hull form and heavy displacement help in this regard. The deep hull also allows room for a large fuel capacity adding range and endurance, while the heavy displacement adds inertia to the tug end of the towing system.

The hull must be large enough to have sufficient volume for storing and rigging the towing connection and spares and for carrying other equipment.

Interior passageways through which crews can reach towing and other equipment during transit will reduce exposure on weather decks.

It is too much to expect the afterdeck of a tug—the working deck—to stay dry. The deck should drain rapidly and have oversized freeing ports. Bulwarks should protect the crew against boarding seas while remaining low enough to work over. Some tumble home protects bulwarks from impact damage when the tug is working alongside other ships.

The tug crew must be large enough to allow putting workers aboard the casualty to help in damage control, and in making the connection to make the hookup aboard the tug while maneuvering the vessel. The crew should be trained in the specific methods of rescue towing and, preferably, experienced in the work.

The towing connection is a vital part of any tow, for it is the means of transmitting the towing force of the tug to the towed vessel. There are four requirements for the towing connection. It must be:

1. Strong enough to transmit the maximum towing load.
2. Elastic enough to absorb dynamic loads without failing.
3. Made up of components that match and work together as a system without introducing unexpected weaknesses into the system.
4. Of such a size that it can be manhandled on both the tug and tow.

Classification society rules specify towing connection breaking strength as a multiple of static bollard pull. They do not specify elasticity.

A tug picking up a tow at sea is necessarily close to the tow in sea conditions that are far different from the sheltered waters where most tows start. When starting the tow and overcoming the inertia of the towed ship, the dynamic loads in the towline induced by the sea are large and the ability of the short scope of towline to respond to the dynamic loads is relatively low. The ability of the towline to accept dynamic loads varies with its elasticity or springiness. A towline may be thought of as a series of springs, each with a different spring constant or stiffness. The towline components respond to sudden increases in load by stretching. The amount each stretches, thus the portion of the increased load it absorbs, is proportional to its stiffness. The load accepted by a component depends upon both the characteristics and *volume* of the towline, as elasticity is expressed as a percentage elongation. A short towline is less elastic and less able to accept dynamic loads than a long one. An all-steel towline generally does not have sufficient elasticity to accept large dynamic loads at short scopes. Several means introduce an elastic response into the towing system. A common means of introducing elasticity into the system is to insert a fiber spring with high stretch into the system. The strength characteristics of the fiber line must match the main tow hawser to avoid introducing a weak link in the system. In some areas, where geography prohibits fiber rope springs, a chain with high inertia may substitute for the fiber spring.

Constant tension winches or winches that pay out under load also contribute to towing system dynamic response. Only the U.S. Navy and some Russian tugs have constant tension towing winches in regular service.

Any of several methods may provide the system elasticity. The choice depends to a large extent on personal or corporate choice, and local practice that often varies with geography. The design details of towing systems can be argued at length without resolution. At the end of the day, it becomes obvious that the details do not matter very much as long as the system's parts are engineered to work together, its strengths and limitations are known by the operators, and it is operated only under the conditions for which it is designed.

Tension members—wire and fiber ropes and chain—lose strength rapidly when bent around fairleads, bitts, rollers, and other surfaces. Work following the *Amoco Cadiz* casualty established that a minimum ratio of bending surface diameter to chain bar diameter (D/d ratio) of 7 is required to maintain chain strength. The strength decrement of wire rope also depends upon the sharpness of the bend as measured by the D/d ratio. The loss of strength does not depend upon the amount of the bend; a bend of a few degrees causes as much loss of strength as a much greater bend. Bending surfaces for the large wire rope in towing hawsers must often be quite large—too large to fit aboard the tug. A reduction in bending strength in towlines is acceptable if the operator understands that towline breaking strength is reduced and that the risk of towline failure under heavy dynamic loads is increased.

Towing is hard service, rescue towing doubly so. First-class, top-of-the-line, well-cared-for equipment throughout, and adequate numbers of thoroughly trained and experienced crew, improve the chance of operational and commercial success.

En route to the casualty the tug master should try to get some basic information to help determine the best course of action. The minimum information he should ask for is:

- The casualty's position.
- The weather at the casualty's position.
- The direction and speed of drift.
- A description of the vessel, her present capabilities, and the extent of the damage.
- Drafts, trim, and heel.
- A description of any towing connections or emergency tow rigging aboard the casualty.
- The nature of the cargo, how it is stowed and divided, and the chance of its shifting.

The status of pollutants and hazardous cargo and the chance of spillage or discharge.

Destination and port facilities required.

Crew on board.

Armed with this information the tug can begin her approach and choose the procedures for hooking up. Upon arrival the master observes the set and drift of the ship, assesses the total scope of the work, and positions himself to make the connection.

To help with either damage control or with the connection, salvage crew must board the casualty. Even when the ship's crew is aboard, salvage crew on board the casualty can save considerable time and frustration in making the connection. Not the least advantage is that the salvage crew speaks the same language with the same terminology as the tug crew. The boarding crew should carry intrinsically safe hand-held radios.

Transferring personnel at sea is seldom easy. Helicopters are an excellent way to transfer salvage crew when the casualty is within helicopter range. Helicopters can operate in almost any weather in which transfers are possible. Personnel also can be transferred in the more traditional ways, by bringing the tug alongside to leeward or in small boats. When the casualty's crew is aboard, they can aid the boarding by rigging pilot ladders or other access. Crews that abandon casualties in a great hurry seldom think of leaving ladders or other means of access for a salvage crew. Some salvors have suggested that permanent ladders or grab irons on the side would be desirable and practical. It is too much to expect owners to provide such things for the convenience of salvors they are sure they will never need. More practically, grab irons would be far too convenient for the pirates who operate in many seas.

Making the connection is a matter of the tug master's shiphandling skill and the efficiency of the crews on the towing deck and the casualty. The first line may be passed by line-throwing gun, rocket, helicopter, or by grappling for a floating line. If the casualty is without power for handling the towline, a graduated messenger line may be passed from the tug, led fair to the towing fitting and bullnose, and returned to power on the tug. The messenger then hauls the towline on board the casualty (figure 4-2).

Many ships, especially tankers and liquefied natural gas carriers, carry rigged emergency towing chains and pendants conforming to IMO Resolution A535[13] or local requirements. They may pass these rigs to the tug. Other types of emergency tow rigs or insurance wires are also found. These systems are intended for easy connection to the tug's towing system to eliminate one of the most difficult and time-consuming steps of an emergency tow.

Ships and barges with emergency towing rigs and insurance wires normally have the end connected on deck, usually to a quick-release type bracket such as the

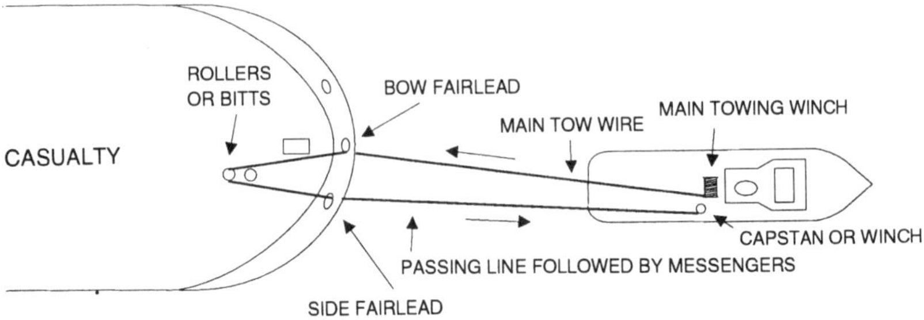

Fig. 4-2. Passing a towline to a ship with no power

Smit bracket (figure 4-3) or an SPM fitting. In other cases the fittings are available on deck with nothing connected. The fittings are sized for chain appropriate to the size of the vessel. Some vessels have nonstandard brackets requiring special fittings or shackles. Alternatively, the towing connection may be made up to a chain stopper on suitably located bitts on the casualty's deck.

A chain chafing pendant at the casualty end of the tow rig reduces the problem of chafe between the towing medium and the casualty's structure. When there is no rigged emergency towing gear, it is usually better for the tug to provide the chain, despite the need for handling its weight, than to use the casualty's anchor

Fig. 4-3. Smit bracket

chain. The choice to rig the latter should be made only if the casualty's master is satisfied in going with one anchor and the anchor is securely stopped off in its hawse before the chain is broken.

There is seldom much choice of fairleads for the towing connection. It is a matter of making do with what is available in either centerline or near-centerline fairleads. Centerline fairleads are preferred. The ideal fairlead is in a direct line from the connection point and has a generous radius in all directions to reduce bending stresses in the chafing chain during the tow.

Beaching

For a ship in danger of sinking near a benign coast, beaching is attractive. A beached vessel is secure against capsizing and sinking but faces the dangers of a stranded vessel. A beaching has a great advantage over a stranding in that the beaching ground and beaching conditions are selected rather than being the result of an accident.

Routing to the beaching ground is chosen so that, should the casualty sink en route, the wreck is not a more severe problem than the floating casualty. Areas to be avoided include harbor approaches, dredged cuts, channels, restricted waterways, environmentally sensitive areas, and hard ledges where the ship might ground, then break. If practical, the ship should be kept in water shallow enough so she may be raised if she sinks, but not so shallow that she grounds. Once these formidable conditions for routing have been met—or the least unsatisfactory route chosen—the salvor can go about selecting a beaching ground.

The selection of a beaching ground is not only technical and operational—it is also political. Administrations with jurisdictions over harbors and coasts may be more than slightly apprehensive about the political and environmental implications of a damaged ship intentionally being put aground on their coast. These authorities should be contacted as soon as beaching is a possibility and wooed with tact and diplomacy. Their cooperation can be invaluable; their opposition fatal to the operation. Governments have refused permission for damaged vessels under the control of competent professional salvors to enter their waters, resulting in the eventual loss of the casualty.

The ideal beaching ground:

- Is firm, but without rock or coral outcrops.
- Slopes gently.
- Is free of strong, longshore currents and heavy surf.
- Is sheltered from heavy weather.

Such a beach reduces the damage to the ship on grounding, keeps the loss of stability that accompanies groundings within acceptable limits, allows emergency work to go forward, and simplifies the retraction. A muddy seabed, such as is often present in estuaries, is desirable for beaching heavily listing ships. The list can usually be brought out quickly.

Some tide in the beaching area is desirable and may be very helpful during refloating. The best time to ground is at high water or on the ebb so the vessel settles slowly onto the sea floor. The vessel should not be driven hard ashore but should be handled slowly and carefully with the ship under positive control. If practical, an anchor should be set to seaward and upcurrent and streamed while approaching the beaching site.

There is seldom much choice of trim for a ship damaged severely enough for beaching. A ship trimmed by the stern may touch first in either the bow or stern,

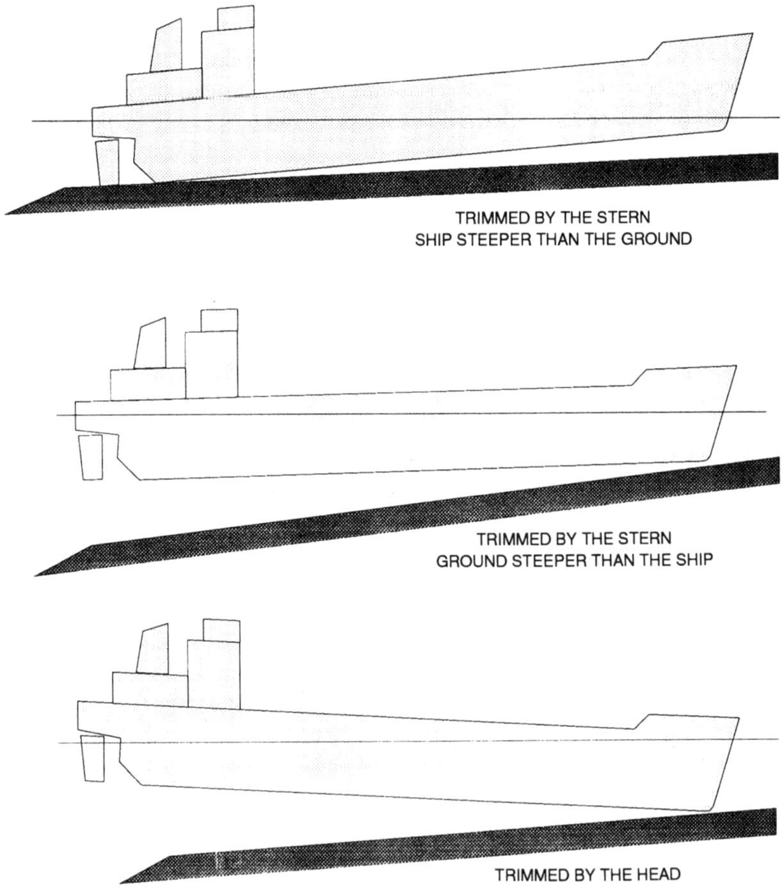

Fig. 4-4. Beaching

depending on the relative slopes of the sea floor and the ship's bottom. A ship trimmed by the head always grounds bow first.

Once she is beached, the ship must be secured in her position by ground tackle laid out both seaward and shoreward and ballasted down, but not so hard that she damages herself.

Strandings and Wreckings

Strandings—unintentional groundings—are one of the most common types of marine casualty. Navigational error, loss of ability to maneuver, anchor drag, or any of myriad other incidents may cause a stranding. No matter what circumstances lead to the stranding, an intelligent assessment of the casualty's situation is a necessary preliminary to seeing the ship safely afloat. In the engineering-seamanship equation that governs salvage operations, strandings require a large proportion of seamanship.

A stranded ship is in a position her designers, builders, and operators never intended. She is immobile and is not floating freely, supported by the sea, but is supported partly by the ground. Thus, she is subject to loads and forces very different from those she sees in normal service. The weight on the ground acts like removal of the same weight at the keel, reducing the ship's stability. High local loads may occur in the way of ground contact, particularly on hard sea floors. These high loads can result in rocks breaking through the skin and impaling the ship. The normal pattern of shear forces and bending loads changes from the pattern the hull is designed to accept. The ship, the sea, the sea floor, the weather, the location, and the conditions of the stranding combine to define the problem and to point the way to its solution. Although the sea and the way the ship lies may prevent accurate determination of many qualities, as much of the situation must be defined as is possible. These situations require that salvors use their technical knowledge, experience, and judgment to estimate the most probable situation. Figure 4-5 illustrates three stranding casualties in very different circumstances.

The complexity of the stranding often depends upon the action taken immediately after the casualty to secure the ship and to define her condition. There is a shock factor in a casualty that militates against prompt and effective response by crews not thoroughly trained and drilled in damage control. The effects of the casualty may become more serious while the crew is "getting it together." Salvors often arrive to find that the crew has done little or nothing to relieve the casualty and may have aggravated the situation. The author was once told by the master of a stranded vessel that he had spent forty years learning how not to go aground and that no one had ever told him what to do if he did. "Nobody told me" is a sorry excuse, but one that serves many, as prompt, effective action is rare. Most books on seamanship have sections on stranding, and excellent advice is offered in *Peril at Sea and Salvage*.[1] For the sake of avoiding redundancy the information is not re-

Fig. 4-5. The three vessels shown above are all stranded but in very different circumstances. The tanker that appears to be lying normally is hard aground on flat sand bottom and is in little danger. The small cargo vessel, although high and dry, is relatively safe and salvageable, while the fish processor broached on a sandy beach is in extreme danger and broke in half shortly after this photograph was taken.

peated here. Well thought-out and prompt action taken after stranding can make the difference between a simple salvage operation and a lost ship.

The crew of a stranded ship should use the time before the arrival of salvors to stop pollution, stabilize the ship as she lies, and assess the condition of the ship. Information that will be useful in developing the salvage plan includes:

Location.
Existing and forecast weather.
Heading, both true and relative to the sea.
Drafts before and after stranding.
Soundings all around the ship.
Trim and heel.
Spillage of cargo or bunkers.
Known damage and flooding.
Bunkers and cargo on board.
Ship's power and ability to maintain it.
Damage control and spill prevention measures taken.

The crew should organize their information and pass it to the salvors when the latter arrive on board. In reality, the probability of getting a good assessment of the ship's condition from the crew is low.

When a ship runs or is driven ashore, momentum carries her up the beach or reef where she is supported partially by her buoyancy and partially by the ground. She loses buoyancy. The amount of buoyancy lost is exactly equal to the weight supported by the ground. The weight on the ground, known as the ground reaction, is of major importance in strandings. Ground reaction is not a constant throughout the operation but alters with any change to weight or buoyancy. At all times the weight of the ship is equal to the sum of the buoyancy and the ground reaction, that is:

$$\text{Weight} = \text{Buoyancy} + \text{Ground Reaction}$$

When the weight is equal to the buoyancy (ground reaction is 0), the ship is afloat. At the other extreme, when the weight is equal to the ground reaction (buoyancy is 0), the ship is high and dry. Most strandings fall somewhere between the two extremes.

Tide is a major factor in strandings. When the tide rises, a stranded ship, unlike a floating one, does not rise with it. Instead, buoyancy increases and ground reaction decreases. On the ebb, the reverse takes place: ground reaction increases and buoyancy decreases. Large ships stranded in locations with great tide range may experience ground reactions on the ebb that cause the weight of the ship to collapse its structure. This damage may not be visible or otherwise apparent to salvors. It may occur on any tide cycle.

Unless the ship happens to strand at a tide station, tides will vary from the nearest tabulated values. The importance of this difference is a judgment call by the salvage master. Local tides may be measured with a homemade tide gauge. Comparison of measured with predicted tides allows establishment of correction factors that, when applied to the tabulated tides, give predictions for the salvage site. A baseline tidal condition must be selected for all calculations to assure consistency. The actual baseline chosen is unimportant, but it must be used consistently, as it provides the basis for determining conditions at other states of the tide.

It is often convenient in salvage operations to know the height of tide during the interval between high and low water. A reasonable approximation may be made by assuming the tide follows a regular cosine curve between high waters and by applying the formula:

$$H_n = \frac{R}{2} \times \cos n\theta + (\frac{R}{2} + H_{lw})$$

where:

H_n = height of tide at n hours before or after high water (feet or meters)

n = hours before or after high water (decimal hours)

θ = tidal phase angle for one hour (180/T degrees or π/T radians where T is the duration of the ebb or flood tide)

R = tide range (feet or meters)

H_{lw} = height of low water relative to datum (feet or meters)

During the salvage operation, salvors manage the ground reaction by varying the weight and buoyancy of the ship and using the other methods described in Chapter 8. The ground reaction may be decreased for refloating or increased to hold the ship securely on the ground until preparations for refloating are complete.

Two qualities of the ground reaction are important: the size and the distribution. At least five means for determining or estimating the size of ground reaction exist. Distribution is not estimated easily. No method of estimating ground reaction distribution has been verified empirically. There are two common theories. The first distributes ground reaction evenly along the grounded length and takes the center at its geometric center. A second distributes ground reaction triangularly from zero at the end of the ground reaction to a maximum at the forward end of the grounded length (assuming a bow on grounding). In a triangular distribution, the center of ground reaction lies one-third of the grounded length from the forward end. A trapezoidal distribution with some portion of the ground reaction distributed evenly and the remainder triangularly is probably likely. The center of a trapezoidal distribution lies at some point between one-third and one-half the distance from the forward end. Exact location depends upon the proportions of the two parts.

The most accurate and most complex method in general use for quantifying ground reaction involves determining the weight and buoyancy distribution in the ship and taking the difference. Excellent accuracy can be obtained with this method by assembling data from the lightship weight distribution, the loading plan, and the curves of sectional area (Bonjean's curves) or lines plan. Hand calculation can be time consuming. A portable computer or programmable hand-held calculator is invaluable for initial calculation and for what-iffing proposed salvage actions.

The weight and buoyancy curves are developed by the methods described in Chapter 3. The waterline of the ship as she lies aground is the basis of the buoyancy curve. Unlike the condition for afloat ships, the areas under the weight and buoyancy curves are not equal. The area under the buoyancy curve is less than the area under the weight curve. The difference is the ground reaction.

The four other means of estimating ground reaction are approximate and give no indication of the center of ground reaction or distribution. The results are usually accurate enough for salvage work. All the methods do not work with all strandings, primarily because vessels trim and rise bodily unpredictably upon grounding. Two of the methods take both trim and bodily rise into account, but require an estimate of the center of ground reaction and may give inaccurate results if that estimate is greatly in error. One of the other methods considers only trim; the other only bodily rise.

The center of flotation, the center of gravity of the waterline plane, appears in many of the equations that follow. While floating, ships trim about the center of flotation, grounded ships do not. The trimming point of a grounded ship is defined by the conditions under which the ground supports the ship. The ground may support the ship so it cannot trim; so it trims around a clearly defined point, such as a pinnacle; or trims about some point that cannot be determined precisely. In the equations that follow, center of flotation refers only to the center of gravity of the waterline plane of the stranded ship.

Most of the methods of estimating ground reaction require knowledge of the ship's drafts before grounding. This information may not be readily available but can be estimated by applying known weight changes to the drafts taken before sailing and recorded in the ship's deck log. The accuracy of drafts after grounding may not be better than ± six inches (15 cm). To reduce the effects of inaccurate draft reading, drafts for salvage calculations are best determined by the mean of quarter means method described below.

Calculation of the mean of quarter means draft involves the seven steps shown in table 4-1:

TABLE 4-1.

1. Measure the drafts forward, aft, and amidships on both the port and starboard sides. This step gives six observed values: T_{fs}, T_{fp}, T_{as}, T_{ap}, T_{ms}, and T_{mp}.	
2. Take the mean of the observed forward drafts.	$\frac{T_{fs} + T_{fp}}{2} = T_f$
3. Take the mean of the observed after drafts.	$\frac{T_{as} + T_{ap}}{2} = T_a$
4. Take the mean of the observed midships drafts.	$\frac{T_{ms} + T_{mp}}{2} = T_{mo}$
5. Calculate the midships draft by taking the mean of the forward and after drafts.	$\frac{T_f + T_a}{2} = T_{mc}$
6. Take the mean of the calculated and observed midships drafts.	$\frac{T_{mo} + T_{mc}}{2} = T_m$
7. Take the mean of the quantity calculated in Step 6 and the observed midships draft.	$\frac{T_{mo} + T_m}{2} = T_{mm}$

The result is the mean of quarter means draft. The additional accuracy of this simple calculation that is more difficult to explain than to do is well worth the time.

The simplest method of estimating ground reaction is by the change in displacement method. The difference between the displacements of the vessel before grounding and after grounding is the ground reaction. Displacement before grounding is determined by entering the curves of form or the displacement scale on the capacity plan with the drafts before stranding. Displacement after grounding is obtained by entering the same sources with drafts after grounding. The drafts after grounding should be referenced to whatever standard tidal datum is in use. Trim corrections to displacements, normally found on the curves of form or capacity plan, should be applied.

$$R = W_{afloat} - W_{aground}$$

In a very simple, frequently used, and reasonably accurate method, the difference in the mean drafts before and after grounding is multiplied by tons per inch (tonnes per centimeter) immersion. This method considers only bodily rise, but is very good for an initial estimate and accurate when the change in trim before and after grounding is 1 percent of the ship's length or less.

$$R = \delta T_M \times TPI$$

Where change in trim is the principal effect of the grounding (trim is more than 1 percent of the ship's length) and the center of ground reaction can be estimated, the change of trim method gives a good estimate of ground reaction. The method determines the force necessary to cause the change of trim only.

$$R = \frac{MT1 \times t}{d_r}$$

where: t = total trim in inches
d_r = distance between the center of ground reaction and the center of flotation in feet

The change of draft forward method is appropriate in any stranding where the center of the ground reaction can be estimated. The method takes ground reaction as a weight removal at the keel that causes both bodily rise and trim. Unfortunately, the calculation results in an equation that is horrible to look at and difficult to use and has two additional drawbacks. The equation is very sensitive to the location of the center of ground reaction. It seldom works well unless:

1. The casualty is grounded on a well-defined position, or
2. The center of ground reaction is "adjusted," often several times, to obtain a realistic result.

$$R = \frac{TPI \times MT1 \times L \times (T_{fb} - T_{fa})}{(MT1 \times L) + (d_r \times d_f \times TPI)}$$

where: T_{fb} = draft forward before stranding
T_{fa} = draft forward after stranding
d_f = distance between the forward perpendicular and center of flotation in feet
d_r = distance between the center of ground reaction and the center of flotation in feet

Four of the five methods give approximate results that are often accurate enough for salvage. All methods have their pitfalls; accordingly, ground reaction should be calculated by at least two methods and the results compared. The results should be reasonably close.

Weight management is critical in dealing with a stranded ship. Weight changes in the ship—additions, removals, and shifts—may increase or decrease the ground reaction depending on the location of the weight and the ability of the ship to trim. The governing principle is the equality of weight and the sum of buoyancy and ground reaction. In all cases:

$$\text{Weight} = \text{Buoyancy} + \text{Ground Reaction}$$

If the ship is supported along so much of her length that she cannot trim, buoyancy cannot change. Thus, any addition or removal of weight results in an equal change in ground reaction.

$$\delta\ \text{Weight} = \delta\ \text{Ground Reaction}$$

If the ship is grounded on a pinnacle or along part of her length that allows trim, additions, removals, or shifts of weight will cause a trimming moment. The ship's trimming causes a change in buoyancy that in turn causes a change in ground reaction. For instance, in a ship grounded forward, moving a weight aft causes the ship to trim by the stern and gain buoyancy. Ground reaction must decrease because the ship gains buoyancy and the total weight is constant. Note that a ship may be supported so she will trim in only one direction.

A grounded ship may have a point where weight can be added or removed without changing ground reaction. This point, the neutral loading point, is the point where the buoyancy change of the parallel sinkage or rise caused by the weight change is exactly balanced by the buoyancy change of trimming. Weight changes that cause the vessel to trim away from the ground decrease ground reaction while those that trim the vessel toward the ground increase ground reaction. A weight *removal* on the far side of the neutral loading point from the ground *increases* ground reaction. A weight *addition* at the same point *decreases* ground reaction.

The neutral loading point can be located by:

$$d_n = \frac{MT1 \times L}{TPI \times d_r}$$

where: d_n = distance from the center of flotation to the neutral loading point

The neutral loading point concept applies exactly to a ship grounded on a pinnacle and free to trim by either end. It is less precise, undefinably so, for other grounding situations. In general, if the center of ground reaction is less than one-ninth the length of the ship from the center of flotation ($d_r < L/9$), the neutral loading point lies off the ship and has no practical significance. The value of the ratio depends upon the fullness of the ship's waterline. When the waterline is full, d_r must be smaller to drive the neutral point off the ship. The formula:

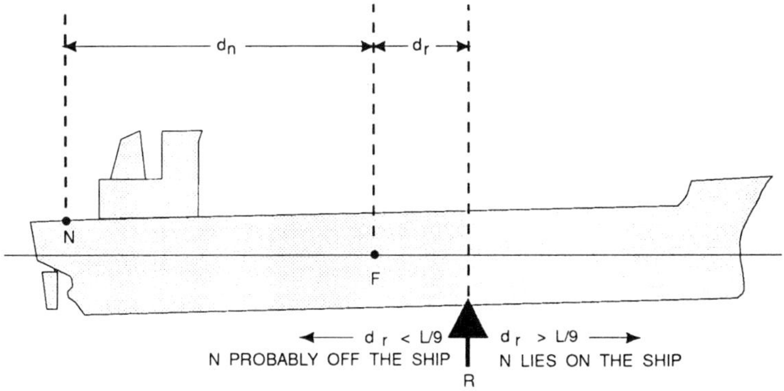

Fig. 4-6. Neutral loading point

$$d_n = \frac{C_{WP} \times L^2}{14 \times d_r}$$

gives an approximate result and may be quicker to apply.

Tide has a major effect on strandings. A stranded ship does not rise and fall with the tide as she does when she is afloat. Instead the waterline and the buoyancy and ground reaction change as the tide ebbs and floods. The significance of the change depends upon the range of the tide. It can be tremendous. *Exxon Valdez*, when she stranded on Bligh Reef in Prince William Sound, had a ground reaction near 25,000 tons. At low water the ground reaction increased to over 50,000 tons, enough to cause the ship's structure to crush.

If the tide range is great and the ship strands near low water, she may refloat on the rising tide or she may become so lively that she is in danger of broaching or being driven farther ashore.

For ships unable to trim, the change in ground reaction caused by a change in tide is exactly equal and opposite to the buoyancy gained or lost. If the ship can trim freely, the following equation applies:

$$\delta R = \frac{R_t \times TPI \times MT1 \times L}{(TPI \times d_r^2) + (MT1 \times L)}$$

where: Rt = tide range in feet

All other quantities are as defined previously.

If the ship cannot trim fully, the change in ground reaction will be less. The change in ground reaction with tide can be estimated by observing draft changes with tide and proportioning them to the changes that would occur with the ship supported on a pinnacle at the estimated center of ground reaction.

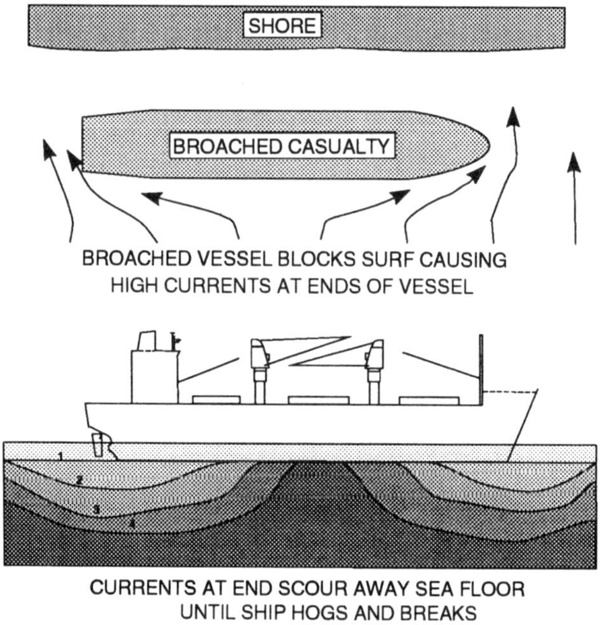

Fig. 4-7. Broaching and scouring. Courtesy of U.S. Navy.

Scouring away of bottom materials by currents is a particular danger to ships stranded on some types of sea floors. Dangerous scouring occurs in two different sets of circumstances. The most common occurs when the ship broaches and goes broad to the sea on a sandy sea floor. Seas and surf encountering the ship are deflected along her side, then sweep around the ends at high velocity, carrying away the sea floor material supporting the ship. The scouring continues working away the sea floor on both ends until very high hogging stresses develop and the ship breaks. Figure 4-7 illustrates this process. In the worst circumstances, only a few hours need elapse between broaching and breaking. It is good practice to prevent broaching by laying ground tackle to seaward, ballasting hard down, or holding the casualty perpendicular to the beach with tugs. If the ship has broached, an extraordinary effort should be made to turn her end on to the sea and to hold her there.

While the end-on position is more secure from scouring than the broached position, there is danger when longshore currents are present. Longshore currents may scour away the sea floor either from under the ends or from under amidships, eventually causing failure in hog or sag. The danger is greater when the tide range is great.

A flat-bottom ship hard aground on a flat sea floor is not going to capsize. No matter how unstable she is, she is constrained by the sea floor. Soft sea floors take the shape of the ship—as do hard sea floors to a lesser degree—and restrain the ship. A ship aground on a pinnacle free to incline in either direction is at the other end of the spectrum—she is in a dangerous situation, one made more dangerous by a large tide range and ground reaction changes.

Ground reaction affects stability in the same way as removing an equivalent weight at the keel. There is a virtual rise in the height of the center of gravity so that the effective height of the center of gravity is:

$$KG_1 = \frac{KG \times W}{W - R}$$

where: KG_1 = the effective position of the center of gravity
KG = the pre-grounding height of the center of gravity
W = the pre-grounding displacement of the casualty
R = ground reaction

The second effect is the change in the metacentric height (GM). Metacentric height decreases in a stranded ship because:

The moment of inertia of the waterplane decreases, as does the underwater volume, usually decreasing the metacentric radius (BM).

With the loss of draft upon grounding, the center of buoyancy moves downward, decreasing the height of the center of buoyancy (KB).

With a lower KB and a reduced BM, the height of metacenter (KM) is lower ($KM = KB + BM$).

The higher KG results in a lower metacentric height (GM).

$GM = KM - KG$.

The reduction in metacentric height may be enough for the metacentric height to become negative. The casualty may then list until restrained by the sea floor or until reaching an angle at which she is stable. A ship grounded on a pinnacle or a fine-lined ship aground only at the bow is likely to capsize.

When the tide range is great, the conditions that contribute to instability are enhanced, and the possibility of capsizing is greater. These situations demand special attention to weight management, free surface, and free communication. Most importantly, a ship that is stable when she is afloat may be unstable while she is aground. The transition from unstable but restrained to stable and afloat must be as quick as possible.

Ships should not be refloated when unstable afloat, except in emergencies or when measures are taken to prevent their capsizing.

Some ships, notably some Asian fishing vessels, are notoriously unstable while aground and take frightening lists during refloating. Stability in these vessels is often difficult to calculate with reasonable accuracy. The only available course of action is to close up every opening, remove all free surface and as much high weight as practical, and refloat them rapidly.

Distribution of weight and buoyancy in a floating ship determines the load on the hull. Grounding introduces a third factor—ground reaction—that changes the load curve. The loading with ground reaction may result in dangerously high bending moments. Types of groundings where high bending moments are probable include groundings on shelves with one end in deep water and grounding with either the ends or middle supported and the other unsupported. Bending moment changes with changes in the tide, with the greatest moments occurring at low water. Large hogs and sags indicate high bending moment. Hog, sag, and changes may be measured by establishing a level line and measuring the distance from the line to the deck.

Collisions

As previously noted, collisions are the third most common type of casualty. The most frequent result of collision is massive hull damage. Fire and sometimes disastrous explosions may follow collisions, especially when cargoes are volatile. Following collisions the most important need is usually damage control to limit the effects of fire and flooding. To be effective in a damage control role, salvors must be on scene quickly after the casualty and must have with them equipment that is easily handled and effective. Usually, the damage control organization aboard merchant vessels is loose and knowledge scant. The situation is normally better on ships carrying LNG, LPG, and other dangerous, specialized cargoes. The shock factor in casualties discussed above in connection with strandings seems particularly prevalent following collisions. It is extremely rare for salvors arriving aboard collision casualties to find that the crew has been actively and successfully controlling the damage.

Salvage damage control actions following a collision stabilize the ship, extinguish fires, limit flooding, and assure adequate stability.

Collisions often set up situations where beaching the ship is necessary to prevent loss of the ship or to allow time to secure it properly. Considerations for beaching a ship following a collision are identical to those discussed earlier in this chapter.

Fire and Explosion

Fires and explosions are just about as frequent as collisions and require the same type of emergency damage control action. Fires often result from collisions; experience in the tanker war in the Arabian Gulf showed that a result of a weapon's strike on a ship is almost always fire.

Even minor shipboard fires are dangerous, as they may become conflagrations if fire fighting is not both prompt and proper. Many shipboard fires start in the engine room or accommodation. Oil fuels most engine room fires initially. This produces hot fires that spread rapidly and require immediate attack with powerful fire-fighting weapons. Because accommodation blocks usually are directly above machinery spaces, engine room fires often spread to accommodations. In accommodations, fire loads can be very high as the rows of rooms and long passageways that form traps quickly fill with heavy smoke, and furnishings, outfit, and personal belongings provide fuel. Ventilation systems and cableways transmit fire and smoke throughout the accommodation.

Cargo fires have different characteristics that depend upon the type of cargo and the ventilation arrangements and fire-fighting arrangements in the hold. Fires in containers, chemical carriers, bulk cargoes of coal, liquefied gas carriers, and tankers require specialized fire-fighting techniques. Marine fire fighting is a very specialized subject; adequate treatment of the subject is well beyond the scope of this book. The reader is referred to the several excellent works on marine fire fighting listed in the Bibliography. Only a few comments on fire fighting as a salvage action are provided here.

Salvors frequently find themselves facing ship fires. Some salvage operators maintain special fire-fighting teams that can respond by air to ship fires anywhere in the world; others respond to fires regionally with all-purpose salvage crews. All members of salvage crews should have basic marine fire-fighting training and most should have advanced training. Although all salvors are trained as fire fighters, some are inherently more capable than others. Fire fighting, like diving and other dangerous occupations, requires a particular psychology. No stigma should be attached to any salvor who is uncomfortable with an attack role in fire fighting.

There are two aspects of salvage fire fighting that differ from the fire-fighting response of shore-based fire departments. The motivation of salvage fire fighters is very different from that of their shore-based counterparts. Shore-based fire departments strive first to extinguish the fire, while salvors put more emphasis on saving the value of the ship and its cargo. For salvors, there is often a matter of choosing between saving the ship or the cargo—a choice predicated solely on worth.

An aggressive attack with the sole purpose of extinguishing the fire quickly not only risks destroying the value of the ship and cargo, but also may endanger the ship. And therein lies the second difference. Shore-based fire departments neither need nor have an understanding of ships or the marine environment. On many occasions, often against sound advice to the contrary, they have poured water into a ship until the sinking or capsizing of the ship extinguished the fire. The wreck removal efforts that have resulted have been some classic jobs. When ships that are afire sink, the casualty response may change immediately from fire fighting to environmental protection, if the ship contains bunkers or cargo that may leak. Figure 4-8 shows such a case.

Cargo fires, particularly in "drugstore" chemical carriers or in ships carrying general cargo in containers or break bulk, are especially dangerous. Normally be-

Fig. 4-8. Aggressive fire fighting aimed only at extinguishing the fire caused this ship to sink and a straightforward fire to turn into a lengthy and costly wreck removal.

nign cargoes may form noxious, toxic, or explosive mixtures or products of combustion. A marine chemist and/or a fire engineering consultant should be employed whenever there is a question about possible fuels or products of combustion.

The history of and potential for horrific fires in the offshore oil industry have led to the establishment of three classes of fire-fighting standards for ships. The fire-fighting technique for platform fires is drenching with huge quantities of water. Accordingly, the classification society Fi-Fi standards are based on water delivery and monitor throw, standards that are not always suitable for shipboard fire-fighting systems. Nevertheless, these standards are upon us and are summarized in table 4-2.

Three classification societies, the American Bureau of Shipping (ABS), Lloyd's Register of Shipping (LR), and det Norske Veritas (DNV), have additional requirements (see table 4-3).

SINKINGS AND CAPSIZINGS

Ships sink because they lose all or most of their buoyancy; they capsize because they lose stability. Often, the loss of buoyancy follows hull damage that complicates the salvage of the ship. Ships may sink completely and be supported totally by the sea floor; or sink so they lie partially above the surface but are supported by the sea floor, or are supported partially by their buoyancy. Capsized ships may come to rest in positions that vary from listed slightly to completely inverted. Refloating

TABLE 4-2.

FI-FI STANDARDS				
Class	I	II		III
No. of monitors	2	3	4	4
Capacity of monitors (m^3/hr)	1200	2400	1800	2400-2500
No. of pumps	1-2	2-4		2-4
Total pump capacity (m^3/hr)	2400	7200		9600-10000
Length of throw (m)	120	150		150
Height of throw (m)	45	70		70
Fuel oil capacity (hrs)	24	96		96

TABLE 4-3.

ADDITIONAL REQUIREMENTS			
	ABS	LR	DNV
Water spraying system for Fi-Fi-I	Yes	Yes	Yes
High-expansion foam generator for Fi-Fi-II and III		Yes	Yes
Foam monitors for Fi-Fi-III	Yes		Yes
Hose connections for Fi-Fi-II and III	Yes	Yes	Yes
Fireman's outfit	Yes	Yes	Yes

sunken ships requires a larger proportion of engineering in the engineering seamanship equation than do most other types of salvage.

Salvage of sunken and capsized ships usually is attempted only when the ship lies in shallow water. The loss of value of the ship and the cost and complexity of raising any but small vessels from deep waters makes deep salvage uneconomical. It is common to remove sunken wrecks that block waterways or port facilities. The removal of these wrecks often requires refloating by the same methods that would be used to salvage the vessel. Disposal rather than return to service follows refloating.

Ships are raised by recovering internal buoyancy lost in sinking or by externally placed buoyancy—lift bags or pontoons—or by mechanical lifting. Ships raised by recovering buoyancy will usually float before all the lost buoyancy is recovered. Water remaining on board can cause dangerous free surface and problems with both transverse and longitudinal stability, list, trim, and hull strength. Raising sunken ships requires not only recovery of the buoyancy lost in sinking but also control of the distribution of buoyancy to obtain satisfactory stability, trim, and strength. Chapter 9 discusses in detail recovering and controlling buoyancy.

Stability of Sunken Ships

The basic principles of ship stability presented in Chapter 3 apply to sunken ships. The stability of a sunken ship resting upright on the sea floor depends to a large extent upon whether the main deck is above the surface, partially submerged, or completely submerged. Stability of the sunken ship depends upon the stability of the ship when she sank—a ship that was unstable when she sank remains unstable unless steps are taken to make her stable. Removing or moving weight during the salvage operation changes the location of the center of gravity and affects stability. The most important determinant of the stability of a sunken ship is whether the main deck is above the surface, or partially or completely immersed.

A completely submerged ship has no waterplane and no metacentric radius (BM). The stability of the sunken hull depends totally upon the center of gravity (G) lying below the center of buoyancy (B) so that a righting moment develops when the ship inclines. Note that, except in submarines that carry permanent ballast to keep the center of gravity low, the center of gravity of most ships lies above the center of buoyancy while the ship is afloat. The size of the righting moment is the product of the distance between the two centers and the displacement of the ship.

As soon as the deck breaks the surface there is a waterplane and consequently a metacentric radius. The metacentric radius may be small because of the small waterplane, consequent small transverse moment of inertia (T), and large underwater volume (V). The center of buoyancy of the hull may be quite high. As the ship is raised, three important things happen: the metacentric radius increases as the waterplane's moment of inertia increases, underwater volume decreases, and the center of buoyancy moves downward. Ideally the ship remains stable during the raising process and while afloat. If the center of gravity (G) has moved upward during the salvage operation, or if a large free surface develops, the ship may become unstable. It is possible that the conditions of the salvage preclude instability. Positive actions must be taken to control the ship and prevent capsizing.

An effective way to prevent capsizing is raising one end while keeping the other end firmly in contact with the bottom. The sea floor restrains the ship from capsizing until sufficient waterplane to assure positive stability develops. A theoretically positive metacentric height during raising of the grounded end does not guarantee stability. Assuring positive stability requires thorough preparation and attention to detail. As much free surface as practical should be removed from the

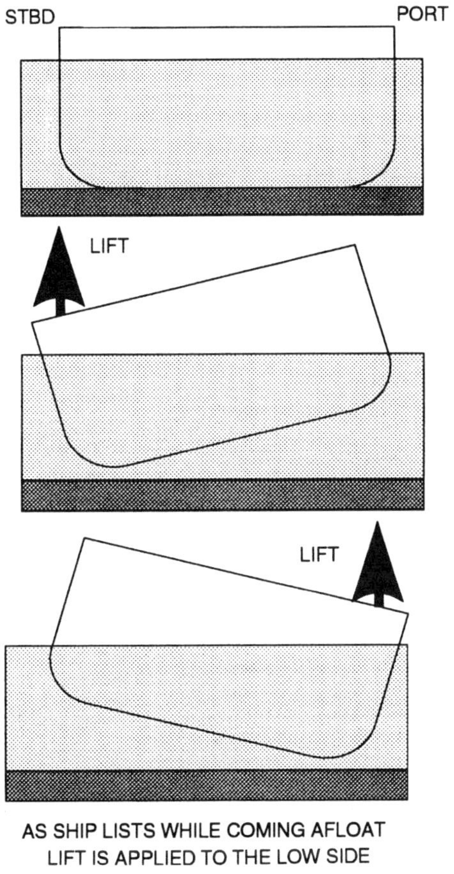

Fig. 4-9. Stabilizing a sunken ship with cranes or tackles

floating end. Low spaces, such as double bottoms, may be flooded and pressed up to eliminate free surface and to keep the center of gravity low. Removing topside weights and moving easily portable weights to places low in the ship also help keep a low center of gravity.

Instead of raising the second end of the ship, it may be kept in contact with the bottom and hauled into shallow water as it is lightened. Hauling gear ashore—winches, linear pullers, or heavy vehicles—or tugs may move the ship.

A force producing a moment counter to the upsetting moment can keep the ship upright. The force must be applied so it can counter an upsetting force that heels the ship to either side. The magnitude must be variable. Figure 4-9 shows typical methods of rigging for application of forces with either cranes or horizontal pullers.

In shallow water, ships have been kept or hauled upright by purchases rigged from their mastheads to anchor points ashore or on the sea floor. Moorings should hold the ship securely, as there is a tendency for ships to kick out from under the force of the masthead purchases.

Barges or pontoons rigged tightly alongside the ship as outriggers perform two functions. They effectively increase the waterplane of the combination and they produce a righting moment from unbalanced buoyancy as the barge on the low side submerges and the barge on the high side rises. The barges must be rigged tightly enough to function as a unit with the ship; if they are free to render, the barges provide only buoyancy and do little or nothing for stability.

The longitudinal and transverse stability of completely submerged ships are identical and dependent solely upon the relative positions of the centers of gravity and buoyancy. As with transverse stability, a sunken ship is longitudinally stable when the center of gravity lies below the center of buoyancy. Two factors make ships with any significant length of waterplane unlikely to capsize longitudinally (plunge) during salvage operations:

1. The length is cubed in the equation for the longitudinal moment of inertia of the waterplane.
2. Length increases rapidly as the ship rises.

The exception, sometimes a very serious one, occurs when transverse subdivision is limited and the longitudinal free surface effect is large. The danger is primarily a combination of a large trimming moment caused by the mass of water that rushes to the low end, and downflooding caused by the trim. Reduction of longitudinal metacentric height is a secondary effect. Keeping one end of the ship in contact with the bottom, stabilizing the ship with external forces, or eliminating large free surfaces by building temporary transverse bulkheads can reduce the hazard.

The most effective bulkheads—and the quickest and easiest to build—are steel or wooden forms filled with concrete pumped in under pressure. The forms should be wider at the bottom than at the top to help move the center of gravity downward.

Strength of Sunken Ships

Sunken ships often have heavy damage with impairment of local, longitudinal bending, torsional, and shear strength. This damage and loss of strength can affect the salvage methods employed.

Local damage seldom leads to catastrophic failure and is usually easy to take care of. Frequently a simple doubler suffices. Patches placed to restore the watertight envelope, particularly steel plate patches welded into the ship's structure, often also serve to restore local strength.

Local cracks in high-stress areas can be dangerous, particularly when cracks are perpendicular to lines of stress and can grow under load. These cracks must be stop-drilled and patched using the methods described in Chapter 9. Welding cracks or plugging cracks to stop leakage does not eliminate the danger of crack growth. Cracks that are not likely to grow under stress may be left alone.

Longitudinal and shear strength of sunken ships are evaluated as described in Chapter 3 for intact ships. If a survey or strength analysis of the hull as it lies shows that failure has occurred or is probable during any phase of the salvage operation, the hull must be reinforced. Any but the simplest reinforcement must be designed by naval architects and installed in strict compliance with their specifications. Failure to follow the specifications may result in inadvertent installation of a fix that is more dangerous than the original damaged condition.

When the hull girder has failed by longitudinal bending, either the deck or bottom plating will be buckled. Buckled structure, characterized by athwartship in-and-out wrinkling of the plate, has very little capacity to carry compressive load, but can carry almost its design tensile load. The ship can be loaded to insure that the buckled plating is in tension throughout the salvage operation.

Ships fail in tension by breaking at the section of highest bending stress. Obviously, the broken section is discontinuous and cannot carry either tensile or compressive loads. Rigid members—structural sections, plate, stiffened plate—tied into the ship's structure to carry tensile and compressive loads may bridge tensile failures. Strict rules discussed in more detail in Chapter 9 govern the installation of rigid bridges. Rigid bridges should be designed and installed under the supervision of a naval architect or salvage engineer whenever possible.

There is often a temptation to tie failed structural sections together with easily handled flexible members such as chain and wire rope. Although this technique has worked, it is normally a bad idea and one suitable only in desperation when no other option is available. The technique is extremely difficult to execute properly and safely and results in a bridge that can carry only tensile loads.

Shear failures are dealt with most simply by adjusting weight and buoyancy to keep shear stresses in the failed area to 25 percent of the design value. Shear wrinkles deform failed plate, making it difficult or impossible to effectively increase the shear area with doublers.

The most difficult case of hull damage is that in which massive hull damage—such as that from a tank explosion in a tankship—leaves the ship in one piece but with a plastic hinge. There are three options to be considered in developing a salvage plan:

1. Cutting the wreck in two and floating each section separately.
2. Refloating by zero-stress/zero-shear techniques.
3. Piecemealing.

When each section can be made watertight and stable, cutting the wreck and handling each section separately is attractive and practical. Different techniques may be used for each section, but the salvor is faced with two or more "ships," neither of normal form and each with characteristics that can be established only by real-time engineering analysis. Sectioning and refloating ships in separate sections can be a very costly and time-consuming process.

Zero-stress/zero-shear techniques are often the most efficient means of floating a badly damaged sunken ship. With these methods the ship is loaded so that throughout the operation both bending moment and shear force are zero at the hinge or at the section where the hinge is likely to develop. Detailed engineering analysis and planning with careful attention to hull loading are mandatory for these techniques to be successful.

Piecemealing is a low risk of failure option that is always open, but depends upon the availability of equipment to cut the ship and lift the pieces.

Capsized Ships

Salvage of capsized ships usually requires detailed engineering analysis and planning. Most capsized ships are raised in two distinct phases: first righting, then refloating. The two operations may flow into one another, in that work to begin refloating may begin as soon as the ship is upright enough for crews to work aboard.

Ships are righted by parbuckling—creating a moment that acts to overcome the moment of weight that holds the ship in place. Both weight and righting forces act about a point that depends upon the shape of the ship but generally lies near the turn of the bilge. Dredging under the ship can move the pivot point and shorten the moment arm of the weight. To keep the righting force as low as possible, the distance through which the force acts should be:

As short as possible for the moment of weight.
As long as possible for the righting moment.

There are many ways and combinations of ways to develop righting forces, some of which are illustrated in figure 4-10. One of the most common methods is to build head frames such as those shown in figure 4-11 to extend the distance through which the righting force acts. Head frames must attach to the hull so they transmit the loads to and spread them throughout the ship's structure effectively. Pulling devices should be equipped with line tension measuring devices to permit adjusting the load as the ship rotates.

The ground under the pivot point must have sufficient bearing strength to support the ship during righting. If not, the ship may sink into the ground or slide. Laying in gravel, crushed coral, rock, or shell in areas of high ground pressure can stabilize soft ground.

The force that rotates the ship may have a horizontal component that tries to move the ship in the direction of the force. A restraining force must be rigged in the opposite direction. The system for restraining the ship against sliding should be rigged to augment, never to act against, the desired rotation of the hull. Restraining tackle also may be required to prevent the ship from moving fore and aft.

When the hull is to be scrapped or sunk, it may be practical to float the ship upside down like the one shown in figure 4-12. Upside-down refloating is most appropriate when the ship is capsized to more than 90 degrees in deep water and the bottom can be made airtight easily. Because the center of gravity of the in-

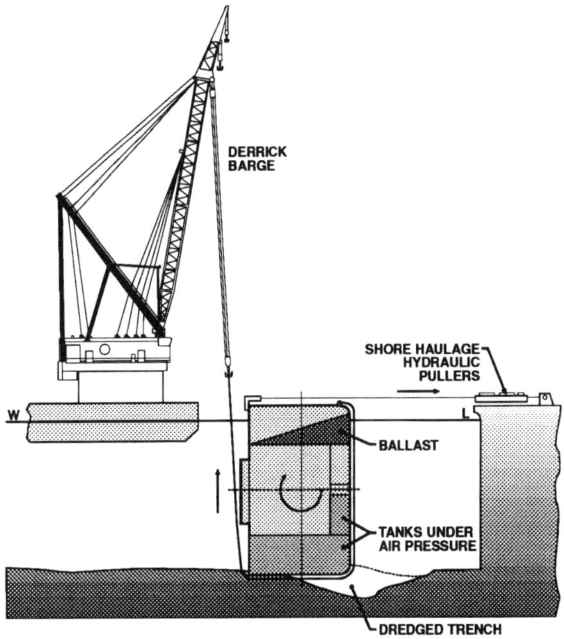

Fig. 4-10. Combination of methods to right a ship.
Courtesy of U.S. Navy.

verted ship usually lies below the center of buoyancy, the ship will be inherently stable—probably more stable than when floating upright. Top hamper and superstructure often are removed before refloating and moving the wreck to decrease the navigational draft of the ship.

Soil Effects

When the weight of the ship on the sea floor exceeds the bearing strength of the soil, the ship sinks into the sea floor until it rests on firmer soil or the soil compacts enough to support the weight. The ship rests in a hole. In cohesive soils, suction holds the ship in the hole and increases lift forces.

Decreasing freeboard is an excellent indicator that a sunken ship is sinking into the sea floor. If the situation warrants prediction of the total depth of sinkage, core samples should be taken and analyzed by a soils laboratory. A ship may sink far enough into the bottom to immerse the main deck and cause loss of stability and downflooding.

The ship may also sink into a hole through the effect of scouring by normal currents or currents induced by the ship changing current patterns. A ship lying in

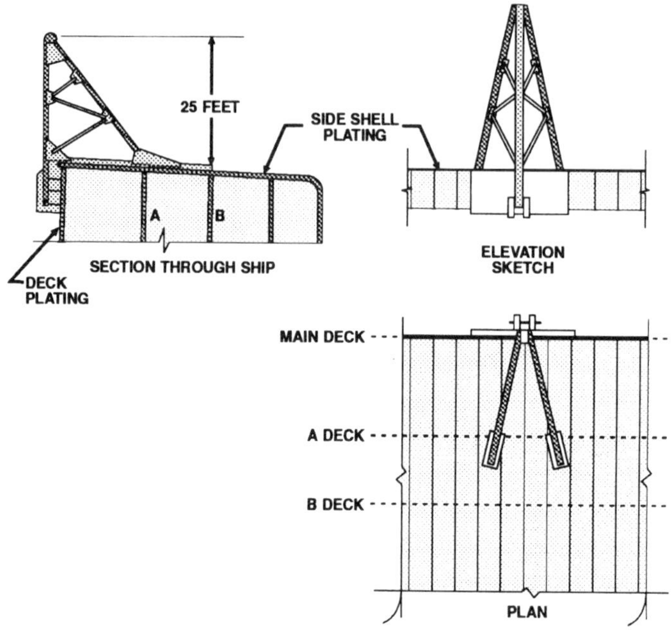

Fig. 4-11. Typical parbuckling head frames. Courtesy of U.S. Navy.

Fig. 4-12. This ship, raised upside down, is being prepared for disposal.

a hole must be lifted clear of the hole when being moved. The shape of the hole usually prevents keeping the ship in contact with the bottom during the move. Ships with critical stability can be stabilized with external forces during the move as described previously. Tidal lifts and mechanical lifts that have a limited range must be able to lift the ship far enough to clear the hole. If it is not practical to do either of the above, a slope may be dredged and the ship moved along it. The latter is expensive.

Scouring also may erode support from portions of the hull and allow development of hull stresses that can lead to hull girder failure. Salvors can do little to prevent scouring other than building barriers to deflect currents. They should be alert to the presence and potential effects of scouring. When scouring is likely, frequent underwater inspections by divers or video help define conditions and changes.

Changes in hull deflection, a sign of changing stresses, can be measured by setting up a long, level reference line, then regularly measuring and recording distances from the line to the deck or skin of the ship.

Cohesive soils create suction that increases the force required to lift ships from them. The amount of suction and the breakout force vary with the sea floor soil and the amount of time the object has been on the bottom. The total upward force required always includes the weight of the object and the weight of soil that sticks to the object. Time and force work together to break objects out of the sea floor. There are two basic methods of breaking objects out of the sea floor:

1. Applying a large force for a short time.
2. Applying a smaller force for a longer time.

Whichever method is chosen, the results are very difficult to predict with any accuracy. The large number of variables and unknowns precludes accurate engineering solutions and generally results in overestimating breakout forces. Large forces may result in the ship breaking out suddenly and beginning to rise out of control. Patient and steady application of a force slightly greater than the calculated lift force usually overcomes suction and allows the ship to rise under full control.

Salvors in the field have several methods of breaking suction and reducing the time and force required to start the ship out of the sea floor. The methods are analogous to breaking a fence post out of its hole by wiggling it or slamming it with a sledge. For ships the methods include:

Dragging a hogging line under the ship.
Breaking down soil layers with a water jet or air lance.
Lifting ends of the ship alternately.
Rocking the ship with a lateral force.
Applying and relaxing lift forces.

Silt is insidious. It enters sunken ships through every possible opening in quantities that defy belief. Silt is weight that adds to the weight to be accounted for during refloating. Additionally, silt and mud are dense fluids that have free surface and reduce stability. The weight of silt and mud varies with the type of soil, averaging about 100 pounds per cubic foot in water. Silting continues as long as the ship lies on the bottom. It can be reduced by blocking major inflows; otherwise removal efforts may be like shoveling sand against the tide. Air lifts, water jets, jet pumps, and clamshells are effective for removing silt and mud. If the silt contains a large proportion of water, slurry pumps or ordinary centrifugal pumps can pump it effectively. Silt is abrasive and wears away pump impellers and casings.

If the ship is lifted or made light and moved along in contact with the sea floor, the slope of the sea floor determines the distance the ship may be moved. A hydrographic survey of routes and set-down locations by a side-scan sonar or simply a fathometer and wire drag determines slopes, locates obstructions, and saves the time, cost, and aggravation of unpleasant surprises.

5

OIL AND HAZARDOUS SUBSTANCES

All ships carry oil and some hazardous substances as cargo, ship's stores, or both. These materials present special problems in salvage. The size and type of problem depend upon the nature of the materials, the quantity, the conditions of carriage, and materials they contact during the casualty or the salvage operation.

The special problems that hazardous substances present led to the development of international design, construction, and equipment codes,[1] operating practices, and safety guides for ships and terminals. When the ship becomes a casualty, the integrity of the systems and safety measures that control the hazards and contain the materials may be breached or destroyed. It may be impossible to follow specified operating procedures precisely. Despite less than ideal conditions, the casualty and its cargo must be salvaged or removed. Salvors may have to rig special handling and other systems either to carry out the salvage operation or to remove a real or perceived hazard.

Various codes now classify more than 50 percent of the cargoes carried by sea as dangerous.[2] A salvor must immediately identify hazardous substances present in a casualty, rate their potential effect on salvage operations, and determine what activity may take place without risk of harm to the salvage crew and the environment. The safety of the salvors and the salvage operation may depend upon the proper identification and handling of the hazardous substances. Preventing or reducing environmental damage from hazardous substances can increase the salvage award. With the myriad materials considered hazardous, salvors cannot be across-the-board experts. The salvors' role is to recognize potentially hazardous situations and to know when to call in experts.

There are several potential types of exposure from hazardous materials in salvage operations that salvors should be prepared for. Chemicals may appear in gaseous, liquid, or solid states and may enter the body by inhalation, skin absorption, injection, or through a cut or other wound. Contaminants can cause localized damage at the point of contact or a systematically toxic effect that affects distant parts or the whole body. The nature and severity of the effect depends upon the chemical, its concentration and entry route, the total exposure, and the individual's physiology and metabolism. Effects of some chemicals may be immediate while others may be delayed or may dull an acute sense, as hydrogen sulfide does with the sense of smell. Chemicals can be found not only in chemical tankers but also in containerships and other types of dry cargo vessels. Incompatible chemicals properly carried in isolated stowage may mix during a casualty to form a material that may present a new chemical, fire, or explosion hazard.

Hazardous and benign gaseous substances may displace oxygen or combine with oxygen in closed spaces causing a localized oxygen deficiency.

Biological hazards can occur from some cargoes but are more likely on ships in which sewage has accumulated or been improperly disposed of. Ionizing radiation is likely only in nuclear propelled ships, ships carrying nuclear weapons, and ships with nuclear materials in their cargoes.

Ship's officers can provide rudimentary information about the presence and locations of hazardous substances and the basic safety precautions. All ships carrying hazardous materials as cargo are required to carry the papers identifying these cargoes by United Nations (UN) number on the bridge. (The UN number is a four-digit identifying number assigned to particular cargoes by the United Nations.) The UN number can be used to enter several publications that give additional information on the cargo, its hazards, and exposure limits for personnel working around the cargo. Manufacturers or shippers of hazardous materials or specialized government services can provide additional information on handling the material. There are three references on hazardous materials that every salvor should have available and know how to use. These references are: The U.S. Coast Guard's *The Chemical Data Guide for Bulk Shipment by Water*, the U.S. Department of Transportation's *Emergency Response Guidebook*, and the NIOSH *Pocket Guide to Chemical Hazards*.[3] With some very valuable, very dangerous cargoes, such as liquefied natural gas (LNG), owners may have special emergency response teams to help salvors.

The United States and some other countries have specific training requirements for working around hazardous materials. These requirements and their applicability to a particular situation change frequently. Wise salvors are aware of the requirements in their principal area of operations and are prepared to look into these requirements when preparing to work in countries in which they do not normally operate.

HAZARDOUS SUBSTANCE CLASSIFICATION

There are several codes for classifying hazardous substances. The most widely used in the maritime world is the International Maritime Dangerous Goods (IMDG) Codes, produced by the International Maritime Organization (IMO). This code divides hazardous substances into nine classes. While different national authorities vary the classifications, the IMDG Codes are a good basis for salvors working internationally. The full text of the IMDG Codes should be a part of every salvor's library. That library should also include local codes that govern local or national shipping in the salvor's area of operation, such as 49 CFR 171 covering the transportation of hazardous materials in the United States.

Class One—Explosives

Explosives and pyrotechnics are solids, liquids, or mixtures capable by chemical reactions of producing gas at temperatures and pressures and a speed that damage the surroundings. Regulations for carrying explosives are extensive and quite detailed. Manufacturers, shippers, and officers of ships carrying explosives usually follow precise storage, declaration, marking, and reporting requirements. Fortunately, few casualties involve explosives. When they do, the salvor is well advised to call in experts in the characteristics, storage, or handling of the particular type of explosive.

Salvors are most likely to encounter large quantities of explosives in military shipments, arms sales, or returning ordnance. Shipments of ammunition include not only the explosives in warheads, but missile propellants and initiating devices. Governments owning or chartering vessels for ammunition shipments or shipping ammunition or explosives normally provide expert advice and technicians. Lacking government assistance, ordnance manufacturers may be called upon for help.

Products, such as some types of fertilizers, that are not normally explosive may become so in casualties when the storage conditions change or the material becomes wet. Salvors dealing with these cargoes should have the services of a marine chemist from the outset.

Class Two—Gases: Compressed, Liquefied, or Dissolved under Pressure

Class Two substances are flammable, combustion-supporting, corrosive, toxic, or noxious gases. They also can be permanently gaseous, liquefied, dissolved, or refrigerated. Rupture of a containment vessel can allow gas to escape with some force and create considerable excitement. Escaping concentrated cryogenic liquid may flash into larger or more concentrated clouds of gas than conventional gaseous products can produce. Gases in the atmosphere may disperse or hang around in all the wrong places—including some quite remote, but always downwind from their source. Alternatively, they may remain within the ship and form an explosive, suffocating, or toxic atmosphere. Liquefied fuel gases—natural gas, MAPP gas, petroleum gas, and ammonia—may form a cloud that can be both explosive and toxic. Factors that influence the hazards presented by gases include: leak rate, physical properties of the gas, ventilation conditions, etc. If time permits, specialists may define the size of the problem. Often, it is best simply to move the casualty well to seaward away from population centers and keep her there until the gases have dispersed or salvage action has stabilized the situation.

Class Three—Flammable Liquids

The IMDG system defines flammable liquids as having a closed cup flash point of less than 61 degrees Celsius (142 degrees Fahrenheit). The U.S. Coast Guard has a more definitive system that divides petroleum products into two categories: flammable and combustible. Eighty degrees Fahrenheit (26.7 degrees Celsius) is the dividing point. Flammable products, those with the lower flash points, are subdivided into three grades (A through C). The basis of the subdivision is their Reid Vapor Pressure (rvp) or the pressure generated when material is heated to 100° F. (37.8° C.) in a closed container. Combustible products are divided into two grades (D and E) by their flash points. Grade D products have flash points between 80° and 150° F. (26.7° and 65.6° C.), Grade E products above 150° F. (65.6° C.). Both Grade D and E products are relatively safe to handle under normal and casualty conditions. Table 5-1 summarizes the classification of flammable liquid products.

TABLE 5-1.

CLASSIFICATION OF FLAMMABLE LIQUIDS		
Grade	*Flash Point*	*Reid Vapor Pressure*
A	80° F. or below	14 psia or above
B	80° F. or below	8.5 to 14 psia
C	80° F. or below	below 8.5 psia
D	80 to 150° F.	not applicable
E	above 150° F.	not applicable

Flammable liquids present the greatest hazard in a casualty when they have both a low flash point and high volatility. When these liquids leak in a closed space, they can produce an explosive atmosphere. Flammable liquids that mix with water, as methyl alcohol and acetone do, present no flammability problem when spilling into the sea. On the other hand, liquids immiscible with water may float and present the risk of a slick fire. The danger is most severe when the flash point of the flammable liquid is below the sea temperature and a layer of very flammable or explosive vapor hovers just above the sea surface.

Petroleum, both crude oils and refined products, makes up a large percentage of the Class Three substances transported by sea. The particular problems presented by a crude oil depend upon such properties as volatility, sulfur content, flammability, paraffins, asphaltic elements, etc. Crude oils have a wide range of properties depending upon their source. Some heavy crudes contain so much wax or asphalt that they are very viscous and require heating before pumping. Other crudes are as light as refined products like diesel oil. Crude oils are the largest type of Class Three substances carried by sea—they are carried in the largest ships afloat, VLCCs and ULCCs.

Petroleum products are classed as either black or white (clean). Black products include furnace oils, fuel oils, asphalt, tars, and similar products. White oils, generally more volatile than black, include benzene, gasolines, kerosene, jet fuels, diesel fuels, and lubricating oils. Petroleum products are usually carried in small to medium-sized product carriers. These ships may be configured to carry a single product or several packages of different products, depending upon their trade.

Hydrocarbon gases—vapors or fumes from flammable hydrocarbon liquids—can be ignited and burn in certain concentrations. Concentrations of vapor lower than the Lower Explosive Limit are too low in flammable vapor content (lean) to burn; those above the Upper Explosive Limit are too high in flammable vapor (rich). The explosive range for petroleum vapors, the most common concern in salvage, is between 1 and 6 percent hydrocarbon vapor in air. Very small quantities of the flammable liquid can produce vapor concentrations within the explosive range. Explosive mixtures cannot form if the oxygen content of the atmosphere is 11 percent or less by volume. Figure 5-1 illustrates the explosive range as a function of oxygen content and hydrocarbon mixture.

Class Four—Flammable Solids

The flammable solids category includes not only materials that are flammable themselves, but also those that are subject to spontaneous combustion or emit flammable gases in contact with water. Some of these materials, such as certain soft grades of high sulfur content coal, are subject to spontaneous combustion and can be dangerous during both ordinary shipping and casualties. These materials are more likely to threaten the vessel than the environment.

A material emitting a flammable gas in contact with water creates the possibility of an explosive atmosphere, particularly in a flooded hold. Burning metal turnings or reduced iron, two cargoes in this classification, are particularly hazardous in contact with water.

Class Five—Oxidizing Substances and Organic Peroxides

Oxidizing agents cause substances that react with atmospheric oxygen to do so intensely. Fires are likely to be more severe in the presence of these materials. These agents usually present a problem limited to the vessel and not greatly threatening to the environment. The problem is quite different with organic peroxides. These chemicals are usually explosive or oxidizing agents or may decompose explosively under impact, friction, or fire and cause damage remote from the ship.

Organic peroxides often require refrigerated storage. If refrigeration machinery is inoperative following a casualty, the material may have to be jettisoned before the temperature rises to the point where violent decomposition takes place.

Class Six—Poisonous and Infectious Substances

Class six substances are cause for serious concern. They may be carried in solid, liquid, or gaseous form; react with other material; decompose in a fire; and generate very toxic gases. The hazard may be confined to the immediate vicinity or may threaten life over a wide geographical area and range of environments. Some spills into the sea do not allow any action other than monitoring and sampling. Salvage actions normally address only reducing the spill. The decision to continue the operation in the face of a poisonous or infectious substance discharge depends on the nature of the material, its packaging, and the requirements of the nation in which the casualty occurs.

Class Seven—Radioactive Materials

Nuclear energy and national authorities maintain tight controls over the transportation of radioactive materials. Despite the precautions and careful packaging, the

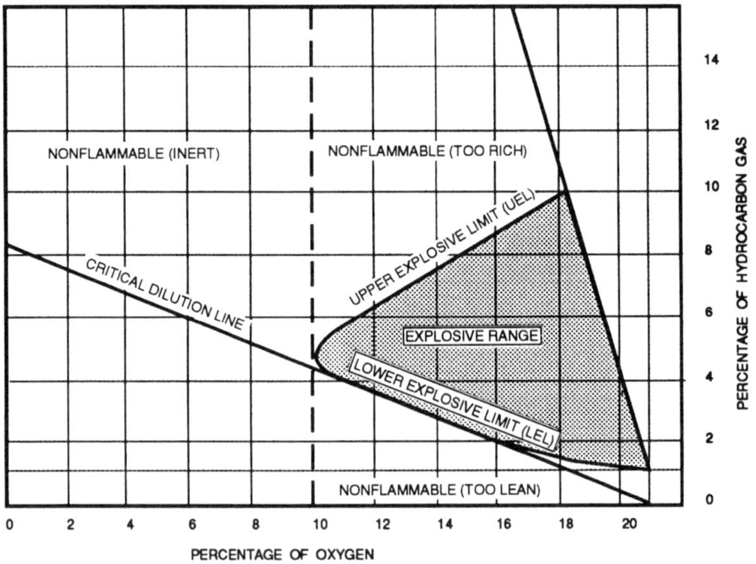

Fig. 5-1. Explosive range diagram

presence of nuclear materials in the cargo of a casualty always causes concern and interest. Perhaps more than with any other substances, including ones that present more serious and immediate dangers, the media exaggerate the dangers of nuclear materials and contribute to the public malaise. During salvage operations, handling and storage requirements should always be met or exceeded. The wise salvor removes the nuclear material from the site as soon as possible.

Class Eight—Corrosives

Corrosives are particularly nasty. These materials present three major problems. They:

1. Destroy human tissue and may cause permanent damage to the body.
2. Can corrode metals, including the ship's structure and the pumps and piping that move them.
3. Can become flammable or produce flammable gases in contact with fibrous materials or metals. Corrosives are the most likely class of hazardous substance to present a danger to the vessel itself. Normally, crews handling corrosive cargoes wear full protective clothing that covers all parts of their bodies. Such clothing is particularly important for crews in salvage where a spill or release is likely. As if the inherent dangers of corrosives were not enough, some corrosives are oxidizing agents.

Class Nine—Miscellaneous

Class Nine substances are those that do not fit into any other category. They present particular hazards that cannot be covered by regulations applicable to other materials, or they present a very low hazard in transportation.

It is extremely unlikely that a hazardous substance fits neatly into a single class. Normally, they are classified by their primary hazard in normal usage, storage, and transportation. In the unusual circumstances aboard a casualty, a secondary danger may become paramount.

Each class of hazardous substance in the IMDG system has specified labeling. Labels are diamond shaped and a minimum of 4 inches by 4 inches (10 cm by 10 cm). Labels on containers and placards for vehicles are at least 6 inches by 6 inches (15 cm by 15 cm). The color and markings are designed to convey the type of danger without need for language. Table 5-2 describes these markings for various classes of hazardous substances.

The system also specifies acceptable packaging for hazardous substances and a great deal of other information, such as requirements for segregation. Table 5-3, a simplified guide to segregation of hazardous substances, gives salvors in the field a general idea of how hazardous substances are stowed. It should be used for general guidance and not as a guideline for stowing hazardous substances.

TABLE 5-2.

MARKING OF HAZARDOUS SUBSTANCES		
Class	*Substance*	*Marking*
1	Explosives	Label with orange background
2	Flammable gas	Label with red background
2	Compressed gas	Label with green background
2	Poisonous gas	Label with white background
3	Flammable liquids	Label with red background
4	Flammable solids	Label with alternate red and white vertical stripes
4	Substances subject to spontaneous combustion	Red and white label split vertically; white on top
4	Substances emitting flammable gases when wet	Label with blue background
5	Oxidizing substance	Yellow label with symbol and words "oxidizing agent" in black
5	Organic peroxide	Yellow label with symbol and words "organic peroxide" in black
6	Poisonous substances	Label with white background
7	Radioactive materials in category 111 with dose rates up to 200 mr/hr at the surface of the package	Label split horizontally, top yellow, bottom white, with three vertical red stripes
7	Radioactive materials in category 11 with dose rates up to 10 mr/hr at the surface of the package	Label split horizontally, top yellow, bottom white, with two vertical red stripes
7	Radioactive materials in category 1 with dose rates up to 0.5 mr/hr at the surface of the package	Label split horizontally, top yellow, bottom white, with one vertical red stripe
7	Relatively harmless shipments	White label with symbol and the word "radioactive" in black
8	Corrosives	Label split horizontally, top white with symbols, lower half black with word "corrosive" in black
9	Miscellaneous	No specified labels
All labels carry the number of the class near the bottom of the label.		

The U.S. Department of Transportation's Hazardous Materials Regulations issued by the Coast Guard delineate regulations in the United States for transportation of hazardous substances. These regulations originated in the early twentieth century when they dealt solely with transportation by rail. An extensive set of regulations pertinent to all forms of transportation has evolved. The regulations contained in the Code of Federal Regulations for Shipping that address *Dangerous Cargoes* and *Certain Bulk Dangerous Cargoes* are of primary interest to mariners.[4] These codes, like the IMDG Codes, should be in the library of every salvor working in the United States or who may deal with cargoes loaded in or bound for the United States. The regulations are generally consistent with international regulation. In general, the policy of regulators in the United States has been to permit international cargoes to comply with IMDG Codes instead of requiring them to comply strictly with DOT rules. The result is that salvors working in the waters of the United States may encounter hazardous substances marked and packaged in compliance with either system.

TABLE 5-3.

SIMPLIFIED HAZARDOUS SUBSTANCES STOWAGE GUIDE

IMDG Code	2	3	4.1	4.2	4.3	5.1	5.2	6	7	8	9
2		C	E	H	E	F	H	A	G	E	A
3	C		B	C	C	C	D	A	C	B	A
4.1	E	B		B	B	C	C	A	B	B	A
4.2	H	C	B		B	C	C	A	B	B	A
4.3	E	C	B	B		C	C	A	B	B	A
5.1	F	C	C	C	C		C	A	B	C	A
5.2	H	D	C	C	C	C		A	C	C	A
6	A	A	A	A	A	A	A		A	A	A
7	G	C	B	B	B	B	C	A		C	A
8	E	B	B	B	B	C	C	A	C		A
9	A	A	A	A	A	A	A	A	A	A	

A – No segregation required
B - Stow away from
C - Separate from
D - Stow in a separate compartment
E - Separate and stow away from flammable gases
F - Stow separately from all flammable gases and other gases
G - Stow separately from flammable gases and away from other gases
H - Separate stowage in another compartment from gases

I'm Here from the Government to Help You . . .

In the United States, three government agencies provide information on hazardous substances to the transportation industry. The agency of primary interest to mariners is the U.S. Coast Guard's Chemical Hazards Response Information Service (CHRIS). This service compiles information on hazardous substances and provides guidelines for identifying and rating hazards. The system has coded hazardous materials for ready identification. The Coast Guard's Marine Safety Information System designates cargoes with these codes on the Certificate of Inspection of U.S. flag ships and the Certificate of Compliance of foreign flag vessels calling in U.S. ports. CHRIS information is available in the form of manuals sold through the Government Printing Office and through on-line systems accessible through subscription services.

The Environmental Protection Agency Oil and Hazardous Materials Technical Assistance Data System is a computerized system with information on more than a thousand oils and hazardous substances. The information allows identification of the substance by observable physical characteristics.

The Chemical Transportation Emergency Center (CHEMTREC), a subscription service that, if work load permits, provides information to nonsubscribers, is oriented primarily toward rail and road transportation spillages, and serves as the liaison between the person with the problem and the shipper or manufacturer of the substance. When contacted by telephone, CHEMTREC supplies information on the hazards of the material to the person with the problem, then contacts the shipper. Services similar to those described above exist in other countries. One of the best is the London Fire Service's Hazardous Chemicals Center. This center responds to telex, facsimile, or telephone requests with a detailed breakdown of the characteristics and hazards of materials in question. Local agents, environmental agencies, fire departments, or companies involved in hazardous substance spill response can provide information on the available services. Where the casualty occurs in or near a loading or discharge port handling the particular material, immediate help may be available from the industries that produce or use it.

Hazardous Substances in Salvage

Codes for transporting hazardous substances are designed to protect the crew during normal operations. The crew may be well be out of the way in a casualty that produces fire, flooding, or other abnormal conditions. Risks for salvors may be high.

Some explosives become unstable with heat or excessive moisture, so that they are extremely dangerous in a ship fire. When there is a fire in a compartment adjacent to one in which explosives are stored, the space with the explosives should be flooded immediately. Because of the possibility of ignition from static electricity, steam smothering systems should never be activated. The cure is not without its price. Decomposing explosives give off highly toxic gases that may or may not go into solution with the floodwater. The liquid to be pumped out of the flooded space may be something quite different from seawater. Expert advice should be sought about handling the floodwater, the atmosphere in the space, and the residual explosives.

Shippers have an obligation to mark their shipments appropriately, but errors occur and hazardous substances may be marked, packaged, or stowed incorrectly.

The marking on the shipment usually is the first indication to salvors that they are dealing with a hazardous substance. Whenever possible, manufacturers should be contacted to clear up uncertainties.

Chemicals are often carried in containers. A properly stowed container is marked with the class of hazardous substance it contains by a six-inch-square (15cm) diamond-shaped label of the type previously described. Only one class of compatible materials is stowed in each container and the container is securely stowed. Containers with the most hazardous materials are carried on deck where they can be jettisoned in an emergency. In practice, containers may be loaded with incompatible materials or poorly stowed so that the materials mix in a casualty or its aftermath. The hazard of the mixture may be greater than the sum of its parts. Salvors should approach damaged containers, and any container known to contain hazardous substances, with great caution.

There is an insidious danger associated with materials that are not hazardous themselves but become so in the presence of other materials, and of the seawater that floods into the ship during the casualty. Benign or other hazardous substances may mix to form a monster. The hazards of the constituents may be not the sum, but a multiple, of the hazards of the constituents. The mixing danger asserts itself in mixed cargoes and breached storage containers. Markings on crated, boxed, drummed, and containerized cargoes may be destroyed in the casualty or in the ensuing flooding or fire fighting. When markings are missing, salvors should not only check the manifest, but study it and think about combinations and permutations. Substances mixed into a potentially dangerous cocktail call for bringing in the best possible advice as soon as possible.

The presence of hazardous substances in a casualty may mean that salvors must set up decontamination stations on board and have specialized medical teams and evacuation helicopters on standby.

The corporate structure of a salvage company may contain a company specializing in hazardous substance cleanup and environmental protection. If so, close liaison between the salvage company and the environmental protection company is advantageous to both. Without such a corporate organization, salvors should set up relationships with companies in their area of operations that can work with them on pollution and hazardous substance problems. Salvors should be equipped with or have immediate access to protective clothing, decontamination materials, and measuring devices for determining toxicity, oxygen levels, and flammability. Salvage crews should be trained to use this equipment.

When casualties contain large quantities of hazardous substances, salvors are well-advised to seek technical advice from the owner, a marine chemist, and government agencies as soon as possible. While the hazardous substances may be safe and secure aboard the intact ship, things are different on a casualty. System integrity may be destroyed. Fumes, often migrating far from their source along seemingly illogical paths, may produce nonbreathable atmospheres in closed and poorly ventilated spaces. Analysis of compartment atmospheres and determination of their ability to support life safely are among the most valuable services a marine chemist can perform in salvage. Determination of the possible effects of hazardous substances on the salvage crew and the necessary precautionary measures should be a matter of the highest priority.

Abandoned casualties known or suspected of containing hazardous substances should be approached very carefully. The presence of hazardous substances, especially fumes, should be determined before boarding and before entering closed or unventilated spaces. It is far better to approach the casualty cautiously and lose a little time than to rush in and risk a personnel casualty.

Gas testing equipment can literally be a lifesaver when toxic gases are present. The tubes for this equipment have a shelf life, but are sufficiently available that tubes for specific substances can be provided to almost any site in a few days. As a stopgap, a polytest tube capable of giving an immediate indication of the presence of toxic or flammable gas may be carried and used for preliminary tests.

Salvors working aboard a vessel that has contained hazardous substances must be aware that the substance can be present on other cargo, in foodstuffs, and in floodwater. Without definitive information to the contrary, all material should be treated as contaminated. Handling should not be done in a manner that will cause pollution or introduction of the hazardous substance into an ecosystem.

LPG, LNG, and Chemical Carriers

Three types of ships, specifically designed to carry hazardous substances, are of particular interest to salvors. These ships are liquefied petroleum gas (LPG) carriers, liquefied natural gas (LNG) carriers, and chemical tankers. These ships are of special interest because their cargoes are hazardous. Much, indeed most, of the salvage effort centers on the cargo and its handling. With all three ships the job remains simple and straightforward salvage while the cargo remains in the vessel.

The principal danger from LPG or LNG cargoes lies in uncontrolled release of a cargo; the most likely time of release is during or in the immediate aftermath of a casualty. Although cargo tanks are located deep within the ship and protected to reduce the possibility of containment vessel rupture during a collision or grounding, rupture is possible. The probable pattern of events is of interest to anyone managing or responding to the casualty.

The most probable effect of grounding is no rupture of the cargo containment; however, there are three situations with a relatively high probability of cargo system rupture:

Hard grounding at speed on a rock, coral, or other hard sea floor.

Grounding by drifting sideways at speeds of 3 to 5 knots onto a hard sea floor.

Grounding in a heavy swell or on a falling tide in such a way that hull stresses become dangerous.

Especially in LPG or LNG carrier groundings, salvage actions must be thought out thoroughly so that they do not exacerbate the danger of rupturing the containment by changing stress patterns drastically during the salvage, and particularly by not setting the ship down harder on the sea floor.

The events following rupture of a cargo tank in a collision depend upon the type of containment system and the location of the rupture relative to the waterline. Rupture of a prismatic tank in grounding is likely to be followed by cargo release into the water until the hydrostatic pressure balances the tank pressure, as in a liquid cargo tankship casualty. Depending upon the geometry of the rupture and with calm seas, an ice plug may form and block flow.

Cargo released to the atmosphere spreads and vaporizes rapidly, but there may be a lengthy release of cargo initially into ballast spaces where it is then trapped. The hull may suffer brittle fracture from the cooling effect of the expanding gas.

Unless the released cargo ignites from the collision, ignition may not be an immediate problem near the rupture because of the richness of the cargo/air mixture. The rich mixture dilutes with time and with downwind drift until it reaches nonflammable, nontoxic concentrations. Drift and dilution can be modeled by computer. Where there is a release of liquefied gas there is little the salvor can do except wait for the cloud to disperse and pray.

Shock of grounding or collision can cause damage to piping and transfer systems that does not cause an immediate release of cargo, but can be a problem during transfers. Before commencing any transfer following a casualty, all piping systems should be checked for damage.

LPG carriers are sophisticated and complex vessels; LNG carriers are even more so. In both ships, cargo transfers are not a simple matter of flanging up and pumping. These operations require specialized knowledge, careful operational and contingency planning, sound procedures, and rigid adherence to safety requirements. The salvor should have specialized professional advice on the cargo, the ship, and the cargo transfer. The Oil Companies International Marine Forum (OCIMF) *LPG Carrier Safety Check List* should be followed as closely as possible in any salvage transfer of LPG. Salvors should not undertake a cargo transfer from a complex and hazardous LNG carrier casualty without the owner's experienced and technically qualified emergency response team's participation.

Chemical tankers transport chemicals in bulk, often carrying small parcels of different products. The very strict segregation of products practiced in normal operations and the safety systems built into the ship may be violated in the casualty and its aftermath. Several products discharged simultaneously may mix to present hazards different from those presented by the individual products. The simultaneous discharge of several products could be very dangerous. The danger depends totally on the characteristics of the products released and their reaction with seawater, air, and other released products. Salvors approaching a chemical tanker casualty should have a detailed list of the cargo, potential mixes, and specialized professional help. The owners of time-chartered vessels may have little or no information on the cargo carried on a particular voyage. It is absolutely essential to take the time necessary to find the information about the cargo, its compatibility, and its hazards before starting salvage actions.

The *Ship to Ship Transfer Guide* (*Liquiefied Gases*)[5] is basically applicable to chemical tankers. Special attention should be given to: handling of static generating or accumulating cargo, hose bonding, quick release couplings on manifolds, fire-fighting gear for specific chemicals, protective clothing and respiration devices, education of all hands in the potential dangers and safety precautions, and the requirements of governing administrations.

In some salvage operations, jettisoning the cargo may be indicated. It is highly unusual for governing administrations and regulatory bodies to permit jettisoning. If permission can be obtained, jettisoning should be below the waterline, preferably through the pump room sea valves, alternatively by hoses led well below the waterline. As the released product may generate gases, the vessel should be shut down, closed up as much as possible, and held up-current and up-wind of the discharge. Personnel should wear protective clothing for the worst case.

Salvage of LPG carriers, LNG carriers, and chemical tankers is a complex, highly technical, and difficult business. In all cases, salvors should seek specialized, professional assistance and not try to go it alone or to improvise salvage methods on their own.

Oil

All powered ships carry petroleum-based oil as bunkers, cargo, or both; thus, any casualty is a potential source of pollution and the very serious liabilities that accompany it. A variety of other liquid cargoes, both oils and other liquids, are also carried. With great public interest and broadly based legislation addressing oil pollution and environmental protection, salvors who in the past dealt with oil and other liquid cargo and bunkers routinely must now give them priority in salvage operations. No bunkers and no cargo, no matter how benign, can be discharged into the sea during salvage operations without the specific permission of regulatory bodies in each case. Anyone doing so faces criminal and civil penalties. Eliminating the environmental danger of a casualty and the handling of potential pollutants has become the first priority in salvage, often taking precedence over actions to refloat the ship.

A ship carries oil as bunkers for its own machinery or as cargo. Ships' fuels make up a narrow range of petroleum products; an incredibly broad range of crudes and products are carried as cargo. Handling bunkers and cargo in casualties requires different techniques and presents different problems. Each type has problems that in some respects are more difficult than the other's problems.

Oil-Water Hydrostatics

Salvors must understand the mechanics of the behavior of oil in ships' tanks when the tanks rupture. A principal determinant of the behavior of oil is its specific gravity. The specific gravity of an oil is the weight of oil compared with the weight of water at the same temperature—usually 60° F. (15.5° C.). The specific gravity of fresh water is 1.00; that of seawater is 1.025; the specific gravity of most oils is less than 1.00. Most oils are lighter than water and float on the surface. Oils that are heavier than water sink to the sea floor. When the specific gravity of the oil and water are equal, the oil may sink or float depending upon temperatures and the amount of oil-water emulsion that forms.

Relative weights of oils also are expressed as American Petroleum Institute (API) gravity (degrees API). The system is common in the petroleum industry and in tanker cargoes. The API gravity system arbitrarily assigns fresh water a gravity of 10 degrees API. Oils that are lighter than water have higher gravities, those that are heavier have lower gravities. API gravities are converted to specific gravity by:

Degrees API = (141.5/specific gravity at 60° F.) – 131.5

Conversely:

Specific gravity at 60° F. = 141.5/(degrees API + 131.5)

Table 5-4 shows gravities and weights of representative petroleum products. More detailed information may be found in the tabulated data published by the American Petroleum Institute. Changes in API gravity with temperature and relative volume changes with temperature are of particular interest to salvors.

TABLE 5-4.

SPECIFIC AND API GRAVITIES AND WEIGHTS OF REPRESENTATIVE PETROLEUM PRODUCTS

Product	*Specific Gravity*	*API Gravity*	*lb/gal*	*kg/l*	*bbl/ton*
Fresh water	1.000	10.00	8.33	0.998	6.30
Petroleum Coke	1.145	–7.97	9.55	1.144	5.50
Asphalt	1.040	4.55	8.67	1.039	6.06
Heavy Crude Oil	0.983	12.40	8.19	0.981	6.41
Lube Oils	0.900	25.72	7.50	0.899	7.00
Benzol	0.882	28.87	7.36	0.882	7.14
Diesel Fuel	0.845	36.05	7.05	0.845	7.46
Jet Fuel	0.813	42.57	6.76	0.810	7.75

Table 5-4 continued on next page

Table 5-4 continued

SPECIFIC AND API GRAVITIES AND WEIGHTS OF REPRESENTATIVE PETROLEUM PRODUCTS					
Product	*Specific Gravity*	*API Gravity*	*lb/gal*	*kg/l*	*bbl/ton*
Paraffin and Petrolatum	0.801	45.26	6.67	0.799	7.87
Light Crude Oils	0.797	46.03	6.64	0.796	7.90
Motor and Natural Gasolines	0.741	59.41	6.17	0.739	8.50
Mineral Spirits	0.731	62.11	6.10	0.731	8.62
Aviation Gasoline	0.708	68.40	5.90	0.707	8.90

Whether oil flows from a ruptured tank or water flows into the tank depends upon the hydrostatic pressure at the hole. If the pressure in the tank is higher than the sea pressure, oil flows out. If the reverse is true, water flows into the tank. When the pressures balance, there is no flow. For no flow:

Oil pressure = Water pressure

The hydrostatic pressure of each fluid is proportional to the specific gravity of the fluid and its depth:

The hydrostatic pressure inside a tank containing oil is:

$$P_{ins} = \frac{SG_O \times D_O}{k}$$

where:

P_{ins} = pressure inside the tank in depth units (feet or meters)
SG_O = specific gravity of the liquid (oil) in the tank
D_O = depth of the liquid (oil) in the tank (feet or meters)
k = 1.025 for a ship in seawater and 1.000 for a ship in fresh water

and the pressure outside is:

$$P_{out} = SG_w \times D_w$$

where:

P_{out} = pressure outside the tank in fsw (msw)
D_W = water depth (feet or meters)

When the pressure balances and there is no flow:

$$P_{ins} = P_{out}$$

Tanks filled well above the waterline spill oil into the sea when ruptured. That is, outflow occurs when:

$$P_{ins} > P_{out}$$

Double-bottom tanks, and other tanks with tops well below the waterline, are likely to flood from sea when ruptured. When low tanks are ruptured oil is forced up vents, sounding tubes, and overflows until pressures balance. Inflow occurs when:

$$P_{ins} < P_{out}$$

When a ship strands and ruptures her tanks, the hydrostatic pressure outside the tanks changes as the tide rises and falls. In deep tanks where flow on tank rupture is out of the tank, the following happens:

Oil flows from the deep tanks until the hydrostatic pressure balances at the state of tide at and immediately after the casualty.

When the tide falls, oil flows out of the tank as the external hydrostatic pressure decreases.

As the tide rises, water flows into the tank to maintain a pressure balance.

If the ship strands at low water, no oil spills following the initial spill. Water flows into the ship during the tide rises. There is always a water bottom in the tank unless the tide falls well below its level at the initial stranding.

Figure 5-2 illustrates the process of oil and water flow in a ruptured deep tank.

In shallow tanks where flow is into the tank on rupture (see figure 5-3), the following happens:

Water flows into the shallow tanks until the hydrostatic pressure balances for the tide at the time of and immediately after the casualty.

Oil is forced up the vents, sounding tubes, and overflows.

As the tide falls, the water level in the tank falls, but no oil is spilled unless the tide level is far enough below the initial tide level making inside hydrostatic pressure greater than external pressure.

If the hydrostatic pressure inside the tank exceeds that outside during the tide fall, oil flows from the tank into the sea.

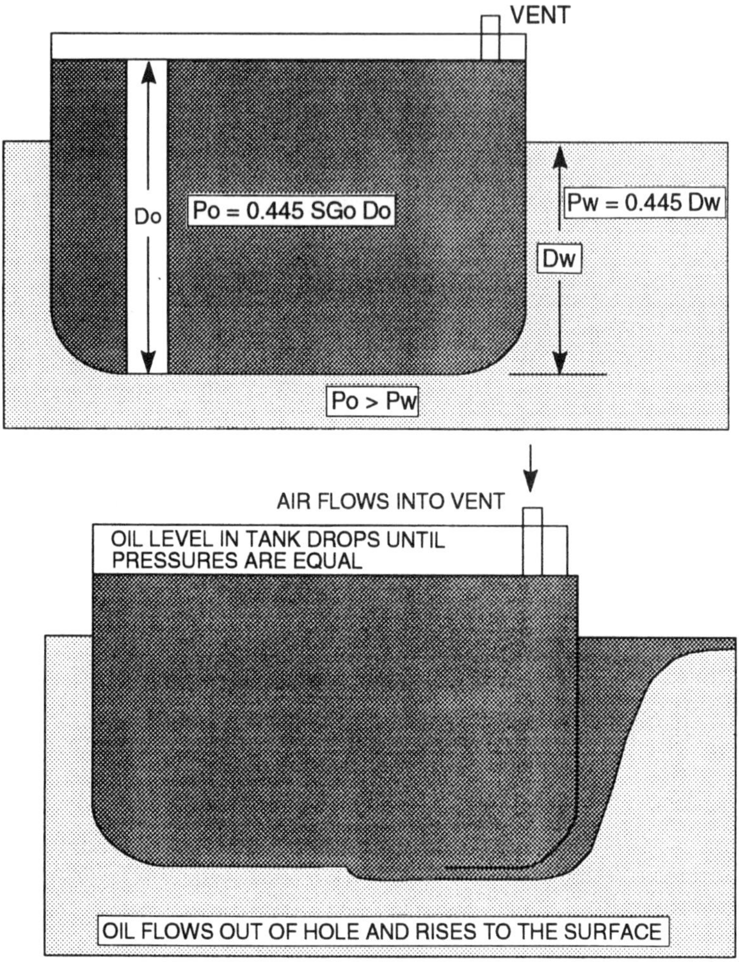

Fig. 5-2. Flow in a ruptured deep tank

In casualties with ruptured tanks, the initial oil spill occurs because the hydrostatic pressure in the tank is greater than that outside. Additional spillage occurs as the tide falls and the external hydrostatic pressure decreases. Spillage may occur on following lower tides with lower external hydrostatic pressures. When the initial internal hydrostatic pressure is lower than the external pressure and remains lower at all states of the tide, there can be no spillage.

Unfortunately, the real world is not as simple as the hydrostatic pressure balance indicates. The turbulence and disruption that occur when a ship strands may cause an outflow of oil, although pure hydrostatics say the flow should be inward. Inward and outward flow can occur simultaneously until the situation stabilizes.

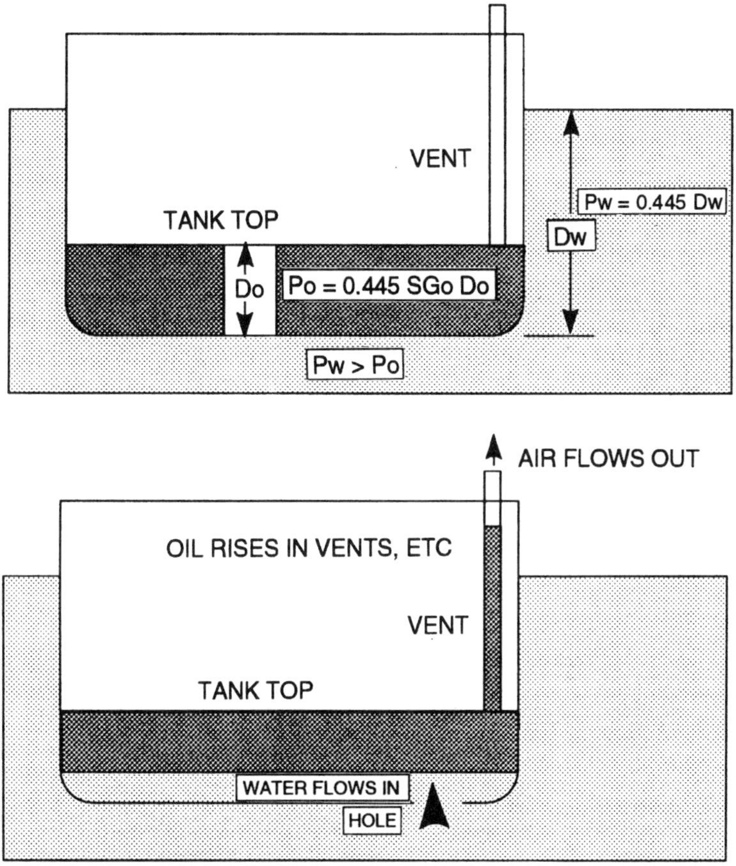

WHEN TANK IS HOLED:

1. WATER FLOWS INTO THE TANK UNTIL THE PRESSURE INSIDE AND OUTSIDE AT THE HOLE IS EQUAL.
2. OIL RISES IN THE VENTS AND SOUNDING TUBES INCREASING THE PRESSURE HEAD OF THE OIL.

Fig. 5-3. Flow in a ruptured shallow tank

Changing hydrostatic heads caused by changing heights of the sea and rotation or other motion of the ship can produce a pumping action that causes oil to spill. The oil-water interchange in the tank and pumping action can work oil, water, and air into an emulsion that is difficult or impossible to pump.

Despite the exceptions, hydrostatic pressure remains the primary determinant of oil spillage or flooding into a tank. Flow in one direction or the other always occurs unless the hydrostatic pressure is balanced. Spillage from tanks with a large hydrostatic head is always greater than from one that's located well below the waterline.

In a casualty, the greatest spillage can be expected immediately after a tank ruptures and on the first tide cycle that follows. Additional spillage can occur on subsequent lower tides, during heavy weather, or if the ship is lively. Unless additional tanks rupture, the spills that follow the first tide cycle should be minor compared to the initial spill. Even after the ship is stabilized and all sources of spillage are secured there may be some visible sheening observed, especially as the ship moves. This sheen often comes from oil that has clung to the hull or has been trapped in upset plate hull irregularities. The spillage from such sources is usually minor and completely unpreventable. When it occurs, every remaining space containing oil must be double-checked to insure it is only minor spillage from clinging and not new leakage.

Water Bottoms

Water flowing into the tank forces oil upward and forms a layer at tank bottom between the oil and the bottom of the ship. This layer, or water bottom, when thick enough, prevents additional spillage and inhibits spillage at any thickness. The water bottom is an excellent tool for the salvor. When oil is pumped from the tank, and the tank bottom is holed and open to the sea, the liquid level in the tank changes only slightly. As oil is removed, water replaces it. The layer of oil becomes thinner and the layer of water thicker. The total pressure at the bottom of the tank continues to balance the external pressure. The depth of the liquid in the tank changes only enough for the combined hydrostatic pressure of the oil and water to keep the pressure balanced:

$$SG_o (D_o) + SG_{w1} (D_w) = SG_{w2} (T)$$

where:

SG_o = specific gravity of the oil

D_o = depth of the oil from the surface to the oil/water interface in feet (meters)

SG_{w1} = specific gravity of the water in the tank

D_w = depth of the water bottom between the oil/water interface and the skin of the ship in feet (meters)

SG_{w2} = specific gravity of the water in which the ship is floating, normally the same as SG_{w1}

T = draft of the ship in feet (meters) at the location of the hole

The top of the water bottom rises as oil is pumped from the tank, giving additional protection against spillage and keeping weight in the tank to secure the ship on the ground or avoid undesired changes in buoyancy. The depth of the water bottom can be calculated.

The pressure in the interior of the tank is the sum of the hydrostatic pressure of the oil and the water bottom, that is:

$$P_{ins} = SG_o (D_o) + SG_w (d_w)$$

where all quantities are as defined previously.

The pressure outside the tank is the hydrostatic pressure at the depth of the tank bottom.

$$P_{out} = SG_w (T)$$

where all quantities are as defined previously.

The water bottom is deep enough to balance the pressure with a known depth of oil.

Tanks that flood on rupture press up so that the water bottom in the tank is approximately equal to the ullage before the rupture. The amount of oil forced up vents and sounding tubes is normally quite small compared to the volume of the tank.

Water bottoms do not form in tanks containing oils with specific gravities greater than 1. After the initial flooding, the oil settles through the water to the bottom of the tank.

Spill Mitigation

Very definite, very positive steps can be taken immediately after a casualty to mitigate the effects of the spill. Spill mitigation procedures are based on the location of the damage and the mechanism by which the spill occurs. Table 5-5 describes eight basic types of spill conditions (damage), the spill mechanisms for each, and mitigation procedures. Actual damage is normally a combination of the seven cases described below. Mitigation action must be structured with the combined effects fully allowed for.

Without air coming into the tanks oil cannot flow out, unless it is deliberately pumped out. Therefore, with underwater damage, closing vents is effective in stopping or cutting down flow. Vents to bunker and cargo tanks do not have valves to close the vents, because there is a possibility of the tank being pressurized or drawing a vacuum and suffering structural damage if the vents are secured. Unfortunately for salvors and those concerned with mitigation of spills, regulators give highest priority to prevention of structural damage, and valves in vent lines are prohibited. Some farsighted shipowners have provided blanks that can be installed in a vent line or can seal a PV valve if the tank is ruptured and leaking oil. Many vents have bolted covers that can be closed. Many of these vents have no gasket or sheet rubber inside the cover; even cloth that would be sucked against the flame screen will assist in blocking air flow. Blocking inflow through the vents of a damaged tank by any possible means helps stop outflow from the tank.

TABLE 5-5.

CASE	*CONDITION*	*SPILL MECHANISM*	*MITIGATION PROCEDURE*
1	Above-the- waterline damage to a wing tank.	Oil under the influence of gravity flows out of the hole until the surface of the oil is below the level of the bottom of the hole.	(a) Release any pressure, such as inert gas pressure, on the tank to reduce the pressure forcing the oil out. (b) With the cargo transfer system, pump the oil out of the tank to lower the level of oil as rapidly as possible. If the cargo transfer system cannot be used, rig a siphon with tank drops to move the oil from the damaged tank to other cargo or ballast tanks. (c) Ballast to list the ship to the side opposite the hole to bring the hole higher out of the water.
2	Hole in the side below the waterline and above the tank top.	(a) Oil flows out of the hole until hydrostatic heads inside and outside balance. Water flows into hole and drops to bottom of tank. Oil flows out and water flows in the hole simultaneously. (b) The oil in the tank floats on the water. It rises and reestablishes a hydrostatic condition where oil flows out of the hole. (c) The process continues and oil continues to flow until the water level reaches the top of the damage. (d) Current, tide, and seas affect the amount and rate of discharge.	Mitigation strategy depends upon the location of the damage. If the damage is low in the ship, the best strategy is to increase the external hydrostatic head by increasing draft by ballasting or transferring cargo. If the damage is near the waterline, the best strategy is to raise the hole by listing and trimming the ship with cargo and ballast. Attempts to remove cargo from the tanks are worthwhile but are likely to meet with no more than moderate success because the water flooding into the hole will soon cover the suction. Portable pumps taking suction near the top of the tank can be effective through the spill period.
3	Damage to a wing tank near the bottom.	This is a special case of side damage because the full hydrostatic head of the cargo forces oil out until the level drops low enough to reestablish hydrostatic balance. Very little water flows into the tank. Less total loss of oil may occur than with damage farther up the tank.	(a) Lower hydrostatic pressure in the tank by venting off inert gas and removing cargo from the tank. (b) Raise the external hydrostatic pressure by putting the hole deeper in the water by ballasting or transferring cargo.

Table 5-5 continued on next page

Table 5-5 continued

CASE	CONDITION	SPILL MECHANISM	MITIGATION PROCEDURE
4	Bottom shell damage.	(a) Single-hull ship: Oil flows out under full hydrostatic pressure of the cargo until hydrostatic balance is reached. No water flows in. (b) Double-hull ship: No spillage because cargo containment is not breached.	(a) Single-hull ship: (1) Lower hydrostatic pressure in the tank by venting off inert gas and removing cargo from the tank. (2) Raise the external hydrostatic pressure by putting the hole deeper in the water by ballasting or transferring cargo. (b) Double-hull ship: No mitigation required.
5	Shell and tank top damage.	Oil floods the double bottom and flows out under full hydrostatic pressure of the cargo until hydrostatic balance is reached. No water flows in.	(1) Lower hydrostatic pressure in the tank by venting off inert gas and removing cargo from the tank. (2) Raise the external hydrostatic pressure by putting the hole deeper in the water by ballasting or transferring cargo.
6	Side shell damage while carrying light cargo.	The higher external hydrostatic head forces cargo up the vent and other openings and causes a spill on deck. Water enters through the damage and continues to rise until hydrostatic balance is restored.	(1) Divert the cargo to other tanks through any piping system. This action may contaminate the piping systems but it is better than spilling the oil. (2) Decrease the external hydrostatic head by raising the ship out of the water as far as possible.
7	Bottom damage with light cargo.	In double-skin ships, the double bottom floods, then the high external hydrostatic pressure forces oil out of vents and other openings in the top of the tank. In single-skin ships, external hydrostatic pressure works directly to force oil out of the top openings.	(1) Divert the cargo to other tanks through any piping system. This action may contaminate the piping systems but it is better than spilling the oil. (2) Decrease the external hydrostatic head by raising the ship out of the water as far as possible.

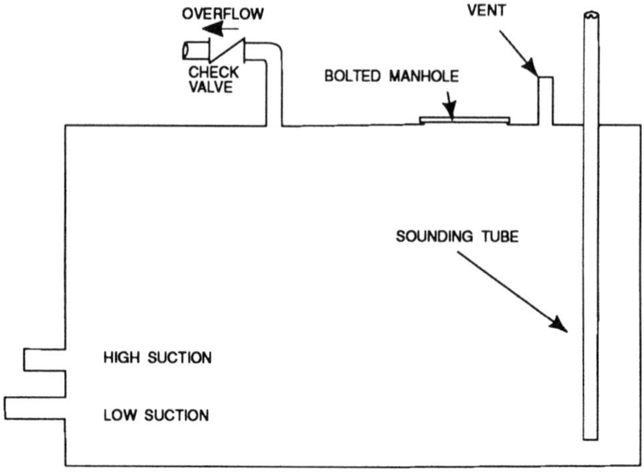

Fig. 5-4. Typical tank and openings

Spill mitigation to some degree, and deliberate removal of liquids to a larger degree, depend upon the designed openings in a tank. The salvor's skill in identifying, understanding the relationships among, using, and controlling these openings determines the effectiveness of the operation. Figure 5-4 shows in schematic a typical tank and its openings.

Bunkers

Bunkers in this discussion includes fuels and all other non-cargo bulk oils carried in tanks in the ship—lubricating oils, hydraulic oils, etc. These oils present a pollution hazard that, although less severe than cargoes because there is less potential pollutant, nevertheless requires positive action. Regulatory agencies often require removal of these oils although the technical aspects of the casualty make removal unnecessary or undesirable and the risk of pollution is low. It is usually most productive to comply with the regulatory agency's demands, unless the action is demonstrably unsafe. In removing bunkers from a casualty, prevention of pollution is the first priority; retention of value is of secondary importance. Often, particularly in remote areas, it may be necessary to place the bunkers in a barge or other receptacle that cannot be cleaned readily and where a suitable temperature cannot be maintained. While putting the oil in such a receptacle causes a substantial loss of its value as fuel, there may be no practical alternative.

Casualties must keep enough oil on board to operate generators during the salvage operation and to use their engines for refloating or transit. They must keep a margin for contingencies and delays, particularly when the salvage site is remote and there is no means of refueling. Ships that burn two types of fuel, such as diesel fuel for maneuvering and heavy oil for cruising, must keep each type in the correct proportion. Damaged tanks and piping systems may require running temporary piping or temporary conversion of tanks to oil storage tanks. The latter action has the undesirable effect of contaminating the tanks that do not normally carry bunkers.

Salvors must be alert to the effects of bunker removal on stability and ground reaction. Weight removal low in the ship adversely affects stability and any weight removal may be undesirable for salvors attempting to hold a stranded ship on the ground until refloating preparations are complete. Seawater is heavier than oil, so that a tank ballasted with an equivalent volume of water contains more weight than it did when containing oil. Partial ballasting should be avoided to prevent the development of free surface; tanks should either be pressed up or empty. Ballasting tanks to restore the weight may have some serious drawbacks. The ballasted tanks contain water contaminated with clingage and other residual oil. The contaminated ballast water cannot be pumped over the side, but must be retained on board or pumped to a suitable receptacle for later disposal. Ballasted bunker tanks require cleaning before filling them with fuel. The cost of cleaning decreases the salved value of the ship. When ballasting of bunker tanks is necessary, the absolute minimum number of tanks should be ballasted.

To remove bunkers from any ship salvors must have: (1) access to the oil, (2) a means of moving it, and (3) a place to put it. There is no cookbook for bunker removal; each case is very different. The first step is always the same: to learn enough about the location, type, and amount of bunkers and as much about the tankage and fill and transfer system as is necessary to remove the oil safely. The location of tank fittings, sounding tubes, overflows, and vents should be noted on a survey.

Bunker tanks may be any size or shape and located in any portion of the ship. Bunkers are carried in deep tanks, double-bottom tanks, wing tanks, engine room tanks, and any other place the naval architect could find that is not desirable for cargo. Break-bulk ships, container vessels, bulk carriers, refrigerated ships, etc., normally carry their bunkers in double-bottom tanks. Roll-on/roll-off ships, warehouse ships, and others that carry cargo high reserve the double bottom for ballast and carry bunkers in deep tanks. Some older tankers carry bunkers in foredeeps—deep tanks located forward of the cargo, but most now carry them in tanks in way of the engine room.

Sound practice is to locate the bunker tanks on a General Arrangement Plan, check the capacity of each on the Capacity Plan, and sound the tanks. For the soundings to be most meaningful, a Soundings Booklet or Table should be acquired. Soundings made without a Soundings Table can be compared with dimensions taken from the General Arrangement Plan, Capacity Plan, or Tank Plan to estimate the quantity of oil in the tank. Assistance from the ship's crew can save much time in finding the sounding tubes and in discovering the ship's idiosyncrasies. Particular note should be made of tanks that soundings show are flooded. Soundings high in the sounding tube or at the waterline are a sign that the tank is open to the sea. Soundings higher than expected, or higher than the precasualty sounding, may suggest slow leakage into the tank from the sea or through a ruptured bulkhead or piping. Oil in damaged ships migrates through damaged boundaries and piping, often to very unlikely places. Lower than expected soundings suggest that oil has migrated through some tank opening to another tank, flooded into the ship, or gone over the side. Water-indicating paste rubbed on the sounding tape shows the location of the oil-water interface.

Insofar as practical, an accounting should be made of all oil known to be in the ship before the casualty before beginning oil removal operations. All soundings with the time taken and any notes must be preserved carefully. The size of civil penalties for oil spills often depends upon the amount of oil spilled. Accurate soundings help establish the amount remaining on board, and are evidence that the salvor is making his best effort to prevent and control pollution. On the other hand, action to stop active or imminent spillage should never be delayed while inventorying and accounting for oil. In structuring his salvage actions relative to oil removal, a salvor must draw a delicate balance.

Tanks have several openings useful for gaining access to and removing oil. These openings include the fill and transfer system connections, normally with high and low connections—manholes, sounding tubes, vents, and overflows.

In salvage, it is always best to use ship's systems for their design purpose. Salvors seeking a solution may overlook the obvious and fail to use intact ship's systems. Every ship has a system designed to receive fuel oil, move it within the ship, and transfer it off the ship. The best way to remove oil from a casualty's bunker tanks is by the designed method of defueling. Even when the system markings are in a language the salvors cannot read and the crew is not available, time spent thinking the system through and tracing it out can pay big dividends in saved time, effort, and risk. Transfer piping in the casualty may be broken or tanks may be flooded above the suction. The situation is evident quickly as only water appears in the discharge; an alternate access must be found. When the ship has power or suitable power can be rigged, the fuel transfer pump can debunker through the transfer system. Debunkering with the transfer pump has one major drawback: the pump is usually of low capacity so that the operation may become a comparatively prolonged affair.

When piping is intact, but the transfer pumps are inoperable or of such low capacity as to be virtually useless, the piping may be broken at a flange, or cut, and a fitting to mate with hoses or piping attached. Pipes containing fuel oil or fumes should be sawn, not flame cut, to avoid the danger of fire or explosion. Pipes or hoses can then be rigged to the suction of portable pumps. The pump suction should be made up to the ship's piping without welding, as welding may ignite the fumes in the tank or piping.

Where the transfer system is totally useless, the first option is to open the tank manhole access by removing the cover, then to put a pump suction or portable submersible pump into the tank. A hydrostatic head in the tank greater than the pressure in the space with the access causes oil to blow out of the open manhole. This process is both messy and dangerous. Tanks should never be opened at a point lower than the sounding. When a reliable sounding cannot be obtained, the bolts should be backed off lightly and the manhole loosened before removal. If oil or water begins to flow out, the manhole can be bolted back in place. Cargo or other material stacked over the manhole is the greatest impediment to removing oil in this manner. Where several thousand tons of bulk cargo, liquid cargo, containers, or other material blocks access to manholes, it is patently impossible to clear and enter the access. Not only must the manhole be clear, but there must be a clear area around it for salvors to work and to handle and rig pumps.

Open manholes allow the escape of fumes that may concentrate in poorly ventilated spaces to form toxic or explosive atmospheres. Sheet rubber gaskets over the manholes or plastic bags filled with sawdust or water seal the access effectively with the pumps in place. Where the ship's configuration permits, it is wise to rig ventilation into the space with the manhole. Prime movers for submersible pumps should be located well clear of potential fume concentrations.

When tanks cannot be accessed from either the fill and transfer system or the manholes, the best options are exhausted. Salvors must use their ingenuity to develop a way to access the tank through other fittings or by cutting through a solid tank boundary.

Tank boundaries may be cut exothermically, sawn, drilled, or chipped. Boundaries possibly backed by fumes should *never* be cut exothermically because of the danger of explosion. Oil- or water-backed plate may be cut exothermically—the head of oil necessary for safe cutting depends on the type of oil. Expert advice should be sought before attempting such a cut. Plates backed by oil, water, or air may be cut mechanically. To eliminate the danger of sparking when cutting air-backed plate in a bunker tank, the deck can be flooded and the cut made through a water blanket.

Hot taps are a modification of an oil field device developed by T.D. Williamson, Inc., of Tulsa, Oklahoma, to allow entry into a flowing pipeline without stopping the flow or spilling the fluid. Hot taps have been used to remove cargo and bunker oils from tanks that cannot be accessed through their normal openings because of the position of the ship or the tank location. These devices allow getting to the tanks by cutting through a solid tank boundary. The hot tap machine consists of a spool piece attached to the tank boundary, a gate valve, and an extendable hydraulically or pneumatically driven rotary cutter much like an ordinary hole saw or boring bar. Figure 5-5 illustrates a salvage hot tap.

The tank boundary is cut through the open valve and the cutter withdrawn, bringing with it the cut coupon. The valve is closed and the hot tap machine removed and replaced with a flange and hose leading to the pump. The hot tap ma-

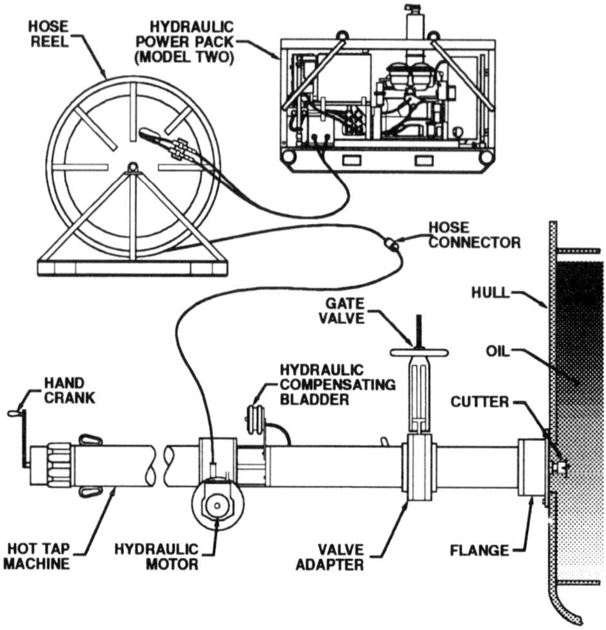

Fig. 5-5. Salvage hot tap. Courtesy of U.S. Navy.

chine works in any position, but, because it weighs more than 250 pounds in the 6-inch size, cranes or lift bags are needed to handle it in the water.

Setting up a hot tap requires the following steps:

1. Clean the surface in way of the hot tap installation.
2. Mark the location of the studs for the flange of the spool piece.
3. Weld, shoot, or drill and tap studs into place. A word of a caution about shooting studs: Shoot stud only when you are *absolutely certain* of what is on the other side of the tank boundary. Shooting into an explosive atmosphere has caused fatal explosions.
4. Mount the spool piece (figure 5-6), with or without the valve and the hot tap machine, and secure it in place. If the hot tap is assembled in place rather than handled as a unit, secure the spool piece, then assemble the other units.
5. Make up power to the hot tap machine.
6. Open the gate valve and manually crank the cutter against the tank boundary.
7. Cut in the power and cut through the hull into the tank.
8. Withdraw the cutter and close the valve.

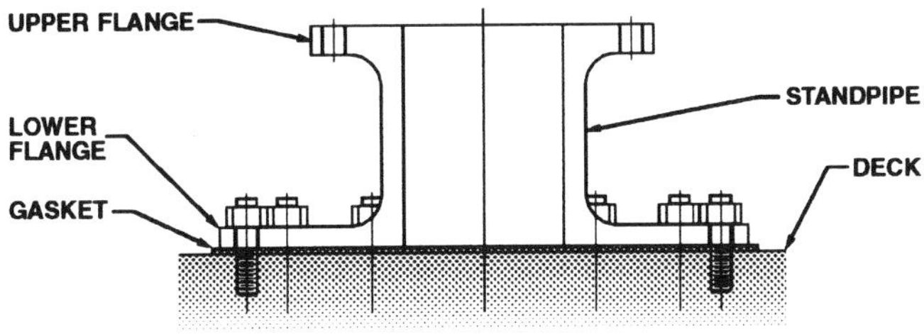

Fig. 5-6. Spool piece with wide flange for hot tapping. Courtesy of U.S. Navy.

9. Remove the hot tap assembly and install a flange and hose.

Often, the hot tap machine may be too much tool for the job. The same principle applies to the poor man's hot tap. With this system there may be a small release of the tank's contents. The poor man's hot tap uses a spool piece with a valve similar to the hot tap machine. A 2-inch valve is about the largest that is practical for divers to handle without lift bags or other aids. The cut is made through the valve and spool piece by drilling, boring, or oxyarc cutting. As soon as the cut is made, the tool is withdrawn and the valve closed. A second short spool piece is set onto the valve and attached to a hose with a Cam–Lok or other fitting. Figure 5-7 illustrates this device.

The flange of the spool piece that fits against the tank boundary should be wider than the outboard flange to make attachment easier and to give stability. A rubber gasket cemented to the inboard flange provides a seal between the hull and the spool piece. Before making up the spool piece, soak some gasket material in the same type of oil that is in the tank to make sure the oil cannot attack the gasket.

Tank entries should always be clear of internal structural members. The location of members may be detected by checking the ship's plan and measuring the locations on the ship's hull, observing the hull for traces of the members, or tapping the hull with a hammer. Tapping with a hammer always applies and is a good backup to other methods. Tank entries should always be below the air-oil interface where the cutting torch or mechanical cutter cannot set off an explosion by sparking into an explosive atmosphere. A location can be confirmed to be below the interface by drilling the hull, confirming that the discharge is in fact oil, and immediately plugging the hole.

Upon completion of pumping, the hole should be blanked so that no residue in the tank can escape. Whether the blank is directly on the hull or attached outboard of the valve depends upon the likelihood of an oil spill as the spool piece and valve are removed. A blank fitted directly against the hull should be gasketed.

Tanks next to the ship's bottom normally have 1½-inch (38 mm) to 2-inch (51 mm) threaded steel plugs to allow draining the tank in drydock. The plugs are re-

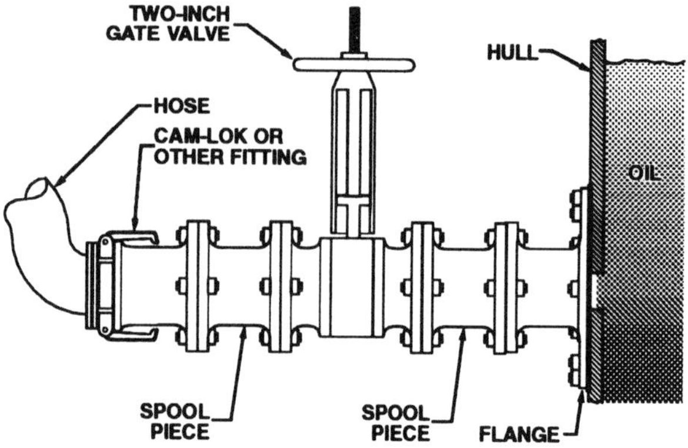

Fig. 5-7. Poor man's hot tap.
Courtesy of U.S. Navy.

moved from the outside with a wrench similar to an Allen wrench. Removal tools fabricated in the field should be made so the plug can be started with a slugging hammer or impact wrench. Keel plugs are a convenient access to tanks in inverted or nearly inverted ships.

Vents and sounding tubes are potential accesses for removing oil from bunker tanks. Sounding tubes are steel tubes at least 1.50 inches (38 mm) outside diameter and 1.25 inches (31 mm) inside diameter. They are often perforated to ensure the fuel inside and outside the tube is at the same level. These tubes lead as straight as possible to the bottom of the tank from some accessible location, usually the main deck. Gate valves are fitted on the upper end of sounding tubes that lie below the freeboard deck. Ships with automatic gauging systems also have sounding tubes.

All tanks have at least one vent located at the part of the tank that is highest when the ship is floating at her design waterline. Vent pipes are at least 2.5 inches (61 mm) in diameter and are commonly 4 inches (101 mm). They lead to weather, extend 8 feet above the main deck, and end in a gooseneck with a flame screen and ball check valve. Vents slope at least 30° from the horizontal and may have sharp bends and end some distance from their tanks. Vent headers sometimes are found, but are uncommon. Because of the small size of the vents and sounding tubes and the considerable head in some ships, removal may be a lengthy process. Vents and sounding tubes have the advantage of being remote from the tank, so direct access to a tank boundary is not required.

Vents end at the top of tanks, so a hose must be run through the vent into the oil. Sounding tubes also require hoses because of the perforations along their length. The oil removal technique depends on the attitude of the ship—upright, heavily listed, on her side, inverted—and the position of the vents and sounding tubes. Each tank must have a way for oil to exit the tank and for replacement air or water to enter.

Overflows lead from all tanks to an overflow tank or a tank with overflow space reserved. These lines have alarms, sight glasses, and check valves. Overflows are not very useful for removing oil because of their routing between tanks and the presence of valves and other obstructions in the line.

There are three basic methods for removing oil: displacing it by pumping water into the tank, pumping it out while water or air flows in to replace it, and blowing it out with compressed air. Water displacement is the safest, pumping the most common. Air, a last choice, is seldom used because of the danger of creating an explosive atmosphere.

Water displacement consists of pumping water into the tank to force the lighter oil from a high fitting. Fumes vent clear so the tank is always completely full of liquid. Whenever possible, gasolines and other Flammability Grade A liquids are removed by water displacement. A water displacement operation consists of the following steps:

1. Place a connection for handling displaced fuel on a fitting in the upper part of the tank. If the ship is inverted or in a position where the fittings are on the bottom, run a hose so fuel is drawn off the top.
2. Seal or blank all fittings through which fuel can escape and gag valves *closed.*
3. Insert a hose through another fitting and run it to the bottom of the tank.
4. Pump water through the hose; fumes are vented and the fuel forced out of the tank. Pump slowly enough that little turbulence and emulsification takes place at the oil-water interface.

When the vent is not at the highest point of the tank, a pocket of fumes remains above the vent. There is absolutely nothing salvors can do to eliminate this pocket other than creating another opening at the high point of the tank, seldom a practical option. Compression of the pocket of fumes can lead to an explosion. To prevent compressing the fumes during water displacement, salvors should watch the discharge, or sample it frequently, and stop pumping when water appears.

Pumping is the most common and usually the most effective method of removing bunkers. Bunkers are always flammable, so the opportunities to ignite either fumes or the liquid fuel itself must be reduced. Fire-fighting equipment and oil absorption and cleanup material should always be ready near the pump, at accesses, and at any point where leakage might occur. Pumping should stop at the first sign of leakage and remain stopped until the leak stops and the cleanup is completed.

Almost any type of pump designed to pump oils and other viscous liquids can pump through a manhole or other access. The best choice is a hydraulically driven submersible pump designed for discharging the cargo of tankers. The U.S. Coast Guard ADAPTS pump is such a pump; there are several equivalent commercial pumps. Pumping bunker tanks with these large, efficient pumps is rapid. Electric submersible pumps that are intrinsically safe and approved by the Coast Guard may be used. Reciprocating steam pumps, common in shipboard or shoreside service, may be brought to the scene and operated by steam from the ship's steam generator, a portable steam generator, or by compressed air. Pumps operate more slowly and less efficiently on compressed air than on steam. The supply pressure of either steam or compressed air should not exceed the design pressure of the pump. Normally, excessive pressure just blows the packing out of the steam end, but catastrophic failure of the pump casing is possible.

Pneumatic double diaphragm pumps such as those made by Wilden are excellent tools for removing bunkers from casualties. These positive displacement pumps are simple, reliable, suitable for all types of liquids, and present no explosion hazard. They are widely available in a variety of sizes and can be rigged into the tank through the manholes or through the vents or sounding tubes. They may operate submerged or dry starting with suction lifts up to 25 feet. Output is a function of the pump size and the volume and pressure of the air supply. These pumps

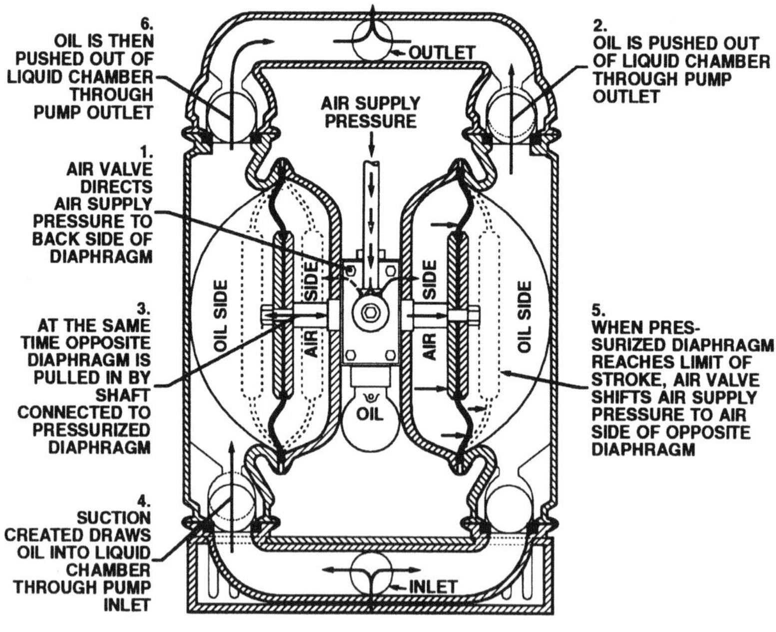

Fig. 5-8. Pneumatic double diaphragm pump. Courtesy of U.S. Navy.

are available in stainless steel and nonmetallic materials for handling corrosive products.

Air is used to remove fuel only if no other means is practical. Sealing a tank to reduce the leakage rate is difficult and introducing compressed air into a tank containing flammable fumes is fairly dangerous. An atmosphere that is otherwise nonflammable because it is too rich may be driven into the explosive range by the introduction of additional oxygen. With care and meticulous attention to detail air can successfully force bunkers from a tank.

The steps to blow oil from an upright, intact tank are:

1. Connect one fitting into the tank and connect an air hose and gauge.
2. Blank or seal tightly all fittings through which air can escape and gag all the valves.
3. Insert a hose through the sounding tube or vent and run it to the bottom of the tank.
4. Open the air control valve and blow air *slowly* into the tank until the predetermined pressure is reached and oil begins to flow through the hose.
5. Continue blowing at the minimum rate necessary to maintain pressure and flow.
6. When air begins to flow through the discharge, shut off the air and vent the tank to atmosphere.

The three basic methods may combine in any way to do the job. The choice of method depends very much on the shape of the tank and the attitude of the ship.

The third basic element in the transfer of oil is a place to put it as it comes off the casualty. Ideally, the oil is delivered into tanks afloat or ashore, designed, intended, and cleaned for the specific type of oil. This type of delivery may be possible when a sister or similar ship can come to the casualty site to receive the oil, when a tank barge that normally carries the same products is available, or when the casualty is alongside a shore facility that handles the same type of oil. In remote areas, oil must often go into whatever tankage is available, including empty tanks in ships or tugs participating in the salvage work. When oil is put into available tankage, the oil probably will be contaminated and have to be disposed of. A near certainty exists that the tanks must be cleaned, sometimes at considerable cost. Costs escalate if the ship or barge must make a special trip to a distant cleaning facility and be out of regular service.

The critical factor in transferring oil from a casualty to another vessel or ashore is the strength of the hose string. Hose strings should be as short as practical and every effort made to keep loads off the hose. The best solution is to transfer the oil to a vessel securely moored alongside. The hose strings are short and lightly loaded; communications are easy. Under casualty conditions it is not always possible to get alongside or remain there. The casualty may be in such a position that there is not enough room or water or the weather may be too bad. Alongside operations in the open sea require that some attention be given to mooring and fendering the vessels. Good mooring practice should be followed with an adequate number of lines, all of the same size and material and made up properly. No alongside operations in the open sea should be attempted without large pneumatic or foam fenders of the Yokohama type, particularly if the casualty is in an area with swell or where frequent weather changes are common. Without good fendering the vessels may be unable to moor safely and to remain alongside in even moderate weather. Few things irritate all the parties more than delaying or aborting a transfer because the ancillary equipment is inadequate. Chapter 12 has a more detailed discussion of fendering and mooring for oil transfers.

Drummed Oil

Ships may carry large quantities of drummed oil in holds, on deck, or in the machinery spaces as cargo or ship's stores. It may be necessary to remove this oil during salvage operations. If so, the drums are handled intact and stored to meet the safety precautions and storage requirements for the particular product. It may not be possible to comply fully with storage requirements under salvage conditions. If this is the case, every effort must be made to comply as nearly as practical to prevent accidents, pollution, and to retain the value of the material. As in the handling of bunker oils, safety and prevention of pollution take priority over retention of value. When very large quantities are present or storage conditions are severe, a specialist in the handling and storage of the particular product is invaluable. Damaged drums may leak. Sorbents, booms, and other environmental protection and cleanup materials should be available for cleaning up spilled oils, and leaking drums should be handled and stored in a containment system that limits the spread of the leakage. To avoid burns or other injury, salvors should not come in contact with the spilled material. The same comments apply to chemicals and other drummed liquids.

Oil Cargoes

The removal of oil or other liquid cargoes from casualties is a very different proposition than removal of bunkers, primarily because of the large quantities and wide variety of materials. These transfers are special cases of routine cargo discharge and ship-to-ship or ship-to-barge transfers of oil cargoes. The major differences lie in one ship being stranded or sunken requiring modification of normal mooring techniques, perhaps including stand-off mooring, and in over-the-top pumping from the casualty. Cargo transfer operations are an integral part of tanker salvage operations, and are discussed in Chapter 12.

Cold Weather

Most oils can be pumped at temperatures at which salvors can work. In cold weather, heavy fuels such as Bunker C or Number 6 fuel oil must be heated to reduce their viscosity for pumping. Usually a temperature increase of only a few degrees in a small volume of the oil is enough to make a difference. A nasty problem can arise if pumping stops with heavy oil in the hoses. The oil temperature can drop enough to cause the oil to solidify and block the hose. Heating the transfer hose with steam traces or electric blankets or insulating it can eliminate this problem.

The most practical way to heat bunker and cargo oil in the tanks is with the installed fuel oil heating coils. Portable steam generators may be brought aboard and rigged into the system if the casualty's steam generators are inoperable. The generators are a potential ignition source and must be located clear of fumes.

Where piping is broken so no steam reaches the tank heating coils, steam hoses or electric immersion heaters may be placed in the tank through an access. Heaters and either looped or open-ended hoses can pass through any large enough access. The heaters must be located so they heat the oil in way of the pump suction. Convoluted steel steam hose gives the best heat transfer. When submersible pumps are rigged through hatches or manholes, heaters or loops of hose may be laid into the tanks near the pumps. Suction hoses may be traced with steam hoses wrapped spirally around the hose or blanketed with electric heaters. Wrapping the suction hose and steam hose or heater with insulation improves heat transfer.

Internal tracing of suction hoses is sometimes desirable. There are at least three practical configurations (see figure 5-9). A loop can be used if the hose is large enough. Six-inch hose can accommodate a 1½-inch loop and have sufficient volume left for pumping. A loop is most efficient for overall heat transfer and water conservation. Open traces either straight into the tank or with a J-fitting that inject steam up the hose take advantage of the tendency of some heavy oils to form low-viscosity emulsions quickly. Open traces contaminate the oil being pumped and should be used when the primary consideration is pollution prevention, not salvage of the oil, or if there is no other option.

The most difficult situation occurs when a heavy oil must be pumped through a vent pipe because there is cargo on top of the tank accesses and the heating system is inoperative. In these cases, an open internal trace may be the only option.

In-Place Destruction

In some environments, particularly remote regions or extremely high or low latitudes, oil may be burned to destroy it. Burning is appropriate when the vessel is a constructive total loss, the whole purpose of the operation is to destroy the oil remaining in the vessel, and removal by more conventional means is prohibitively expensive.

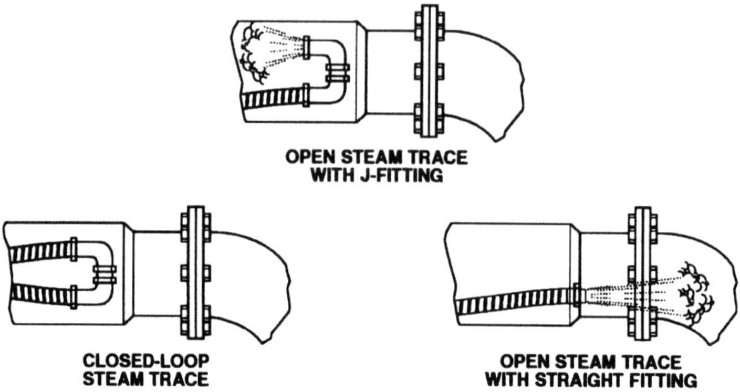

Fig. 5-9. Steam traces. Courtesy of U.S. Navy.

Devices have been built to heat, atomize, and burn oils at casualty sites. These devices have been technical successes and commercial failures. There is simply not enough demand for them to make them a viable product. For effective burning, the oil must be kept within the ship or taken out and transported to a burning site. The former is usually most practical. The burning site must be well ventilated to provide an adequate supply of combustion air and must have a large surface area. Burning the oil in bulk in its tanks can be effective if the tanks are opened and ventilation supplied. The contents of the ship burn with the oil so materials that generate toxic fumes should be removed. Local authorities and environmental regulators must give their approval for large-scale burning operations. Regulators are likely to require measures to prevent the spread of both the oil and the fire.

Open tank manholes do not usually provide enough surface area for burning. Fuel may be pumped or dumped into machinery spaces or holds by breaking fuel piping, and then burned there. Exposed tank tops may be opened to increase the ventilated surface area and deep and wing tank bulkheads may be split vertically to dump oil into holds or machinery space. Holed double-bottom tanks can be opened so oil flows into the hold above. Access to the manholes may require removal of cargo and may not be practical. Some residual oil collects in the structure at the top of the tank and remains after the burning.

The best burning is achieved when both the top and the side of the tank are open and the area of each opening is at least 10 percent of the surface area. If openings can be made only in the top, each opening should be at least 3 feet (1 meter) in diameter.

Explosives can cut openings but there is a danger of premature ignition of the oil or detonation of an explosive atmosphere lying behind a bulkhead or under a deck. Mechanically cutting vertical surfaces below the oil level is possible. If drilling the tank boundary shows there is a head of a few feet of oil, the boundary may be cut exothermally. Horizontal surfaces may be cut mechanically if the tank is pressed up. Even in pressed-up tanks there is a possibility of pockets of explosive gases. The deck over the tank may be flooded to a depth of a few inches and the cut made by sawing, chipping, or drilling. Explosive opening of tanks followed closely by detonation of a series of explosive or thermite devices to ignite the oil as it spreads from the tanks is effective.

Simultaneous explosive cutting and ignition are very practical. Time-fused or remotely fired explosive charges or thermite devices may ignite light fuels, lubricating oils, and hydraulic oils. Heavy fuels may be difficult to ignite, especially in cold climates. Diesel fuel, kerosene, or gasoline spread on the surface of heavy fuel and ignited raises the temperature of the heavy fuel high enough to ignite. An explosive or thermite device strapped to a drum of gasoline, diesel fuel, or other light oil is an effective ignition device.

The potential for air pollution, the loss of considerable value, and other unpleasant effects usually restrict burning of oil to bunkers rather than oil cargoes. The exception is that small packages of contaminated cargo sometimes are burned at a remote burning site.

In-place destruction of oils and other hazardous materials, even in small quantities, should be undertaken only with the full concurrence and written approval of local environmental regulators and authorities. Failure to get this concurrence and approval, even when in-place destruction is obviously the most environmentally sound disposal method, can result in legal action and civil penalties against the salvor.

6

THE SALVAGE PROCESS, SALVAGE PLANS, AND SURVEYS

It is by no means enough that salvors understand the mechanics of salvage. They must do that, of course, but they also must do much more. Salvors must appreciate fully the entire process of salvage, know how to develop salvage plans, how to get information to make these plans complete and workable, and how to put the information into the minds of those who need it.

Although salvage cases fit into general classes, each case has features that make it unique and defy a "cookbook" approach to salvage. Salvage does not defy, indeed it demands, an organized, systematic process of information collection, analysis, planning, and action to reach a successful conclusion. As contrary as it appears, salvors must approach a process innovative in its every aspect with discipline and structure.

THE SALVAGE PROCESS

This systematic process that I have chosen to call simply "the salvage process" consists of eleven steps:

1. Collecting information about the intact vessel.
2. Stabilizing the vessel.
3. Collecting and analyzing information specific to the casualty.
4. Identifying and quantifying risk to and by the vessel and the environment.
5. Selecting appropriate salvage actions.

6. Selecting an appropriate commercial instrument or contract terms.
7. Matching resources—people and equipment—to salvage actions.
8. Sequencing and scheduling the job.
9. Carrying out the salvage actions.
10. Delivering the salvaged vessel.
11. Demobilizing.

The eleven steps delineated above have no neat sequence. They overlap, fall out of order, are iterative, and often require redoing as the job goes along and Captain Murphy takes a hand, as he always does.

Immediately upon notification of a casualty, salvors begin collecting information about the ship and the cargo. This basic information includes:

Location.
Type of casualty.
Name and type of vessel.
Spillage of bunkers or cargo.
Vessel owner.
Vessel builder and year built.
Principal dimensions.
Stability and trim data.
Capacity data.
Cargo type and quantity.
Cargo-handling and safety systems.
Cargo and void space dimensions and centers of gravity.
Ullages or innages and soundings.
Bunker types and quantity.
Liquid load information.
Hull openings and accesses.

Registers of shipping, such as those published by classification societies, contain general information that defines the potential size of the problem. While effective, the registers are expensive and often a little out of date. Lloyd's Register of Shipping provides an on-line response service that furnishes information on any ship directly to the salvor's computer. Charterers or operators can provide details of the cargo. Ship's agents or the terminal operators at the port from which the vessel sailed also can supply details about the cargo. Shippers can provide specific information on cargoes, particularly dangerous or specialized cargoes. Owners or the building yard have the most complete and accurate technical information about the ship. The minimal information that should be requested at once by telex or facsimile from owners or the building yard is:

General arrangement plan.
Capacity plan.
Curves of form.
Midships section.
Trim and stability book or loading and stability information.
Inclining experiment.
Lines or offsets.
Ullage and soundings tables.
Shell expansion.
Deck plans.

Local agents, port authorities, or coast guards are the best sources of initial information about the casualty. Information collection and refinement are continuing processes that end only when all needed information is in hand, obviously unavailable, or no longer needed. The operational personnel—the salvage master and engineer for the job—define their requirements for information about the ship; the backup crew gets the information from the source and passes it to them.

At the casualty site, the ship's crew and salvage crews stabilize the ship by taking the damage control and salvage actions necessary to prevent the situation from deteriorating. In reality, they may only slow the rate of deterioration. Stabilization may include assuring personnel safety, medical rescue, crew evacuation, fire fighting, cargo loss control, stopping or limiting flooding, ballasting, laying out ground tackle to hold the vessel in place, notification and reporting, and any other actions to bring the vessel to a stable, if not secure, situation and fulfill the requirements of government agencies concerned with the casualty.

The process of documenting the operation, described in Chapter 15, should begin in the data collection phase and be in full swing when stabilizing the casualty. When the action is rapid, busy salvors naturally procrastinate about documenting what happened and why it happened. Accurate, complete documentation and records become vitally important before the files are closed and the checks written. This process must never be sloughed aside or given short shrift.

With the vessel secured, salvors continue collection of information specific to the casualty to learn the exact scope of the problem and the methods and resources needed to solve it. This information includes:

Draft, trim, and list data.
Cargo and bunker information.
Cargo and bunker loss definition.
Cargo and handling system integrity.
Hull damage.
Extent of flooding and flooding effects.
Power and machinery available.
Hydrographic information.
Weather information.
Local area marine traffic, access, and site security information.

A competent crew tries to get as much information as possible about the ship's condition and present it to the salvors on arrival. Salvors should neither discount nor accept without verification such information. A combination of physical inspections (surveys) and analyses of the findings of the surveys develops casualty-specific information. Later portions of this chapter discuss types of surveys and methods for making them. Complete surveys and analyses are a prerequisite to development of a good salvage plan and thus to the success of an operation. The analyses that accompany the surveys combine thoughtful analysis of the raw data to determine its meaning with engineering analysis of the ground reaction, buoyancy, stability, and strength. The analyses move from the general to the specific in defining the problem.

Determination and quantification in general terms (low, medium, high) of the risks that the ship, the cargo, and the environment present to one another form a major part of the analyses. The salvor has apparently conflicting responsibilities, such as salvaging the casualty while retaining the maximum value in the hull, salvaging and protecting the cargo while maintaining its maximum value, and protecting the environment. To develop operational plans and priorities he must identify and quantify risks:

Presented by the cargo to people and to the environment.
Presented to the value of the cargo by its situation relative to the casualty and the environment.
Presented by the ship.
To the ship as she lies.
Peculiar to the location.

The surveys and their analysis, complemented by analysis of the risks, provide the basis for determining the specific salvage actions to reduce the risk all around and bring the casualty safely afloat. Salvage actions that deal with the greatest risk first have the highest priority. In general, the priority is:

Reducing risk to human life.
Minimizing damage to the environment.
Reducing risk to the vessel.
Maintaining the value of the vessel and its cargo.

Fighting or containing fires has a high priority and fits almost across the four items mentioned above. Little can be done to get on with the salvage on a burning vessel, but there are occasions where letting the fire burn out minimizes most effectively risk to human life and the environment.

Regulators, rather than technical necessity or desirability, determine certain salvage actions and their sequence, particularly those concerning handling of dangerous or polluting cargoes and bunkers. Usually, the frustration and time lost in going ahead with a perhaps unnecessary action is less than the frustration of trying to reverse a bureaucratic decision, particularly in the heat of an operation. When regulators insist upon action the salvor or any party to the salvage considers unwise or incorrect, they should make their objections known to the regulator and completely document the objection, their action, and the regulator's response.

The next three phases of the salvage process:

Selecting appropriate salvage actions,
Matching resources—people and equipment—to salvage actions,
Sequencing and scheduling the job,

comprise the formulation of the operational plan to see the ship safely afloat and to deliver her to her owner. Determination of the minimum repairs necessary to see the ship safely afloat is inherent in planning salvage actions. The salvage actions must be not only appropriate to the task but also feasible under the conditions of the particular casualty, and economically practical. In selecting proper salvage actions, matching these actions to the resources, and accomplishing them, the salvor's technical skill and knowledge of his trade—and of the maritime industry—come to the fore. Scheduling and sequencing the work similarly shows his management skills.

Salvage action begins when the salvage plan is outlined and sufficient crew and equipment are on hand. Execution of the salvage actions should not wait until all the resources are in place and the plan is filled out in detail. What can be done should be done as quickly as possible. In getting action moving and keeping it moving, salvors must never take shortcuts that endanger the ship or salvage crew, ignore basic safety, or fail to make required analyses and think problems through beforehand. The consequences of poorly thought out actions are great. Often salvors must make a show of doing something, but there is no place for "Do something, even if it's wrong" in salvage.

Delivery of the vessel to its owner must be as meticulously planned in both its technical and commercial aspects as the refloating. Salvors must think ahead to exactly what is to be done with the vessel after refloating: how she is to be physically secured and made safe and where she is to go for delivery. They also must plan the commercial arrangements that precede delivery and secure their payment.

Demobilization deserves as much attention and care as any other portion of an operation. In an effective demobilization, personnel and equipment return to their base quickly and with no damage to either and minimal additional cost. People are tired at the end of the operation and want to go home. They are sometimes a little slapdash during demobilization (and about tending to the gear when it is returned to base). Safety consciousness decreases. Supervisors must take care to assure correct handling and packing of equipment and strict compliance with safety procedures.

SALVAGE PLANS

The salvage plan is the operational plan for the salvage operation. The size and complexity of the salvage plan vary with the size and complexity of the job. It ranges from handwritten notes in a pocket notebook to a complete and detailed project plan. The salvage plan forms the heart of the salvage process by addressing operations directly. It does not stand alone; an entire spectrum of support plans and analyses support it. Some are not nearly as dignified as their names would suggest, but all are part of the total salvage plan.

A good salvage plan:

- Is complete without excessive detail.
- Is technically and commercially viable.
- Balances work with resources.
- Identifies the most economical sources of resources.
- Identifies key players.
- Assigns individual and organizational responsibilities.
- Uses salvage and specialist crews efficiently.
- Schedules target dates, key events, and resources.
- Plans for foreseeable contingencies.
- Plans alternatives and fallback positions.

The resources identified and used may not suit the operation ideally. The choice of resources—both people and equipment—considers not only the suitability, but location and availability. It makes no sense to transport material a long distance when equivalents or near-equivalents can be rented near the salvage site. On the other hand, it is not sensible to rent second-rate or marginal equipment or pay outrageous rates to suppliers whose avocation appears to be piracy. Equipment, along with all other aspects of salvage, justifies a belt and suspenders approach—in the case of supply, this means primary and alternative sources.

Efficient use of resources means not only having the proper mix of types of equipment, skills, experience, and numbers, but also having them available when needed. Expensive equipment or personnel sitting around waiting for their turn to play is inefficient, as is having them waiting for ancillary equipment to arrive. Planning for bringing resources to the site should address not only timing, but also normal and special access to the area and to the casualty.

Target dates often depend upon time, tide, and weather. In scheduling key events and defining the work necessary to reach them, a very basic decision is to work in series or parallel. In this decision the composition and abilities of the salvage crew must be assessed carefully. Scheduling more work than can be undertaken and supervised safely and effectively in the time available is counterproductive. It is also counterproductive to schedule simultaneous work that requires the services of the same individuals simultaneously or results in excessively long hours. Tired people make mistakes; it is a poor leader who plans to drive people to fatigue.

Weather affects salvage as it does every type of operation at sea. The salvage plan should include the systems for weather forecasting—local broadcasts, weather facsimiles, private forecasts, etc. Salvors should be aware of and expect the worst type of weather at the operations site and know its frequency of occurrence and duration. Preparation should be made for weather contingencies. These plans should include securing of the vessel against deterioration and protection of the salvors' ships, equipment, crew, and aircraft.

Contingency planning should include spills of cargo or bunkers, cargo fires, machinery and accommodation fires, and medical emergencies. The last is particularly important in remote areas where evacuation is not simple and facilities for treating major traumatic injuries are hundreds of miles away. It may be necessary to have arrangements in place with air charterers to provide medical evacuation on call.

Salvage is a dynamic process; invariably there are many unknowns and unpredictable quantities. Accordingly, a salvage plan cannot be rigid. Good salvage analyses identify areas of weakness or areas where unknown or unpredictable quantities are likely to affect the success of the salvage action. The planning process should identify alternative action—even if it is recorded only in the brain of the salvage master. Identification of alternative action is not a pessimistic "planning for failure." It is, like contingency planning, preparation before the fact. It is far better to prepare for than to be surprised by failure.

There may even come a time in the operation, as there has many times in the past, when the salvage plan simply is not working and should be abandoned. The decision to abandon a salvage plan is difficult and requires fine judgment. It should be neither premature nor delayed too long.

Two analyses, while not a part of the salvage plan proper, form the basis for many decisions made in its preparation. The first of these is the engineering analysis. The scope of the engineering analysis varies with the type and complexity of the casualty. A straightforward grounding on a mud bank may require only a simple analysis of ground reaction and a cursory look at stability. More complex cases with hull damage, flooding, cargo loss, etc., require in-depth analysis of stability and strength. An initial engineering analysis should be completed before the salvage actions are selected to insure the type and scale of the actions are appropriate and that they carry a reasonable chance of success. An important contribution of the engineering analysis is in the "What if . . . ?" process, an integral part of the salvage plan development. The effects and requirements of proposed actions can be evaluated and actions chosen based on objective results rather than gut feelings. The analysis should be refined as the job goes along and more information becomes available. Throughout the planning process salvors should keep in mind the accuracy of the information serving as input for the analysis and view the results with a jaundiced eye. There is an engineering adage that applies: "If it looks right and feels right, it probably is right."

The second analysis is the hydrographic analysis. Hydrographic information is important input for some basic decisions in the salvage process. The information includes depths, sea floor compositions, relatively fine-grain soundings on routes both the refloated vessel and support vessels may take, tides, and currents. The information should be looked at to decide how the operation may be laid out physically and in what directions and areas vessels may move. Sea floor composition enters into calculation of ground reaction, prediction of the ship's behavior, and prediction of anchor holding power. The latter directly affects ground tackle ground leg makeup.

Tides and currents have a major effect on schedule. Schedules must take advantage of both high and low water. Underwater work must avoid periods of tidal currents of more than 2 knots and must be in segments that can be completed in periods of slack water.

Seven supporting areas require either planning for the specific operation or implementation of standing policies and procedures. These are organization, logistics, communications, documentation, cost accounting, media and public relations, and liaison with authorities. Often, especially for small operations, the plans need not be formal written plans, but the procedures must be understood completely by all parties concerned.

Organization—The organization of a salvage operation is on two distinct, mutually supporting levels: the management of the operation and the work itself.

In any well-organized operation the management organization exists to support the workers in the field. When the opposite situation exists, or seems to exist, the operation is inefficient. A standard casualty management and response organization is an excellent tool because it can be set up quickly. A standard organization for salvage operations should never become Holy Writ. It must be tailored for a specific operation to assure the proper management and operational skills are provided in the correct numbers.

Logistics—The science of moving and maintaining forces in the field is an integral part of any salvage operation. Salvage logistics may vary from two men loading a pump into the back of a pickup and driving to a salvage site, to a major airlift of salvage crew and equipment to an extremely remote site. Regardless of the scale, logistics must be planned carefully and basic logistics procedures be in place before the need for them arises. Logistics preparation includes predetermined sources for special skills and equipment and, where appropriate, standing on-call agreements and price arrangements. Salvage crews should be prepared to travel on short notice. Crews likely to travel internationally should have current international travel documents. Only so much can be done in general preparation; the logistics plan for a specific casualty must be tailored to that casualty. The logistics plan is a joint effort of the salvage master and the logistics coordinator. The salvage master decides what resources he needs and when he needs them. The logistics coordinator then provides the resources when they are needed.

Communications—Both on- and off-site communications must be provided for. Hand-held VHF radios and bridge-to-bridge sets suffice for on-site communications. Intrinsically safe radios must be used on tankers or other ships carrying flammable or potentially explosive cargoes. The channel selected for salvage operations should be one that is not common for other maritime operations in the area. In large, complex operations it may be necessary to ask regulatory authorities to assign frequencies to the operators and to enforce circuit discipline.

Off-site communications between the salvage master at the site and his management and support personnel are required throughout the operation. Satellite communications, facsimiles, cellular telephones, single sideband radio, modems, and all the other wonders of modern communications and data transmission make site-to-base communications a routine matter at the most remote site. Salvage ships and tugs should have satellite communications systems and facsimiles as a matter of routine. Salvage teams operating without salvage ships may use the casualty's communications, bring portable satellite systems to the scene, or contract with local communications companies for facilities and equipment. Communications systems and frequency of reports should be thought out early in the operation and efforts made to see that the correct quantities and balance of communications equipment are provided. The correct balance means enough communications to keep the job moving, but not so much that time is wasted on meaningless and nonproductive blather.

Documentation—The only thing duller than the documentation of a salvage operation is cost accounting, addressed in the next paragraph. Dull as it is, documentation is a vital part of every salvage operation. The salvage award garnered from no cure–no pay salve operations depends on the salvor's ability to reconstruct the operation and present a case based on documentation. Salvage conducted on other contractual bases has a high probability of being litigated. Complete documentation of the salvage effort is a necessary part of being prepared for this kind of litigation. It is a fact of the business that if the salvor wants to make and retain money he documents his work completely. Company policy should provide instructions and directions for who keeps daily logs, the basic information the logs contain, and how the logs are handled and retained. The taking of photographs, motion pictures, videotapes, and audiotapes by the salvor's people at the scene should be controlled as much as possible to ensure all events are documented completely, but that time is not wasted in providing unnecessary documentation. Significant events should be photographed or videotaped as part of the documentation. Audiotapes of meetings and interviews are useful in reconstructing decisions and the rationale that led to them. Planning should assure that critical events are documented. Often, when the fur is flying, people are so involved in the operation that documentation is forgotten.

Control of third-party documentation is virtually impossible. All the parties to the operation as well as government and regulatory bodies have the right to make audio and visual recordings. They can be expected to exercise this right and the salvor has no right to their photographs or recordings unless they are parties to litigation following the operation.

Cost accounting—To the salvor, cost accounting is as dull as death. However, since salvage is a commercial enterprise, cost accounting is a necessary part of the effort. The method of cost accounting for the job should be consistent with standard company policy and should be set up ahead of time. To reduce the work load at the salvage site, on-site salvage management should be responsible only for keeping track of time for salvage crew and out-of-pocket local expenses. Complete and detailed cost accounting should be done at the company headquarters. For large jobs it may be necessary to set up a field office manned and equipped to do most of the cost accounting on site. Whatever the method, the leaders of a crew deploying to a salvage job should know how cost accounting is to be handled and what is expected of them before they walk out the door.

Media and public relations—It is too late to think about how the press should be handled when the red eye of a TV camera is staring you down or the first explosive article has appeared in the local paper. In the current atmosphere of environmental awareness anyone connected with work in which pollution is a problem or a possibility often is treated as a villain whose purpose is to cause rather than to prevent or clean up pollution. Unrealistic as this attitude is, it occurs and affects the attitude of the press toward all the participants in a salvage operation. The public, particularly when under the influence of a hostile or sensational press, also may consider salvors part of the problem. The time spent in preparing for the press and public and in maintaining good relations is well-spent in the long term. Press relations and the relationships with local people should be thought and planned out well in advance. The number of people in the salvage crew who speak for the salvor should be limited and discipline maintained. Lying or shading the truth for the press or public is seldom productive. An open attitude is best and most likely to result in good press relations.

Liaison with authorities—Virtually the entire preceding paragraph can describe the relationship of the salvors with the authorities. Regulatory bodies and agencies have such strong positions that the development of hostile relationships can be not only counterproductive but downright disastrous. How relationships with authorities are handled and who handles them should be established at the operation's outset.

The salvage plan is not just a list of salvage actions but also a plan for all the supporting functions that go into making the operation a success. Whatever its format and degree of detail, the salvage plan lays out the work to be done and the resources for doing it, sequences and schedules work, identifies key people, assigns responsibilities to individuals and organizations. One very important thing: at the risk of playing the same song too often, there is going to be another rousing chorus of those old standards "A Salvage Plan Must Be Commercially Viable" and "A Salvage Job Without a Profit Brings the Blues." No matter how technically perfect the plan and how elegant the execution, the job is a failure if it does not make money.

SALVAGE SURVEYS

Salvage surveys are physical inspections of the casualty and the surrounding area to determine the casualty's condition as she lies and the conditions that affect her salvage. It is vital to both the technical and commercial success of a salvage operation that surveys are thorough, systematic, and are made by people who:

- Understand what they are seeing.
- Fully record their observations.
- Can interpret their observations.
- Can communicate the observations and their interpretation to others.

The most senior and best technically qualified members of the salvage crew should make salvage surveys.

In addition to providing the basic input for the salvage planning process, surveys provide documentary evidence of the "as found" condition of the casualty. This evidence is extremely important for arbitration or in settlement negotiations.

Surveys are dynamic processes that are never truly complete. They begin when the salvor arrives aboard the casualty and continue throughout the operation, with the final comprehensive survey being made after the ship is afloat. Several subsurveys contribute to the complete salvage survey. The subsurveys include:

Preliminary survey.
Pollution and hazards survey.
Topside survey.
Interior survey.
Exterior survey.
Hydrographic survey.
Cargo survey.
Machinery survey.

The *preliminary survey* verifies the information provided by the ship's crew and determines the general condition of the ship. It spotlights conditions for special attention in the detailed surveys that follow and sets priorities for these surveys.

Because of the potential liabilities arising from pollution and the hazards presented by a variety of cargoes, the *pollution and hazards survey* enjoys a high priority. As part of this survey, all cargo and bunker tanks and any void spaces or tanks surrounding them should be sounded or ullaged in the presence of a senior salvor. All the oil aboard, including the "reserve" only the chief engineer knows about, should be accounted for. Once the salvors are aboard and have taken their initial soundings and ullages, no oil should be transferred without their knowledge.

Accesses to bunker tanks that may be used for oil removal should be located and marked during this survey. Important bunker tank accesses include sounding tubes, vent lines, and overflows. Where bunkers are carried in double bottoms with cargo loaded on top, there may be no other way to remove bunkers than through these limited accesses.

The survey also includes all other hazardous material that may be either a part of the ship's outfit or its cargo. The P&I representative may wish to take part in this survey and to keep his own record of hazardous materials and their location. If salvage is not successful, removal of the wreck and the hazardous substances it contains is a P&I responsibility.

The *topside survey* gathers information about the exterior of the ship above the weather decks. In stranded ships, particular attention is paid to prospective attachment points for ground tackle, tugs, and the lead for their lines, and the location, type, and condition of machinery that can be useful in deck operations.

During the *interior survey* salvors inspect all accessible spaces in the interior of the hull to find out in detail the condition of each space, especially if the space is flooded. Several inspections of a space are usually necessary to determine the exact condition of flooding—Is flooding continuing? Is the space tidal? Is the level stable?, etc. The structural condition gets particular attention, especially where either some spaces are inaccessible or an external survey is unfeasible. In these cases, the remote signs of damage have great importance. Equipment or material that may be useful in the salvage is located during the internal survey.

A comprehensive and complete *flooding survey* is particularly important, for water can migrate through the ship in broken pipes and cracks that are not apparent to survey teams. The traditional method of surveying for flooding is to take soundings at regular intervals and compare the soundings. Soundings are made in all spaces, not just tanks. Water-indicating paste is rubbed on sounding rods for taking soundings in bunker and cargo oil tanks and any other spaces showing signs of containing oil. The water-indicating paste locates the interface between oil and water in the space. Subsequent soundings and observations can determine what the flooding is doing. Many cargo holds are easy to sound because the nature of the cargo—containers, break-bulk, unitized, RO/RO, etc.—leaves spaces through which a sounding tape can be worked. Bulk cargoes are not this easy because they fill the space entirely and flooding may be limited to the lowest levels of a mass of cargo. Well points—devices intended to locate the water table ashore—can be driven through many bulk cargoes to locate flooding masked by the cargo.

The *exterior survey* has two parts: a survey of the above-water portions of the hull and a diving survey of the underwater hull. The purpose of both parts is to determine how the ship lies and what damage she may have sustained. When sea conditions make the diving survey impossible or extremely limited, both the topside exterior survey and the interior survey must be unusually thorough. Specific things to be learned in the exterior survey include:

The length and breadth of bottom contact.

Impalement.

The location, extent, and size of structural damage.

The condition of sea suctions, sea valves, fittings, and appendages.

The practicality of diving work and the equipment needed for it.

During the *hydrographic survey*, soundings are taken around the ship and on possible retraction routes, in areas where ground tackle may be laid, in areas that salvage ships may transit or lie in, and in areas that may be refuges for the salvage plant or refloated ship. A few minutes' quiet study of the chart can be extremely enlightening and can give a good indication of how extensive the hydrographic survey must be. Even the largest-scale charts seldom show the local hydrography in sufficient detail for salvage operations. Areas for which the chart shows a great deal of white space between soundings or only a few lines of soundings are not good places to take damaged vessels. Particular care must be taken to locate shoals, rocks, and other hazards in areas where salvage or lightering ships may operate.

Tides are an important aspect of the hydrographic survey, especially since few ships are considerate enough to become casualties near tide stations where excellent tidal data are available. Predictions of tides for a salvage site should be checked by measuring tides at the site. The tidal range should be determined along with the duration of slack water and the relationship between slack water and high and low tides.

Tidal currents impact salvage planning because high currents can limit the hours in which divers can work and affect the maneuverability of assisting vessels and the ability of salvors to handle a refloated vessel.

The hydrographic survey also includes observation of prevailing weather and weather patterns, including the direction, frequency, and size of swells, frequency of frontal passages, and the weather that accompanies frontal passages. In addition to these general observations, specific observations should note the casualty's aspect to the weather and the potential for taking weather damage.

If feasible, bottom samples should be taken around the ship to assist in estimating the coefficient of friction and the quality of the holding ground.

The *cargo survey* includes the cargo, its containment, and means for working the cargo. Information on the cargo itself should include type, quantity, distribution in the ship, damage, residual value, feasibility of transshipping, jettisoning, or leaving it in the ship. Cargo containment systems should be checked to find out if they are still intact or if cargo is being lost. Checks of cargo containment systems should include accesses to cargo for both personnel and for cargo-handling gear.

In ships carrying both solid and liquid cargoes, mechanical means of handling the cargo should be checked to see if they are intact and operable or can be made operable. It is always better to use the ship's equipment to handle cargo than to improvise equipment. Safety systems—such as inert gas systems in tankers—that support the cargo also should be checked.

Part of the cargo survey is done ashore. Facilities and personnel for moving cargo—stevedores, lightering vessels, helicopters, warehousing—can be found only by checking port facilities.

The *machinery survey* checks the ship's main propulsion and auxiliary machinery to decide if it is operable and how it may contribute to the salvage operation. Main propulsion machinery may help in refloating a stranded vessel if there is no damage to the propeller and other running gear and if there is little danger that the engine or its ancillary systems can ingest sea floor material. Electrical generating and distribution systems and electric motors should be checked for the amount and type—voltage, phase, AC or DC—of power. Deck machinery and cargo-handling machinery—anchor windlasses, mooring winches, pumps, and cargo winches—are also checked during the machinery survey.

The dividing line between one survey and another is usually hazy. Union rules do not apply in salvage surveying. The more information collected and the more varied the viewpoints, the better the chance of reducing unwanted surprises. There is no single correct way to make a survey; nor is specific information always critical. When the specific conditions of the casualty prevent obtaining a piece of information, another way can often be found, or the information can be deduced by inference.

For salvors, surveying means wandering around a strange ship—nothing novel for anyone experienced enough to make a worthwhile survey, but nonetheless a potentially dangerous venture. The salvage master or person coordinating the survey must know who is surveying where and what time they can be expected to check in. It is always a good idea for two people to work together to improve both the efficiency and safety of the survey. At least two people should always work together in the interior of the ship, especially when the ship is without power. Everyone entering the interior of the ship should carry a flashlight. Carrying a whistle is not a bad idea. Normal maritime safety precautions for entering closed spaces must be observed scrupulously.

The prudent salvor never accepts the results of his first survey as the complete and unchanging truth—especially in those areas where the results point toward a simple straightforward salvage. Survey results should be constantly rechecked and updated. A salvor can do few better things in his "idle" moments than to walk around the casualty with his eyes open wide enough to see what he sees, not what he ought to see. Prudent salvors are suspicious, inquisitive, and pessimistic.

Most experienced salvors and major salvage companies have developed survey checklists based on their experience. Survey checklists are often tailored to the type of casualty. Appendix C reproduces a survey checklist taken from the *U.S. Navy Ship Salvage Manual*. This checklist is very comprehensive, perhaps so comprehensive it is more comprehensive than practical. Usually, all of the information included in the checklist is necessary. Infrequently, additional information may be needed. For surveying, as for all other aspects of salvage, there is neither a cookbook nor a single right way. Salvors must think the situation through and figure out the information needed.

The salvage surveys and the salvage plan are the heart of the salvage process. The surveys are the first steps in learning the details of the problem. The plan is the layout of the steps to its solution. Both are dynamic and are updated and changed constantly. The probability of conducting a salvage operation that is either technically or commercially successful without good surveys and a good salvage plan is very low.

PUTTING OUT THE WORD

The salvage plan, no matter how carefully produced, is of no use to anyone if it remains in the salvage master's shirt pocket. The information it contains must be put out and into the minds of those who are going to execute it. Regular salvage crews are bright and experienced people; the work goes better when they know what is expected of them and why. No little advantage accrues from reactions from them as the work progresses and what works and what does not work becomes obvious.

Explanation of the salvage problems, the methods chosen for their solution, the priority and sequence of work, allocations of equipment and resources, and estimates of where problems can occur to all the members of a salvage crew may be inconvenient and seem unnecessary. It is not. Time spent bringing the crew up to snuff and keeping them up that way pays big dividends in efficiency and effectiveness. Discussions should be as informal as practical since the best ideas come from general discussions where the people doing the work express their opinions and ideas. Regular briefings and discussions are absolutely necessary to keep an around-the-clock operation going smoothly. The salvage master who can be all places at all times and can be awake twenty-four hours every day is yet to be born. The more everyone involved knows about the salvage plan, the better the job goes. When all hands know and understand the overall plan, meetings can concentrate on changes, and shift foremen can concentrate on the assignments for their shift. As the job goes along, formal briefings can be held less frequently, as long as the senior people talk frequently. All hands in the crew should be encouraged to put their ideas forward in meetings or outside them. Only poor salvage masters or foremen fail to listen to their crews and learn from them.

Surveyors and others representing owners, underwriters, and P&I may be invited to the salvage crew briefings or, if the circumstances make their attendance undesirable, another briefing can be held.

SUMMARY

The salvage process, salvage surveys, salvage plan development, promulgation, and execution are mainly common sense and technical expertise. As is emphasized throughout this book, there is no single right way and no cookbook. The common factor in all successful operations is thinking before doing and paying careful attention to detail.

7

RIGGING

Rigging plays a major part in almost every salvage operation. Most mariners are familiar with rigging hardware and systems, but they seldom put together heavily loaded special-purpose systems from hardware that can be collected on short notice. Salvors do. Adapting available rigging materials to the situation requires knowledge exceeding that of most mariners about what can and cannot be done with specific components. Every competent salvor must have a working knowledge of rigging hardware and of assembling rigging systems. Books far thicker than this one have been written on rigging and a wealth of technical and procedural information is in the public domain, available both from manufacturers and in seamanship and other specialized technical publications. I have no intention of trying either to teach my grandmother to suck eggs or to better the work produced by better riggers than I. Accordingly, this book addresses basic rigging data or procedures only cursorily; it does not provide endless tables of sizes, characteristics, breaking strengths, and safe working loads. Instead it devotes the available space to discussion of specific rigging problems in salvage.

I do not subscribe to the philosophy that there is only one way to do things and all rigging must be made up with only the best possible materials. Sometimes the best method is not practical and the best materials are not available. A good salvor must know how to "make do" and, when he does, he must know how to get the best from what he has and what weaknesses "making do" introduces into the system. He also must know when "good enough" actually is good enough, and when it falls short.

Rigging materials change rapidly as technology changes. Good rigging practice does not change, but points of emphasis do as new materials and technologies come into salvage practice. An excellent example exists in aramid and high molecular weight polyethylene (HMPE) synthetic fiber lines. The advantages of the high tensile strength-to-weight ratios of these lines are realized only when they are protected from abrasion that would be acceptable in more conventional natural or synthetic fiber lines. Salvors must know rigging materials—their strengths and their weaknesses—thoroughly. They cannot rely on either tribal knowledge or rules of thumbs in laying out rigging systems.

Rigging systems are like all other engineering systems, in that a factor of safety is applied to the breaking strength of each component to arrive at the safe working load of the system. Unfortunately, the factors of safety vary widely with the type of material—the factor of safety for wire rope in running rigging is 5; for nylon rope in the same application it is 12. Many salvage applications combine materials and work with loads that may move the system into the gray and unpredictable area between breaking strength and safe working load. Users of these systems are obliged to know the details of the design and the working load the system can carry.

Closely related to the system factor of safety is the system weak link. Every engineering system can be loaded to failure; few, like the wonderful one horse shay, have simultaneous failure of every component. The user of a system, especially a system that is likely to be loaded near its failure point, must know how the system can be expected to fail and what components can be expected to need replacement following failure. Salvage systems should not be so heavily loaded that failure is probable, but the possibility of failure is inherent in every highly loaded system. Salvage rigging systems should be designed so that failure involves as little trauma as possible. In system failure, limiting trauma means limiting hazards to people in the area of the failure and limiting damage to the system to components that can be replaced cheaply and quickly.

WIRE ROPE

Wire rope is one of the most common salvage rigging materials. Salvors need to know the strengths and weaknesses of wire rope so they may use it effectively and do not inadvertently introduce features into the rigging system that weaken it. Wire rope is a forgiving material with a reasonable margin of error acceptable in service. When it fails or becomes unusable, the results can be dangerous, dramatic, and expensive. They can also cause a very serious operational setback. For salvage wire rope systems, efficiency and effectiveness, not long life, are the factors that make the system economical and effective.

A great deal of technical and procedural information appears in the general literature about wire rope. A good general reference that should be in every salvor's library is the *Wire Rope Users Manual*[1] published by the Committee of Wire Rope Producers of the American Iron and Steel Institute. Manufacturers' handbooks usually contain some general descriptive and maintenance information along with technical data on the ropes they manufacture. A good rigging handbook is invaluable in the field.

All wire ropes consist of three basic components: individual *wires* made up into *strands* formed around a *core* to make the rope. There are a variety of types and construction of wire rope in general and specific services. The most common wire rope in marine service is 6-strand right lay rope with either an independent wire rope or fiber rope core (IWRC or FC). Eight-strand ropes are not uncommon; left lay ropes are seen sometimes.

It should be very easy to establish the size of wire rope, but it is not. In the United States, wire rope is measured by the diameter in inches. In Britain, the basic size measurement is circumference—formerly in inches (to which references are still common), now in millimeters. The rest of the world measures wire rope by diameter in millimeters. Whatever the measurement system, the measurement method is the same. Wire rope is measured over its largest dimension as shown in figure 7-1.

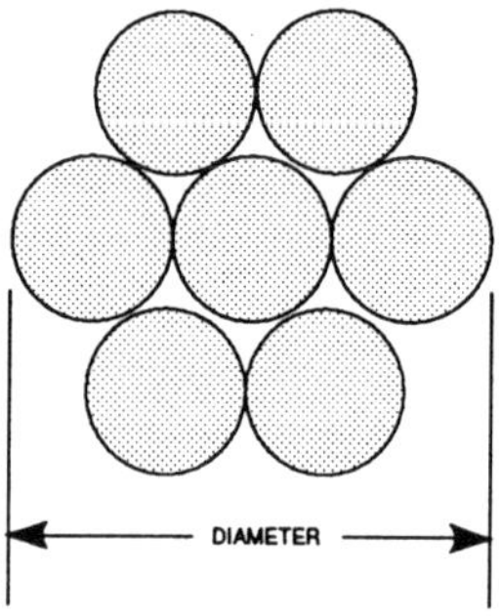

Fig. 7-1. Measuring wire rope diameter

Wire rope is classified by the number of strands that form the rope and the number of wires that form the strand. The designation 6 × 19 describes 6-strand rope with 19 wires in each strand. In practice, the number of wires does not describe the strand exactly; it is a nominal classification. The following table describes the major classifications most often found in salvage work.

TABLE 7-1.

WIRE ROPE CLASSIFICATION			
Classification	*Description*		
	Strands	*Wires*	*Maximum Outside Wires*
6 × 7	6	3 to 14	9
6 × 19	6	15 to 26	12
6 × 37	6	27 to 49	18
6 × 61	6	50 to 74	24
6 × 91	6	75 to 109	30
8 × 19	8	15 to 26	12

As the number of wires in the strand increases, flexibility increases, abrasion resistance decreases, and bending fatigue resistance increases.

The core is the foundation of the wire rope. Its primary function is to support the wire strands and to keep them in the correct relative positions throughout the life of the rope. When wire rope is loaded, the strands exert an inward pressure on the rope. By supporting the strands, the core limits interstrand pressures and wire breakage. The support also allows the rope to bend and move around sheaves and drums without excessive interstrand pressure. Fiber core rope has greater flexibility, 30 percent more elasticity, and 7 to 10 percent less strength than IWRC rope of the same size construction. IWRC rope has less tendency to rotate and greater heat resistance than fiber core rope.

Wire rope is manufactured from several grades of steel. The name and properties of the steel depend upon the standard to which the rope is made. Most wire rope in marine service is made of improved plow steel (IPS), extra improved plow steel (EIPS), or an equivalent. Extra improved plow steel rope is about 15 percent stronger than improved plow steel rope of identical construction. "Improved plow steel" and "extra improved plow steel" are designations used in the United States based on the properties and chemical composition of the steel. Steel designations in other countries may be comparable or may vary somewhat. The salvor is primarily concerned with breaking strength and elasticity.

Wire rope may be galvanized by any of several processes. Galvanizing of any type reduces the wire rope strength about 10 percent below bright rope of the same material and construction. Hot galvanizing increases the elasticity of wire rope by partial stress relieving. Therefore, hot galvanized wire rope is preferred where the rope must carry large dynamic loads.

Breaking strength is the wire rope property of greatest concern to salvors. Breaking strength is the ultimate strength of wire rope as determined in a tensile test. Such a figure is of little use to a salvor in the field without a tensile testing machine and the time to run the tests. Wire rope is manufactured to a nominal breaking strength. This figure appears in manufacturers' data. An allowance of $\pm 2\frac{1}{2}$ percent of the nominal breaking strength is given to account for differences in manufacturing processes. For application in the field the breaking strength of new wire rope should be taken as $97\frac{1}{2}$ percent of the nominal breaking strength. The best source of breaking strength information is the manufacturer's technical data. When no reliable data are available, the nominal breaking strength of wire rope may be estimated by:

$$BS = C \times (\pi \times d)^2$$

where:

BS = nominal breaking strength of the wire rope in long tons
C = a constant that varies with the construction of the wire rope
d = the diameter of the wire rope in inches

The following table gives values of C for wire rope constructions typically found in salvage. The constant is accurate in the midranges of sizes of wire rope, but gives low results for small ropes and high results for large ropes. Table 7-2 also describes the accuracy of C for various sizes. Variation in the accuracy can be taken as linear. Only values for wire ropes up to 2¾ inches in diameter are given. Larger ropes are likely to be used only when the breaking strength is known. All ropes in the table are bright (uncoated) ropes.

TABLE 7-2.

Construction	*C*	*Range of Sizes*	*Accuracy*
6 × 7 IPS FC	4.07	¼" to 1½"	Accurate at ¾" 5% low at ¼" 5% high at 1½"
6 × 7 IPS IWRC	4.37	¼" to 1½"	Accurate at ¾" 5% low at ¼" 5% high at 1½"
6 × 19 IPS FC	4.15	¼" to 2¾"	Accurate at 1½" 6.5% low at ¼" 6% high at 2¾"
6 × 19 IPS IWRC	4.50	¼" to 2¾"	Accurate at 1¼" 6.5% low at ¼" 7% high at 2¾"
6 × 19 EIPS IWRC	5.13	¼" to 2¾"	Accurate at 1½" 7% low at ¼" 6% high at 2¾"
6 × 37 IPS FC	4.15	¼" to 2¾"	Accurate at 1½" 6.5% low at ¼" 6% high at 2¾"
6 × 37 IPS IWRC	4.46	¼" to 2¾"	Accurate at 1½" 6.5% low at ¼" 6% high at 2¾"
6 × 37 EIPS IWRC	5.14	¼" to 2¾"	Accurate at 1½" 7% low at ¼" 6% high at 2¾"
6 × 61 IPS FC	3.91	1" to 2¾"	Accurate at 2" 3% low at 1" 3% high at 2¾"
6 × 61 IPS IWRC	4.20	1" to 2¾"	Accurate at 2" 3% low at 1" 3% high at 2¾"
6 × 61 EIPS IWRC	4.83	1" to 2¾"	Accurate at 2" 3% low at 1" 3% high at 2¾"

While wire rope users, including salvors, usually talk in and often think breaking strength, wire rope is not loaded to or near its breaking strength in service. For normal wire rope design a factor of safety of 4 is used for standing rope and 5 for running rope. This factor of safety (or design factor) not only gives a working margin between working loads and breaking strength but keeps loads in a range that gives the rope a long service life. In salvage work, lower factors of safety can be accepted because efficient accomplishment of the immediate job is more important than a long service life for the rope. The elastic limit for wire rope is usually about 60 percent of its nominal breaking strength. Planned loads should be kept below the elastic limit except in extreme cases.

Elasticity is a measure of a wire rope's ability to stretch under load and to return to its original length when the load is released. This quality assists the wire rope in taking transient dynamic loads and suddenly applied loads without overloading, a very important consideration in salvage. Elasticity depends upon the properties of the steel in the rope and the compaction of the wires, strands, and core under load. Wire rope elasticity is expressed as a percentage of length, 5 percent being a high elasticity for the types of wire rope found in salvage. The elastic stretch of a wire rope is calculated from the usual expression:

$$\Delta L = \frac{\Delta P \times L}{A \times E}$$

where:

ΔL = change in rope length in feet
ΔP = change in load in pounds
L = rope length in feet
A = metallic area of the rope in square inches
E = modulus of elasticity of the rope in pounds per square inch

Since the metallic area (A) and modulus of elasticity (E) are defined by the particular rope construction, a greater change in load can be accommodated by long ropes (greater L) than by short ones. Long scopes in ground legs of ground tackle, towlines, etc., give the system greater ability to absorb the loads put on it by the sea and by surges and jerk loads.

The inelastic and elastic stretch of wire rope under load combine into the total elongation. Constructional stretch is inelastic stretch that occurs when the loads compress and pull together the rope's elements. As expected, IWRC ropes are less compressible and show less constructional stretch than FC ropes. Once the rope has taken its set from constructional stretch it elongates little under its working loads. While considerable stretch of new ropes is expected, a sudden increase in the stretch under load of older rope loaded many times suggests that the metallic area is reduced by wire breakage or that the core is breaking down and the rope is approaching failure.

When wire rope changes direction by passing over a sheave or roller, fairlead, or deck edge, the bending adds bending stresses to the tensile stresses. Carrying combined stresses reduces the tensile load that a rope can carry, causing an apparent reduction of the rope's tensile strength. The amount of reduction depends primarily on the sharpness of the bend expressed as the ratio between the diameter of the bending surface and the diameter of the rope (D/d ratio). A rope bent around a pin of its own diameter (D/d = 1) can carry only 50 percent of its breaking strength, while one bent around a pin about thirty times its diameter (D/d = 30) can carry almost 95 percent of its tensile breaking strength. The amount of bending—whether 180 degrees or only a few degrees—makes little difference. A rough, grooved, or worn surface may introduce local stresses that are equivalent to bending over a knife edge.

When wire rope systems are designed from scratch, the designer can usually increase bending surface diameters to keep bending stresses low. In salvage, this option seldom exists and salvors must make the best they can from the configuration and hardware on site. In setting up systems and in choosing components, salvors must be aware of the loss of tensile load carrying ability caused by bending so they do not set up a system that fails under the planned load. Figure 7–2 is a curve of strength efficiency for wire rope bent over pins or sheaves of various sizes. The curve is empirically derived for 6 × 19 and 6 × 37 classes of IWRC and FC, preformed and non-preformed wire rope, and is only approximate for other wire rope constructions.

A wire rope without an eye, socket, or other termination that allows it to be connected to something is not of much use. Termination efficiency varies with the

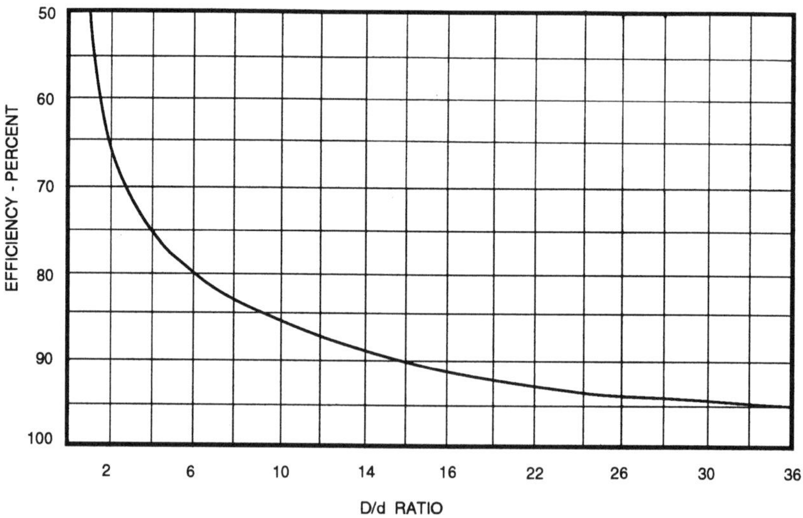

Fig. 7-2. Efficiency of wire rope bent over pins or sheaves

type. The following table gives the efficiency of common wire rope terminations. In all cases the termination must be made properly to develop the maximum efficiency.

TABLE 7-3.

EFFICIENCY OF WIRE ROPE TERMINATIONS		
Termination	*Efficiency IWRC Rope, percent*	*Efficiency FC Rope, percent*
Poured socket (spelter or thermal setting resin)	100	100
Swaged socket	95	not used
Mechanical spliced sleeve	95–90	92½–87½
Eye or thimbled hand splice	90–80	90–80
Wedge socket	75–90	75–90
Wire clips	80	80

Despite their relatively low efficiency, wedge, socket, and wire clip terminations are very useful because they can be made up in the field without special equipment.

Virtually the same words concerning wire rope clips appear in every publication about wire rope because they are important and deserve repetition. They deserve it so much they will be repeated here. Wire rope clips are applied with the U-bolt over the dead (short, unloaded) end of the rope. The memory aid "Never saddle a dead horse" helps keep it straight. Enough wire clips at the proper spacing must be applied to develop the full efficiency. The following table gives the minimum number of clips and torque for various sizes of wire rope. The eye is formed by:

1. Turning back the specified amount.
2. Installing the first clip one base width from the dead end and torquing it.
3. Installing the second clip as near the eye as possible and turning the nuts up firmly but not tightening them.
4. Adding the remaining clips and torquing all the nuts. Spacing is normally about 6 diameters.
5. After the initial loading, and periodically during use, retorquing the nuts.

If the rope is not one of the common constructions or is used, add at least one clip, increasing the amount of turnback proportionately. The information given in the table refers to the common U-bolt (bulldog) clips. Fist grip clips have different spacing and torques that may be gotten from any rigging handbook or a wire rope distributor.

TABLE 7-4.

WIRE CLIP APPLICATIONS			
Wire Rope Size in Inches	*Minimum Number of Clips*	*Amount of Rope Turned Back in Inches*	*Torque lb-ft*
¼	2	4.75	15
⅜	2	6.50	45
½	3	11.5	65
⅝	3	12	95
¾	4	18	130
⅞	4	19	225
1	5	26	225
1¼	6	37	360
1½	7	48	360
1¾	7	53	590
2	8	71	750
2¼	8	73	750
2½	9	84	750

Wedge socket terminations may also be made up in the field. Four major faults occur in wedge socket installation:

1. Welded ends are not cut off to allow the ends of the wires and strands to adjust themselves for the tight bend.
2. The live end of the rope enters the wrong side of the socket. The live end should always be in line with the socket ears.
3. The dead end of the rope is too short. The dead end should be at least 9 rope diameters clear of the socket.
4. The dead end is not made up properly. A short length of rope of the same size is clipped to the dead end with the U-bolt against the dead end. The dead and live ends should never be clipped together.

Salvage is hard service for wire rope; damage that reduces the wire rope's effectiveness can occur in normal salvage service. The wire should be inspected visually whenever possible and should be inspected thoroughly after any job where it has been handled roughly or loaded heavily. The visual inspection locates and identifies gross damage including: kinking, crushing, unstranding, birdcaging, strand displacement, core protrusion, loss of diameter of a short length, unevenness of outer strands, general corrosion, and broken or cut strands and wires. The author is not a proponent of forcing the strands of a wire rope open to examine the core. Forcing the strands open may damage the wires or strands in way of the inspection area and by that do more harm than good.

Electromagnetic inspection techniques for wire rope to locate localized faults and loss of metallic area are proven and available and should supplement very thorough visual inspection following the operation.

The wire rope industry has established criteria for retirement that may be found in any rigging or wire rope handbook and are not repeated here. These criteria are sound and any wire rope meeting the criteria in a post-operation inspection should be retired. The situation is not so clear-cut in the field. It may be impossible or impractical to retire wire rope, although the retirement criteria are exceeded. Retaining damaged wire rope in service requires a subjective estimate of the remaining strength and the service conditions. Loads should be kept well under those that the rope is believed to be capable of carrying. Placing damaged rope in the least strenuous service helps prolong the life of the rope and adds an additional factor of safety. Distinctive paint marks along damaged wire rope serve to remind all hands that the rope may fail and to stay clear.

FIBER ROPE

Just a few thousand years ago a sailor's life was simpler, at least with regard to fiber rope. He had his choice of 3-strand rope in either flax or papyrus. He knew exactly how the rope would behave and how much he could depend upon it. Things changed little for many centuries; all ropes were natural fibers and their performance was well understood by seamen. The primary difference was that until near the mid-twentieth century the major marine ropes were manila, tarred hemp, and coir. Rapid change set in with the development and introduction into rope making of man-made synthetic fibers. The ability of manufacturers to introduce new rope materials and construction outstripped industry's ability to assemble data on rope characteristics, performance, strengths, and shortcomings. The result has been that although seamen now have literally thousands of ropes to choose from—almost all of them synthetic fibers—it is difficult or impossible to select the optimum rope for any particular service. Ropes found at sea vary widely with the service of the ships and the preferences of the owners.

Synthetic fibers have replaced natural fibers for some very sound reasons. In general these include:

Versatility.
High breaking strength, either wet or dry.
High flexing and abrasion resistance.

High strength-to-weight ratios.
Good impact and shock load absorption.
Low water absorption.
Flexibility.
Resistance to mildew and rot.
Ultraviolet and weather resistance.
Good chemical and heat resistance.
Longevity.

The characteristics of synthetic fiber ropes vary widely with material and construction. Trade names and frequent new product introductions confound any attempts to keep current catalogs of ropes and their characteristics. It is inappropriate and futile for this book to attempt to provide a catalog of fiber rope characteristics; instead it will address some principles of fiber rope and their application to salvage.

Seven types of synthetic fiber ropes dominate marine usage. These are nylon, polyester, polypropylene, polyethylene, aramid, HMPE, and blends. It is the blends and the variety of rope constructions that make possible the very wide variety of rope characteristics. The characteristics of the six basic synthetics are tabulated and compared with manila below. Note that these characteristics apply to the *fiber* and not to the finished rope.

Both construction and material determine the characteristics of fiber rope. To make rope, fibers or filaments are twisted into yarns that in turn are twisted into strands. Strands are laid, twisted, or braided into rope. Construction is the way that the strands are laid, twisted, or braided. Constructions most common in marine service are:

3-Strand Twisted: Three strands laid in the same direction with either right or left lay. Rope has a tendency to hockle when a force is applied and one end is free to turn or when wound on a drum opposite to its lay. Hockles are extremely destructive to rope, reducing its strength to 30 percent of its breaking strength, crushing fibers causing fatigue and excessive wear. Crowns (exterior yarns) abrade.

4-Strand Twisted: Has characteristics similar to 3-strand. May be made with or without a center core. Has some advantages in hardness and increased contact area.

8-Strand Plaited: Has 8 individual strands woven together in pairs. Strength is virtually identical with 3-strand, but the rope resists rotation and does not hockle.

TABLE 7-5.

COMPARATIVE CHARACTERISTICS OF MANILA AND PRINCIPAL SYNTHETIC ROPE FIBERS

Fiber	*Nylon*	*Polyester*	*Polypropylene*	*Polyethylene*	*Aramid*	*HMPE*	*Manila*
STRENGTH:							
Tenacity of dry fiber in grams/denier	9.0	8.5	6.5	6.0	18-26.5	30.36	5-6.0
Wet to dry strength ratio	0.85 to 0.9	1.00	1.00	1.05	.95	1.00	Up to 1.2
Shock load absorption	Excellent	Good	Very good	Fair	–	Fair	Poor
SPECIFIC GRAVITY	1.14	1.38	0.91	0.95	1.44	.97	1.38
ELONGATION:							
Percent elongation at break	15-28	12-15	18-22	20-24	1.5-3.6	2.7-3.5	10-12
Creep	Moderate	Low	High	High	Very low	Moderate	Very low
MOISTURE EFFECTS:							
Water absorption of individual fibers (% weight)	8-12	1.0	0	0	3.5-7	0	Up to 100
Resistance to rot, mildew, and marine organisms	Excellent	Excellent	Excellent	Excellent	Excellent	Excellent	Poor
DEGRADATION:							
UV (sunlight) resistance	Good	Excellent	Poor	Good	Fair	Fair	Good
Aging resistance	Excellent	Excellent	Excellent	Excellent	Excellent	Excellent	Good
ABRASION RESISTANCE:							
Surface	Very good	Superior	Good	Fair	Fair	Very good	Good
Internal	Excellent	Superior	Good	Good	Good	Excellent	Good

Table 7-5 continued on next page

Table 7-5 continued

COMPARATIVE CHARACTERISTICS OF MANILA AND PRINCIPAL SYNTHETIC ROPE FIBERS							
Fiber	*Nylon*	*Polyester*	*Polypropylene*	*Polyethylene*	*Aramid*	*HMPE*	*Manila*
WORKING TEMPERATURES (dry ropes) (deg. F.):							
High	300	300	200	150	350	150	300
Low	–70	–70	–20	–100	–100	–200	–100
Melting	480	482	330	285	800	297	–
CHEMICAL RESISTANCE:							
Acids	Decomposes in strong mineral acids: resists weak acids	Resistant to most mineral acids. Disintegrated by 95% sulfuric acid	Very resistant	Very resistant	Attacked by hot or concentrated acids	Very resistant	Disintegrates in hot dilute and cold concentrated acids
Alkalis	Little or none	No effect cold, slowly disintegrated by strong, boiling alkalis	Very resistant	Very resistant	Attacked by hot or concentrated alkalis	Very resistant	Poor resistance, loses strength on exposure
Organic Solvents	Resistant, soluble in some phenolic compounds and in 90% formic acid	Normally unaffected but soluble in some phenolic compounds	Soluble in chlorinated hydrocarbons at 160 deg F.	Soluble in chlorinated hydrocarbons at 160 deg F.	Resistant to most ketone, alcohols, oils, and hydrocarbons	Soluble in chlorinated hydrocarbons at 160 deg F.	Fibers have fair resistance; hydrocarbons remove protective lubricants

12-Strand Hollow Single Braided: Has an excellent strength-to-weight ratio, resists rotation, cannot be hockled, and has low elastic elongation.

Double Braided: Consists of a hollow braided cover over a hollow braided core. The core and cover share the load evenly, giving the rope high strength and low elongation. Ropes are nonrotating, cannot hockle, and wear well.

The rope for a particular job is chosen by matching the characteristics of the rope material and construction to the job requirements with due weight to economics.

In commercial and other literature, breaking strengths are presented as either "average" or "minimum" breaking strength. Average breaking strength is the statistical average of breaking strengths from a number of tests conducted according to the standards and procedures of the Cordage Institute (United States), the British Standards Institution, or similar bodies. Minimum breaking strength is specified by Military Specifications (MILSPECs) in the United States. It is two standard deviations or 16 percent below the average breaking strength. In designing rope systems, minimum breaking strength should be used. Breaking tests are always conducted with new dry rope. Wet rope—especially nylon and to a lesser extent aramid—has less strength than new rope. Old rope, rope that has had long exposure to ultraviolet radiation, and nylon rope that has been exposed to rusting metal may have lost up to half of their original strength.

Quick and very dirty field estimates of the new rope's strength can be made by applying a simple formula:

$$BS = kC^2$$

where:

BS = minimum breaking strength of new, dry rope in pounds
k = a constant that varies with the rope material and construction of the rope
C = circumference of the rope in inches

Astute readers may notice an uncanny similarity between this equation and a similar one appearing a few pages earlier for estimating the breaking strength of wire rope.

Typical constants are:

TABLE 7-6.

Material	*Construction*	*k*
Manila	3-Strand	900
Polypropylene-Dacron	3-Strand	1569

Table 7-6 continued on next page

Table 7-6 continued

Material	*Construction*	*k*
Polyester	Plaited 3-Strand	2319
Nylon	Plaited 3-Strand	2562
Nylon	Double Braided	3462

The constants are not very accurate and should be used with great care. Results are low for small ropes and high for large ropes. Constants cannot be used at all for materials or constructions other than those specified. It is far better, more sensible, and more accurate to keep a table of breaking strengths from the Cordage Institute specifications, manufacturer's literature, or a rigging handbook handy for reference.

The Cordage Institute states that:

> Because of the wide range of rope use, rope condition, exposure to several factors affecting rope behavior, and the degree of risk to life and property it is impossible to make blanket recommendations about working load.

This very cautious statement is also very true. The factor of safety for new, dry, properly spliced rope in noncritical operations properly used varies with the material construction and size of the rope. The following table gives typical figures:

TABLE 7-7.

Material	*Construction*	*Circumference (inches)*	*Factor of Safety*
Nylon	3- or 8-Strand	⅝-1⅛	12
Nylon	3- or 8-Strand	1¼-1½	11
Nylon	3- or 8-Strand	1¾-2	10
Nylon	3- or 8-Strand	2¼-12	9
Polypropylene	3- or 8-Strand	⅝-1⅛	10
Polypropylene	3- or 8-Strand	1¼-1½	9
Polypropylene	3- or 8-Strand	1¾-2	8
Polypropylene	3- or 8-Strand	2¼-12	7
Polyester	3- or 8-Strand	⅝-1⅛	10
Polyester	3- or 8-Strand	1¼-1½	9
Polyester	3- or 8-Strand	1¾-2	8
Polyester	3- or 8-Strand	2¼-12	7
Nylon	Double Braid	⅝-1⅛	11

Table 7-7 continued on next page

Table 7-7 continued

Material	*Construction*	*Circumference (inches)*	*Factor of Safety*
Nylon	Double Braid	1¼-1½	10
Nylon	Double Braid	1¾-2	9
Nylon	Double Braid	2¼-6½	8
Nylon	Double Braid	7-12	7

Some other properties of fiber rope are of major concern to users, especially when the rope is heavily loaded. These properties, like breaking strength, vary with materials and construction.

Elongation comes in three forms. Permanent elongation is nonrecoverable and much like the constructional stretch of wire rope. Recoverable elongation is elongation that is recoverable over a period of time after the removal of the load. The period of time is hours or days. Elastic elongation is recovered as soon as the load is removed. Elastic elongation and thus elasticity is greatest in nylon, less in other synthetic fibers.

Creep is elongation under loads that are applied for a long time. Creep is more evident and occurs at lower loads in polypropylene and polyethylene lines than in ones of nylon and polyester.

Snapback—As a line is loaded it stores energy. The amount of energy stored in the line is a function of the elastic elongation of the line and the load on the line. Parting or sudden releasing of the line frees all the stored energy. This release of energy, called snapback, can cause parting line to recoil with deadly force. The energy in a rope at snapback can be estimated by:

$$S = \frac{1}{3}(BS \times L \times E)$$

where:

S = snapback energy in foot-pounds
BS = minimum breaking strength in pounds
L = length of the line in feet
E = percentage elongation

Snapback energies can be very high. It is basic marine safety to stay well clear of lines that are heavily loaded. Heroics to release or slack lines that are near failure are a good way to get into a hospital—or a quieter establishment.

When fiber rope is subject to dynamic loads from picking up or setting loads down quickly, passing through the air-water interface, ship motions, or snubbing or letting go the line suddenly, all bets are off on factors of safety. Dynamic loads can cause transient loads up to ten times the static load on the line. Accordingly, when dynamic loading is unavoidable, actual working loads must be reduced sharply. How much they are reduced is a matter of judgment that considers the static and dynamic loads, the configuration of the rig, etc. High-elongation lines, like nylon, and long lines are more elastic and better able to accept dynamic loads than low-elongation or short lines.

Just as with wire rope, bending fiber rope sharply under load reduces the load-carrying capacity and can lead to premature or unexpected failure. Bending increases internal abrasion and adds bending stresses to the tensile stresses on the rope fibers. Simple knotting is hard service for rope because knots are a series of tight bends. Knotting generally reduces the strength of ropes by 50 percent or more.

Unlike the case with wire rope, loss of strength of fiber rope cannot be correlated directly with bend sharpness. Some general rules can be laid down:

The chock, bitt, or other surface around which a fiber rope of any material and construction bends 10 degrees or more should have a diameter of at least three times the diameter of the rope. Just as with money, more is better.

Where rope bends over a cleat in a long angle, the diameter of the cleat surface should be at least one and a half times the diameter of the rope.

The length of eyes in eye splices should be between 3 and 5 times the diameter of bitts or bollards over which they are used, to prevent excessive stress at the throat of the splice where the legs join. Thimbles for fiber rope normally have a 3:1 ratio.

Sheave diameters for twisted and plaited rope should be 10 times the rope diameter and for braided rope 8 times the rope diameter.

Fiber rope is often stored in a box or wound on a drum. The question of how much the drum or box can hold often must be asked in the field or in preparing rope for shipment to the work site.

When rope can be carefully stored and faked, the storage volume required is:

$$V = \frac{C^2 \times L}{1090}$$

where:
V = required storage volume in cubic feet
C = rope circumference in inches
L = rope length in feet

Rope that cannot be carefully stowed requires 30 percent more storage volume.

The length that can be stowed on a drum is:

$$L = \frac{0.262 \times (A + B) \times A \times 1}{d^2}$$

where:

L = length of the rope to be stored in feet
l = length of the barrel of the spool or drum in inches
A = depth of the rope layer in inches
B = diameter of the drum barrel in inches
d = rope diameter in inches

In SI units:

$$L = \frac{(A + B) \times A \times 1 \times \pi \times 10^6}{d^2}$$

where:

L = length of the rope to be stored in meters
l = length of the barrel of the spool or drum in millimeters
A = depth of the rope layer in millimeters
B = diameter of the drum barrel in millimeters
d = rope diameter in millimeters

There is no general agreement among rope experts on the criteria for retiring fiber rope from service. The state of the art in rope technology is not such that a rope can be visually inspected and the exact condition of damage determined. Table 7-8 gives conditions to be looked for on visual examination and suggestions as to whether the rope should be respliced and continued in service. These are not firm guidelines. The overall condition of the rope and the experience of the supervisor are factors in the decision to continue use or discard.

Using fiber rope, particularly synthetic fiber rope, is very much a matter of matching the rope material and construction to the application and using the rope in strict compliance with the rope's characteristics. Rope must be matched to the job and associated hardware must be matched to the rope for a fiber rope system to work properly. Any old rope used any old way simply will not do the job. Good basic seamanship is mandatory.

Fortunately, fiber rope is not the material of choice in most salvage applications. When it is, salvors or other users can call upon manufacturers for assistance in fitting the rope to the application. Most manufacturers have good technical departments and want to see their product used correctly.

TABLE 7-8.

ALL ROPES		
	Resplice (Local Damage)	*Discard*
Bulk of surface yarns reduced by 50% or more for a length of 4 rope diameters	Yes	Yes
Cut strands	Yes	Yes
Cut fibers or yarns	Seek manufacturer's advice; if unobtainable set rope aside and do not use	
Rope suspected of having been shock loaded	NA	Yes
Diameter reduced more than 5% below new rope	NA	Yes
Exposure above working temperatures	NA	Yes
Burns or melting over a length of more than 4 rope diameters	Yes	Yes
Abrasion on the inside of an eye with the bulk of yarns or strands reduced by 50% or more	Yes	NA
Rust on nylon	Yes or clean	No
Oily or greasy	Wash in mild detergent	
Progressive heavy fuzz (abrasion)	Look for and eliminate the cause of abrasion	
Rope subject to sharp bending	Yes	Yes
BRAIDED ROPE		
More than four consecutive pulled strands that cannot be worked back into the braid	Yes	Yes
Core of double braids visible through damaged cover	Yes	Yes
Pulled out, abraded, powdered, or melted strands in the core	No	Yes
Damage to the inside of an eye	Yes	NA
FOR 3- AND 8-STRAND PLAITED ROPE		
Damage in the score between strands	Yes	Yes
Cover yarns cut or abraded more than 50% on crowns of rope	Yes	Yes
Powdering between adjacent crown contact surfaces	Yes	Yes
Hockle or backturn	Yes	Yes

CHAIN

Most mariners encounter heavy stud link chain only in their anchoring systems and in the chafing pendant of towing gear. Salvors encounter chain more frequently as a portion of the rode of ground tackle, in heavy mooring, in rigging tows, and in locations where weight, flexibility, and chafe resistance are important properties of tensioned rigging. The stud in stud link chain prevents the chain from kinking and also prevents the sides of the link from deforming under heavy loads.

Chain is heavy and robust, chafe and abrasion resistant, and to all appearances indestructible. Like every other engineered and manufactured product it has limitations that must be respected to use it well. An understanding of these limitations is necessary to salvors, as the mildest effect of unexpected chain failure is embarrassment.

Chain is manufactured by welding, forging, or casting. Modern production technology has led to the dominance of welded stud link chain. In this type of chain, one end of the bar from which the link is formed is bent, hooked through the adjoining link, then the other end is bent and the ends of the bar flash butt-welded. The stud is pressed into the hot link and may be seal welded to the link to prevent crevice corrosion.

Welded stud link chain is made in five grades:

Grade 1—Normal strength
Grade 2—High strength
Grade 3—Extra-high strength
ORQ—Oil Rig Quality
Grade 4—Super strength

Grade 1 chain is no longer manufactured, but some chain remains in supplies around the world. Grade 2 is generally found in most anchoring systems, but Grade 3 is not uncommon. ORQ complies with API Specification 2F for mooring chain and differs from ordinary welded stud link chain by having the stud circumferentially welded on the end opposite the flash weld to prevent stud loss. Grade 4 chain is used primarily for mooring oil rigs. The stud is also welded in this grade and in welded stud link chain manufactured for the U.S. Navy and conforming to military specifications MIL–C–24633 and MIL–C–78096A.

Integral stud link chain is made by casting or forging a stud integral with the link. Arguably, the best-known type of integral stud link chain is Di-Lok chain, forged chain formerly manufactured in the United States by the U.S. Navy and Baldt. Some integral stud forged chain is manufactured in the United Kingdom and Japan.

Cast chain is no longer manufactured, but a great deal remains in service and in stockpiles. The quality of cast chain is always suspect because of its age and the technical difficulties of casting that prevent obtaining optimum metallurgical structure in the link.

Marine chain strengths and dimensions are governed by consistent specifications and standards issued by the International Standards Organization, various national standards organizations, and the American Petroleum Institute (API). Normal, studded links are 6 times the bar diameter long and 3.6 times the bar diameter wide. Chain links are the same size and weight regardless of the grade. The bar diameter of unstudded end links is normally 1.2 times the bar diameter of common links to make up the strength lost by stud removal. Some manufacturers prefer to make these links from standard size bars and heat treat to get the higher strength.

The weight of chain is an important factor in deepening the catenary of mooring or towing lines and in holding drag embedment anchor shanks parallel to the sea floor. The weight per unit length (lbs/ft or kg/m) of chain can be calculated by:

$$w = C_w d^2$$

where:

w = chain weight per foot (meter) in lbs/ft or kg/m
C_w = weight coefficient, 9.92 for Imperial units, 0.228 for SI units
d = chain bar (wire) diameter in inches or millimeters

Breaking strength, proof load, and safe working load for chain are roughly related in the ratio 3:2:1. Conveniently, for Grades 1, 2, and 3 chain the breaking strength of the lower grade is the same as the proof load of the next higher grade.

Approximate breaking strength and proof loads may be calculated by:

$$PL = C_{PL} \times d^2 \times (44 - 2.032 \times d)$$

where:

PL = proof load of the chain in pounds
C_{PL} = proof load coefficient from the following table
d = bar (wire) diameter of chain in inches

and

$$BS = C_{BS} \times d^2 \times (44 - 2.032 \times d)$$

where:

BS = breaking strength of the chain in pounds
C_{BS} = breaking strength load coefficient from the following table
d = bar (wire) diameter of chain in inches

TABLE 7-9.

Chain Grade	C_{PL}	C_{BS}
1	995	1422
2	1422	1991
3	1991	2844
Di-Lok	2020	3058
ORQ	2031	3060
4	3125	3978

The breaking strength in tonnes can be estimated by:

$$BS = \frac{K \times d^2}{600}$$

where:
BS = chain breaking strength in tonnes
K = a constant for the chain grade:

Grade	*K*
1	20
2	30
3	43

d = bar diameter in millimeters

Chain is manufactured in shots of 15 fathoms (90 feet, 27.5 meters) or in continuous lengths of any measurement. Long continuous lengths are common in mooring chains used in offshore moorings, usually ORQ or Grade 4 chains. The continuous lengths reduce the number of connecting links in each mooring leg and thereby increase the reliability of the moor. Baldt- or Kentner-type connecting links connect chain lengths, particularly where the chain is hauled by a wildcat or passes over a grooved roller, but the failure rate of connecting links is much higher than the failure rate of common links or end links. The failure rate can be reduced by ensuring the links are made up properly, in good condition without excess wear, and sealed with a lead plug. The next larger size link or a higher-grade link can help reduce failure.

Salvors often confront piles or pieces of chain that have no identification or certification. While ends of each shot or continuous length are normally marked with the test loads, certificate number, and grade after manufacture, the marking may have become illegible with time. The grade of the chain can be determined by a Brinell hardness test. Grade 1 has a Brinell hardness of about 111, grade 2 about 163, and grade 3 about 207. The strength of the chain may be proven by subjecting it to proof testing in a tensile test machine. Soundness of the chain may be determined by measuring the length over five links to determine if there has been permanent deformation of the chain and by magnetic particle and ultrasonic inspection to determine the soundness of each link.

In the real world of salvage such procedures to identify chain are seldom practical because of time constraints or the distance from testing facilities. Chain can be tested quickly in the field by inspecting it visually for wear, cracks, and missing studs. The presence of defects can be determined by sounding each link with a hammer. A sound link will ring clear and true while a cracked one will emit a dull thunk. Several measurements of the length over five links should be made along the length of the chain with particular attention to sections that show wear. The length over five links should lie between 22d and 22.55d. As these inspections identify only the condition of the chain and not the grade, all chain inspected this way should be treated as grade 1 chain and loaded accordingly. Treating chain as grade 1 chain, a relatively weak tension member, may cause difficulties in designing systems for salvage, particularly when the system is a composite of wire rope and chain. The ultimate design and use of the system is heavily dependent upon the judgment of the salvage master and salvage engineer and the urgency of the work.

Visual inspection of chain in the field helps in establishing its soundness if not its grade. Chain should be inspected link by link before and after each operation. Damage to be looked for in chain inspection includes:

- Links bent out of plane by more than 3 degrees.
- Heavy wear in the grips that reduces a single diameter to 90 percent or less of the original diameter or that reduces the average of two diameters to 94 percent of the original diameter. Serious wear in the grip is often characterized by metal displacement that looks like a smear of rusty butter on the link.
- Cracking at the toe of the stud weld extending into the base material.
- Missing studs or studs that can move more than ⅛ inch laterally or 3⁄16 inch in any direction.
- Gaps of more than ⅛ inch between the stud at the end opposite the weld and the bar.
- Gouges or cracking.

Gouges or cracking may be ground lightly, but grinding should not reduce the bar diameter more than 10 percent. Damaged links may be cut out and the chain sections joined by appropriate connecting hardware (connecting links or shackles).

Pressed-in studs may come loose from chain or studs may be knocked out or cut out to get sufficient space to pass a shackle pin to connect the chain to some other member. Empirical evidence about the effect of a missing stud is inconclusive and the loss of strength of the link is difficult to quantify. Logic indicates that the strength of the link is reduced because the design geometry is destroyed and the side of the link is unsupported. Exothermically cutting a link out leaves unpredictable metallurgical structure in the heat-affected zone. Intentionally removing studs reduces the chain strength by an indefinable amount. The best practice is not removing studs. Sometimes the best practice is not possible. The second-best practice is to treat the chain as though it is one grade lower than its actual grade.

No attempt should be made in the field to reweld loose studs. Studs may be rewelded, but only with instructions from the manufacturer.

Often the choice is joining chain links with connecting links and accepting some loss of reliability or cutting out studs and joining chains with shackles. The choice is not always clear-cut and must be made after balancing loss of strength, connecting link condition, the geometry of the application, and the results of a failure at a critical time.

Like other tension members, chain performs best when carrying pure tensile loads, but it is often necessary to bend chain around some surface, such as a chock, deck edge, or bilge bolster. Bending chain can reduce load-carrying capacity. There are three general cases in chain bending:

1. Chain bends over a smooth, ungrooved surface, such as a chock, where the links alternate in one direction then the other in an X configuration. All links are subject to bending.
2. Chain bends over a shallow grooved surface that holds alternate links vertical but does not support the horizontal link; only the vertical links are bent.
3. Chain bends over a deeply grooved surface where the vertical links are clear of the bottom of the groove and only the horizontal links are bent.

Only the first case is of interest to salvors, as it is the case most likely to come up in the field. Grooved surfaces are more probably found in purpose-built systems, where chain bending has been factored in during design. Empirical and experimental work in chain bending has been limited, but the results indicate that if the diameter of the surface over which the chain is bent is at least seven times the bar diameter of the chain, bending causes little reduction in load-carrying capacity.

MISCELLANEOUS HARDWARE

A variety of miscellaneous hardware connects, stoppers, terminates, or otherwise forms a part of a rigging system. Whatever the type of hardware, it must form a true system with the tension members. The strengths and characteristics of the miscellaneous hardware must be not just compatible but must match other components of the system. In the heavily loaded rigging systems found in salvage, use of any convenient piece of hardware—rather than the proper one—can introduce a weak link into the system that can lead to failure at a critical time. System compatibility is best achieved by matching components by safe working load, *not* by breaking strength.

Shackles are arguably the most common type of joining hardware. Shackles come in two basic shapes—anchor (bow) and chain (straight)—with several pin types. The most common pin types are:

Screw pin with a threaded round pin that screws into the body of the shackle.

Round pin with a pin that passes through both sides of the shackle and is secured with a cotter pin.

Bolt type with a threaded round pin that passes through the body of the shackle and is secured with a nut.

Screw pin shackles are most common. In heavily loaded systems, the pin in screw pin shackles may loosen and eventually fall out under load, particularly if the load constantly varies. The pins of screw pin shackles should always be seized to the body of the shackle with a few turns of baling wire. Bolt-type shackles with double-locking nuts and through bolts on the outer nuts are the most secure type of shackle and are preferred in critical applications. Shackles should never be welded because welding causes metallurgical changes and loss of strength in the heat-affected zone.

Shackle-to-shackle connections, especially with chain shackles, are not desirable because shackles may jam and fail at low loads from unusual asymmetrical loading. This type of connection is often unavoidable in salvage. Whenever shackles are connected to one another the connection should be bow-to-bow or bow-to-pin, never pin-to-pin.

Shackles are classified and sold by their safe working load, normally one-fourth or one-fifth of the breaking strength. If shackles are matched to tension members by using shackles with a rating (safe working load) of one-third the required breaking strength of the tension member, an additional factor of safety is provided for asymmetrical loading—a condition almost impossible to avoid in salvage.

The safe working load of newer shackle is marked on the shackle in raised or indented letters along with the manufacturer's name and size of shackle. If the shackle is not marked and the origin of the shackle is unknown, safe working load may be conservatively estimated by:

$$SWL = 3.6 \times d^2$$

where:

SWL = safe working load in tons

d = diameter of the bow of the shackle in inches

Sometimes salvage ground tackle systems and heavy lift systems use plate shackles. These are simply two plates spaced an appropriate distance apart and bolted together. Plate shackles can be built in the field, but they must be designed, not just made up of convenient components. The holes in the plate are sized and placed by the same methods used in designing bolted connections. The pin is sized to preclude bending under loads that can be carried by the system. Through bolts or cotter pins should be passed through the pin to prevent the nut securing the pin from backing off.

Hooks are considerably weaker than shackles and should be eliminated in heavy lifting and pulling systems wherever possible. As is the case with shackles, the safe working load of newer hooks is marked on the body. The strength of older hooks can be estimated by:

$$SWL = \frac{2}{3} \times d^2$$

where:
SWL = safe working load in tons
d = diameter of the hook at the back of the hook below the eye in inches

Hooks with a safety latch should be used when possible. When safety hooks are not available, hooks should always be moused with small stuff. Neither the mousing nor the safety latch contributes to the strength of the hook; their function is solely to help retain the load. Shackles across a hook can prevent the hook from spreading under a heavy load. This method should be used only when heavier hooks are not available and there is no other choice. Hooks set up with shackles may have been overloaded and the integrity of the hook destroyed although the shackle prevents spreading and physical evidence of failure. Hooks set up with shackles should be discarded after the operation.

Wherever there is a possibility that the rig or load may twist, a swivel should be inserted. Swivels are somewhat stronger than shackles the same size. The tendency of tackles to twist can be accommodated by reeving the tackle with reverse bends as described below. With this type of rigging the swivel may be redundant.

Earlier, this chapter briefly mentions Baldt- and Kentner-type connecting links in association with chain. The principal use of these devices is to connect lengths of chain or to connect chain to other components. They may also serve as other connections, but shackles are more reliable and, therefore, preferred for most service.

Connecting links and anchor-joining (pear-shaped) shackles that connect chain sections and other components can be taken apart and then reassembled and secured. Pear-shaped links connect chain of different sizes or fittings of different dimensions. Kentner shackles are slightly larger than the corresponding chain size. Baldt-type detachable links are the same size as the chain. Baldt and Kentner links are less likely than anchor or chain shackles to hang up when hauled over taffrails.

The Baldt-type link has a configuration that allows hooking it through the fittings being connected while assembling the link. The links must be fitted individually to assure proper load distribution; parts are not interchangeable. Baldt-type links should be marked for identification and matching. A drift pin secured by a lead pellet driven into a cavity above the pin holds both types of connecting link together. The lead pellet must never be omitted. Baldt-type connecting links and pear-shaped links may be fitted with a hairpin to further secure the link. The hairpin was originally intended for links in anchor and mooring chains subject to impact with the sea floor. In practice, they are seldom necessary and rarely used.

Detachable links should never be welded closed. Welding in the field can produce crack-susceptible hard spots and hydrogen embrittlement in the heat-affected zone. Both may lead to premature failure of the link. Both Baldt- and Kentner-type links may be obtained with breaking strengths equaling the breaking strength of chain in the various grades and sizes. The fittings are forged and have the manufacturer's name and size on the side of the link. Manufacturers can supply certificates of proof loading, break testing, and ABS approval.

Analyses of various systems failures have shown that while overall failure rates are low, a disproportionately high percentage of failures in chain systems start in connecting links.[2] A high failure rate of connecting links compared to common chain links, shackles, or wire rope is logical because of the relative complexity of the connecting links. Properly selected connecting links are acceptable in salvage rigging, but each connection should be considered individually to ensure selection of the most appropriate connecting device.

Carpenter stoppers (illustrated in figure 7-3) are sliding wedge block wire rope stoppers that have undergone a long evolution until now. In their forged form, they are able to hold the full breaking load of the wire rope for which they are sized without damaging the rope. The stoppers have the advantage of quick and easy release. Carpenter stoppers are used in ground and lifting tackle to hold the hauling wire to the purchase and to hold the main wire under load while the tackle is overhauled. Several types of Carpenter stoppers are in circulation. The older ones are cast and may fail before the wire rope. Failures have a way of being spectacular and dangerous. The forged alloy steel Carpenter stoppers are identified by four transverse ribs on the cover plate and long ears.

The wedge for Carpenter stoppers is specifically sized for each size of wire and is made to fit the lay of the wire. To obtain good performance from the stopper and to prevent damage to the wire, the size and lay must match. Wedges for any lay other than right regular lay are rare.

To pass a Carpenter stopper:

1. Open the cover of the stopper.
2. Lay the wire rope in the stopper.

Fig. 7-3. Carpenter stopper in the ground leg of a salvage ground tackle system. The four transverse ribs show this stopper is the forged steel type.

3. Close and secure the cover.
4. Tap the wedge home.

As load comes on the wire, the wire moves the wedge more tightly into the stopper.

Bullivant clamps are bolted, two-piece, cast steel shells that join large wire ropes in a way similar to the way wire clips join small wires. Figure 7-4 illustrates a Bullivant clamp. Bullivant clamps are heavy and cumbersome but clamp wires securely without damaging them. They are well suited to tidal lifting and to other applications where quick release is not necessary. They are normally fitted in pairs or threes.

Bullivant clamps are normally lined with "grass" made of unlaid natural fiber rope yarns to soak up lubricant squeezed from the wire rope by clamping. In these days when one rarely sees natural fiber rope, other absorbent material can be substituted for the natural rope yarns. The grass should not be omitted.

To set a Bullivant clamp:

1. Frap the two parts of wire rope together.
2. Fit the bolts through the lower shell of the clamp. Note that there are recesses on the bottom shell to hold the heads and prevent the nuts from turning as the bolts are tightened.
3. Grass the lower shell.
4. Set the ropes into the lower shell; add more grass.
5. Set the upper shell in place.
6. Put washers and nuts on the bolts and run thc nuts up by hand.
7. Run the nuts up tight with an impact wrench, adding spacers as necessary until the wires are clamped tightly.

Figure 7-5 shows Bullivant clamps in use.

TACKLES

Tackles, or purchases, are force multiplication systems that allow low-powered pulling machines to develop large amounts of force. Tackles multiply force because each rope part in the tackle exerts the same force on the traveling block as

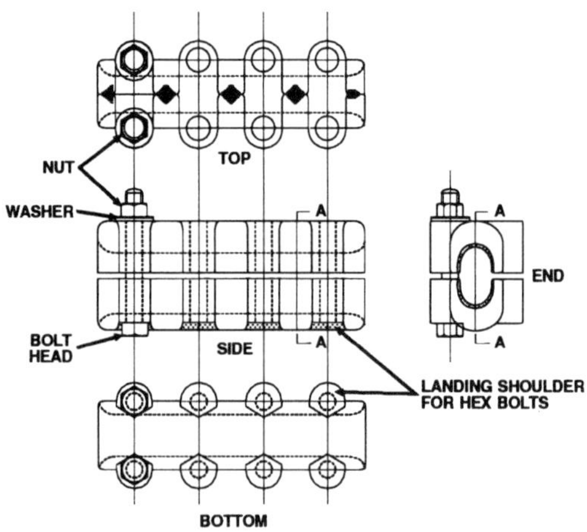

Fig. 7-4. Bullivant clamp. Courtesy of U.S. Navy.

Fig. 7-5. Bullivant clamps in use. The clamp in the background is being set with a pneumatic impact wrench. Note the clamps on deck have been grassed with unlaid manila.

the winch exerts on the hauling part. Both large and small tackles have wide applications in salvage.

The mechanical advantage of the tackle is the ratio between the total pull by the tackle and the line pull on the hauling part. Disregarding friction gives a mechanical advantage equal to the number of rope parts at the traveling block. Mechanical advantage is gained at the expense of hauling speed. The speed of the traveling block is the quotient of the speed of the hauling part and the number of rope parts at the traveling block.

A tackle is *rove to advantage* when the hauling part comes off the traveling block because the number of parts at the traveling block, and thus the mechanical advantage, is greater. When the hauling part comes off the standing part, the tackle is *rove to disadvantage.*

In practice, the friction of the sheaves diminishes the mechanical advantage. The amount of friction depends upon the type of bearing or bushing in the block, its condition, the amount of rope in contact with the sheaves, and the weight of the rope. As the number of parts increases, the overall efficiency of the tackle decreases because the total friction increases. Also, as the number of parts in the tackle increases, the effect of having low friction or roller bearing sheaves becomes greater. The actual mechanical advantage is approximately:

$$\text{AMA} = \frac{\text{TMA}}{1 + (k \times n)}$$

where:

AMA = actual mechanical advantage

TMA = theoretical mechanical advantage (number of rope parts at the moving block)

k = friction factor:

0.10 for wires bending not more than 180 degrees on the sheave and bronze bushings in good condition

0.06 for roller bearing sheaves in good condition

0.15 to 0.25 for blocks in poor condition or of unusual construction

n = *total* number of *sheaves* in the system

Tables abound for calculating line pull and number of parts of tackle rope. These tables depend upon the ratio between the weight and the line pull applied. The tables differ principally in the application for which they were developed. Table 7-10 applies primarily to crawler cranes that have larger-diameter sheaves than are common in salvage. The table can be generalized by giving the results a little latitude, or applying a few percentage points of salvage fudge.

Ratios are calculated by:

$$\text{Ratio} = \frac{w}{P}$$

where:

w = weight or pull in pounds or tons

P = line pull in pounds or tons

To find the number of parts of line required to generate a particular force with a known line pull:

1. Calculate the ratio.
2. Enter the figure for the correct type bearing. Find the same or next higher ratio.
3. Read left to the number of parts of line.

To find the pull attainable with a given line pull and tackle:

1. Enter the figure with the number of parts of line in the tackle.
2. Read the ratio for the correct type of sheaves.
3. Multiply the line pull by the ratio to find the force that can be generated.

The two most common applications for heavy multipart tackles in salvage are tackles working vertically for lifting and tackles working horizontally for pulling or for lifting with lines fairled to the vertical.

TABLE 7-10.

LINE PARTS AND LINE PULL		
Number of Parts of Line	*Ratios Bronze Bushed Sheaves*	*Ratios Roller Bearing Sheaves*
1	0.96	0.98
2	1.87	1.94
3	2.75	2.88
4	3.59	3.81
5	4.39	4.70
6	5.16	5.60
7	5.90	6.47
8	6.60	7.32
9	7.27	8.16
10	7.91	8.98
11	8.52	9.79
12	9.11	10.6
13	9.68	11.4
14	10.2	12.1
15	10.7	12.9
16	11.2	13.6
17	11.7	14.3
18	12.2	15.0
19	12.6	15.7
20	13.0	16.4
21	13.4	17.0
22	13.8	17.7
23	14.2	18.3
24	14.5	18.9

The methods of rigging tackles for the two applications differ. Blocks in a tackle may be rove either in the same plane or at right angles to one another, depending upon their use. A primary concern is avoiding lateral forces on the wires, working them hard against the sheaves and abrasion between wires in contact. Figures 7-6 through 7-8 show representative methods of rigging multipart tackles.

Four sheave blocks rigged to work as the hauling tackle for ground tackle should be rigged with the blocks perpendicular to one another as shown in figure 7-6, to avoid wires working heavily against the sheaves. It sometimes suits the situation better to rig the blocks in the same plane. This reeve should have two reverse bends (figure 7-7) to relieve the twist and to distribute the loads better.

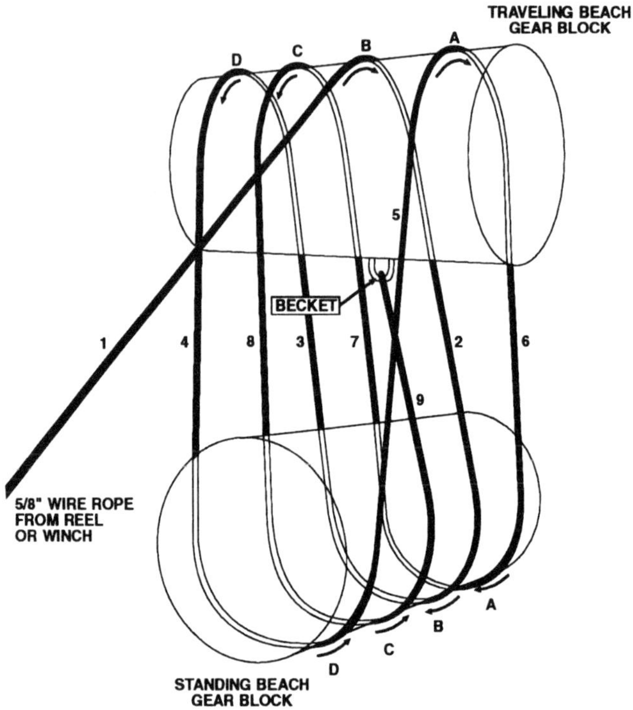

Fig. 7-6. Center-to-center reeving of four sheave blocks. Courtesy of U.S. Navy.

Luff on luff, a term correctly used for rigging two simple luff tackles so that the first hauls the second, has become generalized to describe any set of tackles rigged in series. This type of rigging works better in theory than in practice with large heavy tackles. For a safe and effective rig the second tackle must be rove with rope large enough to carry the full output of the second tackle with an acceptable factor of safety. A quick calculation shows that this results in a very large second tackle and a huge main pulling or lifting line. For heavy pulls or lifts, rigging with the Spanish Burton principle shown in Figure 7-8 is more practical.

Enough fairlead blocks should be provided to give the hauling part a straight run or very small fleet angle as it comes onto the drum. Not just any old blocks will do as fairlead blocks. The fairlead blocks must be so small that they introduce bending stress in the rope and must be in good condition so they do not introduce unnecessary friction losses.

There is a temptation to leave frequently used tackle rove with the regular purchase wire. This is poor practice, as wire rope damage eventually and inevitably results. Good practice is to marry a wire gantline to the purchase wire and

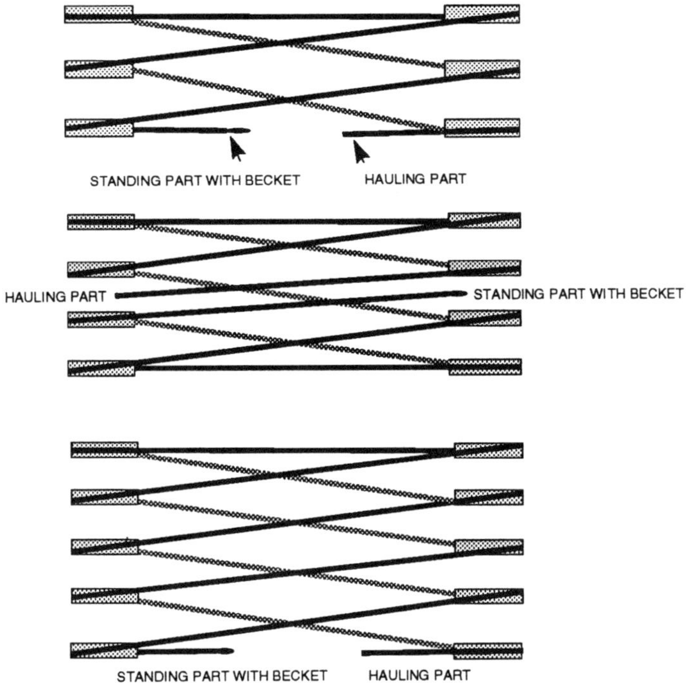

Fig. 7-7. Three, four, and five sheave blocks rigged in the same plane for either vertical or horizontal use

heave it through the purchase to preserve the reeving sequence. At the next use the process is reversed to reeve the blocks with the purchase wire.

Salvors often improvise tackles from materials that can be collected at remote sites. In doing so, compromise is inevitable, and only equipment in poor or worn condition may be available. A subjective decision on site is necessary as to whether the equipment is satisfactory, if it is likely to hold up through the operation, and if the damage worn or scored sheaves, for instance, can cause to wire rope is worth the risk.

Unconventional tackles are sometimes rigged by running the main hauling wire through blocks rigged to the ship or anchored on the sea floor.

Chain falls and their wire rope equivalent, comealongs, have largely replaced the simple rope tackles seamen traditionally used for lifting and skidding loads. Both these devices are convenient and efficient, allowing one man to move a load of several tons and to position it accurately. Any salvor's tool bag should contain a selection of these devices.

Chain falls are available in a variety of types and sizes with mechanical advantages between 5 and 250 and capacities from ½ to 40 tons. There are four general types of chain falls: differential, spur gear, worm gear, and ratchet, with

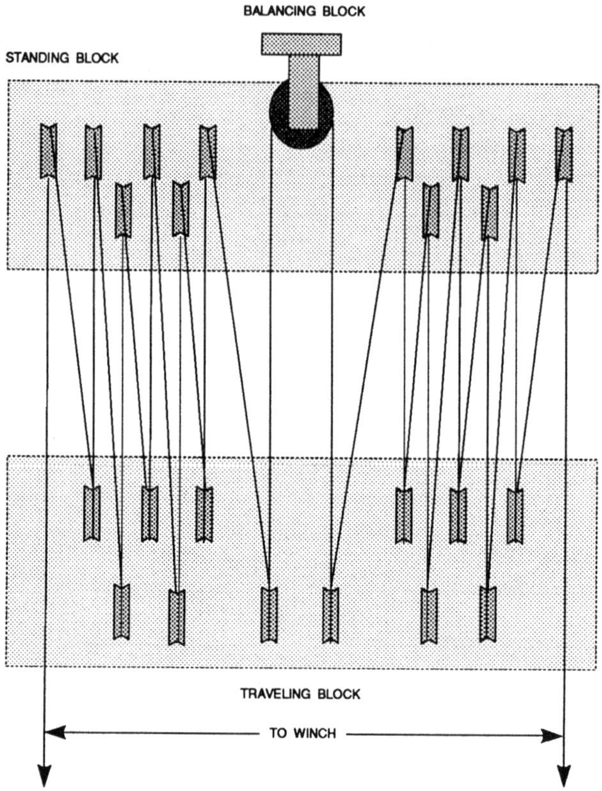

Fig. 7-8. Spanish Burton principle for heavy purchases

differential and spur gear being the most common. The spur gear is both the most efficient and the most expensive. Ratchet falls are suited only for light service.

Comealongs are more lightly constructed and have less capacity than chain falls. They are ratchet operated.

The capacities of both comealongs and chain falls are marked on the case. Both devices are designed to fail by the hook spreading. Hooks, chains, and wires should be inspected frequently and the device discarded if excessive wear or spreading of the hook is found.

SLINGS

Slings are in common use, and the theory of slings is well known among riggers. Enough accidents continue to happen from incorrectly sized or rigged slings to call for a few words of reminder.

The load is divided evenly among the legs of the sling so long as the legs are equal in length and rigged at the same angle. For equal length slings, the portion of the load carried by each leg is:

$$T = \frac{w}{n}$$

where:

T = portion of the weight carried by each leg of the sling
w = weight being lifted
n = number of legs in the sling

The portion of the weight being carried by the leg equals the tension in the leg only when the legs of the sling are vertical or make an angle of 0° with the vertical. When the legs make an angle with the vertical, the vertical component remains equal to the portion of the weight the leg carries but the tension in the leg increases, until at 90° the tension is theoretically infinite (figure 7-9). Sling angle is critical to sling tension. It is easy to overload slings if attention is not given to the angle the sling makes with the vertical. Unless the sling hangs straight down, the tension in each leg of the sling is greater than its share of the load. Slings are normally rated at an angle of 60°, where the tension in each leg of the sling is twice the leg's share of the load. Good practice calls for limiting the sling angle to 45° to provide an operational factor of safety of 1.4. When the situation requires rigging at a greater angle, heavier slings sized for the angle and the resulting tension should be used. Slings of equal length prevent unequal tension in the slings. Sling tension can be calculated from the formula:

$$T = \frac{w}{n \times \cos\theta}$$

where:

T = tension in each sling leg
w = weight being lifted
n = number of legs in the sling
θ = angle at the top of the lift

HIGHLINES

Highlines are practical and effective for transferring loads between a ship and the shore. The basic concept shown in figure 7-10 (a) is simple: a span line is rigged between the ship and the shore and a tailed block or trolley is hauled back and forth by inhaul and outhaul lines. All seamen can immediately devise methods for varying the rig and modifying the system to fit the conditions at the salvage site. A heavier-duty rig such as that shown in figure 7-10 (b) is usually required in salvage work. Figure 7-11 shows the shore end of a highline.

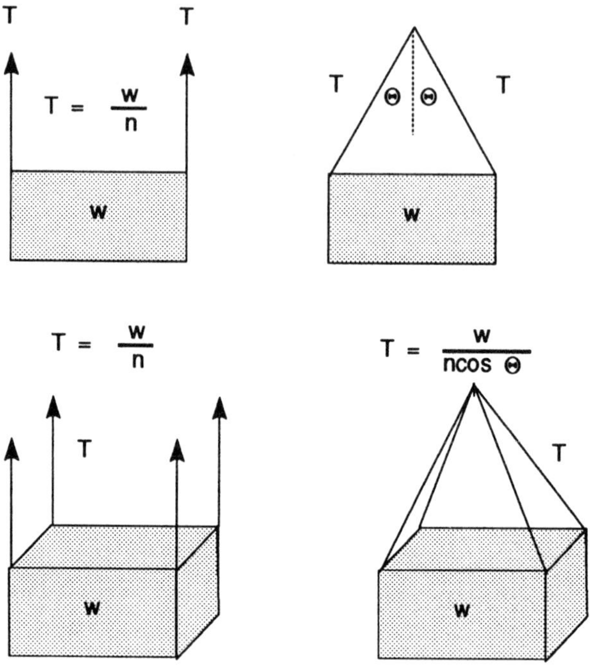

Fig. 7-9. Sling loads

Getting the correct amount of tension in the span line takes some trial and error. The amount of tension in the span line and thus the load in the connecting hardware and on the booms or masts at either end varies with span line tension. If the span line is bar tight, the theoretical tension in the line is infinite. Tension increases in compliance with the principles that apply to slings as the line is slacked and sags. Mother Nature is well known for being perverse; she does not fail here. As the tension is increased and the line sags, the load becomes harder to haul. The correct tension is one that balances the load in the span line and its terminals with ease of hauling. Tension can be maintained from either end, with weights, tackles, or winches. Outhaul and inhaul lines can be hauled and slacked from either or both ends. It is usually preferable to handle both from the shoreward end. Exact configuration and method of operation depends upon the situation at hand. Wisdom calls for building the rig to carry loads of ten times those that are to be transferred.

Trees or other insubstantial structures may anchor the shoreward end of the rig for very light transfers. Lines should be fixed low on the trunks of trees to avoid setting up moments that may uproot the tree and dump the load. A well-designed and securely anchored A-frame or mast anchorage and heavy-duty trolleys are necessary to carry significant weights. As with many items described through-

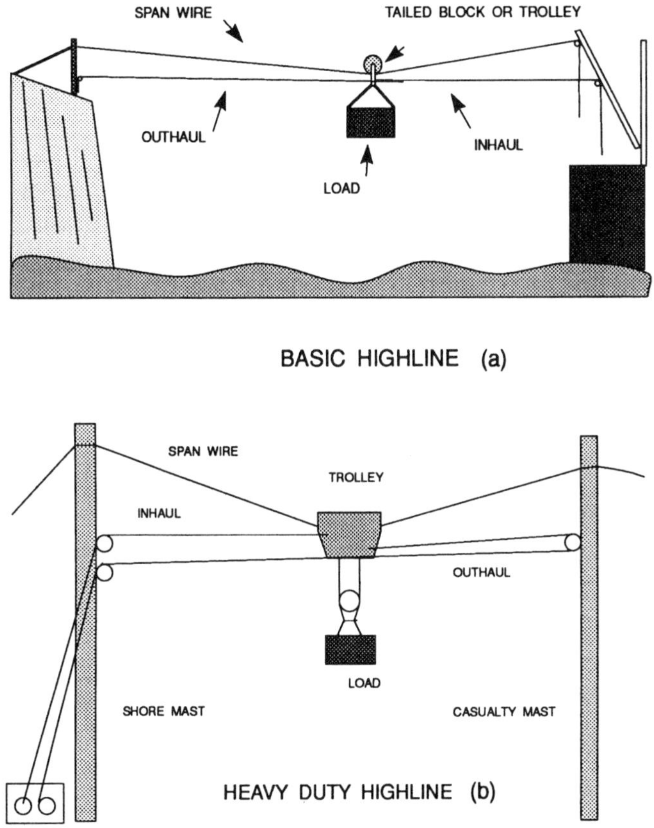

Fig. 7-10. Salvage highlines

out this text, salvors must look outside the marine industry for such equipment. Masts suitable for anchoring the shore end and trolleys capable of carrying significant loads are available in the logging industry. Figure 7-12 (a) illustrates one such trolley. Naval vessels also use suitable trolleys for replenishment at sea operations. Figure 7-12 (b) also illustrates this type of trolley. The naval trolley is lighter and less rugged than the logging trolley.

CONCLUSION

Rigging pervades salvage. This chapter has provided an overview of a few of the important factors in salvage rigging. It does not cover everything. No one knows all there is to know about salvage rigging. Good salvors learn on every job; poor ones repeat their mistakes. In salvage rigging three things are very important:

Fig. 7-11. Shore end of a salvage highline. Note how sheer legs are dug in and guyed. Courtesy of Captain David Hancox.

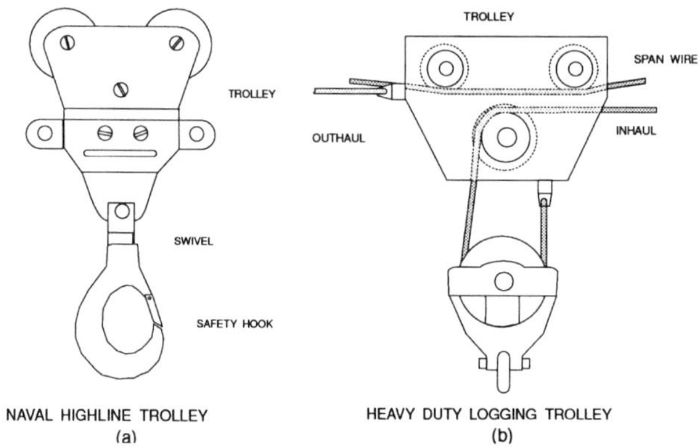

Fig. 7-12. Highline trolleys

1. A thorough understanding of the relationship between safe working load and breaking strength for each type of rigging component.
2. An appreciation that rigging systems work as systems of matched components where one inappropriate component can destroy the integrity of the entire system. The components to be matched must be matched on safe working load.
3. Common sense.

8

STRANDINGS

Historically, strandings make up about 20 percent of marine casualties. Most are minor incidents resolved quickly with a small number of resources and a cost to match. Major strandings can lead to lengthy, complex, and costly salvage operations. The frequency of such events has decreased with the common use of GPS and other electronic systems that take much of the uncertainty out of navigation. Fewer ships at sea also means a decrease in the number of strandings. Despite the factors improving safety, ships continue to strand with human error as the most common cause. Cahill, in his excellent analyses of strandings and their causes,[1] shows that major strandings are seldom the result of a single failing. Instead, they are at the end of a chain of inattention to the principles of good seamanship, poor navigational practice, and inadequate supervision. Although the causes of strandings are of professional interest to mariners, they are of no specific interest to salvors. Salvors' interests are limited to the condition of the ship and the process of seeing her afloat.

Strandings are serious because a disabled and immobilized ship lies at the mercy of the wind and sea. Initially, a stranded ship retains most of her value, but her condition always deteriorates as she lies aground. Salvage of a ship is time-critical. Stranded ships usually present a threat of pollution from bunker or cargo tanks rupturing on the initial stranding or as the ship continues to lie aground.

Three actions are necessary immediately following a stranding:

1. Action to assess intelligently the condition of the vessel and the probability of a successful salvage.
2. Action to free, stabilize, or reduce deterioration of the vessel.

3. Action to assess realistically the pollution threat and to assign it proper priority among salvage actions.

INITIAL ACTION ON STRANDING

When a ship strands, sailors instinctively react by making an effort to refloat her immediately. Immediate floating is usually the wrong action. Only a structurally sound ship, lightly aground on a soft bottom, warrants an immediate attempt to refloat. In any other circumstances, determination of the vessel's condition precedes any refloating attempt. Prompt refloating reduces hull stresses and eliminates changes in loading caused by tide cycles and deterioration of the weather. A ship with a ruptured hull is a less severe pollution hazard when it is safely afloat than when it is stranded. Drafts afloat are deeper than stranded so the hydrostatic pressure outside the hull is greater on the floating ship. If the hull became damaged in the stranding, a prematurely refloated vessel may flood, capsize, or sink. A ship aground on rock or coral probably does not have sufficient power to rip the hull while refloating with her engines, but may batter herself against the ground and extend the damage. A floating ship may flood rapidly, but while the ship lies aground in contact with the sea floor, the ground may partially plug the holes. Refloating with the intention of regrounding, if the ship behaves badly, is fraught with peril. The ship may sink or capsize, with greater chance of pollution before regrounding again. In any but the simplest case, attempting to refloat without determination of the seriousness and extent of the damage is dangerous and foolish.

Large ships, even when operating at low speeds, have large amounts of energy and momentum that can carry them very hard aground. The chance of a minor stranding is low. Any stranding carries the risk of hull damage and a ground reaction large enough to defeat simple methods of refloating.

In newly stranded ships, discharge of cargo or other weight to lighten the ship is dangerous to the point of folly. Lightening unsecured strandings permits the sea to drive them further ashore. Unplanned, precipitous weight removals from stranded ships have led them from "lightly aground" to "constructive total loss."

Immediately upon stranding the crew should:

Stop the engines.

Shift all sea suctions to the high suction to prevent ingestion of bottom material into machinery, piping, and heat transfer equipment.

Sound the general alarm. This action makes all hands aware of the emergency. To assure no one is missing, the crew, any industrial hands, and passengers should muster at a central place with their survival suits and other emergency equipment and stay there until the extent of the emergency is known.

Determine if pollution is occurring and take the shipboard mitigation measures appropriate to the resources on board.

Begin the determination of the ship's condition.

Inform interested parties.

Determine the need for help.

Show the proper visual signals.

Communications

All parties who have an interest must be informed of the existence and nature of the emergency. Any method of communication is proper for a ship in peril. Speed is essential. Satellite communications or single-sideband voice systems may be the most rapid means. Governments of coastal states may require VHF voice radio communications. Ships without power may arrange with ships in the vicinity or nearby shore stations to relay messages from battery-powered radios. Brevity and directness characterize good messages. After establishing communications, messages without distress prefixes are sent on working frequencies to keep calling and emergency frequencies clear.

Owners who have good information on the complexity and nature of a casualty are best able to make logical decisions. Simple drawings such as those shown in figures 8-1 and 8-2 for a product carrier convey a great deal of information in a readily understood form. The drawings can be faxed to owners or agents.

All discharges of oil or other harmful substances require reports to the authorities in the nearest coastal state as soon as possible. The report allows cor-

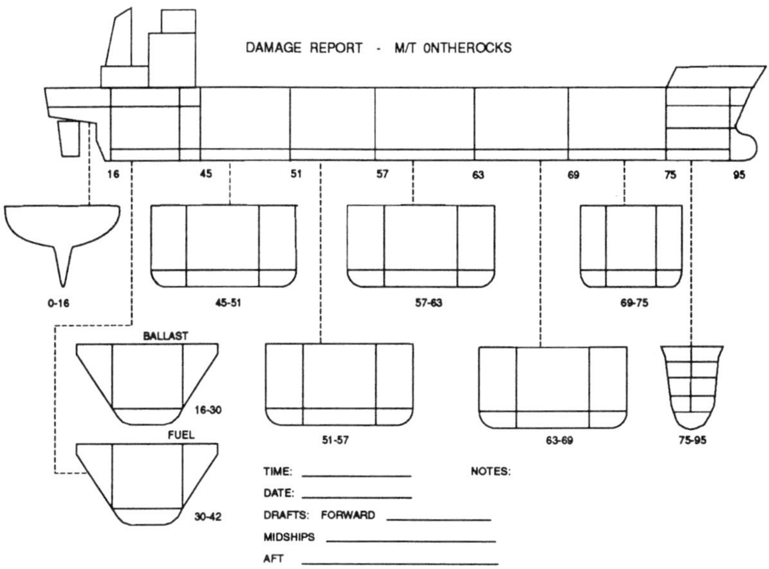

Fig. 8-1. Sample damage report

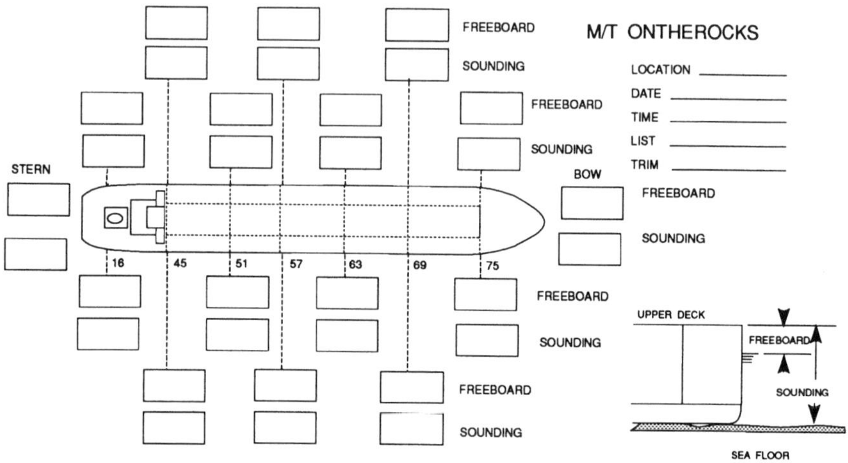

Fig. 8-2. Soundings report

rective action to begin and prevents civil and criminal penalties for failure to report. The master must make such a report under the *International Convention for the Prevention of Pollution from Ships* (MARPOL 73/78) and the laws of various coastal states. It is vitally important that ships operating near or in the waters of the United States make reports to both federal and state agencies. Failure to make the reports required by OPA-90 and the supporting state legislation, even in the midst of a life-threatening crisis, can bring draconian results. The contact information should be available in the ship's Vessel Response Plan or other documentation. Agents in departure or destination ports should also be prepared to make reports for ships they are servicing. As reporting requirements may change and vary locally from both the MARPOL and the International Maritime Organization (IMO) requirements,[2] this book includes no specific guidance on reporting. The periodically updated *Peril at Sea and Salvage, A Guide for Masters*,[3] a booklet that deserves a place on the bridge and under the Master's pillow in every ship, has an excellent discussion of communications in a casualty.

Determining the Ship's Condition

Only after a full determination of the damage and how the ship lies can a reasonable assessment of the probability and effects of refloating be made. The extent of the damage depends upon several factors—the type and slope of the sea floor, the speed of stranding, the construction of the ship, and the condition of the ship. In a laden ship, determination of the exact extent and nature of the damage may be impossible or impractical because of cargo blocking accesses. As much information as possible should be sought. Two sets of soundings have immediate interest.

The first set are those depths alongside the vessel taken at short, regular intervals all around the ship. These soundings help determine the extent and nature of the stranding. The set always includes bow, stern, and midships soundings. Averaging three soundings at each location compensates for the effects of surf and swell. In seas too rough for reliable readings, even by averaging, measuring the distance from the main deck to the sea floor and plotting it to scale on a profile of the ship gives a good picture of the sea floor and how the ship rests on it. The time of each set of soundings and the state of the tide are logged on the same sheet as the soundings. Soundings are repeated at the same locations at regular intervals until the ship is stable and only tidal effects cause changes in sounding. Hourly soundings are appropriate through the first two tide cycles. To accommodate watch changes, stations for soundings can be clearly marked by a spray of paint or other means. From the soundings and drafts calculated by the Mean of Quarter Means method (Chapter 4), an estimate can be made of the length and breadth of the ship in contact with the ground. Ground reaction may be approximated by the Change in Displacement or Tons per Inch (Centimeter) Immersion methods (Chapter 4). The records of all soundings and calculations made from them are preserved and given to salvors on arrival.

The second set of soundings—internal soundings of all tanks, double-bottom spaces, voids, holds, chain lockers, and other compartments—is to get a rough idea of the extent of the damage to the ship and where the hull is breached. This set of soundings is approached with extreme caution. Hull damage may cause flooding that drives water or the contents of tanks up sounding tubes and vents. The space may be pressed up or may be contaminated with cargo or bunkers. Opening a tank, sounding tube, or ullage plug, etc., may cause a release of the contents, a loss of buoyancy, or the release of toxic fumes or an anoxic atmosphere. Bunker or cargo oil carried in double-bottom, wing, or deep tanks may migrate to unexpected places as the result of damage. Every space is treated as though it is damaged and contaminated with toxic fumes or is oxygen deficient until proven sound and safe. Both wet and dry spaces are sounded at regular intervals to determine progress and rate of flooding. Spaces dry for one set of soundings may not be dry on subsequent sounding sets. Successive sets of soundings are compared for inconsistencies or improbable indications.

A third set of soundings is taken later only if the weather permits and a boat can be put in the water and operated safely. These soundings are taken astern. It is axiomatic in salvage that the best direction to refloat a ship is along the reciprocal of her grounding course. Thus, soundings are taken between the ship and deep water along that bearing. Soundings made alongside the ship determine if the area is safe for boat operations and for lightering vessels to come alongside to load. In determining the latter, it must be remembered that the lightering vessel will have a deeper draft on departure than on arrival.

Tides have great importance in strandings. As discussed in Chapter 4, ground reaction and, to some extent, buoyancy change with the tide. In an area of large tide ranges, a rising tide can refloat the ship and a falling tide can cause additional damage and pollution by impalement or crushing. The state of the tide at the time of stranding is calculated as well as the tide through the next few cycles. Tidal corrections are applied to all depth soundings to bring them to a common basis.

The strength and direction of tidal currents also should be calculated to determine what forces they exert on the ship. Longshore currents that encourage broaching present a serious danger.

The composition of the sea floor is estimated or sampled. Samples may be obtained with a lead, or composition can be estimated from chart notations, pilot publications, sailing directions, local knowledge, and inspection of the foreshore.

Immediate note is made of pollution and its source. A maximum effort must be directed to stopping the pollution as soon as possible. Efforts include moving pollutants from damaged tanks into undamaged tanks and voids. There should be no hesitation to move pollutants from damaged tanks into spaces not intended for their carriage. The additional complication to the salvage operation or expense of cleaning the space is far offset by the savings in fines and cleanup costs. Careful records of the amount of oil moved to other tanks and spaces are very important as are estimates of the quantities of oil spilled. Quantities of oil spilled form the basis for fines and penalties for spilling in many coastal states. Spill figures and fines can easily become inflated if poor records or no records at all exist of the oil transferred or of the soundings in ruptured tanks from the beginning of a casualty. Arriving salvors need accurate locations and quantities of oils and other potential pollutants.

Present weather and sea conditions, forecasts, and weather faxes for the area should be studied and analyzed for their potential effect on operations.

Go or Stay?

With a rough idea of the condition of the ship, a rational decision can be made either to attempt refloating with available resources or to call for salvage assistance. The ideal situation for an immediate refloating attempt occurs when the tide is rising, the sea floor is mud or sand, the ship is lightly aground with her hull intact, and there is tug assistance to help refloat and control the ship. Any of these conditions being less than perfect can affect the decision to attempt immediate refloating or to secure the ship and await professional assistance.

All the available, potentially effective resources are applied to the refloating attempt. Saving a few hundred dollars by not hiring a tug that can spell the difference between success and failure is false economy.

Not calling for salvors as soon as determining that help is needed is equally false economy. There is a period of denial following a casualty when ship's companies—and often shipowners—do not admit they are in trouble and are sure they can solve their problem. The denial period is very dangerous for the ship if it leads to delays in asking for help, or in accepting it when offered. Such delays, often characterized by haggling over contract forms or terms, have contributed to the loss of ships. In a world of very high values of ships and extreme penalties for pollution it is more foolish than ever to delay acceptance of help.

Before attempting any refloating, serious thought must be given to how the ship is to be handled immediately after she comes afloat and where she is to go. Arrangements should be made to enter a nearby port where inspections can be completed and necessary additional work undertaken. The permission of the port authorities to enter the port must be obtained. Authorities may ask the ship to enter a nearby sheltered area to complete an underwater inspection and determination of the pollution hazard before entering a port. It is often unwise to take a casualty into such a place because of the chance of another grounding, perhaps more serious than the first. Any safe refuge should be well charted and commonly visited by vessels of deeper draft than the refloated casualty. Similarly, casualties should not transit poorly charted areas when doing so is avoidable. After becoming a casualty, a ship has some degree of reduced stability and strength. It makes no sense to take a ship with reduced capability to withstand damage into a poorly charted area where the risk of becoming a casualty again is high.

Refloating should take place around high water when the ground reaction is lowest. The effort begins well before high water—at least two, more usually three hours—and held well after high water so maximum power is available and applied steadily when the tide is rising and at or near its peak.

The behavior of the ship as it comes off in the existing weather and with the layout of shoal water around should be thought out carefully. The situation may be such that although the ship could back off, she should not, because the combination of backing and weather may put her back aground—probably in a new location, but still aground. Although the ship may be perfectly capable of backing off, it may be preferable to wait for tug assistance to assure control of the refloated ship.

If the decision is not to attempt an immediate refloating, or the attempt does not succeed, securing the ship on her strand reduces deterioration until the salvors arrive and begin work.

Securing the Ship

There are three primary dangers to a stranded ship:

1. Pounding on the bottom and sustaining progressive hull damage that may result in fracture of the hull girder.

2. Broaching, with the dangers described in Chapter 4.
3. Being driven farther ashore by the seas causing additional hull damage and increasing the difficulty of refloating.

All three dangers can be reduced by securing the ship to eliminate liveliness at any state of the tide and with it the danger of easily broaching or being driven farther ashore. Ballasting down as hard as possible is the simplest step in securing a ship. Ballast in addition to that normally carried may be added by filling voids and empty tanks to put as much weight into the ship as possible. Fire hoses down the vents can fill such spaces in the absence of suitable piping. Ballasting also increases the bottom contact, spreading the load, and reduces stresses caused by the ship working on the ground.

There is a downside to ballasting, particularly on hard sea floors, such as rock and coral. Ballasting increases the ground reaction by the tonnage of ballast added. In large ships—PANAMAX and larger—this can be a very large amount. The increased ground reaction on an unyielding bottom can be enough to cause high local stresses that increase the damage to the ship's bottom. In double-hull ships the high stresses can force floors and other internal structures to punch through the skin or tank top, complicating the salvage problem and reducing the value of the ship and cargo. Ballasting on large ships, particularly those lying on hard bottoms, should never be undertaken as a matter of course, but only after analysis of the increase in ground reaction and the probable consequences. When such casualties are ballasting, the minimum amount of ballast necessary to secure the ship should be added and the minimum number of tanks ballasted.

Ground tackle also may secure stranded ships by anchors attached to heavy wire rope and deck purchases to seaward and up current to secure the ship against broaching and being driven further inshore. Alternatively, lines may be run ashore and secured to a simple log deadman, such as that illustrated in figure 8-3.

Standard works on seamanship describe methods of running out anchors with boats and kedging off stranded ships. Most of the methods have historical interest only, as most modern ship's boats, particularly enclosed lifeboats, are not only unsuited but dangerous for this work. With the disappearance of masts and booms, many ships have neither the means of moving anchors about easily nor the winches to haul the anchor purchases. Bower anchors may be walked out and hung off onto floats or rafts constructed for the purpose. The raft is then towed into position by a lifeboat as the chain is paid out. When the anchor is in position, the stopper is set and the raft towed out from under the anchor.

Tugs may hold the ship in position, normally only until ballasting is complete and ground tackle is laid. When necessary, tugs can secure a ship against broaching or being driven ashore for relatively long periods. A tug may either lay along and push as necessary or lay off with a light strain on her hawser. The tug master

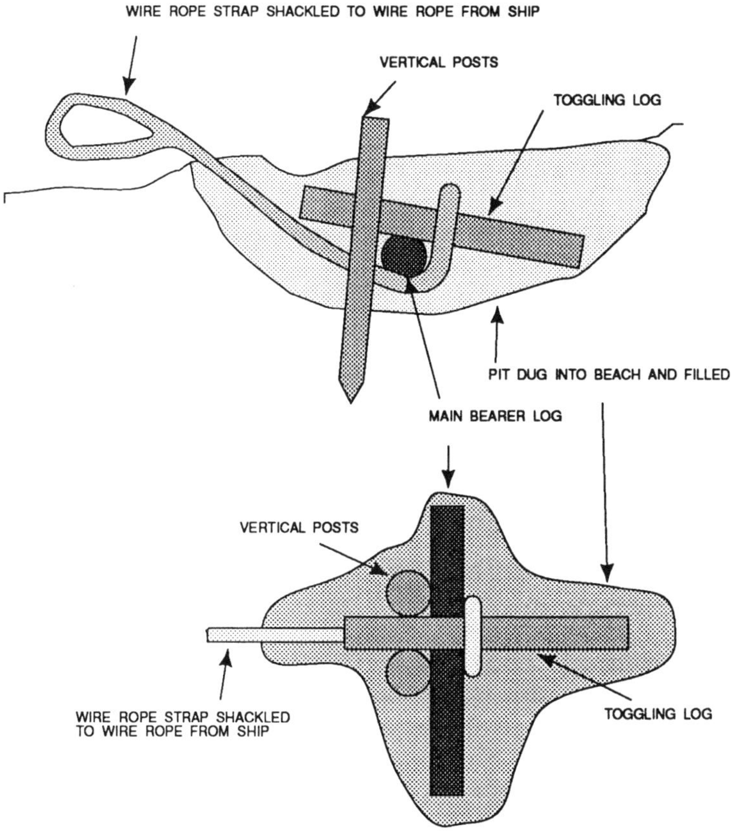

Fig. 8-3. Log beach anchor

must be alert to changes in tide, tidal current, and weather that may cause the stranded ship to move. Night operations need particular attention, as small changes may not be obvious immediately. If no tugs are available in the area, other boats, such as fishing boats, may act as tugs. Fishing boats, while better than nothing, do not make very effective tugs. They seldom have enough power nor are their lines the right size and strength for heavy towing.

SALVAGE OR CONSTRUCTIVE TOTAL LOSS?

Before salvage operations begin, the parties who have an economic interest in the casualty must decide if salvaging the vessel is technically and economically feasible. Shortly after word of the stranding goes out, various parties with an interest in the casualty begin to make their way to the site. The crowd includes surveyors for hull and cargo insurers who will recommend to their principals that the vessel either be salvaged or declared a constructive total loss. One or more surveyors also represent the owners' Protection and Indemnification Clubs at these early stages. The P&I club surveyors have the responsibility of setting up pollution control and cleanup operations proportional to the pollution that has occurred and the seriousness of the threat. They also represent P&I interests during the salvage operation and insure that the salvors' actions do not incur liability for the club. P&I has a direct interest in the decision to salvage. They have responsibility for removal of potential pollutants, hazardous substances, and the wreck itself when the vessel is declared a constructive loss.

The decision to salvage the vessel is purely economic. Technically, almost any vessel can be salvaged; economical salvage is another sort of bird. Along with technical feasibility, inputs to the decision are:

Availability of salvage resources—To conduct a successful salvage, competent salvors with the proper equipment must be available. They also must be close enough to get their workers and equipment to the site in a reasonable time at an appropriate cost, able to work in the coastal state, and be willing to work on a contract satisfactory to the shipowners and insurers. More frequently now than in the past, coastal state authorities must approve a salvor before he may work on a particular job.

Salvage costs—Sufficient data exist for knowledgeable surveyors to predict costs of salvage on both no cure–no pay and other types of contracts. As salvage operations normally contain many surprise factors, margins for escalation are normal.

Hull damage and repair costs—The type and location of hull damage affect the technical feasibility of salvage, the risk of a transit, and the cost of repairs. Hull surveyors routinely make repair cost estimates based on historical data from shipyards where the refloated vessel may go.

Transit to repair yard—Depending upon the condition of the refloated vessel, she may make the transit to the repair yard on her own, with a tug escort, or under tow. The availability of suitable tugs must be determined along with the costs of towing. Weather plays a major part in the decision, as it is unwise to expose a damaged vessel either under way or under tow to severe seasonal weather.

Cargo—The relative value of cargo and the hull must be weighed. It may be entirely reasonable to save the cargo while abandoning the vessel, or vice versa.

Government intervention—The laws of the particular coastal state must be taken into consideration along with the regulations and restrictions they are likely to impose on the salvage operation. The likelihood of government intervention that may stop or interrupt the operation is particularly important. Where a high likelihood of government intervention prevails, the salvor should avoid open form no cure–no pay contracts that do not fully protect his investment if government intervention prevents him from completing the job.

When all factors have been weighed and the decision made to salvage the vessel, cargo, or both, the principals can sign the contracts and the salvage operation can begin. On the other hand, if the decision is to declare a constructive loss, a whole new ball game with a very different set of rules begins.

When the vessel is declared a constructive total loss, the hull underwriters pay off and are out of the picture. Cargo underwriters may choose to recover the cargo and hire salvors for this work. Alternatively, they may consider the cargo lost and pay the owners. Once their obligations are paid, the hull and cargo insurers no longer have any responsibility for or interest in the ship. Not so the owner. The owner remains responsible for the wrecked vessel and its contents. The owner looks to his P&I club for indemnity in dealing with the wreck and any materials that present an environmental threat.

In practice, the club normally determines the action with the advice of their correspondent and the surveyor at the scene. A salvor employed for a wreck removal or environmental cleanup operation may find himself billing the owner but reporting directly to and taking direction from the club's representative at the site.

Local law and regulation and the position of the wreck very much govern the necessary action. Some jurisdictions, particularly those in heavily populated areas, have and enforce laws that require complete removal of the wreck. Others may temper their requirements to consider the location of the vessel and the problem it represents to the environment and the population. Some jurisdictions allow the wreck to be abandoned but will remove it and litigate to recover removal costs. The days of owners simply abandoning a vessel "as is, where is" have passed. At the least, the owner and his club can expect to remove all hazardous substances and potential pollutants from the wreck. They also can expect a broad interpretation of "hazardous substances." Removal of nonhazardous, persistent materials may be necessary, as may removal of small quantities of hazardous materials and materials in forms where release is improbable.

Representative of materials whose removal authorities may require from constructive total losses are:

Cargo, bunker, lubricating, cooling, and hydraulic oils.

Gasoline, greases, and other petroleum products.

Paints, thinners, white lead, and preservatives.

Refrigerant, fire-fighting, and other industrial gases.

Asbestos insulation, and some other insulating materials.

PCBs in electrical and electronic equipment.

Halides and other materials in vapor lights.

Radioactive nuclides in radar cathode-ray tubes.

Depending upon the location of the wreck and the nature of the materials, the skills required for the removal of hazardous materials may differ from those required of salvors. Hazardous substance workers should be trained to the level required for handling the materials they are removing and should have the proper personal protective equipment. Handling, storage, and disposal regulations must be followed strictly. Handling of hazardous substances offers great peril not limited to the immediate hazard presented by the substance, but including great potential liability if the materials are mishandled.

Wreck removals are usually undertaken as planned operations and become time critical only when their location blocks traffic, a berth, or other facility. Even when expedited by every feasible means, wreck removals are often long, complex, and expensive operations. There is an immense amount of work and coordination required to remove a structure as large and complicated as a ship. Chapters 10 and 14 discuss techniques for wreck removal in some detail. The contract for wreck removal varies considerably from that for time-critical stranding salvage. Strandings are usually done on an arbitrated no cure–no pay basis under standard terms or on a day rate. Wreck removals have historically been on a lump sum no cure–no pay contract. The latter is changing toward a day rate or lump sum contract with definite milestones at which agreed partial payments are made, similar to most construction contracts. Chapter 15 discusses the contractual basis for salvage and the features of different types of contracts.

SALVAGE OPERATIONS

When the decision to salvage the vessel has been made and an appropriate contract is in place, planning and mobilization can begin in earnest. The purpose of the operation is to restore the buoyancy that the vessel lost in grounding by moving her into deeper water, or to reduce the weight of the vessel so she floats as she lies.

Specific refloating techniques depend upon the equipment available and the conditions of the grounding. Too much emphasis cannot be placed on the fact that, in general, grounded vessels are best refloated by managing weight and buoyancy so the ship lies clear of and parallel to the sea floor. Tugs and ground tackle are invaluable, even indispensable in the salvage of stranded ships. They have two functions: to control and position the ship, and to provide the tractive force needed to overcome the residual ground reaction and physically drag the ship into deep water.

A portion of the art of salvage is achieving the balance between weight management and pulling forces that refloats the ship most efficiently and to the greatest economic advantage for the salvor. At the risk of being repetitious, the most elegantly structured and technically correct salvage operation fails if it does not make money for the salvor.

When a ship grounds and goes from steaming through the water to aground and stopped, the kinetic energy of the moving ship is expended by:

1. Lifting the ship bodily.
2. Tearing and deforming of the ship's plating and bottom structure.
3. Stopping the ship by friction with the sea floor.
4. Compacting the sea floor.

It is impossible to determine, or even to estimate, the amount of energy absorbed by each mechanism. It is unimportant to do so, for only the easily observed or measured results hold any interest. The salvor is interested only in the lifting of the ship as an indicator of how hard the ship is aground, the bottom damage as an indicator of the work needed to refloat the ship, and the composition of the sea floor as an indicator of the characteristics of friction between the ship and sea floor.

The amount of buoyancy that the ship loses in grounding, exactly equivalent to the weight of the ship supported by the ground, is the most important single quantity in the salvage of grounded ships. Chapter 4 describes various ways of determining ground reaction. Ground reaction should be calculated early in the operation and a system set up to track the variation with tides and the removal, addition, and movement of weight. While ground reaction calculations should be made with the best available information, attempts to calculate ground reaction with extreme accuracy waste time and effort. Anyone thinking they can acquire information at the site that will permit exact determination of ground reaction is living in a dream world. A calculation within 5 to 10 percent of the actual ground reaction is close enough, as prudent refloating plans normally allow for a larger margin of error. Errors should be on the side of high ground reaction. It is far more pleasant to find a ship refloating with less effort than predicted than to restructure the operation because of overoptimistic predictions.

Ground reaction must be reduced so the ship either refloats without tractive force or so the tractive force available can overcome the ground reaction. The required tractive force is the product of the ground reaction and the coefficient of friction between the ship and the sea floor.

$$F = \mu \times R$$

where:
F = tractive force required to free the ship in long tons (tonnes)
μ = coefficient of friction between the ship and sea floor (dimensionless)
R = ground reaction in long tons (tonnes)

The coefficient of friction between the ship and sea floor cannot be measured and can be determined only within broad limits through lengthy and costly experimentation done only in the rarest of circumstances. In practice, the coefficients of friction given below are well established through experience and have proven accurate enough for salvage work.

TABLE 8-1.

SHIP–SEA FLOOR COEFFICIENT OF FRICTION	
Type of Sea Floor	*Coefficient of Friction*
Mud or silty soil	0.2 to 0.3
Sand	0.3 to 0.4
Coral	0.5 to 0.8
Rock	0.8 to 1.5

Most sea floors do not fall neatly into one category. Good, conservative practice chooses the sea floor material constituent that gives the highest coefficient of friction, then applies common sense and judgment to choose from within the range. Pessimism and conservative assumptions pay in choosing coefficients of friction as they do in other aspects of salvage.

The coefficients of friction given above are static coefficients. When the ship begins to move, a much smaller dynamic coefficient applies. Less force is required to keep the ship moving than to start the movement. Once the ship starts to move, it should be kept moving until floating, for when it stops, the coefficient reverts to the higher static value.

For rigid bodies, friction is independent of areas in contact. This is not true of grounded ships, unless they have grounded on rock or dead coral. Most soils and living coral act more like a very dense fluid than a rigid body. Thus, the coefficient of friction may decrease when the unit pressure on the sea floor is high. Often, trimming fine-lined ships aground on fluid sea floors down hard by the bow increases the total and unit pressures on the ground. The decrease in coefficient offsets the increase in ground reaction and allows refloating with a smaller tractive force.

Damage to the ship's bottom and irregular surfaces that impede smooth sliding effectively increase the coefficient of friction. If the bottom is rough or damaged, the coefficient of friction should be increased by the larger of 0.5 or half the value of the estimated coefficient of friction.

The extreme case occurs when rocks or coral heads impale the ship and act as an anchor. If the ship cannot be floated off the impalement, trimmed so it is free, or the rock or coral head removed, it is usually impossible to generate enough force to float the ship. It may be possible to pull hard enough to do considerable damage to the hull.

Stimulating a dynamic condition between the ship and sea floor reduces the effective coefficient of friction. Dynamic conditions may be stimulated by:

Running the ship's machinery to set up hull vibrations. This technique is most effective when the machinery is in way of the grounded area.

Moving large weights on the grounded ship. Unless there are large weights that can easily be moved quickly and repeatedly, it is usually a better use of resources to remove the weights to lighten the ship.

Wrenching the ship with tugs or ground tackle. The force normally required to rotate a ship is about one-third of that required to cause it to move fore and aft. Wrenching rotates the ship and sets up a dynamic friction so the ship moves fore and aft more easily.

Swell that varies the buoyancy and thus the ground reaction along the length of the ship. Swell may be natural or induced by ships running racetrack patterns parallel to the beach. The latter practice is more apt to be found in naval than commercial practice, where cost-benefit ratios have greater importance.

Inducing sea floor movement with the shock waves from nearby explosions. This method is more likely to be tried by naval than commercial salvors. The possibility of shock damage to the vessel's hull and machinery and a concomitant diminution in salvage value should not be ignored.

A unique condition distantly related to friction occurs in mud sea floors. The mud, a mixture of clay and water, breaks down unevenly under pressure along the bottom of the ship. The clay forms layers that restrict the movement of water and prevent the hydrostatic pressure under the ship from changing. The effect is to hold the ship to the sea floor. This effect may be overcome by breaking up the layers by dragging a hogging line under the ship, blowing air under the ship, or washing with a fire hose and nozzle.

With the ground reaction and basic information about the ship and how she lies known, more detailed plans are made and preparation for refloating can move ahead.

Preparation

The choice of refloating method is one of the first and most important decisions. The desirable method refloats the ship promptly with minimum additional damage. There are only three classes of action to be considered:

1. Managing weight and ballast so the ship comes afloat in her present position.
2. Refloating with tractive force alone.
3. Removing the ground under the ship.

Any two, or all three, of the methods may be—and usually are— combined in a particular stranding.

A careful look at the ship and her movable weights quickly determines the feasibility of weight and ballast movement and removal as a refloating method. Determination of the drafts of the floating ship is made by normal draft and trim calculations with the prestranding drafts as a starting point. Structure of a vessel hard aground with no cargo or cargo easily removed may be cut away to reduce her weight for refloating. The benefit gained by weight removal must balance the cost and effort of the removal. It may be desirable to hold the vessel in position until she is lightened and trimmed enough to float, or it may be better to lighten her just enough to refloat with tractive forces. Each stranding is different; each requires thoughtful analysis.

The adequacy of tractive forces can be determined quickly. With ground reaction known, freeing force is calculated by assuming a coefficient of friction and multiplying ground reaction and freeing force. Comparison of the result with available tractive forces shows whether the tractive forces alone can float the vessel or if floating requires some other method or combination of methods. Tractive forces should have a margin of at least 25 percent above the required freeing forces to allow for uncertainties in force development and application. Methods of developing tractive forces and of quantifying tractive forces developed by various means are discussed later in this chapter. It is seldom practical to develop a tractive force of more than a few hundred tons.

As soon as a salvage contract is in place and any assets are on scene, the pressure begins for an immediate refloating attempt. The salvor may know full well from his surveys and calculations that only levitation can refloat the ship without more salvage actions. Despite this knowledge, it is sometimes easier and politically smarter to go ahead and make the attempt than to argue the point. There is usually no harm or time lost in the attempt. However, the ship's equilibrium and security on her strand are disturbed and may not be restored without some efforts and unsettling moments. Should the attempt unexpectedly succeed and the ship refloat, any salvor worth his salt can pull out a story about how he knew it would. If it fails he can go ahead and do what he wanted to do in the first place—often with much less second-guessing.

The third option is removing the ground under the ship and often along the route to deep water. Ground removal varies from scouring away some types of sea floors with propeller wash to very complex dredging and ponding operations.

While the cost of the more complex operations may be high, sometimes no other choice exists.

Very early in the process of casualty resolution the question of dealing with the ship's bunkers and any hazardous or potentially polluting cargo arises. Hazardous cargoes and oil secure in intact stowage tanks should not be moved where there is a high probability of successful salvage without moving it. The chance of a release into the environment is greater during handling than while the material lies in its design stowage. Probability of a release during a salvage transfer is particularly high because salvage transfers by their nature are compromises of normal transfer procedures.

Salvors cannot always leave oil and hazardous materials in secure storage in the casualty for the duration of the salvage operation, particularly in a casualty that has high visibility and media attention. The increase in environmental concern, legislation, and regulation means that regulators have a presence at and strong influence on salvage operations. Although removal is not always the best technical choice, regulators may insist on removal of oil and hazardous materials. While regulators' direction may be open to appeal, salvors are usually well advised to follow such direction rather than to waste time and opportunity in argument. Salvage management may make a parallel appeal to senior regulators that does not take the time of salvors in the field. In all cases, salvors should keep detailed notes of direction given by regulators, should log the direction and their objections, and should make their objections known to regulators—in writing, if the work directed is likely to affect the operation's schedule or cost.

Chapters 5 and 13 respectively discuss bunker and cargo oil removals while Chapters 5 and 12 address hazardous cargo.

Ships often suffer damage upon grounding, particularly when they ground on rock or other hard sea floors. The surveys described in Chapter 6 identify this damage. Analysis of the information obtained in the surveys identifies hull repairs that must be made before refloating. Restoration of the watertight envelope and restoration of buoyancy to flooded spaces may be considered as part of the weight and buoyancy management scheme for refloating the vessel. Some repairs may not be possible with the ship upon the ground and must either be made after refloating, but before the ship undertakes her voyage or voyage-in-tow to the repair yard, or in the repair yard. Chapter 9 describes methods of patching the hull and restoring buoyancy to flooded spaces.

Preparation for refloating includes a stability analysis of the ship both as she lies aground and afloat. Ground reaction acts like a weight removal equal in size to the ground reaction at the keel. The ground reaction produces a virtual rise in the center of gravity (G) that may cause instability in the grounded ship. In addition, a change in metacentric height results from lowering the position of the center of buoyancy (B) and changing, usually decreasing, the moment of inertia of the waterline plane and the underwater volume of the ship.

The new position of the center of gravity above the keel may be calculated by:

$$KG_1 = \frac{(KG \times W)}{(W - R)}$$

where:

KG_1 = effective height of the center of gravity above the keel when the ship is aground

KG = height of center of gravity when the ship is afloat

W = new displacement of the ship

R = ground reaction

The height of the metacenter above the keel with the ship aground (KM_1) is taken from the Curves of Form by entering with the grounded mean draft. Extreme trim may cause inaccuracies, but these are normally acceptable for salvage calculations. The grounded metacentric height may be calculated by:

$$GM_1 = KM_1 - KG_1$$

As the tide changes, the stability of the ship changes, with the condition of minimum stability coinciding with low water, the condition in which ground reaction is maximum and waterplane inertia and underwater volume are minimum. On an ebbing tide, negative stability can develop in a ship that is stable in the upper portion of the tide range. The same condition can occur as draft increases with sea floor washout under the ship.

The importance of stability in a grounded ship depends upon how the ship rests on the ground. On a flat sea floor—especially a soft one that takes the shape of the ship—the chance of capsizing is low. An unstable ship may take a list, but will come to rest on the ground, unable to capsize. On a pinnacle or in another situation in which the ship can incline without restraint, she may capsize. Particular care must be taken with ships aground on pinnacles. Weights must be carefully calculated and handled to prevent inducing or worsening negative stability. Liquid loads and flooding require thorough attention to prevent free surface development.

Sometimes, a ship is unstable when ground reaction is low enough to refloat her with tractive forces. The salvor may be unable to reduce ground reaction more and may be forced to refloat from the unstable condition. He must analyze the casualty's stability before she grounded, and her stability after refloating. A ship that was stable before grounding and that has had no major weight changes passes from negative to positive stability during refloating and has positive stability when again afloat. With major weight changes, free surface, or free communication, the negative metacentric height (GM) aground is not totally attributable to ground reaction. The casualty may then be either stable or unstable upon refloating.

In all cases, as much free surface and high weight as possible must be eliminated to have the ship as stable as possible before the refloating attempt. The refloating attempt should have a high probability of success, so the ship moves smartly off the ground and passes quickly to the stable condition. When avoidable, ships unstable on refloating should not be refloated. Sometimes, it is unavoidable. An unstable ship may capsize on refloating, causing the loss of the ship and a much more severe salvage problem. Careful and detailed plans for stabilizing the ship by low weight or restraining her should be made before refloating. Filling small, low tanks adds low weight quickly, but the free surface effect while the tank fills may offset the weight advantage.

Ground reaction in ships grounded along one side or on an off-center ledge acts like removal of an off-center weight at the point of contact. The resulting upsetting moment causes the ship to list. Both the upsetting moment and the list can be calculated, but the accuracy can be no better than the accuracy of the ground reaction. The calculation does indicate whether the entire list comes from the off-center grounding, or if another cause contributes to it.

It is axiomatic that a ship should come off the ground in the reverse direction she went on. Like all axioms, this one is only usually true. The ship should refloat in the direction in which the way to deep water is short and clear. When the ship has gone straight ashore and not rotated or been driven to a new position after grounding, the best direction to refloat is normally the reciprocal of the grounding course. Ships that drift ashore sideways, broach, rotate on a pinnacle, or are driven into often improbable positions require some thought. The time to find the clearest way to deep water and to rotate the ship so she refloats in that direction is well spent. Refloating in the direction of stranding is particularly important on coral and other environmentally sensitive sea floors. In areas where governments may assess penalties for sea floor damage, care in reducing sea floor contact and damage can reduce these penalties. Minimizing sea floor contact almost dictates refloating along the grounding course reciprocal.

Ships often take considerable damage when they ground, especially when the grounding is on a hard sea floor. The damage can result in breaches in the hull and may flood into the double bottoms or into the holds or tanks of the ship. Ships carrying bunkers in double-bottom tanks may lose bunkers into the sea, liquid cargo may flow into the sea, and the hull may flood. Either discharge of oil or other pollutants or flooding of the ship adds another dimension to the stranding.

Hull damage taken in stranding has two possible effects:

1. It reduces either the longitudinal bending strength or the shear strength of the hull so much that the hull cannot carry normal loads and may fail catastrophically.
2. It allows flooding of the hull with:
   a. additional loss of buoyancy that must be restored before the ship can sail and
   b. loss of watertight integrity that endangers the ship.

Either situation requires temporary repairs. The second situation is less serious. Repairs need be only patches that form a watertight—or near watertight—boundary, so the ship may be dewatered. In the first case, the repairs must restore not only watertight integrity but also some portion of the structural strength. Salvors have neither interest in nor obligation to make complete, permanent, and elegant repairs. Their job is to make the minimum repairs necessary to see the ship safely afloat. There are neither extra points nor more dollars in salvage for salvors who make unnecessary or overly complex repairs during salvage operations. Conversely, salvage history contains many examples of inadequate patching or salvage repair efforts. Determining necessary repairs for a stranded ship should never be a shot in the dark. Instead, it should begin with a careful analysis by an engineer who knows and understands ships' structures and should lead to practical repairs made on-site. Chapter 9 discusses techniques for patching and restoring buoyancy to damaged hulls.

Earlier, this chapter discussed the need for securing a vessel on her strand so she stops pounding and will neither broach nor be driven farther ashore. This need continues throughout the operation, particularly if salvors lighten the ship to facilitate refloating or if weather is likely to drive the salvage forces away for a time. The method for securing cannot be difficult or time-consuming to release at the proper time.

Ballasting all available tanks, including bunker tanks, and even flooding selected holds and cargo tanks is a quick and convenient way to add weight to a ship to secure her. Flooding introduces free surface into partially filled spaces, but this is of little consequence unless the vessel rests on a pinnacle and the flood water should be removed before refloating. Ballasting presents the problem of dirty ballast—or dirty floodwater disposal. Authorities are unlikely to permit the discharge of dirty water into ports or coastal waters. The method of disposing of dirty water must be firmly in hand before deciding to ballast.

Adding liquid weight in bladders, built-for-purpose tanks, or in clean spaces is a variation on ballasting. Such temporary weight additions have two primary requirements: enough unencumbered space to add an adequate amount of weight and a method of getting rid of the weight quickly. Weight in bladders and tanks on deck or high in the ship can drain by gravity through large gate valves. Larger-than-normal pump batteries provide for rapid pumping of liquid weight that cannot gravity-drain.

Ground tackle laid in the direction of prevailing seas and weather is an excellent tool for securing the ship. Ground tackle has the additional advantage, when rigged to a purchase or linear puller, of developing tractive forces during refloating operations. It is common practice for salvors to rig ground tackle for pulling, although its primary purpose is to hold the ship in position. Ground tackle may either be rigged directly to the ship or to a salvage ship or pulling barge attached to the ship. A more detailed discussion of ground tackle in salvage appears later in this chapter in the discussion of tractive forces.

Weight and Buoyancy Management

Management of the quantity and distribution of weight and buoyancy, the salvor's primary tool for refloating stranded ships, puts the ship in a suitable attitude for refloating. The most desirable situation occurs when salvors can lighten a ship until she is floating and trimmed almost parallel to the sea floor. A ship in this condition can be hauled into deep water without potentially damaging drag along the sea floor. The second most desirable situation occurs when the ground reaction can be reduced enough that the ship can be dragged to deep water by tractive forces. Weight and buoyancy management play an important role in almost every major stranding. The historical importance of tractive forces has decreased as large ships grounded to the same percentage of their displacement as small ships have ground reactions too large for tractive forces to overcome.

The calculations for weight and buoyancy management are nothing more complex than the calculations for weight changes that every mariner is familiar with. The approach is normally "what if." That is, "What if I removed 1,000 tons from Number One—what would my drafts be?" Investigation of several possibilities is likely. A simple form, similar to the one on page 745, is convenient for making numerous calculations. The ship's load calculator is more convenient, and a computer is even more convenient. With a computer, a spreadsheet tailored to the situation may be set up or a simple program written. A little study of the arrangement of the casualty and the location of weights and buoyancy usually leads to simplification of the calculations. Several excellent books, among them *Stability and Trim for the Ship's Officer* by La Dage and Van Gemert, edited by William George,[4] provide complete discussions of trim calculations.

Usually, many combinations of weight removals from various places result in the same drafts. Candidate combinations should be checked to be sure that the bending moment remains satisfactory with the new weight and buoyancy distribution. The combination chosen has a practical basis considering ease of handling; availability, cost, and handling of transshipment vessels; retention of value of the cargo; and operational practicality.

Chapter 12 discusses salvage cargo handling in some detail. As weight other than cargo may be removed, some of these weights, as well as some other issues about cargo, warrant discussion here. Weights removed in salvage may include bunkers, stores, passengers, outfit, and portions of the ship. Most of these items are small and limited in effect when compared to cargo. Although regulatory agencies sometimes insist on the removal of bunkers as a pollution prevention action, bunker removal may be exactly the wrong action for bunkers carried in low tanks. During the removal of bunkers, every effort should be made to retain the value of the fuel. If at all practical, the debunkering barge should be set up and cleaned for the type of fuel involved and should be equipped to keep the fuel at the proper temperature and to handle it properly to retain its value. The labor and cost of removing stores and outfit may outweigh the benefit gained. Removing passengers is well worth the effort. When passengers leave, not only a weight but also a source of irritation, interference, and, most importantly, potential liability is removed. Removal of portions of the ship's structure is the last resort, primarily because it involves massive work that usually requires a shipyard to reverse and that decreases the salved value of the ship. Structure cut away should be kept so it can be put back aboard the ship. Removal of structure for anything but a wreck removal is rare.

Jettisoning of cargo to reduce weight was more acceptable in the past than today. Authorities look very carefully at materials jettisoned in coastal waters, harbors, and waterways. No assurance exists that they will grant requests for jettisoning even the most benign materials. In matters of "jettison or lose the ship," authorities may not grant permission to jettison. If they grant permission, they may also impose civil and criminal penalties for laws broken in jettisoning pollutants. Salvage plans based on jettisoning are not conceived in wisdom.

Tugs or ground tackle to hold the ship in position, or the replacement of weight by quickly removed, compensating weight, must accompany removal of large weights to bring a ship lightly aground or afloat. Without a means to hold her, the lightened ship is in danger of driving up harder on the beach. Later, this chapter discusses ground tackle for this purpose and for hauling the ship. Suffice it to say at this point that even ground tackle intended solely for positioning the ship must be capable of being tensioned to accommodate changing conditions.

Weight and buoyancy management is most practical in casualties with large quantities of easily moved cargo. Tankers and bulk carriers are especially easy in this regard. Some ships, particularly service and industrial vessels and some warships, do not have enough weight that can be removed under salvage conditions. In these ships and in many others, management of the weight and buoyancy of the hull alone may not be enough to permit refloating, or to bring the ship to the point where tractive forces can move her. Externally applied buoyant or lifting forces can reduce the ground reaction further so she may move.

Pontoons or barges rigged alongside can supply external buoyant forces. The pontoons or barges are brought alongside, ballasted down, rerigged to hold them in position vertically, and deballasted. The pontoons and their lift move with the ship and are removed after refloating.

Where space and water depths permit, cranes, derricks, or sheer legs may be rigged alongside and lift to reduce the ground reaction. With all lifting equipment, but especially with sheer legs, the refloating should proceed very slowly under full control so when the ship comes afloat and the center of buoyancy shifts, no sudden, high, transient loads come onto the lifting equipment.

Jacking, a somewhat archaic practice that requires a very labor-intensive effort, occasionally proves worthwhile on rock or very hard sea floors. This method is always combined with pulling by some means.

To implement the method, jacking pads are prepared on the sea floor and on the side of the ship, and jacking beams topped by jacks of at least 60 tons' capacity and 30-inch risers are placed between the jacking pads. The pulling system is brought up to full tension two hours before high water and the ship jacked. As the ship begins to move, pressure is maintained on the jacks until the jacking beam topples and the ship either floats or again rests on the ground. The process repeats as many times as necessary to bring the ship afloat.

The jacking pad on the sea floor can be a smooth place on a rock or coral bottom or a heavy steel plate laid over rougher spots to spread the load. In very rough spots, timber crush pads may lie under the plate. Weldments placed at strong parts of the hull side structure make up the jacking pads on the side of the ship. Ideally, the pads are distributed symmetrically about the center of ground reaction.

The jacking beam is a section of 12-inch or larger, Schedule 120 pipe or a comparable I or wide flange section fitted with a plate pad on each end to distribute the load and support the jack. A lazy wire rope strap, shackled to an eye of the beam and stopped off on deck, catches the beam when it topples.

The jack, bolted to the pad on top of the beam, sits between the jacking beam and the pad on the ship. Actuating lines lead to a central operating location on the ship, so all jacks can operate simultaneously. Figure 8-4 illustrates this type of jacking.

Another method of jacking is well suited to refloating small to medium-sized ships broached on rocky beaches where the roughness of the beach and the high coefficient of friction of rock makes dragging the ship across the beach impractical. The method simulates side launching of the ship by jacking the ship up, placing launching ways under the ship, and sliding her down the ways. The number and location of the ways depend upon the ship's weight and her weight distribution.

Jacking points are built at each way, preferably on either side of the way on both sides of the ship so there are four jacking points at each way. The most practical way of building jacking points is to place concrete over roughly cleared areas of beach rock. For reasons that are soon to be obvious, the jacking points on the shoreward side are built to carry the horizontal loads as well as vertical loads equal to the full jacking force. Starting at one end and working toward amidships, the ship is jacked up enough that the ways can be built under one end and the ship is blocked and cribbed in place.

Simply driving the fixed way under the ship, leaving it supported by the beach rocks, is not a good idea. As the ship slides down the way, the uneven support may allow the way to fail and leave the salvor with more of a mess than he had before. A solid, even support for the way must be prepared, much in the same way as the

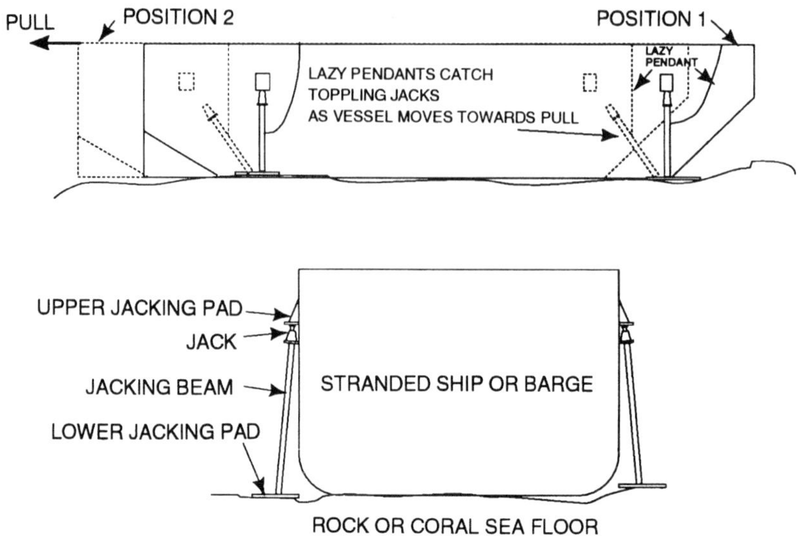

Fig. 8-4. Jacking a stranded vessel

jacking point, by placing concrete over beach rock and riprap. The fixed way—either heavy timbers or steel plate—is greased and driven under the ship, then fixed securely to the foundation. The heavily greased sliding way is driven in on top of the fixed way. The ship is set down on the ways and the process repeated at the other end.

Ground tackle laid to seaward is attached to the vessel. Attachment of the ground tackle should be given some special attention. Ground tackle attached at the deck or above on the seaward side may produce an undesirable upsetting moment. Leading chains from the ground tackle leg under the vessel and up the shoreward side may counter this moment and help bring the ship down the ways more evenly. The jacks are now placed horizontally in the shoreward jacking points. The forces of the jacks pushing and the ground tackle pulling move the ship down the ways like a side launch.

On hard, flat beaches, the same general technique may raise small ships enough to put trailer, aircraft, or railway car undercarriages, wheel assemblies, or trucks under the ship to roll her into the sea.

Tractive Forces

Tractive forces are horizontal forces that attempt to move the ship in the direction of application of force or to produce a moment that changes the ship's heading. In salvage tugs, pulling or pushing systems and the casualty's propulsion plant develop tractive forces. The forces always act in a straight line in the direction of application. Both the magnitude and direction of tractive forces are important. The

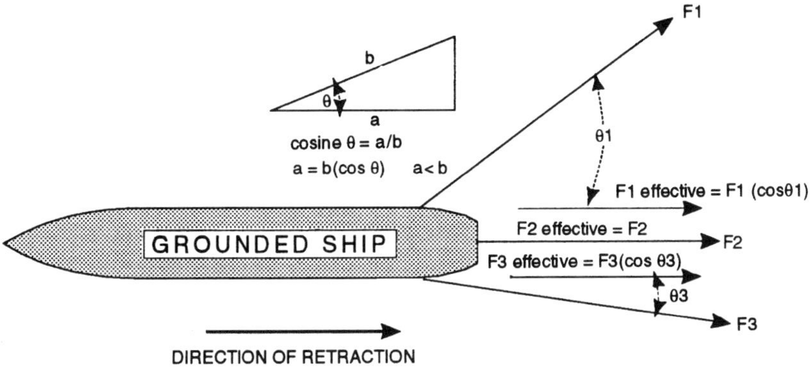

Fig. 8-5. Loss of effectiveness in an angular pull

importance of magnitude is obvious; a large pull has more effect in retracting the ship than a small one. The direction of the pull should be as nearly parallel to the direction of retraction as possible. A force at an angle to the desired direction of retraction has a component in the direction of retraction that is less than the total force. The effective force, the force acting in the direction of retraction, equals the product of the force and the cosine of the angle between the direction of retraction and the direction in which the force acts, or:

$$F_{effective} = F \times \cos\theta$$

where:

$F_{effective}$ = the force in the direction of retraction

F = the magnitude of the applied force

θ = the angle between the desired direction of retraction and the direction in which the force is applied

For small angles the loss is small, but it reaches about 14.5 percent of the applied force at 30°, 30 percent at 45°, and half at 60°. Obviously, lines to the vessel will interfere with one another if they do not have enough angular separation. There is no rule for how close is too close. Seaman's eye and the adage that if it looks right it probably is right apply. Part of the art of salvage gained only by experience and thought is arranging tractive forces to produce the greatest possible effect.

Tugs. Tugs develop their tractive force, called bollard pull and measured in tons (tonnes), through their propulsion systems. Static bollard pull, the greatest towline force the tug can develop, occurs when she is making full power at zero speed in calm water. As the tug speed increases, the amount of power required to propel her also increases, and the proportion of total power available for bollard pull decreases. As tugs pull on stranded vessels at zero speed, static bollard pull is the quantity of interest to salvors.

Five main factors affect a tug's bollard pull: the brake horsepower of the tug's engines, whether the propeller is fixed or controllable pitch, whether or not the propeller is shrouded, the water depth, and power losses caused by overheating of machinery. Both controllable pitch propellers and propeller shrouds increase the low hull speed efficiency of the propulsion system and increase bollard pull significantly.

The most reliable measure of bollard pull is a standardized full-scale trial run under the supervision of a classification society when the tug is new or has had major changes. Certificates carried on board document such tests. No requirement exists for tugs to have these tests or carry the certificates. Most quoted bollard pull figures are estimates from the characteristics of the propulsion system. Tug owners, in their enthusiasm for their tug, sometimes inflate bollard pull figures and horsepower. Bollard pull of tugs may be estimated by:

$$BP = K \times bhp$$

where:

BP = static bollard pull
K = a factor that considers the propeller type and shrouding
bhp = the total brake horsepower of the tug's propulsion engines

K factors for the equation above are:

Propulsion System Type	*K Factor*
Open, fixed pitch propeller	0.011
Open, controllable pitch propeller	0.012
Shrouded, fixed pitch propeller	0.013
Shrouded, controllable pitch propeller	0.016

Most tugs use standard marine diesels with the rated output quoted in brake horsepower (bhp) or kilowatts (kw). The latter converts easily by multiplying kilowatts by 1.34 to obtain bhp. Multiplying shaft horsepower (shp) by 1.05 gives a good estimate of brake horsepower. Indicated horsepower (ihp), a measured quantity somewhat equivalent to brake horsepower for reciprocating steam engines, has no meaning in diesel propulsion. Another ihp, installed horsepower, is sometimes quoted. This figure does not relate directly to the main propulsion system, as it includes all the horsepower installed in the ship for any purpose. Multiplying either ihp by 0.75 gives a very rough estimate of bhp.

Certified or estimated bollard pull is reduced by as much as 50 percent by: rough seas, constant rudder, shallow water, or the towline not leading directly astern.

An older method of estimating bollard pull by allowing 1 ton for each hundred horsepower has enough accuracy for open, fixed pitch propellers and gives a convenient quick and dirty estimate. Equally quick and dirty estimates can be made by increasing the estimate by 10 percent for a controllable pitch propeller, 20 percent for a shroud, and 40 percent for both.

The figures above clearly show that even the highest horsepower tugs will develop only about 200 tons of bollard pull, far from enough to refloat a ship several thousand tons aground.

While tugs can be connected and can commence pulling quickly, salvors should normally avoid the temptation to hook up all available tugs and make an immediate—and usually fruitless—pull. The time is better spent in actions likely to contribute to successful refloating. Tugs are most appropriate in strandings to:

Control the position of the ship as she is being prepared for refloating.

Augment other pulling systems or provide the pull needed when the ship is lightly stranded.

Take charge of the refloated vessel and assist her in moving to her next destination.

High horsepower tugs effectively wrench stranded vessels by swinging in an arc of about 60 degrees as they pull. The combined wrenching and pulling action helps set up dynamic conditions between the ship and sea floor more effectively than either would do separately. The most desirable position for any tug wrenching and pulling is directly in line with the desired direction of retraction. A small tug holding the larger tug's head can enhance maneuvering, especially in longshore currents.

The towing hawser of a properly equipped tug is sized to accept the full static bollard pull with a reasonable margin of safety. In a few very large, high horsepower tugs a single wire of adequate strength would be too large to be practical and the tug is designed to tow with two wires. Such vessels can break a single hawser by application of full power. When pulling with two hawsers from the same tug, a load cell must be incorporated in each hawser system so the tension can be measured and controlled; otherwise the majority of the load falls on the stiffer of the lines. Some very experienced seamen with the best of intentions and the greatest confidence in their seaman's eye have various ways of estimating tensions in towlines or other loaded tension members. They do not work. Correctly installed and calibrated load cells are the only way to measure the tension in a system. Load cells are not common in salvage systems because the normal practice is to load all systems to the maximum. Whenever loads are balanced between two or several lines, load cells are mandatory.

Complete dependence on tugs for holding stranded vessels in position has a severe drawback. Often weather takes a hand in salvage operations and requires salvage forces to seek shelter and wait the weather out. When tugs providing the securing force—or a critical portion of it—abandon the vessel, the weather may drive the casualty farther ashore or broach her.

Work around strandings in shoal water has inherent dangers. Tugs frequently touch ground during salvage operations, but it can be disrupting. The hydrographic survey should include all the areas in which tugs may work. Shoal areas, uncharted rocks, and coral heads should receive particular attention and, when in the way of operations, be marked. Tug masters and salvage masters can spend a few minutes well by flying over the operations area in a helicopter and noting changes in water color and such signs of varying depths. They mark their observations on charts and give them to all who have a use for them. A mariner in a helicopter can guide tugs through difficult waters.

During all operations tugs must neither interfere with one another nor foul ground tackle. For the pulling operation, they must be in position to maximize their effective pull.

In a multi-tug operation, towlines that place the tugs at the same distance from the casualty prevent fouling if the tugs drift together. With such an arrangement, the tugs may bump, but cannot overrun and damage one another's towlines. The tugs should rig fenders to prevent damage should they come together. Where tugs combine with ground tackle, the towlines should be long enough to place the tug well outside the ground tackle, and the towline catenary should be shallow enough to prevent towlines and ground legs from fouling. Long tug towlines have the additional advantage of having greater elasticity than short lines. When pulling, tugs statically load towlines as heavily as they can. The greater elasticity gives the line better ability to absorb the dynamic loads superimposed on the static pull and reduces the probability of towline failure.

In cases of more tugs than space, tugs may be rigged in tandem. The lead tug helps control the head of the inboard tug as well as providing additional direct pull. From the preceding statement, the reader could infer that the tug with the least ability to control her direction—absent or inadequate bow thruster—should have the inboard position. This is conditionally true. The towline of the inboard tug transmits the towing force of both tugs to the casualty. That towline must be able to transmit the bollard pull of both tugs without failing. The overall factor of safety for towlines is normally 4 or 5 to 1 based on the bollard pull of the tug in which it is installed and the breaking strength of the wire rope. In salvage operations, particularly in tandem pulls, it is permissible—even necessary—to operate with a reduced factor of safety. The overall factor of safety, the ratio between the breaking strength of the wire rope and the total static bollard pull of the tugs pulling in tandem, should never be less than 2 to 1, and should be greater if the tow wire is not in first-class condition or if the weather is bad.

Tugs in tandem are less maneuverable than those operating singly. A lead tug that loses propulsion may drag the second tug aground. Towlines should be rigged for quick release and anchors kept ready for letting go.

Salvage masters and others who have prime concern in the casualty must bear in mind that the tug master remains responsible for his vessel's safety. Tug masters unaccustomed to salvage operations may need occasional reassurance. It is far better to appreciate the tug master's position and devote the time to get his cooperation than to have him decide he has had enough and break off in the middle of the operation.

Ship's Propellers. The casualty's engines and propulsion system can generate tractive force. Rare is the case where a ship can drive herself off the beach. Ship's propellers do not produce maximum thrust at low hull speeds and high powers as tug's propellers do. They produce significantly less force backing than going ahead. The result is that ship's propellers do not operate at high efficiency under stranding conditions and cannot produce the tractive forces their horsepower would indicate possible. The amount of force that the ship develops is impossible to calculate with any realism or accuracy. Prudent salvors design their refloating efforts without the ship's propulsion system and count on it only for an extra margin.

Ship's propellers are most effective when augmenting tugs and pulling systems. In addition to supplying some tractive force, operating ship's engines at high powers in stranded ships can set up hull vibrations that help simulate dynamic conditions under the ship.

Propellers should be inspected before attempting to operate the engines to be sure they have not been damaged and that they are clear and free to rotate. Sand and mud from the sea floor can enter sea suctions and be ingested into cooling systems. What goes in does not always go out, but may build up and impair efficiency in these systems. Operating with high suctions open and frequent cleaning of strainers reduces this problem, but the concentration of particulate matter may be so heavy that operating the engines is not warranted.

Ground Tackle

Whether ground tackle leads or follows weight and buoyancy management in a salvor's parade of tools could be argued far into the night without resolution. In reality, they work together in a symbiotic relationship. As a tool, ground tackle is as old as going to sea. Its application in salvage evolved from the use of kedge anchors in early salvage operations.

In salvage, ground tackle applies a force to a ship to: (1) hold it against other forces, (2) move it linearly, or (3) rotate it. Salvage ground tackle normally consists of a heavy anchor; a ground leg of chain and wire rope; a multipart purchase that acts as a force multiplier; a winch or linear puller to tension the system; and connecting hardware, stoppers, and other miscellaneous bits and pieces to put the system together and make it work. There are many variations on the basic system and many ways of deploying a system. The result is the same—a force in a particular direction.

The size of the force generated and thus the effectiveness of the system depends upon the components and their strength. The holding power of the anchor and the force the winch or puller can put on the ground tackle system determines its basic power. A good ground tackle system is a true system with components sized and working together to develop the design strength of the system. The size and strength of the system also define the primary system failure mode. One of the dangers of cobbling a system together in the field lies in the inadvertent introduction of a weak link that makes the system dangerous. Failure in a salvage system in the field, often far from sources of rapid resupply, should leave it intact with the minimum damage. For this reason, anchor drag is the failure mode of salvage ground tackle. The anchor of a ground tackle system should drag before any other component fails. A dragging anchor can be reset and steps taken to improve the holding. Changing the anchor for a larger one may solve the problem of anchor drag, but also may cause another failure mode—perhaps ground leg wire rope failure—to become primary.

Some of the variations on salvage ground tackle are:

- Standardized systems that may be laid from any of several platforms, normally the casualty. These systems consist of an anchor, ground leg, purchase, and winch.
- A system in which the heavy tackle is laid from a barge or ship and hauled either through purchases or by direct pull.
- A dynamic system whereby the pull is made from a moored barge or tug hauling on wire rigged on blocks aboard the casualty.

The U.S. Navy's standard beach gear is an excellent example of the first type of system. American salvors developed the system between the world wars; the U.S. Navy standardized it as part of their huge salvage effort in Wold War II and has made incremental improvements since. Easy mobility, one of the primary design criteria, allows rigging the gear aboard any tug of opportunity or aboard the casualty. The system is based upon the 8,000-pound Eells anchor (a comparatively high holding power anchor when the system originated), a 2¼" chain, a 1⅝" wire rope ground leg, a four-sheave purchase rove with ⅝" wire rope, and the winches and lifting capacity of a 5-ton cargo boom. The resulting system has a maximum pull of 50 to 60 tons. Anchor drag is the primary failure mode of the standard Navy beach gear system. In practice, dragging of imperfectly set anchors has been common. In the system's most modern configuration, lighter anchors with higher holding power per pound have replaced the Eells. Although catastrophic failure in the system is unlikely unless the anchor fetches up on an object too heavy to move, catastrophic failure occurs first in the 1⅝" wire rope in the ground leg. All the components of the Navy beach gear system are transportable by boat and helicopter, so the system can deploy from a variety of platforms. The system has done yeoman's work over the years and continues as a useful tool, although its relatively low pull limits its effectiveness in refloating large ships.

Commercial salvors have also standardized ground tackle systems, fitting them to their areas and styles of operations, the types of casualties they encounter, and their preferences. These systems are usually similar in configuration, but heavier than the U.S. Navy's standard beach gear. Being heavier, they produce proportionately more pull.

The anchor, the heart of the ground tackle system, develops the holding power of the system. Almost any type of anchor is suitable when laid correctly and not expected to hold more than its capability in the sea floor at the site. Drag-embedment anchors are the most common type in salvage, although deadweight, direct-embedment, and piled anchors have been used. Anchors designed for mooring have higher holding power than the same weight ship's anchors. The utility of mooring anchors in salvage ground tackle depends on the practicality of handling them aboard and laying them from the salvage platform.

Overall holding power of drag-embedment anchors depends upon the anchor weight, fluke area, and soil type. These anchors penetrate the bottom when dragged by the tension in the ground leg. When properly laid and with a pull parallel to the sea floor, the anchor eventually reaches the depth at which it develops its maximum holding power. This depth depends upon the soil type, fluke angle and smoothness, and anchor streamlining.

Anchor performance varies with sea floor soils:

In *firm sand and clay*, the anchor becomes embedded firmly so it can develop its nominal holding power. This type of soil is the standard for establishing nominal holding power.

Anchors must penetrate *medium density sand and clay* more deeply than firmer soils to develop the same holding power. Depending on the depth of penetration and the density of the soil, anchors can develop between two-thirds of their nominal holding power and their full holding power.

Anchors must penetrate *soft mud* deeply to develop much more than about one-third of their nominal holding power. Underlying substrata of rock, hard clay, or peat may limit penetration. Conversely, anchors may penetrate the substrata and develop near their nominal holding power.

Anchor performance in *loose coarse sand or gravel with large rocks* is unpredictable. Holding power may vary from one-third to far above nominal holding power depending upon penetration and the chance engagement of a large rock.

Rock, coral, peat, or shale resist penetration, so that the holding power of drag-embedment anchors is theoretically no more than their weight. In fact, anchors that fetch up on large rocks or coral heads or fall into a crevice develop very large holding forces.

The holding power of a drag-embedment anchor in any type of soil can be estimated only within reasonable limits. It cannot be calculated with engineering certainty for a salvage situation. Since the soil is such an important and unpredictable variable, the salvor can reduce the overall uncertainty by (1) choosing the hardware for best performance, (2) designing the ground leg for maximum holding power, and (3) employing the highest standard of seamanship in laying and setting the gear.

Holding power of an anchor is often taken as a simple multiple of its weight. This method of determining holding power is quick and convenient, but not very accurate. A more accurate determination may be made by:

$$H_M = k_R \times \left(\frac{W_A}{10{,}000}\right)^b$$

where:

H_M = the holding power of the anchor in kips (thousands of pounds)
k_R = a coefficient from the following table
W_A = anchor weight in thousands of pounds
b = an exponent from the following table

TABLE 8-2.

Anchor Type	*Soft Soils (Soft Clays and Muds)*		*Hard Soils (Sands and Stiff Clays)*	
	k_R	b	k_R	b
Boss	210	0.94	270	0.94
Bruce Cast	32	0.92	250	0.80
Danforth	87	0.92	126	0.80
Flipper Delta	139	0.92	-	-
AC14	87	0.92	126	0.80
LWT	87	0.92	126	0.80
Moorfast	87	0.92	100[1]	0.80

Table 8-2 continued on next page

Table 8-2 continued

Anchor Type	*Soft Soils (Soft Clays and Muds)*		*Hard Soils (Sands and Stiff Clays)*	
	k_R	b	k_R	b
Stato	210	0.94	250[2]	0.94
Stevin	139	0.92	165	0.80
Stockless (fixed fluke)	46	0.92	70	0.80
Stockless (movable fluke)	24	0.92	70	0.80

[1] For 28° fluke angle.
[2] For 30° fluke angle.

For an anchor to embed properly in any soil, the pull on the anchor shank must be parallel to the sea floor. Elevating the shank 6° reduces holding power 15 percent; at 12°, the decrease rises to 38 percent; and at 20°, 50 percent. The function of the chain in the ground leg is twofold:

1. It provides a heavy member next to the anchor so a pull equal to the anchor's nominal holding power cannot lift the shank off the sea floor and, thus, holds the shank parallel to the sea floor.
2. It resists chafing and abrasion from the sea floor more than wire rope.

Wire rope, lighter and easier to handle than chain, makes up the greater portion of the ground leg. The catenary of the wire rope and its elasticity gives the ground leg the ability to carry the dynamic loads that the sea superimposes on the static pulling load. This quality of the ground leg is much more important with the ground tackle rigged from a floating platform—a salvage ship or barge—than from a nearly motionless stranded ship. In a properly assembled ground leg, the wire rope is tangent to the sea floor where the wire rope joins the chain with the system loaded to the nominal holding power of the anchor. This scope is approximately:

$$S = \sqrt{2 \times h \times \frac{T}{w} - h^2}$$

where:

S = scope of wire rope in the ground leg
h = height from the sea floor to the deck edge
T = tension in the ground leg
w = weight per unit length

If the bathymetry of the area does not permit laying out the most desirable scope of the ground leg, adding chain allows a shorter scope. A portion of the chain lifts to form part of the catenary, but the chain will remain parallel to the anchor shank where it joins the anchor. In depths to 25 fathoms, addition of a second shot of chain permits shortening the scope by about 25 percent; a third shot permits shortening the original scope by 40 percent. These reductions do not include the amount of wire rope on the deck of the casualty or the amount that allows for travel of the casualty. In practice, a minimum ground leg of about 1,500 feet (460 meters) is the shortest that will have enough elasticity to respond to dynamic loads. About 2,400 feet (730 meters) is the practical maximum for shallow waters.

An alternative method of shortening the ground leg is to include a closely coupled weight—a clump or anchor—at the inboard end of the chain. A clump or anchor added in this manner cannot be counted on for additional holding power, although it undoubtedly contributes some. The weight's primary function is to hold the chain on the sea floor.

The anchors should be laid in water deep enough to prevent the refloated casualty overriding the anchor and impaling herself. The water should not be so deep that a large vertical angle causes a large vertical force component and loss of effectiveness. Where deep water lies close to the shore, as in many places in the Pacific, a spring buoy included in the system gives a nearly horizontal pull on the casualty. The spring buoy is any large buoy with a buoyancy of 15 to 20 tons rigged into the ground leg about 600 feet (180 meters) from the casualty. The wire rope between the casualty and the buoy lies almost horizontally while that between the buoy and anchor is more nearly vertical. The pull on such a system is optimum when the buoy just submerges.

On narrow, shallow reefs with deep drops, tandem rigged anchors laid to fall over the edge of the reef give good holding power. Anchors laid this way are very difficult to recover.

With limited scope or poor holding ground, a second anchor added to the ground leg improves holding power. Two anchors rigged in parallel from a flounder plate—or preferably with an equalizer—are "doubled." Each of the doubled anchors acts independently. The combination develops up to 15 to 20 percent more than the sum of the holding powers of the individual anchors. To prevent the anchors from moving together and fouling, the chain between one anchor and the flounder plate is at least four fluke lengths longer than the other chain. Doubled anchors are more likely to perform well when placed than when dropped.

Anchors in series or "tandem" can develop twice the holding power of a single anchor. As the anchors set, the far anchor drags in the track of the near anchor and penetrates deeply. The weight of the near anchor holds the shank of the far anchor down. Tandem anchors may be rigged from either the crown or shank of the near anchor to the shank of the far anchor. Crown-to-shank rigging is more convenient for handling rigging and laying. The near anchor must be well stabilized to prevent it from rotating and becoming ineffective. The shank of both anchors carries the total load; accordingly, the near anchor must have enough strength for this load. Unless the flukes of the near anchor can rotate freely, line tension from the far anchor may hold the flukes parallel to the shank. When this happens, the near anchor does not penetrate, but breaks out and slides along the sea floor, preventing deep penetration and development of its full holding power by the far anchor. The distance between anchors should be at least three fluke lengths for the anchors to be able to function properly. In practice, this distance is too short for laying and handling the gear. A better figure is 125 percent of water depth.

When the anchor of an anchored ship drags, normal practice is to veer chain and allow the anchor to reset itself with the increased scope. In salvage, anchors are not likely to reset properly. Time-saving practice is to skip the initial step and go directly to resetting. Rarely is a properly set anchor overloaded, but heavily loaded anchors drag during salvage operations for a number of reasons, including:

Anchors incorrectly set.

Wrong fluke angle.

Soil balled on the flukes preventing penetration.

Rotation of an ineffectively stabilized anchor.

Anchor fouled by chain.

Recovering the anchor and laying it again without attempting to discover and remedy the cause of drag makes little sense. Often, divers in the water can inspect the anchor and identify the cause of drag before recovering the anchor. Divers may also inspect an anchor before setting to insure it is lying properly and is not fouled. They may also wash or blast holes ahead of the anchor to direct it in setting.

Carpenter stoppers, sliding wedge block wire rope stoppers that allow wire rope loading near the breaking strength without damage, are best for connecting ground legs to purchases. Two Carpenter stoppers sized to the ground leg wire are necessary: one to attach the ground leg to the purchase, and one to hold the ground leg while overhauling the purchase. A Carpenter stopper sized for the purchase wire holds that wire. Toggles make the best substitute for Carpenter stoppers with skilled crews and the proper equipment. Wire rope clips, plate clamps, or chain stoppers do not hold as well and can damage the wire rope at high loads.

A buoy large enough to carry the weight of the crown wire is attached to the crown of the anchor with a wire rope about the same size as the ground leg. The rope should be long enough for the buoy to lie easily on the surface and watch in a tight circle. The primary purpose of the crown buoy is to hold the crown wire vertically. Recovery by picking up the buoy and lifting with the crown buoy wire is much faster and more positive than running a chaser down the leg to the anchor. The buoy also provides a means of tending the anchor.

At the extreme other end of the ground tackle from the anchor is the device for hauling the gear. The winch or puller puts a static tension on the system to prevent the ship from moving under the influence of outside forces or causes it to move in the direction of the tension. Almost any type of winch can haul ground tackle. The primary requirement is enough line pull to tension the gear to the holding power of the anchor through the force multiplier of the purchase. The casualty's cargo winches or anchor windlasses are first choice. Salvors may put portable winches aboard ships that have no winches or very few of them. These winches must tie into the ship securely. Purchase wires must be led fair as necessary to approach the winch drum perpendicularly.

Occasions arise where there are more legs of ground tackle than winches. There are at least two methods of dealing with this problem; neither of them is very satisfactory:

1. The first leg is tensioned, then the ground leg wire is hung off a standing stopper while the purchase is disconnected, fleeted, and used to haul the second leg. The process repeats as necessary.
2. The first leg is tensioned, and the purchase wire hung off a standing stopper while the second purchase is hauled. Again, the process repeats as necessary.

Linear pullers of the type developed for hauling bridge cables have been applied to ground tackle systems. These machines pull directly on the ground leg wire rather than on a purchase, thus eliminating fleeting and other disadvantages of purchases. The U.S. Navy has adopted them, but they are not widely accepted in commercial stranding salvage.

Navy standard beach gear has four-sheave purchase blocks. Many commercial systems employ either five- or six-sheave blocks. The importance of the purchase lies in its ability to multiply force so a modest pull on the purchase wire results in a much larger pull on the ground leg. The theoretical mechanical advantage (TMA) of a purchase is the ratio of the pull on the purchase wire to the pull on the ground leg. Conveniently, this ratio is the same as the number of parts of wire at the moving block. In practice, blocks have friction losses that make the actual mechanical advantage (AMA) less than the theoretical mechanical advantage. The AMA can be calculated by:

$$AMA = \frac{TMA}{1 + (k \times n)}$$

where:

k = a friction factor taken as: 0.10 for ordinary sheaves in good condition with wire bending 180°, 0.06 for low friction blocks, and 0.25 for poorly lubricated blocks. The friction factor includes the friction of the wire rope moving on the sheave.

n = the number of sheaves in the purchase system. In a system of 2 blocks, each with 5 sheaves, n = 10.

The most common and effective way of using ground tackle is to place the purchases on the ship, pass the bitter end of the ground leg to the ship, connect it, and lay the anchors steaming away from the casualty along the selected bearing. The anchors may be laid first with the ship steaming toward the casualty and passing the bitter end as the final step. The choice is largely one of personal preference.

The salvage ship may also haul ground tackle. The salvage ship lays her tackle steaming toward the ship on a selected bearing. The entire leg is let go with the bitter end of the ground leg made up to a retrieving buoy and wire. The salvage ship is free to do other tasks until the time comes to pick up the ground leg and pass the tow wire. There are some disadvantages to the latter method: the salvage ship is locked into position and cannot slew or wrench to use her bollard pull most effectively; if she is forced off site by weather the ground tackle is of no use in restraining the casualty; the gear must be rigged for letting go quickly to allow the salvage ship to move out of the way of the refloated casualty; and the ground legs are subject to dynamic loads caused by the sea-induced motions of the salvage ship.

A salvage ship, or any vessel acting in that role, should be prepared to lay two legs of ground tackle on arrival at the casualty. If weather does not hamper passing lines and gear to the casualty, the two sets should be connected, laid, set, and hauled taut in 6 hours.

Only equipment availability and working space limits the number of sets of ground tackle in a salvage operation. Four sets suffice for most strandings, but many more have been rigged.

The number of sets required depends upon the role of the ground tackle in the refloating. If the purpose of the ground tackle is to refloat the vessel unassisted, the total number of legs is the force required for retraction divided by the force realistically expected to be developed by each leg. When the ground reaction is reduced by lightening or ground removal, or when tugs also pull, the contribution of the ground tackle and the number of legs is decreased appropriately. Determining the balance among the methods of refloating is an iterative process driven heavily by the particular resources available and the geography and conditions of the stranding. If the ground tackle is primarily a means of holding the ship in position, the number of sets and their layout are determined by the environmental forces on the ship. Ground tackle for holding is addressed in more detail later in this chapter.

Purchases laid out on the salvage ship normally are set up in predetermined locations and patterns; not so when the gear is rigged on the casualty. Ideally, the casualty has sufficient deck space to lay out as many purchases as desired, all with long fleets, and all directly in line with a convenient fairlead. Deck space may be extremely limited on container vessels and vessels such as log carriers that carry large amounts of deck cargo. In passenger vessels, car carriers, and similar ships, holes cut through the side shell may be necessary to reach a location that allows enough fleet length. The edges of the cuts that the tensioned wire rope contacts should be well rounded to prevent cutting and introducing high bending stresses in the rope. Purchases should be separated by setting them in troughs or on bridges, if necessary. Putting a timber or pipe through purchases inhibits twisting.

Standing blocks and standing stoppers must be securely connected to the structure of the casualty (figure 8-6). Strong deck pad-eyes are acceptable. Pad-eyes, welds, and surrounding structures should be inspected for cracks and deformation before connecting them into the system and each time the wire is tensioned. Chain or wire rope can be figure-eighted into bitts. Loaded members should lead from the bottom of the bitts and a preventer rigged to prevent the tensioned member from jumping off the bitt. Connections to bitts should be backed up to a second set, made up tightly, then hove taut. It is poor practice to lay the eye of a line or the bridle of a Carpenter stopper over bitts (figure 8-7). When limited space makes it necessary, a preventer should hold the eye or bridle down on the bitts. Sometimes, especially when rigging several sets of gear, the ship simply does not have enough fittings. Chains are passed around foundations, masts, kingposts, deckhouses, or through holes burnt in the deck or hatch coaming. Holes should be separated so the bight of the chain passes around one or, preferably, two structural members that run perpendicular to the direction of pull. Timber balks should pad sharp corners.

Pulling of ground tackle, like pulling with tugs, should start two to three hours before high water so that all legs are completely taut well before high water. The legs cannot be hauled taut and allowed to stay because the tension drops off with time. They must be touched up to restore full tension frequently. When tensiometers are in use, the tension can be read directly and a low tension limit set. With no tensiometers, wires are hauled periodically until they show signs—stalled winches, singing wires, or dripping lubricant—that the tension is again high.

Ground Tackle Layout. The layout of the ground tackle depends primarily upon the geography of the stranding area and the primary purpose for which the ground tackle is laid—pulling, rotating, or holding. To get the maximum effect from each set of ground tackle, it should be laid as nearly as possible along its desired line of action. Ground tackle to:

Pull the ship should be laid in the direction of intended movement.

Rotate the ship should be laid to give the largest possible rotating moment.

Rotate then pull the ship should be laid along the final line of intended movement, because pulling requires more force than rotating (figure 8-8). If the angle is not large enough to produce enough rotating moment, separate sets of ground tackle may be set for rotating and pulling.

Fig. 8-6 (a). A heavy purchase block attached to the ship's structure with heavy turns of wire rope. The three sheave blocks on either side are pinned to purpose-built pads.

Fig. 8-6 (b). A pulling system secured with chain

Fig. 8-7 (a). A poor way to secure a ground tackle leg with a Carpenter stopper without a preventer to hold it near the base of the bitts

Fig. 8-7 (b). The same bitts after failing in a heavy swell. The Carpenter stopper passed through the Panama chock when the stretch came out of the ground leg.

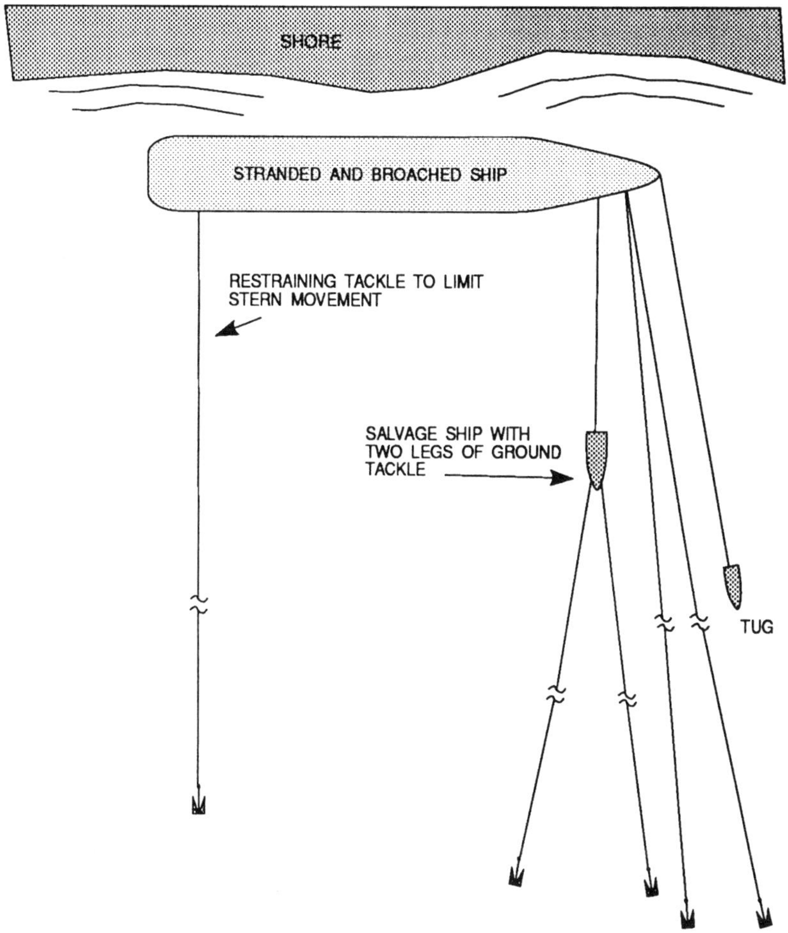

Fig. 8-8. Representative ground tackle layout to rotate ship and retract by the bow

Ground tackle holding the vessel should be laid in the direction from which the most severe weather is expected and directly opposite the direction in which movement is not desired.

Hauling Ground Tackle. Skillful handling can enhance the effectiveness of properly laid and set ground tackle. Primarily, skillful handling means tensioning the ground tackle to the maximum the system allows and holding it there. Reaching the maximum tension is easiest when there is a load cell or tensiometer in the system and the system can simply be hauled until the desired tension is reached. Tensiometers are uncommon in salvage ground tackle. There are a number of other ways of determining when tension is near maximum. One that is infallible is simply to pull until the winch stalls out. Other indications of heavy tension in the line are grease oozing from the wire rope as it contracts with tension and the rope itself singing. Kicking a tensioned rope, although sworn to by many, has been shown on load cell-equipped systems not to provide a reliable indicator of the tension in the rope.

Ground tackle must be tended to assure the tension remains near maximum. With load cells, this is simply a matter of watching the load cell and touching up the system when the tension begins to drop. When the system is tensioned by stalling the winch, tension can be maintained by hauling until the winch stalls every so often. Experience with the particular system helps determine the proper interval for hauling. Indications of a need for tightening up the system are less singing or oozing grease, or chalked marks on the wire rope and deck moving apart. If the ship begins to move it seldom is possible or necessary to maintain tension, but it is a good idea to continue to tension the system while there is still slack in the purchase.

On Refloating. Ships that are trimmed parallel to the bottom and properly lightened refloat quietly. Those depending more on tractive power for refloating are likely to refloat quickly and accelerate off the strand. Plans for this type of refloating must be made before refloating the ship. These plans must include:

- Clearing salvage vessels from the casualty's path.
- Handling ground tackle by either letting it go or using it to gain control of the casualty.
- Tug placement and use of tugs or other vessels to control the movement of the casualty as she refloats.
- The destination of the refloated casualty.

Holding a Ship with Ground Tackle. Ground tackle for pulling or rotating a ship develops a force on the ship by pulling against an anchor. The maximum force developed is a function of the holding power of the anchor and the mechanical characteristics of the pulling system. The purchases or pullers provide a part of the means of developing the force in the system. With ground tackle holding a ship, the situation is different. Forces on the anchor are developed by environmental (wind and sea) loads on the ship, much as in normal anchoring. The ground tackle must develop enough force to resist these loads. The purchases or pullers in these systems serve to keep the slack out of the ground tackle legs and thereby to limit motion of the ship.

Determination of the ground tackle needed to hold a ship requires calculation of environmental forces acting on the ship. For purposes of laying out ground tackle to hold ships in salvage, this calculation has no need of being complex or more than approximate. The two environmental forces affecting the ship most are current and wind. Major factors in each are the velocity of the wind or current and the projected area exposed to force. Wind force on a ship is calculated by:

$$F_w = C_w \sum (C_s C_h A)\, v^2$$

where:

F_w = wind force in pounds (newtons)
C_w = 0.0034 lb/(ft^2 × kt^2), (0.612 Nsec^2/m^2)
C_s = shape coefficient
C_h = height coefficient
A = projected area of each surface exposed to the wind, ft^2 (m^2)
v = wind speed, knots (m/sec)

The following tables give shape and height coefficients.

TABLE 8-3.

WIND FORCE SHAPE COEFFICIENTS	
Exposed Area	*C_h*
Cylindrical shapes	0.50
Hull surface above the waterline	1.00
Deckhouses	1.00
Isolated structures (cranes, etc.)	1.50

TABLE 8-4.

WIND FORCE HEIGHT COEFFICIENTS		
Height of Centroid above Waterline		
Between (feet)	*Between (meters)*	*Height Coefficient*
0–50	0–15.3	1.00
50–100	15.3–30.5	1.10
100–150	30.5–46.0	1.20

As the areas of several different portions of the hull and superstructure must be taken into account, a tabular or spreadsheet format is most convenient for wind force calculations. A sample calculation appears in Appendix A.

The formula given above applies to winds that are either parallel or perpendicular to the centerline of the ship. Where the wind is at an angle to the centerline, a formidable-looking equation applies:

$$F_w = F_{wbow}\left(\frac{2\cos^2\theta}{1 + \cos^2\theta}\right) + F_{wbeam}\left(\frac{2\sin^2\theta}{1 + \sin^2\theta}\right)$$

where:
F_{wbow} = wind force on bow or stern (parallel to the centerline)
F_{wbeam} = wind force on the beam (perpendicular to the centerline)
θ = the angle between the wind direction and the centerline

Current force is calculated in a similar manner by the two equations:

$$F_{cbow} = C_{cbow} S v_c^2$$

and

$$F_{cbeam} = C_{cbeam} S v_c^2$$

where:
F_{cbow} = current force on the bow or stern (parallel to the centerline), lbs (N)
F_{cbeam} = current force on the beam (perpendicular to the centerline), lbs (N)
S = wetted surface of the hull, ft^2 (m^2). May be approximated by:

$$S = C_B LB + 1.7\,LT$$

v_c = current speed, knots (m/sec)

The force of an oblique current is given by an equation of the same form as that for an oblique wind force:

$$F_c = F_{cbow}\left(\frac{2\cos^2\theta}{1 + \cos^2\theta}\right) + F_{cbeam}\left(\frac{2\sin^2\theta}{1 + \sin^2\theta}\right)$$

where all quantities are as previously defined.

Wave drift also produces a significant force on the ship, but calculation of its magnitude is tedious and difficult. It is best accounted for in salvage by allowing a generous margin between the sum of the wind and current forces and the holding power of the ground tackle laid to hold the ship.

When lightening a ship, the ship cannot stay in place if ground tackle is laid only in one direction. Ground tackle or lines ashore also must be provided to keep the ship from drifting afloat before all is ready for her to do so.

The layout of ground tackle also depends on the geography of the area—where it is possible and practical to put the gear—and other operational requirements. Lanes must be left clear to bring lightering vessels alongside for cargo removals or for mooring them in standoff moors. There is always a requirement for some workboats or craft to work alongside the stranded vessel; they should be able to do so without interference from ground tackle legs. The legs should be far enough apart that the threat of their fouling one another is reduced as much as practicable.

Pulling Vessels and Dynamic Systems. Some vessels—both self-propelled and dumb barges—are rigged as pulling vessels. These vessels normally deploy several 6-ton or larger anchors and haul them with heavy purchases or directly with winches. One or more wire ropes connect the opposite end of the pulling vessel to the casualty. The arrangement may allow hauling both the wires to the anchors and the wires to the casualty. Ground tackle systems deployed from pulling ships and barges can be placed, set, and tensioned quickly. When the casualty refloats, the pulling vessel may have to slack her gear quickly or have highly geared winches and move—or be moved—to prevent being overrun.

In dynamic systems, the pulling force is provided by the tug pulling on the ground tackle wire against an anchor laid astern of the ship through one or a series of sheaves, as shown in figure 8-9. The dynamic loads associated with this system are very large and the load-carrying ability of the wire rope is reduced by bending unless very large cumbersome sheaves are used. Conventionally rigged ground tackle coupled with pulling, wrenching, or pushing is a more efficient use of equipment.

Tensioned ground tackle stores a large amount of energy that may be released suddenly if any part of the system fails. Large pieces of equipment moving very rapidly normally follow failures closely. Movement is in the direction of tension, but whipping or other movement cuts a wide swath. All hands should stay as clear as possible of and never step over or cross under tensioned ground tackle.

Recovering Ground Tackle. The exact means of recovering ground tackle depends upon the vessels and equipment doing the recovery. In general:

The crown buoy is recovered on board, taken to power, and hauled, breaking out the anchor. Hauling the anchor against the direction in which it was set is normally adequate to break it out. In very cohesive sea floors or with tandem anchors, it may be necessary to run a chain chaser down the ground leg to lift the inboard anchor shank.

The crown wire is hauled until the anchor is on the surface and can be brought on board and secured.

The remainder of the ground leg is hauled aboard.

An anchor handling tug supply vessel (AHTSV) with a stern roller, low freeboard, large open deck, and good winches is ideal for recovering ground tackle. Vessels with fewer of these features suffice as long as they have the appliances to handle the weights and the deck space to store the recovered wire rope, chain, and anchors. Salvage vessels that regularly lay ground tackle have their own systems and procedures.

Ground Removal. Sometimes, no choice exists other than taking some ground to allow the ship to sink deeper in the water, to have a pond to float in, or to have a

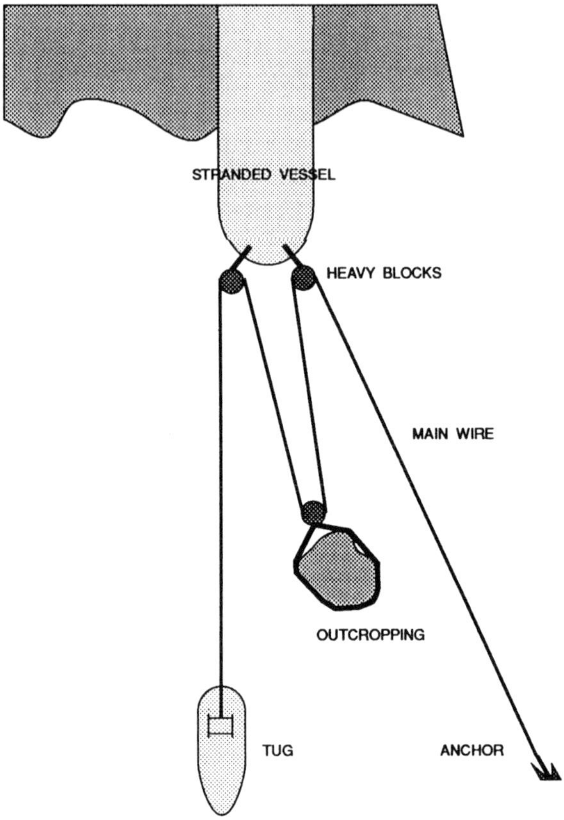

Fig. 8-9. Dynamic pulling system

channel to deep water. Sand and clay sea floors move comparatively easily. Hard sea floors are another matter altogether, and very soft sea floors that fill in immediately are a source of frustration. Dredging, blasting, or scouring can remove ground under and near partially floating ships. If the ship is high and dry, earth-moving equipment may dig a pond around the ship or a dredge may cut a channel in from deep water. The most suitable method for a particular job depends upon the equipment available, the site conditions, and the quantity of ground to move.

Scouring is the simplest and most common means of ground removal in salvage. It is appropriate for moving small to medium quantities of earth. Natural currents diverted by the salvors, propeller wash from the casualty or tugs, air injection, or jetting pumps have been successful scouring tools.

Natural longshore currents directed by groynes built perpendicular to the beach are a slow but sometimes effective means of preventing buildup of sea floor material around the ship or helping to move it away. Often, groynes must be adjusted to achieve the desired effect.

The casualty's propeller running ahead sets up currents along the axis of the ship that can move moderate quantities of the sea floor in way of the propeller. The same action can remove material deposited near the stern of the ship by the sea. When the ship's propeller is turning over to scour, the high suctions should be opened to avoid taking sea floor material into the machinery, piping, and heat exchangers, or, as an extreme measure, water brought to the machinery from another source that has little or no suspended particulate matter. Controllable pitch propellers should never scour because sand can work its way into the mechanism and play hob with it. Ships scouring with their own propellers should be secured against driving ahead by laying ground tackle astern. Scouring with engines running astern is counterproductive in that sea floor material is driven under the ship.

Controllable pitch propellers and tractor tugs with mechanisms sensitive to sand have made scouring with tug propellers almost a historical practice. The technique works, and with proper tugs, suitable sea floor conditions, and safe water depths alongside the casualty, it is a useful technique. Scouring tugs trim by the stern as much as possible to point the wash downwards. The tug, secured amidships by stern and head lines at an angle of about 50° to the casualty, works up to full power and gradually walks toward the end of the ship with winches. The technique may be repeated on the other side of the ship and on the other end. Two tugs may scour simultaneously on opposite sides, but preventing unbalanced forces from swinging the ship requires careful attention. Tugs made up alongside on the same or opposite heading as the ship do not scour effectively because their propeller wash does not cut in below the turn of the bilge. Overall, scouring with tugs is a poor second choice with dredges available.

At least one pulling ship has adopted a variation on scouring. Hydraulic rams position a large flap extending across the stern of the ship in the propeller wash, diverting it downward. The diverted wash digs a trough under the ship. This system has dug channels shoreward for the ship to approach stranded vessels and seaward for pulling and burying pipelines.

Diver-operated hoses fed by jetting pumps can scour away small amounts of sea floor material. The best location for jetting pumps is a float, barge, or small tug alongside the casualty.

Dredges are the best choice whenever they are available and substantial amounts of material are to be moved. Profile dredging along and under the wreck is far more efficient than scouring. Dredges also can dig a pond for a ship to float in, then dig a channel in from offshore. In these operations, it is usual to leave columns or ridges of ground supporting the ship much like drydock blocks, partially jet away the blocks, and let tidal wash complete the job of lowering the ship into position. Alternatively, systematic profile dredging may lower the ship into the pond.

Rock removal is very different from—and more difficult than—soil removal. Explosives remove rocks most effectively. Explosions close to the ship are likely to have unexpected and invariably detrimental effects on the ship. Cutting channels in hard sea floors at distances where the explosive effects are dissipated is effective. Jackhammers are effective for removing impaling rocks inside the ship and hard sea floors close to the ship. As they are essentially hand tools, they are very slow when sizable amounts of rock and coral must be moved. There is often little choice, especially when impaling rocks must be cut down within the ship.

SECURING AFLOAT

The job is far from over when the ship is newly afloat and under command. She must be moved—under her own power, with or without a tug escort—or towed to a safe location to define her condition fully. This location and alternatives should be chosen and inspected before the ship refloats. The selected location should be sheltered, have no shoals or navigational hazards, and, preferably, be used regularly by ships larger and with deeper drafts than the casualty. Local fishermen make excellent sources of information about sheltered areas and can provide information not found on the chart or in the *Coast Pilot*. Routes to the sheltered area should avoid poorly charted waters. There is little gain in removing a ship from a well-defined shoal only to locate an uncharted rock the hard way. When a choice exists, moves should be made in good weather. In moving a damaged ship, you can't be too careful—belt and suspenders on a tight pair of trousers is the only sensible rule.

Definition of the pollution hazard with the ship afloat is particularly important. With a real or perceived pollution hazard, local authorities may resist the ship entering their waters. Salvors should be prepared to present the detailed condition of the casualty and their evaluation of the pollution hazard, thoroughly substantiated by fact, to local authorities. They should also have an alternative plan in mind for use when their complete and well-reasoned presentation falls on deaf ears.

Immediately after the ship comes afloat, salvors should make a complete survey to assure themselves the ship contains no surprises. Damage concealed while the ship lay upon the ground should be checked carefully. As a minimum, the following should be checked during the survey:

Overall seaworthiness.

Stability, list, and trim.

Machinery and piping systems.

Systems needed for the transit.

Patch security and pumping arrangements.

Towing bridles, anchors, and day and night signals.

Anchorages for an underwater inspection should be selected before refloating. Current should be slight and underwater visibility good for effective underwater photography and video.

Anchors should be made ready for letting go before refloating. If the towline parts, anchors should be used to anchor the ship in shallow water or to arrest the drift of the ship in deep water until the towline is reconnected.

A badly damaged ship in danger of sinking after refloating can be beached at a suitable site. When there is any danger that the casualty will refloat in a sinking condition, beaching areas should be selected and inspected beforehand. Beaching areas should be chosen along the route to the haven as well as near the stranding. Ideal beaching areas have neither rocks nor obstructions and slope gently with weak currents and surf. Public and private bathing beaches are not suitable, no matter how ideal the geography or how pleasant the scenery.

Before beaching, the ship should be trimmed so she touches bottom seaward end first at near zero speed. Trim should be slightly steeper than the beach slope so the ship settles gently onto the sea floor. When conditions allow a scheduled beaching, it should occur on the ebb just before low water. The falling tide helps the ship settle gently; the tide rise helps refloating. If the tide fall is needed to expose a portion of the ship, it may be necessary to beach near the top of the tide. Prudent salvors who do not wish to create work for themselves avoid beaching at unusually high water.

The beached ship should be secured by her own anchors dropped and streamed to seaward as she approaches the beaching ground and by other ground tackle to hold her against broaching or running farther ashore.

A ship with no or low remaining value may be scuttled in deep water by blowing holes in her hull with explosives. The quantity of explosives is defined by the quantity P, known to explosives technicians to represent "Plenty." Plenty of explosives coupled with redundant firing circuits assure the ship will sink and not become a derelict. It is very dangerous for a crew to return to set more explosives after a failed attempt. It should not be necessary. Ships also may be scuttled by opening piping systems, venting a bubble, or otherwise opening the ship to the sea. As with explosives, overkill is the rule. Finesse does not scuttle ships.

In these days of environmental concern, ships cannot be sunk on the high seas without the proper permits and permissions. These should be obtained as soon as there is the whisper of an idea that sinking is desirable. Without permits and permissions obtained promptly, the salvor may find himself husbanding a beached or sinking ship while his dollars dwindle and lawyers argue.

In stranding salvage, as in all other types of salvage, there are no hard and fast rules and there are no limits to the potential solutions for problems. Common sense, imagination, good seamanship, and good judgment in the employment of proven tools and adoption of new ones combine with knowledge of the construction and behavior of ships to lead the way to success.

9

RESTORING BUOYANCY

The preceding chapter addressed restoration of buoyancy to ships that have stranded and lost buoyancy through bodily lifting, by returning them to suitable depths. This chapter discusses restoring buoyancy to ships whose hulls are breached and flooded.

There are two basic steps in restoring buoyancy to flooded ships. The first is to restore the watertight envelope of the hull—or part of it. The second is to remove the water. The method of removing the water often determines the method of patching or sealing the hull. In its turn, the method of patching and sealing depends upon the nature and location of the damage.

Water is either pumped from the hull or blown out with compressed air. For pumping, the hull is made watertight from the bottom up; for blowing, it is sealed from the top down. When the deck lies beneath the surface, cofferdams around the entire hull, or a portion of it, may extend the watertight envelope above the waterline.

Whether raised by pumping or blowing, ships come afloat before restoration of all the buoyancy lost in sinking. They often float with considerable free surface. The rising ship may develop problems of transverse and longitudinal stability, list, trim, and local and longitudinal strength. Raising the ship requires not only restoration of buoyancy, but also management of the distribution of buoyancy and of free surface.

Pumping offers advantages of control that are absent when blowing with compressed air. Unsatisfactory situations during pumping operations develop slowly and signal their presence, and salvors have time to take corrective action. Ships floated with compressed air are difficult to control because the air leaks from small openings and migrates through the ship. They come afloat suddenly, gaining buoyancy as they rise and external hydrostatic pressure drops, and may float in unusual attitudes.

Displacing water with a buoyant material also may restore buoyancy. Placing air bags or sealed drums in the ship to displace water is a fairly common and practical salvage method. Securing the buoyant object in place assures it and its buoyancy stay where they are wanted. Placing buoyant objects is likely to be labor-intensive and consume large amounts of diver time. Other induced buoyancy systems—chemical foams, pressurized spheres, and expanded polystyrene granules—have been applied in salvage with some success. All are either very expensive, technically complex, require large amounts of equipment on-scene, or have other disadvantages. Although they have succeeded in a limited number of cases, they are seldom the answer.

PART 1—PATCHING AND COFFERDAMMING

Patches are coverings, fillers, or sealing devices applied to a ship to limit flooding and form a watertight boundary. In addition to forming a watertight boundary, patches may restore the structural strength and continuity of the ship. Elegance and beauty are not factors in patching. The correct patch is whatever works, lasts as long as necessary, and is quick and easy to install. There are no extra points for overbuilding patches; there are severe penalties for underbuilding them. Salvage patches range in size from wooden plugs and wedges, to steel plates or plywood sheets, to massive steel, wooden, or concrete structures. Whatever their size, patches must be installed at the salvage site with the handling equipment and manpower available there. Handling the patch on-site may influence the patch design and require building large patches in sections.

The rate of flooding through a hole has some pertinence in any discussion of patching. In practice, salvors make patches as tight as possible to be as certain as they can that the ship does not flood uncontrollably and the patch remains secure during the salvage operation and voyage to a repair port. The rate of flow through a hole depends upon the area of the hole and the velocity of the liquid flowing through it. Velocity in turn depends upon gravity and the hydrostatic pressure. The theoretical flow through a hole is:

$$Q = K_1 \times K_c \times A \times \sqrt{D}$$

where:

Q = flow rate in various units

K_1 = a constant depending upon the units of Q. The table below gives values of K_1.

K_c = contraction coefficient, discussed below

A = area of the hole in square feet or meters

D = depth of the center of area of the hole below the surface

TABLE 9-1.

VALUES OF K_1			
A in square feet *D in feet*			
Volume units	*Second*	*Minute*	*Hour*
Cubic feet	8.02	481	28,890
Tons (seawater)	0.229	13.74	825
Gallons	60	3,600	216,000
A in square meters *D in meters*			
Cubic meters	4.43	266	15,960
Tonnes (seawater)	4.32	259	25,570

The contraction coefficient, K_C, accounts for contraction of the stream of water flowing through the hole. The coefficient can vary from about 0.60 to 1.00, depending upon the geometry of the hole. Assuming $K_C = 1.00$ gives the maximum flow through the hole. When the interior has flooded above the depth of the hole, D becomes the difference between the external and internal depths. Figure 9-1 is a graphical representation of flow through a 1-square-foot hole at various depths.

In practice, the flow is very difficult to estimate or calculate. Accurate estimates of flooding rate have little practical function. Flow rates are reduced as much as possible as quickly as possible. The point of interest is that very large amounts of water flow through holes in a very short time.

Most patches are simple barriers intended to prevent flooding through the hole. The primary requirement for these patches is watertightness. Absolute watertightness is not necessary to the functioning of the patch, but a leaking patch means difficulty and extra work for salvors as long as the patch is in place. Barrier patches require only enough strength to prevent collapse or some other type of failure of the patch itself. The scantlings of a barrier patch may and should be only as heavy as necessary for the patch to be an effective barrier. Barrier patches do nothing to renew the strength of the ship's structure in way of the patch. An exception to the last statement occurs with welded steel patches that may make a contribution to continuity and strength and may reduce the stress-concentrating effects of the hole.

Patches that are intended to restore the strength and continuity of the ship's structure are very different from barrier patches. These patches must have scantlings comparable to the structure being patched and must be tied into stiffeners in a way that restores the continuity of the stiffener. The most effective structural patches are welded; however, bolting with proper joint design provides an acceptable degree of continuity.

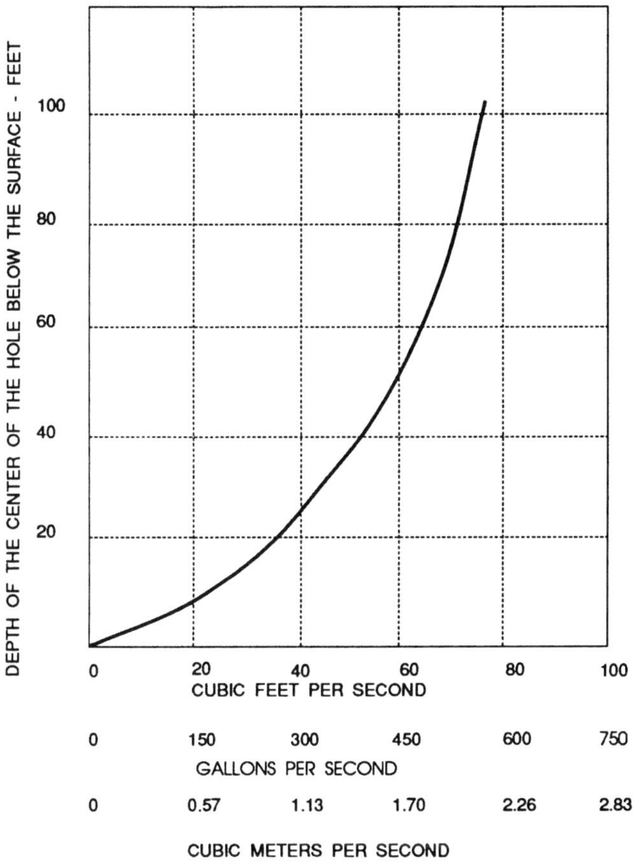

Fig. 9-1. Flow through a 1-square-foot hole

Pressure can help seal a patch. Externally placed patches for pumping allow the hydrostatic pressure of the sea to seat the patch against the hull. Internal pressure in compartments blown with compressed air seats internally placed patches. Holes below the waterline in spaces to be blown can be double-patched to seat on the inside with air pressure and on the outside with hydrostatic pressure. Figure 9-2 shows these patching techniques. Seating with pressure is not a consideration for welded steel patches, a minor consideration for well-seated bolted steel patches, and a major consideration for wooden patches.

Ships' crews with no means to reach the outside of a ship necessarily install damage control patches internally. Damage control patches are always suspect and should be inspected carefully to ascertain if they are to be left alone, reinforced, or replaced. If the operation is likely to be lengthy, damage control patches are usually replaced.

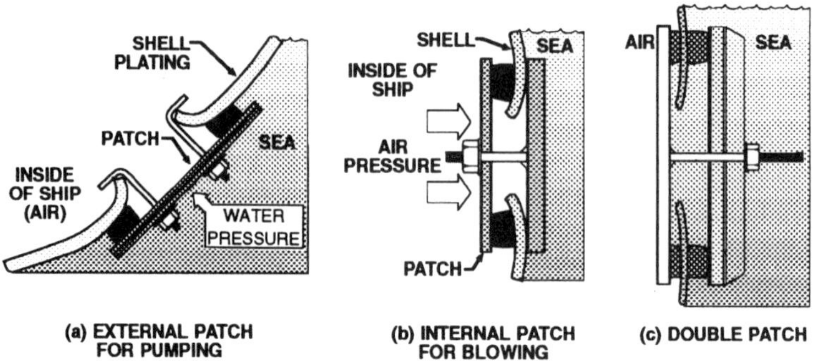

Fig. 9-2. Placement of external, internal, and double patches. Courtesy of U.S. Navy.

Determination of the types of patches and the materials for making them begins with the initial survey. The initial survey gives enough of an idea of the nature and extent of the damage to indicate appropriate patching methods. Videotape of the damage is invaluable to the salvage master and engineer planning patching. A particular advantage is that it allows them to determine how much damaged structure and debris must be cut away to clear the patch area. The videotape also documents the "as found" condition.

The nature of the job impacts the selection of patching methods and techniques. Hastily assembled plywood patches are appropriate on a fishing boat that will be salvaged and on dock in a few days, whereas they would be totally inappropriate on a large, badly damaged ship where the salvage operation is expected to take weeks. There are no hard and fast rules for selecting patch materials and attachment methods; the choice depends upon the judgment and preferences of the salvage master.

The quality of the patching job also depends on how much the flooding rate must be reduced, that is, if the patch must be absolutely tight or only tight enough to reduce the flooding rate enough so that pumps can overcome the flooding. This decision requires some knowledge of the flooding rate through the hole.

The size and shape of holes must be defined in three dimensions for a patch to fit properly. Measurements of length and height provide all the information necessary to patch holes on flat portions of the hull. Where there is a contour to the hull, small and medium patches can be shaped by bending plywood or sheet metal to fit the hole. Alternatively, a mock-up of a box patch can be made with ¼- or ⅜-inch plywood for the sides. The mock-up is test fit to the hole and shaped with saws or rasps until it fits satisfactorily. It then becomes a template for patch construction.

Large holes and holes on curved portions of the hull must be defined fully so patches can be built with a minimum of lost motion and wasted effort. Plumbed lines over the side at frames just forward and aft of the damaged area—not only the hole but back to fair plating—define the overall size of the patch. Square marks or direct measurements on additional plumb lines spaced at convenient intervals between the end lines define the upper and lower limits of damage.

There are four methods for determining the contour. All employ a window frame made up of light timbers, welded steel angle, or PVC pipe diagonally braced to prevent racking. The fourth method described below is the easiest, simplest, and quickest. The methods are:

1. Snug-fitting steel rods (⅝ to 1 inch diameter) are fit into holes drilled at regular intervals around the perimeter of the wooden or pipe frame. The frame is positioned in the place of the patch and held in place by J-bolts or hogging lines. A diver taps the rods until they contact the hull. The line of rods then corresponds to the contour of the hull. The snug initial fit of the rods and the swelling of the wet wooden frame hold them in position while the frame is brought carefully on deck and the contour taken.
2. The wooden window frame is positioned over the hole and secured. A diver nails picket-shaped battens to the frame at marked intervals along its edge with the points against the hull. The frame is brought on deck and the contour taken.
3. The frame is made of steel angle or PVC with the dowels replaced by threaded rod with two nuts for positioning. Because of the manipulation of the two nuts required, this is the hard way. However, the rods are not likely to come out of position during handling.
4. Any type of frame with marks at predetermined intervals is fit in place. The diver measures the distance between the hull and frame and reads the measurements to his tender who records them.

Steel Patches

Modern methods of underwater metalworking make mild steel plate and shapes the preferred patching material for most applications. Steel plate and structural sections are widely available, comparatively easy to work, and can be attached to the hull easily. Welded steel-plate patching both above and below the waterline allows semi-permanent repairs in the field. The apparent permanence of the repair makes it extremely important that all parties be aware that, despite its appearance, the patch may be a simple barrier, not a restoration of the ship's structure.

The patch must be strong enough not to fail under the pressure the sea puts on it. The scantlings of the patch—thickness and stiffener size and spacing—are a function of the maximum depth under water of the patch and the allowable stress in the material. Normally in salvage, the depth of the patch and the thickness of the available material are knowns. The quantity desired is the distance between the stiffeners given by the equation:

$$d = 1.73 \times \sqrt{\frac{\sigma \times t^2}{D}}$$

where:

d = distance between stiffeners in inches
σ = allowable stress in psi (28,000 psi for mild steel)
t = patch thickness in inches
D = water depth in feet

With the allowable stress for mild steel, the equation simplifies to:

$$d = 289 \times \sqrt{\frac{t^2}{D}}$$

The same formula applies to determine the maximum width of hole that can be closed by an unstiffened plate. Figure 9-3 gives the stiffener spacing for steel patches.

Stiffeners should be tee sections or angles of about the same thickness as the plate and with the height of the web and breadth of the flange about six times the thickness. Patch stiffeners may be welded to either side of the patch and may be tied into existing sound stiffeners. When patch stiffeners do not tie into hull members or are on the other side of the plating, ends are snipped at a length/height ratio

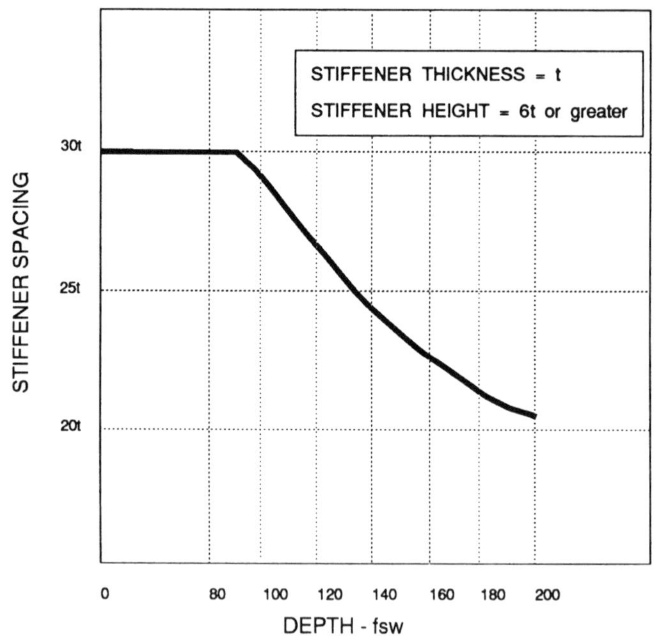

Fig. 9-3. Stiffener spacing for steel patches

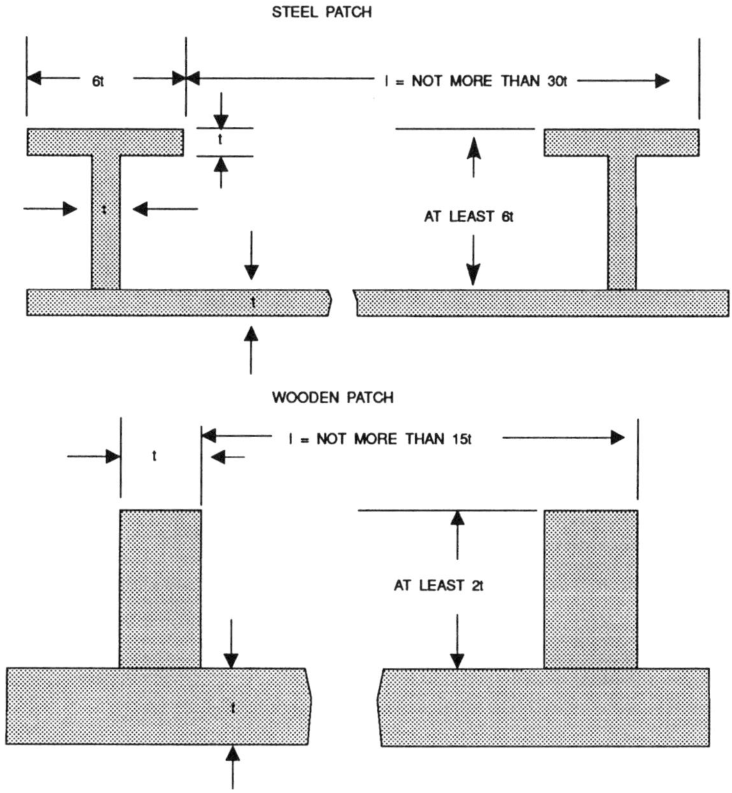

Fig. 9-4. Patch stiffener proportions

of six to one. Figure 9-4 illustrates typical stiffener proportions for both steel and wooden patches.

Experienced salvors standardize patching materials. Mild steel plate in ⅛-inch (3 mm), 3⁄16-inch (5 mm), and ¼-inch (6 mm) thicknesses is an excellent general patching material. Thin plates can be plug welded face to face to form a thicker plate for patching. Standardized stiffening materials, say 3 × 4 × ¼-inch steel angles, make patch fabrication easy and routine. Materials chosen as standard should be common so they can be obtained in areas that are not exactly industrial centers.

If material for patches runs out and cannot be resupplied or for some other reason becomes unavailable at the salvage site, an alternative always exists. Steel can be cut from structure on the casualty and used to make patches. Such cuts should be from deckhouses, superstructure, and other noncritical areas. They should also be cut from areas where exposure through the resulting hole does not damage valuable equipment or cargo.

Patches are normally constructed aboard the salvage ship, a barge, the casualty, ashore, or any place where there is sufficient space and the proper facilities. Small, flat, or nearly flat single plate patches are most common. These are steel plates cut to size from the divers' measurements, bent to fit when necessary, and bolted or welded to the hull. Small patches will work only if they are sufficiently larger than the holes they cover to land on sound structure.

The corners of welded plate patches have radii of at least three inches (76 mm). In patches larger than 2 feet (61 cm) in any direction, the radius is one-eighth of the largest dimension.

Bolted patches have rubber gaskets glued to the inside. Bolt holes are burned in the plate. When the gasket is firmly in place, bolt holes are burned in it with a red-hot rod. A white circle painted around each bolt hole assists divers in finding the holes for fitting up and installing the patch. Figure 9-5 illustrates typical flat steel patches.

Large patches may be prefabricated in a shipyard or other fabricating facility and brought to the casualty site for installation. Prefabrication reduces diving work and has the advantage of design and construction in an industrial facility rather than on-scene. Alternatively, patches may be built on-site by divers fitting, bolting on, and welding together individual plates.

Whatever the size of the patch, it is hung off and handled from the casualty rather than from any craft alongside. It is very dangerous and almost impossible for divers to fit and install patches when the patch-supporting vessel and casualty have different sets of motions. The time and effort spent in setting up a handling system from the casualty is worthwhile, shortens installation time, and increases safety markedly.

Hole preparation includes cutting away damaged plating to give surfaces that are practical to work with. Steel patches are positioned, then wedged in position in angle clips welded to the hull while the patch is welded, studs are fired into the hull with velocity-powered tools, or holes for hook bolts are cut. It is not a particularly good idea to fire studs or burn holes in oil-laden tanks or fume-filled spaces. In these cases, holes can be drilled, but this is usually unacceptably slow. Attaching the patch to the edge of the damage with some form of hook bolt often is an acceptable solution. A power tool for final bolting assures the bolts are taken up as tightly as possible and the gasket is compressed. When no power tools are on hand, butterfly nuts that can be slugged up with a heavy hammer can be made by welding round stock to regular nuts. Butterfly nuts are a poor second best; getting pneumatic or hydraulic tools is a better idea. If the irregularity of the shell makes the patch fit a little leaky, the edges are sealed with epoxy or silicone rubber.

Wooden Patches

Wood was the primary material for salvage patches before advances in underwater welding technology and tools made steel the preferred material. Sometimes

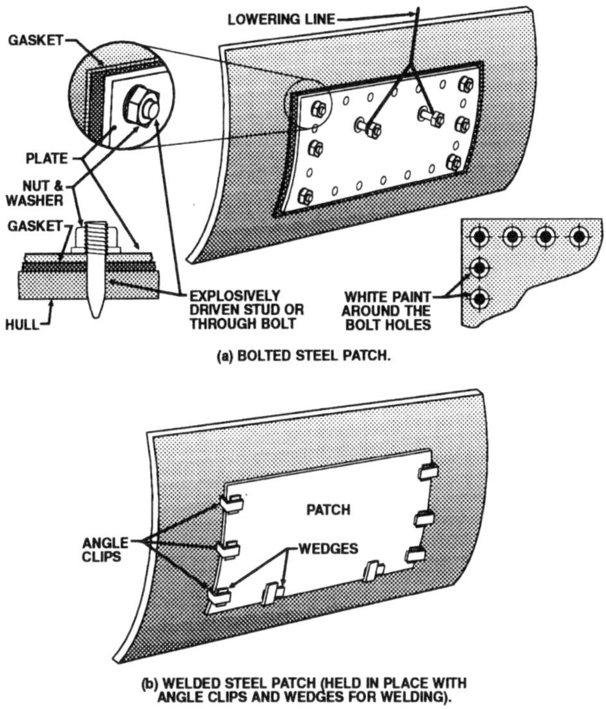

Fig. 9-5. Flat steel patches. Courtesy of U.S. Navy.

wooden patches are appropriate in modern salvage; accordingly, they are discussed here in some detail. Wooden patches vary from plugs and wedges driven in cracks and small holes, to small plywood and medium-sized plank-on-plank patches, to very large box or built-in-place plank patches. Wood is available in most places, easy to work with simple hand tools, and both crushes under pressure and swells when wet to aid in making seals. On the other hand, wood is buoyant, not as strong as steel, and rots in relatively short exposures. Wooden patches must be weighted with scrap to make the patch negatively buoyant so it sinks and can be handled under water. The specific gravity of common structural woods runs from about 0.41 for Douglas fir to about 0.63 for white oak.

Plywood patches with soft gaskets are suitable for small holes as deep as 30 feet, but cannot be left in place for long periods, as the plywood may delaminate. As shown in figure 9-6, the size of the hole that can be patched depends upon the thickness of the plywood and the depth. Modern plywood patches are built and installed in the same way as the small steel plate patches discussed previously.

Small to medium-sized patches are built of planks, usually 2 × 6s, laid edge to edge, covered with plywood, painted canvas, or synthetic fabric, and reinforced with flat bar or angles screwed or bolted to the planking. Soft gaskets are placed along the edges. Box sides of the same planking as the patch and shaped to fit the hull in way of the hole may be added when appropriate.

Thanks to the effectiveness of modern underwater welding, steel patches have superseded the historically important large wooden box and built-in-place patches. There may be times in remote locations when wood is available but steel is not. Salvors may then have no choice other than to build wooden patches for even the largest holes.

The same basic patch design formula used for steel patch design applies in wooden patch design.

$$d = 1.73 \times \sqrt{\frac{\sigma \times t^2}{D}}$$

where:

d = distance between stiffeners in feet
σ = allowable stress in psi (1,500 psi for structural woods)
t = patch thickness in inches
D = water depth in feet

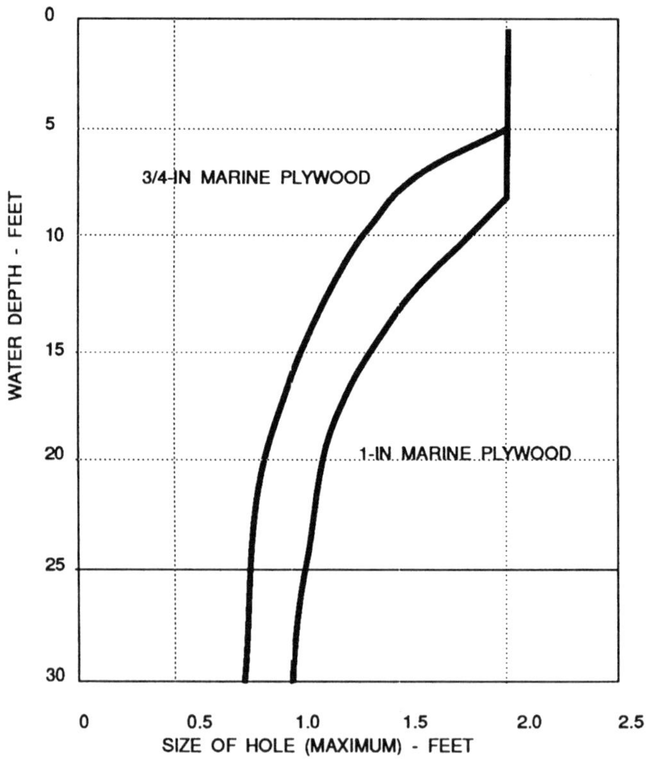

Fig. 9-6. Patching with unstiffened plywood

With the allowable stress for structural woods the equation simplifies to:

$$d = 67 \times \sqrt{\frac{t^2}{D}}$$

Figure 9-7 shows stiffener spacing for wooden patches. Note that the finished size of planking in the United States and some other countries is less than the nominal size, whereas in some countries it is the same. American standard yard lumber and timber is ⅜-inch less than nominal size in 2-, 3-, and 4-inch sizes and ½-inch less in larger sizes. The thickness of the patch in the calculation is the actual thickness of the planking. Doubled planking is nailed, screwed, or bolted.

Wooden stiffener depth is at least twice the thickness of the planking on the face of the patch. Stiffener thickness is equal to patch thickness. The maximum dimension of the hole is substituted for the stiffener spacing in the design of small to medium unstiffened plank patches.

Concrete reinforces large wooden patches for long-term service. If concrete reinforcement is not possible, the allowable stress is 1,000 psi and extra bolts secure the patch.

The large box patch, or American patch, has a long history of success in salvage. It is surface-built and requires little work by divers. The patch is heavy and cumbersome. Templates for the patch are made with the window frame technique described early in this chapter. The window frame is made from the timbers that

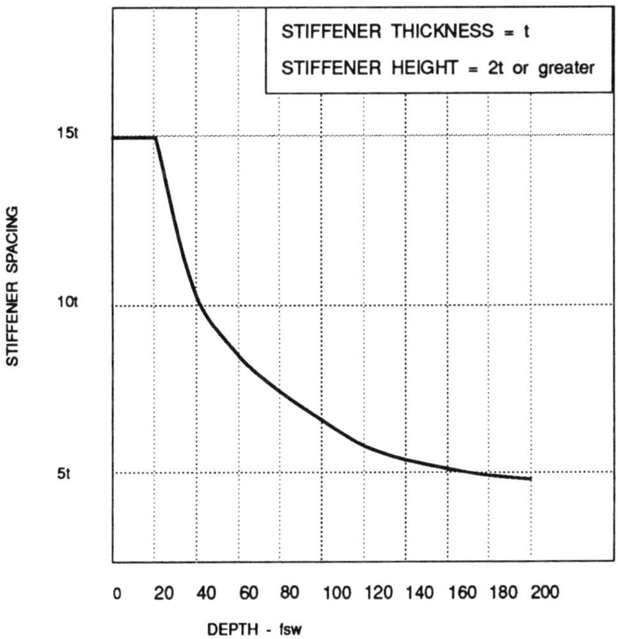

Fig. 9-7. Stiffener spacing for wooden patches

will form the side frame of the patch. When the contour is determined, the window frame timbers are trimmed to match the contours with chain saws. Planking is installed across the back and caulked with a sealing compound or covered with canvas and painted. Many of the large American patches in the past were built with tongue-and-groove planking to help make the seal. Tongue-and-groove planking is not commonly available now and, where it is, it is too expensive for building patches. Caulking the seams of the patch with industrial caulking materials or epoxies provides a satisfactorily tight patch. Weights added to the patch make it slightly negatively buoyant. The patch is lowered over the side and hogged into position. Normally, when the patch is nearly in position, tackles are attached to the internal side of the patch and haul it against the shell. The patch is attached by a large number of hook bolts and seated by the pressure differential that develops upon dewatering the space. With the space dewatered, the hook bolts are tightened to assure they are as snug as possible. One of the major disadvantages of the large American patch is that it almost always requires access from the inside to haul the patch into place, secure the inboard end of hook bolts, or build the forms for concrete reinforcement. When cargo and interference block access to the inside of the patch, some other type of patch should be chosen.

The plank-on-plank patch is a diver labor-intensive alternative to the American patch. These patches are built of 4 × 8 to 8 × 10 timbers bolted to the hull beginning at the top and working down. This unusual method of construction is best because buoyancy overcomes gravity and pushes planks being installed up against those previously installed, helping to make a tight seal.

Plank-by-plank patches are built by:

Fitting two heavy angles down the entire length of the patch to act as guides for the timbers.

Fitting false frames connected to a sound portion of the casualty's structure at intervals appropriate for stiffening the patch.

Individually placing the planks in the guide, slugging them up against the higher plank, and bolting them to the end plating and false frames.

Wooden patches are appropriate on wooden hulls where they may be bolted, screwed, or nailed directly to the hull planking. Wooden hulls are often in such poor condition that the general leakage between planks makes it desirable to wrap the hull in plastic sheeting secured to the hull along the edges. The plastic sheeting is drawn into the leaks when pumping begins.

For steel ships, the advantages of steel patching over the laborious and archaic wooden patching techniques are obvious.

Concrete

Concrete applications in salvage include sealing small holes from the inside, backing up externally placed patches, and reinforcing or final-sealing moderate to large patches. Concrete is a dense slurry that conforms to contours and flows—or can be forced to flow—into inaccessible areas. It is, therefore, particularly good on badly distorted structure. The weight of concrete, its compressive strength, and its bulk reinforce large patches. Concrete has the additional advantages of being obtainable almost anywhere in the world, requiring minimum surface preparation, and adhering well to steel (except oily steel). It can be placed on the surface or under water without skilled labor or precision fitting.

While high in compressive strength, concrete has almost no tensile strength. Reinforced concrete has steel reinforcing bars set in the concrete mass to provide tensile strength. In civil engineering applications, reinforced concrete design is precise; in salvage it is not. However, a somewhat systematic approach is desirable to assure the desired strength. Adding wire mesh or reinforcing bars inside the mass in any practical manner gives concrete some tensile strength. Hooking the bars or mesh into existing structure and the forms improves the overall effectiveness of the reinforcement.

Concrete boxes are particularly good for sealing off scuppers, broken pipes, valves, and small holes.

A cement-rich mix in concrete for salvage facilitates development of high strength in a short time. The rich mixtures cause the concrete to set in about forty-five minutes, but full strength does not develop for about four weeks. Concrete is not expected to develop its full strength in salvage. The mixture recommended for salvage is:

Portland cement	1 part (by volume)
Sand	1 to 1½ parts
Gravel or aggregate	1½ to 2 parts
Water	4 to 6 gallons for each 94-pound bag of cement

The ingredients are measured carefully and mixed in a watertight container. If mechanical mixers are not available, the concrete is mixed by hand by pouring the sand into the container, layering the cement over it, and mixing them dry. Sand, cement, and aggregate must be mixed thoroughly before stirring in the water. The aggregate and water are added and the mixture turned until it is homogeneous. The amount of water specified in the instructions is added to a ready mix. The setting time can be shortened by adding a setting gel, or, for concrete placed under water, warm water with a cup of soda dissolved in it. Salt water and beach sand produce an inferior concrete. The final mix should be stiff—just pliable enough to flow or be worked into place.

The greatest strength results when concrete is placed in a dry space, but this is seldom practical in salvage. The cement-rich mixture described above is suitable for wet placement.

A concrete patch is laid in with a good overlap all around the hole and a temporary patch over the hole to reduce leakage. To assure that the concrete patch is as tight as possible against the hull, the shell in way of the patch is cleaned thoroughly to remove dirt and oil and wirebrushed to remove loose paint and scale. Reinforcing rods or scrap metal can be welded to the shell around the hole to improve adherence. A couple of inches of a rich mixture of cement mortar, composed of equal parts of Portland cement and sand, against the skin helps make a better bond.

Concrete must always be placed in a form that constrains it to a particular place and shape. The form may be either steel or wood and must be reinforced to support the weight of the concrete and to resist the hydrostatic pressure of the wet concrete. Good marine concrete weighs about 150 pounds per cubic foot (1,500 kilos per cubic meter). The form encloses convenient structural members in the vicinity to improve the anchorage of the concrete. Shoring to sound structure reinforces the patch against hydrostatic pressure and prevents it from being dislodged by the ship's motions. Shoring directly in way of the hydrostatic pressure reduces bending loads on the patch. If the patch cannot be shored, it must be extra-thick and encompass as many structural members as practical. Figure 9-8 shows a typical concrete patch.

Patches placed in the dry to support a small patch that is weeping must have a small drain fitted with a sheet metal funnel at the outboard end to collect and carry off seepage. A pipe with threads on the inboard end is best for this service, as it can be capped when the concrete sets. Large concrete patches must have a sealing box with a drain and drain hose to carry away leakage (figure 9-9). Normal practice is to put a fitting on the drain that fits onto a salvage pump suction hose. The sealing box can be kept pumped out with a salvage pump until the concrete is thoroughly set; then the drain can be plugged or capped.

Concrete may be poured from buckets or a mixer, shoveled in, blown in with a concrete gun, pumped in, or placed in paper or porous fabric bags. Obviously, only small quantities can be shoveled in or poured from buckets. Buckets for passing concrete underwater are covered to prevent the light cement from washing out, leaving a non-setting mixture of sand and aggregate. The buckets have a canvas bottom closed by a slip knot. Buckets are placed in contact with previously laid concrete before opening the bottom. Concrete poured in reasonably large amounts in the dry may be poured through a simple trough or chute. When concrete is placed underwater a *tremie* is preferred (figure 9-10). A tremie is simply a large funnel with a long discharge. For the pour, the tremie is nearly vertical, but pivoted so the bottom can move horizontally over the area being filled. The lower end

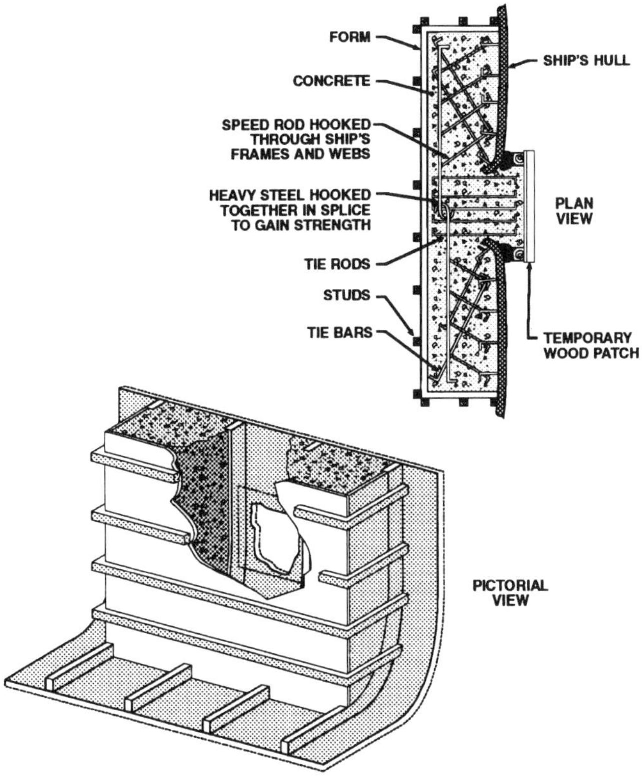

Fig. 9-8. Concrete patch. Courtesy of U.S. Navy.

rests on the bottom of the form until the tremie is filled. To pour, the lower end is raised and kept in motion so the concrete does not pile up. The tremie is raised as the pour proceeds, but always remains below the surface of the wet concrete. The tube remains full throughout the operation. A tremie requires a relatively wet mixture. Whenever possible, pours are continuous. If no concrete is poured for a considerable time, *cold joints*—laminations caused by the early pours setting—develop. Cold joints seriously reduce the strength of the concrete mass.

A concrete gun (figure 9-11) is a device for driving concrete against water pressure with air pressure. This device is particularly good for forcing concrete into jammed valves. The heavy, cumbersome gun must always have pad eyes for handling and positioning.

One common method of making concrete patches has little elegance and is likely to offend those obsessed with technical precision. It works and saves time—

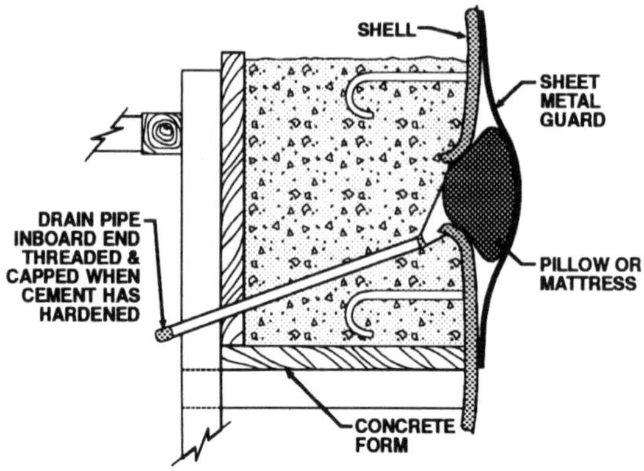

Fig. 9-9. Drainpipe installation.
Courtesy of U.S. Navy.

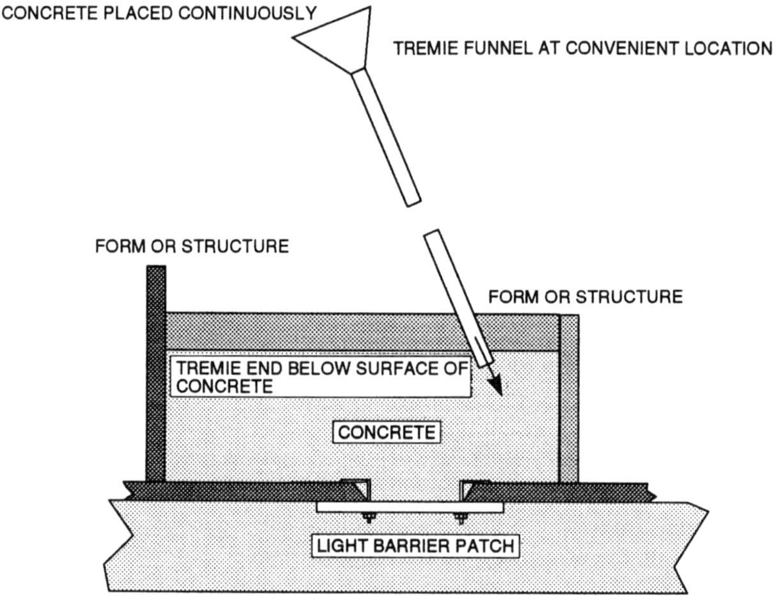

Fig. 9-10. Placing concrete with a tremie

two very big advantages in salvage. The completed form is loosely filled with crisscrossed bags of cement or ready mix and bits and pieces of steel plate, structural shapes, wire rope, and other junk. Concrete is poured on top of the resulting mass. This expedient is appropriate when sealing a hole; inappropriate when strength is a major factor.

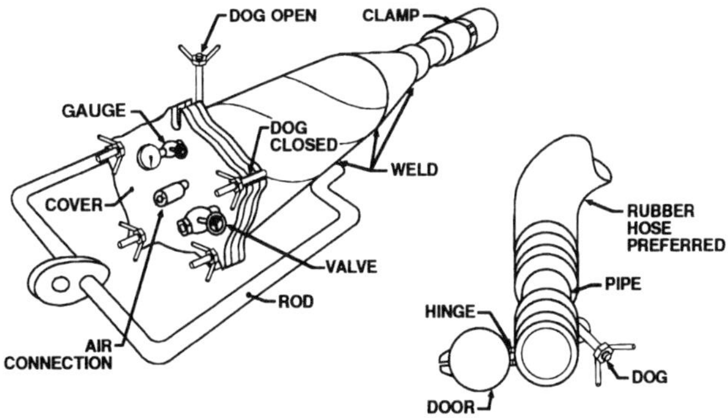

Fig. 9-11. Concrete gun. Courtesy of U.S. Navy.

When very large amounts of concrete are placed, it is well worthwhile to truck or barge concrete to the site and pump it in with pressure grouting pumps. The logistics of bringing pumps and trucks of concrete to the salvage site may be nightmarish, but the efficiency of the operation and the overall saving in labor and time offset the nightmare.

Concrete backs up large wooden patches that are to remain in place for some time or are to be in place for a long tow or other transit. As the concrete reinforcement not only strengthens the wooden patch but acts for it in case of failure, it must be strong and made well enough to withstand the hydrostatic pressure plus the additional loads of swells and impact from tugs or ships alongside. The clearance necessary to clear damaged hull plating by 6 inches (15 cm) to 1 foot (30 cm) usually determines the depth of reinforcement.

Epoxies

Epoxy resins find broad applications in salvage as a sealing and patching material under water and for small repairs on deck. Epoxies smeared around the edge of patches give an almost perfect seal that is easy to make and economical.

Most common marine epoxies are medium- to high-viscosity liquids that when mixed with a hardening agent or catalyst harden quickly into a strong solvent-, acid-, and salt water–resistant solid. Epoxies adhere well to roughly cleaned shipbuilding and patching materials, making them useful for sealing around patches where hydrostatic pressure acts to force the epoxy into the seal as it sets.

Epoxies are selected carefully to insure they are suitable for the environment. Some materials have critical curing times while others may release toxic or noxious gases during curing or mixing. Most epoxies sold for general marine use, notably Splash Zone Compound, are suitable. If marine epoxies are not available, automobile body filling compound is suitable. When the choice for sealing lies between stuffing the space with rags and sawdust or sealing with an epoxy, a trip to the local ship chandlery or auto parts store is well worthwhile.

Collision and Salvage Mats

Collision mats are an outgrowth of the old practice of *fothering*, a method of stopping a leak at sea wherein a basket was filled with rope yarns and ash and covered loosely with canvas. The basket on the end of a long pole was plunged over the side near the leak. Yarns shaken through the basket gradually filled the holes and stopped the leak. The process is more suitable for wooden ships that have lost their caulking than modern casualties. A variation of fothering in which material such as sawdust is released to be sucked into small leaks is sometimes seen when more efficient methods are not available.

Collision and salvage mats are seen infrequently in modern salvage, but are available as limited-effectiveness patches that may suffice until a more suitable patch can be rigged. A collision mat is nothing more than canvas or synthetic fabric, usually doubled and stuffed with soft material (figure 9-12). Steel or wooden battens laid horizontally and stitched into the fabric may stiffen the mats. The mat is handled by lines at the corners. The lower corners are fitted with chains or are otherwise weighted to assure negative buoyancy. Lines haul the mat into place over a hole. When the lines are hauled tight, pressure forces the mat into the hole. Collision mats are better suited for stopping leakage through several small holes and cracks in a limited area than through a single large hole.

Salvage mats in turn are an outgrowth of collision mats. They are heavier mats of stuffed canvas or other gasketing stiffened with timbers or heavy steel bars and capable of being hogged over a hole as a patch. The British standard patch, made of a pudding with chamfered planking and through-bolted to the hull, was developed during World War I for salvage of torpedoed ships. This patch is really a heavy-duty, more permanent salvage mat. The British standard patch was applied widely until developments in underwater welding made patching with steel quicker and more effective.

Collision or salvage mats may reduce the leakage enough so that a concrete patch can be placed inside.

Gaskets

Patches other than steel patches welded into or over the hole must have some sort of gasket or packing to make a tight seal between the hull and the patch—two surfaces that have little chance of fitting precisely. The thickness of the gasket depends upon the fit of the patch to the hull and the amount of tightening the method of attachment allows. Often a diver test fits small patches and takes measurements that allow the gasket to be custom made. A thickness of about 1 inch (25 mm) is adequate for most small patches. Where the hull has little or no curvature—on the

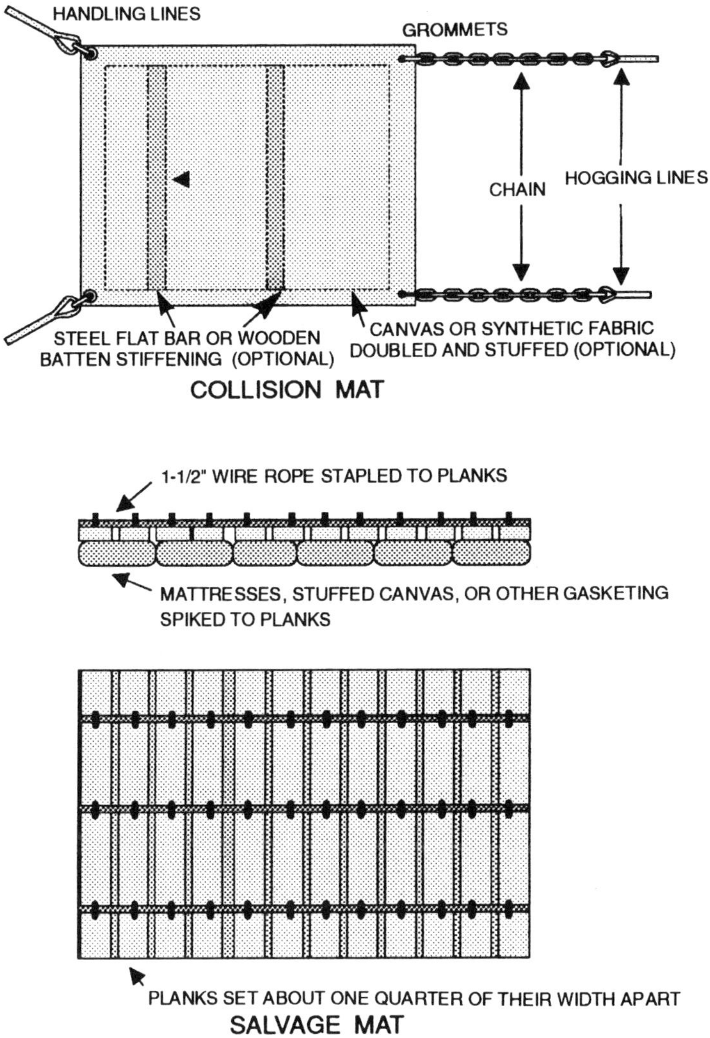

Fig. 9-12. Collision and salvage mats

bottom or in the parallel midbody—gasket thickness can be reduced. Quarter-inch (6 mm) rubber sheeting or a double thickness of thin sheet lead may suffice.

Closed-cell rubber foam or sheet rubber, cut and glued to fit, is a very satisfactory gasket material. Historically, a variety of rather prosaic common shipboard materials have been made into gaskets. These include canvas, oakum, rolled mattresses, fiber mooring lines, shaft packing, fire hose stuffed with soft material, industrial gasket or packing material, and sheet lead. These gaskets do not provide very tight seals and are most suitable for wooden patches. The cargo or casualty's stores may contain suitable materials. The primary requirements are that the gasket be nearly waterproof or impervious to water and soft enough to compress and conform to surface irregularities.

Gaskets for large patches may be built up to whatever thickness the irregularities of the surfaces demand. Often, the irregularities of the hull in way of damage make it impossible to make a good seal or to give confidence that the patch can survive a tow. In these cases the patch is backed up with concrete.

Cracks

Cracks can be patched effectively in three ways:

Welding. One of the stupidest things a salvor can do is to fill a crack with weld metal and consider it repaired. The crack almost invariably opens through the weld and runs past its original length. Proper welding repair of a crack requires either:

1. Cropping out the cracked area, making generous radius curves at each corner, and inserting a plate or welding on a doubler, or
2. Cleaning of the cracked area to determine where the crack ends, drilling the ends to stop additional propagation, and welding on a generously radiused doubler plate that extends at least 6 inches (15 cm) beyond the crack in all directions (figure 9-13).

Plugs and Wedges. Cracks may be patched by driving plugs and wedges into the crack to fill it as much as possible (figure 9-14). Softwood—white pine is best—plugs and wedges are preferred because softwood swells when wet and helps fill the crack. Hardwood wedges, if not driven carefully, may split or, worse, extend the crack. The seal is improved by wrapping the plugs and wedges in canvas. Sheet lead and oakum, traditionally very suitable materials for this purpose, are seldom found in modern ships. Better yet is a filler of epoxy or an industrial caulking compound worked into the patch and smoothed to form a single solid mass. A near perfect seal can result. For a particularly elegant job, suitable to remain in place for a long time or survive a long tow, the plugs and wedges are cut off evenly nearly flush with the skin of the ship. A coarse wire netting like poultry wire, pig wire, or hardware cloth is stapled to the wooden plugs and wedges. Epoxy is worked into the crevices and built up so that plugs, wedges, wire, and epoxy form a single, solid mass.

Concrete. Bags of ready-mix or of cement are laid against the crack and jammed into it. An internal concrete box patch backs the rough patch, as shown in figure 9-15.

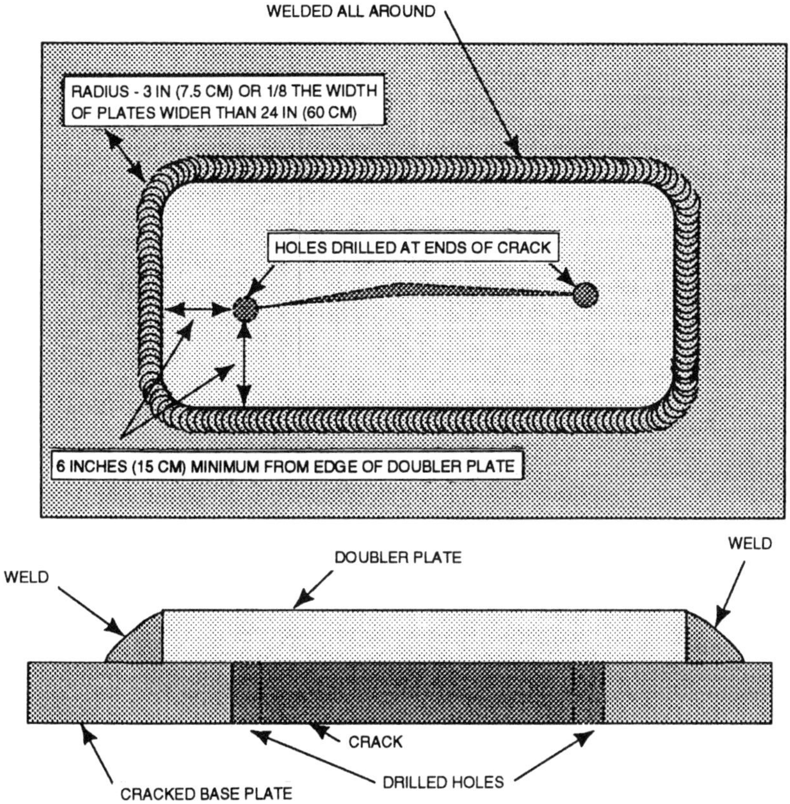

Fig. 9-13. Crack repair by welding

Bridging of athwartships cracks to tie two parts of the ship's structure together often seems like a good idea. And so it is, done correctly. Done incorrectly, it is a very bad idea that can lead to the loss of a ship.

Doubler plates of the same thickness as the hull and stiffened by stiffeners the same size as those in the damaged structure are the best bridges. This type of bridge is more suitable as an emergency repair than as a salvage fix at a remote site. In salvage, bridges may be built of either flexible tension members like chain or wire rope or of rigid structural shapes. Tension member bridges have a limitation that their name implies—they can carry only tensile loads and offer no help with compressive loads. Without tension-measuring devices and machinery for measuring the tension in the bridge, it is almost impossible to balance the load among the members. One member usually winds up carrying the great majority of,

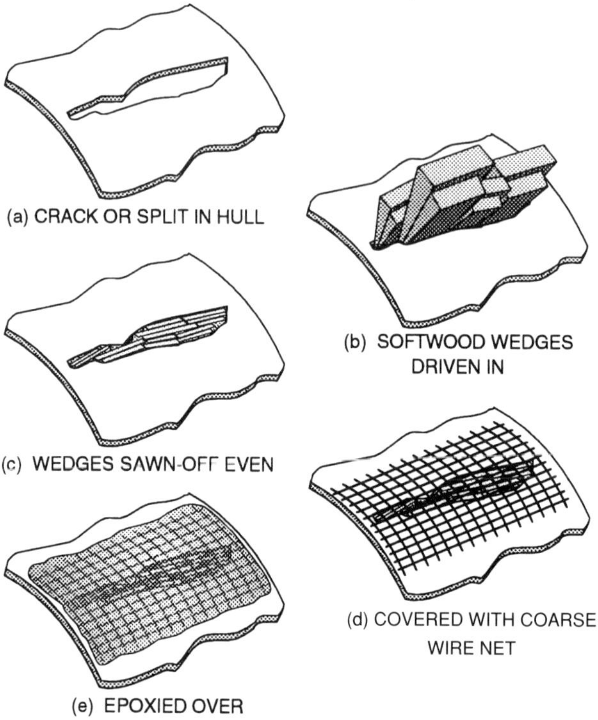

Fig. 9-14. Sealing a crack with plugs and wedges. Courtesy of U.S. Navy.

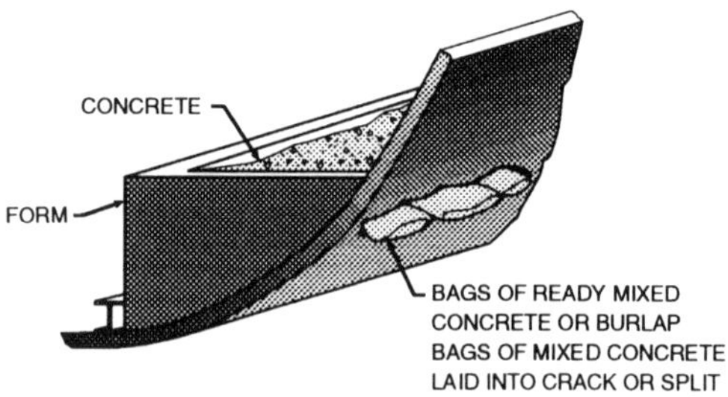

Fig. 9-15. Concrete crack repair. Courtesy of U.S. Navy.

if not all of, the load. Bridging with flexible members is better suited to wreck removals than to salvage cases, where long exposure to the loads of the sea are probable. In all cases, bridging with flexible members is a desperation technique.

Bridges of rigid structural members are reliable when installed in conformance with some rather stringent rules. Ignoring the rules produces a cosmetically satisfactory bridge that can induce stresses leading to massive failure and loss of the ship. The basic rules for bridging with longitudinals apply to the number of longitudinals and their length, positioning, attachment to the ship's structure, and termination.

Hull damage in the surrounding area usually accompanies cracking. The bridge must restore not only the continuity of the cracked structure, but also the strength. The number of longitudinals must be large enough so that the cross-sectional area makes a significant contribution to restoring the section modulus lost in the damage and keeps the stress in the members below the failure stress of the bridged section. The only way to determine the correct number is by an iterative series of section modulus calculations.

Bridges must have sufficient length to tie into sound structure on both sides of the crack. They must extend at least four times their height into the sound structure and must terminate on a major structural member, such as a bulkhead or web frame.

Main bridging longitudinals must be continuous and lie in the same longitudinal plane as existing sound longitudinals. Additional smaller longitudinals placed between the main bridges at narrow intervals—say 6 inches (15 cm)—are effective in replacing the strength of the damaged plating.

The most suitable bridging sections are I or wide flange sections or channels with the lower flange intact, with 100 percent full penetration fillet welds along both sides of as much of their length as possible. The lower flange reduces the stress concentration at the weld and contributes to the restoration of the section modulus of the damaged structure.

Proper termination of bridging longitudinals prevents development of high stresses at the end. Both the web and the upper flange of the longitudinal are sniped. The web slopes for two frame spaces or has a slope of 6 to 1, whichever gives the least slope. Web cuts are at least 45 degrees. In addition to landing on a major sound structural member, the longitudinal should have a soft toe. The soft toe is a plate about the same thickness as the longitudinal's web and at least 30 times as long and wide, with corners radiused generously, say 3 inches (7.5 cm) or about the size of a 36-ounce coffee can.

Cofferdams

When all or part of the main deck is submerged, flooded spaces cannot be pumped until sources of flooding are closed and the watertight boundaries extended above the water surface. One method of extending the watertight envelope is to build cofferdams—watertight walls or fences—around deck openings or the entire hull. There are three principal types of cofferdams:

1. *Small cofferdams* allow access or pumping spaces that are under water at some stage of the tide.
2. *Partial cofferdams* fit larger openings, such as cargo hatches or small deckhouses.
3. *Complete cofferdams* are erected in place all the way around the ship, a major engineering and construction effort.

Small cofferdams (figure 9-16) may be purpose-built of steel plate, planks, or plywood, or adapted from small structures. Cofferdams can be made from anything that works. Only the salvor's imagination and ability to scrounge limit the possibilities. Makeshift cofferdams of the past include:

Standard 20-foot ISO containers with the doors welded up, the bottoms removed and the tops cut away.

Cylinders—fuel tanks, air volume tanks, boiler drums, steel drums, large-diameter pipe.

Discarded structures, such as small deckhouses.

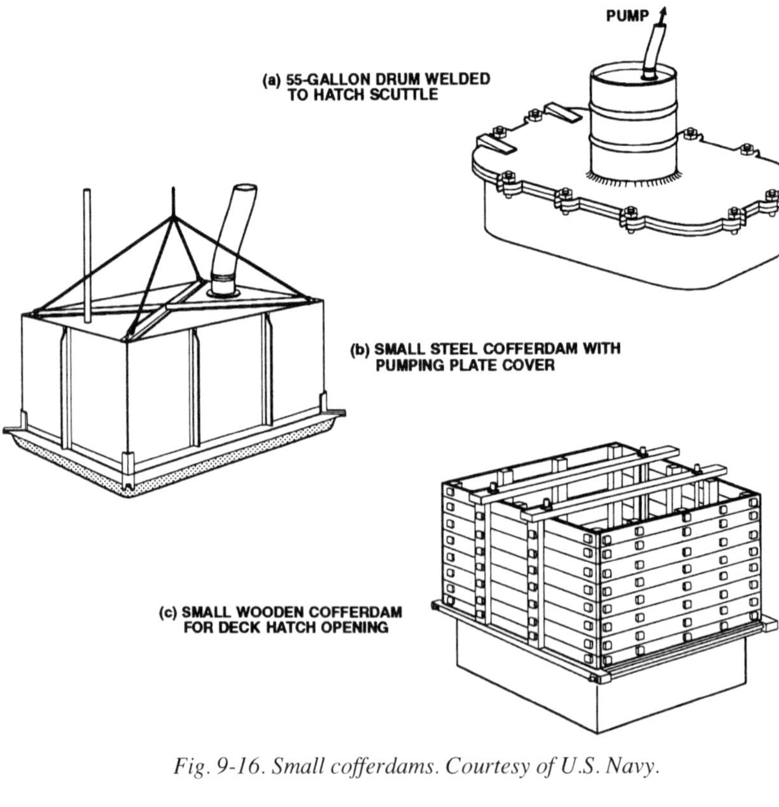

Fig. 9-16. Small cofferdams. Courtesy of U.S. Navy.

In its simplest form, a small cofferdam is a small box with a flat bar flange and rubber gasket on the bottom. Small cofferdams may be secured to the hull by welding or bolting the cofferdam to the hull, securing the cofferdam with lines hauled tight with turnbuckles and comealongs, or weighing them down.

Partial cofferdams (figure 9-17) are built from steel, wood, or a combination, either as complete units or as sections that can be erected in place. These structures are very often applied on cargo hatches where they fit completely around the hatch. Normally, hatch cofferdams fit outside the coaming with their faying surfaces welded to the deck. Partial cofferdams must be designed and constructed as carefully as large patches. Theoretically, partial cofferdams are heavy enough to be held in place by their own weight. In practice, they are welded, bolted, or secured with rigging.

There are two problems with partial cofferdams. Metacentric radius develops slowly while the partial cofferdam is pumped and the waterplane is confined to the cofferdam. Not only is there free surface in the space being pumped, but the water trapped on the deck outside the cofferdam acts as free surface. The result is that the ship is almost always unstable as it comes off the sea floor. The greatest

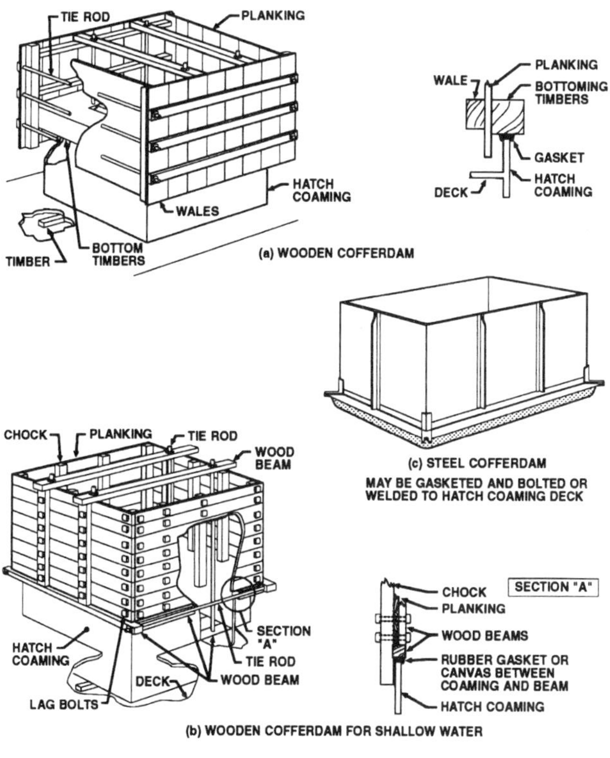

Fig. 9-17. Partial cofferdams. Courtesy of U.S. Navy.

instability occurs just as the ship starts to rise and just before all the water is pumped out. Good practice is to install large, quick-acting valves in the cofferdam to allow the ship to be reflooded and set down if stability becomes dangerous. Cranes for steadying are normally placed on either side of a ship being raised with partial cofferdams; one end is kept securely grounded, or the vessel dragged into shallower water as she becomes light. Secondly, hydrostatic pressure from the sea acts upon the deck outside the cofferdam, becoming most severe as the water level drops below the main deck. If the deck is submerged more than 4 to 6 feet (1.3 to 2 meters) the deck must be shored to prevent collapse (figure 9-18). Shoring, discussed in more detail below, is a difficult and time-consuming operation that must be factored into the decision to use partial cofferdams.

As with all things at sea, weather is a factor in cofferdam design and construction. Good practice is to design and build cofferdams for the worst weather expected at the site and then add a bit for an extra margin of safety.

Complete cofferdams are extensions of the shell plating built all around a ship sunk on a more-or-less even keel. When one end or side of the ship is submerged, only the submerged portion need be cofferdammed. This practice may require less

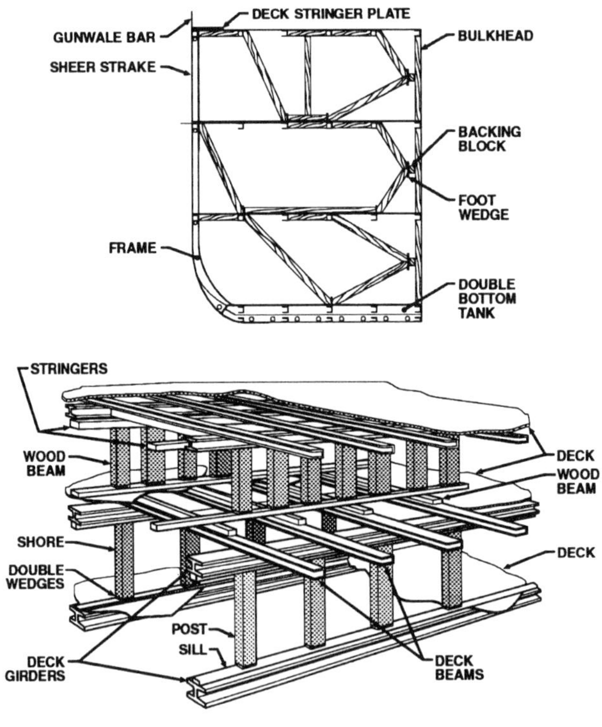

Fig. 9-18. Shoring with partial cofferdams.
Courtesy of U.S. Navy.

effort and time than the construction of several partial cofferdams around hatches or other openings.

Complete cofferdams are difficult and expensive to build. While massive structures have been built and proved successful in the past, complete cofferdams are seldom built in modern salvage. They are appropriate when:

The ship is sunk in protected waters where loads from seas and swells are low.

The ship is in such poor condition that making temporary repairs and sealing the deck is clearly impractical. This condition is often found in old, poorly maintained ships that are wreck removal rather than salvage cases.

There are so many openings in the deck that the combination of sealing, partial cofferdams, and shoring requires more work and time than complete cofferdams.

The decision to build complete cofferdams is a combined technical and operational decision requiring analysis from the two sometimes opposing, usually complementary viewpoints. Individual analyses are made. The operational analysis looks at the feasibility of building the cofferdams and overcoming the accompanying problems with the manpower and resources that can be brought to bear. Perhaps more importantly, it looks at and develops plans for dealing with potential failure of any portion of the plan. One of the most important elements of the latter is the development of reasonable contingencies for dragging the ship if she cannot be brought afloat.

The engineering analysis considers the heavy side loading on the cofferdam during dewatering and methods of controlling or countering the instability that occurs when large free surfaces develop during dewatering. A thorough analysis that delves deeply into complete cofferdams for a particular application often shows that what is apparently an attractive alternative may be neither practical nor sensible.

Complete cofferdams, like partial ones, may be built of steel, wood, or a combination. Steel structures are relatively simple structures of stiffened steel plate, welded or bolted to the hull and braced with diagonal braces tied to the ship's structure. Wooden structures are more complex because they require an elaborate system of diagonal bracing and weighting to keep the buoyant material in place. Wooden cofferdams are difficult and time-consuming to build. The internal structure of a wooden cofferdam occupies a great deal of deck space. Whatever the material, complete cofferdams are normally built ashore in sections.

Two practices have been followed in landing complete cofferdams. Practice in Europe has been to bolt cofferdams to a heavy timber strake attached to the side plating, while American practice is to land the cofferdam on the deck edge. Both systems work; the American system requires less time and labor. Steel cofferdams can be welded to either the deck or side shell.

With any type of complete cofferdam, as much top hamper as possible is removed to clear working areas for salvage rigging and structure. Large deckhouses may be removed. Removal of unnecessary structure removes high weight and improves the stability of the casualty.

Cofferdams resist external pressures only. Good practice is to keep these loads as low as practical and to apply them for as short a time as possible. Bracing of cofferdams against lateral pressures is very important. The best practice is to overbrace with bracing carried to deckhouses and other strong points in the ship's structure and to pick up hard points in the ship wherever possible.

To keep the loads on the cofferdam structure low during construction and preparation, the interior of the cofferdams are kept tidal. Large valves are placed in each corner and wired open. Before pumping begins, the valves are closed, but not wired closed, in case they must be opened to flood the hull and set it safely on the bottom.

Pumping Plates

Pumping plates (figure 9-19) are closed, steel, wooden, or combination cofferdams with fittings for pumping through the plate and for venting the space and taking soundings. They are fitted across hatch coamings, tank accesses, or other deck openings and welded or bolted in place. Pumping plates are suitable for either ships sunk so they do not require shoring or for installation after shoring is complete.

Either surface-mounted or submersible pumps may pump through pumping plates (figure 9-20). The best mounting for surface pumps is on a float or ship alongside so the rising tide does not flood them out. Pumping plates for submersible pumps must have a cofferdam or access built into them. The access allows rigging the submersible pump into the space and access for personnel.

Air vents are generous and monitored regularly to insure they are not blocked or closed accidentally and a vacuum drawn that collapses the structure.

Sealing for Blowing

Cracks and holes must be more thoroughly sealed for blowing than for pumping because air as a low-density, compressible fluid under pressure leaks through even the smallest openings at rates four to six times that of water, and can migrate through the ship. Unwanted migration complicates and confuses buoyancy distribution management and can result in longitudinal stability problems if air leaks into long, narrow tanks. Small cracks and holes that could be left for pumping must be sealed for blowing. Liberal epoxy sealing of small holes and the periphery of well-made patches is called for.

Air Locks

Air locks (figure 9-21) are a variation of cofferdams that have been used infrequently on sunken ships refloated inverted and sometimes on upright ships. Air locks allow the water level to be blown down in the hull and men to work inside

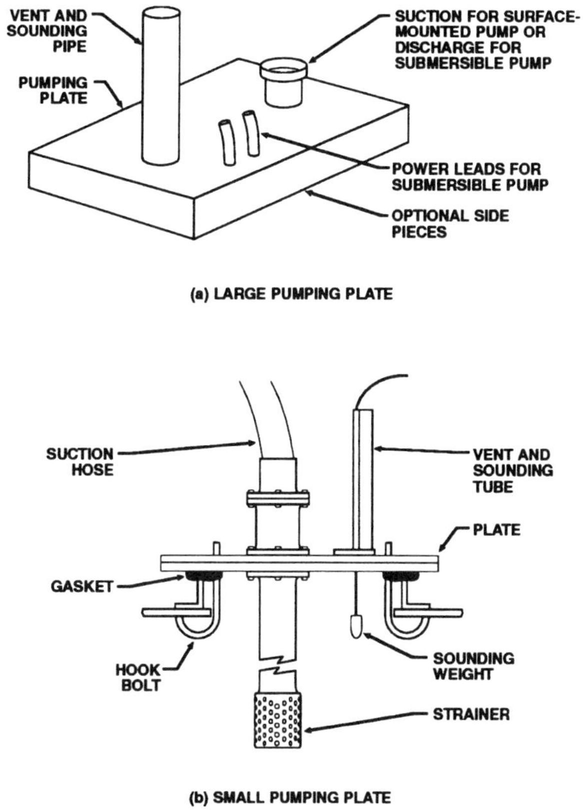

Fig. 9-19. Pumping plates. Courtesy of U.S. Navy.

the hull in the dry. With air locks, supporting equipment is normally mounted on a barge or ship moored securely at the site. Men working inside the ship incur the same decompression debt as divers working at the same depth. While most exposures can be kept well within no decompression limits, a recompression chamber and operator should be available at or near the salvage site.

Shoring

Shoring in salvage refers to addition of steel or wooden braces to support weakened structures or structures exposed to loads greater than they can carry. Steel shores—either adjustable steel shores with ball and socket or shoe ends and integral screw jacks, or pipe or rolled structural sections cut to fit and welded in place—have greater strength than the traditional wooden shores. The adjustable steel shores are very quick and easy to install and allow rapid changes to the shoring pattern.

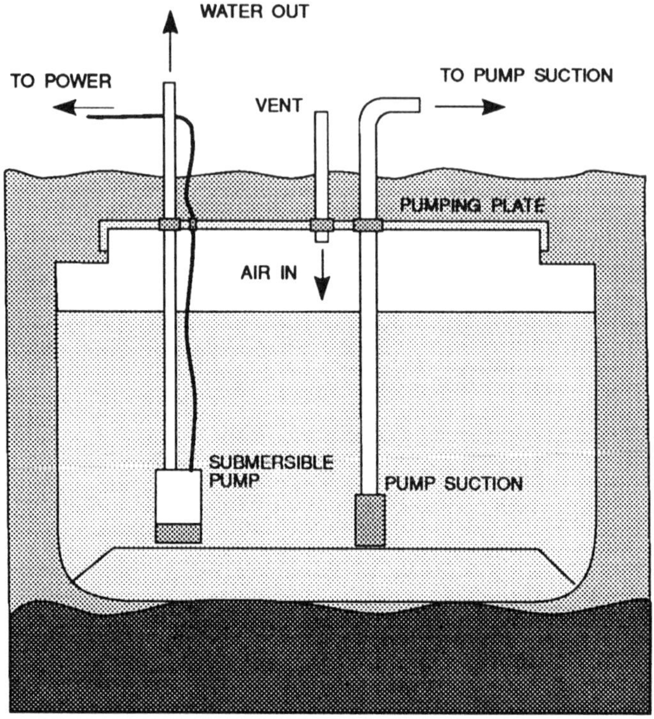

Fig. 9-20. Pumping through a pumping plate

The shoring patterns for wooden and steel shores are the same. Some general principles apply to both:

The length of shores must not exceed thirty times their minimum dimension or diameter. The smaller the length-to-thickness ratio, the stronger the shore.

Shores have their greatest strength when in direct compression.

Shoring is laid against stiffeners or other hard points in the structure on both ends.

Shoring is installed to distribute the load over as large an area as possible.

The pressure of shores on a bulkhead is applied at about one-third of the bulkhead height.

Considerable strength is lost if the angle between shores exceeds 90 degrees.

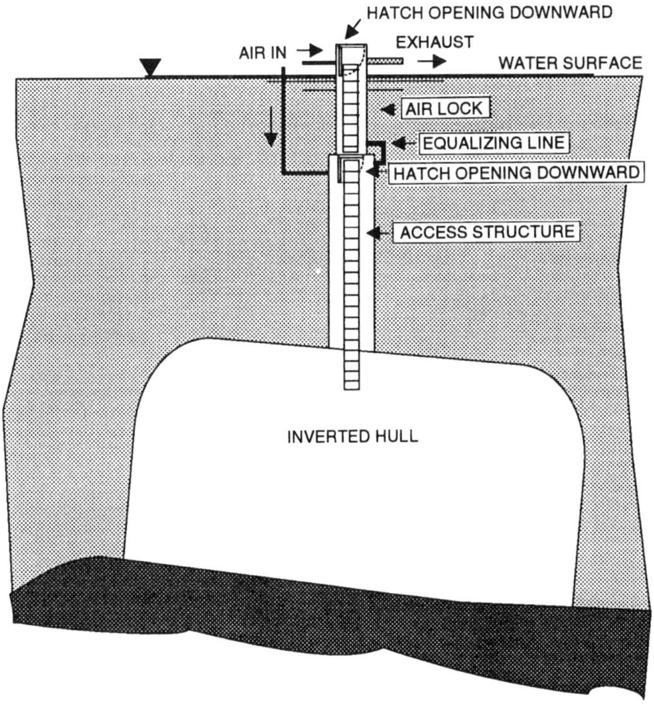

Fig. 9-21. Air lock for an inverted ship

Some additional considerations apply to wooden shores:

Relatively straight-grained woods, such as pine, oak, or fir, are chosen for shores.

Shoring loads should be as nearly parallel with the grain as possible.

Twelve-by-twelve timbers are excellent shores.

Wedges for shoring are about the same width as the shoring timber and six times as long as the butt thickness.

Pairs of wedges are driven simultaneously under the shores.

Sholes or strongbacks should never be less than 1 inch (25 mm) thicker than the shore. Preferably, they are larger in breadth and width to assist in spreading the load.

Cleats secure ends against slippage, as shown in figure 9-22.

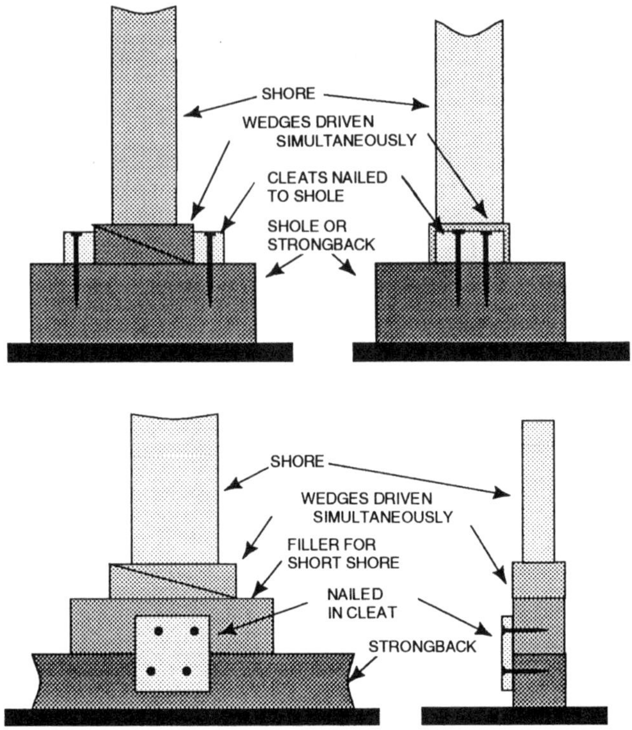

Fig. 9-22. Shoring secured against slippage

Stiffening Bulkheads

Stiffening bulkheads, while not truly either patching or cofferdamming, is closely related enough to include in the same discussion. Bulkhead stiffening ranges from expedients like piling bagged cargo against the bulkhead, to shoring, to false bulkheads built near the bulkhead with the intervening space filled with concrete.

Bulkheads should be stiffened when they are adjacent to flooded compartments or when they have been damaged or bulged. Access to bulkheads is difficult in loaded holds. To reach the bulkhead for shoring or the construction of temporary bulkheads, cargo must be discharged. In some cases, cargo can provide the stiffening. Bagged cargo can be stacked tightly against the bulkhead or bulk cargo can be trimmed against the bulkhead and held in place with shifting boards. Empty holds in multideck ships can be shored easily with metal or wooden shores. The depth of holds in modern dry bulk and wet cargo vessels produces such a long span for the shores that shoring is impractical. If the cargo cannot provide simple reinforcement, temporary bulkheads can be built. When bulkheads are badly damaged or have failed structurally, temporary bulkheads may be quicker and easier than patching.

Temporary bulkheads are normally steel or wooden structures built in place on one or both sides of a damaged or weakened bulkhead. The temporary structure may be made significantly lighter if the space between the temporary and structural bulkhead is filled with concrete. Sand, mud, bagged or bulk cargo, debris, or anything else at hand may also fill the space. Concrete gives the strongest and most reliable structure. Tie rods through the entire structure help hold it together and reinforce the concrete. For a strong structure, if the temporary bulkhead cannot be landed upon and supported by a heavy member of the ship's structure, it should have a heavy steel or I beam or timber footing with a concrete footing poured over that. The most efficient way to place the quantities of concrete required for major bulkhead stiffening is by pumping with a pressure grouting pump through accesses cut in the deck. The upper end of the temporary bulkhead is secured to the ship's structure by welding or by otherwise securing it rigidly to a deck beam.

Figure 9-23 shows stiffening of a bulkhead by both the very basic means of piling cargo against the bulkhead and by the "all up" means of building temporary bulkheads on both sides and filling with concrete. Most salvage requirements fall between these two extremes.

Marking of Patches

All the work of designing, building, and installing patches under water can come to naught if a tug operator bumps the patch and ruptures it or knocks it off. There is no way of totally preventing this possibility, but clear marking of the patch reduces the risk. Clearly marking patch locations by painting on "Patch Below" or something similar in large letters that contrast with the hull is a very good idea.

Summary

A patch, cofferdam, or patching plate is only as good as the workmanship that went into it. Every patch must be carefully thought out, made and installed with care, and well-secured. The structure in way of the patch must be prepared for patching by removing jagged plate that may interfere with a proper seal. Work areas for making and handling patches and shores are kept policed to increase productivity and reduce fire hazards. Patching, cofferdamming, and shoring are critical to the overall salvage work. They must be done well.

PART 2—PUMPING

There are two basic requirements for pumping in salvage: removal of floodwater and moving liquid or semiliquid cargoes, bunkers, and ballast. This chapter addresses only pumping of floodwater to restore buoyancy and the pumping equipment appropriate for this purpose. Chapter 12 addresses cargo, ballast, and bunker movement. The line is not always clearly defined, so some pumps can find applications in both services.

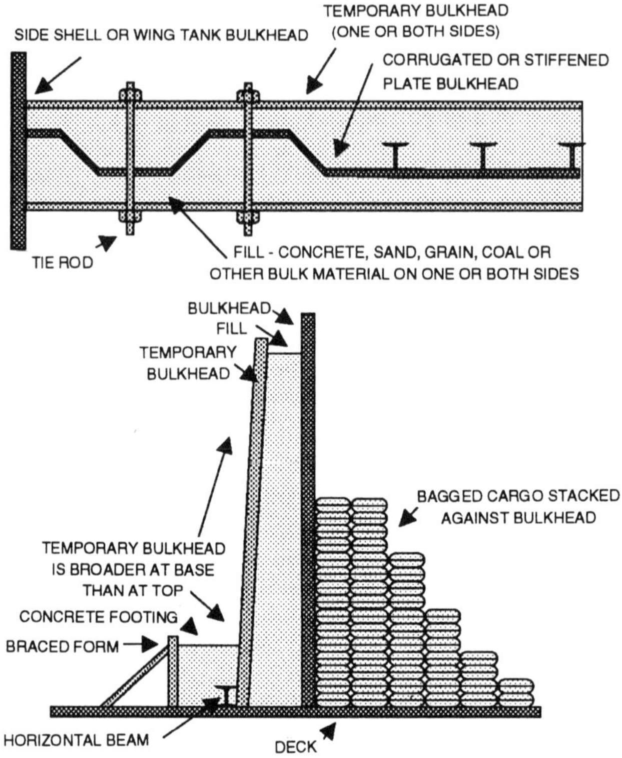

Fig. 9-23. Bulkhead stiffening

Pumping is usually the preferred method of restoring buoyancy because:

- Water levels and pumping rates can be controlled with some precision.
- The attitude of the ship can be adjusted.
- Problems tend to telegraph their presence early, giving adequate time for corrective action.
- Pumps move large volumes of water efficiently.
- Pumps are relatively easy to use and quick and easy to rig.
- The hull does not need to be sealed as thoroughly as it does for blowing.
- Pumps and pumping accessories are cheaper to buy, operate, and maintain than air compressors and their accessories.

Welded and bolted steel patches and epoxy sealants have influenced salvage pumping practice. Steel patches welded or bolted to the hull have low leakage rates compared to wooden patches hook bolted to the hull. Low leakage permits smaller, more efficient pumping plants than were common in the past.

Pumping Theory

Pumping theory is based upon head pressure. Head is the pressure exerted by the weight of a column of liquid expressed in any of several units; in salvage, the unit is normally feet or meters of seawater.

Suction head is the difference between the height of the liquid level and the height of the pump impeller. For reasons discussed later, it is the most important head in salvage.

Static discharge head is the distance between the pump impeller and the point of free discharge of the pumped liquid.

Static friction head is the loss caused by the drag of the liquid on the suction and discharge hoses expressed in head units. It is a function of flow rates and the types and length of hoses. In salvage, friction head is approximated as 20 percent of the total suction and discharge hose length.

Total head is the sum of the suction, discharge, and friction heads.

Figure 9-24 illustrates pumping heads.

Pumps for salvage work by creating a vacuum into which the water flows. They are limited by the irrefutable laws of physics to a maximum vacuum of 1 atmosphere or 33 feet of seawater. Therefore, salvage pumps cannot pump with a theoretical suction head of more than 33 feet. In practice, losses associated with

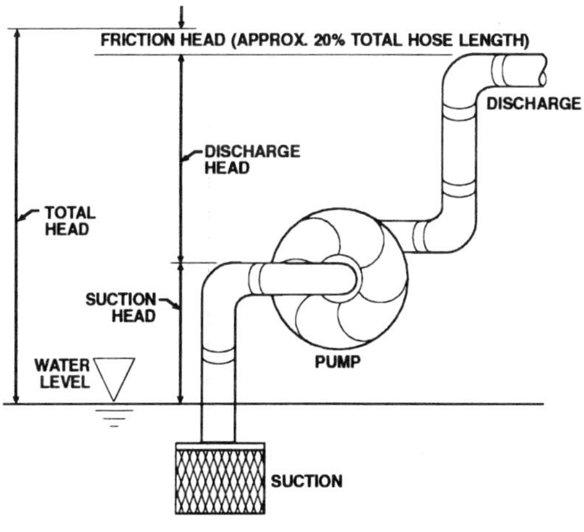

Fig. 9-24. Pumping heads. Courtesy of U.S. Navy.

friction, leaks, and gases and solids in the pumped liquid reduce the *maximum achievable* pumping head to 25 feet. Pump capacity varies with suction head, increasing as head decreases. Performance curves available from manufacturers show capacity as a function of total head and suction head. As a rule of thumb, halving suction head decreases capacity about one-third.

Pump manufacturers usually express pump capacities in gallons per minute (gpm) or cubic meters per minute (m^3/min). Neither unit is as convenient as (long) tons per hour for salvage work, where the intent is to pump for long periods of time to recover tons of buoyancy. Dividing gallons per minute by 4.37 yields tons per hour, or its near equivalent, tonnes per hour. Because one cubic meter of seawater is equivalent to one tonne, multiplying by 60 converts cubic meters per minute to tonnes per hour. If the pump rating is unknown it may be approximated by:

$$Q = 5 \times D^2$$

where:

Q = discharge in tons per hour at 25-foot suction head
D = pump suction diameter in inches

Pump Types

The primary requirement for salvage dewatering pumps is to move large quantities of water with no specific requirements on discharge pressure. The most suitable type of pumps for this service are self-priming centrifugal pumps with open, trash-type impellers capable of passing solid objects up to 25 percent of the nominal size of the pump.

The most common and most versatile pumps are diesel engine–driven pumps in sizes ranging from 3-inch to 12-inch. The usual sizes in salvage contractors' inventories are 4-, 6-, and 8-inch. The 4-inch size is convenient and highly portable. Most salvage ships carry these pumps. The larger sizes are normally shore-based, but are often aboard salvage ships in limited quantities. Military organizations and construction contractors normally hold 10-inch pumps. These large pumps move great quantities of water in a short time, but are so heavy and cumbersome, primarily because of their large diesel engines, that handling is difficult.

Pumps are subject to rough handling on a salvage site. The pumps and engines should be skid-mounted and encased in a pipe or angle frame that protects them from casual impacts and damage to accessories. The frame also has pad eyes at each upper corner for lifting slings and on each corner of the skids for attaching skidding slings. Boxes of hand tools and high usage spares welded to the frame are full whenever the pump goes aboard a casualty.

Pumps advertised as self-priming and not requiring a foot valve rate a skeptical look. Reliable operation of a self-priming feature on pumps larger than 4-inch at heads greater than 12 feet (4 meters) is questionable in salvage. Pumps should be treated as though they always require priming and foot valves. If they are not

Fig. 9-25. A pumping operation with a number of large engine-driven pumps discharging over the side

treated so, the situation is bound to be one in which they cannot properly self prime.

Gasoline engines drive some 3- and 4-inch pumps. These pumps, smaller and lighter than their diesel-driven counterparts, are easy to transport and rig. They are particularly good where pumps must be rigged and put into operation quickly, and where conditions for moving and handling the pumps are more than difficult. Gasoline-driven pumps are never appropriate where explosive atmospheres are possible, or for pumping flammable liquids.

Electric Submersible Salvage Pumps

Electric submersible salvage pumps, available in the same sizes as engine-driven pumps, have two advantages over their engine-driven cousins: they are easier to handle and, because they are submerged in the fluid they are pumping, they always operate at zero suction head. Many electric pumps come with high-volume/low-head impellers that limit their effective discharge head to about 50 feet (15 meters). Manufacturers may be able to supply impellers that can pump to higher heads. Submersible pump impellers, like those in engine-driven pumps, should pass objects about 25 percent of the suction diameter. The pumps are subject to severe impeller damage when pumping slurries or water with high percentages of solids in suspension.

Electric pumps must have a compatible power supply. "Compatible" is the most important word in the preceding sentence. Voltage, frequency, and phase of the power supply and pump must match. The power supply, if correctly sized, can serve several pumps. The high, short-duration starting current of the last pump in a series may trip the breakers on a generator that can easily carry the running load. It may be necessary to tie down the breaker or hold it in manually while the last pump starts. Portable generators, rigged with frames and lift points like engine-driven pumps, are part of the pumping plant. It is unwise to rely upon providing power to pumps from a salvage ship or from the casualty.

Electric pumps intended for salvage dewatering may not be intrinsically safe. Those that are not should never be used for pumping petroleum products or in spaces where concentrations of hydrocarbon vapors are present. The intrinsically safe requirement applies not only to the pump but also to all associated switch gear and accessories.

Miscellaneous Pumps

Pneumatic centrifugal sump and double-diaphragm pumps find application in salvage although neither type is available in sizes and capacities that suit them for primary dewatering pumps. Centrifugal pumps are especially suitable for removing fire-fighting water and for pumping out small tanks and spaces with limited accesses. These units may pump small spaces containing water contaminated with oils or chemical cargoes.

Pneumatic double-diaphragm pumps are among the most versatile small pumps a salvor can have. The pumps can be applied in the same ways as centrifugal pumps, and have the additional advantage of being able to take suction at remote points and of easy tandem connection for high discharge heads. The action of these pumps causes them to vibrate and jump in normal operation; they should always be well lashed upright with matting under them.

Eductors (figure 9-26) are jet pumps that derive their power from a stream of water. Eductors have no moving parts and consume no power directly. Pumping small enclosed compartments containing water contaminated with fuel or chemicals with eductors is safe and convenient. The capacity of the pump depends upon the pressure and flow rate of the water supply, the suction head, and the discharge head. All eductors have a minimum pressure and flow rate below which they do not function at all. In operation, regulation of the inlet pressure and flow rate regulate the discharge. The best discharge of a good eductor is between 1.5 and 2.0 times the quantity of water supplied. Proper function is obvious by the quantity of the discharge.

Fire hoses and fire-fighting water supply can drive 4-inch and smaller eductors. Larger eductors require the greater volumes that only large pumps can supply. Driving eductors with the discharge of large engine-driven or submersible pumps

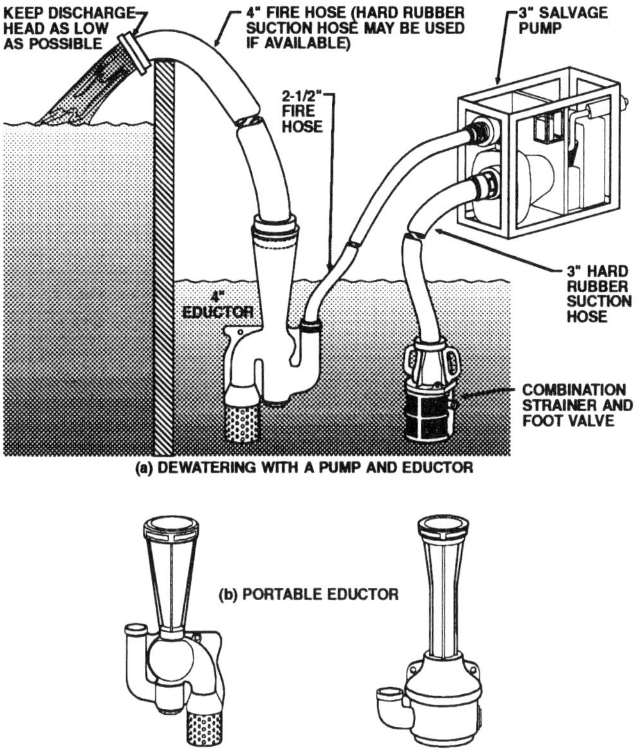

Fig. 9-26. Eductors. Courtesy of U.S. Navy.

substantially increases the total output. The effectiveness depends upon the particular situation. It may be easier to bring in another pump than to rig and adjust.

Salvors should not overlook the possibilities of dewatering with, or supplementing portable pumping plants with, the casualty's installed pumps. Even when the normal power is not available or piping systems are damaged, it may be possible to rig alternative or temporary power and to restore piping with jumpers. As discussed in Chapter 5, defueling with the installed systems and pumps is always a good idea.

Salvors may find themselves in situations where they have no salvage pumps conveniently available or do not have sufficient pumping capacity for the job. Blank looks may meet local inquiries for salvage pumps. There is nothing magic about salvage pumping; almost any type of pump can work. Suitable pumps are in agriculture, mining, construction, fire departments, or other services. Often, they can be hired from their owner-user or from industrial supply companies. Guarantees of replacement for lost or damaged equipment invariably are part of the deal.

Hired pumps may not be set up as the salvor would choose nor be as convenient, but they offer a very fine alternative to no pumps or an inadequate pumping plant.

Pumping Calculations

Pumping calculations in salvage usually are limited to determining the number of pumps required to dewater a space in a given time or determining the time required to dewater a space with a particular pumping plant. Both calculations are simple and straightforward.

Calculating the number of pumps to dewater a space in a specified time requires three steps:

1. Determining the number of tons a single pump can pump in the specified time. Pump capacities in tons per hour are obtained from the performance curves or estimated by the methods discussed earlier in this chapter. If the pumps are old or worn, an arbitrary factor may be included to account for decreased performance. The rating for each pump is multiplied by the number of hours available for pumping.
2. Dividing the volume of the space, allowing a permeability factor or deduction for cargo or equipment in the space, by 35 to determine the total tonnage to be removed. Either increasing the volume or decreasing the calculated capacity can account for leakage.
3. Dividing step 2 by step 1 to get the number of pumps.

Time to dewater a space, a variation on the above, is determined by:

1. Determining the capacity of the entire pumping plant in tons per hour.
2. Determining the tonnage of water to be removed.
3. Dividing step 2 by step 1 to get the number of hours of pumping.

Either calculation yields only approximate results, as the pumping rate varies as suction and discharge heads change during pumping operations.

Pumping Operations

The discussion of pumping operations that follows is not a cookbook on how to pump. It is not highly technical; rather it is a collection of notes, based on experience and good practice. The notes may seem conservative. They are. Pumping operations are usually a critical phase in the overall salvage operation; they deserve a belt-and-suspenders approach because the result of inattention to detail or a half-hearted approach may be failure and a major setback.

The size of the pumping plant is a major decision made early in the operation. Sometimes the number of pumps available either in the salvor's immediate inventory or that can be hired is the limiting factor. When this is the case, the structure and sequence of the operation must employ the available plant most effectively. At other times, adequate plant may be available to structure the operation in any manner the salvor chooses.

If pumping is to be completed in one tide cycle, overall capacity of the plant is critical. In other circumstances, time to dewater and the size of the plant may be a matter of convenience and coordination with other functions. The pumping plant should always have excess capacity to allow for overcoming leakage, breakdowns, clogged suctions, and the other unforeseeable events that Captain Murphy visits upon even the best-planned salvage operation. The size of the reserve capacity depends upon the time criticality of the operation and the anticipated reliability of the plant. There is no rule of thumb for excess pump capacity; 100 percent may not be excessive.

It is most embarrassing to forget that diesel engines driving pumps or generators require fuel and lubricating oil at regular intervals. A copious supply of both, much more than enough for the planned pumping operation, should be aboard the casualty before starting to pump. The pumps and their fuel supply are checked regularly.

Six- and eight-inch salvage pumps and their hoses are not small pieces of machinery, but they must be placed aboard the casualty and moved around on it. Far and away, helicopters are the safest and fastest means of placing a pump and its accessories aboard a casualty. The next choice is lifting the gear off the deck of the salvage ship or barge lying alongside with a crane or boom on either vessel. Least desirable are snatch lifts off the deck of a salvage vessel or high line transfers. The means is seldom the salvor's option; whatever means is necessary, it should be thoughtfully planned and conducted as safely as possible. Poorly made transfers can damage both workers and equipment; neither type of damage contributes to a good operation. One of the easiest and most effective precautions is to be sure all lifts except helicopter lifts have tag lines attached. With tag lines, the receiving crew can steady the lift and help place it without standing under it or so near as to be struck. Tag lines are seldom necessary with helicopter lifts. It is better to let the pilot set the load on deck and make the release.

Most electrical submersible, pneumatic, and engine-driven pumps up to 4 inches can be manhandled to where they will be used. Large skid-mounted pumps can be dragged along the deck by rigging attached to their frame or moved on rigid or inflatable rollers. Lifting pumps over hatch coamings or up a deck level requires sheer legs or similar arrangements.

The casualty may seem rock-steady, but when she comes afloat she may move suddenly. Pumps should be secured so they do not begin to slide about with the ship's movement.

Power leads, connection boxes, switch gear, etc., for electric and hydraulic submersible pumps are designed for hard use. Nevertheless, they must be protected against accidental damage. Leads and boxes should go where they cannot be damaged and do not present a danger to themselves or personnel. They should never lie in a jumble resembling a nest of snakes. Although designated intrinsically safe, power leads and switch boxes should be kept clear of the tank decks of tankers or other locations with possibly explosive atmospheres.

In ships with 'tween decks or in multideck ships that trim and list during pumping, free surface exists in water pooled on the deck. Holes cut in the deck in the corners of the holds allow this water to drain and eliminate the free surface. Alternatively, small pumps or eductors can strip the pools out as they develop.

Centrifugal pumps have an optimum speed above which the pump cavitates and excessive wear damages the prime mover. Optimum speed is normally about two-thirds of rated engine speed. Operating at higher speed gives a greater discharge head and is sometimes necessary.

The rated maximum suction head of most diesel-driven salvage pumps is about 25 feet (8 meters). Few, if any, salvage pumps do any effective work at this suction head. Suction heads for diesel-driven salvage pumps should be limited to 15 feet and kept lower if possible.

Placing the pump close to the free surface of the water effectively limits suction head. Suction hoses should be as straight and as short as possible and should never lead above the pump suction inlet, to prevent the formation of air pockets at high points. For various reasons, among them reducing the suction head, it may be desirable to pump from a ship or barge alongside or to hang the pump over the side and pump though holes cut in the shell for suction lines. If the pump is neither on nor supported from the casualty, the tide and the rise of the casualty during pumping can change the relative positions of the pump and hole for the suction hose. It may be practical to place pumps on platforms suspended from cargo-handling gear or purpose-rigged sheer legs. As the water level drops, lowering the pump and platform maintains a low suction head. Note that the discharge head increases, but this increase has less effect on output than increases in suction head.

Pumps may operate in series by leading the discharge of one to the suction of the other when the discharge head is high. This is not a particularly easy or efficient mode of operation. It is difficult to balance the pumping rate of the two pumps so the upper pump is neither starved nor overwhelmed by the discharge of the lower pump. If the upper pump starves, cavitation damages the impeller and casing. If it is overwhelmed, a back pressure develops on the lower pump. Pump speeds are adjusted by trial and error to reach a combination that works.

Engine-driven pumps should be as level as possible during operation. Pumps placed in ships whose attitude is expected to change during pumping have been placed on hinged platforms to keep them nearly level.

Pumping of spaces filled with cargo presents some special problems. Holds containing a large amount of tightly packed solid cargo, such as containers or crated or bagged cargo, may be pumped through the bilge suction line. It is much easier and more efficient to manhandle small diesel or pneumatic pumps into the engine room and connect them to the bilge system than to work suctions down through the cargo. In some ships it is possible to drain holds into adjacent tanks or shaft alleys and to pump from there. It is usually better to pump bulk cargoes or other cargoes that are likely to clog pump suctions over the side with air lifts as described in Chapter 11.

In enclosed spaces there must be arrangements for ventilating engine exhaust fumes. The best way is flexible exhaust extensions that carry engine exhaust to the atmosphere. If the exhaust run is long and produces appreciable back pressure, removing the muffler reduces total back pressure.

When water is flowing, pump discharges can flail around and whip wildly, causing a hazard to men and equipment and dumping the discharge where it is not wanted. To prevent whipping, all pump discharges, especially the large ones, should be lashed securely.

Sometimes it is most efficient to manifold pump discharges so there is a single final discharge for two or more pumps. The manifold piping must be large enough to prevent a back pressure on the pumps discharging into it. The area of the manifold must be larger than the sum of the areas of the discharges of the pumps feeding it or:

$$A_M > \Sigma \; (A_{P1} \ldots . A_{Pn})$$

where:
A_M = cross-sectional area of the manifold
A_P = cross-sectional area of the pump discharges

Since the cross-sectional areas are directly proportional to the *squares* of the diameters of the sections:

$$D_M^2 > \Sigma \; (D_{P1}^2 \ldots . D_{Pn}^2)$$

where:
D_M and D_P are the diameters of the manifold and the pump discharges respectively

It is also possible to manifold pump suctions so separate suction lines can run into two or more compartments. To prevent starvation of the pump, the total area of the suction hoses should be greater than the area of the pump suction, or:

$$D_P^2 > \Sigma \; (D_{S1}^2 \ldots . D_{S2}^2)$$

where:
D_P and D_S are the diameters of the pump suctions and suction lines respectively

When pumping a partial cofferdam with engine-driven pumps, it is often advantageous to place the pump inside the cofferdam. There are at least three ways to do this:

1. Mount the pumps on platforms at the top of the cofferdam. This method has the disadvantage of a constantly increasing suction head as the water level drops and is not practical in deep ships.
2. Hang the pumps off a boom or purpose-built A-frame above the cofferdam and lower them as the water level drops. The discharge line and exhaust hose must be long enough at the beginning of the operation so pumping does not have to stop for their adjustment. Pumps hanging off a boom are difficult to reach for refueling. It is generally best to bring them back on deck to refuel and check.
3. Mount the pumps on floats that fit inside the cofferdam and are guided by lines at the corners. The suction head remains low while the water level drops. Discharge and exhaust leads must be long as with hung-off pumps. Ladders are necessary for crews to reach the pumps for refueling and regular checks.

Pumps for complete cofferdams are either mounted on platforms attached to the cofferdam or set upon floats.

Before the actual pumping operation, all pumps are run in a test pumping. This test has a number of purposes, among them:

To be sure that the pumps are operable.

To be sure the pumps are rigged correctly and are properly secured with all connections and fittings tight. Air leaking into suction hoses can reduce pump efficiency. Questionable hoses are put in discharge rather than suction strings. A coat of sealing compound or varnish usually stops persistent suction hose leakage.

To be sure the pumps can actually dewater the space. With patches tight and pumps pumping, a constant or too slowly falling water level is a sure sign of another hole.

To allow divers to check patch integrity and mark leaks. Past practice was for divers to carry sawdust and similar materials with which to fother leaks during the test pumping. Marking the leaks for later sealing with epoxy is much more effective.

As soon as the space is accessible, survey teams enter the space to inspect the structure, bulkheads, patchwork, and shoring. Spaces that contain or contained decaying organic material may still contain weak sulfuric acid and some hydrogen sulfide gas. The same precautions followed in entering closed spaces are followed in entering recently dewatered spaces.

After dewatering, spaces frequently have a quantity of mud resulting from silt entering through openings in the hull. This mud is high weight, extra weight, and free surface that should come out. Washing the space down with fire hoses and stripping it with a small pump, eductor, or air lift can remove this mud.

Frequently, the salvage contract calls for delivery at a repair port remote from the salvage site. A pumping installation aboard the casualty for the voyage in tow is very important for a safe voyage. Submersible pumps must have a generator and enough fuel. A second generator or engine-driven pumps—rigged and in backup to the primary generator—is the first backup. A backup system for the backup system consisting of engine-driven pumps that can be rigged into any space quickly is not overkill.

The amount and location of buoyancy as each space is pumped and the trim, list, free surface, and bending moment that result from pumping each space and the spaces collectively are all considerations in determining the pumping sequence. Free surface and the stability of the vessel are particularly important when the casualty is starting to float and before her fully afloat stability develops. It is often better to pump and secure one space at a time.

Past practice was to pump floodwater and whatever it may have contained over the side. It is highly improbable that environmental authorities would allow such discharges now. If salvors cannot demonstrate that the pump discharge is purer than pure, they can expect to provide barges or other materials to carry away the floodwater and to dispose of it as hazardous waste. Disposition of pollutants is particularly important in pumping out engine rooms that are invariably flooded with a mixture of oil, water, and other materials. For convenience, pumping of engine rooms, although applicable to all types of ships, is discussed in Chapter 13, Tanker Salvage.

Pumps and pumping accessories are some of the most frequently used and most valuable tools that salvors have. They are worthy of thoughtful selection, good maintenance, and careful handling. Good pumping operations come together when good equipment combines with attention to myriad details, *only a few of which are described above.* The preceding pages are not in any way a complete treatise on pumping. It behooves every salvor to have one or more of the excellent books on pumping mentioned in the Bibliography in his library. The book gains in value when removed from the bookshelf and studied before its information is needed.

PART 3—BLOWING

Despite the extra preliminary work and difficulty of control, there are situations in which blowing with compressed air is preferable to pumping. These situations in-

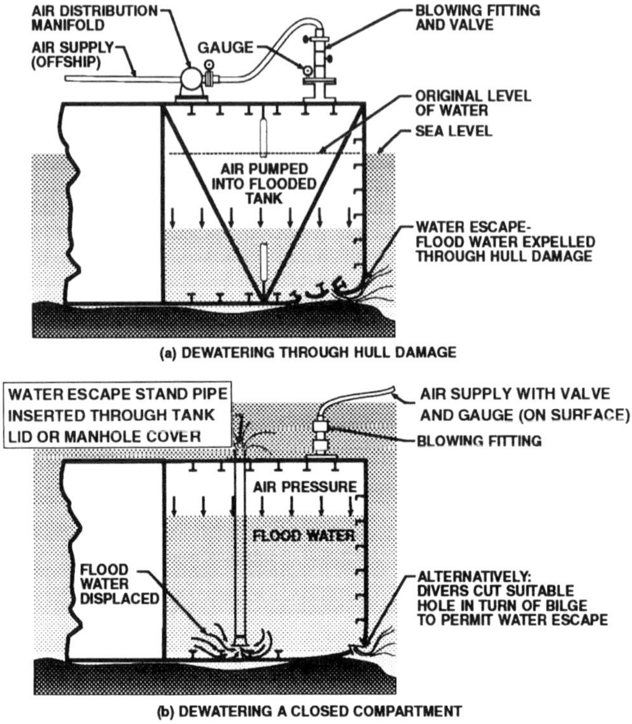

Fig. 9-27. Blowing operations

clude tankers and other single-hull ships with few deck openings, barges aground on rocky bottoms, and other cases of severe bottom damage. Older books on salvage discourage compressed air dewatering; this one does not. Improvements in underwater welding technology and in epoxies and other sealing compounds give salvors better tools for sealing for blowing than were available some years ago. Concurrently, through improved air compressor and blower technology, higher-volume, lighter-weight, more reliable compressors and blowers have become available.

Blowing a space with compressed air recovers buoyancy by replacing floodwater with compressed air (figure 9-27). The floodwater is either forced out of damage or other openings at the bottom of the space or blown up standpipes. The top and at least part of the vertical sides of the space to be blown must be airtight. A significantly higher degree of tightness is required than for pumped spaces, because air leaks through small holes much more rapidly than water does. A statistic accepted by salvors is that air leaks four to six times as fast as water through the same hole. The space must either have damage in or near the bottom or have a standpipe that reaches very near the bottom. Neither buoyant volume of the space below open damage on the vertical sides nor buoyant volume below the end of a standpipe can be recovered. In any space containing unrecovered buoyancy there is free surface.

Compressed air has the disturbing habit of not staying where you put it. It migrates to the high side of the casualty and can find its way out of apparently perfectly sealed spaces. Migration of air can destroy planned buoyancy distribution, give rise to free surface in unexpected spaces, and even result in disruption of longitudinal stability when it enters long, narrow tanks.

In salvage, spaces are blown with compressed air when that is the most efficient, cost effective, technically feasible, and least labor-intensive method of recovering buoyancy. On many occasions blowing is the obvious choice and considering other methods serves no purpose. At other times, blowing is a doubtful starter. Whichever is the case, in a particular casualty the salvage plan must be subject to a thorough and detailed engineering and operations analysis of structure, stability, and feasibility.

Salvage Compressed Air Theory

Air compressors or blowers are rated by discharge pressure in pounds per square inch gauge (psig) and flow rate in standard cubic feet per minute (scfm). The conditions defining a standard cubic foot of air are:

Pressure:	14.7 psig
Temperature:	68 degrees F.
Relative humidity:	36 percent
Density:	0.0750 lbs/cu ft

The behavior of air with changes in pressure or temperature conforms to Charles's Law and Boyle's Law. Volume varies directly with temperature and inversely with pressure. That is, at constant temperature:

Volume *decreases* as pressure *increases.*

Volume *increases* as pressure *decreases.*

At constant pressure:

Volume *decreases* as temperature *decreases.*

Volume *increases* as temperature *increases.*

Blowing Calculations

Blowing calculations in salvage are generally limited to calculation of:

The number of standard cubic feet needed to blow a space.

Blowing pressure.

The number of compressors or blowers.

Time to blow.

Unfortunately, conditions on a salvage site do not always match standard pressure and temperature conditions. One of the first steps in sizing the compressors or blower plant is converting the volume of the space in actual cubic feet (acf) at ambient temperature and pressure to standard cubic feet.

$$scf = acf \times \frac{D + 33}{33} \times \frac{T_A + 460}{T_W + 460}$$

where:

scf = standard cubic feet required to fill the space
acf = volume of the space in cubic feet
D = depth of water in feet
T_A = air temperature in degrees Fahrenheit
T_W = water temperature in degrees Fahrenheit

Omission of the temperature correction in the preceding equation introduces an error of only a few percent—usually less than 5.

The blowing pressure is normally a function of only the depth of the hole or standpipe through which the space vents. The pressure calculated is the maximum for the blowing operation. In a space venting through damage, the pressure to blow remains constant as the external hydrostatic pressure remains constant until the vessel rises. If a closed compartment vents to atmospheric pressure through a standpipe, blowing pressure decreases as the water level falls. Pressure must increase to allow for air line losses and friction. The pressure loss allowance is normally 2 psi.

$$P_B = 0.445 \times D \times P_L$$

where:

P_B = blowing pressure
D = depth of vent holes or standpipe inlet in feet
P_L = pressure loss allowance (usually 2 psi)

Calculation of the minimum number of compressors or blowers to dewater a space has three steps:

1. Calculation of the number of standard cubic feet of air to dewater the actual volume of the space under ambient conditions by the method described above.
2. Division of the quantity of air needed by blowing time to determine the necessary flow rate.

3. Division of the total flow rate by the flow rate of individual compressors or blowers to determine the number of compressors or blowers.

Three steps are also necessary to calculate the time to blow with a particular compressor or blower plant:

1. Calculation of the number of standard cubic feet of air to dewater the actual volume of the space under ambient conditions by the method described above.
2. Calculation of the total capacity (scfm) of the compressor or blower plant.
3. Division of the actual volume by total capacity to determine the blowing time.

Blowing Operations

This section, like the equivalent one on pumping operations, is a collection of notes describing practices proven by experience. Blowing a ship with compressed air is not an easy undertaking. Even more than pumping, blowing demands an orderly approach and meticulous attention to detail.

Making the ship tight enough to hold air is the first step of any blowing operation. All leaks must be sealed. The cumulative effect of many small leaks can become serious and affect the outcome of the operation. Tankers and other ships with relatively few deck openings can be sealed with less work than general cargo ships, bulk carriers, RO/ROs, and other types where cargo handling requires large hatchways. Making ships airtight is time-consuming, labor-intensive, expensive work, particularly if the ship is submerged. The labor requirements and expense often are the prime factors in a decision against salvaging with compressed air. Hatches and other large openings are very difficult to seal and require heavy structures designed for the purpose to resist the air pressure acting upon them.

Whenever possible, the hatches should fit under the deck and close with pressure. A patch similar to a Tooker patch can be built for single-entry spaces, but it is not easy to get a good seal with these patches. A bead of silicone rubber sealant under the seating surface, around the inside of the top of the patch, and across the hinged surface helps. In practice, such patches are likely to be more trouble than they are worth. If it is not practical to put replacement hatches under the deck so they seat with pressure, hatch replacements can be fabricated and fit to the outside. A simple hatch replacement can be made from flat steel plate—½-inch plate is usually sufficient with pipe couplings welded in for blow/vent and discharge fittings. The most practical way to attach the hatch is to weld studs to the deck and bolt the hatch down; if welding on deck is not possible, J- or L-bolts may be used. For hatches up to about 24 inches, eight ¾-inch bolts are enough. To effect a seal, a soft neoprene gasket about 1 inch square (for hatches up to 24 inches) is glued all around the hatch. A heavy bead of silicone rubber sealant laid under the gasket makes a better seal, particularly where the deck surface is rough or uneven. Larger hatches should have proportionately thicker plate, more bolts, larger bolts, and heavier gaskets.

The basic fitting for blowing (figure 9-28a) consists of:

A spool piece fitted to a vent pipe or set over a hole cut in the compartment boundary.

A flange normally bolted to the spool piece and fitted with a pipe nipple and a gauge.

A valve, usually a quarter-turn valve, but often a gate valve, for precise control, connected to the pipe nipple.

A second pipe nipple on the valve with a Chicago, Cam-Lok, or other suitable air fitting on the end.

A gauge fitted to the flange. Gauges should be fitted to the flange rather than the inlet line. On the inlet line they register incorrectly when air is flowing. The gauge is very important for indicating pressure in the compartment and preventing overpressurization. The gauge must be located at the point where air flow is controlled, so that the person controlling the air knows the pressure in the compartment.

Compressed air delivery systems must be planned thoroughly. Delivery of air from the compressors or blowers to volume tanks, and distribution from the volume tanks or directly from blowers by manifolds serving groups of spaces and giving central control, is highly recommended. Manifolds are of two types: (1) those that serve solely as a distribution header and (2) those that are both distribution and control devices (figure 9-28b). Both types have check valves on the inlet side of the manifold. Inlets may be on one or both ends as the air supply system indicates. The distribution and control manifold has both control valves and gauges and is intended to be used for blowing a group of spaces from a central location. Note that the gauge is mounted on the discharge and readings can be affected by flow. Accurate readings are obtained by closing

Fig. 9-28(a). These blowing fittings consist of a blank flange tee with a gate valve connected by a European-style fitting to a low-pressure hose. The gauge is mounted clear of the air flow so that readings will not be affected by the flow.

the valve, then taking the reading. Steel rather than PVC is the preferred material for manifolds—particularly control manifolds that have heavy valves and fittings—both because a steel manifold is more rugged and because PVC pipe working pressure is derated if the temperature of the working fluid is greater than 73.4 degrees F. For instance, allowable working pressure of PVC pipe at a temperature of 90 degrees F. is derated by 25 percent and at 110 degrees F. by 50 percent. The working pressure also decreases with increasing size and is halved if threaded ends are used. PVC pipe suppliers can supply technical data on their pipes.

Hoses, pipes, or a combination carry air from the manifold or volume tank to the spaces being blown. Hoses are preferable for higher-pressure systems. Schedule 80 PVC piping, 3 inches and greater in diameter, is usually quicker, easier, and cheaper to set up and use than hoses when low-pressure blowers supply air and large volumes of air are flowing at low pressure and the control valve is on the manifold. Hoses attached to one or both ends by Cam-Lok fittings give the system some flexibility and eliminate the need to fit the system together precisely. Metal or plastic tags with identifying codes should mark both hoses and valves. Identification marks can be painted directly onto pipes. After all connections are made, the lines are traced individually and the tags double-checked before admitting air.

Fig. 9-28(b). Distribution and control manifold used with the blowing fitting shown in figure 9-28(a). Flow may be controlled from either the manifold or at the fitting. It is usually better to open the valve on the manifold and control the flow where the gauge is. Gauges may be ganged at the manifold and the flow controlled there with the valve on the fitting left open. Valves on the manifold also permit using only a few connections on the manifold.

Hoses and pipes are kept as clear as possible of open deck spaces and high traffic areas to prevent damage. Hoses and pipes running along together are bundled and always lashed down.

Installed piping systems, such as bilge and ballast piping or tanker inert gas piping, make excellent air distribution or venting systems.

There is a danger of overpressurizing and damaging or rupturing the space. This danger is greatest when blowing starts and air space is limited. Pressure can build rapidly in the limited space with the admission of a small amount of air. The air control valve should be just cracked open to begin, not opened either widely or abruptly. Pressure should build slowly and should be monitored carefully. The vents must be large enough to allow water to flow out as rapidly as an equivalent volume of water flows in. If they are not, pressure increases in the space and may cause damage to or even failure of the structure. If pressure begins to build past the planned point, blowing is secured until the outflow can catch up and the pressure drops to within limits. Venting is particularly important in sunken ships, as an increasing air volume vents as the ship rises. If there is any question about the adequacy of the vents, make some more.

Perhaps a sound measure of the hazards of blowing with compressed air is the very sound and highly recommended practice of putting compressors or blowers, controls, and receivers on a platform alongside rather than on the casualty. The reason for doing this is simple and practical. If the casualty goes out of control on rising, the compressors or blowers on the casualty can be lost. A corollary is that the hoses between the receiver and blowing connection must part, or have a fitting, rather than dragging the receiver, compressor or blower, and control station over the side—an event sure to cause anxiety and to delay the operation. The practice is seldom necessary on large, stable vessels.

As with pumping operations, blowing operations call for a high level of redundancy in the air compressor or blower plant. The degree depends upon the circumstances and the type and reliability of the machines. It is false economy to have too little redundancy. The machines are not the entirety of the pumping plant. More than enough fittings, hoses, gauges, tools, spare parts, fuel, and lubricating oil must be present—not just at the salvage site, but where they can be found and used.

The temptation to jack up the blowing pressure to drive water out faster is always present. There is little point in doing so. Jacking up the pressure does only that; it does not increase the volume of air entering the space with time. Volume is controlling; one cubic foot of air replaces one cubic foot of water. For fast displacement of water, low-pressure, high-capacity compressors or blowers are a better choice than high-pressure, low-flow machines.

Even with the most careful and attentive sealing program, some leaks occur when air is first admitted. These leaks are difficult to plug because of the pressure. They can be marked and sealed with epoxy, sealing compounds, or a concrete wash when the pressure is off the space. If leaks must be sealed under pressure, a solid plug driven in firmly is likely to be better than a semiliquid that the air can blow through.

Stability, particularly the development of free surface, is a major consideration in determining the sequence of blowing compartments. It is seldom possible to remove all free surface from a space by blowing. Worst case assumptions should be made about stability and precautions taken whenever the possibility of a stability problem exists. Pneumo-fathometers, water levels, or vertical poles painted in horizontal bands mounted at both bows and quarters of the casualty and monitored at the central blowing station make changes in list and trim obvious early. Cranes alongside taking a strain or barges lashed in tightly to serve as outriggers add additional stability.

Blown ships normally rise one end first; sometimes as planned, sometimes out of pure orneriness. Limiting trim prevents air from spilling from vent holes in high end compartments losing buoyancy and perhaps causing the ship to sink again.

Stopping the blow before the water level reaches the vent holes or standpipe can limit the buoyancy in a space. The volume remains about the same on ships sunk in shallow water, but in deep water expands as the external hydrostatic pressure decreases, adding buoyancy without any control.

Just as a sunken ship is about to rise, large numbers of bubbles appear in a rough outline of the ship. The ship will probably leave the bottom quickly, accelerate, and come to the surface with great ebullition. Workboats, barges, and other surface craft should be pulled clear and secured to prevent collisions with the rising casualty.

Capsized ships may be refloated upside down. Sealing the bottom of a ship is much easier and quicker than sealing the deck because there are so few openings. Spill pipes are located on the centerline to reduce the likelihood of off-center pockets of buoyancy developing. Tests have shown that the stability of inverted ships is good, but some effort must be expended to keep it that way. Although inverted ships may be brought quite high out of the water, it is best not to raise them higher than their tank tops. With this low freeboard, the center of buoyancy is high and the metacentric height positive.

Removal of top hamper from inverted ships may be necessary for towing out of ports and through channels. This can be time-consuming work, but it is better to take the time to do it well rather than to bring the ship so high that her stability is low. It is practical to raise the ship temporarily to pass shoals.

Some very large ships have been raised inverted. In some cases, air locks similar to those described in Part 1 of this chapter were fitted and the ship was divided into sections. Salvors' crews working under pressure inside the ships prepared one section at a time. When all sections were ready the ship was raised. These were remarkable operations. It is highly doubtful anything like them will ever be repeated. Technological improvements in underwater cutting and the availability of large lifting equipment make cutting up wrecks and lifting them out piecemeal more practical and less expensive.

Air locks have been fitted to upright ships to allow salvors to enter the spaces and work inside to prepare them for blowing. This, too, is a rare practice in modern marine salvage.

A ship floating on a bubble always loses some air while it is under tow. Air is lost through an imperfectly sealed small leak or leaks opened in the seaway or through the bottom as the ship rolls and pitches and pressure changes. Some way of replacing the lost air must be provided. Ways of furnishing additional air include:

- Compressors, blowers, or air banks on board tended by riding or boarding crews.
- Hoses made up into the space and stopped off and supplied from compressors or blowers in a workboat. This method is a fair weather method, for it requires the workboat to come alongside to pick up the air fittings and to remain tethered to the casualty while the air is refreshed.
- Hoses made up to the spaces and tracing or paralleling the towline to blowers on the towing vessel. This method requires particular attention to be sure the hoses remain longer than the towline and that none of the towing load comes on the hoses. Towing loads on air hoses can quickly cause the hoses to fail with catastrophic results.

The choice of method depends upon the particular job, including place, length, season of the tow, equipment on hand, and preferences of the salvage master. A means of refreshing the air in the tow is always provided for a tow on a bubble.

Blowing operations have two critical phases. The first, planning the operation and selecting the equipment, is completely controllable and requires only time, thoughtfulness, and thoroughness. The second, the period from the casualty breaking ground until it is secure on the surface, has some element of chance. Thoroughness in the first critical phase and throughout the operation can reduce the role of chance.

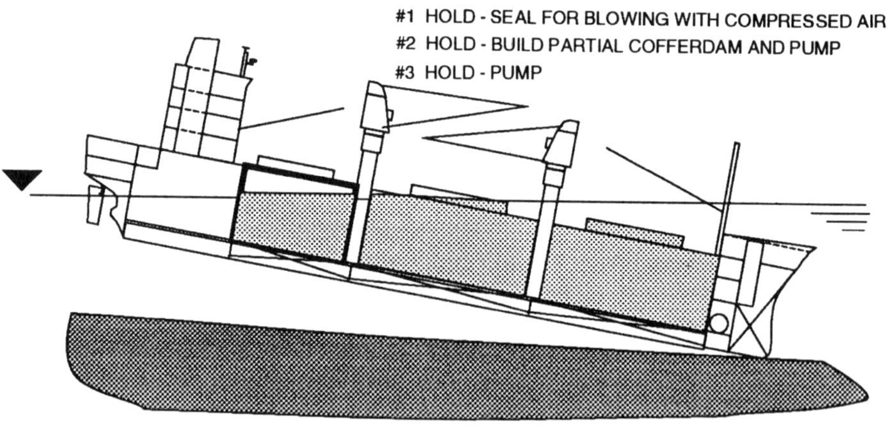

Fig. 9-29. Pumping and blowing in the same operation

On occasion, the position and condition of the ship may call for pumping in one space while blowing in the other. These are cases such as that shown in figure 9-29 where the work involved in preparing the spaces is quite different. As with almost everything in salvage, there are no hard and fast rules; each case has its own merits.

Pumping and blowing together also may limit the differential pressure in adjoining spaces. Such combined pumping and blowing operations are difficult to conduct and coordinate. A good preliminary analysis and appreciation for all the factors is mandatory.

Additional information on blowing operations, specifically those on tankers with inert gas systems, appears in Chapter 13.

10

LIFTING

In salvage lifting a vertical force, other than self buoyancy, acts on the casualty to stabilize it, augment its buoyancy, or to raise it bodily. Only two means can produce this force: (1) mechanical lifting or (2) another vessel rigged so its buoyancy acts on the casualty. Historically, pontoons were the best way to generate large vertical forces. Pontoons have taken many forms—flexible and rigid bodies, purpose-designed salvage pontoons, ad hoc pontoons, and special lifting craft usually set up for tidal lifts. Pontoons, like wooden patches, remain in salvors' bags of tricks but now run second in importance to mechanical lifts. The evolution came as technology developed to allow construction of derricks and sheer legs with thousands of tons of lifting capacity, and the production of wire rope and other rigging that make heavy lifts possible.

Because pontoons lift with buoyancy, the amount of lift is a function of the volume of the pontoon minus its weight. Large lifts require very large pontoons, or a very large number of smaller ones. Unfortunately, the difficulty of handling pontoons appears to increase exponentionally with size and number. The difficulty of rigging and handling the units is a major consideration in selecting the type of lift. Mechanical lifting is normally much easier and more positive than dealing with large pontoons or a group of pontoons.

While most salvors operate some lifting equipment, salvage and wreck removal applications alone do not justify the capital outlay required to build and operate large cranes. These vessels find their primary employment in offshore and marine construction. Offshore construction cranes and sheer legs are very expensive. A well-planned operation keeps them on site no longer than absolutely necessary. Planning the lift includes planning passing wires and lift slings and doing as much other rigging as possible before the arrival of heavy lift equipment.

Lifting by buoyant or mechanical lift, or both, can combine with restoration of buoyancy. The bases for the choices are: the least work to accomplish the job, availability of lifting equipment, its suitability for the particular work, and economics. The percentage of the vertical force that lifting supplies is critical to the decision. Lift forces of 25 percent or less of the total vertical force act primarily as stabilizing and control forces that supplement self-buoyancy. When the lift force reaches about 70 percent of the total vertical force, self-buoyancy supplements lift by reducing the external lift required and providing a margin of safety.

In combined operations, unless very unusual conditions exist, self-buoyancy is recovered first and the lift applied second. With this sequence, patching and pumping or sealing and blowing, work with a high level of schedule unpredictability is under control before expensive lifting equipment comes in. The same principle applies in combined pontoon and mechanical lifts. Pontoons, devices often possessed by demons, are rigged and tested before rigging mechanical lifts. The same sequence of self-buoyancy, pontoon lift, and mechanical lift is followed in both the preparation and the actual lifting operation.

LIFTING BASICS

Size and Distribution of Lift

The size of the lift and self-buoyancy must be great enough for the job and have a margin to allow for unknowns. The size of the margin depends upon the type of lifting equipment, its availability, the method of rigging into the casualty, and the degree of accuracy of the total lift calculations. No hard and fast rules exist for determining the margin. Selecting it is a matter for the combined professional judgment of the salvage master, salvage engineer, and lift equipment operator. The absolute minimum margin over maximum lift is 10 percent. A more judicious margin is near 25 percent.

Sunken vessels gain weight between the time of their sinking and the time of their refloating. This weight gain can have a profound effect on any lift. It can easily eat up and exceed the planned margin. It cannot be avoided. The source of the weight gain is sand, silt, and mud settling out of suspension in the water inside the ship. Silt is surprisingly insidious; it enters the hull in large quantities through every possible opening.

During the surveys of the wreck and planning for the lift, an estimate is made of the volume of mud or silt in the wreck or section. Siltation of the wreck can be expected to continue at about the same rate between the time of the initial estimate and the lift. The best way to obtain a weight on the material in the wreck is to take a sample and weigh it. In the absence of the weight of a sample, a density of 100 pounds per cubic foot (1600 kg/m^3) is a reasonable estimate.

When lifting equipment cannot raise the casualty bodily, it can lift one end as a step in recovering additional buoyancy.

Engineering and operational considerations combine for choosing the location of lift points. Lifts should:

1. Center on structure inherently strong enough or easily reinforced to carry the lifting loads.
2. Be distributed to give satisfactory shear forces and longitudinal bending moments in the hull of the casualty.
3. Be distributed along the length and across the breadth of the casualty to give the desired trim and heel.

The shear force, longitudinal bending moment, trim, and heel during the lift depend upon the combined action of weight, buoyancy, and lift. In longitudinal bending moment calculations, lifts should be considered as point or distributed, upward-acting, vertical loads applied at the point of lift. Often, the age and condition of a wreck being lifted is such that detailed structural data for the wreck are not available. A reasonable approximation of the section modulus or allowable bending moment can be made by starting with the minimum section modulus or maximum bending moment allowed for a ship of that size by a classification society. If the hull is damaged or badly deteriorated, the chosen number should be reduced by a factor reflecting a subjective judgment of the condition of the hull. Trim and heel depend upon the position of the lift forces relative to the centers of gravity and buoyancy of the hull. Suitable locations for lifts may be calculated by summing moments of weight and buoyancy about any convenient point. The initial planning points for lift location are determined by compromising between ideal solutions for local strength, longitudinal strength, heel, and trim.

Operational considerations such as water depth alongside the casualty, and restrictions on passing lifting slings may limit placement of lifts. Flexibility in varying the size or placement of individual lifts gives a greater chance of success in lifting at the desired trim and heel.

Passing Lifting Slings

In most large lifting operations lift wires or slings pass under the hull of the casualty. The cranes or pontoons apply the lift force to the slings. Passing lift wires is usually diver-intensive work, thus it also can be the most tedious and time-consuming part of the entire operation. As with all diving operations, current and tide may limit the hours when work is possible and stretch out the operation. It is good practice to pass all lift slings before the arrival of lifting equipment to reduce the amount of time the expensive equipment is on site.

The particular requirements of company-owned equipment are known to the salvors, but that of hired equipment may not be. It is imperative these requirements be determined before starting to pass slings and that they be complied with exactly. Whenever conditions force changes, the changes should be checked out with the company operating the lifting equipment before the work is undertaken. A delay to do things properly the first time is much less expensive than a delay to redo them.

The way the vessel rests and the type of sea floor are the major factors in determining how to pass lift slings. As with just about everything else in salvage there is no single right way to do the work. Imagination and ingenuity backed by common sense, good seamanship, and good engineering practice always have a place.

Direct reeving is the easiest and usually the quickest way to pass lifting slings. Stern apertures and hawses are convenient and very strong points with built-in restraints for reeving slings. When the wreck rests on a rocky or very uneven sea floor, there may be locations where the ship is proud of the sea floor and slings can be rove through the gap. Such a situation is extremely fortunate with other than small wrecks. If the opportunity is there to reeve any lifting sling directly, take it.

Lift slings are usually passed through tunnels or sawn into place rather than rove directly. Sawing and tunneling are hard work and hard service for the sling. A small messenger should be the first line through, both because it is easier and faster to handle and to spare the lift line the abrasion accompanying the first passage.

Sawing is the one method of passing slings that is not diver-intensive. The messenger is hauled back and forth under the wreck while being moved longitudinally toward its planned position. Sawing requires a relatively soft sea floor, a ship without impalement or bottom damage that can stop the progress of the wire, and a more-or-less upright ship with one end clear of the sea floor to allow the sawing to get started.

One method of sawing uses two small tugs or workboats. After divers place the messenger in starting position under the ship and shackle in lines from the workboats, the workboats run at full power to haul the line as far under the ship as possible. When they are brought to a halt by the resistance to passage, the boats go ahead alternately sawing the wire into position.

In a second method, vessels with winches moored on each side of the casualty and past the location of the lift wire haul the working line back and forth while keeping a tension in the direction of sawing. The process usually works best when a shot or two of chain is shacked into the center of the messenger so the chain does most of the actual sawing. This method is suitable for harder soils and for moving obstructions like debris.

There are also two methods of placing wires by sawing. The first is to saw all messengers in from one end to the farthest position first and work backward toward the starting end. Sawing the first wires is more work, but this method gives assurance of no impalements or instructions to stop sawing the wire all along the length. The second method saws wires in from both ends, placing the wires near the midships section first. The best solution is to saw wires from one end as far as possible. When further sawing is blocked, then saw wires in from the other end. Where obstructions block wires from both ends, wires can be passed by tunneling.

Tunneling is by far the most difficult way to pass lifting slings. The principle of tunneling, like that of most salvage operations, is simple; the execution is difficult. Tunnels are usually constructed by divers jetting away sea floor material with water pressure. The bottom of the ship forms the tunnel overhead so there is no chance of the tunnel roof collapsing on the diver.

A means of removing the spoils—usually air lifts—is a necessary part of the tunneling operation. Jetting in a tunnel creates a large quantity of material that must be removed from the immediate area. The sides of the tunnel, never as cooperative as the roof about not collapsing, also generate spoils that must be removed. It has been practice in the past to carry spoils down current and return them to the sea. In the existing environmental climate, this may not be possible as the sea floor soil may be polluted. This condition prevails primarily in harbors with a history of dumping or inflows of pollutants. When return of the sea floor material to the sea in the immediate vicinity is not permitted, spoils must be taken to scows or barges and disposed of at sea or in landfills. The large amount of water carried along by airlifts further complicates the problem and may require a drying operation to reduce the mass of material being handled.

The initial step in tunneling is excavation of a pit 6 to 7 feet (2 meters) deep alongside the wreck from which tunnels can be driven under the wreck. The width and depth of the pit depends upon the type of sea floor soils; mud and other soft soils that flow easily into the pit require a larger pit. The angle of the sides of the pit must be less than the angle of repose of the sea floor material. Soft soils allow a more gradually tapering side than clay or hard sand sea floors. The pit can be cut away with jetting nozzles and the spoils carried away by airlifts. If time is of the essence, it can be most cost-effective to bring in a suction cutter dredge to dredge a trench the length of the wreck and as far under the wreck as practical.

When the pit is complete, a working face is jetted on the side under the ship and gradually worked forward by washing away soft soils or cutting away the base of the tunnel and undermining the remainder in hard soils. A second airlift is brought in to remove the spoils from the tunnel. A hose attached to the end of the airlift pipe can be carried into the tunnel by a second diver and swept back and forth carrying the spoils away as they are generated.

In some soils it speeds up the tunneling operation to jet through a 1- or 2-inch pipe forced 10 or 15 feet (3 to 5 meters) into the working face. The jet through the

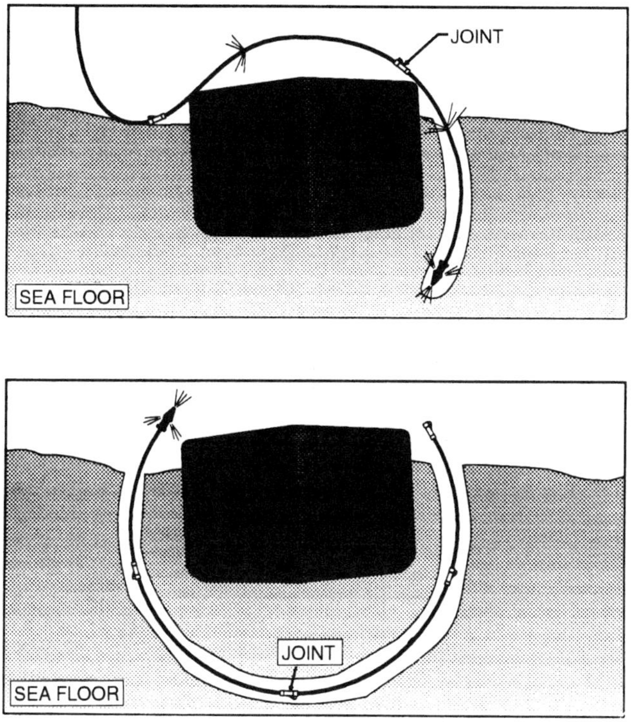

Fig. 10-1. Tunneling lance operations

pipe starts to break up the sea floor material. For the last section the pipe can carry a messenger wire that a diver on the far side can pick up.

Tunnels may also be driven by attaching a reaction nozzle to a pipe and driving the pipe through the tunnel face. For long tunnels, sections of pipe are screwed together to make up the correct length. A messenger wire can be shackled inside the pipe and led through each successive section so the messenger arrives at the far side as soon as the tunneling lance does. The messenger is stopped off on the far side and the lance withdrawn with the messenger as a guide. Alternatively, the messenger may be made up outside the lance and run through shackles welded on successive sections. On the far side the messenger is stopped off and the lance pushed on through the tunnel with each guide shackle being released as it comes through.

The reaction nozzle deserves some discussion. The principle of the reaction nozzle is that a portion of the water flow is directed away from the jetting stream to balance forward and after flow through the nozzle. In most commercial reaction nozzles (figure 10-2a), a slight majority of the flow is to the rear so the nozzle has

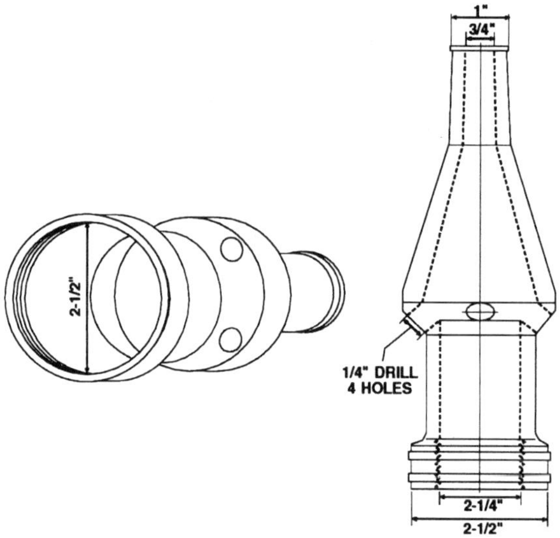

Fig. 10-2 (a). Jetting nozzle. Courtesy of U.S. Navy.

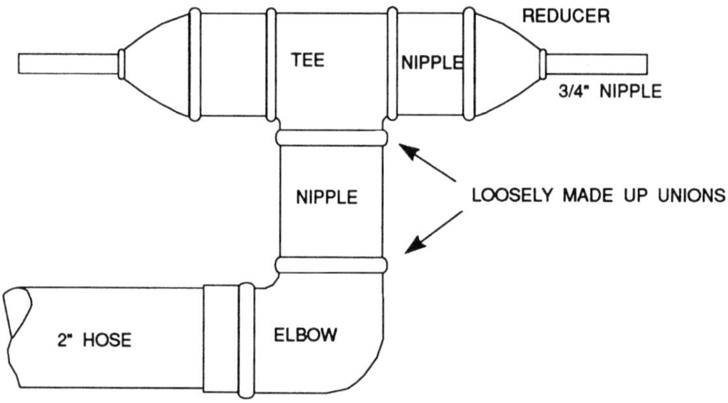

Fig. 10-2 (b). Simplified jetting nozzle.

a net forward thrust. These same nozzles distribute the flow around the periphery of the nozzle so at least one jet is directed at the diver. Divers generally do not find this pleasant. A simple combination of pipe fitting can be made into a tee-shaped nozzle that is very efficient in hand-held jetting (figure 10-2b). The commercial-type reaction nozzle is better for lancing because the forward thrust helps drive the lance.

Once the messengers have been passed, they can haul the main lift wires through. Single wires are passed by connecting their eye to an eye in the end of the messenger with a Baldt- or Kentner-type connecting link (preferably) or a shackle.

The wire and the connecting hardware are likely to have a pretty rough ride under the wreck. To prevent screw pin shackles from coming unscrewed the pin should be seized to the shackle or a safety shackle with a nut and cotter key used in lieu of a screw pin shackle.

It is often convenient to pass more than one lifting wire with a single messenger. The most convenient way is to shackle two lifting lines and a messenger to an ordinary flounder plate. Theoretically, the wires should hold their position but there is a tendency for the plate to roll and the wires to become twisted as the plate bounces between the sea floor and the ship's bottom. If the two wires are a twinned pair, the twisting makes little difference. If, however, the wires are to be moved away from the passing location, it is better to pass them individually and avoid the hassle of twisted wires. Reeving plates for passing more than two wires may be made by cutting holes in triangular plates or welding eyes to them to accept shackle pins (figure 10-3).

Lift wires that have lifting eyes may be shackled directly to the messenger or reeving plate. Wires that are to be secured with Bullivant clamps need no eye. A reduced eye made with half the strands of the wire rope can be made in these wires and shackled to the messenger wire or reeving plate. The reduced eye has only a fraction of the strength of the original wire rope and should never be used for lifting.

PONTOONS

The principle of pontoons is simple. A buoyant body, flooded or collapsed, and rigged tightly onto the casualty, is blown dry or inflated until it provides buoyant lift to the casualty. In a variation, the tidal lift, the combined buoyancy of the casu-

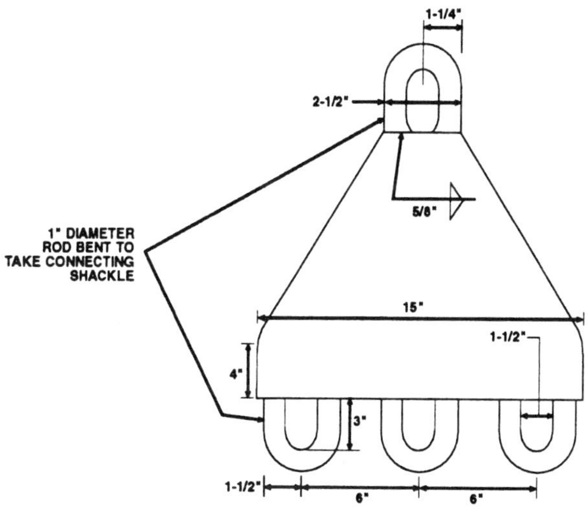

Fig. 10-3. Reeving plate with three welded-on eyes. Courtesy of U.S. Navy.

alty and lift craft, acts so they rise together with the tide and move to shallower water where the casualty again grounds and the process repeats. In both pure pontoon and tidal lifting, the pontoon or lift craft and the wreck form a single system of buoyancy and weight that must be treated as a single vessel.

Pontoons are available in two types: collapsible pontoons or lift bags, and rigid pontoons. Lift bags are the more modern, while rigid pontoons have a long history in major salvage operations. Rigid pontoons are quite heavy for the buoyancy they provide, are difficult and unpredictable to handle, and are labor-intensive—usually diver-intensive—to rig.

Collapsible Pontoons

The bulk and handling difficulties inherent in rigid pontoons make the idea of light, easy-to-rig, collapsible pontoons very attractive. Many types of collapsible pontoons, most made of rubberized fabric, have been tried since the early twentieth century with varying success. One of the outstanding successes was the raising of the tug *Hero* in Sydney Harbor with twelve Brizay 30-ton capacity lift bags. Following World War II, the U.S. Navy sponsored a development effort that led to the purchase of 15-, 25-, and 40-ton parachute-type pontoons. The devices proved practical in field tests, but found little use in field salvage and were eventually disposed of. Later events led the U.S. Navy to develop and keep in its salvage inventory a collapsible, cylindrical rubber pontoon with a lift capacity of 8.4 tons. This pontoon—some 10 feet (3 meters) long and 7 feet (2.1 meters) in diameter when inflated—folds to a package 54 × 70 × 20 inches (137 × 179 × 51 centimeters) for storage. It weighs 750 pounds, a little heavy for a collapsible pontoon of this capacity. The pontoon is a fully enclosed bag; therefore, a relief valve is fitted to prevent overpressurization as ambient pressure decreases on ascent. Despite its considerable weight and size, the pontoon is much easier to handle and rig than rigid pontoons.

The development of tough, impregnated, and coated fabrics has led to construction of collapsible pontoons that are lighter and more easily handled than the 8.4-ton pontoon. These pontoons, made in the enclosed and open bottom (parachute) types, are available in standard sizes from 1 to 35 tons with larger sizes available on custom order. Figure 10-4 shows typical inflatable lift bags.

The transfer of load between the pontoon and the lifting sling is of major con-

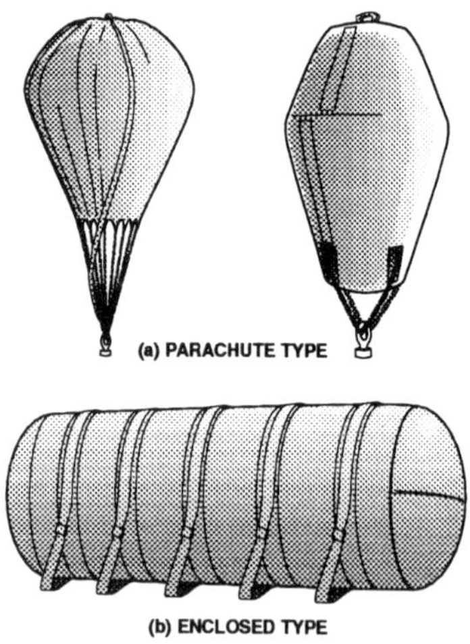

Fig. 10-4. Typical inflatable lift bags. Courtesy of U.S. Navy.

cern in collapsible pontoon design. Early pontoons used elaborate harnesses laid over the pontoon bag. The Navy pontoon has a plate with an eye bolted to a flange through the pontoon. A chain running the length of the pontoon connects and carries the load to the far end. Modern stitching and fabric bonding techniques allow fabric harnesses integral with the bag structure. Pontoon harnesses are set up to be shackled directly into lifting slings or onto pad eyes welded onto the casualty.

Enclosed bags that float horizontally and have two securing lines are best rigged to pad eyes. It is well nigh impossible to get two lines passing under the wreck to carry the same load. Without perfect load distribution, enclosed collapsible pontoons will trim, distort, and lose efficiency. Parachute bags rigged in pairs with a single line are preferable for most other lifts. No more bags than necessary to make the lift should be rigged. Excessive lift can produce very rapid ascent rates that can, in turn, result in loss of control, distortion of the bags, instability, and buoyancy dumping.

The total quantity of air to fill the collapsible pontoons may be calculated by:

$$V = 1.3 \times (\Sigma W \times p_a)$$

where:

V = total air requirements in cubic feet

1.3 = a constant multiplier to allow air loss

ΣW = the total displacement volume of the collapsible pontoons in cubic feet

p_a = pressure at depth in atmospheres

With the total air required known, the time to fill the bags from a specific compressor plant or for the compressor plant to fill the bags in a specific time can be calculated by solving the equation:

$$v \times t = V$$

where:

v = total compressor capacity in cubic feet

t = time in minutes

for the desired quantity

Enclosed bags are best suited for shallow lifts where venting is relatively minor and for tows where the forward motion of the tow distorts parachute bags and may dump buoyancy. In almost all other cases, parachute bags provide a smoother and easier operation as their buoyancy and overpressure are more easily regulated than the enclosed bag type.

The lightness and relative ease-of-use of collapsible pontoons come with a price. That price is fragility. While the material in collapsible pontoons is tougher than in the past, it is not as tough as the steel of rigid pontoons. Collapsible pontoons can snag, tear, and puncture. Pontoons should be handled with their fragility in mind. Layout areas should be cleared of objects that may damage pontoons, and pontoons should not be dragged more than absolutely necessary. Best practice is to keep them off the ground as much as possible. They should be rigged clear of objects such as pier structure or damaged plating that may reach out and get them. Collapsible pontoons are not a good choice for placement inside the casualty because of their propensity to snag when inflated.

Rigid Pontoons

Salvage companies and military salvage organizations throughout the world built rigid salvage pontoons in varying sizes up to 500 tons (figure 10-5). The U.S. Navy developed 60-, then 80-ton steel salvage pontoons for the classic submarine salvage operations undertaken between the world wars and kept them well into the 1970s. When operations showed their shortcomings, these pontoons underwent the constant evolution that only governments can afford. Most pontoons built for salvage no longer exist. A considerable number of pontoons suitable for salvage, but built for other purposes, do exist. Many structures—almost any sturdy cylindrical structure—can serve as improvised pontoons.

This chapter contains several disparaging remarks about the behavior of pontoons and the difficulties of handling them. These remarks are justified. Anyone who has handled rigid pontoons can testify that they are truly the spawn of the devil. They come by their bad behavior honestly. It derives primarily from their shape and construction. A thorough understanding of the bases of the behavioral

Fig. 10-5. Large (500-ton capacity) rigid pontoon of Russian design. Photo courtesy of Captain David Hancox.

problems in pontoons can save any salvor who would undertake to improvise pontoons or use purpose-built pontoons hours of grief and frustration.

Most pontoons are right circular cylinders because that shape gives the maximum practical volume in the smallest and lightest structure. Vessels of circular cross section are special shapes in naval architecture. The metacenter of a circular cross section always lies at the center because the shape of the waterplane does not change with inclination. A homogenous section, like a log or an empty cylinder, has its center of gravity at the same spot so that no righting arm develops as the cylinder inclines. To develop some amount of transverse stability and to give a floating pontoon a positive metacentric height, weight must be distributed to move the center of gravity below the center of the cylinder. Achieving this effect may mean adding significant amounts of weight that pound-for-pound reduce the lift of the pontoon.

In modern submarines, placing the center of gravity below the center of buoyancy under all conditions assures continuous stability. The stability of a submerging pontoon is analogous to that of an older submarine, in that the center of buoyancy rises from its initial position below the center of gravity until it passes and lies above the center of gravity. When surfacing, the reverse occurs. The pontoon is stable in both cases, but undergoes a moment of instability when the centers of gravity and buoyancy coincide. In practice, this must happen so quickly that the instability does not take effect. The salvor cannot dawdle when surfacing or submerging a pontoon.

Dry, floating pontoons are usually very stable longitudinally on the surface because of their large longitudinal metacentric height. When they are fully submerged, longitudinal stability, like transverse stability, totally depends on the separation between the centers of gravity and buoyancy.

Free surface is a serious hazard to the stability of pontoons. Because pontoons lose their buoyancy by flooding the interior rather than external ballast tanks, a large free surface exists throughout the flooding process. Where no transverse watertight bulkheads divide the waterplane, both the transverse and longitudinal moments of inertia of the free surface are approximately equal to the corresponding moments of inertia of the waterplane. Free surface in an undivided pontoon virtually destroys both the transverse and longitudinal stability. In both divided and undivided pontoons, the free surface effect increases until the water level reaches the centerline of the tank; then it begins to decrease as waterplane rises and the surface area decreases. Whether the free surface completely disappears depends on the configuration and subdivision of the pontoon.

An additional problem occurs when an undivided pontoon pitches and a mass of water moves the length of the pontoon and impacts on the low end. The dynamic effects exacerbate the longitudinal instability caused by free surface.

Some pontoons are divided so that some compartments are completely full and others dry when the pontoon is about neutrally buoyant. This arrangement can eliminate free surface when the pontoon is flooded completely, reduce the free surface effect on both transverse and longitudinal stability during the flooding process, and reduce the dynamic effect of the sloshing water. In pontoons not so divided, the initial position of the center of gravity must lie far enough below the center of the pontoon that it stays below the center during the greatest virtual rise caused by free surface. When the situation permits, it is an excellent idea to install transverse bulkheads in improvised pontoons.

Rigging pontoons tightly to the casualty restrains them so they cannot roll or pitch dangerously or capsize either transversely or longitudinally.

Pontoons are by design large-volume, light structures. They float at shallow draft with great sail area. The result is predictable. They wander from wherever they are wanted with the slightest breeze or current. Unless the pontoon is constructed so that one compartment can be flooded completely, the pontoon should not be flooded to increase draft. The stability decrement from free surface can more than offset the gain in handling.

Under water, pontoons handle most easily when they have either slight negative or slight positive buoyancy. The correct amount of buoyancy is difficult to realize; the pontoon is usually too heavy or too light. Even when the ideal state is achieved, tender stability makes pontoons difficult to handle.

Their size, handling difficulties, and stability combine to give pontoons their evil reputation. Operations with pontoons require careful attention to detail, meticulous planning, great care, and the favor of the gods.

Pontoons are necessarily rugged. Their difficult handling characteristics mean that they will routinely impact other pontoons and craft. The structure of pontoons should be heavy enough to withstand casual impacts and should have wood, heavy rubber, or energy-absorbing plastic strip sheathing to resist heavier impacts and prevent holing by concentrated loads. The structure and sheathing mean additional weight, but the weight is small penalty to pay for the ruggedness. Rigid pontoons can absorb mistreatment, contact, and damage that would destroy flexible rubber or fabric collapsible pontoons.

There are several methods of rigging and placing pontoons. No hard and fast rules apply. Pontoon placement and attachment are tailored to the particular casualty and the conditions at the site. Figure 10-6 shows three of the most common methods of rigging pontoons. In the first, slings passing under the casualty hold the pontoons together. The casualty and pontoons do not function as a unit; the pontoons act like a buoyant craft lifting an unattached load. The casualty is free to render and adjust itself to its equilibrium position in this arrangement. Unless the pontoon has a centerline hawse through which the lift wires run to securing devices on top of the pontoon, it is difficult to rig the pontoon tightly to the wreck. A loosely rigged pontoon will work in any seaway, impacting the casualty and creating a risk of ripping away hoses and lines.

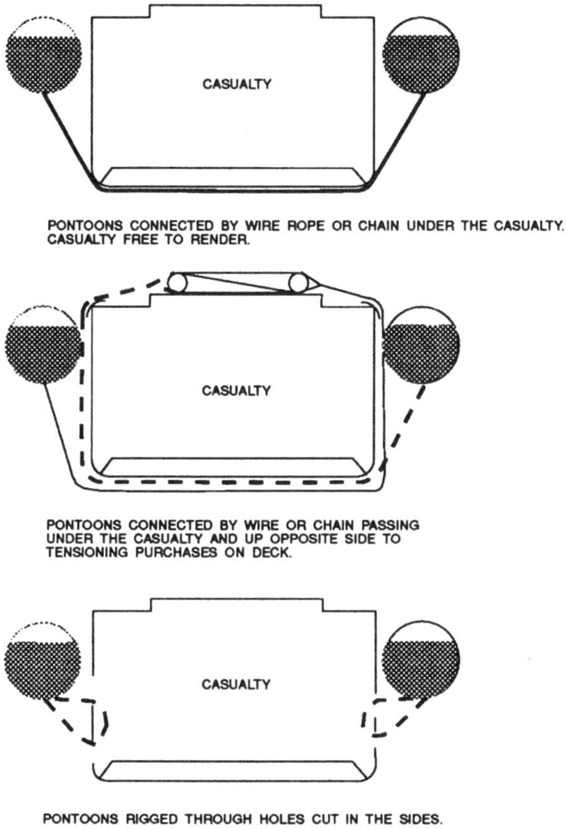

Fig. 10-6. Some methods of placing pontoons

The second method shown solves the tight rigging problem by having the pontoon lifting wire led under the wreck and up the opposite side to purchases that can be hauled to cinch the pontoon in tightly. The pontoons and casualty act like a single craft, the pontoon behaving like a sponson, increasing the stability of the unit. The method is suitable when the wreck has sufficient dry deck space to accommodate the purchases and winches, or when a false deck can be built above the surface for them.

The third method suits wreck removals that allow holes in the hull for reeving lift chains. Lines from the pontoon to deck fittings hold the pontoon against the wreck and prevent excessive relative motion. In a variation of this method, the lifting wires or chains are shackled to pad eyes welded to the hull or attached by purpose-built brackets or gussets.

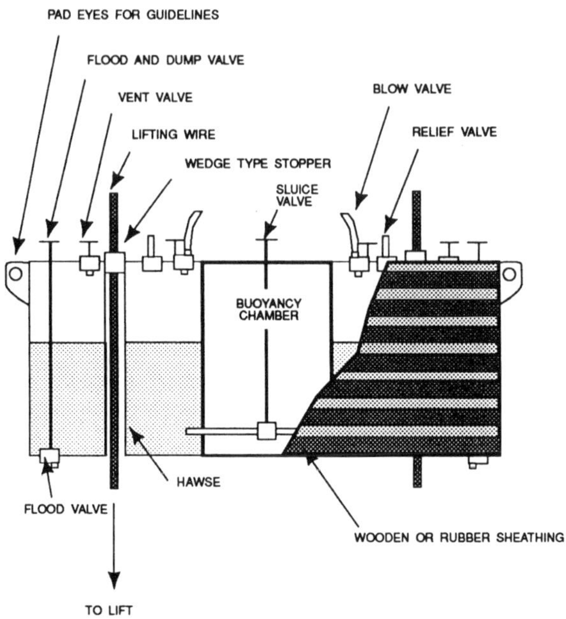

Fig. 10-7. Rigid salvage pontoon schematic

The methods illustrated in figure 10-6 are far from the only means of rigging rigid pontoons. They may be placed inside cargo holds or other large open spaces where self-buoyancy cannot be restored. They can be doubled up the side of the ship. The only limitations on their placement are the room available, practical handling and rigging, and work necessary to place them. Normally, when placed alongside, pontoons work in pairs rigged together or to the ship to prevent inducing asymmetrical buoyancy.

Figure 10-7, a simplified schematic, shows some features common in purpose-built salvage pontoons. The pontoon shown has two major floodable end compartments and a center buoyancy compartment. Other arrangements may include a larger number of compartments and tanks to control trim.

The two floodable compartments are operated independently, through individual flood, vent, and blow valves. The flood valve, which also serves as the discharge for blowing water from the space, must have a large port area for both flooding and discharging rapidly. The flood valves that double as vents are large enough to accommodate the expansion that takes place during an uncontrolled rise of the pontoon without permitting over-pressurization. Each compartment also has a pressure relief valve to prevent over-pressurization of the compartment. The relieving pressure of the valve should be easy to reset at each depth of use. While the compartments normally operate independently, a valved sluice line allows balancing the water level in the two compartments.

The pontoon shown in figure 10-7 has centerline hawses through which wire lifting ropes secured by wedge-type stoppers pass. This is only one of several possible arrangements. Lifting chains and suitable stoppers, including bars through links with the stud removed, may replace the wire ropes. Chains and wire ropes may be shackled directly to pad eyes on the bottom of the pontoons or to lifting bridles made up to pad eyes on the sides or top of the pontoons. Hauling tightly before setting the stopper can take almost all slack out of slings passing through a centerline hawse. Slings made up to pad eyes or bridles necessarily have more slack than those passing through hawses. If the slings are not equally tight, the tighter sling carries a larger share of the lifting load. The attachment point transfers the load on the lifting slings to the pontoon structure. It is very possible that a disproportionate part of the lifting load will fall upon a single attachment point. Therefore, each attachment point must be strong enough to carry the full lifting load of the pontoon.

As they are lowered into position, lines attached to pad eyes fore and aft guide and steady the pontoons. Each of these lines should have a breaking strength great enough to permit it to carry the submerged weight of the sinking pontoon. Markers on the lines show the pontoon's trim during lowering. Nylon, because of its stretch and potentially dangerous snapback, is not the best choice for these lines.

As much preparation as possible should be completed before bringing the pontoons to the scene. Towed pontoons should be especially well secured, for even in the finest weather, they tow poorly. Less than perfectly secured fittings and rigging may be carried away. Similarly, the salvage site should be prepared to receive the pontoons with lifting slings passed and all preparatory rigging done.

In keeping with their irascible behavior patterns, pontoons sometimes submerge very slowly. Air pocketing away from vent valves usually causes this behavior. The remedy is to blow some air through the vents to move the air around and to rock the pontoon longitudinally to move the pocket toward the vent.

Deep Lifts with Control Pontoons

Rigid and collapsible pontoons may lift completely submerged ships and other objects. In water depths much less than the length of the vessel, one end is raised while the other end remains on the sea floor (figure 10-8). The raised end is stabilized before bringing up the other end. In the water depths that would result in an inclination of more than about 30 degrees, it is usually better to raise the vessel in stages with pontoons rigged at different levels. The still-submerged vessel is moved into shallower water for the final raising.

The technique of raising with pontoons at two levels (control pontoons) (figure 10-9) came about through unhappy experience with ships raised in one step

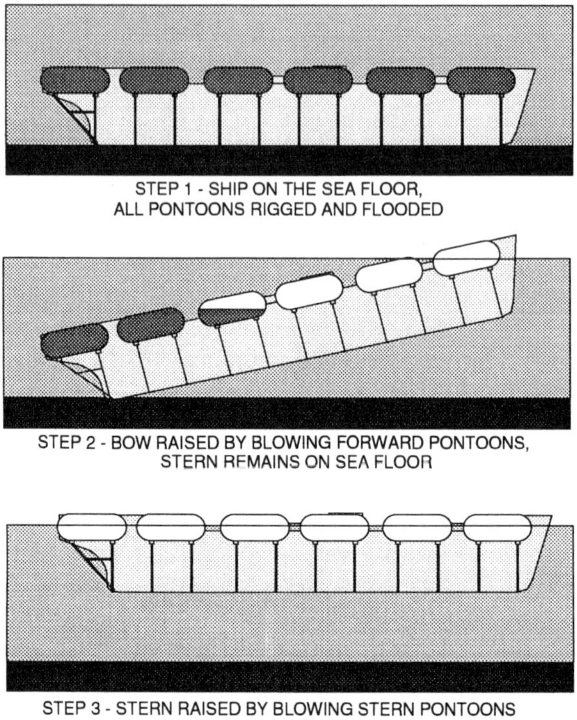

Fig. 10-8. Raising a ship in shallow water with pontoons

rising out of control, sometimes surfacing in unusual attitudes, or even sinking again in a mare's nest of rigging. The total buoyancy of the surfaced control pontoons and the main lifting pontoons equals the weight of the vessel so that the vessel-pontoon combination is in equilibrium on the surface.

TIDAL LIFTING

Tidal lifting, a variation of pontoon lifting, finds application where a large tidal range gives a significant lift distance and allows moving the casualty into shallower water in one tide cycle. In tidal lifts:

1. A cradle of wire ropes passed under the casualty and clamped on deck make one or more securely moored, ballasted lift craft fast to the wreck.
2. The craft are deballasted so the regained buoyancy of the lift craft equals or exceeds the total weight of the lift craft and casualty.
3. Tidal rise lifts both the lift craft and the casualty off the sea floor.

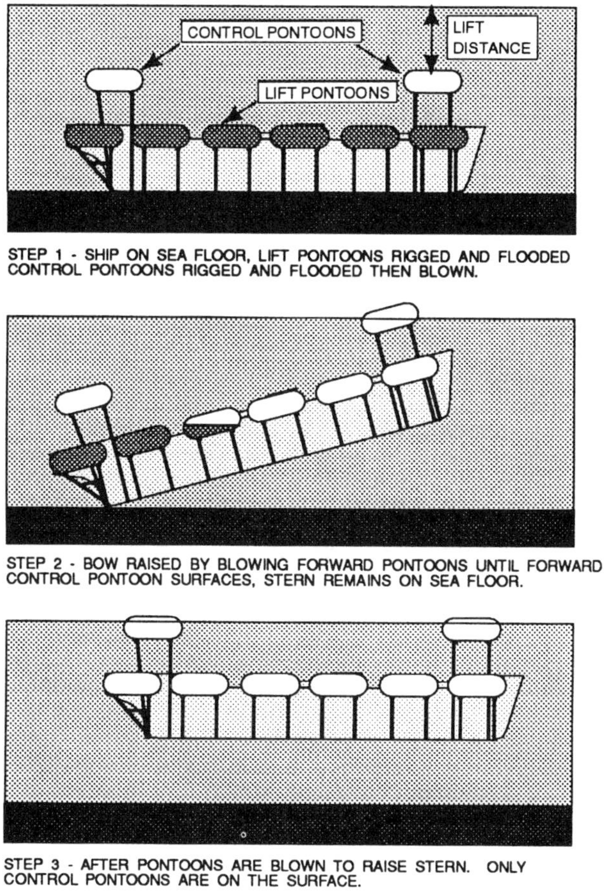

Fig. 10-9. Raising a ship with control pontoons

4. When the vessels float, the lift craft slip their moorings and move to shallower water to ground the casualty. The casualty can move again in a series of tidal lifts to water shallow enough for refloating by pumping.

Figure 10-10 illustrates the tidal lift process.

Salvors, operating in regions where conditions favor tidal lifting, built special craft with lift capacities of up to 2,400 tons. The craft normally operated in pairs, one or two on either side of the wreck. Some larger craft had deck tackles for mechanical lifts. Most of these craft disappeared with the increasing availability of heavy lift derricks and sheer legs. The tidal lift technique still has value, as barges

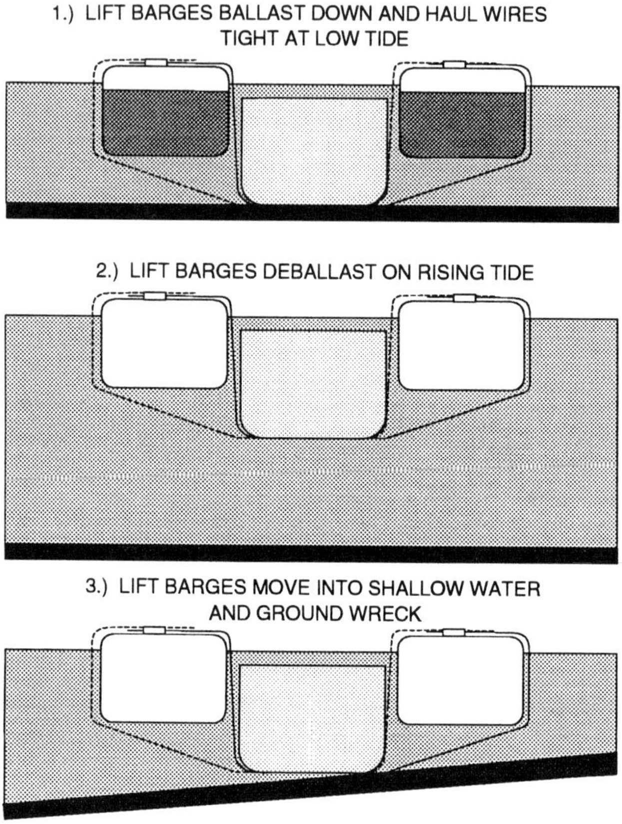

Fig. 10-10. The tidal lift process

or floating drydocks can be converted to lifting craft as a solution to a particular problem. Figure 10-11 shows a tidal lift with four 750-ton lift craft.

While lift craft normally operate in pairs, a single craft can make a lift directly under herself—a belly lift (figure 10-12). The bottom of the lift craft limits the belly lift as the lift craft must clear the wreck. The lift craft must set the wreck down in a new position and move clear before the tide falls away and sets her on the wreck. Without an unusually great tide range, it can be very difficult to find a location to set the wreck where she is dry enough for pumping at low water.

Operating tidal lift craft is not as simple as it appears above. The operation requires very careful and thoughtful coordination to make sure everything goes reasonably well. Ideally, the crew should be trained and practiced in operation of the lift craft. This ideal cannot always be reached with converted lift craft and crews who do not make tidal lifts frequently. Many things can go wrong and many details require coordination; it is foolhardy to try a tidal lift without as many rehears-

Fig. 10-11. A tidal lift being made with four 750-ton lift craft, two on each side of the sunken dredge

als and as much practice as it takes to give a good level of comfort for the real thing.

In the most common practice, lift craft moor on either side of the wreck with the wreck between them. The mooring must be heavy enough to support the entire nest of lift craft and wreck in the tide and current conditions expected during the operation. If the lift craft have the necessary winches, the wreck can be moved a short distance in the moor. This type of move is a very touchy operation that must be well coordinated and carried out with utmost care. For most moves, the moor should be rigged with pelican hooks for easy slipping. The vessel must be under positive control by enough tug power to control the nest in the currents at the site. The moor at the destination should be in place before the lift and configured for rapid pickup and securing.

A cradle of wire ropes supports the casualty. In side lifts, the wires run over the inboard (wreck) side of one lift craft, under the wreck, under the other lift craft, and up the outboard side. The wire twins with a second wire run just opposite. Bullivant clamps clamp the twinned wires together on deck. Clamping the twinned wires with Bullivant clamps leaves the lift vessels and the wreck free to render and find an equilibrium position in the bights of wire rope. Some lift craft had deck edge clamps to secure the lift wires. While the author prefers that the lift vessels be free to render, either method can produce satisfactory results.

Rope yarns of any convenient absorbent line—manila is best, but difficult to find—pad Bullivant clamps to absorb the grease squeezed from the wire rope dur-

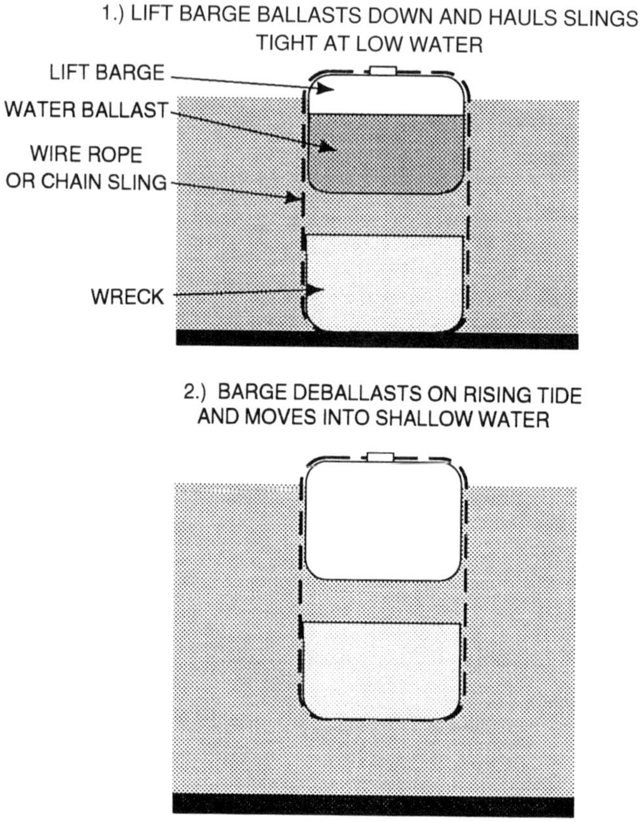

Fig. 10-12. Single craft belly lift

ing the lift. Unabsorbed grease lubricates the clamp, allowing wire slippage and load shirking.

Wires are tensioned as evenly as possible to distribute the load properly among them. The usual method is to:

1. Ballast the craft down.
2. Haul the wires tight as quickly as possible and set the Bullivant clamps.
3. As the tide starts to rise, and the wires begin to surge, set the clamps hard.

The entire pinning-down procedure and the setting of the clamps takes time. Even with perfect coordination and an expert crew, there is simply no possibility of achieving an absolutely even load distribution. The unevenness of the load distribution should not be so great that some wires are overloaded, but unbalanced forces that the craft accommodates by rendering can be expected.

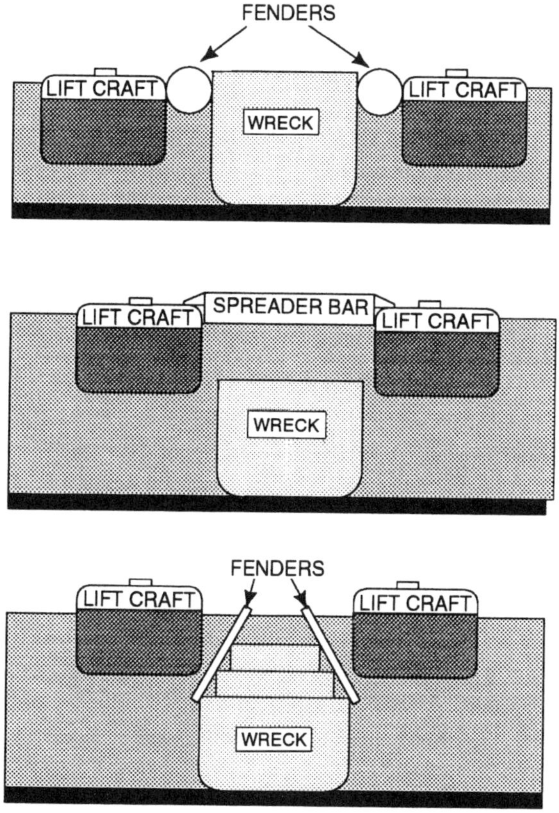

Fig. 10-13. Three methods of fendering or spreading lift craft

During the lift, the craft acting under unbalanced forces tend to move together. Some type of fendering keeps the lift craft apart. Figure 10-13 shows some methods that can keep the craft in the proper position. Spreader bars placed beyond the limits of the lift are one of the most effective methods, but are impractical if the lift is longer than the lift craft. Note that the relative position of the wreck and lift craft do not change during the entire procedure.

When handling large-diameter lift wires on improvised lift craft, a long boom crane on a flat deck barge is a great help in moving and positioning wire rope bights and ends.

Deballasting should begin promptly on the turn of the tide or just before if the craft is pinned down. The craft do not begin to rise until ballast equivalent to the weight of the lift has been removed. This amount of ballast must be removed before the tide rises over the lift craft deck.

When the wreck is in her new location and the lift craft moored securely, the clamps are slacked on all craft so the wreck cannot hold the lift craft down on the rising tide. One crew considering the day done and going off to supper without releasing the lift wires could have disastrous results. On purpose-built lift craft, the lift wires are made up to large bollards provided for this purpose and the Bullivant clamps slacked. On improvised lift craft without the large bollards, the Bullivant clamps are slacked carefully and the wires surged slowly so the wire does not run away with the ends scything across the deck. Emergency release of the wires can be very dangerous. Flame cutting of tensioned wires is stupid; it is far better to have small charges that can be placed quickly and detonated remotely to cut the wires. Whenever wires are released in an emergency, all hands should stay well clear, because the ends may flail about with immense energy.

MECHANICAL LIFTING

In mechanical lifting, mechanical force replaces the natural forces of buoyancy and tidal rise used in pontoon and tidal lifts.

Two methods of lifting are seldom seen in modern salvage, but are described here because, like tidal lifts, an opportunity to use them occasionally arises. These methods entail jacking and lifting with winches from two barges made into a sort of catamaran pontoon by the addition of a bridging structure.

A pure jacking method passes chain slings through centerline hawses and under the wrecks. The chains are stopped off to the upper jacking plate. As the system reaches the limit of jacking, the chain is stopped at the lower jacking plate and the upper plate and jack reset for another go. When applied in the past, these jacking systems were slow and labor-intensive. If the work allowed development and construction of an automated system, jacking systems might find new life. The idea is not dead; jacking has been employed in setting bridge sections, but the author knows of no recent applications of jacking in salvage lifting.

For small wrecks two roughly equal-size barges can be bridged with a structure—beams, logs, bridge trusses—that can carry the full lifting load (figure 10-14). Purchases can then be hung off the bridging structure and hauled by winches on the decks of the barge. The bridging structure must be soundly landed and secured on the barge and must extend all the way across the barge to reduce upsetting moments.

Many ships built as salvage ships, many salvage barges, and lifting barges have rollers on the bow for lifting. With these vessels the lifting wire makes up to the sling and to a purchase on deck. Winches haul the purchase. In variations of this type of lift, two Dutch salvage barges have hydraulic rams that replace the purchases and winches and some U.S. Navy ships haul the wires with linear hydraulic pullers. On most of the salvage barges, the same system can pull horizontally.

The principle of the deck purchase lift is so simple and so universally understood that it is possible to convert almost any seagoing flat deck barge to a lift barge that can make a suitable alternative to more expensive equipment. The

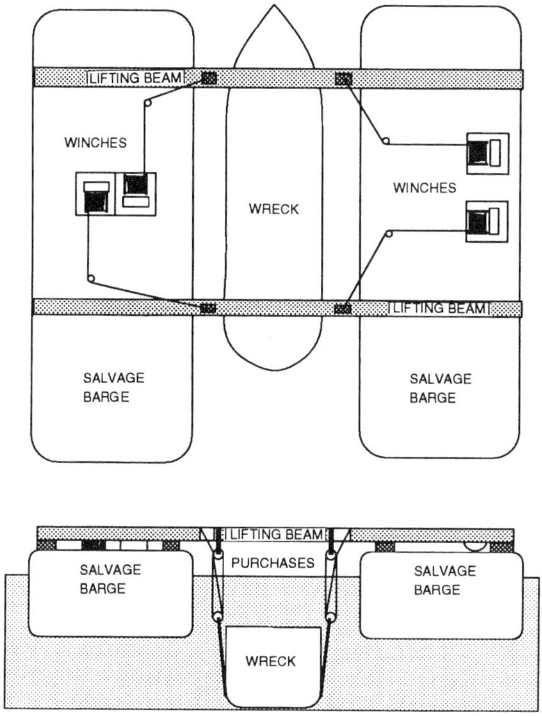

Fig. 10-14. Mechanical lifting with two barges

amount of lift that the barge can produce depends on the power of the lifting system and the reserve buoyancy of the barge. Installing a very powerful lifting system on a barge that will be pulled under by a load equalling only a portion of the lift system capacity is not recommended. In addition to size, overall hull strength to carry the lifting loads and local strength to support the winches and rigging is critical in barge selection. Bow lifting craft and ships normally have sheaves sized for the lifting wire over which the wire bends. The sheave makes a suitable bending surface for the wire and a low friction roller over which the wire moves with few losses. Ideally, sheaves can be constructed for the barge and fitted before taking the barge to the site. Sheaves may not always be practical. When they are not, a section of pipe of the proper diameter to bend the wire over may serve. A three-quarter section of pipe is welded across the forward deck edge and vertical pipe guides are placed to keep the wires from sliding transversely. A pipe installation has more friction loss than a sheave. Undersized pipe giving a sharper bend in the wire than is desirable can be used, but the load-carrying capacity of the wire rope decreases as a function of the ratio of the diameters.

The number of purchases, the number of sheaves in the blocks, the reeving wire, and the winches should all match the lift and the size of the barge. Four sets of purchases on each barge are about the maximum that can be managed effectively. A separate double drum (waterfall) winch should haul each purchase. The best winches for this service come packaged with engine and gearbox on a single foundation. These packages are available from industrial equipment suppliers and equipment rental firms with almost every major manufacturer's winches. It is highly desirable that the winches and purchases be identical. A mishmash of equipment assembled ad hoc in the finest tradition of the practical salvor is very likely to lead to an operational nightmare for a heavy lift.

Because of their experience, most salvors think primarily in terms of purchases for pulling and lifting. Linear hydraulic pullers, common in civil engineering projects such as bridge building, and all types of hydraulic rams provide some interesting alternatives and are worthy of consideration in designing pulling and lifting packages.

Two tools—salvage sheer legs and offshore construction derricks—when used properly for the proper job are superior lifting devices for salvage. Both are products of modern technology that has allowed their construction. The sheer legs are built for salvage and find utility in other work. The offshore construction derricks were a necessary outgrowth of offshore oil and gas exploration and production. For them, salvage is an aside.

Sheer legs have been used in ports and harbors and in salvage work in protected waters for a very long time. Since the mid-1960s a number of salvage sheer legs mounted on self-propelled barges have been built (figure 10-15). These sheer legs are an evolutionary development of the fine salvage lifting craft that were built in northern Europe in the first half of the twentieth century. Like their distinguished predecessors, these sheer legs combine deck tackles and cranes to develop their total lift. The crane on the sheer legs is a self-erecting, boxed A-frame with two main hooks and, usually, a flying jib. The flying jib may or may not combine with the main lift, depending on the particular design.

While lifting sections of, or entire, sunken wrecks is the primary job of sheer legs, they have proven suitable for a number of jobs involving heavy weights in salvage operations, including chain cutting of hulls, demolishing wrecks with grabs, making stabilizing lifts, lifting to reduce ground reaction, and furnishing parbuckling forces.

Sheer legs have greater operational flexibility than tidal lifting craft because they are not constrained to wait for tides or forced to rush to be ready for a lift on a tide. If slings are passed and ready, sheer legs can begin hooking up as soon as they moor and rig their A-frame. The A-frame itself is a rugged structure built to accept the racking and misalignment that can occur in open sea operations. Figure 10-16 shows typical working arrangements on salvage sheer legs.

*Fig. 10-15. A salvage sheer leg making a lift.
Photo courtesy of Captain David Hancox.*

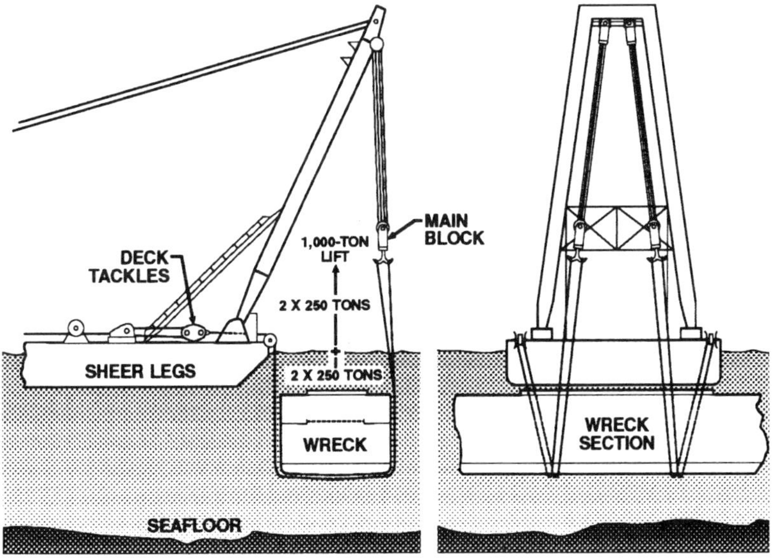

*Fig. 10-16. Typical working arrangements on salvage sheer legs.
Courtesy of U.S. Navy.*

Sheer legs are not huge and ungainly craft. The propulsion system gives sheer legs considerable freedom at the site and allows close work around the wreck without tug assistance. Tug assistance is needed when moving while supporting large lifts and for moves at sea. Relatively simple moors are adequate for holding sheer legs at the lift site.

The seagoing derricks that have developed as a result of offshore construction requirements can be excellent salvage lifting tools, or they can be inappropriate white elephants. These derricks are available in monohulls with capacities from 200 to 3,000 tons. Catamaran and semisubmersible cranes have capacities into the double-digit thousands. The barges required to support the cranes are so large that they easily support fabrication and construction facilities and accommodations. The results are large, integrated, floating industrial complexes. It is something of a paradox that the broad capabilities of these vessels militates against their use in some salvage operations. There are times when smaller, single-purpose tools can be combined into a more efficient and cost-effective salvage system.

Most derricks have a large, single boom whirly crane mounted on the stern. The crane normally has three hooks; the main hook has the rated capacity of the unit at a short radius, normally very near the barge. The auxiliary and whip hooks have substantially smaller capacities at greater radii.

Capacities can be increased by 15 to 20 percent in tied-down lifts, where the derrick is trained directly astern and secured so it cannot rotate. While the tied-down method gives a large lift capacity, it eliminates one of the major advantages of the whirly crane and one of the major advantages of the offshore derrick over sheer legs—the ability to rotate and reposition the load.

A number of other things limit derrick operations in salvage:

- Large derricks normally operate from a multi-point moor; moving them to reposition the lift is a major operation. Anchor-handling tugs are needed to lay, pick up, and reposition the moors, and tugs are required to move the derrick barge.
- The size and draft of a derrick barge may limit its ability to approach the lift and position itself where the derrick can be effective.
- Strict limitations on list, trim, and sea state can easily be exceeded in salvage.
- Offshore derricks are normally part of carefully planned, engineered, and structured operations that bear little resemblance to salvage operations. They are out of their element.
- They are hellishly expensive.

All of the above notwithstanding, they are wonderful tools—in the right application, such as that shown in figure 10-17.

Operating sheer legs and derrick barges is a very specialized business requiring a high degree of technical knowledge of lifting in general and of the specific

Fig. 10-17. Offshore derrick making a salvage lift

equipment. Salvors who hire in sheer leg and derrick operators should pay careful attention to what the operators tell them about how their equipment can be used and should be used in the specific situation.

Heavy lifts with this type of equipment require a great deal of detailed planning. In their normal operations, planning and preparing for a single lift may take months. In salvage, such periods are not available. Lifts must be planned and carried out quickly. Only by careful attention to detail, sound engineering, and following the plans in detail can the situation work. The modification of planned rigs in the field to make them fit the situation is common and necessary in salvage, but totally inappropriate in heavy lifting. Field modifications should be checked by engineers and planners no matter how much delay it causes—doing it over after a failure is more likely to be more expensive both in time and money than the delay necessary to do it right.

PREVENTING HULL AND LIFTING SLING DAMAGE

All lifts should be set up to reduce damage to the hull by the lifting slings and damage to the lifting slings by the hull. Critical points occur where lift slings bend over the deck of the lift craft or around the bilge of the vessel being lifted. There are two potential problems:

1. The pressure of the sling on the hull of the casualty may be so great that the sling slices through the hull, or
2. The bend in the sling may be so severe that bending stresses add to the tensile stresses in the lift sling and significantly reduce the load the sling can carry. If the load-carrying ability of the sling is reduced enough, the sling can fail—a potentially expensive failure in time and money.

While hull slicing can occur only where the sling contacts with the hull of the casualty, excessive bending stress can occur wherever the lifting sling bends. Increasing the radius of the bend and increasing the thickness of the plate against which the sling bears solves the hull slicing problem. Slicing is of most concern on lightly built vessels and those with tight bilge radii—vessels like small warships, pleasure craft, workboats, dredges, and inland and seagoing barges. It is exactly these types of vessels that are particularly good candidates for lifting. Increasing the bending radius of the sling and thereby increasing the ratio of bending surface diameter to wire rope diameter reduces the bending stress in the lift wire.

SLICING

The slicing problem is the most difficult to detect and to evaluate. Solution of the problem is in two parts. The first part determines the tension in the lifting sling, while the second part applies that tension along with the scantlings of the wreck to the particular problem.

Determination of the tension in the slings of cranes, derricks, sheer legs, and pontoons with vertical lifts is straightforward. Load-measuring systems form an integral part of most deck purchase, derrick, and sheer leg systems. When measuring devices are not part of the system, off-the-shelf load cells, strain gauge systems, or hydraulic tensiometers can be fitted. Any measuring device should be calibrated before use. Because lifting units may have a different capacity or their intended lifts differ, each should be considered individually.

Where there are no tension-measuring devices, the lifting tension in each sling is estimated as the total lift divided by the number of slings.

Tidal lifting craft present a more complex problem because each lifting sling has four parts, only two of which are vertical. Figure 10-18 shows the general arrangement of a tidal lifting sling. The sling is composed of two wires clamped together to perform as a single sling. Because one part of each wire is vertical and the other inclined, the tension in the two parts is not equal. The tension in parts 1 and 4, the vertical parts, equals T, while that in parts 2 and 3 is less, and equals $T\sin \Phi$, where Φ is the angle between the bottom of the lift craft and the wire rope. Φ cannot be measured easily in practice, but it can be obtained from quantities that can be determined: the depth of the bottom of the wreck below the lift craft at its deepest draft, that is, when ballasted at low water, and the beam of the lift craft, that is:

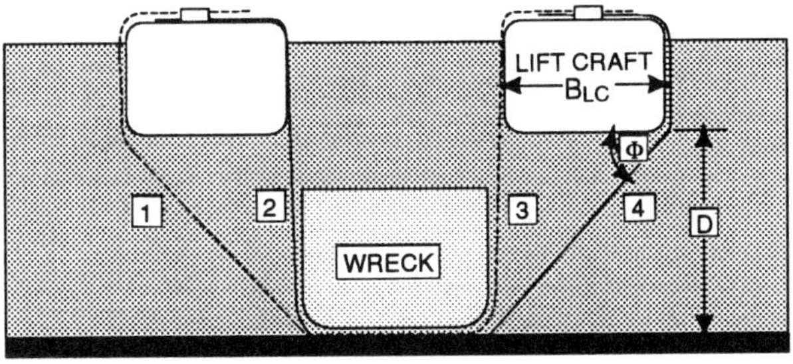

Fig. 10-18. Tidal lift tension diagram

$$\tan\Phi = \frac{D}{B_{LC}}$$

The total tension in the sling equals the sum of the tension in the parts or:

$$\frac{W}{n} = T_1 + T_2 + T_3 + T_4 \ldots. T_n$$

where:

W = the total weight of the lift in pounds

n = the number of *pairs* of lift wires

Then:

$$\frac{W}{n} = T + T\sin\Phi + T + T\sin\Phi$$

$$\frac{W}{n} = 2T + 2\sin\Phi$$

$$\frac{W}{n} = 2T\,(\sin\Phi + 1)$$

$$T = (\frac{W}{n})(\frac{1}{2\,(1 + \sin\Phi)})$$

The quantity:

$$\frac{1}{2\,(1 + \sin\Phi)}$$

is the tension factor. In any tidal lift, the weight, the number of pairs of lift wires, the beam of the lift craft, and the depth of the lift are known. By first calculating Φ, the tension factor can be calculated. The tension factor (figure 10-19) multiplied by W/n then gives the tension in each wire.

In any lift, hull stress can be shown by thin shell theory[1] to be the product of the wire tension, T, and a stress factor, S, or:

$$\sigma = T \times S$$

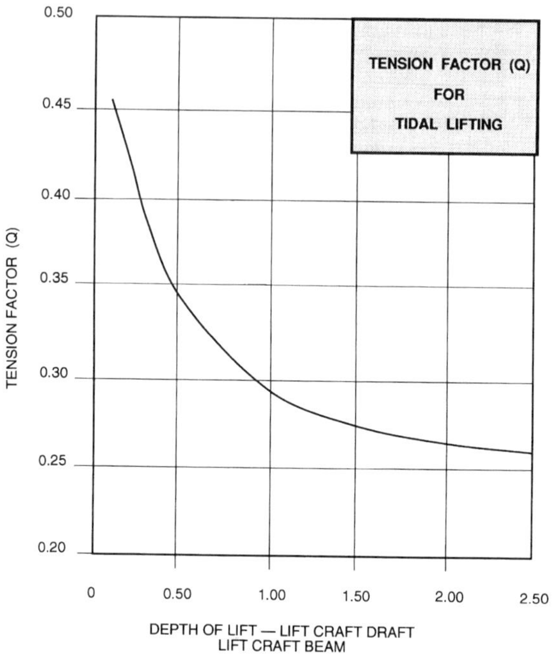

Fig. 10-19. Tension factor in tidal lifting

where:

σ = the hull stress in psi

S = the stress factor

The stress factor is defined by the expression:

$$S = \sqrt{\frac{9.470}{r^3 \times t} + \frac{0.203}{r^2 \times t^2} + \sqrt{\frac{22.42}{r^6 \times t^2} + \frac{0.959}{r^5 \times t^3}}}$$

where:

r = the bilge radius in inches

t = the plating thickness in inches

The expression for the stress factor appears daunting, but inspection shows that it is easy to calculate, especially with the help of a calculator or computer. Note that the stress factor decreases rapidly as bilge radius and hull thickness increase. Bilges with radii greater than 24 inches (61 cm) *and* thicknesses greater than 1 inch (25 mm) are unlikely to be sliced.

To prevent slicing or deformation of the hull, the stress, σ, must not exceed the yield strength of the hull plating. For most shipbuilding steels, a yield strength of 33,000 psi is a good value. In practice, a factor of safety of 1.5, giving a working stress of 22,000 psi, is recommended. With these criteria:

$\sigma = TS > 33{,}000$ psi	failure is probable
$22{,}000 \text{ psi} < \sigma = TS < 33{,}000$ psi	failure is possible
$\sigma = TS < 22{,}000$ psi	failure is improbable

Either increasing the bilge radius by fitting a larger radius bolster or increasing the effective hull thickness by fitting a doubler plate between the hull and lift slings can reduce the chance of hull damage. Figure 10-20 illustrates some typical bolsters that can be fabricated in the field.

Most purpose-built lift craft have heavy scantlings and well-rounded deck edges to prevent wires from slicing the lift craft. Slicing or plating deformation at the deck edge should be considered in outfitting barges or other vessels of opportunity for tidal lifting. It may be necessary to fit bolsters at the deck edge. The same type of bolsters are suitable for deck edges and bilges.

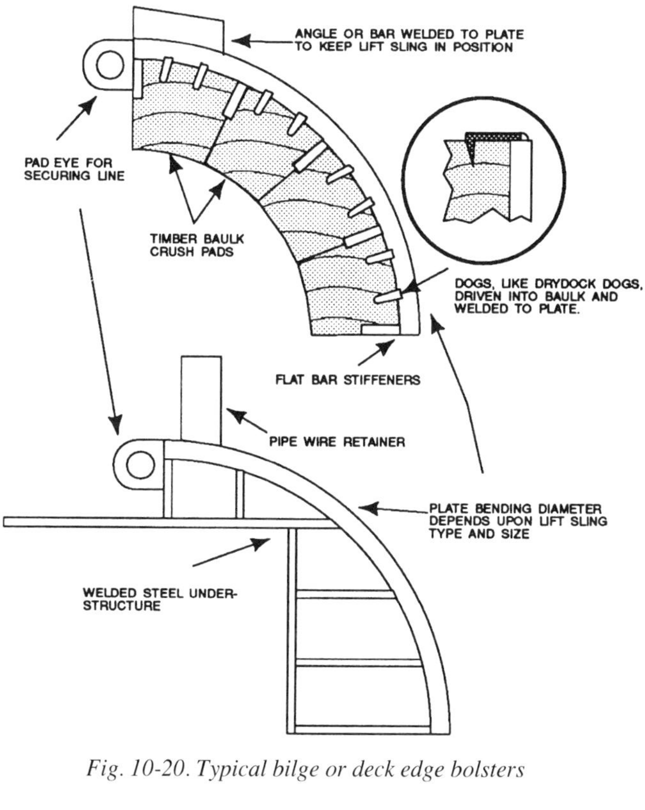

Fig. 10-20. Typical bilge or deck edge bolsters

Sling Bending

As discussed in greater detail in Chapter 7, any bending of wire rope, even by a few degrees, around a sharp radius significantly reduces its ability to carry tensile loads. Bending effects are local and are not cumulative. The overall strength reduction depends upon the sharpest of multiple bends.

To maintain wire rope lifting capacity at near 95 percent of its rated strength, the ratio of the diameter of the bending surface to the diameter of the wire rope (D/d ratio) should lie near 30. It is not always possible in marine applications, particularly when working with large ropes, to provide large radius bending surfaces. Sharper bends are acceptable if the breaking strength assumed for the wire rope is reduced to account for the bending and the acceptable loading is determined by applying an appropriate factor of safety. For instance, a bend with a D/d ratio of about 6 results in approximately a 20 percent loss of rope strength, a condition that may be acceptable for the planned loading. Chapter 7 discusses reduction in strength for bending quantitatively and the selection of factors of safety in wire rope applications.

Bolsters installed at deck edges and bilges where the rope bends can increase bending radius.

Chain also is susceptible to tensile strength reduction by bending. With chain, the minimum D/d ratio should be 7, based on the chain size.

MOVING AND SETTING DOWN A LIFT

A complete lifting operation has two distinct movements, a vertical movement to raise the casualty from the sea floor and a horizontal movement to take it to a new position. The foregoing parts of this chapter have addressed the vertical movement—the heart of any lifting operation. The horizontal movement deserves some small attention, for if this portion of the operation is not correct, all that went before may have been a waste.

Candidate locations for setting down the wreck should be selected during the preparation for the lift and all steps taken to insure the site suitability. The owner's permission to use the site must be obtained. Environmental regulations must be checked for restrictions on the use of the site for industrial purposes and for the possible interference with fish or wildlife habitats. Permission and concurrence of environmental regulators is a necessary part of the preparation to move a wreck, whether the wreck is to be disposed of there or just pass through the site.

Suitable sites must be surveyed for rocks, old wrecks, cables, pipelines, or other items that can cause damage or be damaged. When depositing the wreck in the dry on the bank, a walking inspection of the site suffices. Wet sites should be checked by divers or with wire drags or side scan sonars. Where the presence of buried wrecks or installations is suspected, sub-bottom profiles should be run. Accurate sea floor and sub-bottom surveys are particularly important in areas that have supported considerable industrial effort, as installations capable of damaging or impaling the wreck may have subsided into the sea floor. Sites used for legal or illegal dumping are especially prone to contain surprises. Such sites should be sampled and samples analyzed for contaminants that are likely to be a problem when moving the wreck again or disposing of the scrap.

Investigation of a site includes determination of depths, tides, currents, channels, sea floor installations, and traffic patterns between the original location and the relocation site. The effect of local and transient conditions on the transit should be planned and alternatives arranged.

Permission to move must be obtained from local authorities and arrangements made to close the area to traffic, or at least restrict traffic, during the move. Local authorities or coast guards may provide for policing traffic closures and keeping sightseers clear of the operation.

Some sort of hydrographic survey of the routes—primary and alternatives—between the original location and the set-down site is necessary to find any obstructions, shoals, hummocks, or the ilk that can impede or halt the movement. The surveys do not need to be sophisticated because of wide margins of operational safety; wire drags are adequate. In situations where wide margins are not possible and some refinement is required, side scan sonar surveys of the routes are advisable.

Lifting operations are fairly straightforward; they deserve, in truth they demand, careful planning and supervision to be sure they go as planned. Inattention to detail can result in a large, expensive, almost successful operation turning into an expensive fiasco in the blink of an eye.

There is simply no way all the methods of lifting in salvage and the nuances of their employment could be discussed in this short chapter, or in one many times its length. Salvage lifting is simple in principle but more complex in execution. The first secret lies in realizing that no one lifting tool is perfect for the work at hand; select the tool that best fits all the conditions. The second secret is in meticulous planning and attention to every detail; be flexible in carrying out the plans.

11

TOOLS AND TECHNIQUES OF SALVAGE

The other chapters of this book focus on narrow aspects of salvage and casualties. This one picks up the pigs and chickens—the miscellany that contributes to a salvage operation and fills the bag of tools salvors bring. The order of discussion does not reflect the importance of the subject. In fact, the order has no significance at all. What may be very important in one casualty may not even be a matter for consideration in another. All the subjects discussed here come to the fore eventually. The list of subjects in this chapter is incomplete because it is, in reality, infinite. Competent salvors expand it on every casualty.

SALVAGE SHIPS AND CRAFT

Salvage ships and craft range from "vessels of opportunity," a term applied to whatever salvors can come up with on short notice, to purpose-built ships. Purpose-built and converted salvage vessels vary widely in their characteristics and capabilities because those quantities depend very much on the work that ship does and where she operates.

The services any ship performs determine her characteristics. Nowhere is this more true than in salvage ships. Although both carry out salvage services and the specific services may overlap, a rescue tug differs from a multipurpose salvage ship; both differ from specialized vessels. Overlaps in services are very important in vessel design because they inevitably lead to compromises to give vessels broader capabilities at the expense of optimized characteristics for a specific service.

The economics of the salvage business prevent operators from having rescue tugs or multipurpose salvage ships waiting on station devoted to salvage operations. Salvage ships must earn their keep in routine workaday operations to be economically viable. This very real necessity also leads to compromises in the ship's design, usually at the expense of optimization for salvage tasks.

Other publications document the history and development of salvage ships and present articles[1] discussing salvage ship characteristics for specific services or regions.[2] This section repeats neither but discusses characteristics of good salvage ships and the advantages and shortcomings of some types that may be candidates for conversion or for use as vessels of opportunity. But, first, one comment on history and development. Economics have historically dictated converting existing hulls to salvage ships rather than building purpose-built vessels. The list of clever and very effective conversions is long and includes vessels ranging from gunboats to amphibious vessels to offshore supply vessels. Well thought-out new buildings have set high standards. *Salvage King,* built in 1925, became effectively the prototype for the British Admiralty's *King Salvor*-class ships and the U.S. Navy's *Diver*-class ARSs. More modern salvage ships show the influence of its good design for purpose.

Laymen and many mariners equate salvage with tugs for good reason; tugs are important in salvage operations for towing and ship handling, and to a lesser extent for pulling. Small tugs make convenient general service workboats. However, tugs lack the deck space needed to support salvage work or the accommodation required for salvage crew. Tugs also seldom have the space or deadweight capacity to carry quantities of or large individual pieces of salvage equipment. The characteristics of a good tug are not always compatible with those of a good salvage ship. On the other side of the coin, some salvage ships have good characteristics as towing vessels; others do not.

Most tugs optimized for a particular service move out of their element when pressed into salvage service. A large oceangoing tug designed for point-to-point towing service may be of little use in rescue towing and salvage service because of details of her design. These details include:

Deck machinery and appliances—Rescue tugs have a large complement of capstans, gypsy heads, gogging winches, Norman pins, fairleads, rollers, etc., to permit efficient handling of lines while attaching to and starting the tow. They also have a minimum of avoidable interferences—such as towing bows—so men may work effectively on the deck.

Bollard pull—A rescue tug calls for a high static bollard pull during the ship's most difficult operation: picking up the tow, stopping her drift, and getting her under way under tow, all in severe weather. High bollard pull is important in point-to-point tows because it translates into towing speed. Propulsion efficiency, so that a good pull is maintained through a broad speed range, is also a factor. In practice, bollard pull in point-to-point tows is a compromise between towing speed and fuel efficiency. Rescue towing permits no such compromise. Effectiveness in handling the tow is all-important and cannot be compromised.

The towing connection—A rescue tow must be specifically designed to have higher elasticity, particularly at short scope, than that of a point-to-point tug to absorb the dynamic loads that occur when picking up and streaming the tow in bad weather. Means of passing lines to ships that may have areas of explosive or inflammable atmospheres and of boarding casualties at sea—emergency systems on most tugs—are everyday working systems on a rescue tug.

Maneuvering systems—A rescue tug must maneuver at close quarters under the distressed vessel while connecting the tow. The tug must hold position at low and zero speed and apply small amounts of power that are converted to thrust efficiently. Most important, from the control stations the captain must see the afterdeck—the working end of his ship.

Arrangement—Point-to-point tugs rig their gear in port; rescue tugs rig theirs en route to a casualty. Accordingly, rescue tugs should have rigging and equipment stowed below deck for protection and interior access so crews may reach the gear and rig it in transit. Working decks should be as dry as possible without such high freeboard as to give excessive towline nip or such high bulwarks that the crew cannot work over them. Superstructures must be set back from the hull so they do not roll into the casualty with the tug lying alongside.

Crewing—Point-to-point tugs carry no more crew than needed to operate the ships. Rescue tugs must carry extra hands to make the hookup and to put crew aboard the casualty when necessary.

It follows that, while a good point-to-point tug does not make a good rescue tug, a good rescue tug in its turn does not make a good salvage ship.

A multipurpose salvage ship is a heavily built, shallow draft, self-propelled work platform capable of doing a variety of tasks and of withstanding hard usage. The ship must be configured and equipped to:

Fight fires.

Refloat stranded vessels.

Conduct diving operations.

Lift objects from the sea floor.

Handle weights on and off both herself and the casualty.

Lay, enter, position herself in, and recover heavy moors.

Tow.

Provide tankage for oils and other liquids removed from the casualty.

Carry out repairs and various metal fabrication and industrial tasks.

Serve as headquarters for a salvage operation.

Accommodate and feed salvage crew, project staff, divers, and others in attendance at the salvage operation, along with her own crew.

Act as a logistics and communications center.

Carry a substantial amount of salvage equipment.

Operate helicopters.

The type of salvage—coastal, offshore, harbor, fishing vessel, large ships, tankers, etc.—that the vessel engages in and how large and complex a vessel the owner desires strongly influence any hull's ability to do the listed tasks.

Two specialized American salvage vessels deserve special mention. These vessels are *Salvage Chief* (figure 11-1a) and *American Salvor* (figure 11-1b). Both ships are pulling vessels designed to operate in the surf refloating stranded vessels by deploying heavy anchors and hauling them with winches. They operate in the Pacific Northwest where any stranding salvage must be conducted quickly to have a chance of success. The vessels are fitted out and equipped as multipurpose salvage vessels with helicopter decks. They are excellent examples of vessels optimized for a particular type of salvage, but having good flexibility.

Fig. 11-1 (a). M/V Salvage Chief *is pulling a ship converted from an amphibious assault craft. Winches located below the weather deck provide pulling power. Note the helicopter deck. Salvage equipment is stowed immediately below and passed to the helicopter deck for transfer. Photo courtesy of Fred Devine Diving and Salvage Co.*

Fig. 11-1 (b). M/V American Salvor *(ex-*Arctic Salvor*) is a pulling ship converted from an OSV. Pulling machinery is located out of the weather below the large open deck. Photo courtesy of Crowley Maritime Salvage.*

Offshore supply vessels (OSVs) and anchor handling tug supply vessels (AHTSVs) have been converted into excellent salvage vessels. The large open deck area of these vessels makes them particularly attractive to salvors. The U.S. Navy's *Narragansett* (T-ATF-166)-class, oceangoing tugs, and sometimes salvage ships are an OSV-type hull. Extensive modification of the converted vessels was necessary to provide winches, versatile cranes, fire-fighting and diving capability, and extra generating capacity. AHTSVs have some advantages over pure OSVs because they start with some heavy winches, rollers, and other fittings for handling heavy ground tackle.

Both OSVs and AHTSVs have some shortcomings when used as vessels of opportunity—the principal ones being lack of salvage fittings forward and often lack of suitable weight-handling equipment for moving equipment onto, off of, and around the deck. AHTSVs are more likely to have heavy rigging and mooring equipment forward than are pure OSVs. When using either of these types as vessels of opportunity, salvors should bring everything they expect to need and not count on the vessel to have large amounts of rigging equipment. While most of these vessels have extra accommodation for project crews and passengers, there may not be enough for salvage crews. The large open deck allows accommodation vans to be set aboard. The deck space on these vessels is eaten up rapidly during a salvage operation. Careful thought should be given to deck use and conflicts that may occur.

Almost any vessel can be a vessel of opportunity for salvage. The most important requirements are that the ships have characteristics that enable them to make a contribution to the work envisioned for the particular job at hand.

Landing craft, because of their shallow draft, large open deck space, and high deadweight, make excellent salvage support craft. These vessels are often found in cargo service in island groups or in remote areas where ports are not well-developed. Figure 11-2 illustrates such a vessel.

Barges have wide applicability for pulling, equipment transportation and storage, workshop and workspace, tankage, helicopter basing, accommodation, and any other service that does not require self-propulsion and precision maneuvering. Some salvage companies have fitted out barges for salvage, but these vessels are now rarer than dedicated salvage ships.

Despite the advantages salvage ships possess for salvage work, economics are driving them from the seas in favor if multipurpose ships and vessels of opportunity. Salvage ships once waited on station astride major shipping lanes and at shipping choke points awaiting casualties. No company can afford this in the existing economic environment. "On station" in a company's fleet status sheets means the ship is between jobs. Salvage ships flying house flags of salvage companies no longer mark the professional salvor; that distinction now belongs to a trained and

Fig. 11-2. This landing craft with its large open deck is an excellent salvage support craft. The large open deck provides working space for diving, fabrication, and a place to put cargo removed from the casualty.

experienced cadre of professionals accompanied by select salvage equipment deploying on short notice to a casualty.

Rather than keeping ships on station, many salvage companies operate in a flyaway mode, where personnel and equipment are flown away from the home base to the salvage site, and use vessels of opportunity or vessels that can be chartered for the operation.

SALVAGE MACHINERY AND EQUIPMENT

Just as salvage borrows many of its techniques from other industries and modifies them to fit its needs, so, too, it borrows equipment and machinery. Very little machinery is made especially for salvage. The only example that comes immediately to mind is the hydraulic pumping equipment made expressly for over-the-top pumping of tankers. This is not to say that salvors do not modify machinery for their use or assemble driven ends and prime movers for particular purposes. They do, usually to good effect.

No list of best or mandatory salvage machinery and equipment can be laid out. The choice depends upon the type of work the salvor does, the geographical area of operations, experience, and preferences. Arguments could be carried on until sunrise about whether a few large pumps are better than many small pumps, and many similar subjects. There is no "right answer" and there is no "right" inventory of salvage machinery and equipment. For these reasons, but primarily because there is no such thing, no attempt is made to provide a comprehensive list of must have, should have, or be nice to have salvage machinery and equipment. Rather, the following pages address some of the principles and considerations in collecting a salvage inventory.

Economics is a major factor in selecting the equipment that is purchased, maintained, and warehoused. In these decisions, salvors must balance capital expenditure and maintenance costs against return on investment as determined by frequency of use. Unless the equipment is so unique that it cannot be obtained other than by purchasing it, and there is no other way to do the work, there is little sense in buying expensive, infrequently used gear.

One- (or a few)-of-a-kind pieces of equipment are often made up for a particular job. Where they are successful, they are usually kept for the next time—no matter how rare their potential use. Salvors making up these devices frequently soon find themselves with a warehouse that resembles a museum. The decision to keep special-purpose machinery or equipment should not be automatic. It is often better to break special machinery down than keep it for a next time that never comes.

Salvage Machinery

Much salvage machinery is equipment adapted from the construction industry. The most common modifications are provision of a heavy pipe or angle frame to protect the machine and allow easier lifting and lashing, replacement of inlet and outlet fittings with the salvor's choice of fittings, and movement of frequently serviced components for better accessibility for maintenance.

It is entirely practical to rent equipment for salvage operations—pumps, compressors, generators, etc.—from construction firms or equipment rental companies. This equipment is of course not modified to the salvor's likes so it is advisable to rent an entire set of hoses, fittings, etc., rather than taking the chance of not having the correct adapters and fittings. Digging around most locations with eyes open is likely to turn up a range of equipment suited to a particular job. The cost advantage between bringing in the salvor's equipment and renting equipment locally often lies with the local equipment.

Large equipment can bring a very great capacity to a task in a few units, but is heavy and more difficult to handle than smaller units. U.S. Navy data[3] show that under design conditions their 10-inch pumps have about nine times the capacity of their 3-inch pumps and twice the capacity of their 6-inch pumps. This capacity carries with it a weight that is almost five and a cube, that is, more than five times that of the 3-inch unit. Comparable figures for the 6-inch unit are 1.35 for weight and over 1.5 for cube. Selecting equipment often means balancing capacity against practical considerations of handling and positioning units at the site and aboard the casualty.

As with most things in salvage, there is no simple answer for the best size or mix of sizes of equipment. What is right for one operator or for one casualty may be altogether wrong for another operator or casualty. Most salvors have a mix of equipment tailored to their operations and the type of work they are most likely to be doing. For instance, an operator who depends on helicopter transfer may opt for many small units to be sure that even very small helicopters can carry them. Small equipment is easy to position and move about on a casualty. Large units may be prohibitively difficult depending upon where they go and the handling equipment on the casualty. General practice, although not cast in gold, is to carry small equipment in salvage ships with large units retained at the base for deployment when needed.

Small numbers of large units require less tending than large numbers of small units during an operation. On the other side of the coin, breakdown of a single large unit can reduce the total plant capacity below the minimums for the job, whereas breakdown of several small units may be acceptable.

There is really little choice as to whether salvage machinery engines should be diesel or gasoline. The most all-around useful engines are diesel with hydraulic or pneumatic starters. These units can be taken aboard and operated on any type of ship, including tankers, because elimination of an electrical system makes them as safe as an internal combustion engine can be made. The heat of the engine itself still warrants considering the engines as an ignition source, locating it clear of possible fume locations and upwind of fume sources, and taking frequent explosimeter readings of atmospheres near the engines.

Because of the potential for ignition, gasoline-driven pumps should not pump flammable fuels. Where there is no other choice, the pump engine should be in a very well ventilated area, preferably in the open. All pump and hose connections should be especially tight. Leak-off through pump glands should be as little as possible. The pump should be shut down frequently to clean up leak-off and spillage and to check all connections. Naturally, the pumps are always set upwind from sources of flammable fumes.

Gasoline engines are lighter and more portable and perfectly safe for environments without flammable fumes. They are particularly suitable on smaller vessels, such as fishing boats, and where hauling the machinery aboard and placing it is difficult. Gasoline-driven machinery is often less expensive than diesel machinery, but a supply of fuel may be a problem in remote areas and aboard ship where diesel fuel is common and gasoline is not.

Electrically driven machinery has some advantages in weight over engine-driven machinery, but aboard tankers or in other ships where there are likely to be explosive atmospheres, electrical machinery must be intrinsically safe. Making any electrical equipment intrinsically safe increases its cost and causes maintenance to be both more difficult and more expensive. Hydraulically driven equipment is gaining favor with salvors. This equipment is reliable and rugged, lighter than comparable electrical machinery, and eliminates any explosion hazard because there is no ignition source inherent in the equipment. Both electrically and hydraulically driven equipment require engine-driven sources of power that can be located a considerable distance from the driven unit, either on the casualty or on a vessel alongside.

Standardization of salvage machinery is desirable, but not always practical. Machinery is often purchased at different times, from different sources, and on short notice. Sometimes different units are purchased for side-by-side evaluation and both types wind up in the permanent inventory. All the equipment for an operation or aboard a salvage vessel should be as standard as the total inventory permits. There are few things more likely to inspire language that turns the air blue than machinery and fittings that cannot be used together.

Standardization of hoses and hose fittings is easy and productive. Cam-Lok fittings are common, easy to connect, and, when properly wired, secure. Fittings should be arranged with male fittings on discharges and female fittings on inlets.

There is no substitute for reliable well-maintained equipment that performs to its specifications. Machinery that does not operate reliably competes with mismatched machinery and fittings for blue air honors. It is certain to fail at the worst possible time. The only way to be sure machinery is ready to operate is to operate it regularly and maintain it carefully in compliance with the manufacturer's directions, modified by practices learned in the hard school of experience. Routine maintenance and checkout should be carried out not less than biweekly for warehoused equipment. Equipment carried aboard ship should be checked out and run every week. This much attention to machinery is expensive and consumes a large amount of time. It is, however, the only way to ensure that the equipment operates when it is needed.

Salvage equipment should always be stored in a ready-to-go condition with a full set of accessories and spare parts. Mobilization for a salvage operation bears a great resemblance to feeding time at Bedlam. There is ample opportunity for error and for forgetting critical bits. Captain Murphy can be counted on to take an active role. Completely inventoried equipment, shipping containers suited to the probable mode of transportation, checklists, and standing arrangements with shippers, especially air freight carriers, reduce the possibility of error and increase the chances of a successful deployment. All of these arrangements should take into account that the equipment requirements for no two jobs are exactly the same. Figure 11-3 shows typical well-maintained, ready-to-go salvage equipment.

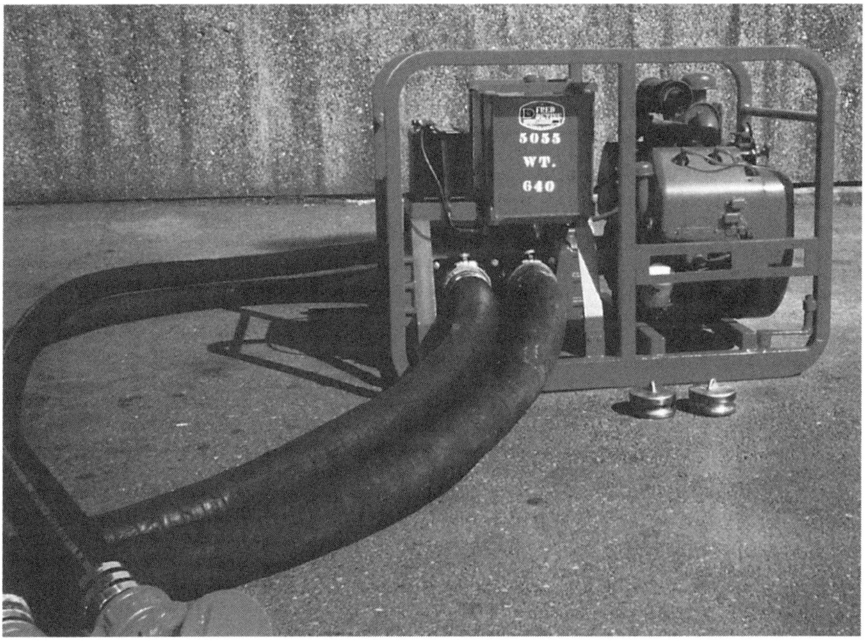

Fig. 11-3. This diesel-driven, low-pressure blower, with its accessories, is a good representative of portable salvage equipment that is well maintained and ready to go to the next job without delay for repair, maintenance, or a search for fittings.

Machinery returning to the warehouse following an operation gets a heavy dose of maintenance before going back to the warehouse routine. This maintenance includes correction of any problems, change of lubricants and filters, at least one hour's operation at design operating conditions, and correction of deficiencies found. Finally, the machinery should be thoroughly cleaned and the paint touched up.

Paint may sound like a minor matter for a piece of machinery in severe service like salvage. It is not. A well-painted and clean piece of machinery is not likely to last longer but creates a positive impression on the job site. With machinery looking good and well cared for and the crew professional, shipowners are more likely to be sympathetic about breakdowns than with equipment looking like junk and a crew looking like refugees from Rent-A-Bum Temporary Services, Inc.

The same philosophy applies to warehousing and storage. Visitors to a salvage warehouse and yard go away with a warm feeling from equipment that is well-stored and maintained. A yard full of machinery with weeds growing through the frames does not impress prospective customers.

Other Equipment

A remarkable variety of equipment—in addition to large machinery and accessories discussed above and items mentioned in other chapters—finds application in salvage—some rarely, some on almost every operation, none always. The necessity for having ready access to such a wide variety of equipment makes salvage a potentially very capital-intensive business. It is often said there are two types of knowledge: knowing it and knowing where to find it. The same philosophy applies to salvage. Salvors can either have equipment or know where to get it on short notice. The decision as to which falls into each category is the decision of the individual salvor and is a function of his ideas about what equipment is important for his operations. All of the potentially needed equipment cannot fall in the "knowing where to get it" category. Some must be on hand in the salvor's warehouse. Mobilization for a salvage operation usually does not include time to go to Sears or K-Mart to fill up the equipment locker.

The equipment taken to any job depends primarily on the nature of the job. It also depends on how equipment is transported to the job and the time sequence of work. There is no need to transport heavy equipment by very expensive charter aircraft if the schedule can accommodate slower, less expensive transportation. A major factor in making up the equipment list is the location of the operation relative to industrial suppliers. In the Pribilof Islands the salvor should take everything he may need; in the Houston Ship Channel he can easily obtain supplies and expendables in the local area.

A number of items of salvage equipment are listed below. The list is representative rather than all-inclusive. Depending upon the nature of the geographic area and the casualties encountered there, priorities may vary. The list that follows is divided into general categories with some overlap and no particular order.

Machinery and Accessories

- Pumps of various types with hoses, fittings, tools, foot valves, and spare parts
- Compressors with hoses, fittings, tools, and spare parts
- Low-pressure blowers
- Air distribution manifolds
- High-capacity ventilation blowers, preferably the water turbine type
- Gauges
- Generators or alternators
- Hydraulic power units and hoses
- Welding machines, leads, electrode holders, and electrodes
- Air tuggers
- Winches
- Adapters for matching various types of hose and pipe fittings, including gender change and same-gender fittings and reducers
- Oxy-arc and oxy-acetylene cutting rigs
- Lights
- Sounding tapes
- Water-indicating paste
- Steel and PVC pipe in various sizes from 1" (25mm) to 8" (200mm), nipples, unions, reducers, elbows, gate and globe valves, etc., in various sizes

Rigging and Materials Handling

- Wire rope
- Chain
- Anchors
- Grapnels or hawk anchors
- Connecting hardware
- Tackles
- Pelican hooks
- Carpenter stoppers
- Bullivant clamps
- Shackles
- Turnbuckles
- Wire rope clips
- Wire rope straps
- Nylon straps
- Hydraulic wire rope cutters
- Hydraulic jacks and rams
- Fiber rope working lines
- Light line
- Heaving lines
- Line-throwing gun
- Chain falls
- Comealongs
- Cargo nets
- Cargo hooks
- Highline trolleys
- Snatch blocks
- Strapping tools
- Small floats
- Jacob's or pilot ladders
- Extension ladders

Tools

- Mechanic's tools in both Imperial and SI sizes
- Electrician's tools and instruments
- Rigger's tools
- Carpenter's tools for rough carpentry
- Welder's tools and supplies
- Pipefitter's tools
- Pneumatic or electric power tools with compressors or hydraulic power source and hoses and fittings
- Stud drivers
- Jackhammers
- Impact wrenches
- Explosives and powderman's tools
- Explosives magazines
- Reaction nozzles
- WD-40
- Knives

Patching Materials

- ⅛" and ¼" steel plate
- Various sizes of steel angle

Threaded round stock
½" and ¾" marine plywood
Epoxies
Plastic steel
Gasket material
Foam rubber sheets
Sheet rubber
Wooden plugs and wedges
Shoring material
Bolt cutters
Nails
Nail guns
T-, L-, or J-bolts

Diving
Diver-worn equipment
Diver's umbilicals
Diving stage with hoist
Diving ladder
Diver's primary and backup air supplies
Diver's communications equipment
Thermal protection equipment
Recompression chamber and outfit
Aviator's breathing oxygen
Underwater tools

Boats
Inflatable boats or aluminum skiffs
Outboard motors
Oars or paddles
Fuel
Fuel cans
Spare parts and tools
Patching kits
Personal flotation devices

Instruments
Portable echo sounder
Multigas detector
Interface indicator
Explosiometer
Oxygen analyzer

Oil Cleanup
Dispersants
Dispersant eductors
Detergents
Sawdust
Sorbent pads
Sorbent boom
Tyvek coveralls
Rubber booties
Duct tape
Heavy-duty trash bags

Personal Protective Equipment
Level B protective clothing for hazardous substance handling
Tyvek coveralls
Rubber booties
Rubber gloves
Duct tape
Respirators with cartridges
Resuscitator
Medical kits
Work suits
Survival suits
EPIRBs
Work vests and helicopter life jackets
Hard hats

Fire-fighting Gear
Fireman's outfits
Fire hose
Fire-fighting foam
Fire extinguisher
Fire nozzles

Communications
Hand-held VHF radios with extra batteries and chargers
Hand-held UHF radios with extra batteries and chargers
Portable satellite telephone equipment

- Cellular telephones with extra batteries and chargers
- Fax machines

Record-keeping and Administrative

- Salvage contracts
- Notebook computer with modem, fax card, extra batteries, chargers, diskettes, and power adapters
- Miniature printer and printer paper
- Engineer's hand-held calculator with extra batteries
- Cassette recorders with extra tapes and batteries
- Charts
- Tools for chartwork
- Writing instruments
- Scratch pads
- Graph paper
- Checklists
- Notebooks
- Seamanship, engineering, and salvage references, including a copy of this book
- Cameras with film, videotapes, 35mm, Polaroid, and video film, underwater camera or waterproof case
- Timekeeping materials
- Extra batteries for everything
- Battery chargers
- Voltage and plug adapters for electrical equipment

Weapons

Weapons may be desirable in areas where piracy or banditry flourishes. Hiring reasonably reliable local security or enlisting the aid of the local military is preferable to arming the salvage crew. In areas where it is necessary to arm salvage crew, the consent and cooperation of the local authorities should be obtained. Many nations, including some of those whose day-to-day life is marked by chaos, do not smile upon armed foreigners. Jails in these countries usually are not comfortable. Semiautomatic shotguns and rifles are the preferred weapons.

EXTREME WEATHER OPERATIONS

Salvage takes place in any weather in which men can work. Operations are stopped only by storms that produce seas and winds that physically prohibit work. Operations in extremely hot and cold weather are routine. These conditions put stress on both men and equipment, so that some precautionary measures must be put into effect to keep the efficiency of both within acceptable limits.

The effects of both hot and cold weather operations are in some ways similar. Machines and equipment bear the extremes better than the people. People are subject to debilitating injury from both, and their efficiency drops markedly in both conditions.

Prevention of weather-related injuries and loss of machinery is not simply sound operational practice—it is good business practice. On-the-job injuries are expensive and increase insurance rates. Loss of skilled or key personnel to preventable injury or loss of effectiveness of men or machinery, especially in remote areas, can mean the difference between failure and commercial success in an operation.

Hot Weather

People working in hot weather are subject to three forms of injury from becoming overheated. Overheated bodies attempt to compensate by increasing blood flow and perspiration. The former causes the skin to redden, the latter causes loss of electrolytes and a chemical imbalance in the body. Perspiring and drinking large quantities of water without replacing the body's salts dilutes the remaining electrolytes and causes cramping of fatigued skeletal muscles. Heat cramps are the least serious of the effects of heat; heat exhaustion, characterized primarily by extreme weakness or fatigue, dizziness, nausea, headache, moist clammy skin, and either paleness or flushing, is the next most serious type of heat injury. This condition is caused primarily by loss of fluids exacerbated by the body continuing to sweat. Heat stroke is a very serious condition caused by breakdown of the body's temperature regulating mechanism. Loss of consciousness, mental confusion, and convulsions may occur. Heat stroke can result in permanent brain damage or death. The potential for a heat injury is greatest when people are wearing personal protective equipment as protection against hazardous materials.

All types of heat injury require medical attention and can take key people off the job for days—or permanently. Taking preventive measures to preclude heat injury is sound practice. Good acclimatization is necessary for effective work in hot conditions. Workers coming into hot conditions after being away from them longer than two weeks should start work at about 50 percent of their normal work rate and work up to their full rate gradually in about a week. In salvage, this kind of acclimatization is more theoretical than practical. Supervisors should be aware that people who are not well acclimatized to hot weather are at greater risk of heat injury and are not able to work at full effectiveness. During the acclimatization period, rest periods should be more frequent than normal.

A good supply of drinks should be on hand and both workers and supervisors should pay particular attention to their liquid consumption to avoid dehydration. Salt consumption also must be watched to keep electrolytes balanced. Taking salt through food or drinking commercially available products that balance salt and water is preferable to taking salt tablets.

The temptation to remove shirts should be resisted, as a wet shirt is a good cooling device and shields against debilitating sunburn. Some sort of headgear should be worn. The best kind is probably some kind of broad brimmed floppy hat that keeps the sun off the back of the neck. Reasonably thick-soled work shoes help prevent foot burns on steel decks heated by the sun. Wearing shorts and rubber sandals, no matter how strong the temptation, is not good practice, as it increases the chance of traumatic injury. The last is noted without a strong recommendation. Making that recommendation would be a matter of "Do as I say . . ." and pure hypocrisy.

Machinery is much more resistant to environmental heat than people, but there are limits. High ambient air and water temperatures limit the temperature differential available for cooling. The machine continues to produce heat but less heat is carried away, causing the temperature to rise. Exceeding the manufacturer's maximum operating temperature may cause lubricants to break down with resultant machinery damage. If the temperature rise cannot be controlled, the machine must be throttled back until the temperature drops into the acceptable range. When machinery is operating at high temperatures, attention must be paid to the lubricants to assure that the quantity is adequate and the lubricant shows no signs of breakdown. Lubricants that show any sign of breaking down should be changed. Awnings over machinery protect against temperature rises caused by direct sunlight. Awnings should not restrict ventilation of machinery.

Electronic equipment is very sensitive to overheating and should be kept in the air-conditioned comfort of the accommodation or, at least, the shade. Portable units such as hand-held radios, cellular telephones, calculators, and computers are not to be left lying around in direct sunlight.

The properties of wire rope and metal rigging components are not much affected by temperatures in which people can work. Metal items do become hot enough to burn the skin, especially when in direct sunlight. Wire rope lubricants in ropes lying on deck in the sun may become fluid and run out of the rope. Some synthetic fiber rope, especially nylon, is sensitive to and loses strength when exposed to the ultraviolet radiation of sunlight.

Cold Weather

People and equipment must be protected, perhaps more thoroughly in cold weather than in hot. Two types of injury occur from extreme cold: frostbite and hypothermia. Frostbite is local freezing of tissue, most likely to appear in the hands and feet. Hypothermia, characterized by numbness, weakness, drowsiness, and shivering, results from depression of the body's core temperature. Severe depression of the core temperature can cause the body's temperature-regulating process to malfunction and lead to death. A third type of injury occurs when bare skin touches extremely cold metal and freezes almost instantly. Protection against cold stress is provided by adequate warm clothing, preferably layered, and frequent work breaks in warmer, wind-sheltered places. Hot drinks should be taken during the breaks. The body expends great amounts of energy working in low temperatures. Larger than normal quantities of food are consumed by crews in cold climates. Considering the normal appetites of salvage crews, the prospect of feeding them in cold climates can be daunting.

Cold weather is harder than hot weather on machinery. The problems with cold weather include icing of fuel, freezing of pump and compressor, high cranking resistance because of high lubricating oil viscosity, poor battery performance, and poor fuel atomization. Most machinery can be winterized to operate in temperatures far colder than men work in.

With diesel engines, the goal is to preheat the engine fluids to get the engine started and to keep it in an operating environment that prevents excessive heat loss and maintains as near normal operating temperatures as possible. To do this, diesel engines are winterized. Winterizing diesel engines includes coolant heaters to help starting by reducing cranking resistance, covers to reduce circulation and heat loss from radiators, enclosures to hold engine heat near the engine, battery heaters, and lube oil, fuel, and air heaters. The specific steps taken in winterizing vary with the engine and the temperatures expected. To be sure of reliable operation, the engines should be operable in colder weather than that actually expected. Manufacturers' recommendations and instructions should be followed closely.

Pressures in hydraulic starting units are increased as the temperature drops. Below 0 degrees Fahrenheit (–18 degrees centigrade) pressures are normally about twice those at 40 degrees F. (4.5 degrees C.) because of the greatly increased cranking resistance. The manufacturers' instructions for cold weather operation should be followed without exceeding allowable pressures. Glow plugs in the combustion chambers and, that old standby, a little ether in the air-fuel mixture also assist starting. The safest means of ether injection is by placing an ether-filled metallic capsule in the injection port and piercing it. Many engines have been started with acceptable safety by more traditional methods.

Arctic diesel fuel (DFA), a mixture of ordinary diesel fuel and kerosene to give a minimum cetane number of 40 and a slush point of –70 degrees F. (–57 degrees C.) is desirable at temperatures below 20 degrees F. (–7 degrees C.). About half a pint of denatured or isopropyl alcohol or an equivalent amount of other water-absorbing chemicals should be added for 10 gallons of fuel each time the tank is filled. Normal Number 2 fuel oil (DFM) is satisfactory above 20 degrees F. (–7 degrees C.). Straining fuels for low-temperature operations through felt or chamois removes paraffin that gums up engines and injectors.

Lacking other instructions from manufacturers, series 3 SAE 10W lubricating oils with an API service rating of CD or CD-II should be used for operations below 10 degrees F. (–12 degrees C.). Enclosed gear drives should be filled with SAE 90 gear oils and all bearings and bushings lubricated with cold weather greases to reduce drag. Oils should be changed at about half the normal interval.

Gasoline engines suffer from fuel starvation from incompletely vaporized fuel in cold weather. This problem can be eliminated by choking to give a rich mixture or by heating the air intake manifold or cylinder walls. The usual problem with gasoline engines is fouling of the spark plugs from condensed water or an excess of liquid fuel. Winter grade gasolines commercially available in the region with a Reid vapor pressure of 12 to 14 are satisfactory in temperatures in which men can be expected to work.

Most rigging materials are satisfactory at practical working temperatures. Wire rope is derated by 20 percent below 20 degrees F. (–7 degrees C.) because of its stiffness. Carbon steel shackles and fittings may become brittle below –20 degrees F. (–29 degrees C.). Rubber goods should be brought up to a temperature of 32 degrees F. (0 degrees C.) or they may show signs of brittleness. Below 20 degrees F. (–7 degrees C.) cranes are derated by 20 percent to allow for brittleness of the boom and stiffness of the wire rope.

Operations can be carried out in temperatures of –20 degrees F. (–29 degrees C.) and, perhaps, in slightly colder temperatures with careful attention to detail. The operations are bound to be inefficient and expensive; a thoughtful commercial evaluation of the practicality of the operation should be made before a contract is accepted.

HELICOPTERS AND FIXED-WING AIRCRAFT

Both helicopters and fixed-wing aircraft have very important functions in salvage operations. Fixed-wing aircraft primarily transport personnel and equipment to the salvage site rapidly; helicopters serve as general workhorses in three dimensions around the salvage site. At remote sites a fixed-wing aircraft on charter gives salvors easy access to nearby major industrial areas and airports and frees them from dependence on scheduled airlines and air freight services for critical transportation of personnel and equipment.

The large distances from salvors' bases to salvage sites and the time criticality of response make deployment of salvage crews and equipment by air almost mandatory. It is often most practical to deploy a salvage master and cadre of salvage crew by the first available commercial flight while the remainder of the crew and equipment follows on chartered flights. Smaller aircraft may be chartered for the cadre to get close to the salvage site. A chartered aircraft allows the cadre to fly over and observe the casualty and the nearby waters from the air, giving a perspective that is very different from that from the surface.

Moving salvage equipment efficiently in cargo aircraft requires a great deal of preparation. Preparation begins with selection of aircraft that have the volume and lift to carry the salvage equipment and that can land and unload at an airfield near the salvage site. At times, it may be necessary to pick an airfield farther away from the site than desirable to get the necessary facilities. The transportation job is not over when the airplane lands. Equipment must be unloaded and transported to a port for transshipping or prepared for helicopter lift to the casualty. The transportation system and equipment must match. Air-transported equipment should fit onto standard aircraft loading pallets or break down into packages suitable for air transport and handling in remote, even primitive, airports. Air transportability is a major characteristic that should be considered when purchasing or building equipment.

Helicopters (figure 11-4) have become so nearly indispensable that one wonders how salvage was ever done without them. They are true workhorses at a salvage site, finding employment in:

Transporting people and equipment.

Serving as a platform for aerial observations and surveys.

Guiding support craft through unmarked channels.

Removing cargo and other weight.

Passing lines.

Helicopters are primarily transportation devices and find their major employment in moving people and equipment between the shore and the casualty and between floating units. They are faster, safer, and more efficient than boats in the same service. Moving people and equipment across a high or dumping surf, where a boat transfer would be, at best, inefficient and most probably dangerous, is particularly good service for helicopters.

Tankers and gearless bulk carriers seldom have more than two small cranes and derricks for stores handling. These devices are not of much use when large, heavy equipment must be moved about the deck—such as relocating over-the-top pumping equipment on tankers. Helicopters fit admirably into this kind of service.

The aircraft are very good platforms for viewing the wreck from above and getting a total picture of the situation. When the only perspective is from the surface, the picture is incomplete and distorted. A helicopter in the air during critical phases of a refloating attempt with an experienced salvor in VHF communication with the salvage master can be invaluable. The airborne observer can see movement and changes in attitude that are not in any way apparent to people on the casualty.

Water depths are often easily discernible by color differences in the water. Current patterns can also be distinguished and casualty drafts read by an airborne observer.

Helicopters are indispensable in oil spill operations as they can range over broad areas to find where the spilled oil is located and to survey areas requiring protection. In a combined operation where a limited number of helicopters serve oil spill responders and salvors, great care—sometimes the wisdom of Solomon—is needed to allocate the transportation resources. The attention and priorities given the spill response may result in short shrift for the salvors, even when attention to the ship can produce the greatest long-term benefit.

The ability to discern water depths and clear channels allows a mariner in a helicopter to guide tugs and other vessels toward the casualty. Helicopter guidance is no substitute for a hydrographic survey of the channels to properly define depths and the position of obstructions that may not be apparent from the air.

Just as helicopters can deliver equipment aboard casualties, they can remove cargo and other weight from the casualty. Removal of cargo by helicopter is most practical with packaged, frozen, or unitized cargo that can be easily made up into packages for sling loading. Large helicopters can lift off containers and vehicular

A B

C D

Fig. 11-4. This montage shows helicopters in some of their principal functions in salvage: (a) landing on board with personnel and light cargo, (b) transferring people by hoisting, (c) delivering or removing sling-loaded cargo, and (d) passing lines. Photo courtesy of Fred Devine Diving and Salvage Co.

cargo. It may be necessary to partially discharge containers or trim them to get their weight and weight distribution within limits that the helicopter can handle.

Passing lines is a routine operation for helicopters. When the casualty has power, it is usual to pass the light end of a graduated messenger that the casualty can haul aboard. A helicopter with enough lift capacity may pass large wire ropes, up to a tug's main tow hawser. Light lines are usually laid across the deck and dropped. Heavier wires are winched down and released only after the deck crew is positioned to control them.

Helicopters are expensive machines to operate and maintain. That expense translates directly into expensive hire. An economic decision must be made about the specific uses of a helicopter in salvage. In most situations, an analysis shows that so much can be accomplished in a short time or the technical advantages are so great that helicopters are economical despite their apparent high cost.

Salvors maintain lists of helicopter operators and aircraft in their operating area so they can obtain equipment as close to the casualty as possible. Often, a salvor prefers to deal with an operator with whom he has had satisfactory experience or who has helicopters suited to the operation. The decision is both economic and operational. With satisfactory service from a nearby operator, it makes sense to hire him and avoid the charges to bring distant equipment to the site.

Ship-helicopter operations have become routine enough that the International Chamber of Shipping has published a *Guide to Helicopter/Ship Operations*[4] that lays out guidance and practice for operations between ships and helicopters. Most of the procedures and practice in this publication are applicable to casualty helicopter operations. There are some differences that warrant discussion.

Most of the differences come about because conditions that prevail in casualties are by definition not normal. The operational aim should be to approach normal operations as closely as possible, allow no unsafe conditions, and get the pilot's concurrence with every variation from optimum practice. It is important to safe operations that the helicopter operators and salvors understand the limitations under which each is operating. Understanding of the weather conditions—visibility and wind—that the pilots feel comfortable in is particularly important, especially in situations where the weather is consistently bad and emergency evacuation of the casualty may be necessary. Normally, helicopters can operate with 0.5 miles of horizontal visibility, 150-foot ceiling, and wind velocities of 50 knots, depending upon the wind direction and the configuration of the landing area. Landing on moving ships with crosswinds and on landing areas where eddies and crosswinds can occur can limit the weather in which pilots are willing to operate. Such winds are serious, as they can affect a helicopter and cause the pilot to lose control quickly when he has little margin for recovery. The decision about when to operate is always the pilots'; attempts to push them to fly in conditions they feel are unsafe are not smart.

Many ships have designated and marked landing areas for helicopters. Most do not. Some have winching zones where landing is not allowed, sometimes over accommodation areas. Winching is a poor choice for personnel and equipment transfers. Landing is always preferable. Helicopter decks or landing areas marked on deck should be used wherever they exist. On casualties it is usually necessary to select a landing area. The best landing areas have the widest variety of approach angles to give the pilot as much choice as possible to accommodate different wind conditions. Landing areas near the side of the ship are practical on tankers and other ships with large open deck areas. On most ships, the most practical landing areas are hatch tops. It may be necessary to land on top of container tiers, leaving passengers with the problem of getting off or onto the tier.

Ships that do not operate helicopters regularly are not likely to have landing areas laid out and marked, particularly when helicopters land on casualty hatches. When helicopters are operating frequently from the same location in salvage operations, the landing area may be temporarily marked to assist the pilot. Figure 11-5 shows the "all up" markings of first-class landing areas. These markings are a goal in salvage, but a conference with the pilots operating from the ship soon reveals what marking they consider reasonable and are comfortable with. A can of spray paint and the concurrence of the pilots can turn a hatch cover into a helipad in short order. All irregular fittings that could foul helicopter skids should be painted to increase their visibility. Booms and cranes serving the area should be brailed up and secured and obstructions more than 18 inches (0.5 meter) high removed to provide the largest possible clear area. Landing areas should not be exposed to spray and boarding seas, for helicopters are extremely sensitive to both. Chapter 7 of the *Guide to Helicopter/Ship Operations* gives an interesting discussion of helicopter operations and potential landing areas on various types of ships. Readers of this information should keep in mind that salvage operations are extraordinary, not routine, operations and that extraordinary procedures are appropriate. They should not allow what should be done to prevent them from doing what can be done.

Loose gear around a helipad invariably makes a beeline for the rotors of arriving or departing helicopters, where it can do serious damage. The area all around the helicopter landing area must be kept policed and free of material that might be sucked into the rotor. An inoperative helicopter can be more than a major inconvenience during a salvage operation, especially if it is sitting on the only hatch suitable for a landing area, or maintenance and repair personnel and equipment are a long way away.

Twin-engine helicopters are preferred in all-over water operations and are mandatory for hovering and for all salvage operations. The helicopters and their equipment must comply with all the national standards of the country they are working in.

Communications are very important. The helicopters should be equipped with international maritime VHF radios with Channel 16 and at least two working channels. Often, the most practical way to do this is for the salvors to supply the pilot with a hand-held VHF marine radio.

Communications have a broader meaning than meaningful radio conversations. Helicopter pilots must understand exactly what the salvage master wants them to do; they should not be shy about operational limitations or about suggesting other methods. Most helicopter pilots are bright and flexible, with ideas that are well worth listening to.

When operating more than two helicopters, hiring a helicopter pilot to coordinate helicopter operations is well worthwhile. The coordinator is responsible for schedules, liaison, and load arrangements throughout the operation. A professional helicopter person in this role gives the pilots a degree of comfort, but more importantly, assures productive and economical aircraft operation.

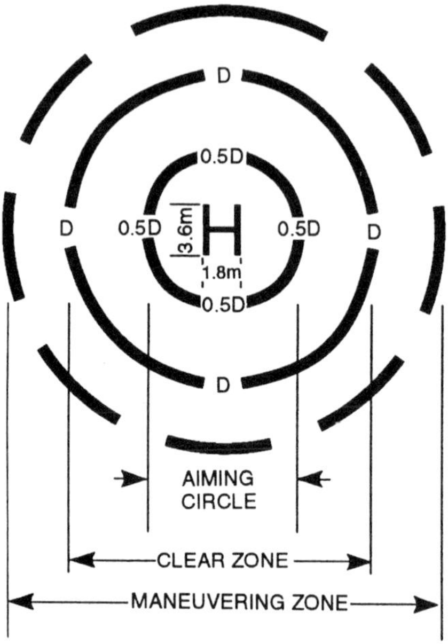

AIMING CIRCLE - NO OBSTRUCTIONS HIGHER THAN 0.1m.
BACKGROUND IN CONTRASTING NONREFLECTING COLOR.
"H" PAINTED IN 0.4m WIDE LINES.
CIRCUMFERENCE 0.2m WIDE YELLOW LINE.

CLEAR ZONE - NO OBSTRUCTIONS HIGHER THAN 0.25m.
DIAMETER (D) EQUAL TO OVERALL DIMENSION OF HELICOPTER WITH ROTORS TURNING.
CIRCUMFERENCE 0.2m WIDE YELLOW LINE.

MANEUVERING ZONE - 1.3 D.
NO OBSTRUCTIONS MORE THAN 1.25m HIGH.
CIRCUMFERENCE 0.2m WIDE BROKEN YELLOW LINE.

Fig. 11-5. Helicopter zone markings

Casualty operations near population centers attract attention that may bring additional fixed-wing aircraft and helicopters into the airspace near the casualty. These aircraft may present a hazard to helicopters working on the casualty. If the aircraft in the area become a problem and collision risks grow, the local air traffic control authorities should be asked to declare a restricted zone around the casualty. No helicopters, except those directly connected with the salvage operation, should be allowed to land on board. Regulatory authorities may operate aircraft in the area, may transfer equipment aboard for their use, and may land on board. Their landings and time on board should be coordinated with the salvors, as their helicopters may block the landing area or otherwise interfere with the operation.

Underwriters and others not familiar with the true economies of helicopters in salvage operations often object to "the expense of helicopters." Sometimes the objections are farfetched. Objections to cargo removals with helicopters have been heard because some think it is not possible to work in helicopter downdrafts. This objection is typical of the ignorance of inexperience. Helicopter downdraft velocities at the rotor are, by industry rule of thumb, about 60 knots. They decay quickly with distance. There is absolutely no difficulty in working in helicopter downdrafts to transfer cargo, pass lines, pick up or hook up loads, or conduct any other kind of operation.

The lack of suitable bases is also cited as a limitation on helicopter operations. The most desirable base is a full facility airport, but the lack of one is not a serious problem. Helicopters can operate successfully from temporary facilities set up ashore or aboard any ship or barge with sufficient open deck space. Low freeboard ships, like OSVs or AHTSVs, while they have adequate deck space, often allow too much spray for reliable helicopter operations. The casualty is not a good base because there is enough going on aboard without the additional confusion of operating and maintaining a helicopter base.

Economically, technically, and practically, helicopters are invaluable salvage tools. They bring much to the party and have proven themselves in many operations. A decision to bring them into any operation should be made after a realistic and knowledgeable appraisal of what they can do and how much they cost. The decision should never be made in ignorance; to do so is to risk throwing away one of the most valuable tools a salvor has.

COMPUTERS

Computers are wonderful tools that have rightfully earned a place in salvage operations. However, the fastest, most powerful supercomputer cannot salvage a ship. Appropriate work for computers in salvage depends upon applying the capabilities of these tools to the correct problem. The principal advantages of computers in salvage lie in rapid calculation of many variations and in retrieval of data from stored information.

The calculations that are necessary for and appropriate to salvage have been identified for a long while. Salvage calculations fall into two primary categories: stability and strength. Draft and trim, oil outflow, and a miscellany of other calculations also may be done by computer. In design offices and on salvage sites, such calculations were made by hand or with the help of mechanical or electronic calculators for many years. Hand calculations are tedious, arduous, and time-consuming. The number of cases that can be examined in any period of time is limited. Computers in salvage are tools that allow more what-iffing of problems and solutions than is possible without them. They do not introduce revolutionary techniques or methods. The ability to make calculations of a particular type and the need for these calculations are easily confused. Calculations that do not contribute directly to the operation are unnecessary and should not be made. In particular, calculations should never be made simply because computers give the capability to make them on site. The fascination with computers is such that computer results can become confused with reality. Salvors can become bogged down to the point that they fail to apply common sense, good seamanship, and the capacity of that very powerful computer on which they wear their hat.

As availability of more powerful personal computers has grown, so has the availability of programs designed to make salvage calculations. Several ship salvage programs are available as commercial products. Some of these programs are adapted from naval architectural design programs; others are specially written salvage programs. The latter usually provide the most satisfactory results. No attempt is made here to list or describe the various programs available to shipowners and salvors. Instead, the characteristics of useful salvage programs are discussed below. One of the most valuable characteristics is common to both good salvage programs and good salvors—flexibility and the ability to deal easily with a variety of difficult situations.

A program must create a model of the ship to make salvage calculations. The most accurate models are created by putting naval architectural data that describe the ship exactly—such as offsets—into the computer. This type of modeling has two disadvantages.

1. Data for actual casualties may be difficult to come by, despite the existence of repositories for ships' characteristics. Salvors often find themselves working with only a Capacity Plan and little hope of getting anything else, particularly when the casualty is an older ship, has had several owners, flies a flag of convenience, and was built by a defunct yard.
2. Putting the large quantities of tabulated numerical data into the computer may take more time than is warranted in the early stages of an operation. The option of how the salvage engineer can most profitably be employed is the salvage master's. He should exercise this option by specifying what calculations are to be computerized and the degree of accuracy that is acceptable. The salvage engineer should reciprocate by advising the salvage master as to how his requirements can be met.

Comprehensive computer analysis is not necessary on every casualty. Sometimes, accurate observation, common sense, good seamanship, and cursory analysis are enough. At other times, parametric modeling, with the relations described in Chapters 3 and 4, or broad assumptions, can often produce results quickly and with enough accuracy for all but very complex salvage cases.

Some ship operators are now providing salvage programs with their ship's characteristics included in the ship or in their offices. Such ready-to-run models can give the salvor a leg up on accurate modeling.

The problem of accurate information in salvage is not limited to initial naval architectural data. Information acquired at the scene is often estimated or so difficult to measure that large margins for error exist. These potential sources of error and inaccuracy and their effects on calculation results must be recognized in evaluating the worth of results. Computers, like the alchemists of old, cannot make gold from base metals. Calculations based on poor assumptions or data cannot produce accurate results, whether made by computer or on the back of an envelope.

Ground reaction in stranded ships is a basic calculation that can easily be computerized. While reasonable estimates of ground reaction may be made by hand, computers applying weight and buoyancy distribution to determine ground reaction and distribution can make complete estimates. The salvage master must decide if the input data are accurate enough and if the grounding is serious enough to warrant a detailed computer solution.

To determine ground reaction and track it during changes in hull loading, a salvage program must be able to distribute naval architectural information from detailed data, parametric sources, or estimates and to modify the information as better information becomes available or the situation changes. The program must be able to change variable solid and liquid loads, such as cargo and bunkers, and calculate the effects on trim, list, stability, shear force, longitudinal bending moment, and free surface effects.

The program should be capable of making intact and damaged stability calculations for at least two different conditions—grounded and afloat, or sunken with the main deck submerged and afloat. It should also be able to identify the stability during the transition from one condition to another.

One of the most important and useful functions of a computer in salvage is the determination of longitudinal bending moment and shear force for different conditions of loading. In many ships, this function is done by the on-board load computer for an intact floating ship. The program may have a grounded condition, but the assumptions of the program should be checked to ensure the grounded condition of the program at least comes close to the actual conditions of the casualty. Often the load computer's output of shear force and longitudinal bending moment is in some form like "percent of allowable" rather than in absolute units. Such figures are of little use to salvors who do not know what factor of safety was used in determining the allowable bending moment and may have to work in the grey area between allowable bending moment and the bending moment that causes catastrophic failure. Most on-board load computers have no editor whereby section modulus can be adjusted to allow for loss of section modulus from damage. Such an editor is an absolute requirement in a salvage program.

Salvage computer programs require an engineering background and a considerable amount of computer competence to operate them. Not all key salvage personnel have the computer competency of salvage engineers, but they need the information developed by the computer. The output of the program must be presented in a way that the essential information can be read and understood at a glance. Tables and columns of information are not useful. Where information is presented in simple forms such as Go, No-Go, backup data supporting the presentation should be easily accessible and understandable to people with low levels of computer literacy.

The salvage engineer operating a program should be thoroughly familiar with the assumptions and weaknesses of the particular program. He must analyze how these assumptions and weaknesses apply in the casualty he is dealing with, and present the results of the analysis. Computers are fine tools, but they do not make more accurate calculations than can be made by hand, just more rapid ones and more of them. There is a tendency to treat anything produced by computers as though it is cast in gold. This practice is dangerous in salvage; computer-produced information should be given no more and no less value than its accuracy and applicability deserve.

Other uses of computers on-site include rapid stored-data retrieval on equipment, contractors, meteorology, tides, and a variety of other items. A word-processing program is handy for keeping records, notes, and logs and for producing letters and other communications and records.

PHOTOGRAPHY AND VIDEO

Photography and video play two important roles in salvage operations. The first is recording "as found" conditions for reference during planning; the second is documentation of the work done by the salvors. Documentation serves three purposes. If the contract is to be arbitrated, photographic and video documentation is a valuable tool for the arbitrator. The same footage may contribute to excellent advertising and training tools. Work for arbitration should be a factual narration of events with no boasting. Film produced for an advertising tool may contain some boasting, for it is the purpose of an advertising tool to present the salvor as the biggest and most powerful gorilla in the jungle. The training tape should emphasize the specifics of techniques and should show mistakes made during the operation. The three tapes can be produced from the same footage by careful editing.

Early in the operation the salvor should decide if the job is major enough to produce a high-quality videotape. If he decides yes, he should hire a professional to tape the operation and produce the final product. To obtain good tapes, everything should be videotaped and photographed and attempts made to obtain footage from local television stations and any amateur tapes that may have been made. The salvor should retain the right to final editorial approval of the work to ensure that his purposes are fulfilled and the producer does not get carried away with the artistic opportunity and produce the kind of symbolic work no one understands.

Photography and video are tools for during the job and also after the job. A Polaroid camera is invaluable during surveys to document conditions for the planning sessions around the table—clear Polaroid prints with good contrast. They can be marked up and faxed to the home office to supplement reports and requests. Thirty-five-millimeter photographs of the same material make a better permanent record. In cold weather, both Polaroid and 35-mm cameras should be kept as warm as practical. Keeping warm is particularly important for Polaroids, as the cold inhibits the development process. Film is cheap; many photographs should be taken.

Whether or not a professional video team is on site, videos should be taken by the salvage team. Rather than relying on the chance that some team member is likely to bring one, the salvage team's equipment should include a video camera. A format that plays on an ordinary VHS videotape player without an adapter is preferred, as other types of players and adapters may not always be available to parties with a legitimate interest in the tapes. Video, like Polaroid photography, should be backed by 35-mm photography.

Divers should take underwater videos during surveys, paying particular attention to damaged areas. These videos help surface personnel to visualize and define the work and can be an aid in planning underwater work. Often a second or even third video of areas of interest may be necessary to define required work. Color video is almost universal for underwater work, because color gives a more meaningful picture than the shades of grey of black and white video. High-resolution black and white video can give a more detailed picture, but the higher degree of detail is seldom needed in salvage. Any video camera has better resolution under water than the diver's eye.

Underwater work in progress and finished work should be videotaped. Thirty-five-millimeter photographs should also back up underwater video.

Processing facilities for 35-mm film can be found almost anywhere. Many produce finished work in an hour. In regions without commercial processors, a commercial photographer or a local photography buff may have a darkroom, there may be a government darkroom, or a newspaper may have facilities. With any of these facilities, including commercial film processors, submitting a test roll for processing before giving them the whole batch may save grief.

AIR LIFTS

Air lifts are pumping devices in which air is introduced into the end of a submerged pipe. The air mixes with the water and expands as it rises to the surface, reducing the hydrostatic head in the pipe. Water flows into the submerged open end of the pipe carrying with it solid material in way of the suction.

Air lifts are not particularly efficient but are easy to make in the field and, if a reasonable amount of attention is paid to their construction and setup, are easy to use. They have proven themselves in salvage for moving cargoes that can be slurried, including small solids, for demudding spaces, and for dredging in some types of soil.

Depth of water and the ratio between the lengths of lift pipe above and below the surface affect the efficiency of air lifts. Air lifts become more effective with increasing water depth as the velocity and expansion of the air flowing up the pipe is greater at greater depths. They are virtually useless in less than 11 feet (3.3 meters) of water, as the height they can lift is too low.

The above-water pipe should not be much longer than one-third of the submerged pipe length. The air does not expand above the surface and the energy present is lost in overcoming the head and friction losses. When the ratio drops below one-half, efficiency drops very quickly. It is usually desirable to move the material some distance from the location where it is being picked up. Usually, it is enough to incline the air lift.

Theoretically, any pressure over bottom pressure can drive an air lift. Practically, a driving pressure at 20 to 30 psi over bottom pressure works best. In air lift operation, as in blowing compartments, volume is more important than pressure.

A flow in gallons per minute of 12 to 15 times the pipe area can be expected from an air lift operating at a typical (good) efficiency of 33 percent.

There are several ways to approach sizing of air lifts and air-lifting equipment:

Start with the air lift size, estimate the flow in gallons, and divide by 2.5 to 4 to get the cubic feet of air required.

Start with gallonage, divide by the capacity of available compressors, and multiply by 3 to get the air lift size in inches.

Calculate the air flow in cubic feet per gallon directly, starting with the conditions at the site. The equation is:

$$Q = 0.1337 \times \frac{L}{(D + 33) \times \log\left(1 + \frac{(D - d_1)}{(D + 33)}\right)}$$

where:

Q = air flow in cubic feet per minute
L = total lift in feet
D = water depth at the sea floor in feet
d_1 = distance from the sea floor to the air entrance in feet

Compressor capacity should be twice the air flow calculated by the foregoing formula to assure a steady flow.

Most calculations for air lifts are approximate. Approximate is good enough, because some experimentation and adjustment are always necessary to get the best performance.

Air lifts can be made as simply as inserting and securing an air hose in the open end of a pipe or inserting an air pipe through the side of the lift pipe. Results are better when air entry is distributed around the lift pipe by an annular collar and the holes are angled up at 45 degrees. Working ends of air lifts can easily be made in sizes that can be transported to the site and connected to air supply and discharge piping or hose. Table 11-1 gives details of construction of well-engineered air lifts. The quantities in the table are defined in figure 11-6.

Once an airlift is set and producing a good output, it requires little attention except moving it back and forth and into the material being moved. Divers and remotely operated vehicles (ROVs) can position small lifts; larger ones are handled by cranes or lines rigged near the mouth of the air lift. It is practical to cap the lower end of the air lift with a cap with one or two openings fitted with Cam-Lok fittings. Lightweight hoses or flexible ducting with mating fittings are attached and swept over the area being cleared. This method causes losses in efficiency and is suitable only for light work.

When the air is turned on to an air lift and flow starts, there is a kick from the reaction that may cause the air lift to jump. ROVs should be moved clear and div-

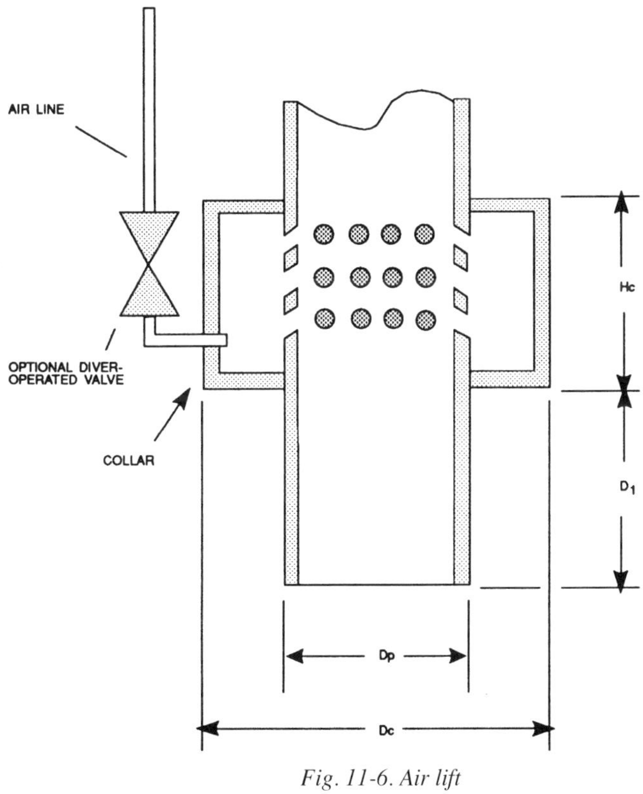

Fig. 11-6. Air lift

TABLE 11-1.

AIR LIFTS						
Nominal Pipe Diameter Dp (inches)	*Collar Diameter Dc (inches)*	*Air Line Diameter (inches)*	*Collar Height Hc (inches)*	*Distance from Bottom to Collar D_1 (inches)*	*Output (gpm)*	*Hole Details All Holes Angled up at 45 Degrees toward Center of Lift BC = Between Centers*
3	5	½	6	16	85-105	3 rows of eight ¼"-holes 1.147" BC horizontally 1" BC vertically
4	6	¾	6	18	150-190	3 rows of eight ⅜"-holes 1.57" BC horizontally 1" BC vertically
6	8	1¼	7	20	334-400	3 rows of sixteen ⅜"-holes 1.17" BC horizontally 1 row of eight ⅜"-holes 2.35" BC horizontally All holes 1" BC vertically
8	10	1½	9	23	600-725	6 rows of sixteen ⅜"-holes 1.57" BC horizontally 1" BC vertically
10	12	2	10	25	900-1150	5 rows of sixteen ½"-holes 1.96" BC horizontally 1.25" BC vertically
12	14	2	10	28	1350-1650	6 rows of twenty-four ½"-holes 1.57" BC horizontally 1.25" BC vertically
14	16	2	12	30	1800-2500	7 rows of twenty-four ½"-holes 1.83" BC horizontally 1.25" BC vertically

ers should climb the air lift a few feet when starting. Both divers and ROVs should stay clear of the suction of larger airlifts or they may be drawn into the pipe.

Heavy cohesive or clayey soils must be broken up before they can be air lifted. Heavy-duty air lifts have been picked up and dropped onto the clayey soils. This method works but may damage the air lift. Jetting the soils is more efficient.

INDUCED BUOYANCY

Induced buoyancy is the technically inaccurate term used in this text to describe the introduction of buoyant material into a space to displace or exclude water. All too often suggestions to raise a sunken ship by filling it with Ping-Pong balls or freezing the water inside the ship are heard. If life were only that simple and we never had to worry about things like hydrostatic pressure, density, the laws of physics, and economics, salvage would be simpler. Because of the real world factors we worry about, induced-buoyancy systems have had mixed success. Widespread acceptance and adoption of any one system has not followed the successes that induced buoyancy has enjoyed in salvage.

All of the systems described below are less efficient than air for making a space buoyant. Air occupies the space fully and restores all the available buoyancy. Some induced-buoyancy systems have large volumes of dead space from which they cannot exclude water, and all have weight that reduces the total buoyancy available. Induced-buoyancy systems are best suited for large open spaces and spaces in which damage is severe and the mass of induced buoyancy can be contained easily.

The Foam-in-Salvage system is a cast-in-place polyurethane foam system developed by the U.S. Navy in combination with Murphy Pacific Marine Salvage Co. and used with some success. Application of the foam results in a single water-displacing mass of foam with a density about half that of water. The foam is produced on the surface or under water by mixing chemicals in a mixing chamber and then blowing the liquid into the space with a fluorocarbon gas. It sets up quickly into a solid adhesive mass. Unfortunately, the chemicals that make up the foam are toxic and flammable. Components must be mixed to suit water and air temperatures or an inferior quality foam of little use is produced. Removal is difficult and expensive and accompanied by the release of flammable gas.

The foam contributes an undefinable amount of strength to the hull girder. The cured foam has good compressive strength that contributes to the compressive strength of the structure to which it adheres. Any quantification of that contribution is purely seat-of-the-pants.

Foam-in-Salvage is no panacea. It is expensive, difficult, and tricky to use, difficult and dangerous to remove, and has all sorts of unpleasant properties. It is not a very useful salvage tool.

An expanded polystyrene sphere system developed by Karl Kroyer A/S in Denmark expands polystyrene granules with steam and pentane to about fifty times their original size. The resulting spheres, about ⅜ to ½ inch (9 to 12 mm), are dried, aged, then pumped into the flooded space where they build up and displace water. The spheres displace 60 to 65 percent of the water in the space with a noncohesive foam mass whose density is about 60 percent that of water.

Removal of the spheres is difficult only in that the spheres migrate and become oily and dirty in the process. Depending upon the location, the spheres may require disposal as hazardous materials—an expensive process.

In the pressurized sphere injection system, plastic spheres about 5¼ inches in diameter are pressurized to bottom pressure and blown into the flooded space. The spheres displace the water in the space. As the vessel begins to rise, a relief valve opens to keep the pressure in the sphere near ambient. The system sounds ideal, but it is not. The spheres and their storage and blowing equipment make up a very large plant, and there is a large quantity of unfilled space—usually about 50 percent of any actual space.

All the major induced-buoyancy systems were developed some years ago and inspired a flurry of interest and excitement. These systems did not develop into major salvage systems and no comparable systems have been introduced in recent years. The disadvantages offset the advantages in all but a few cases that do not occur frequently enough to make the systems economically and technically viable.

UNDERWATER WORK

Underwater work forms a significant part of most salvage operations. The work ranges from simple inspections, through complete detailed surveys, to heavy industrial work of cutting, welding, fitting, drilling, milling, etc. Diving is usually the best and most efficient way to accomplish underwater work. Sophisticated robotics and remotely operated vehicles cannot replace the discrimination of the human eye and the dexterity of the human hand in salvage diving. Divers (figure 11-7) in all shapes and sizes and of different skills form an invaluable part of the salvage team. Good salvage divers must understand ships, the diving conditions in and around ships, and the work. SCUBA diving as popular sport has given many the misconception that diving is easy. Putting on self-contained (SCUBA) gear and swimming around is easy; working under water, particularly in salvage, is not.

The following paragraphs discuss the place of underwater work in salvage and means for its accomplishment. They address the place of diving in salvage and how the two interface. This book is not a manual for divers; an adequate number of those—several listed in the Bibliography—exist. The information that follows is a bare minimum for supervising or planning underwater work in salvage operations.

In many countries, government-imposed regulations address equipment, techniques, training, and qualifications. Salvors working in their own country should follow their national regulations as a matter of course. Those working in other countries should be aware of local regulations and follow them, especially when they are more stringent than their own. The regulations are usually not onerous; complying saves hassle, usually increases diver safety, and avoids hefty penalties and possible shutdown of the job.

Fig. 11-7. This diver dressing out in surface-supplied gear is equipped for heavy underwater work. Photo courtesy of Diving Systems International, Inc.

Thorough planning, essential in any salvage work, is doubly so for underwater work. Underwater work is difficult by nature, difficult to inspect and control, and difficult to redirect when it starts to go wrong. A rule of thumb, developed through long experience, states that underwater work takes at least three times as long as the same task on the surface; when conditions are unusually difficult, the three can grow to a much larger multiple. The best planning minimizes the amount of work under water and allows prefabrication, subassembling, and as much other work as practicable to be done on the surface. The same detailed work planning should make the underwater tasks as simple and straightforward as possible.

Conditions under which divers must work affect the practicality of the work and the quality of the final product. The first step in planning underwater work is, then, to define the conditions under which divers are expected to work. The following factors affect planning of diving work:

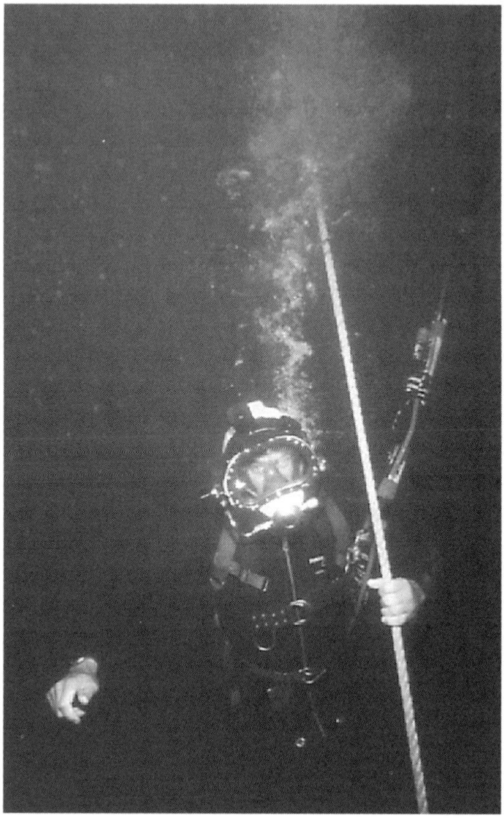

Fig. 11-8. Decompression, not a particularly fun time for anyone, is a necessary part of diving operations that cannot be omitted or cut short without risk. Photo courtesy of Diving Systems International, Inc.

Depth plays a major role in planning work because it determines how long a diver can work without incurring a decompression debt. Despite the belief of some supervisors, divers did not invent decompression so that they can hang on a line in dark, cold water (figure 11-8). Decompression requirements are absolute physical facts. Decompression can neither be cut short nor hurried. Anyone trying to rush or shortcut decompression takes a stupid risk. Decompression sickness is bad stuff that hurts divers, causes operational delays, and costs a lot of money in the long term. Some countries require a recompression chamber on site for all decompression diving. While a chamber at the site is always a good idea, it increases the complexity of the diving plant.

Operations requiring decompression diving are always more complex, longer, and require more plant on-site than diving within the no-compression limits. Decompression requires care and attention in planning to use divers' time well and to prevent delays because divers are decompressing or burned out of time too soon.

Divers doing heavy work or working in cold water have a high probability of decompression sickness if they are near the no-decompression limits or making decompression dives. Safe practice in these cases is to jump to the next longer and deeper table than the one called for by the dive depth and duration to give the diver additional decompression.

Current impedes work by driving divers off their work site or forcing them to spend much of their energy and attention just staying in place. Commonly, currents prevent any diving or limit diving to slack water periods in the tidal cycle. In the latter case, diving becomes the major force in scheduling because divers must make the best of slack water to get their work done. Schedules for all work must be adjusted to let the divers get into the water when they can.

Surface currents do not necessarily suggest currents near the sea floor. Divers may be able to drop through strong surface currents and find more benign conditions at their working depth. SCUBA divers normally lose most of their effectiveness at currents greater than 1.0 knot. Surface-supplied divers can work in currents up to 2.5 knots by wearing extra weight; beyond that all they can do is hang onto their down line.

Temperatures that may be quite comfortable on the surface can cause hypothermia to divers. A resting, unprotected diver may become uncomfortably cold in water as warm as 88 degrees F. (31 degrees C.) and shiver in water only a few degrees colder. Even without hypothermia, chilled divers lose the ability to concentrate and to work efficiently. Divers in cold water tire quickly and are in greater danger of decompression sickness if they are near no-decompression limits or in the range requiring decompression. The need to wear gloves decreases divers' dexterity and increases the time for them to do a task. Except for rare circumstances in the tropics, divers should always have some thermal protection. The degree of thermal protection should increase as the temperature drops. In very cold water, divers may need external heat for long exposures. Supervisors must balance the equation of extra complexity at the site against the increase in diving efficiency.

Under rare conditions that seldom apply in salvage diving, divers can become overheated in the water. It is easy for divers to become overheated in decompression chambers if the chamber is in the sun. A simple awning or roof rigged over the chamber makes a world of difference.

Visibility in the waters where salvage operations usually occur generally varies between poor and none whatsoever. Divers, particularly good salvage divers, find diving in the dark commonplace rather than daunting. Nevertheless, poor visibility slows work and increases the time required for a diver to do a particular task. Low visibility also limits the effectiveness of video, especially when turbidity causes the poor visibility. Where low visibility comes from lack of light rather than particulate matter in the water, video cameras, especially the low-light-level kind, can see more than the diver.

Divers should play a major role in planning underwater work. Experienced salvage divers can best judge the equipment and tools they need to carry out a task. Unless very special techniques are involved, salvage supervisors should tell divers what to do, not how to do it. Divers' ideas on setting up the work and selecting tools and equipment should carry great weight. Most salvage divers are excellent, hard-working, intelligent people with great ability. They invariably have a high regard for their own abilities and a desire to show those abilities to advantage. They may try to push themselves beyond reasonable limits and, at times, may need reining-in.

Salvage dives are usually shallow enough that the primary choice is between SCUBA and surface-supplied equipment with air as the breathing medium. Both types of equipment have their place in salvage diving. The choice to a large degree is governed by the type of work the divers are going to do.

SCUBA has the advantages of mobility, portability, and ease of employment. Divers usually are not tethered to the surface and can move considerable distances along the ship. Most SCUBA systems have only through-water communications, which may be no better than marginally satisfactory in noisy environments. A SCUBA diver carrying a tethered video camera, tool, or other device loses much mobility, but perhaps the greatest limitation of SCUBA is that the diver-carried air supply limits the duration of the dive. With a limited air supply, any situation in which the diver is fouled or unable to surface is particularly dangerous.

Surface-supplied diving is normally the better choice for most salvage diving, especially if the diver must go into the casualty where he can easily become fouled. This type of gear is normally the equipment of choice when doing heavy work and when coordination with the surface or other divers requires good communications, and when diving in current.

Diving safety is the overall responsibility of the diving supervisor. He must have the full cooperation of the salvage master and should not be reluctant to stop diving if unsafe conditions prevail. Like salvage itself, diving is inherently dangerous; it is simply foolish to make it more dangerous than necessary. Safety measures for divers and areas calling for the salvage master's cooperation are:

- Keeping boats and other craft away from divers and the area in which divers are working.
- Assuring that no heavy loads are handled over the area where the divers are working and that the divers are well clear of loads that are being put into or taken from the water.
- Allowing the divers adequate room to set up their gear and work without interference from other work or material on deck.
- Providing shelter for tenders, standby divers, supervisors, and others working at the diving station on deck.
- Displaying proper diving signals.

Divers perform a variety of underwater work. One of the most important types is underwater surveys that define both the condition of the hull and how the ship sits on the bottom. Underwater video is an excellent tool for these because it provides real-time information to supervisory and technical people topside. Exact locations can be marked by tending lines or hogging lines and measurements taken and recorded on the videotape. In the absence of video, divers must make the survey by describing what they see or feel to the tender who records it either in writing or, preferably, on tape. Good communications and real-time video allow the salvage master and diving supervisor to direct the diver in his survey and to have him return to locations to get all the information obtainable. Even with the best videotape or photographs, a diver should be thoroughly debriefed after the dive and asked to make sketches of what he saw. Still photographs, preferably in color because of the better definition, are extremely useful in recording specific conditions and the sequence of patching or repair. Survey reports must be accurate and complete, for their use is seldom confined to the salvage crew. Complete reports are often required by various surveyors and others with interests in the casualty. Written and recorded reports should always contain a description of the underwater visibility at the time of the dive.

Salvage divers often must work inside wrecks. The greatest danger in working inside a wreck lies in working in limited areas where things may be displaced from their expected positions and divers may become fouled and unable to work their way back out. In such situations the limited duration of SCUBA can be a distinct disadvantage. Working inside casualties, even in such confined spaces as a duct keel, need not be extraordinarily dangerous nor should it be taken lightly. Surface-supplied gear with voice communications gives the diver the advantages of a long-duration air supply and the ability to talk to his tender. If SCUBA is the only choice, only a diver with a death wish enters the wreck without a tether he can follow back to his point of entry. A second diver tending at the point where the first enters the ship is nice to have but often impractical, unless the first diver must penetrate far into the wreck in a complicated access pattern.

Remotely operated vehicles have proven to be excellent tools for underwater work, particularly as they do not expose men to the hazardous underwater environment. In the shallow depths of most salvage work, ROVs have no advantage over divers. In depths deeper than divers can work or at depths where diving is very complex and expensive, ROVs are a viable and practical choice. In shallow depths ROVs are not affected by decompression or temperature. They may be unable to work if their thrusters cannot hold them in position against the currents, or if the vehicle's video cannot see the work area with enough clarity for the operator to guide the vehicle and its manipulator.

Underwater Tools

Almost as many tools are suitable for underwater work as for surface work. All of the normal hand tools may be used under water, although the diver has to be firmly in place to use a rotary motion tool like a wrench effectively and may find that swinging a hammer through the water does not produce the same effect it does on the surface. Most of the problems of hand tools under water are minor and are familiar to experienced divers who have developed means of living with the problems and of using the tools to good effect.

Power tools are another matter. Electric power tools have been built for underwater use, but the complexity associated with making them electrically safe resulted in large, heavy, expensive tools with low power. Electric underwater tools have not been commercial successes. Pneumatic tools are another matter altogether. Pneumatic tools designed for surface use may be used under water, suffering only because of the loss of efficiency caused by the air exhausting at ambient pressure at the depth of use. Surface pneumatic tools require little special maintenance other than operating the tool submerged in a bucket of oil following the dive to purge the operating mechanism of seawater.

By far the most efficient tools for underwater work are hydraulic tools especially designed for underwater service (figure 11-9). A variety of wrenches, grinders, linear and rotary impact tools, saws, and the like are available. These tools are powered by or can be adapted to be powered by the same hydraulic power sources that drive other hydraulic equipment on the salvage site.

Velocity powered tools that drive a stud into steel plate with an explosive cartridge are effective at making attachments. Studs are available for various grades of normal and high-yield steels and are threaded for attaching screwed fittings, hollow for attaching air fittings, or configured for simply punching holes in plate. Stud guns do have a muzzle flash and on at least one occasion have ignited the gases in a tank containing an explosive atmosphere. The guns, while designed to be safe and containing some fail-safe features, must be handled carefully and treated like any other loaded firearm. Accidents can occur, especially with divers who are not experienced with the equipment or who are so experienced they are cocky and careless. I know a diver who managed to attach his foot to the side of a dredge with a stud gun, but in over twenty-five years have been unable to figure out how he did it.

What makes one underwater tool good and another poor is more than a matter of diver preference. Good design can make a world of difference in the tool and in the effectiveness of the diver. A few design principles apply to all underwater tools:

Underwater tools should be as small as possible, both for handling and for minimizing viscous drag.

Controls should be easily operated by divers wearing heavy gloves and located so they cannot be easily operated accidently.

The same applies to tool changes. Snap-in tools are preferable to those requiring rotary chucks.

Tools should be as nearly neutrally buoyant as possible with the centers of gravity and buoyancy placed for easier underwater handling and use.

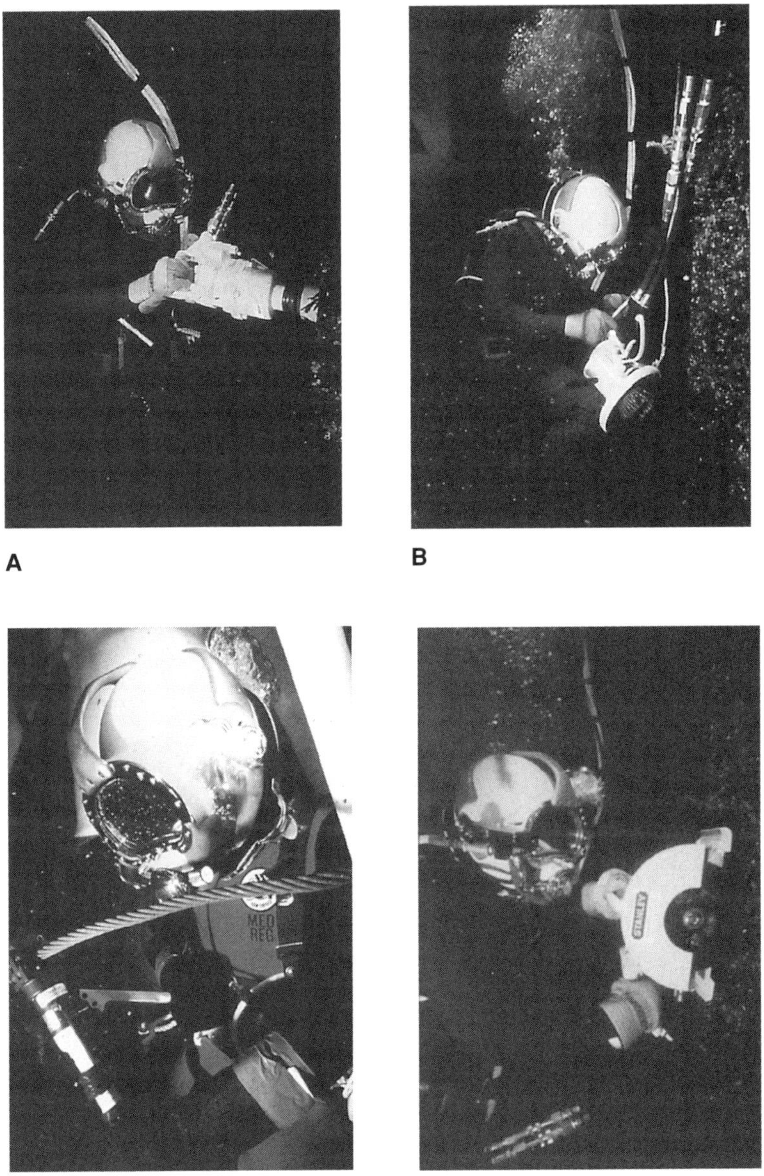

Fig. 11-9. This group of photographs shows a variety of hydraulic power tools designed and built for underwater use: (a) rotary tool, (b) wire brush, (c) cable cutter, and (d) saw. Photos courtesy of Diving Systems International, Inc.

The umbilical should be flexible and nearly neutral near the tool.

The reaction forces generated in the tool are absorbed by the tool and not passed on to the diver, who already has enough forces to hold himself against.

Tunneling with high-pressure water jets (see figure 11-10) is a common underwater task and a good example of the need to counter reaction forces. A diver attempting to jet with an ordinary hose nozzle, particularly straight (suicide) nozzles, can easily be driven off the work site by the reaction of the water stream. The situation can be improved by weighting the nozzle heavily, but the solution is almost worse than the cure, as the heavy nozzle is difficult to handle. A number of commercial nozzles exist which balance the flow and thus the reaction fore and aft. Jetting nozzles are discussed in Chapter 10.

Fig. 11-10. Diver jetting. Photo courtesy of Diving Systems International, Inc.

Underwater Metalworking

Almost any type of metalworking that can be done on the surface can be done under water. Specialized metalwork, such as milling for close tolerances or drilling, cutting, or sawing a large number of holes, may require the adoption or construction of special tools, jigs, or fixtures. In salvage it is better to avoid building special tools or to simplify the task as much as possible to save time and prevent deterioration of the exposed casualty.

Cutting, burning, and welding are the most common underwater metalworking tasks. Development of reliable methods of making sound welds under water changed the basic material for salvage patches from wood to steel and saved millions of man-hours in salvage operations. Very sophisticated underwater welding techniques producing very high quality welds have developed in the oil patch. Such sophisticated techniques are seldom appropriate in salvage, where old-fashioned methods with a modern flair and attention to detail get the job done. Techniques for making underwater salvage welds differ little in principle from the very early welds. Underwater welds can be made in all three positions: horizontal, vertical, and overhead. As with surface welding, vertical and overhead welds are more difficult than horizontal. Undercutting and convex beads are hard to avoid in overhead welds. Good welders are the secret to obtaining good underwater welds. No matter what his other underwater skills may be, no diver can be a good underwater welder without being a good welder on the surface and practicing, practicing, and practicing some more.

Wet welding uses the same basic manual shielded-arc technology as surface welding:

An arc is maintained between the work and an electrode dragged along the weld path.

The arc burns in a cavity inside the flux covering the electrode.

Gases vaporized from the flux—plus superheated steam from the surrounding water—surround and protect the arc and heat the surrounding water.

The diver keeps a steady pressure on the arc to keep the arc length constant.

Metal from the arc is deposited along the arc's path.

In poor visibility a groove that can guide the electrode helps assure the weld is where it is wanted.

Several types of electrodes have proprietary waterproof coatings for underwater welding. When these electrodes are not available, surface rods can be substituted by applying any of a number of waterproofing compounds. Surface welding electrodes cannot be used without waterproofing because water seeping or leaking into the flux turns to steam and blows the flux off the rod.

Wet welding does not produce the same quality weld as an equivalent surface weld, because the large heat sink surrounding the weld quenches the weld. Both ductility and tensile strength drop below surface welding standards. Also, rapid cooling in the huge heat sink surrounding the welds causes loss of fusion defects and underbead cracking. Wet welding is restricted to mild and low carbon steels that do not require special treatment. Despite the numerous shortcomings, a skillful welder can make underwater welds that are more than satisfactory for salvage work.

Wet welding electrode holders are heavier and specially insulated to protect the diver from shock. Electrode holders, cables, and all connections should be inspected frequently for current leakage. In addition to having good equipment and operating it properly, the diver must keep all the parts of his body out of the electrical circuit and should wear gloves with no rips, tears, or holes, and even in low light levels must wear a welding shield. Metal parts of the diving gear and electrode holders are subject to electrolytic deterioration during welding operations and should be inspected regularly.

The same D.C. welding generators used topside are used for underwater welding. There are two important differences in operation:

Current settings are about 25 percent higher.

Straight polarity is always used.

Because the currents are always high, the welding generator should have at least a 300-ampere rating. Lower ratings slow the work dramatically. Even with the best equipment, any underwater welder makes underwater welds much more slowly than equivalent surface welds.

Despite the foregoing litany of shortcomings, underwater welding is an invaluable tool for salvors and one that salvors' divers should practice regularly to maintain and improve proficiency.

Specialized devices are available for welding studs to hulls as an alternative to the velocity powered stud gun described previously. One such device welds electrically with a special welding gun that requires very high amperage (2,000 a). Another type produces welds with the friction generated between the work and a rotating stud with a pneumatic gun. The friction welding device requires no surface preparation and eliminates many of the problems with conventional welding, but requires locking in place with mechanical, vacuum, or magnetic clamps.

Credit for the first practical underwater thermal cutting torch usually goes to Commander Edward Ellsberg, U.S. Navy, for the oxy-hydrogen torch he developed during salvage operations on the submarine S-51 in the mid-1920s. Whether this credit is correct or not we shall probably never know; it doesn't matter. The oxy-hydrogen underwater cutting rig has given yeoman service. Although largely displaced by oxy-arc and other electrical equipment, the oxy-hydrogen torch still has a place in salvage operations. That place is for quick and dirty cutting jobs where a minimum of equipment can be brought to the scene or where the work cannot produce or sustain an arc. A number of other fuel gases have been used under water but are generally not very effective. Aside from hydrogen, MAPP gas (stabilized methyl-acetylene propadiene) is most effective for underwater cutting.

All the oxy-gas torches for underwater cutting use the same principles as surface torches, except that a shield is provided to keep water away from the tip. An artificial combustible atmosphere is created by the gases inside the shield.

Oxy-arc is the most common underwater thermal cutting method and by far the one most likely to be seen in salvage. For oxy-arc cutting, oxygen flows through the electrode holder and a hollow electrode into the arc. The heat of the arc brings the base metal to its melting point and the jet of oxygen increases the

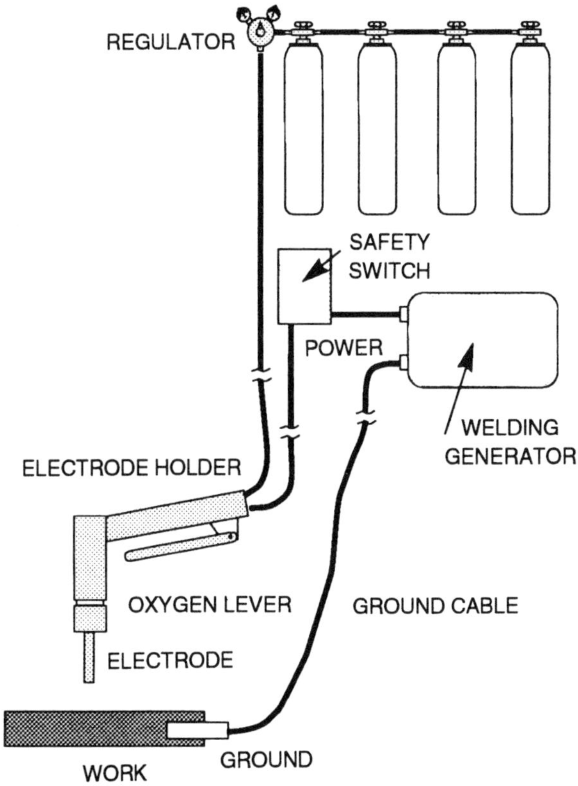

Fig. 11-11. Typical oxy-arc setup

temperature, oxidizes the base metal, and blows the molten metal out of the cut. The process consumes electrodes rapidly. Figure 11-11 shows a schematic of a typical oxy-arc cutting setup.

Amperages for oxy-arc cutting are in the 300- to 400-amp range, requiring a 400-amp generator. Oxygen consumption is also high. Seventy cfm delivered at an over bottom pressure of about 90 psi is required. Efficiency drops off rapidly with decreases in oxygen purity. High-purity aviator's breathing oxygen normally is supplied for underwater cutting.

Three types of electrodes are used:

Tubular steel
Tubular ceramic
Exothermic

Exothermic electrodes such as the Broco Ultrathermic and Arcair Sea Jet sustain arcs when electric power is secured as long as oxygen flow continues. Maintaining current provides more heat and enhances the burning process.

The Broco Ultrathermic rod consists of seven small mild steel rods in thin steel tubes. The seven rods burn independently when an arc is struck and oxygen is flowing. The Arcair Sea Jet is a mild steel tube enclosed in a spiral mild steel springlike wrapping in still another steel tube.

Nonferrous metals, concrete, and sea growth may be cut with oxy-arc, but there is no oxidation of the base material and thus no requirement for high-purity oxygen.

Thermic cutting devices can also be used under water. These devices consist of bundles of wire in flexible tubing (Kerie Cable) or rigid piping (burning bars) with oxygen supplied down the tube. Great heat is produced. Kerie Cable can burn through almost anything except concrete and rock. Burning bars can burn through those materials.

All of the exothermic cutting devices produce enough heat to dissociate water into its components of hydrogen and oxygen. These components may mix and combine in bubbles or mix in confined spaces where they form an explosive mixture. Explosions on the surface may be harmless and great fun to set off. Explosions in confined spaces are less humorous. They can be and have been fatal.

EXPLOSIVES

Due to the technical complexity of salvage, this book can give no more than an overview of explosives and their work. The following paragraphs address explosives in salvage concentrating on principles. Explosives are powerful and effective tools. They also are dangerous and expensive. Their power, effectiveness, safety, and economical use depend upon skilled application by thoroughly trained and experienced people. As with most things, the devil is in the details of explosives operations and safety. Knowing the operational details is specialized knowledge; safety is everyone's business.

Skilled salvors should be able to cut and break steel plate and shapes with explosives; more complicated work requires experts. No one should handle or attempt to work with explosives without formal training. Self-education in explosives is, at the very best, unwise. Knowledge acquired through training helps prevent accidents, but care, practice, and attention to detail assure explosives are used properly and do not create more problems than they solve.

Because the actual explosion is fast, explosives work has a reputation for speed. This reputation is wrong. Effective explosives work requires such careful planning and preparation that the complete job is often slower than one accomplished by other means.

Work with explosives requires much administrative and technical planning to assure that local regulations are met. Things that must be considered include:

The types and quantities of explosives allowed in the area.

The quantity of explosives in any one shot.

Storage, magazine, and security requirements and precautions.

Transportation requirements, including import requirements for introducing explosives into another country.

Site licensing.

Operator licensing.

Environmental concerns.

Explosives produce four major disturbing effects: air blast, water shock wave, ground movement, and noise. Air blast can rattle or break windows. Water shock wave damages underwater structures, including underground pipelines. It can rattle nearby structures, and kill or injure marine life. The latter is a sensitive issue with environmental groups. Ground movement shakes, rattles, and can damage structures. All the effects upset the populace and cause complaints.

The effects are interrelated. Measures to control any of them usually reduce the others. The importance of each effect at any site varies with the characteristics of the explosive, the setup, and local political concerns. The severity of all the effects decreases with decreasing charge size. A balance has to be struck between sizing the charge to achieve the desired effect and limiting the side effects.

A careful public relations effort may help reduce the problem, but even the best program is not likely to win many friends. The best solution keeps the effects listed above and the noise levels as low as possible.

The effects discussed above generate the most concern in areas with moderate to heavy population densities. In even the most remote areas, environmental concerns can be a major problem and hindrance to working with explosives. Environmental impact statements may be necessary for major operations. If they are, an alternative solution is probably the most reasonable recourse. Delay in approval of an environmental impact statement can make salvage or wreck removal operations commercially impractical. Environmental concerns usually focus on danger to marine life and are so great that time spent on calculating fish kill ranges and planning attenuation methods form a part of planning any explosives operation.

The means by which explosives kill or injure marine life is not defined fully. It is known to vary with the type of life. Fish with well-developed swim bladders are most vulnerable. Overpressures in the 40 to 70 psi range kill free-swimming fish of all types, but lethal range seldom exceeds 650 feet. Shellfish of all types are completely resistant to shock effects beyond about 50 to 80 feet. Practically, the range of the potential kill zone is the distance at which 90 percent of marine life survives. This range is defined by the equation:

$$R=Kw^{k}$$

where:

R = range in feet at which 90 percent of marine life survives
K = coefficient from the table that follows
w = weight of the charge in pounds
k = exponent from the table that follows

TABLE 11-2.

Fish Weight	*Depth of Blast (feet)*	*K*	*k*
1 oz	10	328	0.220
1 oz	50	385	0.256
1 oz	200	475	0.262
1 lb	10	174	0.264
1 lb	50	235	0.275
1 lb	200	272	0.299
30 lb	10	86	0.284
30 lb	50	131	0.314
30 lb	200	139	0.342

Unfortunately, if even one dead fish is found after the explosion, that fish can be expected to make the nightly news with scathing comments by local environmental groups. Keeping fish kill down deserves some measures to diminish blast effects. Explosions have no long-term effects on marine life; fish return to the site almost immediately.

Bubble screens effectively attenuate blasts and reduce the fish kill radius. These screens surround the area containing the shot with perforated pipe and blow air through the pipe. The bubbles absorb the energy of the explosion by compressing in milliseconds. Upon reexpansion—also occurring in milliseconds—the bubbles generate a much lower overpressure than the pressure of the explosion. The minimum flow for significant attenuation by a bubble screen is about 2.5 cfm for each linear foot of pipe. The attenuating effect of the screen increases dramatically with the air volume. The rule of thumb for air volume in a bubble screen is "more is better."

Explosives come in many types and forms—block, plastic, liquid, sheet, cord, slurry, tape, etc.—with widely varying characteristics. With shaped charges added, the list grows longer. Selection of the form and type of explosive for a major operation is work for specialists. In their routine work, properly trained salvors should limit themselves to a few explosives and forms that can cut steel and blast rock or coral.

Basic Types and Characteristics

The two main types of explosives are high explosives and low explosives. The chemical change in high explosives, a detonation, moves faster than the speed of sound. In a low explosive, the chemical change, a deflagration, moves slower than the speed of sound. High explosives are further divided into initiating, primary, and secondary based on sensitivity or ease of initiation of a detonation.

Explosives are compared based on nine characteristics:

1. Brisance—The rate of rise of pressure during a deflagration or detonation. Brisance is a measure of potential for work.
2. Rate of detonation—The speed at which the explosive reaction moves through the charge.
3. Power—Results produced by detonation. Used in selecting the most suitable explosion for a particular situation.
4. Strength—Amount of work a specific explosive is capable of. In dynamites it indicates the percent of nitroglycerin and is *not* linear.
5. Sensitivity—Measure of the amount of energy necessary to initiate the explosive reaction. A measure of stability.
6. Sensitiveness—Tendency of an explosive to detonate sympathetically.
7. Relative effectiveness—Effectiveness compared to TNT rated at 1.00.
8. Density—Weight per unit volume expressed in g/cc. Higher density means more explosive power per unit volume.
9. Water resistance—Measure of an explosive's ability to withstand degradation or desensitization after getting wet or while under water.

Safe Distances

Personnel in the area of explosives need protection from the explosion's flying debris. On the surface the safe distance from an explosion in the open can be calculated by the equation:

$$d = 300 \times \sqrt[3]{w}$$

where:

d = minimum safe distance from the explosion in feet

w = weight of the explosive charge in pounds

People in the open at the minimum safe distance have some risk from falling debris and the odd bit of flying debris. Good practice means increasing the distance and getting under and behind cover. This advice comes directly from one who has heard a few fragments zing by at "safe" distances.

Divers must get out of the water for safety. There is never any reason in salvage work for firing explosives under water with divers in the water.

Cutting Steel

Salvors in the field should be able to make simple cuts in steel plates and shapes with explosives. Explosives can make clean, efficient cuts, but usually all except the simplest cuts require some combination with manual cutting. Manually cutting the entire structure is often more efficient. Chapter 14 discusses explosives in the context of major cutting of wrecks.

So many variables affect explosions, particularly underwater explosions, that only general and approximate rules are appropriate. The equations in this section give guidelines and approximations only. Test shots at the site with the explosives for the job are always desirable.

Cutting effectiveness varies with both charge weight and placement. Effectiveness is greatest with the charge in intimate contact with the work. Thus, a plastic explosive, like the common military explosive C-4, is excellent for cutting steel because it can be molded into close contact. Linear, ribbon, diamond, and shaped charges also can cut steel plate and shapes.

The quantity of explosive, based on an untamped charge of C-4, is:

$$P = \frac{3}{8} \times A$$

for surfacing cutting, and for underwater cutting:

$$P = A$$

$$P = \frac{3}{4} \times A$$

where:

P = weight (quantity) of explosives in pounds

A = cross-sectional area of section being cut in square inches

An equivalent expressions for cutting steel bars, wire rope, and chain, where good contact is not always possible is:

$$P = 2 \times A$$

The simplest way to cut chain is to pack the link with the calculated quantity of plastic explosive.

Charges placed on one side of the steel along the cut line can cut steel plate and shapes. Dividing the charge in two and placing the two parts on opposite sides makes a more efficient cut. The two parts of the charge are offset from one another by a little more than the thickness of the steel, as figure 11-12 shows. Cutting from both sides is practical only when workers can reach both sides, a condition that does not always occur in salvage.

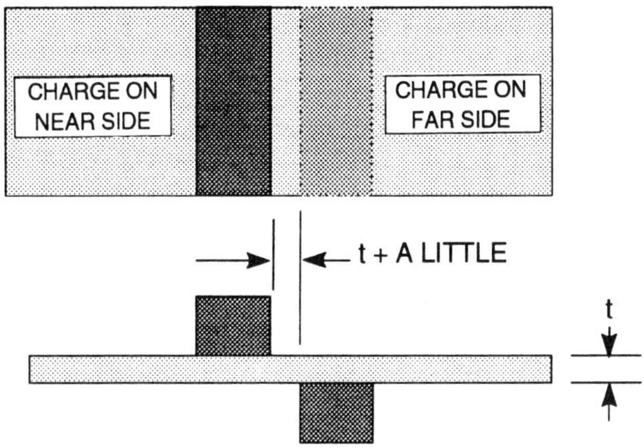

Fig. 11-12. Cutting steel with charges on both sides

Ribbon charges, long thin charges made from plastic or sheet explosive, should be half the thickness of the plate being cut and must have a minimum thickness of one-half inch. The width is three times the thickness. Charges are detonated from either end or the middle. Ribbon charges may be prepared in advance and wrapped in aluminum foil until placed. Charges should always be cut rather than molded to avoid affecting the density of the explosive.

Diamond charges cut by collision of two shock waves produced by simultaneous initiation from two ends of a diamond-shaped charge. The charge should be one-inch thick with equilateral sides for plate cutting. The charge is placed on the plate with two points of the diamond on the cut line. Detonation starts at the other two points. To cut pipe or a hollow round section, the long axis of the charge equals the circumference of the pipe; the short axis is half that length. The charge wraps completely around the pipe and detonation starts at the corners that lie along the pipe axis (figure 11-13).

Shaping a charge improves cutting performance dramatically. Where a flat-ended charge only dents a surface, a hollowed-out charge concentrates the force of the charge to produce a crater that mirrors the cavity in the charge. A liner in the cavity further concentrates the effect and produces a jet of particles from the liner, making a deep narrow cut. Figure 11-14 shows these effects. Shaped charges are as effective under water as on the surface, as long as they have dry cavities.

The charge must have a standoff from the work to allow the jet to form. Manufactured charges have the standoff built in. Shaped charges can be made in the field from readily available materials. The standoff should be manufactured to fit the charge. The proper standoff depends upon the apical angle of the charge. This angle is normally between 40 and 60 degrees (figure 11-15). For angles of 45 degrees or less, standoff equals charge diameter. Each 15-degree increase in diameter requires increasing the standoff one half width.

Figure 11-16 illustrates some typical field-fabricated shaped charges. Efficient operation of a shaped charge depends on the material and precise shape of the liner. To compensate for shortcomings in these areas, field-fabricated charges should contain a generous quantity of explosive.

All charges must be held tightly against the work by lashing them, tamping them with sandbags, or securing them to studs shot into or friction-welded to the hull. The charges must remain in place until the shot is fired.

No matter how water resistant the charge, immersion does not help it. Long immersions increase the chance of misfire. When lengthy immersion is unavoidable, explosives

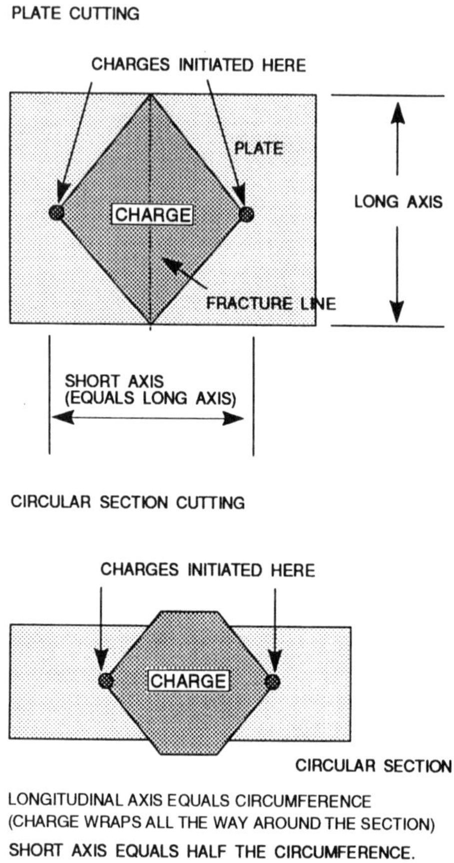

Fig. 11-13. Cutting with diamond-shaped charges

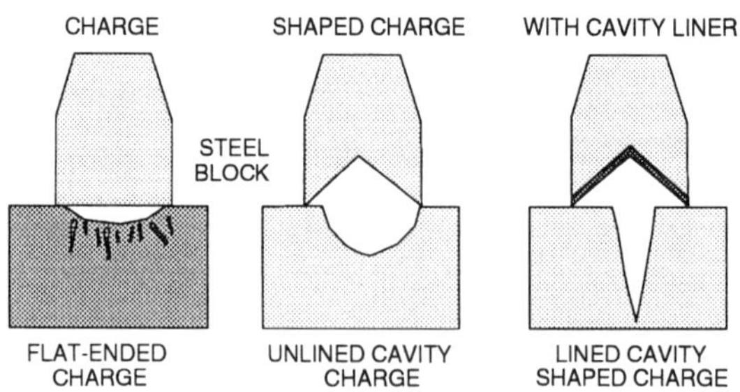

Fig. 11-14. Effect of charge shape

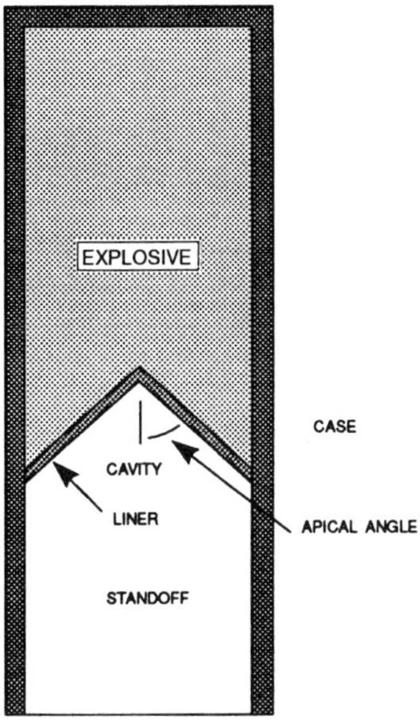

Fig. 11-15. Shaped charge

should be protected from direct contact with water, preferably by a factory-supplied submarine wrap, and firing circuits doubled.

Breaking Rock and Coral

Salvage work may include the removal of sea floor obstacles, normally rock and coral, to provide the casualty a clear path into deep water. Explosives do this work effectively. Alteration of the sea floor with explosives is environmentally sensitive. Beyond the factors discussed before, the amount of damage to the sea floor is a major concern, especially on a living coral reef. Officials may not allow the use of explosives on such a reef and may otherwise restrict salvors' actions to prevent damage to the coral. Damage to the casualty may occur from the effects of blasting nearby obstacles.

Rock

Rock blasting, a specialty within a specialty, requires knowledge of geology expanded by experience. Drilling and blasting characteristics of rock depend on hardness, toughness, density, and structure. Rocks of similar composition vary widely in their characteristics. Rock characteristics determine the type of explosive that works best for any particular shot. All rock blasting requires fast, brisant explosives. Heavy, tough rock needs a fast, high-gas-producing explosive; light, tough rock needs a fast, lower-gas-producing explosive to break and move it. Onsite testing is the only sure way to select an explosive for rock blasting, especially under water.

Underwater rock blasting, because of the weight of water moved by the shot, takes two to six times as much explosive as the same work on the surface. The quantity of explosives also varies with the technique. There are four basic techniques and countless variations for rock blasting. The four techniques are:

1. *Contact blasting*—A charge placed on and in intimate contact with the rock acts much like a high-velocity sledge, cratering or shattering the rock. A high-velocity, high-gas-producting explosive in a conical pile in intimate contact with the rock works best. Contact blasting is the least efficient technique in explosive per volume of rock and the most efficient in diver time.

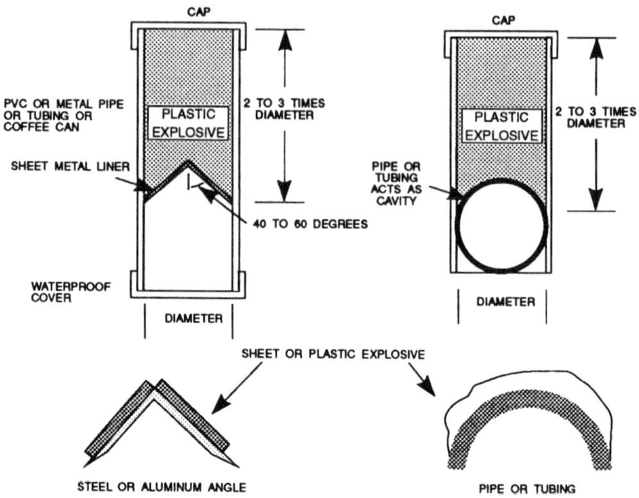

Fig. 11-16. Typical field-fabricated shaped charges

2. *Mudcapping or tamping*—Either clayey mud or sandbags tamp the charge and help direct the energy downward. An increase in efficiency over contact blasting results.
3. *Snakeholing*—Buries the charge under boulders or rock formations that are themselves buried or partially buried. The technique is very effective but its practical application depends on drilling quickly and efficiently under the rock and placing the charge in intimate contact with the rock.
4. *Blockholing*—Explosive is loaded into holes drilled into the rock. The confined charge gives efficiency in explosive consumption. Greatest efficiency occurs when the blockhole is near the geometric center of the rock.

Figure 11-17 illustrates the four techniques.

The quantity of explosive varies with technique. Relative values for quantity, or *powder factors*, are expressed in pounds of explosives per cubic yard of material. The following table lists powder factors for underwater blasting with the four basic techniques.

The actual powder factor depends upon the density and toughness of the rock, whether individual boulders or formations are blasted, and the water depth.

Calculation is an iterative process with some empirical information:

1. Estimate the volume of rock being blasted.
2. Select a powder factor.
3. Select an explosive.

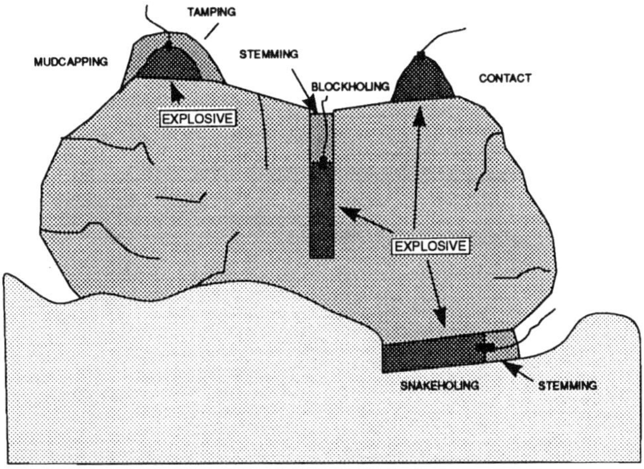

Fig. 11-17. Rock-blasting techniques

4. Adjust the powder factor by dividing the selected figure by the relative effectiveness of the explosive.
5. Multiply the volume of rock by the adjusted powder factor to determine the quantity of explosives.
6. Fire a test shot and make adjustments suggested by analysis of the results.

Shearing charges are good for removing pinnacles (figure 11-18). External charges are placed on opposite sides and different heights—one at the base, the other about halfway up. When detonated from the top, the charges push the material away, toppling the pinnacle away from the upper charge.

TABLE 11-3.

POWDER FACTORS FOR UNDERWATER ROCK BLASTING	
Technique	*Powder Factor (lbs/cu yd)*
Contact	6 to 20
Mudcapping	4 to 15
Snakeholing	3 to 10
Blockholing	2 to 6

Coral

Coral is a hard deposit built up by coral polyps that live in waters that never cool below 68 degrees F. The colonies form heads that grow into reefs. Cementation of reef fragments also forms reefs. Reef coral may be porous or dense, depending

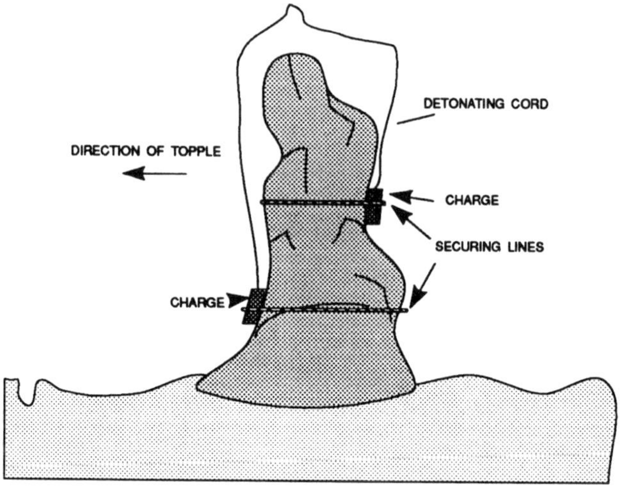

Fig. 11-18. Shearing a pinnacle

upon its cementation, and can vary in hardness. Both the coral polyp and the reef are vital portions of the local ecology. Coral reefs repair themselves, but over such a long period that any damage to a reef or coral colony is severe environmental damage.

The probability of any local authority allowing coral blasting in any salvage operation is not high. Coral blasting would probably never be allowed unless the alternative would result in very severe environmental damage. Coral blasting, like oil jettisoning, is unlikely to happen.

Coral does not blast well. Driving powder points (pipe filled with explosive) into the coral and washing the waste away with jetting hoses does the best job. Shearing and shattering charges are alternatives.

Impalement

Impalement of a ship on a rock or coral head always poses difficulties for salvors. Floating the ship off the impalement is the preferred method of removal, but is not always possible. The only other choice is removal of the impaling rock from the ship. Jackhammers are slow and labor-intensive. Explosives represent an option, albeit one that carries with it a high risk of more damage to the ship. The only feasible procedure is to begin with very small shots and check the results after each. Any attempt to speed the process up beyond dead slow is likely to cause damage to the casualty. Destroying an impalement with explosives is only an option when no other choice is possible.

The pinnacle can seldom be reached easily. Cargo may bury it, or fuel or torn structure surround it, limiting access from the interior. The ship probably sits on the sea floor, her hull blocking access from the outside.

Explosives may be used either inside or outside the ship, depending upon access. In attacking the pinnacle from inside, a series of a few shallow blockholes are drilled; about half are left unfilled to allow the pressure a place to vent. Charges of no more than $\frac{1}{8}$ to $\frac{1}{4}$ kilogram per blockhole are fired with a delay to keep the pressure low. The process continues with a series of very small shots followed by inspections until the impalement disappears.

Virtually the same procedure of chipping away little bits removes pinnacles from outside the ship. A large concrete patch around the impalement gives a material that absorbs some underwater shock, allowing larger charges. The explosives' effect and their potential are not calculable because of the large number of variables. Going slowly and considering each shot a test shot is absolutely mandatory.

Concrete may cement the rock into the hole for shearing off slowly outside the hull. Coral impalements must be removed because they do not have enough tensile strength to form part of the patch.

WATER DAMAGE PROTECTION

Actions taken to preserve and protect machinery, equipment, and cargo exposed to salt water is water damage protection (WDP). Water damage protection can help retain the value of equipment and cargo and by that increase the salved value.

The danger to exposed material comes not while the material is in the flooded space, but when the floodwater has been removed and air reaches the material. Serious damage can occur within forty-eight hours. Water damage protection consists of cleaning, removing salt water and other residue, drying, and preserving the material. This degree of protection requires opening, partially disassembling, cleaning, and preserving machinery and other equipment under the less-than-ideal conditions found in recently dewatered spaces in ships under salvage.

Machinery necessarily must be protected in place. Salvors should remove containerized, unitized, and break-bulk cargoes—the types that usually benefit most from water damage protection—from the ship and protect them ashore whenever possible. Some bulk cargoes also benefit from water damage protection programs that save at least a part of their value.

Hiring water damage protection contractors is normally preferable to trying to do the job with salvage crew. Not only does the work divert salvage crew from the salvage of the ship, but it also engages them in work they may be poorly prepared and equipped to do. Water damage specialists bring their own equipment, tools, personal protective equipment, and respirators or breathing apparatus. They may need salvage crew help to rig lighting and ventilation into the space. WDP contractors should be encouraged to be as independent as possible.

Salvors performing water damage protection should keep the work as simple as possible. Salvors do not have specialized knowledge of the tasks and should settle for drying equipment and applying WD-40 liberally. Electronics should be dried only; WD-40 does not do electronics much good.

The process of triage or establishing priorities applies to water damage protection. Those items that produce the greatest retention of salved value should get the most attention and highest priorities. The water protection damage plan and the salvage plan must coordinate so that crews are employed to advantage and material is not exposed to the atmosphere longer than necessary while awaiting protection. In some cases, where the requirements of the salvage work permit, a space may stay flooded with its contents immersed rather than skipping or skimping on water damage protection. This, the priorities, and integration of water damage protection into the salvage plan, like many other things in salvage, are judgment calls by the salvage master. There are neither hard rules nor simplistic guidelines.

SUMMARY

This chapter has covered several widely varying subjects that at one time or another are important in salvage operations. No doubt any experienced salvor could add to the list. The variety of subjects that arise during salvage operations emphasizes that the salvor must have versatility and open-mindedness about adding to his storehouse of information and keeping up to date. Everyone, salvors not excepted, likes sea stories. Salvors who become absorbed in the glories of the past rather than seeking new knowledge and new ways to operate soon find new glories elusive. Salvage is about keeping up to date on a broad front, maritime and otherwise, and adding more pigs and chickens to the next edition of this chapter.

12

CARGO HANDLING IN SALVAGE

To salvors, the job includes saving both the ship and the cargo. Cargo is money as a part of the total property at risk—the basis for the award under an arbitrated agreement. It is also weight to be managed during the salvage and can be a potential pollutant that, released to the environment, could have dire consequences. More significant than either of the above, cargo often becomes the dominant factor in salvage operations, dictating the salvage methods used and determining the length of the operation. It is common for cargoes to have greater value than the bottoms that carry them.

Salvors have a duty to maintain cargo in good condition for delivery to the consignee. Refusal of delivery by the consignee can result in: (1) cargo interests not posting security, (2) a reduction of the salvage award, or (3) a charge of negligent salvage. The salvor has a parallel duty to prevent the release of a polluting cargo into the environment. The salvor's requirement to manage the cargo in the salvage operation complicates the situation and provides a basis for dichotomies among the parties.

Other parties have differing interests. The primary interest of charterers, cargo owners, and their underwriters lies in saving the value of the cargo and in seeing it reach its consignee. Regulators and environmental groups may view the cargo solely as a potential pollutant. They may have little sympathy for other viewpoints and little tolerance for commercial concerns. The salvor has to handle the cargo safely and efficiently, integrate cargo management into the overall salvage plan, prevent pollution, and balance the concerns and legitimate interests of other parties—not always an easy task.

The first step in cargo handling is identification of the cargo in as much detail as practical. The salvor should collect and review bills of lading, mate's receipts, the cargo plan, and any other documents associated with cargo to determine the types of cargo, its location, and the conditions of stowage. Cargo plans can vary from simple papers for a homogeneous single cargo to voluminous computer printouts for general cargoes and containers. Salvors finding an old-fashioned stowage plan showing approximate volumes of cargo and the positions of pillars, beams, doors, and other interference are lucky indeed. Cargo documentation is useful not only in cargo handling, but also in valuing the cargo for determination of security or salved value.

Hazardous and obnoxious cargoes, their characteristics, and locations should be identified in as much detail as possible. Segregation requirements based on not creating dangerous mixes and on not decreasing values for both hazardous and nonhazardous cargo are determined before moving any cargo. The current editions of specialist publications such as *Thomas's Stowage*[1] and *The Storage and Segregation Guide to the IMDG Code*[2] are excellent tools for planning cargo movements and stowage during salvage operations.

When the ship carries hazardous cargoes or cargoes requiring special handling, an early decision must be made to call in marine chemists and other specialists in the particular materials and to identify safety measures for handling and storing. Decontamination stations suitable for the particular hazardous cargo must be set up and operable before handling that cargo.

The second step in cargo planning is to determine the quantity of cargo to remove. Normally, the best procedure is to salvage the cargo by salvaging the ship. No more cargo is removed than is absolutely necessary to put the ship in condition for refloating or to access that part of the ship blocked by cargo. There are two reasons for this. The first is obvious—moving a small amount of cargo is less work, time, and cost than moving a large amount. The second one is that undamaged cargo is safer and more likely to keep its value in its normal stowage than it is when handled and transhipped. Low-value, rugged cargo is almost always the leading candidate for discharge in salvage. Cargo that returns good results by removing large amounts of weight from the right places for little work is also a prime candidate. Deck cargo, where the return in weight removed per lift is high, fits the latter category. It is usually better to keep polluting or hazardous cargo aboard the casualty when it is safe to do so. Handling cargo under casualty conditions may carry a much higher risk of release than leaving it in its proper, intact stowage on board. Because of the high risk of release during transfers, extraordinarily safe handling procedures are appropriate. Regulatory authorities or good salvage practice may require the removal of all hazardous materials or pollutants to prevent their accidental discharge or to remove the hazard from the area.

Stowage factors in cubic feet per ton (cubic meters per tonne) describe the volume any commodity occupies in storage. It is not the actual measurement of the material, as it includes broken stowage, dunnage, irregular packaging, etc. Different stowage factors apply to commodities carried under refrigeration and other special conditions requiring an allowance for air circulation, etc. At best, and particularly in salvage, stowage factors are a rough guide, useful for estimating lightering requirements.

The type and nature of the cargo and its location in the ship affect the salvage methods. In the large majority of cases, some handling and discharge of cargo is a necessary part of weight management. Cargo may either be moved within the ship or removed from the ship entirely. Whichever is the case, cargo movement must be part of a plan integrated into the overall salvage plan and done in an orderly manner and sequence. While experienced salvors can begin making plans for cargo with very scant preliminary investigation, firm plans cannot coalesce until on-site surveys supply detailed information. Usually, the time required to arrange for receiving vessels and to get them on-site is enough to secure the ship and make internal preparations. Even when receiving vessels are available immediately, cargo should not be removed until the casualty is secured and can be expected to remain in position while the weight decreases.

Receiving vessels must be chosen carefully with an eye toward efficient stowage and movement of the cargo. A later section of this chapter discusses choosing and preparing receiving vessels in more detail.

The source of the labor for cargo handling must be settled at the outset. The rules of the port may require hiring local stevedores to handle all cargo. One of the principal advantages of using local stevedores is that most stevedoring firms provide labor, supervision, and cargo-handling equipment. One-stop shopping for forklifts, slings, spreader bars, platforms for unitized cargo, and similar materials not in the salvors' inventory may save considerable time. Several alternatives exist when the rules do not require local stevedores or the ship is outside a port. Salvage crew may make up the cargo gang, although it is not a very good use of their time. They are normally more profitably employed on other work requiring their skills as salvage mechanics. The casualty's crew is seldom a good source of labor. Casualty crews often dissociate themselves from salvage work and go about their normal routine. Extra cash pay, negotiated between the salvage master and the vessel's master or owner's representative, can make the extracurricular stevedoring work suddenly very attractive. Usually, salvors need some help from the crew in providing information on the cargo and power and other services for discharge. With liabilities resulting from casualties and the value of ships increasing, more owners are providing specially trained and qualified emergency or crisis management teams to casualties and supporting them from the home office. Very specialized cargoes like liquefied gases require help from a member of the ship's crew who has expert knowledge of the ship's system and the products. Owners of these vessels almost always have emergency teams that can be invaluable to salvors in handling very specialized and dangerous cargoes. Local pick-up crews, available through labor contractors or more informally in remote areas, are suitable when no special qualifications are necessary or when technical assistance can be provided by a single knowledgeable surveyor. Hiring crews intact with their own supervision is preferable to assembling crews from off-the-street hires. If the situation demands off-the-street hires, providing strong, dedicated supervision is necessary to form the individuals into an effective crew. When crews are unaccustomed to the work, there is a learning curve, but usually a steep one, as the work is simple.

When local stevedores do the work, union rules or local custom may set the working hours. The salvage master sets them for other crews. The number and length of shifts depend upon the number of workers available and the ability to supervise second and third shifts effectively. Sometimes, especially when crews do not subsist on the casualty, hours of daylight and transportation may limit work hours. Without such limitations, the author prefers one twelve-hour shift with two breaks, two ten-hour shifts with one break each, or three eight-hour shifts with one break each. Overall, the two ten-hour shifts often are the most productive. Efficiency usually decreases if the shifts extend to twelve hours and the job goes more than a few days. When conditions warrant, the number of breaks can be increased or short breaks and spelling set up.

Cargo can be handled in three basic ways. Two preserve its value and integrate cargo into the weight management plan; the third destroys the value but gets rid of the weight.

The first method is to move the cargo to another location in the casualty. This method retains the cargo and, through proper handling and protection, its value. The ship must have space to receive the cargo located so ground reaction is reduced and the trim changed in the desired direction. Seldom is there enough room in the ship to move much cargo about effectively. Additionally, ships' cargo-handling gear is built for loading and discharge, not for moving cargo about the ship. Cranes and booms may serve only one hold. Exceptions exist in RO/RO ships, where the cargo itself is mobile and fore and aft access reasonably clear, and with liquid cargoes that can move through piping systems. Liquid cargo must not be put into a tank where reactions can occur with the coating, or the corrosion products in uncoated tanks contaminate or react with the cargo. The aid of a specialist in the chemistry of the particular product should be sought before putting liquid cargo in a tank not set up for it. A way akin to the normal methods for moving bulk, break-bulk, or unitized cargo between ships can usually be rigged for same-ship transfers. For instance, it may be possible to bring up break-bulk or unitized cargo from one hold, run it down the deck to another with a forklift, and stow it in another hold; to blow bulk grain from one hold to another with a vacuum evacuator (vacuvator); or pass bulk ore or coal between holds with a conveyor or auger.

The second, and most common, method is to discharge the cargo into a lightering vessel or directly ashore for storage or disposal. Much of the remainder of this chapter is devoted to discussion of methods for handling various types of cargoes in salvage.

The third method of dealing with the cargo is jettisoning. Jettisoning is most suitable for cargoes with low values that do not justify the labor and expense of saving them, and when it is the only possibility for getting the cargo off the casualty. Most jettisoned cargoes have been ore, coal, rock or stone, grain, or similar dry bulk materials. Many cases exist of jettisoning deck cargoes of logs to improve stability. Even oil has been jettisoned in some rare cases. Because jettisoning involves only discharging the cargo without providing any means of retaining or transshipping, it is the quickest and easiest action, particularly when the ship can discharge her own cargo.

Even though jettisoning may be the best solution to both the cargo and the overall salvage problem, there are two big "buts . . . ." The first is loss of the total value of the jettisoned cargo. The salvor must prepare for allegations that jettisoning was expedience and not the best solution. He must prove jettisoning was reasonable and necessary. Potentially far more serious, jettisoning is release of the cargo to the environment. In most countries, permission of local authorities and environmental agencies is a prerequisite to jettisoning any cargo. Cases are on record where local officials have denied, or been extremely slow to grant, permission to jettison benign cargoes ranging from oranges to iron ore, coal, and china clay. Other cases show peripheral issues—usually environmental or wildlife management–based—have complicated jettisoning of benign materials. Some of the issues defy logic and have an "Alice in Wonderland" quality. It may be well worthwhile to seek permission to jettison benign cargoes, but it is optimistic to expect permission to be granted. The wise salvor hedges his bet by planning a way to lighter the cargo.

When the cargo is oil, chemicals, or any material that can be even mildly polluting, the probability of getting permission to jettison is practically nil. The mechanism for granting permission to jettison pollutants may not be defined in any particular governmental jurisdiction. Jettisoning of pollutants is not an issue in routine salvage operations. The question may arise when jettisoning a portion of the cargo may prevent even greater pollution than certain breakup and release of the entire cargo. The philosophical and legal aspects of this question have been and are expected to be argued ad nauseam. The answer depends upon the country in which the casualty occurs and the circumstances of the case. It is difficult to conceive of a bureaucracy that could move rapidly enough to make a sensitive decision in time to do any good.

Cargo Types and Handling Methods

Life for salvors was far simpler in the past when ships had derricks, booms, and steam-powered deck machinery that could always somehow be made to work.

Those days are gone and unlikely to return. Today, ships and cargoes are highly specialized. Many ships have no capability for loading or discharging cargoes; others have such specialized equipment that they can load and discharge only at specialized terminals. As casualties, these ships present salvors with complex problems. Despite the difficulties, salvors have consistently improvised methods of handling cargo under the very worst of conditions. This improvisation has been done without the benefit of forethought and research, simply because the variables are so many that too many credible scenarios can be put together. Considering Captain Murphy's strong penchant for salvage, one can reasonably expect the situations gamed in practice not to be those faced in the field.

Considerable experience in handling cargo under casualty conditions has built up within the salvage industry. Cargo and its handling in salvage can be broken down by the general types of cargo.

Whatever the type of cargo, the purpose of the discharge is threefold:

1. To remove the weight from the proper place in the casualty.
2. To save the value of the cargo.
3. To remove a potential pollutant.

All cargo operations should be structured with these three goals in mind. The circumstances and overall requirements of the particular case determine the priorities.

The traditional boomed yard and stay rig that served dry cargo vessels well for years has nearly disappeared in favor of more efficient handling methods. Sticks are still found on older vessels—the type that statistics show are most likely to become casualties. These ships also are likely to be poorly maintained. Cargo gear should be inspected before use and dangerous deficiencies corrected. It would be foolish to insist upon fully certified cargo gear for salvage operations, but it is good practice to reduce loads and not overwork the rigging.

Stuelcken booms and other heavy-lift booms with long outreaches and capacities up to several hundred tons are common, particularly in log and timber ships. These booms can reach any portion of the hatch served.

Most modern geared bulkers have post-mounted whirly cranes capable of operating through 360 degrees, fitted so they may work in pairs to double the lifting capacity. Other ships may have gantry cranes fitted or various types of bridles for handling different cargoes. Self-supporting containerships and barge carriers have similar gantries designed for their cargo. The crane operator and the cargo supervisor should check and understand the crane capacities at different outreaches before starting to move cargo. They also should understand any limitations that list places on the cargo gear.

Modern shipping carries very little break-bulk cargo. Most of the cargo that was carried as break-bulk is now containerized or at least unitized. Be that as it may, break-bulk cargo is encountered and must be dealt with. Break-bulk cargo can consist of almost anything packed in almost any manner.

It is general practice to place heavy cargo low in the hold with lighter cargo atop it and in 'tween decks. Accordingly, when a hold with break-bulk or unitized cargo is to be partially discharged, it is most efficient to clear the light cargo in way of the hatch square and remove the heavy cargo stowed deep in the hold. Preslung cargo, often placed in the hatch square for rapid removal at the discharge port, also can be discharged rapidly during salvage.

Mechanical equipment, usually forklifts, is best for moving unitized, palletized, bagged, drummed, crated, or other packaged cargo aboard the casualty from its stowed position to the hatch square. Forklifts also are required to position the cargo in the receiving vessels. Cases may arise when it is impossible to get forklifts. In such cases purchases will have to be laid out to move the cargo. Greasing the decks can make the job go much faster by reducing friction, but carries a penalty. Grease on weather decks is a potential pollution hazard, particularly where rain may wash some of the grease into the sea. Scuppers must be plugged and provision made to handle runoff. In a listing or extremely trimmed ship, restraining tackle may be necessary to prevent the cargo from running away.

Pallets are so common in cargo operations that the International Standards Organization (ISO) has set some standard sizes. These sizes can be used to plan and lay out palletized cargo stowage in the receiving vessel.

TABLE 12-1.

ISO STANDARD SIZE PALLETS	
Inches	*Millimeters*
40 by 32	1,000 by 800
48 by 32	1,200 by 800
48 by 40	1,200 by 1,000
48 by 64	1,200 by 1,600
48 by 72	1,200 by 1,800

Other sizes may be found in some countries, in stevedoring and warehouse operations, and for cargoes such as bagged materials where the pallets support standard packaging. Lacking more specific information, ISO sizes are good for planning.

Bagged or baled cargo can be removed from break-bulk or bulk storage and dump stowed on the receiving ship. Dump storage saves time and exertion without an unacceptable loss of cargo value. Bags are loaded and dumped into the receiving vessels where the resulting pyramid can be broken down to provide more efficient storage. Labor and time for cargo removal can be reduced significantly by this type of handling, but it may take some persuasion to talk stevedores into accepting dump storage as a salvage expedient. Bagged and baled cargo should be put into underdeck storage or covered and not exposed to moisture unless it is in impervious bags. Drummed and crated cargo does not have the resilience of bagged or baled cargo; it should never be dumped. The chance of cargo damage and possible spillage of pollutants or hazardous materials is simply too high.

Helicopters may move break-bulk, bagged, baled, drummed, crated, frozen, or unitized cargo. Because helicopter flying time is very expensive, a major goal is to move the maximum amount of cargo per flying hour. The normal method is to sling load the cargo under the hovering helicopter and drop it and return for another load without landing. The maximum transfer rate can usually be achieved when the flight is as short as possible and the cargo is delivered to a nearby lightering ship or barge. The economics and geography of the particular situation may dictate that the cargo be delivered to a more remote shore site. Cargo-handling crews at both ends must be large enough to assure the helicopter is not delayed waiting for a load to be prepared or for cargo to be moved out of the landing zone.

Containers have become ubiquitous in modern non-bulk dry cargo shipping. Vessels—ranging from containerships, all of whose cargo is in containers, to ships that carry containers on deck and RO/RO or break-bulk cargo below, and barges—carry containers. Most pure modern containerships, especially those on liner service between well-developed ports, rely on shore cranes to handle the cargo. Containers are a difficult problem in salvage because large, sometimes heavy boxes must be handled.

Containership capacity is described in TEUs—20-foot equivalent units. Several sizes of ISO standard containers are in service; table 12-2 contains a listing of those intended for intercontinental service.

While 20- and 40-foot ISO containers make up 95 percent of the container population, there are several variations, among them:

Sea-Land containers that are 35 feet by 8 feet 6½ inches high and 8 feet wide with a gross rating of 49,500 pounds.

Other lengths on specific trade routes. In the United States, a number of sizes have been developed as "domestic containers" for road and rail service. The lengths, widths, and depths may exceed ISO sizes. These containers have top and bottom fittings with apertures the same as the 40-foot ISO container. The European Economic Community has brought about a family of containers called "swap bodies." These units, like those in the United States, are designed around the truck size and weight limits of highways. These containers come in large sizes that have lashing and securing fittings at the bottom corresponding to ISO 40-foot boxes. They also come in half-size units with bottom fittings corresponding to ISO 20-foot containers.

Containers that are 9 feet and 9 feet 6 inches high.

Twenty-foot containers rated at 24 tonnes.

TABLE 12-2.

ISO SERIES 1 FREIGHT CONTAINERS (INTERCONTINENTAL)				
Desig.	*Length × Height × Width*		*Maximum Gross Weight*	
	feet	*mm*	*lbs (thousands)*	*tonnes*
1A	40 × 8 × 8	12,000 × 2,438 × 2,438	67.2	30.48
1AA	40 × 8 × 8.5	12,000 × 2,438 × 2,591	67.2	30.40
1B	30 × 8 × 8	9,000 × 2,438 × 2,438	56	25.4
1BB	30 × 8 × 8.5	9,000 × 2,438 × 2,591	56	25.4
1C	20 × 8 × 8	6,000 × 2,438 × 2,438	44.8	20.32
1CC	20 × 8 × 8.5	6,000 × 2,438 × 2,591	44.8	20.32
1D	10 × 8 × 8	3,000 5 2,438 × 2,438	22.4	10.16
1E	6 8" × 8 × 8	2,000 × 2,438 × 2,438	15.7	7.1
1F	5 × 8 × 8	1,500 × 2,438 × 2,438	11.2	5.08

Many types of container other than the basic closed box with end doors fit within the basic container size and weight limitations, among them:

Open-top containers with doors at one end and a removable roof, for very heavy cargoes that can be loaded into the container only with an overhead crane and for tall cargoes.

Open-sided containers for cargoes that must be side-loaded or that require ventilation.

Ventilated containers similar to dry cargo containers except for small openings to allow air circulation.

Dry bulk or hopper containers with loading hatches in the roof and discharge hatches opposite the doors or in the doors.

Tank containers suitable for a variety of liquids. These units may have means to heat the liquids.

Refrigerated containers or closed box containers with refrigerating plants or fittings for cooling by the ship's refrigeration system.

Flat rack containers similar to a flatbed trailer for heavy or oddly shaped items.

Auto-carrier containers carrying two to four vehicles.

Half height containers for high-density cargoes.

Livestock containers.

Collapsible containers.

Closed-box containers may carry large bags of liquid cargo or, with a temporary bulkhead, in way of the doors, dry bulk cargo. Liquid cargoes suitable for carriage in bulk bags have specific gravities of between 0.80 and 1.20, with the exception of a few products whose specific gravities reach up to 1.47.

Weights of containers in a casualty are difficult to estimate accurately because the manifested weight of the container may be the weight of the goods only and not include that of pallets, packaging, packing materials, or the container itself. Uneven weight distribution in the container may cause a balance problem when lifting the container. The problem is not made any easier by the propensity of shippers to overload containers and the willingness of shipping companies to accept them.

In the past, structural failure of containers was rare because container design was conservative. Nowadays, competition has driven container designers and manufacturers to reduce the margins to economize in construction materials. The result is a reduction in the reserve strength that requires extra care in handling containers in salvage.

Containers holding hazardous materials should be suitably placarded and the contents noted on the shipping papers. The location and nature of all hazardous materials should be in the hazardous materials information relative to that cargo. The papers should be on the bridge and with the chief mate. Don't count on it. Surveys have shown that a remarkably high percentage of containers are incorrectly placarded and contain materials other than what is indicated on the manifest. When purple smoke and green fumes are coming out of a container it is not the time to play hero or to take action on the chance the manifest may be right. Every reasonable effort must be made to identify the material and the hazard it presents. No action, even jettisoning, is safe or reasonable until the material is identified.

Discharging containers with the ship's container cranes when the ship is floating and rolling and pitching is a slow and tedious process because of the loads placed on the handling equipment by the sea (figure 12-1). It can be done, but care is needed not to damage the handling equipment, thereby hampering the container-handling operation. Care should also be taken not to damage containers during handling. Damage and rough handling can make the containers difficult to handle, exacerbating the original problem, causing damage or loss of cargo.

Cranes set on deck are not usually suitable for handling containers. There is seldom enough deck space to accommodate the crane, and the crane can reach

Fig. 12-1. This container is being lifted from the hold of a stranded ship with the casualty's container crane and a four-legged chain sling.

only a few containers. Placing a crane atop a tier of containers is satisfactory only if a foundation strong enough to support the weight of the crane and a loaded container is practical.

Where the depth of water alongside permits and the equipment is available, a floating whirly crane or sheer leg can come alongside to handle containers. The crane or sheer leg must have enough outreach to lift containers vertically out of their cells. Very large equipment is often necessary to reach the top tier of containers. Sheer legs are rather slow in this kind of work, as they must be repositioned to set each lift down and repositioned again to make the next lift.

Helicopters may lift containers, but should be reserved for very high value cargoes or for situations where no other options exist, as helicopters with enough lift capacity to handle loaded containers are very expensive. The weight and balance of the container is much more critical when lifting with helicopters than when lifting with cranes.

Slings for lifting containers should be similar to the slings in normal loading and discharge. Single-point-lift, four-leg slings, with hooks that fit facing outward into the fittings on the lower corners of the containers, are preferred. Simple four-leg slings connected to the fittings at the upper corners of the containers are acceptable. For 20-foot and smaller containers the slings can lead directly to a ring or to a vertical spreader. Slings for larger containers are made up to a frame so the legs are vertical and slings from each corner lead to a central, single lifting point. For helicopter lifting, slings should be as light as possible, as sling weight is part of the total lift weight. Various patent devices, similar to that shown in figure 12-2, are available for lifting containers lying in unusual positions. With such devices and judicious rigging of slings, containers can be picked up from almost any position, damaged containers can be picked up, and containers can be picked up with a single lift point.

There are no standard, proven methods that always work for discharging containers in salvage. If helicopters are not available and a crane cannot be brought alongside, the salvors' ingenuity must come into play to design and build some workable device to cope with the situation.

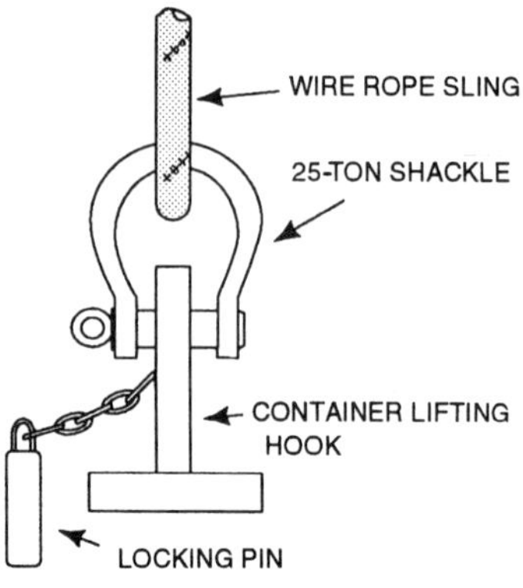

Fig. 12-2. Hook for lifting containers in unusual positions

Unstuffing containers for transfer is slow and labor-intensive, both because of the time to unstuff and restuff them and the nightmare of keeping track of the cargo. It is sometimes necessary to partially unstuff containers to get their weight and balance within the lift limits of helicopters or other equipment. The practice should be held to an absolute minimum. The comments for containers apply equally to trailers and barges, except that the latter are larger and heavier.

The barges carried by LASH, Seabee, and BACO ships are loaded and discharged with break-bulk, bulk, or unitized cargo or containers. Ships carrying these barges normally have gantry cranes with capacities of about 450 tons, elevators capable of lifting 2,000 tons, or arrangements for floating barges on and off. In salvage situations where the shipboard systems are inoperative, a discharge method must be improvised or the barges discharged individually.

Heavy-lift ships normally have gear that can handle their cargo; however, the attitude of the ship may prevent using the ship's gear. Where the ship's system is used, the help of the casualty's crew who know their ship's rigging and limitations is invaluable. The only options are to bring a piece of heavy-lift equipment alongside to remove the cargo or to call upon the ingenuity referred to previously.

Bulk carriers make up a sizable proportion of the world's fleets and carry a wide variety of products with stowage factors that range from 11 cubic feet per ton (0.31 cubic meters per tonne) to 100 cubic feet per ton (2.81 cubic meters per tonne). Bulk cargoes may liquefy and shift transversely, may have hazardous or obnoxious properties, or may emit gases. Salvors preparing for work on a bulk carrier should check the properties of the particular cargo, as they may affect the approach to the operation. Smaller bulkers have cranes or derricks for handling their own cargoes; larger ships are typically gearless.

TABLE 12-3.

SPECIFIC GRAVITIES FOR TYPICAL BULK CARGOES	
Cargo	*Specific Gravity*
Oats	0.35 to 0.49
Linseed	0.61 to 0.63
Barley	0.46 to 0.61
Grain Sorghums	0.63 to 0.71
Rye	0.63 to 0.72
Corn	0.59 to 0.72
Wheat	0.64 to 0.77
Raw Sugar	0.78
Coal	0.75 to 0.85
Phosphate	1.12
Salt	1.20
Bauxite	1.03 to 1.28
Chrome Ore	2.09 to 2.72
Manganese Ore	1.79 to 3.15
Iron Pellets	1.84 to 3.49
Iron Ore	1.91 to 3.49

Mariners traditionally load bulk carriers in any manner not specifically proscribed by the loading manual. On the other hand, classification societies intend that only the loading conditions shown in the manual are acceptable. Salvors need not become party to this argument; they have an "as found" condition they must deal with. The condition may or may not be found in the ship's loading manual. In any bulk carrier casualty, the hull shear and bending stresses for the condition in which the casualty is found should be calculated and a generous margin below the allowable stress maintained whenever possible. The size of this margin is a subjective judgment that takes into account the age and condition of the ship. The margin should be increased wherever evidence of wastage or damage appears. Calculations of hull stresses should be made before moving any cargo, with care taken that transient high stress conditions do not develop.

One of the simplest methods of discharging a gearless bulk carrier is to put cranes with grabs or clamshell buckets on board on the deck abeam the hatch and discharge over the side into the receiving vessel or the sea. Space limitations and the height of hatch coamings often dictate building foundations so cranes can rotate without interference from the hatch cover. It is sometimes possible to use the cranes and derricks on the receiving vessel to handle the cargo. As the receiving

Fig. 12-3. Discharging a gearless bulk carrier by cranes mounted on the receiving vessel

vessel is normally smaller than the casualty, the reach of her cranes or derricks may not be enough to make this method practical. As illustrated in figure 12-3, crawler cranes can be mounted on the lightering vessel to gain the necessary reach. The ship-to-ship transfer must be worked out carefully, taking into account the amounts of cargo to be transferred, crane access to the holds to be worked on both ships, hold capacities, and the development of bending moments and shear forces in both ships. Cranes should be placed to work with as little booming as possible during transfers.

Belt conveyors, augers, or endless chain bucket conveyors set into the hold of the casualty and discharging to a dump chute are very good tools for discharging bulk cargoes. Bobcats or other small bulldozers placed in the holds of both the discharging and receiving ships are invaluable for keeping the operation moving smoothly. Their function in the receiving ship is to move the cargo into position for cranes with a limited reach and to feed augers and conveyors. In the receiving ship, they trim the cargo and move it to fill the hold. It is normally most practical in the receiving ship to trim the cargo out evenly without regard for the angle of repose.

While grabs are normally faster and more efficient, skip boxes or intermediate bulk containers (IBCs) can be used for moving small quantities of cargo. Garbage dumpsters can easily be converted to skip boxes for this purpose. Cargo nets with canvas laid in to form a solid sling are faster than skip boxes, as they can be laid out on top of the cargo and filled by the Bobcat, or, where no small bulldozer is available, by building and dragging trimming boards. The slings are rigged so the contents may be dumped into the receiving vessel.

The grab that does not leak has not been made. The cargo-handling setup must include arrangements for preventing cargo that falls from the grabs from entering the water by falling between the ships or being washed off the deck by rain. Heavy-duty tarpaulins rigged over the rails of both ships under the grab paths deflect cargo that falls from the grabs (figure 12-4). Sweeping up the cargo prevents accumulations that may run off in rain, and plugging all scuppers but one and screening that one reduces the possibility of polluted runoff.

Cargoes that can be wetted without loss of value and cargoes that are being jettisoned can be slurried with seawater and pumped overboard or to the receiving vessel with slurry pumps. The slurry water pumped into the receiving vessel can be returned to the casualty to form more slurry (figure 12-5). Some slurries are very abrasive and can cause rapid wear on pumps not specifically designed for pumping them. A good supply of pump repair parts or extra pumps is needed to keep the operation running.

Grains, grain pellets, and other cargoes of fine discrete particles are most effectively discharged by grain evacuators, suction devices that are common in bulk grain–moving operations. Portable grain evacuators are available in most ports where bulk grain is handled and from special companies that move grain between

Fig. 12-4. The tarpaulin rigged between ships, over the rails of each and under the grab path, prevents bulk cargo from falling into the sea.

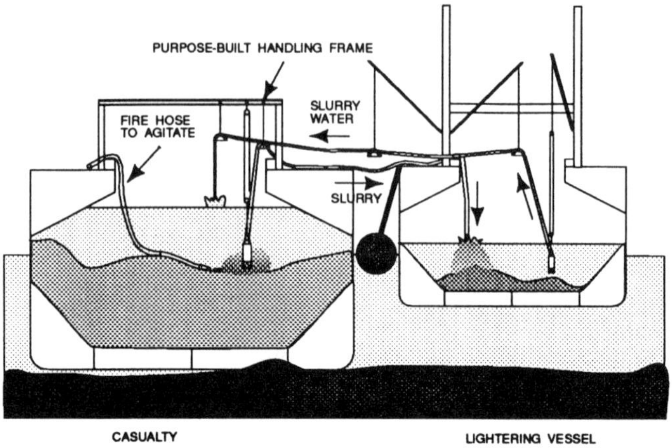

Fig. 12-5. Lightering bulk cargo by slurrying

storage and railway cars or barges. Water-driven eductors can move grain but, because wet grain loses its value, eductors are practical only when jettisoning the cargo.

Refrigerated cargo normally is carried either in containers or in refrigerated holds where it may be boxed or frozen in blocks. The key to handling refrigerated cargo is to keep it contained in a cooled, insulated space at the proper temperature as much as is possible and to minimize the temperature rise and exposure to ambient temperatures.

Refrigerated containers with their own cooling plant are the simplest problem. As long as power can be supplied to the container from the ship's supply or from salvage generators, the temperature should stay down. The box should be moved quickly out of direct sunlight and the power reconnected immediately. If necessary to help keep the temperature down, liquid oxygen or nitrogen or solid carbon dioxide (dry ice) may be introduced into the box unless the cargo is chilled vegetables or other living cargo. A warning should be spray painted on the container door that the atmosphere inside is not breathable.

Refrigerated holds normally hold their temperature a long time even without power if the hold is not opened. Holds should be kept closed except when cargo is actually handled. The cargo should be handled through the ambient temperature as quickly as possible and kept out of direct sunlight. Refrigerated containers, another refrigerated vessel, or fishing vessels with a freezing plant cooled when the cargo comes on board are preferred for receiving the cargo. This is not always possible. When it is not, the cargo should be packed into a solid block to limit thawing damage to the outside of the block and the block should be covered with any available insulating material. Ice or dry ice can be packed around the cargo to help keep the temperature down. If dry ice is used, the concentration of gaseous carbon dioxide in the space may become dangerously high. No one should enter the space until it has been well ventilated. Only short transshipments followed by careful inspection of the cargo are acceptable with dry-ice packing.

Stevedoring gangs handling frozen cargo and working in freezer holds should have freezer gear and other personal protective equipment. The casualty may have caused rupture of the refrigerant system and leakage of the refrigerant into the hold. The hold should be checked for a breathable atmosphere before the crew enters it, following the same procedures used for entering any closed space. Most modern ships use an odorless chlorofluorocarbon (CFC) refrigerant, but ammonia systems that warn of system damage with the characteristic smell of ammonia are still around and may be around in the future if chlorofluorocarbon systems are phased out as an environmental measure.

In theory, vehicular cargo in RO/RO ships, including those incredibly ugly car carriers, is quick and simple to discharge—just drive the vehicle down the ramps and off the ship. Like most things that are simple in theory, handling cargo on RO/RO casualties can be difficult in practice. RO/ROs are notoriously tender. Great care is necessary in sequencing cargo discharge and maintaining ballast in the ship to keep a positive metacentric height and righting arm. Particular attention must be paid to ships carrying containers on deck. Such a ship can easily become unstable by discharging vehicular cargo with the containers in place. The stability situation in a grounded RO/RO is made more critical by the reduction in normal stability that accompanies grounding. No cargo should be removed from a RO/RO or car carrier, particularly from a grounded one, before detailed stability analyses and careful and full study of the discharge sequence.

When the stability situation is in hand, discharge is a relatively simple matter. The simplest and most practical method is to bring a barge and moor it so vehicles can drive off the casualty onto the barge. Vehicles are either parked on the barge and taken to a standoff moored receiving vessel or ashore or driven across the barge onto a receiving vessel moored alongside. The particular arrangements depend upon the circumstances of the case and the arrangements of the ramps.

When placing barges to act as transfer platforms, the height of the barge and that of the ramp of the ship must be aligned within workable limits. The barge may have to be ballasted quite heavily to allow the ramp to land properly. If the change in slope between the ship and barge is too great, trailers may strike the ship or all vehicles may bottom out with some damage as they move across the ramp. It is altogether possible that ballasting the barge to fit the discharging ship may make a fit with the receiving ship impractical. In these cases, the receiving ship may go into a standoff moor or two barges rigged. The former is usually more practical.

Logs deserve a few words because they are often deck cargoes and are easy and efficient to discharge and restow without any loss of value. Logs are buoyant; they can simply be put over the side and ponded or rafted with a simple boom made of the logs themselves. Once rafted, they may be towed away, floated ashore, or held and reloaded and restowed upon completion of the refloating. There is a glitch in this simple time-honored operation. In recent years, environmental authorities, concerned about chemicals that leach from woods not native to the area, have prevented putting some types of logs into the water. The message is clear: anytime any cargo goes into the water, permanently or temporarily, the permission of cognizant environmental authorities must be obtained or civil penalties may follow.

Although crude oil and petroleum products are the best known, and probably the most common, liquid cargoes, a wide variety of liquid and semiliquid products are carried in tank ships or in tanks aboard other types of vessels. Many of the cargoes are benign—neither polluting nor hazardous—others are one or the other, or both. Because huge liabilities can result from spilling polluting liquids, especially petroleum, more owners are prepared to assist salvors and more tanker crews are better trained and prepared for salvage operations. All the liquid and semiliquid cargoes are pumped with either the casualty's installed system or over-the-top with portable equipment. Chapter 13 describes in some detail pumping of oil cargoes from tanker casualties. The principles of discharging oil cargoes apply to discharges of all liquid and semiliquid cargoes. The differences are in the cargo-specific details. While salvors are familiar with petroleum transfer operations and most of the other common cargoes in their area of operations, they cannot be knowledgeable in the details of precautions and equipment for transferring all the liquid and semiliquid cargoes they may encounter. They must be prepared to call in experts in particular cargoes. By sticking to the principles of transferring oil cargoes and modifying the procedures and equipment to fit the conditions extant, a successful transfer of any product can be improvised.

The final cargo type discussed is probably the most dangerous cargo at sea—liquefied gases. Liquefied gases transported by sea fall into two categories—those whose vapors are flammable when mixed with air and those whose vapors are both flammable and toxic. The first group, composed of hydrocarbons—natural gas, butane, propane, butadiene, propylene, and ethylene—make up the bulk of liquefied gas cargoes. Fire and explosion are the primary hazards of these cargoes. Cargoes in the second category are chemical liquefied gases—vinyl chloride monomer, methyl chloride, ammonia, and propylene oxide. Fire, explosion, toxicity, and asphyxiation are the main hazards of these gases. Because the gases evaporate rapidly at ambient pressures and temperatures, there is little or no water pollution problem. Chemical gases may be corrosive and ammonia is very soluble in water.

The characteristics of the particular liquefied gas govern the type of containment and conditions for carrying the cargo. The following table gives typical conditions under which liquefied gases are transported at an ambient temperature of 30 degrees Celsius.

TABLE 12-4.

Liquefied Gas	*Fully Pressurized up to 19 bars*		*Semirefrigerated up to 7 bars*		*Fully Refrigerated up to 1.7 bars*	
	Press bars	*Temp. deg. C*	*Press bars*	*Temp. deg. C*	*Press bars*	*Temp. deg. C*
Methane					1.0	–161.5
Ethylene			6.0	–66.5	1.0	–104
Propylene	13.2	30	6.0	1.0	1.0	–47.7
Propane	10.8	30	6.0	8.5	1.0	–42.8
Ammonia	11.6	30	6.0	9.5	1.0	–33.4
Butane or Propane	7.5	30	6.0	26	1.0	–32.0
Methyl Chloride		30			1.0	–24.3
Vinyl Chloride	4.7	30	4.63	30	1.0	–13.4
Butadiene	3.3	30	3.3	30	1.0	–4.5
Butane	2.9	30	2.9	30	1.0	–0.6
Ethylene Oxide		30		30	1.0	23-28
Propylene Oxide	1.0	30	1.0	30	1.0	30
Isoprene	1.0	30	1.0	30	1.0	30

Fortunately, the operators of liquefied gas carriers are among the most responsible of owners. As noted previously, many operators have detailed, well-organized contingency plans and emergency teams. Some have the cryogenic hoses and other materials needed for ship-to-ship transfers in their emergency kits. Salvors should take advantage of every source of assistance for liquefied gas transfers.

Despite the fact that technical assistance normally is forthcoming from the owner, a few general words about liquefied gas transfers in salvage are in order. As with other polluting and hazardous cargo carriers, the primary salvage problems with LPG and LNG ships are associated with safe handling of the cargo.

Emergency transfers should approach, as closely as possible, normal ship-to-ship transfer procedures. Accordingly, some knowledge of basic cargo-handling procedures makes good background for developing modifications. When a fully or semipressurized LPG carrier discharges, compressors take suction on cargo vapor in the top of the tank and pressurize the tanks with gas vapor. The pressure forces liquid cargo to the suction side of a pump through a liquid line in the bottom of the tank. The pump raises the pressure of the liquid and discharges it through the cargo manifold into the liquid line of the receiving tank.

Fully refrigerated vessels normally have individual deep well pumps for discharging to a booster system and then into precooled tanks. In neither case is cargo transfer simply a matter of flanging up and pumping.

The OCIMF booklet *Ship-to-Ship Transfer Guide (Liquefied Gases)*[3] and the International Chamber of Shipping *Tanker Safety Guide (Liquefied Gas)*[4] provide excellent information on the procedures and concerns in these operations. These booklets furnish basic guidelines. Normal procedures are modified as little as possible by unusual conditions caused by the casualty. Any variations from normal ship-to-ship transfers should be agreed to between the salvage master and the owner's emergency team leader before gas is transferred.

The greatest hazard of LPG operations comes from release of highly flammable, possibly toxic cargo. Liquefied natural gas in cryogenic storage presents no pollution problem but is dangerous because of the cargo's flammability, toxicity, and low temperatures. Brittle fracture of the structure from exposure to cryogenic cargo is one of the major problems of LNG handling in salvage. LNG carriers under salvage must be protected from bumps and knocks from other vessels. In both fully refrigerated LPG vessels and LNG ships maintaining the reliquefication plant, close control of the cargo and keeping links and sharp bends out of the transfer hose are absolutely mandatory when transferring cargo.

The need for expert assistance in cargo handling from the owners cannot be emphasized too strongly. Salvors, for all their initiative, imagination, and ingenuity, are simply over their heads with the technical complexity of LNG and LPG vessels and the hazards of their cargo.

Expert assistance has equal importance in chemical tanker casualties. *The Tanker Safety Guide (Chemicals)*[5] is a good basic reference for the salvor, as are the Material Safety Data Sheets for each chemical in the cargo. The three books mentioned in Chapter 5, *The Chemical Data Guide for Bulk Shipment by Water*, the U.S. Department of Transportation's *Emergency Response Guidebook*, and the NIOSH *Pocket Guide to Chemical Hazards*, are invaluable. As good as all these books are, they are not enough; expert knowledge is mandatory.

During normal commercial operations, several chemicals are frequently discharged simultaneously. Simultaneous discharge of several chemicals in salvage is more than poor salvage practice; it is dangerous and stupid. Discharging several products spreads the attention of senior salvage people too thin and increases the probability of an accident dramatically.

The LPG *Ship-to-Ship Transfer Guide* is a solid reference for chemical ship emergency transfers. In addition to the procedures contained in this guide, particular attention should be paid to hose compatibility with the product, quick-release couplings on the manifolds, appropriate fire-fighting equipment and agents for the chemicals being transferred, and proper personal protective equipment.

LPG, LNG, and chemical transfers are the most serious cargo work that salvors undertake. The margin for error ranges from zero to tiny. There is no place in these operations for the big, hairy-chested, macho salvor filled with bravado. Technical knowledge and meticulous care are necessary.

Removal of any but bulk cargo from flooded holds is diver-intensive, complex rigging work. The work can be particularly difficult when the cargo contains chemicals or products that react with water or organic matter that decays and forms hazardous or noxious products with the floodwater. It is usually better to leave the cargo in place, or remove only as much as absolutely necessary, pump the hold, then work the cargo.

The same methods—grabs, slurries, augers—may discharge bulk cargo from flooded holds as well as from dry holds. It may be necessary for divers with jetting hoses to drive the cargo into the removal equipment, agitating slurries with fire hoses both to keep the concentration of cargo in the slurry high and to supply water to the slurry. Air lifts are very effective for moving grain and almost any cargo that can fit through the air lift suction. During one classic case on the West Coast of the United States, air lifting salvaged a valuable cargo of canned salmon. Air lifts can normally be rigged so the suction may be moved about to assure a constant flow.

Fire, flooding, or oil leakage may make a cargo valueless. Even worse, flooding may start a decomposition process that can result in swelling and production of dangerous or obnoxious gases (figure 12-6). With the concurrence of the surveyor representing cargo or general average, if one is on board, the cargo can be disposed of. Disposal means either jettisoning, with the appropriate permissions, or taking the cargo ashore for disposal at a landfill or by incineration. Bulk cargoes in partially flooded holds are often well handled by finishing the job of flooding and discharging the cargo with slurry pumps or air lifts. Grabs can haul out frozen blocks, unitized cargo, bagged cargo, and cargo too dense or too cohesive for slurrying. Combinations of methods must remove some cargoes, such as thawing fish in deteriorating cartons in flooded holds. Disposing of cargo requires no finesse. The most economical, expeditious, and effective methods consistent with strict compliance with environmental regulation are best. Working closely with local environmental officials to obtain agreement on the method and place of disposal is mandatory in such cases. Failure to comply with local regulations, no matter how onerous, can result in civil penalties and long and costly administrative or legal procedures.

Rates of cargo handling achieved at terminals are seldom, if ever, reached during salvage operations. The conditions just do not permit; there are far too many variables and irregularities. This being the case, it is difficult to impossible to estimate the time required for cargo removals. The most practical method is to start pulling cargo out and see how the work goes. Inevitably, times improve as crews get used to the work and methods change to eliminate inefficiencies.

Fig. 12-6. This break-bulk cargo, damaged by fire followed by flooding, is being removed by portable materials-handling equipment. Photo courtesy of J.H. Leitz.

Lightering Ships

Large marine operators operating a salvage company may have divisions that can supply lightering vessels from their fleets, but usually salvors charter lightering vessels. Ideal vessels are seldom available; make do is the order of the day. Owners and their underwriters seldom display wild enthusiasm for exposing vessels to the rigors and inherent dangers of salvage operations. They are likely to make their less-than-first-line equipment available and charge premium prices for it. It is incumbent upon the salvor to select the vessels most suited for the cargo and conditions—often from a collection of poor choices. Vessels outfitted as lightering vessels and fully equipped for mooring alongside and transferring are found in ports that are substantially shallower than the roadstead serving the port. These vessels can be ideal, but they usually have quite heavy schedules. They are usually very expensive, especially if away from their normal operating area.

For any vessels selected, the charter party specifies the terms and conditions of the charter. The charter party must address any special or unusual equipment the owner provides. Fenders and dunnage are excellent examples. When the lightering vessel provides either or both, aggravation and significant delay can result if the lightering ship or barge arrives at the casualty without proper equipment. This book discusses neither charter parties nor the attendant surveys, other than to emphasize the wisdom of on- and off-hire surveys to establish the condition of chartered vessels at the beginning and end of the operation. An independent surveyor should make the surveys. Independent surveys are not always possible, as the ship may arrive at the site without a port call. If it does, the salvage master and the vessel's master should conduct joint surveys and agree to the conditions found. Checking bunkers, lubricants, and other consumables is an integral part of these surveys. Vessels receiving bulk cargo should have a draft survey before loading, after loading, and frequently during the ship-to-ship transfer.

Preservation of the cargo requires development of a simple cargo stowage plan for the lightering vessel. The plan does not need to be a full-fledged load plan, but should assure that incompatible cargoes are not mixed and that dangerous combinations of materials are not formed. A load plan also helps to get the maximum amount of cargo in the ship.

The complexity of mooring vessels alongside one another increases with the size of the vessels. Mooring a small ship or barge alongside a larger ship is normally a routine and straightforward operation. Mooring large ships together is more complicated, as is mooring in restricted waters, such as when one ship is aground. When a lightering ship or barge goes alongside a grounded vessel, tugs should assist. The price of tug assistance is much less than that of having two ships aground. Good seamanship, common sense, and a belt and suspenders approach should be present in all mooring operations.

Tugs for assisting during berthing must be efficient in that service. This usually means passing over any oceangoing tugs at the scene and having tugs come out for ship assistance from a nearby port. While this may seem inefficient, it is sound practice and good economy. Oceangoing tugs and salvage ships are not good ship assistance tugs. They are too big, too heavy, and too slow to respond. Often, they cannot work alongside because of design features. Before using oceangoing tugs to berth lightering vessels alongside a casualty, the salvage master should review the operation carefully with the tug masters. If the tug masters have severe reservations or the salvage master on reflection has doubts about the usefulness of the tugs, other tugs should be brought in. The potential consequences of a botched operation are too great to take unnecessary and avoidable risks.

Fendering and mooring, two very important issues for alongside cargo transfers, are discussed in some detail later in this chapter.

The lightering ship must be suitable and prepared for the cargo so that the transshipment does not decrease the value of the cargo. Overall ship size is important for two reasons: the ship must be large enough to carry a reasonable amount of cargo yet small enough to come alongside and remain there without grounding as her draft increases during loading. Point loads from heavy loads, laden forklifts, and distributed loads from dense bulk cargo may overload the structure of some ships. Laying timbers or steel plates on the deck of the hold allows carrying heavier loads. Bulk loads, especially high-density loads of ore and concentrate, must be spread evenly to limit longitudinal bending moment during both loading and the passage.

Significant cargo value can be lost if cargo, particularly bulk foodstuffs, is put into holds that have not been cleaned for it or have not been fumigated. Salvors must make an economic judgement between loss of cargo value and delay in arrival at the salvage site if time is taken to clean or fumigate holds before leaving port. It is reasonable for salvage crew to clean holds when the vessel arrives at the salvage site.

The length of the trip to the discharge site and the expected weather can influence methods of securing cargo in the lightering ship. For a short trip, in sheltered waters, or in assured good weather, securing does not have to be as thorough as for a long deep-sea voyage; some judicious shortcuts are permissible. For instance, securing the free surface of grains and trimming bulk cargo may be omitted. The decision to take shortcuts should be made deliberately after careful consideration of the situation and of the potential results of being wrong. Securing the hatches properly for even short voyages should never be ignored. No shortcuts that risk damage to cargo in transit or threaten the vessel should be taken. It is wise to obtain the concurrence of the attending cargo surveyor in any shortcuts made to expedite cargo transfer.

Barges

In some areas, barges are plentiful and easier to hire than lightering ships. Finding suitable barges may take an effort, for they may serve the offshore oil or the construction industries rather than the marine transportation industry. The comments made for lightering ships apply to barges as well.

Tank barges, especially in service carrying the same cargo taken from the casualty, are very useful in salvage. Cleaning is not required and the barges have heating systems appropriate to the product. Other tank barges may be capable of carrying either single or multiple cargoes. The latter may be able to individually control the temperature of each product. All tank barges have ullaging or other gauging devices suitable to their normal service. Those intended to carry light petroleum and certain chemical products that have noxious fumes may have vapor control systems.

Often, salvors may use any tank barge that is available to take bunkers and cargo from the casualty. This practice may result in a significant, if not total, loss of the value of the products loaded through their contamination by residues. It may also result in a large cost for discharging the barge, cleaning it, and disposing of the contaminated product. This is not to disparage the practice. As frequently occurs in salvage, such a selection may be the best of a collection of poor choices.

Covered barges that can protect the cargo from moisture are best for bulk cargoes, steel coils, and products subject to corrosion damage, and any cargo that requires underdeck storage. When covered barges receive cargo other than bulk cargoes, they should be equipped with forklifts or other equipment for moving the cargo within the barge.

Open-deck barges are very good for receiving containers, vehicles, and some forms of unitized or packaged cargo. All cargoes, except containers put onto flat-deck barges, should be covered and protected from weather. The barge itself should be protected against damage from the cargo by dunnage or steel plates laid over the deck. Cranes, forklifts, and small bulldozers are invaluable for moving cargoes about barges and assuring efficient stowage. If bulk cargo is put aboard, sturdy side and end walls, preferably of steel, should be built to contain the cargo. Containers make fine side walls. It is often necessary on deck barges to add tie-down points and pad eyes to secure cargo.

Mooring

The decision of how and where to moor the lightering vessel is an important one in any salvage operation. A well-sited, secure moor contributes to the success of the cargo transfer. A successful cargo transfer can spell the difference between success and failure of the salvage operation. The same principles and general procedures apply whatever the types of ship and cargo transferred.

Ship-to-ship transfers of both solid and liquid cargoes have become routine operations. There is nothing routine about a casualty ship-to-ship transfer, but no magic, black or otherwise, governs casualty mooring operations. That honor belongs to first-class seamanship, attention to detail, and meticulous preparation. There is no margin for relaxation in planning and carrying out a moor in a casualty situation.

As soon as possible, all the details of a normal ship-to-ship transfer should be worked through by the masters of the two ships at a conference chaired by the salvage master. When the ordinary details are in hand, variations for the specific operation are discussed until the salvage master is satisfied everyone knows the situation and their role. Specific items to be discussed include:

- Maneuvering to approach the casualty.
- Tug assistance.
- Vessel supplying mooring lines, fenders, etc.
- Mooring lines—type, number, size, and arrangement.
- Passing lines.
- Fendering.
- Ground tackle off the casualty and its position.
- Communications, including VHF working channels.
- Emergency and abort procedures.

For normal ship-to-ship transfers, moors usually are made with the ships under way or one ship at anchor headed into the wind. Salvage operations seldom allow the luxury of choosing the transfer site, let alone the heading for the transfer.

Tug assistance is likely to be required for casualty transfers; there should be no hesitancy about providing these tugs.

Mooring maneuvers are carried out slowly and carefully. Mooring operations are a playground for Captain Murphy. Once things begin to go wrong they are likely to continue to deteriorate until a serious accident takes place. If things begin to go wrong, no one in a position of responsibility should hesitate to break the operation off and begin again.

Night mooring operations in particular are an invitation to disaster. Sometimes they cannot be avoided. In these cases, extra attention must be paid to the details of planning and extreme care used throughout the operation. The berthing side should be well illuminated with spotlights on fenders. The lights should be directed so personnel on the maneuvering ship are not blinded. If the plan begins to break down in any way, it is far wiser to abort and try again than to continue the operation.

Positioning

In the preferred position for ship-to-ship transfers, the ships lie alongside one another, either bow-to-bow or Chinese, with the manifolds in tankers aligned as nearly as practical, and the gear in dry cargo vessels in the best position to work the holds. There are many situations in which alongside transfers are impractical—the casualty lying stranded where the lightering vessel cannot safely go alongside because of weather, water depth, surf, swell, heavy cargo leakage, etc. In these cases, stern-to-stern and other standoff moors that fit the geography and meteorology of the salvage site are set up. Figures 12-7 and 12-8 show typical mooring setups. Standoff moors are most common when liquid or slurried cargo can be pumped between the casualty and lightering vessels. They are also practical where the cargo is transferred by helicopter or barge between the two ships.

Floating hoses for transferring liquid cargoes make the long hose runs in standoff moors practical. Good practice calls for keeping the portion of the hose in the water short. Floating hoses can be a blessing in calm weather but can behave badly in heavy weather, strong surf, or currents. Several parallel floating hoses can be used, but the problems associated with many hoses in the water in heavy weather or strong surf or current often outweigh the advantage of a faster transfer.

In some cases, hoses supported by a span wire between the ships may be better than floating hoses. Wire-supported hoses are used in cases where the ships can lie close enough together to make wire support of the hose practical or where the seas are so rough that floating hoses are impractical.

The exact location of the lightering ship in stern-to-stern or standoff moor depends upon the geography of the site and the location of critical ground tackle. The ships should be as close together as safety permits. A booster pump for liquid cargoes or slurries may be required in the transfer system if the ships are too far apart.

Inserting a booster pump is a minor inconvenience and should be subordinated to assuring the ships are soundly and securely moored.

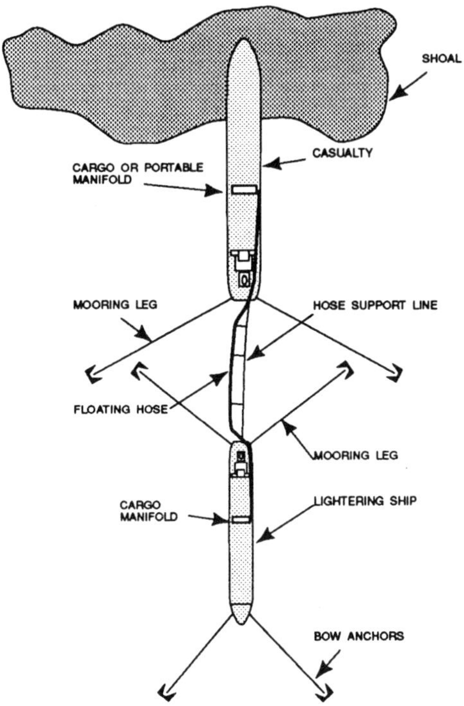

Fig. 12-7. Stern-to-stern moor for liquid cargo transfer

Mooring Lines

Casualty cargo transfers demand a thorough understanding of how mooring lines work and what they do not do. A lot of voodoo and old wives' tales appear in sea stories about mooring. As with many things, what seems obvious about moors ain't necessarily so, and less can work better than more.

Good seamanship requires that mooring lines all be of the same material and construction and that the moor be tended and adjusted regularly to accommodate tide and weather as well as the increasing draft of the lightering vessel. Weather should be watched with lightering vessels alongside a casualty. When the weather is likely to deteriorate beyond acceptable conditions, the operation should be broken off early enough to have the lightering vessel clear before maneuvering in restricted or shoal waters becomes too dangerous.

The moor is an elastic connection between ships that holds them in position relative to one another while accepting and responding to dynamic loads from the sea and wind. Both wire and fiber rope mooring lines obey a basic rule of the sea: you can't push on a rope. They only accept loads in tension. Other principles of mooring lines are well known, but bear repeating:

Breast lines provide most of the restraint against transverse forces.

Springlines provide most of the restraint against longitudinal forces. Springlines provide restraint, either forward or aft, depending upon their direction of lead, but only one set of springs carries load at any time.

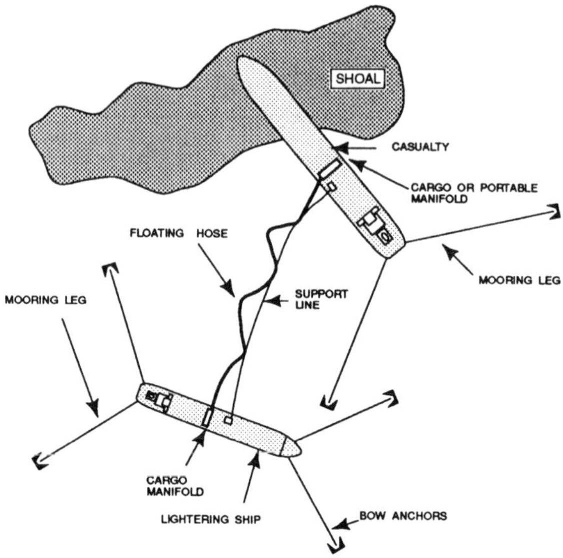

Fig. 12-8. Standoff moor for liquid cargo transfer

Head and stern lines, because of their angle of lead, provide some restraint against both transverse and longitudinal forces. Their effect is less than generally assumed for two reasons:

The direction of the largest forces is usually almost completely transverse or completely longitudinal, therefore in directions where the breast and springlines carry most of the load.

Head and stern lines are normally much longer than breast and springlines and thus carry a reduced proportion of the load.

Short lines carry proportionately more load than long lines and are more affected by dip—the angle the line makes with the horizontal. The effectiveness of the line equals the cosine of the dip; a line at 30 degrees to the horizontal is 86.6 percent effective, one at 45 degrees 71 percent effective, one at 60 degrees 50 percent effective, etc.

Multiple lines at the same location add little to the strength of the moor because the load is not distributed evenly between all the parts of the lines. The tightest lines carry nearly all the load.

Load is distributed among mooring lines in direct proportion to their stiffness. For two ropes of the same size, stiffness is a function of the material, construction, and length of the rope. Figure 12-9 shows the effect of length and material on typical mooring lines.

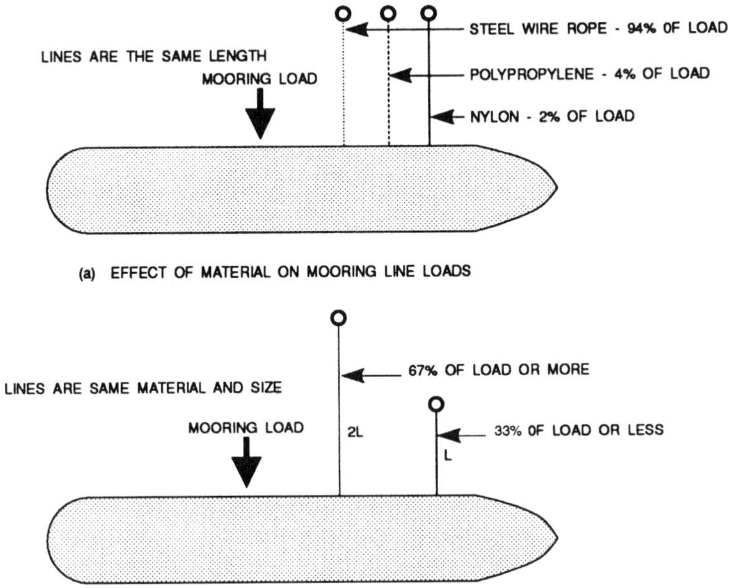

Fig. 12-9. Effect of material and length on mooring line loads

Understanding of the basic principle that stiffer lines accept a greater proportion of the load leads to an appreciation of how moors work and some basic rules for good mooring. Mooring lines should be of the same material and construction; otherwise, disproportionate load sharing occurs throughout the moor. Mixing wire and fiber ropes in the same portion of a moor has little point, as the wire rope carries almost all the load. The exception lies in fiber lines backing up wire rope lines. If wire and fiber ropes must be mixed, the breast and spring lines should be wire rope, the head and stern lines fiber. Wire ropes require lubrication; otherwise they lose strength rapidly and unpredictably with corrosion. However, many owners do not lubricate wire mooring ropes because when the rope goes in the water the lubricant can leave a sheen that can incur a fine. Accordingly, synthetic fiber ropes often back up wire rope mooring lines. Another wire rope should replace parted wire rope mooring lines immediately.

Some very large ships have replaced wire rope mooring lines with aramid or HMPE lines. These lines have about 98 percent of the strength of the same sized wire rope. Abrasion is the primary enemy of these lines, so all surfaces they pass over must be as smooth as possible. Smooth surfaces can be expected on the ship owning the lines, but the other ship should be checked carefully to insure the very expensive lines are not abraded needlessly.

The effect of dip can be significant as freeboards change during lightering. If the casualty is grounded, its freeboard does not change, but that of the lightering vessel decreases as she is loaded. However, if the casualty is afloat, her freeboard increases while that of the lightering ship decreases. It may be necessary to add mooring lines to accommodate the dip that results from large freeboard differences.

During ship-to-ship transfers, normal good mooring procedures should be followed with regard to making up mooring lines and fitting chafing gear and preventers. Automatic tensioning mooring winches should not be set in automatic, as the winches may begin to work against one another. Winch brakes should be set and the winches taken out of gear.

A special warning concerns transfers made with ships at anchor. A ship's anchor is designed to hold one ship in good holding ground in moderately bad weather. Two ships on a single anchor can easily load the anchor system near its design point and cause failure of the anchoring system. Ship anchor systems fail by anchor drag. Two ships moored on a single dragging anchor can provide more excitement than most mariners are comfortable with. Whenever two ships are moored to a single anchor, a sharp eye should be kept on the weather and the moor to make sure it is not broken, or a second anchor should be set at any sign of deteriorating weather.

Fendering

Fendering is an important component in any alongside cargo transfer. As with mooring, the principles and procedures discussed for fendering apply equally to all casualties.

Fendering in alongside cargo transfers serves three purposes:

1. The primary fenders along the parallel midbody absorb impact loads during mooring and prevent ships that are moving with the sea from contacting one another.
2. Secondary fenders forward and aft of primary fenders absorb loads and prevent contact during berthing and unberthing and when ships do not lie parallel.
3. Tertiary fenders protect overhangs and other places where contact is likely.

Potentially large contact forces require substantial fendering systems. Fender systems for casualty oil transfers are tailored to the casualty, the lightering ship, and the situation by considering the sizes of the ships and the energy to be absorbed in berthing.

Three types of heavy fenders suitable for use in cargo transfers are available: foam-filled fenders and high- and low-pressure pneumatic fenders. Fenders may be obtained from several specialty equipment and rubber products manufacturers. The following table gives descriptions of the characteristics of each type.

TABLE 12-5.

FENDER CHARACTERISTICS			
	Foam Filled	*High-pressure Pneumatic*	*Low-pressure Pneumatic*
Construction	Closed cell polyethylene foam covered with neoprene or a polyurethane elastomer	Reinforced rubber containing air at 7 to 10 psi filled through a filling valve on one end	Rubber cylinders containing air at about 1 psi
Cover	Sometimes tires with galvanized chain net	All but smallest have tire net	Protective tire nets on special order only
Diameter	20 inches to 14 feet (508 millimeters to 4.25 meters)	20 inches to 20 feet (508 millimeters to 6 meters)	3 to 15 feet (1 to 4.6 meters)
Length	Less than 5 to more than 28 feet (less than 1.52 to more than 8.5 meters)	39 inches to 40 feet (1 to 12 meters)	Shortest practical length is 2.5 times the diameter, maximum practical length 100 feet (30 meters)
Weight	75 to 28,000 pounds (34 to 12,725 kilos)	112 to 29,000 pounds (51 to 13,200 kilos)	88 to 16,000 pounds (40 to 7,275 kilos)

The three major types of fenders have advantages and disadvantages related to their construction. Foam fenders have high-energy absorption, are easy to repair, but are bulky and heavy to transport. Pneumatic fenders may be deflated for transportation and partially deflated to reduce standoff distances, but require a compressed air source for inflation and are effectively lost if punctured. Ease of transportation makes the low-pressure pneumatic fender particularly suitable for casualty transfer operations. Salvors seldom have the luxury of choice when setting up a fender system. Individual preferences and prejudices enter the selection of fenders, but ruggedness is always a major factor. Fenders, like all other equipment in salvage operations, are subject to hard knocks and unpredictable accidents. Rugged fenders are likely to be around at the end. That having been said, it is worthwhile to note that it is not really necessary to baby fenders, but they should be treated with reasonable care when moving them, launching them, or setting them up. They should not be dragged when any way to lift or carry them exists. High-pressure pneumatic fenders are more rugged but still subject to puncture damage. A hose spraying water on pneumatic fenders prevents heating, expansion, and possible rupture during long operations in hot climates.

In emergencies, fenders can be improvised from scrap heavy equipment tires by ganging them over an oil-filled pipe core or a core of timbers as shown in figure 12-10. To increase energy absorption, the tires should have inflated inner tubes or a stuffing of old fiber line. No matter how carefully they are assembled, tire fenders are never better than marginally satisfactory. A salvor may have no choice.

The particular fendering system for a job depends upon the ships and conditions for the transfer. Figure 12-11 shows a typical-ship-to-ship transfer fendering system with primary, secondary, and tertiary fenders. Note that the primary fenders are located abreast bulkheads so that bulkheads transmit impact loads from berthing to the structure. The high-pressure pneumatic fenders could be replaced with low-pressure pneumatic fenders at a moderate cost in efficiency. Either ship may carry the fenders. Commonly, the lightering ship carries the fenders, but rigging the fenders from the casualty is a security measure to prevent collision damage if something goes awry during the approach.

In general, primary fenders are rigged along the parallel midbody with one at each end and others at about 100-foot (30-meter) intervals centered on the carrying ship's transverse bulkheads. Two-fender arrays suit only small ships (under 5,000 deadweight tons). Three- and four-fender arrays are more usual with four fenders being most common. Figure 12-12 shows a typical fender string in place.

Major factors in selecting fenders for cargo transfers include:

Energy absorption.

The ships' freeboards.

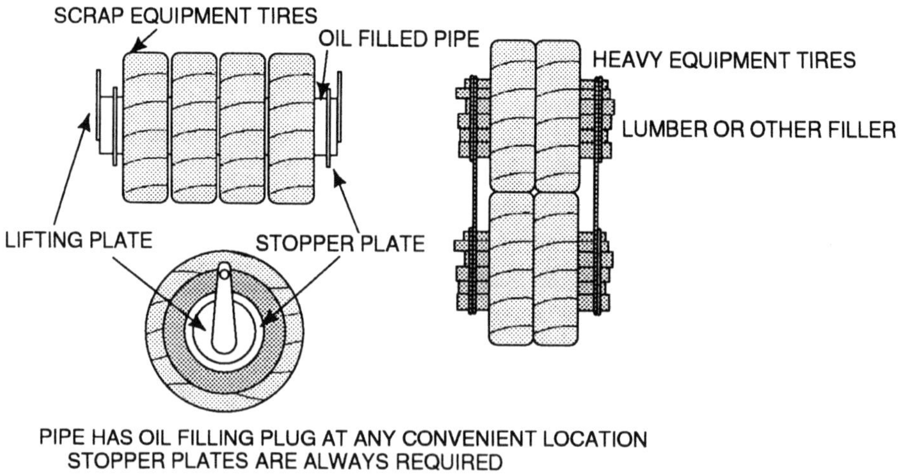

Fig. 12-10. Improvised fenders

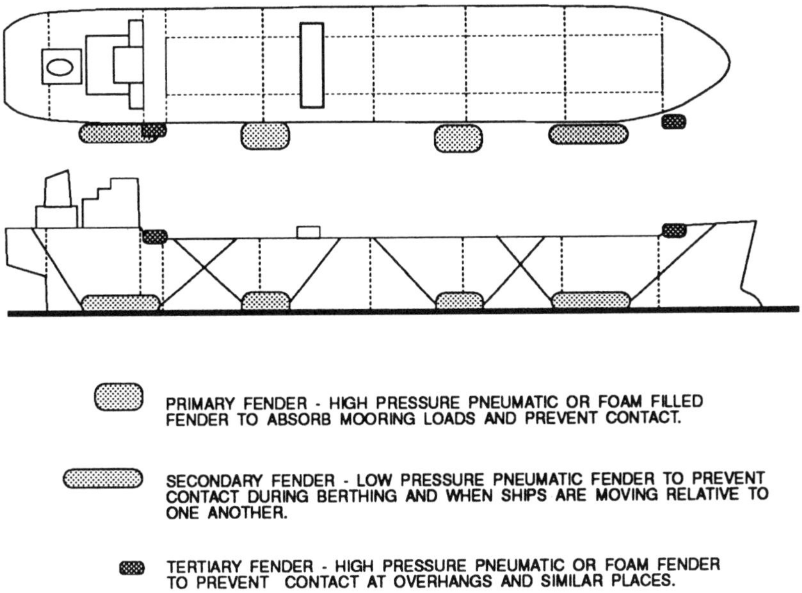

Fig. 12-11. Typical fendering for ship-to-ship transfer

Fig. 12-12. Fender string in place

Overhanging structure.
Local hull strengths.

Fenders compress as they absorb energy, flattening themselves against the sides of the ships. The maximum compression for salvage berthing is 50 percent. This percentage gives a reasonable factor of safety against fender failure. Compression of 50 percent also halves the standoff distance. Fenders must be chosen that keep the ships apart at this compression. As the fender compresses, a larger area of the fender contacts the ships' sides (figure 12-13). The flat width of any circular fender is directly proportional to the percentage of compression and can be calculated by:

$$\text{Flat width} = 0.0157 \times \%\ \text{compression} \times \text{fender diameter}$$

One primary fender is assumed to absorb all the berthing energy. A fender system that can absorb the berthing energy is adequate in any sea where the transfer is possible. The energy absorbed depends upon the size of the ships and the speed with which they move toward one another (berthing velocity).

Table 12-6 is a guide to minimum fendering arrays based on deadweights and berthing velocity. The figures in the table are recommendations only and should always be checked to be sure the energy absorption and standoff fit the actual situation and equipment. If there is any doubt, good practice is to go to the next larger

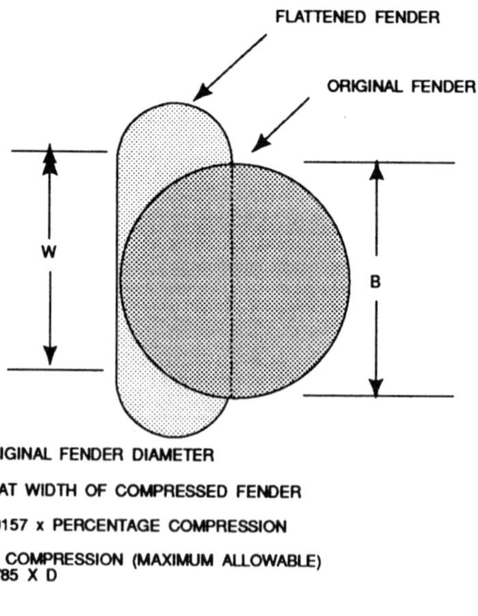

Fig. 12-13. Fender compression

size fendering system. When the lightering vessel moors alongside a heavily stranded ship, the table is entered with only the deadweight of the lightering vessel. If both ships are afloat or the casualty is lightly aground, an equivalent size must be calculated for entering the table. The equivalent size is:

$$C = \frac{2AB}{(A + B)}$$

where:
C = equivalent size (tons)
A and B = deadweight tonnage of the two ships (tons)

When A and B are the same, C = A or B.

The berthing velocities given in the table are the maximums allowable without damage to the fendering system or ship. Low berthing velocities mean low berthing energy and low loads on the fendering system.

TABLE 12-6.

FENDER ARRAYS						
C	*Berthing Velocity*	*Effective Berthing Energy*	*Fender Array HP Pneumatic or Foam*		*Fender Array LP Pneumatic*	
dwt 1,000's	*ft/sec*	*tons*	*D × L feet*	*No.*	*D × L feet*	*No.*
1	1.00	3	3 × 6	3	4.4 × 13	3
3	1.00	8	4.5 × 9	3	6 × 20	3
6	1.00	14	6 × 11.5	3	7.5 × 26	3
10	0.82	15	6 × 11.5	3	7.5 × 26	3
25	0.82	37	8 × 18	3	9 × 40	3
50	0.66	46	8 × 18	4	9 × 40	3
100	0.50	49	11 × 15	4	10.5 × 40	3
200	0.50	93	11 × 21	4	9 × 52	3

Fenders should be floating throughout the operation, but they have such a light draft that they are easily tossed about by the sea and may be thrown up on deck. Repeated loading followed by incomplete relaxing can allow fenders to crawl up the ship's side. To keep the fender where it is effective, fender diameter should not be more than about half the least freeboard of either ship. Because of their small diameter, low-pressure pneumatic fenders are often the best choice when freeboard limits fender size.

Overhanging structure can be protected by using large-diameter primary fenders to increase the standoff distance, but it is usually more effective to place smaller tertiary fenders.

Ideally, fenders are set athwart bulkheads on both ships. In practice, this ideal is seldom possible and fenders are set at bulkheads on the ship on which they are rigged. Low-pressure pneumatic fenders are good choices if the structure of the casualty is weakened, because these fenders spread loads over larger areas of the hulls. When freeboard is very low, as is likely with heavily damaged ships, fenders small enough to meet the 50 percent of freeboard requirement may not have enough energy absorption capacity. In these cases, fender diameter can be increased to 70 to 80 percent of freeboard, but the fenders must be tended with extra care.

In all cases, fenders are tended through the operation to assure they remain in place as the operation proceeds and displacements and freeboards change.

Ships that frequently conduct lightering operations usually have fenders semipermanently rigged and davits and other devices for handling fenders. The fenders may be set for particular classes of ships with which the lightering ship works regularly and should be checked in port or at arrival to be sure of correct placement for the operation. Fenders on the lightering vessel may be rigged in port, but preferably are rigged at the site when long transits are required. Launching and rigging fenders from a large ship at the site should be attempted only in reasonably calm weather where workboats can operate safely.

Rather than attempting to rig fenders from the lightering vessel, a string of fenders can be rigged and launched from a workboat and brought alongside the lightering vessel at anchor or steaming ahead dead slow. This method is particularly effective with two or more sequential lightering operations. Workboats can haul the string clear of the first vessel and move it to the next quickly and easily. Figure 12-14 shows rigging for a typical fender string.

The rigging of fender strings is particularly important, for it is hard service for the rigging components, and shortcuts or expedients in rigging can lead to rigging strings coming apart. At least some disruption of the operation follows fender strings breaking apart; damage to ships and equipment and major disruption are likely. Even in reasonably quiet weather the space between the ships is likely to be quite turbulent, with fender rigging being exposed to high dynamic loads as the fenders are tossed about or become caught between the hulls and suddenly fall back into the sea. Some specific features of the rigging are worthy of note:

The nylon rope pendants are placed in the rigging to allow the rigging to respond to dynamic loads. They are very important and should never be omitted.

The rigging should have a swivel at each connection to the fender to allow a maximum amount of freedom of motion.

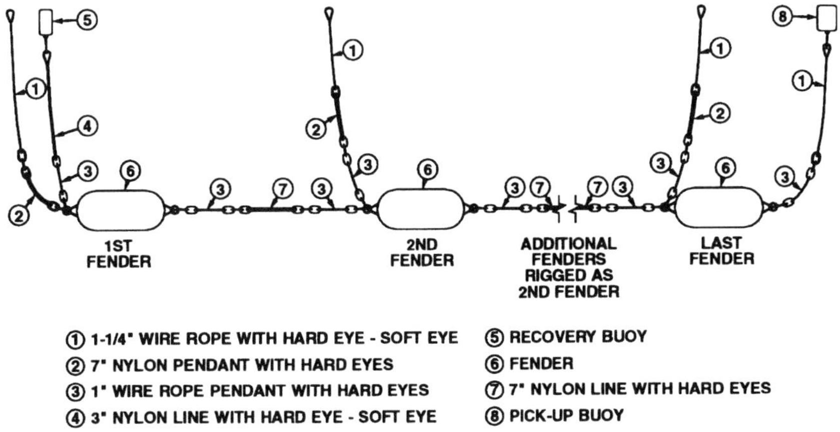

Figure 12-14. Typical rigging for fender string passed by support vessel

All shackles should have nut and bolt type pins properly secured to eliminate the possibility of the shackle coming apart in service. If only screw pin shackles are available, they should be seized securely to prevent the pin from backing out.

Close-link chain may be substituted for wire rope between fenders.

Every fender must have a line on deck and this line must be tended so the fender cannot move too far out of position if the fender string does come apart.

Casualties in the Surf

Casualties lying in the surf present a difficult problem because lightering vessels cannot be brought alongside. At least three possibilities exist for removing cargo.

Helicopters shuttling cargo to a lightering vessel lying offshore is a good method when the value of the cargo justifies the expense of the helicopter, when the exposure to the ambient environment must be minimum, or when authorities require its removal and access from the shore side is not practical.

A highline either ashore or to a ship standing off is also suitable. On rare occasions, cargo has been removed from the casualty and dumped into a barge between the casualty and the offshore terminal of the highline on a salvage ship. Transfer by highline is slow and labor-intensive. It is practical only for cargoes of very high value or cargo that must be removed from the vessel for environmental reasons.

The third method depends upon the shore configuration. If the shore permits and the ship provides shelter to the shoreward side, a causeway can be built from the shore out to the ship and the cargo discharged across the causeway.

Cargo transferred ashore is often landed in rough undeveloped areas. A secure area must be provided for the cargo as it lands, and trucks and trailers to receive the cargo must be set up to transfer the cargo to suitable warehousing. Rough terrain forklifts may be needed to move cargo ashore.

Protection during Transportation, Handling, and Storage

The salvor's responsibility for the cargo continues as long as it is in his custody. Rain and spray protection must be provided for cargoes that moisture harms. This protection must be provided not only during transportation but also while the cargo is stored ashore. Cargo that had underdeck stowage at sea should be stored under cover ashore. Containers may be stored in the open. Sometimes, cargo is landed at one location then transported to its final storage; neither place may be part of the normal port. Any storage, no matter how temporary, must be secure against pilferage and damage. It may be necessary to hire a security service and to build and later remove fences around the storage area.

Cargo removed from flooded holds deserves special consideration. Flood damage to cargo varies from practically no damage to complete destruction of the cargo's value. Some cargoes, such as machinery, may suffer little from immersion but lose their value if removal is not followed by a water damage protection program immediately after discharging the cargo from the vessel. Effectively retaining the value of cargo removed from flooded holds requires specific planning and attention. Determination of the number of hands needed for the work and their specific skills, along with the materials needed for their work, is a part of the planning. Foodstuffs, as well as manufactured goods, may be salvaged by a water damage protection program, usually one consisting of washing and drying. A portion of the value of some products made unfit for their primary purpose by wetting can be retained by converting the product to a secondary use. As an example, grain unfit for human consumption can be converted to animal feed.

Salvors need not attempt to become experts in water damage protection for all the cargoes they are likely to find in casualties. It would be unwise to do so. Expert advice in handling and salvage of cargoes can be obtained from specialist cargo surveyors, water damage protection contractors, suppliers, manufacturers, users, and, in the case of foodstuffs, government departments of agriculture.

Surveys and Documentation

Good documentation of cargo handling is essential to salvors' obtaining the most profitable results. When a cargo surveyor hired by the salvor or by the cargo or general interest is on site the salvor should work closely with him and listen closely to his opinions and recommendations. The surveyor should be asked to examine the cargo as it lies in the casualty and note any conditions that contribute to loss of value. Methods proposed for handling the cargo right through the time it is the salvor's responsibility should be discussed with the cargo surveyor. The surveyor also should be asked to inspect any lightering vessels before cargo is loaded and to give his recommendations on stowing and securing. He should inspect shore facilities and be advised of the details of the water damage protection program. He should inspect the lightering vessel before it leaves the site. If he makes recommendations for changes in the stowage arrangements, a second inspection of compliance with these recommendations is in order. All of the surveyor's reports and recommendations should be made in writing and become a part of the salvor's records. Sometimes the surveyor may appear to be overly fussy or even obstructive. This is seldom a true impression. A surveyor's recommendations are based on special knowledge and experience that he may not communicate well to the salvor. The overall good is achieved by following the surveyor's recommendations. When damage occurs during handling, surveyors are unlikely to forget recommendations that were not followed.

When the lightering ship discharges in a port remote from the salvage site, the salvor should hire a surveyor in that port to survey the cargo upon arrival.

Accurate records of the quantities of cargo handled and any damage occurring during handling are absolutely necessary. Photographs and videotapes are very useful in documenting cargo condition. They should be made whenever any damage appears, whether it is caused by handling or by salvage actions.

Tally men (checkers) provided by the casualty ship's crew, the receiving ship's crew, the salvor, or the stevedoring or labor contractor should be a part of every team handling cargo and should maintain a complete record of the cargo handled by hold and shift. Tallies should also be made on both discharging and receiving holds or locations whenever the cargo is transferred as long as it is the responsibility of the salvor. Bulk cargo quantities are determined by draft surveys of the lightering vessel before and after loading. Confirming draft surveys should be made of floating casualties. Draft surveys of grounded ships have no meaning. Salvors must have copies of all cargo records including tally sheets, ullage sheets, temperature logs, mate's receipts, and draft surveys to refute any claims of cargo loss.

Cargo always has value; it may have more value than the ship—either in its own intrinsic value or in the damage and liability that may result from its release to the environment. Salvors who realize the most from their work put as much into the handling and preservation of the value of the cargo as into salvage of the ship.

13

TANKER SALVAGE

Tanker casualties generate great interest not only among those with direct and legitimate interests but also among the public. The public interest has little to do with the ship or the conditions of the casualty; it centers on the cargo and pollution damage from actual or potential release of cargo into the environment. Mariners have long recognized tanker salvage as a special type of an already highly specialized maritime activity. Salvors attended tanker casualties long before pollution and environment became buzzwords. They devoted serious attention to preventing the release of oil both as a safety measure and because the oil, whether cargo or bunkers, had value. Emphasis on preventing the release of oil, large liabilities, and severe penalties have changed the nature of tanker salvage by subordinating ship salvage to cargo release prevention. These changes have affected the structure of tanker salvage operations.

The hazardous and potentially polluting cargo of tankers is the primary factor complicating salvage of these ships. In another way, the nature of the cargo simplifies salvage operations. Liquids are easy to handle and move in salvage by methods that parallel or emulate conventional cargo handling.

The importance of tanker salvage has grown in recent years because of: (1) the size of modern tankers, (2) the amount of oil transported by sea, and (3) the publicity given casualties like *Torrey Canyon, Amoco Cadiz, Exxon Valdez,* and *Braer*.

Tankers face the same types of casualties as do other ship types, but tanker casualties have some unique aspects.

TANKER CASUALTIES

Breakdowns

Tankers are as susceptible to mechanical failure and breakdown as any other ship type. A peculiar danger lies in the breakdown as the first event of a string leading to a more serious casualty. *Amoco Cadiz* makes an excellent example; a steering failure led to total loss of the ship and her cargo. Breakdowns are most serious in or near ports or other places with little sea room because of the short time for reaction between the casualty and disaster. Many oil ports lie in remote but environmentally sensitive areas. The need for responding rapidly to breakdowns, and controlling them before they become more serious, has led to requirements for escort tugs and special towing packages in many oil ports.

Strandings

The simplest strandings, those in which the tanker rests on a benign bottom with no breaches in the cargo containment system and no cargo spillage (figure 13-1), make the kind of jobs with which generous gods reward virtuous salvors—a high-value ship and cargo, intact, with little real danger of polluting. Double hulls increase the percentage of strandings that do not include breaching of the cargo

Fig. 13-1. This tanker, stranded on a gently sloping sea floor with no breaches in the hull and no spillage, is an easy salvage job, but is of concern to regulators and environmental interests because of the nature of the cargo.

containment system. Securing the vessel on her strand with ground tackle, lightering enough cargo to reduce her draft until she is afloat, and moving her clear with tugs can normally refloat these casualties. Regulators may insist upon measures to reduce an inflated pollution threat. Some of these measures may have value, while others only delay the operation. Delay means danger, because the probability of the casualty becoming more severe increases while it remains in a hazardous position.

Strandings with breached or threatened cargo containment and cargo release are much more complex. Crew and salvors must stop cargo release and reduce the potential for release as the first order of business, if possible. Measures to reduce additional pollution often take precedence over salvage of the ship. A danger lies in giving all the attention to the cargo and the pollution, reducing the attention given to the ship. Many times attention to and salvage of the ship may be the best way to limit pollution. The dynamic condition of the ship may worsen, perhaps to the point of sinking or breaking up. Weather and location can make a stranding, like that of *Braer* in the Shetlands, so severe that nothing can be done about either the ship or the cargo.

Large tankers, even moving at low speeds, have high momentum and typically strand with ground reactions of several thousand tons. *Exxon Valdez*, still building to sea speed when she struck Bligh Reef, had an initial ground reaction of more than 25,000 tons. Hauling off ships with such large ground reactions with tugs and ground tackle may be possible theoretically, but impractical. Any attempt to do so wastes time and effort. Dragging the ship along in contact with the bottom can cause additional damage that can lead to cargo loss and pollution in single-skin tankers. Lightening the ship to reduce ground reaction enough to refloat her makes up the primary effort. Tanker groundings on any but the softest sea floors usually cause heavy bottom damage that inevitably results in oil spillage from single-hull tankers. Spillage also follows severe damage, including rupture of the inner bottom of double-hull tankers. Damage to any tanker may cause flooding that threatens the strength and stability of the vessel. Cause for concern remains until the extent of the damage and the effect on strength and stability are defined. Precipitous action taken in ignorance is more likely to exacerbate than help the problem. The critical early hours of a stranded tanker casualty are best devoted to securing and preparing for lightening.

Collisions

Collisions can occur anywhere along a tanker's route, but, logically enough, experience shows they are most likely in a port area or in the approaches to a port. Tanker design considers the possibility of collision, in that the location and breadth of segregated ballast tanks results from studies of collision damage. Collisions may not always follow the scenario set by the studies and may be the first event in a chain leading to flooding, loss of power, cargo spillage, fire, stranding of a drifting vessel, or sinking with later cargo and wreck removals. Getting control of the situation may require very rapid response followed by longer-term response to control and clean up pollution, lighter cargo, fight a major fire, refloat a stranded or sunken ship, or even remove a wreck.

Fires

Engine room and accommodation fires occur much more often than cargo fires in tankers. Eventual cargo involvement is the greatest danger of engine room and accommodation fires. Cargo fires usually start in the pump room or from spills. They have resulted from sparks and heat generated by collisions, and in at least one case by the ship's bow falling off. Experience in the Iran-Iraq war in the Arabian Gulf showed very clearly that neutral merchant shipping is no longer safe from attack in war zones. It also showed that a missile strike almost inevitably causes a fire—exactly as the missile designers intended. Whatever the source or size, tanker fires are serious. Marine fire fighting, especially tanker cargo fire fighting, is a very specialized science beyond the scope of this book. Salvors should stay aware of the potential for and dangers of fire in tanker casualties and during salvage operations. They should prepare to fight and extinguish any fires in the early stages and have contingency plans for bringing in additional resources if fires get out of hand.

Properly operated inert gas systems help reduce serious cargo fires and eliminate the horrendous explosions and fires from lightning strikes on tankers.

Terminal Accidents

Terminal accidents that do not fall into one of the categories above are usually small spills associated with loading and discharging or catastrophic events like explosions during tank cleaning or from a lightning strike.

PLANNING AND PREPARATION

Planning and preparation for tanker casualties is not limited to salvage companies. Tanker operating companies can do a great deal to mitigate the effect of a casualty and speed up the salvage operation. Legislation in the United States[1] has been construed to require tanker operators to have standing arrangements with salvage and fire-fighting operators. These arrangements provide a certain level of readiness that training crews and preparing ships can raise.

Peril at Sea and Salvage, A Guide for Masters,[2] published and prepared principally for tankers and liquefied gas carriers by the OCIMF and ICS, contains much advice that applies to all types of ships. This publication, updated regularly to reflect changes in environmental and salvage law and other factors affecting salvage operations, should be in every ship—particularly tankers. It provides practical advice for masters faced with a casualty. The advice is of little use if it remains only in the publication without absorption into the heads of those likely to need it.

Training in casualty response for ship's officers begins with the information contained in this booklet.

Trained officers in a casualty can carry out cargo release mitigation before the arrival of salvors. Understanding cargo release mitigation requires only a thorough understanding of oil-water hydrostatics and spill mitigation principles discussed in Chapter 5, and knowledge of the casualty ship and its cargo. Casualties may involve several tanks or several types of damage in the same tank. Successful mitigation requires thinking, not reaction, and tailoring the response to the conditions that exist.

ORGANIZATION

Tankers demand a more complete and knowledgeable salvage team than any type of ship except LNG carriers. The initial team should include not only the salvage master and salvage engineer, but cargo and other specialists, and supervisors down to the salvage foreman level. Salvors remain generalists. They cannot be as expert in day-to-day tanker operations as those who sail in tankers. They should know the principles of construction and operations of tankships. Salvors' reference libraries should include one or more of the specialist books for tanker officers such as Marton's *Tanker Operations*[3] and Baptist's *Tanker Handbook for Deck Officers*.[4] The OCIMF publication *International Safety Guide for Oil Tankers and Terminals*[5] (ISGOTT), while designed for normal transfer operations, applies to tanker casualties. A salvor benefits from experience sailing in tankers as an officer or tankerman.

Tanker salvage carries some unique commercial risks. The most serious of these risks emerged when governments became concerned about pollution and passed laws that allowed them to intervene in tanker salvage to reduce environmental risk. Potential intervention by administrations means that salvors operating on a no cure–no pay contract could find themselves without a job after having spent a great deal of money. Several evolutionary steps have provided a solution to this problem. The principal open form salvage agreements and the 1989 Salvage Convention deviate from the strict no cure–no pay principle and allow payment of special compensation to salvors who cannot complete work because of intervention. This special compensation consists of the salvors' costs plus a percentage of those costs.

Chapter 1 discussed the parties to a salvage operation and their roles. In tanker salvage, the environmental hazard of the cargo increases the number of diverse and conflicting interests. Bureaucratic representatives from every level of administration, observers, lawyers, journalists, and all sorts of out-of-town experts are present at the scene or have their say from some distant location. As the situation develops, any attempt to sort out the players or draw an organization chart becomes an exercise in frustration and futility. Salvors may feel that the presence of so many people hinders their work. Difficult although it may be, they must not show their irritation, particularly with regulators and journalists.

Tanker casualties call for a closer relationship between the senior management of the salvors, insurers, and owners than in salvage of most other ships. One manifestation of cooperation is a united position when dealing with the administration of the coastal state, regulators, journalists, and others interested in the casualty. A plan for dealing with these people should be developed as a matter of high priority. Dealing with the varied interests can be as complex and time-consuming as work on the ship.

Regulators have a legislated job to do. A very big stick comes with the job. Few regulators hesitate to use the stick. Normally, the back-up team ashore or the salvage master should handle dealings with regulators. Surveyors and pollution specialists provided by P&I can deal with regulators whose primary concern is pollution cleanup and protection of fish and wildlife. Salvors should not hesitate to seek the aid of such experts. While they represent different parties, their interests lie in rapid, efficient, and economical resolution of the casualty. Good relationships with the administration of the coastal state may be very important when taking a damaged tanker into coastal waters for lightering or repair or into a port for delivery.

Journalists see tanker casualties as media events and focus on aspects of the work that sell newspapers and television time. The amount of journalistic attention is directly proportional to the often exaggerated quantity of oil spilled and the perceived threat of environmental damage. The journalistically perceived threat may bear little resemblance to the actual threat. Coverage of the *Exxon Valdez* spill provides an excellent example of what to expect in a major tanker casualty. The tanker owner and his representatives should take the lead in media relations. Salvors should not speak to the media but should refer journalists to the owner and his representatives or to the salvors' home office. Press statements by the salvors are proper late in the work when they can refer to solid accomplishment rather than intentions.

Salvors should never be brusque or rude with either regulators or journalists, no matter how strong the temptation. Courtesy and tact are the order of the day: hostility from either can make the salvors' lives very difficult while good relations can open many doors.

SAFETY

Risk exists during any tanker casualty; more in older, poorly maintained tankers that have drifted from owner to owner, flag to flag, classification society to classification society, and have sailed under a variety of names. In any casualty, some systems are inoperative or not operating at the top of their performance with full capacity and safety. In older ships, owners may have abetted the development of unsatisfactory, even criminally unsafe, conditions. The degree and nature of the risk depend largely upon the nature and characteristics of the cargo. Fires and explosions involving the cargo supply the primary risk, but fumes of some crudes and products may be toxic in high concentrations. Salvors cannot be expert in all the oil cargoes they may encounter. Any but the simplest tanker casualty with a single, common product warrants bringing in a safety specialist who can judge the risks of the specific product(s) and the effects of systems degradation. A safety specialist properly devotes his time solely to safety. The salvage master delegates attendance to most details of salvage safety to the safety specialist. The additional cost of a safety specialist is small in comparison to the benefits of his presence.

Comparable in importance to the salvors' safety specialist are the owners' oil transportation expert and the pollution specialists provided by P&I. The former is thoroughly familiar with the characteristics of the cargo and with the ship's details, the latter with the pollution threat of the cargo and practical cleanup measures. The pollution specialists can relieve the salvage master of concern with cleaning up the initial pollution from the casualty and let him concentrate on the full-time business of salvage and preventing additional pollution.

One of the most important functions of the safety specialist is to create a safety plan based on the conditions of the casualty and the location at which it occurs. The safety plan should combine salvage safety practice with tanker safety practice and must include local site-specific requirements. The most complete safety plan is useless unless promulgated and implemented. The safety specialist starts this process and the salvage master makes sure it gets done. Practices that deviate from normal salvage and tanker safety practice must be thoroughly explained to and understood by the crew.

Most salvors have developed a Tanker Safety Checklist to help assure safety during salvage operations. These lists are more extensive and cover more items than covered by tanker operations checklists, generic checklists appearing in manuals and publications, and lists required by regulators for normal operations. A representative checklist appears in Appendix C. This checklist is not the ultimate—just representative of such lists to serve as a rough guide to salvors preparing their own.

Salvage crews on any casualty should be no larger than necessary, but tanker salvage has some requirements that redefine "necessary." Crews must be large enough to maintain a full cargo transfer watch on each ship during the transfer and to stand taut watches without incurring needless fatigue. While fatigue has not been directly connected with increases in casualties, anyone with operating experience knows that tired people make mistakes and are accident-prone. One of the requirements of OPA-90 is limitation of work hours for tanker officers. During tanker salvage, good salvage practice calls for sticking to these limits and adding crew as necessary to assure all hands get proper rest.

Tanker salvage requires outfitting the crew with some specialized equipment. Throughout, this chapter will discuss the use of special equipment in conjunction with particular hazards. General-purpose equipment must include a number of items:

Self-contained breathing apparatus of a type the salvors know thoroughly must be available aboard the casualty. The primary purpose of this apparatus is rescue of people overcome by toxic or anoxic atmospheres. Trying to use unfamiliar apparatus at a critical, stressful time can be dangerous to life.

Similarly and for the same reasons, the *resuscitator* must be one the salvors know how to work and can use right out of the box.

The salvor should provide the *rescue stretcher* and rig it as agreed with the helicopter operator beforehand.

Safe practice usually proscribes synthetic fiber clothing aboard tankers because some materials melt and cause severe burns when exposed to high temperature. Salvors should make a practice of wearing natural fiber clothing on the job and should avoid shoes of synthetic material. Some oil companies require flame-resistant (Nomex) coveralls on all hands at their terminals and facilities. A stock of these garments is handy at times.

RESCUE TOWS

Because of the urgency of immediate effective response planning, equipping and training for rescue tows must take place before a casualty. A ship that must break out or improvise a towing system after she is in trouble has much less chance of survival than one better prepared.

Many oil ports require tugs or oil pollution response vessels to escort tankers through the port and its approaches so they can control the ship should she lose mobility. The size, type, and use of these tugs depends upon the size of the tanker and the conditions in the port and approaches. Discussion of handling large tankers with escort tugs is now active, filled with controversy, and beyond the scope of this book. Of more interest here are preparations for conventional hawser tows of tankers in emergencies.

Following the *Amoco Cadiz* casualty in 1978, the problem of making a suitable towing connection in an emergency received much attention. A near stranding of the *Prince William Sound*, appropriately, in Prince William Sound, and practically every tanker breakdown since has inspired additional study. These studies addressed both equipment and methods for making connections. The independent results of the studies showed an emergency towing package aboard the tanker that the tug could pick up and connect to was the most sensible solution. Specifications for such a system were issued by the OCIMF[6] and later adopted as IMO Resolution A535[13]. The Trans Alaska Pipeline System (TAPS) trade adopted a similar package known as "The Prince William Sound Towing Package." Several European salvors developed and marketed equivalent packages. The packages consist of connection points on the bow and stern, a chain pendant, a suitably sized and rounded bow chock, a wire rope towing pendant, and a buoyant fiber rope pick-up line and buoy. Experience with the packages has shown that they work as intended, but for effectiveness they must be connected and not stowed in the forecastle. The weight of the components requires several crewmen to deploy the system. The development of high-strength, low-density high molecular weight polyethylene (HMPE) synthetic fiber rope offers a solution to the weight problem. With this type of line replacing wire rope, one man can deploy an emergency towing system. Because of the danger of cargo fire limiting access to the forecastle, the best installation has emergency towing systems permanently installed on both thc bow and stern.

A tanker emergency towing system allows the tug to maneuver to pick up the buoy, haul the towing package aboard, attach it to his towline, and steam away as he pays out his towline. The time to get the tanker under control is in theory, principle, and fact much less than if the tug passes the entire towing connection to the tanker for making up on deck.

The bollard pull to control a tanker depends upon the hydrodynamic characteristics of the tanker and the weather at the time of the casualty. Various formulas for finding the minimum amount exist. Optimum figures are convenient for planning. When emergencies occur, any power that can help arrest, change, or delay the drift of a tanker toward a lee shore should be used. There is never too much power as long as the towline and deck connection have enough strength to transmit the power from the tug to the tanker.

The master of the tug knows his ship, her capability, and his crew better than anyone else. Others involved in the casualty should forgo directing him and let him do his job.

INITIAL ACTION

The first order of business in any tanker casualty is to secure the ship. Extinguishing or at least getting any fire under control is the first step in securing. Every effort must be made to keep the fire away from the cargo. The tanks should be kept inerted as a matter of high priority. Engine room fires can involve bunkers and oil stored in tanks under or alongside the engine room. Where possible, fire fighters should prevent involvement of these oils in a fire.

With the fire out, attention can turn to the next major item, spill mitigation. Spill mitigation procedures (Chapter 5) should be put into effect immediately.

While informing appropiate authorities about any spill as soon as possible is an important necessity, spill mitigation procedures take precedence over reports.

With the urgent emergencies of fire and oil spillage under control, attention can turn to determining the effect of the casualty on the ship and to securing her pending the arrival of salvors.

Chapter 8 describes procedures for this work. An unusual circumstance applies to tankers and to other very large ships. Large ground reaction and concentration of ground reaction in a limited area allow ground reaction to grow during the tidal ebb until the ship's structure crushes under its weight. The same effect can be achieved by ballasting the ship too heavily. Such crushing is very expensive damage. In double-hull tankers, it may rupture the double bottom and cause cargo spillage that would not happen otherwise. An estimate of the ground reaction should be made by one of the methods described in Chapter 4 before ballasting to secure the ship. If the ground reaction is high—5 percent of the ship's deadweight for ships over about 50,000 displacement tons, 10 percent or more below that displacement—ballasting should be attempted only if severe forecast weather is likely to set the ship farther ashore or broach her.

STABILITY AND STRENGTH

The determination of stability and strength is important in any casualty, but even more so in a tanker casualty. Stability is always important in stranding casualties, with the critical period being refloating. Free surface effect in a tanker's large, partially filled cargo tanks can be significant. Longitudinal bending strength is of particular concern with hull damage or when cargo must be moved within or off the ship. The straightforward calculations require a computer and a damage stability program tailored to the ship for complete and accurate results.

Stability and strength calculations are made whenever the ship strands, structure has damage, or weight distribution changes. Updating stability and strength continues throughout the operation. Ignoring stability and hull strength is foolhardy; doing so invites capsizing or structural failure.

The extent of the damage and loss of section modulus may remain hidden when the ship lies on the damage. Estimates of lost or ineffective structure in these cases should assume the worst case until better information becomes known.

Tankers have some form of load computer that allows calculation of stability and strength for various conditions of loading in the intact ship. These devices have limited usefulness in salvage because normally they do not allow for the effects of grounding or hull damage. Many of the devices read out in percentage of IMO or other stability standards and percentages of allowable shear force and bending moment. Readings in this format have meaning for ship's officers. Salvors, however, need absolute values for decision making.

In the not very distant past, technical data went to a remote computer that used builder's data to make or check salvage calculations. At the time, this way worked best because calculating on site would have occupied the naval architect full time and would have produced results neither as complete nor as accurate as needed for salvage of large tankers. Computer technology prevented bringing a sufficiently powerful computer to the scene. The rapid advances in computer design have made it possible to have computers capable of making all the necessary calculations on-site. Sufficient input for these computers can usually be found in the plans aboard the casualty.

Several programs for salvage calculations exist, some specifically for tankers. A few ships carry ship-specific programs on board, loaded into computers in the cargo control room. Some of these are standard salvage programs with the characteristics of the ship already loaded. Extreme accuracy in salvage calculations is ultimately impossible. Even the most careful analysis is rendered approximate by the quantity of unknowns and information which must be assumed.

Interested parties sometimes exert pressure to fit strain gauges to monitor the casualty's hull. These gauges give an indication of changes in strain and rates of change of strain. This information is of interest, but because no zero point or baseline exists for strain, absolute strain readings and stresses cannot be obtained. For an intact hull with a known section modulus, changes in stress levels can be calculated from changes in strain. For a damaged hull, loss of section modulus cannot be determined precisely. The imprecision in section modulus passes along as imprecision in stress change estimates. In my opinion, a level line for measuring hull deflections as an indication of stress and strain changes makes a more practical and useful tool than strain gauges.

Legend tells of a salvage crew that routinely fit an impressive-looking set of well-maintained, shiny brass gauges that measured absolutely nothing in important-sounding but meaningless units. The crew made a great show of collecting and studying the readings much to the satisfaction of the surveyors wanting data and the amusement of the salvage crew.

SECURING A STRANDING

The cargo has priority in any tanker casualty. Usually, regulators insist upon removal of cargo before allowing salvage to move forward. The earliest efforts of the salvors should assure the ship lies securely upon her strand. If additional ballast and ground tackle must go in, this work can move ahead while beginning preparations to deal with the cargo.

A hydrographic survey of water around the casualty and of approaches should be an early order of business as well as layout and marking of approaches and anchorages for lightering vessels, selecting sites for laying ground tackle, and choosing the direction for refloating the casualty. A simultaneous detailed diving survey determines the condition of the hull. Information from this survey complements that gotten from ullage readings, water cuts, and cargo tank surveys. Spaces in the ship thought suitable for filling with cargo from damaged tanks should be checked. With this basic information, the salvage master can begin to formulate a salvage plan and the naval architect can begin to work out the supporting calculations.

Weather, especially tides and currents, should receive particular attention. As a salvage plan and schedule evolves, tidal-dependent key events, such as taking off a lightering ship or refloating the casualty, should be compared with predicted tides and tidal currents. Casualties to tankers and liquefied gas carriers require more planning than those to other types of ships because of the ship's size, the cargoes' nature, and the operation's complexity. Changes occur daily as in any salvage operation, but the salvor who does not plan and prepare completely for a tanker salvage operation can expect that operation to jump up and bite him on the backside.

Ground Tackle

In tanker salvage, ground tackle has a primary function of holding the ship in position and preventing her from broaching, rotating, or moving up the beach during cargo discharge, not to haul the ship off her strand. Ballasting as weight replacement for removed cargo often does not hold the casualty alone. Tankers are likely to ground so heavily as to make refloating with ground tackle as impractical as refloating with tugs. Lightening by removing cargo has far more likelihood of success, but the casualty must be held in place during lightening or the situation may worsen.

The ground tackle system should be laid out according to the discussion of ground tackle in Chapter 8. The particular equipment and its layout should take account of the environmental forces acting on the casualty at the site, the size of the casualty, the equipment, laying vehicles, and access lanes to the casualty for all the vessels that must work alongside and in the vicinity. Ground tackle must be set up for hauling to keep it taut as conditions change throughout the operation.

Properly watched and tended ground tackle is both much more reliable and economical of resources than tugs for holding stranded vessels.

CARGO REMOVALS

This chapter has stressed that cargo removals make up a major part of almost every tanker casualty operation (figure 13-2). Vessel-to-vessel cargo transfers are common commercial operations. The *Ship to Ship Transfer Guide (Petroleum)*[7] first produced by OCIMF in the mid-1970s and updated periodically covers basic operations and safety for normal transfers between undamaged vessels. Salvage situations have dimensions and complexities beyond those of normal operations;

Fig. 13-2. In this cargo-removal operation, cargo is being transferred from a VLCC casualty to another VLCC. Note the difference in freeboards at the beginning of the operation.

they are emergencies that require more than normal care and attention to safety. The salvor must remain in total charge of salvage operations and must insist that his working procedures and safety practices always be followed precisely.

Emergency oil transfers from casualties have three purposes:

1. To remove a potential pollutant.
2. To remove weight from the vessel.
3. To save the cargo.

The primary purpose and the priorities depend on the viewpoints of the parties. Relative priorities may vary during the operation. Before starting the transfer, all parties should determine and agree to the amount of oil for transfer. Oil transfer from a casualty is a technical operation and the quantity transferred rightly a technical decision. To expedite the operation and to keep the pollution potential low, the correct amount for transfer does not exceed the minimum amount of oil to achieve the purpose(s) of the operation. A greater chance of spills or other accidents is probable during transfer operations than when the oil remains in intact tanks or well buffered by a water bottom in damaged tanks. Despite the inherent danger in transfers of oil under salvage conditions, some regulators insist on removal of all cargo before moving the ship.

The emergency operation should simulate a routine ship-to-ship cargo transfer as nearly as possible. Every practical way of using installed pumps and piping systems should be explored—and discarded only for sound reasons—before resorting to over-the-top pumping or jury-rigging piping systems. Over-the-top pumping arrangements suit only real emergencies where there is broken piping or hull damage preventing any use of installed systems.

Lightering Vessels

Salvors may locate and charter a suitable lightering vessel or the owner may provide such a vessel. The latter arrangement may have financial advantages for the owners, but sometimes results in a less desirable vessel than the one salvors would choose. A safe and efficient lightering operation is short; transfers to several small vessels are much less efficient and much more likely to result in accident than a single transfer to a large vessel. Captain Murphy, with his usual skill, invariably assures that sister ships make poor lightering ships that are very difficult to moor under salvage conditions.

Often the salvors' first look at the lightering vessel comes when she steams into the area. When the lightering vessel appears, considerable pressure often builds to get flanged up and pumping. Usually, this is exactly the wrong action. Careful planning and orderly procedures can make the difference between a safe and efficient operation and a fiasco.

An inspection and conference with the master should follow the lightering ship's arrival. The salvage master and safety officer inspect the vessel to determine, as a minimum, that:

- Her certificates are present and current.
- She is in generally satisfactory condition.
- All her safety equipment is aboard and operable.
- Her cargo system is safe to operate.
- She actually has the capacity and is in condition to receive the cargo.

Under no conditions should the inspection stop with an examination of certificates. Many a ship has complete and up-to-date certificates but is in no condition to participate safely in lightering operations. The truth and the route to safe and successful operations lie in physical inspection and critical evaluation, not in reliance upon certificates. No unsatisfactory ship should ever be accepted despite its being fully classed and apparently well-maintained. The salvors cannot afford to take unnecessary risks. Pressure by owners, government agencies, or other parties to force salvors to accept an unsuitable vessel is at best inappropriate and, at worst, very dangerous.

Following a satisfactory inspection, the master and mate of the lightering vessel should accompany the salvage master on an inspection of the casualty. No matter what pressures for moving ahead exist, these inspections should never be omitted. Neither should there be any hesitancy in rejecting clearly unsatisfactory or marginal ships.

Few mariners find themselves as lightering shipmaster during casualty operations. Fewer still immediately feel comfortable with the situation. The post-inspection conference lays out the operation for the master, allows him to voice his ideas, and allays his concerns. The master of the lightering vessel has very serious responsibilities. His concerns are real, not side issues to be pooh-poohed and set aside. In a poorly done lightering operation, one tanker casualty can easily become two. Failing to assure that the lightering shipmaster understands the planned operation and his role can easily put both ships ashore.

Barges are perfectly satisfactory and, in some locations, preferable to tankers for lightering. Virtually all the considerations for lightering ships described throughout this chapter apply equally to barges and tankers.

Regulators and environmental people, never salvors, often suggest dracones as suitable receptacles for cargo from tanker casualties. These devices—flexible, elongated bladders made of woven nylon proofed with acrylonitrile rubber and coated with neoprene—were designed specifically to carry liquids lighter than water in port areas and the open sea. They load and discharge the single compartment through a hose connection in the stern. While dracones have transported petroleum products in some parts of the world, they are now seldom found in anything but government pollution response operations. Dracones are difficult to fill, handle, and empty; they are relatively easy to rupture. I fail to see the advantages of taking oil from a sound steel tank and putting it into a rubber bag in the open sea, especially in a remote area.

Mooring and Fendering

The preceding chapter discusses mooring and fendering in some detail. All the principles and procedures laid out in that chapter apply to tankers as to other ships, but tankers have some unique considerations. Some come purely from these ships' size and the forces generated on their moorings and fenders. Although standoff moors can be used for any cargo, they are more efficient for tankers because of the flexibility in transfer systems their liquid cargo offers.

The discussion in Chapter 12 about the unsuitability of salvage tugs for ship assists is true for tankers as well as other ship types. A very large ship entering or leaving a moor alongside or near another ship must be under positive control. Good, maneuverable tugs can give positive control; salvage tugs cannot.

Nylon tails on wire rope mooring lines increase the total elasticity of the line, a quality that helps counter the dynamic forces that occur during ship-to-ship transfers. The tails should be no longer than about 35 feet (11 meters) and should extend about one-third of the distance between the ships with the moor made up. For normal service, good tails are about 25 percent stronger than the wire rope to account for aging. In salvage operations, where the tails are used only once, they may have the same strength as the wire rope. Normally, special joining shackles designed to reduce wear, rather than ordinary chain or anchor shackles, join wire rope and tails. Plastic or leather sheath tail eyes. Both these precautions may be omitted in emergency operations, but the tails should be checked frequently for wear, particularly for chafing of the nylon. With ordinary shackles or no sheathing, compromising on the strength of the tail is not good seamanship.

In stern-to-stern standoff moors, floating hoses run down the decks from the manifold—or just from the stern connection in ships having them—and go over the side at the sterns to reduce the length of hose in the water as much as possible.

In fendering as in mooring, for much the same reasons, tanker casualty operations present the most severe problems, both because of the ships' size and because of the unusually serious potential of failure. The principles and procedures for fendering discussed in Chapter 12 are totally applicable to tankers.

Cargo Transfers

Mooring, fendering, and ground tackle, important in themselves, are preparation for the critical act of cargo transfer—a prerequisite for further salvage action. Two distinct routine operations, discharge and loading of cargo, make up ship-to-ship cargo transfer operations. Unusual conditions can occur aboard the casualty, where systems may be degraded or nonstandard methods of handling the cargo used. On the discharging ship, with the situation far from routine and the salvage crew overseeing the discharge, the level of vigilance remains high. On the lightering ship where the operation appears nearly routine, attention by the ship's officers maintains the higher standard of alertness casualty operations require.

Although routine leads to complacency, the transfer operation should simulate a normal transfer insofar as possible. The procedures should follow as nearly as possible those established in the ships' cargo transfer procedures books. Deviations should result from conscious decisions. Transfers begin slowly with very low pumping rates and thorough systems checks as they work up to the intended pumping rate. Whenever a problem occurs, the transfer operation shuts down to address and solve the problem.

The primary factor in choosing the sequence for discharging tanks is the effect of loading on the structural strength of the ship, especially when the hull is weakened by damage causing a large loss of section modulus. Also, it is highly desirable to get the oil out of damaged tanks early in the operation. The two major considerations are not incompatible. Water replaces oil removed from damaged tanks, resulting in little change to hull loading. The sequence for the transfer is worked out by evaluating possible or desirable sequences with the ship's on-board load computer or a salvage or damage stability program that includes strength calculations, accommodation of hull damage, and effects of grounding.

Regulatory authorities are very likely to require that administrative procedures for routine transfers apply. This normally means filling out and filing the U.S. Coast Guard's Declaration of Inspection (DOI), an equivalent form in other countries, or an OCIMF checklist. Salvors' checklists for emergency transfers are much more comprehensive than the DOI forms, but no one gains by arguing over the matter.

Static Electricity

Static electricity and the sensitivity of the cargo to it is of concern in every tanker casualty because of the fire and explosion hazard in handling petroleum. Explosions occur when *all* of the following conditions are met:

- Enough static charge has accumulated to generate a hydrostatic spark.
- There is a spark gap.
- An explosive atmosphere fills the spark gap.

Following sections discussing inert gas and vapors are oriented toward preventing the formation of or eliminating explosive atmospheres. Although theory says a properly inerted tank cannot contain an explosive atmosphere, common sense and good safety practice demand taking precautions to reduce static electricity generation.

Dissimilar metals coming into contact with one another generate static electricity. Typical sources in tankers include:

- Fluids flowing through pipes and hoses.
- Solids or nonmiscible liquids settling through a liquid mass.
- Particles or droplets from a nozzle.
- Splashing against a solid surface.
- Rubbing and separation of some synthetic polymers, such as gloves and synthetic fiber lines.

Water entrained in petroleum is a particular concern in casualty operations because of the friction between the water and petroleum within the fluid mass. Charges may be limited by keeping flow rates and the drop distance into the receiving tank low. As many foreign objects as possible should be kept out of tanks. Only necessary manual ullaging should be done, and then *only* with *linen* ullaging tapes in small tankers with no inert gas systems or large tanks that have lost their inert gas. In inerted tanks, manual ullaging should be done *only* with MMC-type metal tapes with built-in interface detectors inserted through a vapor control valve.

End fittings should be cut off hose ends put into the tank and the hose and any other metal object put into the tank continuously grounded to a common ground.

The sensitivity of a particular oil depends upon its internal conductivity. Any petroleum distillate with an internal conductivity of 50 picoSiemens/meter is classified as a static accumulator oil. The internal conductivity of a product is not likely to be known; therefore, all distillates, unless specifically known to be treated with antistatic additives, should be considered static accumulators and treated accordingly. Normally, antistatic procedures go into effect when a volatile static accumulator is handled at or above a temperature equal to its flashpoint minus 10 degrees C. and the tanks are not inerted or gas-free. In casualties with degraded conditions, safe practice calls for following antistatic procedures whenever handling static accumulator oils. The primary danger with these oils occurs during the initial transfer. To limit the hazard, flow velocities should not exceed 3 ft/sec (1 m/sec) until the level of cargo in the receiving tank has reached the point where all surface disturbance and splashing have stopped. During and for thirty minutes after loading, no metal objects may go into the tank. When metal equipment goes into the tank it must be continuously grounded to a common ground while it is in the tank and after it comes out. Nonmetallic equipment going into the tanks must be lowered on natural, not synthetic, fiber. Micropore filters can generate high static charges inappropriate in casualty transfers.

Large electrical currents can flow through piping, hoses, and mooring lines. These currents result from DC impressed current or sacrificial anode cathodic protection systems, galvanic potential differences between ships, and current leakage. Incendiary arcs may result from sudden interruption of the current path. Procedures for reducing the dangers from these currents differ, depending on whether or not the static accumulator oils are being transferred.

When transferring *nonstatic accumulators* the ships are *isolated electrically* from one another by nonconducting mooring lines—wire ropes with nylon tails, nonconducting hoses, or hose strings with insulating flanges. Impressed current systems are shut down.

When transferring *static accumulators* there should be a nonconducting hose between the ships. A length of hose isolated by two insulating flanges should be avoided, else a static charge may build in the isolated length. Impressed current cathodic protection systems should continue to operate when both ships have impressed current systems or one ship has impressed current and the other sacrificial anodes. Systems are shut down if they are not operating properly or if one ship has no cathodic protection.

Hose Strings

Strings of hose through which the oil flows connect the casualty and lightering ship—for normal loading, discharge, and lightering operations, two strings of 12-inch or larger hoses. Vessels that routinely conduct lightering operations normally carry hose strings and have handling systems for them. Alternatively, a support vessel may bring the hoses to the site and pass them to one of the ships, or, in standoff moors, to both ships. In casualty operations, smaller hoses may suit ad hoc handling arrangements better. Eight-inch hose strings are as large as men can manhandle readily. Ten-inch strings are difficult to manhandle but higher transfer rates may justify the effort. Saddles, radiused to at least six times the nominal hose diameter, must support hoses to prevent kinking and pinching.

Strings must be long enough to handle all the expected motion between the vessels without halting the transfer to add or remove sections. In standoff moors with floating hose, the string should have enough slack to allow it to ride easily in any sea in which the transfer can continue. Sections of stiff nonfloating hose fitted as tail strings where the hose comes aboard both vessels prevent kinks and sharp bends that occur with floating hose in these locations.

The diameter of the hose string must be compatible with the manifolds or adapters on both ships.

Three types of hose are available. They vary in construction and ruggedness:

1. Rough bore hose (Type R)—heavy, very robust hose with an internal steel wire helix.
2. Smooth bore hose (Type S)—lighter than rough bore without the steel helix.
3. Lightweight hose (Type L)—lighter still, and normally suitable for discharge and bunkering only.

Types R and S hoses normally are found in cargo service at terminals and on specialized lightering vessels. Lightweight hose is excellent for casualty operations where flexibility and weight are important. All three types come in sizes from 6 to 30 inches and as floating and other specialty hose. The floating hose has enough buoyancy to float when full of seawater. When nonfloating hose must be used in standoff moors, the portions of the hose in the water buoys or foam blocks can support the portions in the water. Lines for tying on buoys may choke collapsible hose. Spool pieces between hose sections in the string and with buoys attached at the spool pieces can eliminate this problem.

Hoses anywhere in the cargo transfer rigging must comply with the specifications of API, ASA, British Standards Institute, Japanese Industrial Standards, the OCIMF, or comparable organizations. The hose should be marked with the manufacturer's name, a serial number, the specification or standard of manufacture, test pressure, date of most recent pressure test, and whether the hose is electrically continuous or discontinuous. The pressure test date should be within one year of the use date.

No matter who supplies the hose string, salvors should inspect the entire string visually before use. Disqualifying faults include blisters larger than about 2 inches, kinking, cracking deeper than 3/64-inch (1 millimeter), severe abrasion, flattening, leaks, and badly corroded flanges.

Good operational practices include:

- Never exceeding test pressures, recommended flow rates, and oil temperatures of 180 degrees F. (82 degrees C.).
- Avoiding surge pressures on the hose.
- Segregating hoses for white and black oils.
- Selecting hoses for chemicals and specialty products compatible with product characteristics.

Most hydraulic salvage pumps discharge through 6-inch-diameter lightweight, fabric-reinforced, collapsible rubber hose. This hose coupled with easily handled transfer hose can support a velocity of 40 ft/sec (12 m/sec). Pumping with main cargo pumps calls for more heavily constructed hose rated at 50 ft/sec (15 m/sec).

Most salvors in preparation for a tanker salvage make up both adapters that can connect Cam-Lok fittings to standard ASA or API flanges and manifold reducers in several sizes. The stock of associated equipment includes bolts, nuts, washers, gaskets and packing, blank flanges, hose caps, and Cam-Lok fittings.

This discussion has carefully and intentionally avoided any mention of transfer rates. Transfer rates are a measure of efficiency in normal loading and discharge operations. In salvage operations priorities lie with safe, secure, pollution-free transfers from degraded systems rather than achieving high transfer rates. Attempting to approach transfer rates reached at terminals or in normal ship-to-ship transfers is foolish.

Inert Gas

Flammable vapors from liquid hydrocarbon cargoes can mix with the atmosphere in the ullage space to create an explosive mixture. Chapter 5 briefly discusses explosive range and how flammable vapors and oxygen must lie within certain limits to ignite. Hydrocarbon cargoes cannot burn in atmospheres containing less than 10 percent oxygen. Vapors must fall within certain limits to make a flammable or explosive mixture. The table below gives the approximate upper and lower percentages at which common liquid hydrocarbon cargoes form explosive mixtures with air. Atmospheres with percentages by volume of hydrocarbon gas that fall outside these ranges are either too lean (too little hydrocarbon gas) or too rich (too much hydrocarbon gas) to burn or explode. In a tanker casualty, a rich atmosphere is more dangerous than a lean one because atmospheric air may dilute the former into the explosive range.

TABLE 13-1.

FLAMMABLE LIMITS FOR TYPICAL LIQUID HYDROCARBON CARGOES (Percent by Volume in Air)		
Product	*Lower Limit*	*Upper Limit*
Crude oils (average)	1.0	10.0
Gasoline	1.3	7.6
Kerosene	0.7	6.0
Propane	2.1	9.5
Methane	5.0	15.0
Benzene	1.4	8.0
JP4	1.4	7.6
Ethylene oxide	2.0	100

Figure 13-3 is a representative explosive range diagram for hydrocarbon cargo. The percentage of oxygen in the atmosphere is plotted along the horizontal axis while the percentage of hydrocarbon vapor is plotted along the vertical axis. An explosive mixture exists when the intersection of the vertical line representing the oxygen percentage and the horizontal line representing the hydrocarbon vapor percentage lies within the shaded area. If the intersection lies outside the shaded area, the mixture is either too rich or too lean to explode. The shape and size of the

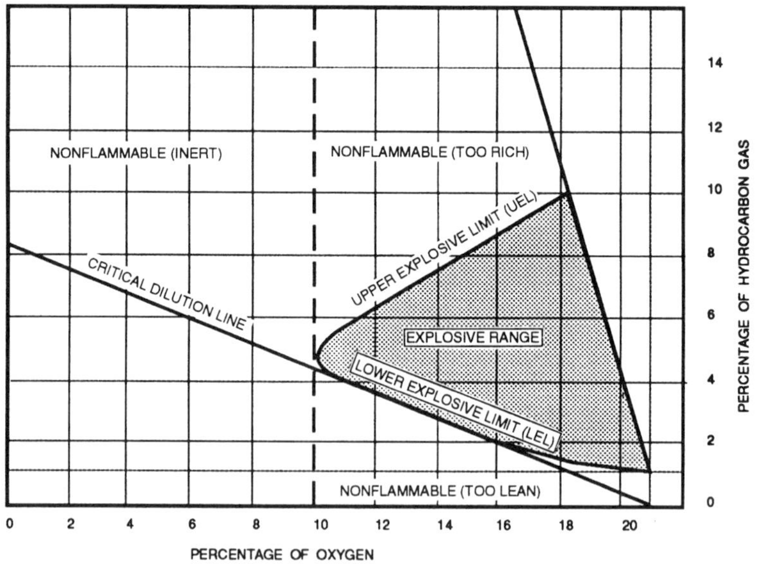

Fig. 13-3. Explosive range diagram

explosive range depend upon the type of liquid hydrocarbon cargo. The diagrams are not interchangeable. Decisions made with the wrong diagram are likely to be wrong and dangerous.

Assuring that the atmosphere in the ullage space remains outside the explosive range can significantly improve safety in carrying and handling liquid hydrocarbons. The hydrocarbon vapor production and vapor content of the tank atmosphere is very difficult to control; the oxygen content is not. Inert gas systems fill the ullage space in cargo tanks with gases containing little or no oxygen, so the mixture in the tank remains outside the explosive range. Inert gas systems have proven so successful in improving tanker safety that they are required on most tankers. Exhaust gases from the ship's boiler or a separate inert gas generator provide the inert gas through a scrubbing system (figure 13-4). Scrubbers and driers remove oxygen and water vapor until the gas theoretically contains only nitrogen (85 percent) and carbon dioxide (15 percent).

Inert gas has a place in salvage as both a safety measure during transfers and as a fire-fighting mechanism. The ship's system or portable systems can supply the gas. The most common inert gas generator is the diesel oil–fueled HOLEC Portinert 1000 that provides 6,000 scfm of inert gas at 2.1 psig. Gas provided by this device contains less than 1 percent oxygen, and less than 200 ppm carbon monoxide with a trace of soot. The gas leaves the generator about 10 degrees C. over the seawater temperature. The unit consists of two parts weighing between a ton and a half and 2 tons each and requiring a total of about 50 square feet of deck space. It delivers gas through a 6-inch outlet. The inert gas generator as an ignition source should be located where hydrocarbon vapors do not accumulate (figure 13-5). The system includes 6-inch heat-, age-, and seawater-resistant hose, but almost any type of hose or ducting can be pressed into service.

Inert gas generated by the casualty's system can be distributed through the inert gas system in the normal manner. Some tankers have 10-inch (250 mm) bolted flanges on the inert gas main for connecting emergency inert gas supplies. The flange is located forward of the deck seal, isolated from the inert gas main by a valve. Although difficult, rigging a distribution system without such a fitting warrants the first-class jury-rigging it requires (figure 13-6).

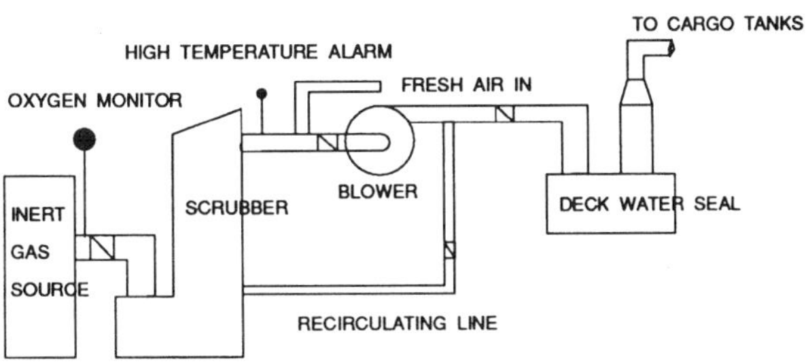

Fig. 13-4. Inert gas system components

Crude oil tanks always should be inerted during cargo transfers. Products are another matter. Many products have greater flammability than crudes. Inerting the tanks enhances handling safety with these products. Some products are color sensitive so the product may lose its value if even slightly contaminated by soot. A rough cost-benefit analysis and expert technical advice on the particular product are necessary prerequisites to a decision to inert tanks carrying refined products.

Fig. 13-5. This portable inert gas generator system (the two outboard units) aboard a tanker casualty is located clear of the tank deck, to remove an ignition source from areas where explosive fume concentrations are likely. Photo courtesy of Captain David Hancox.

Inert gas, heavier than air at the same temperature, should enter a space low to form a layer and force the tank atmosphere out the vents. Vents should be at the high point of the space and preferably well away from the point where the inert gas enters. These locations provide good flow through the tanks and prevent short-circuiting.

Inert gas presents a hazard to personnel because of its low oxygen content. It has no smell and can suffocate anyone entering an inerted space. When inserting, lowering, or adjusting the position of portable pumps in inerted tanks through the Butterworth openings, the only choice is to open the tanks and allow the inert gas to escape while handling the pump. A pocket of inert gas may form in way of the opening. Normally it disperses rapidly, but may linger in still air, and salvors may accidentally get a whiff. In very still air serious pockets develop, requiring rigging blowers or wearing breathing apparatus while handling pumps. Such occasions are very rare.

Good practice requires checking the oxygen content of inert gas at both the outlet from the machine and in the inerted tanks. Atmospheres less than about 10 to 11 percent oxygen by volume do not support combustion. Eight percent, the figure recommended by OCIMF, allows a margin of safety. Many tanker operators normally carry their tanks at 5 percent or less.

Normal precautions for grounding and spark prevention apply when lowering anything into cargo tanks. These include removing unneeded metal fittings from

Fig. 13-6. Portable inert gas hose (a) crossing the deck of a casualty tanker and (b) tapped into the inert gas main. Photos courtesy of Captain David Hancox.

hose ends and continuously grounding metal connections to the inert gas generator.

All normal tanker safety precautions concerning opening tanks, using explosive-proof or intrinsically safe equipment, etc., are mandatory during casualty cargo transfer operations with inerted tanks.

Vapors

Two types of vapors generate concern during casualty oil cargo transfers: the potentially explosive and toxic vapors coming from the cargo, and the non-life-supporting inert gas. Ideally, both remain within the tanks and the transfer system. Casualty situations are not ideal.

The mechanisms for release of vapors and the potential dangers differ between the casualty and lightering ship. In the discharging ship, inert gas flows into the tank as the cargo comes out. Adding gas too slowly allows a vacuum to be drawn in the tank and the PV valve to open and admit oxygen-rich air to the tank. Conversely, adding inert gas too quickly allows pressure to build up and causes the PV valve to open and vent the inert gas-vapor atmosphere on deck. The tank atmosphere also vents on deck when an opening to the tank is open for any reason, such as rigging in hydraulic submersible pumps or taking hand ullages.

In tanks receiving cargo in the lightering ship, a combination of cargo vapors and inert gas vents from the tank as the cargo enters. To reduce the release of aromatic hydrocarbons into the atmosphere, many ports require a vapor control system by which the vapors go ashore to the receiving facility for incineration. During ship-to-ship transfers of any type, gases normally vent to the atmosphere. Theoretically, vapor balancing, a process used when discharging and ballasting, is possible during ship-to-ship transfers. The practicality of such an operation is questionable; it is not a proven practice. Attempting to set up for vapor balancing in a casualty situation adds another complication to an already complicated operation. Inert gas significantly reduces the explosion potential of vented gases by changing the composition of the gaseous mixture. It would be foolhardy to belittle the problem in salvage planning and to fail to prepare to deal with the worst possible situation. Instead, salvors must prepare to deal with the presence of gases that are explosive, toxic, and suffocating, and always behave as though the risk is extreme.

In double-hull tankers, double-bottom tanks may contain explosive vapor mixtures. Unless cargo is leaking into these tanks from the cargo tanks, as may happen when tank boundaries rupture during casualties, a single flushing of the double-bottom tanks usually suffices to remove the hazardous vapors. Frequent explosimeter readings of tank atmospheres detect vapor buildup before atmospheres become explosive and dangerous. Readings are taken in all tanks, even those remote from apparent damage, as heavy shocks—such as those occurring during groundings and weapons strikes—can crack structure some distance from the shock. Oil in casualties migrates in unexpected ways.

The vented gases with their high hydrocarbon gas content must enter the atmosphere as high as practical above the deck and well away from accommodations, machinery space intakes, and salvage machinery that are potential ignition sources. Neither vented gases nor oxygen-deficient inert gas should accumulate on deck. Wind usually disperses and mixes gases so the air-vapor mixture remains below the Lower Explosive Limit (LEL). The dispersing effect of the wind depends upon the volume of gas and the rate of venting, but winds of 5 knots (2.5 m/sec) and better dilute gas to a safe level 15 to 30 feet from the vent. Winds above 10 knots (5 m/sec) disperse the gases quickly enough to remove concern. Equipment kits for salvage operations on tankers or other vessels should include a hand-held anemometer. Structures and ships alongside may alter wind patterns and local velocities. It is far wiser and safer to take the time to measure local wind velocities than to accept the general conditions as prevailing all around the ships.

Gases rise in a plume, bend to leeward, and settle toward the surface. They may collect behind deckhouses and structures, under the break of the forecastle, in doorways and recesses, between the ships, and in other places where there can be a still atmosphere. Figure 13-7 shows a typical dispersion pattern for gases venting on deck. Undiluted gas mixtures from petroleum liquids all have greater density

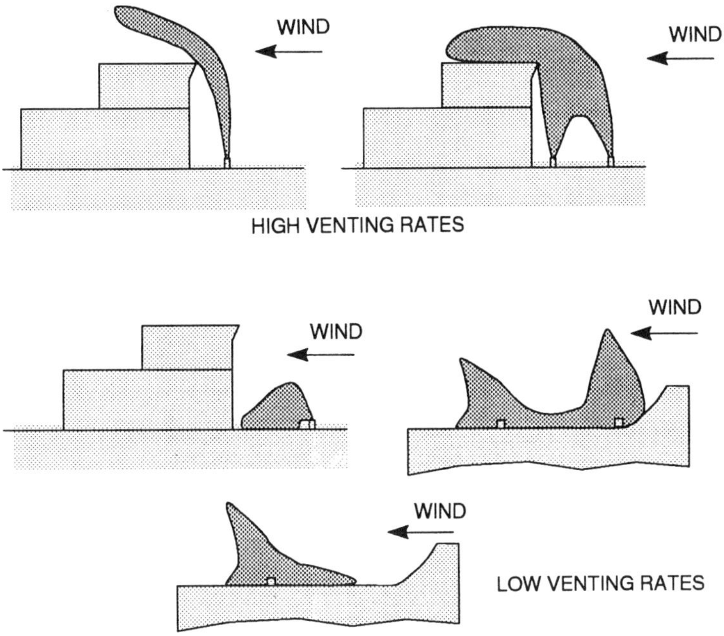

Fig. 13-7. Typical flammable zone plume patterns for vented gases

than air. Vapor densities vary from about 1.5 to about 2.5 times the density of air. The gases not only lie along the deck and sea surface, but can layer. When mixed with air, they can form pockets and layers of explosive gases. Blowers, either intrinsically safe electrical blowers or, preferably, water turbine–driven blowers, effectively disperse stagnant pools of gas.

Dealing with the vapors and dangerous atmospheres possible in tanker salvage requires the correct instruments to measure gases in the atmosphere—instruments not only to measure atmospheres thought to contain vapors, but also to measure atmospheres in closed spaces and those in which combustion has taken place. Every salvor's tanker salvage kit ought to contain at least:

An *explosimeter* or *combustible gas indicator* to show the flammability or explosivity of an atmosphere in a closed space or an area of stagnant air. The device chosen should measure both the oxygen level and the LEL of combustible gases simultaneously and should have a battery-operated pump. Explosimeters are accurate only for the gas on which they were calibrated. Most use methane or butane for calibration. The manufacturer's instructions should contain curves for converting readings for other gases. These instruments do not indicate either toxicity or the presence of enough oxygen to support life. Every man on the salvage crew must be aware that an atmosphere, while not explosive, can be fatal to breathe.

An *oxygen analyzer* to measure the oxygen content of atmospheres. This instrument permits checking the oxygen content of inert gas and inerted tanks and checking breathable atmospheres.

A *multigas detector* to show the presence of hydrogen sulfide, carbon monoxide, carbon dioxide, nitrogen dioxide, and chlorine in tank atmospheres, and vented gases in burned-out spaces and areas where rotting organic material may generate these gases.

This instrumentation is of little use if it remains in its shipping container. Areas where gas buildup is suspected or probable are measured frequently with all three types of instrument. When the wind shifts, new places where the gases may lie are sought and checked.

Keeping doorways, ventilation intakes, ports, and other possible gas intakes into the accommodation, pump rooms, and other interior spaces closed bars fumes from entering these spaces. Air-conditioning systems should recirculate, not act as intakes for potentially fume-laden air.

Areas in which vapors may accumulate are cleared of potential ignition sources. Locating portable salvage machinery clear of the tank deck on the forecastle or stern, on platforms atop tank deck centerline pipelines, and upwind keeps it clear of fume sources. Shutting down machinery at least once every twenty-four hours to blow the exhaust through with compressed air removes carbon buildup and reduces the chance of sparking. Poor-quality fuel requires more frequent blow downs. Machinery should operate within its normal operating temperatures with no overheating. Use of electrical equipment should be minimized. All electrical equipment, regardless of size or power source, must be intrinsically safe. This requirement very definitely includes the UHF and VHF hand-held radios, loud hailers, flashlights, and any other portable electrical equipment that the salvors carry. As far as possible, boat and helicopter operations are stopped during transfer operations. Total shutdown may not be practical, but boat and helicopter operations should be limited to only those that are absolutely mandatory.

A pocket or layer of explosive gas anywhere in the ship calls for shutting down until the gas disperses. Toxic or oxygen-deficient gas is another matter. Shutting down with these gases aboard is a matter for the judgment of the salvage master and his perception of the hazard.

Pumps and Pumping Systems

There are three basic ways to handle cargo in a tanker casualty:

First, and all-around most preferable—taking suction through the ship's pipelines with the ship's pumps and discharging though the casualty's manifold into the lightering ship's cargo-handling system.

Second, running well behind the first, and actually third choice from the standpoint of operational desirability—putting portable submersible pumps into the tanks and pumping over the top into the lightering ship. Portable submersible pumps have low capacities compared to tankers' installed cargo pumps. Over the top is unavoidably a slow process.

Third, some combination of over-the-top pumping and the installed system allows salvors to take advantage of the operable parts of the casualty's cargo-handling system and limit over-the-top pumping to situations where no other option exists. The ability to use some part of the installed cargo system with its inherent safety and higher transfer rates makes combined systems the operational choice before over-the-top pumping.

Discharge with Installed Systems

Installed systems of pumps and pipelines are by far the fastest and safest way to handle tanker cargo. These systems have all the pipelines, pumps, gauges, and control for a safe, effective transfer. The casualty's crew, with the advice and assistance of the salvors, performs these discharges most effectively. The casualty's crew is not only qualified to operate the system, but also knows all its quirks and idiosyncrasies. When the casualty's crew is not available for the discharge operation, the salvage crew should study the cargo transfer procedures book and walk the system out until they understand it completely before attempting a transfer. Some repairs may be necessary.

In casualties without power and operable pumps, steam or electricity for powering pumps may come from a lightering or salvage ship, or portable generators or boilers. Salvage crews can usually repair electric deep-well and reciprocating steam cargo or stripping pumps with a reasonable amount of effort. Burned out, flooded, or misaligned steam turbine–driven pumps are more difficult. Restoring turbine-driven pumps, if even possible, seldom justifies the time and effort required. Reciprocating pumps are well worth the time and effort to put them in service. Deep-well pumps found most often in product carriers are particularly good in casualties. Electrically driven deep-well pumps serve individual tanks, with their motors mounted on deck, not concentrated in a single pumproom.

With the main cargo system, discharge should follow normal procedures insofar as possible. Sequencing the discharge of the tanks, always important, is especially so when the hull has damage and some loss of hull strength. Discharge sequence should be worked out in advance of starting to pump and should consider not only removing as much cargo from the ship as practical, but also hull strength at each step of the discharge. The ship's installed load computer, adequate for calculating stresses on an intact hull, probably does not contain a section modulus editor that allows factoring in hull damage. Normally, it is as quick and more accurate to make discharge sequence calculations with a salvage program that allows consideration of the loss of section modulus.

Over-the-Top Pumping

The heart of over-the-top pumping systems is portable, hydraulically driven pumps that enter cargo tanks from the top. The entire pumping system includes power sources, power supply lines, and discharge hoses. Pumps go into the tanks through the Butterworth opening and/or tank hatch and can be suspended at any level in the tank; therefore, they can pump oil floating on a water bottom. When pumping a tank open to the sea, the liquid level in the tank changes only slightly because water enters the tank as oil is pumped out, maintaining the hydrostatic balance. Over-the-top pumping is also appropriate where broken pipelines in the tanks prevent the main cargo pumps from getting suction, and with main cargo pumps beyond practical repair. Over-the-top pumping equipment is first-class, and good techniques have been developed and proven in practice, but over-the-top pumping remains a jury-rig with inherent dangers and many violations of design pumping system integrity. Although a standard salvage technique, over-the-top pumping is the system of no other choice. Nothing in this section implies that over-the-top pumping is either unsafe or ineffective. It can be both, but making it so requires a low level of knowledge and competence.

Several manufacturers make hydraulically driven pumps suitable for salvage use (figure 13-8). In a small market, these complex pumps with high safety standards are expensive and readily available only through salvage operators or specialty rental companies.

Fig. 13-8. A submersible cargo pump with handling tripod, lightweight discharge hose, and power hose

Most pumps fit through a standard 12.5 inch (318 mm) Butterworth opening, the preferred entry for portable pumps because there are no obstructions in way of the opening. When pumps cannot go through Butterworth openings, they may go into the tank hatches. If they do, the pump, hydraulic hoses, discharge hose, or rigging can foul on the ladder. Some poor soul must go into the tank to free a fouled pump. To make the tank hatch even more unappealing, it is practically impossible to secure the hatch against gas leakage from the tank.

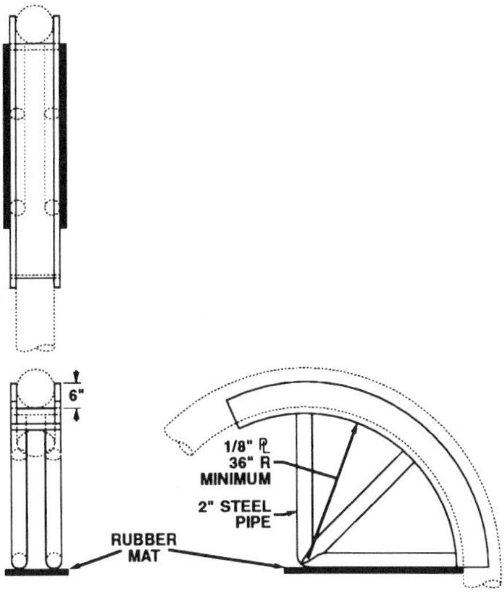

Fig. 13-9. Pump discharge hose guide

Either a rubber hose collar or sheet rubber wrapped around and lashed to the discharge hose and the hydraulic hoses can seal Butterworth openings satisfactorily against gas leakage. A discharge hose guide and saddle at the tank exit prevent kinking, take the hose into the tank perpendicular to the deck, and keep side thrust off the collar (figure 13-9). The saddle should be secured to the studs for the Butterworth opening cover with two nuts on each stud and set on a rubber mat.

No matter how effective sealing appears, atmospheres near any opening in a non-inerted tank are monitored frequently for explosive and toxic gas. Keeping tanks inert during over-the-top transfers is practical, but some gas always leaks out, particularly when putting pumps into or taking them out of tanks.

Portable, hydraulically driven, over-the-top pumps should be treated with the care and respect expensive, complex machinery deserves. The pumps should never be banged or dropped. Special care should be taken not to bang hydraulic couplings when handling pumps into the tanks. Pumps should not be operated on their side or at an angle of more than thirty degrees from the vertical and should not be allowed to thrash around or vibrate excessively while pumping.

Marrying the lifting line and hoses at 3-foot (1-meter) intervals with a timber or rolling hitch in fiber line prevents the lowering line from wrapping around and choking the hose and makes it easier to haul the pump and hoses out of the tank.

Rigging, moving, and handling equipment for over-the top pumping is fairly heavy, labor-intensive work. Adding to the physical work in moving heavy equipment around in very large ships is the work of maintaining a taut pumping watch. Casualty crews seldom, if ever, help with any part of over-the-top pumping except heavy labor—hardly ever even that—because of the specialized nature of setting up, watchstanding, and breaking down.

Lessening work requires care during sequencing planning. Sequencing for over-the-top transfers calls for considering how many times and how far equipment must move, as well as stresses in the ship's hull caused by the changing load. Failing to consider the work involved in moving equipment may turn a straightforward operation into a nightmare. Although tanker salvage equipment is as light as possible, the equipment is still large, heavy, and difficult to manhandle—especially when on a ship the size of a VLCC. The sequencing plan should be walked through as a check on its practicality. A system that works well is to draw up the plan, mark the routes out on deck with paint, and walk through it dragging a piece of 3-inch (circumference) line. The line shows up bottlenecks and problem areas.

The diesel-engined prime mover must be placed on or near the casualty's tank deck. Near is preferable. The forecastle, poop, and midships house top make the best locations, but sometimes require such long leads that hydraulic pressure losses affect pump performance. Platforms built over the pipelines on deck accommodate prime movers close to pumps. Diesel engines for over-the-top systems have hydraulic starting, nonsparking exhaust, and efficient cooling systems to increase their safety aboard tankers. With proper attention to their siting, operation, and maintenance, they are safe on the tank deck.

Engines on the tank deck should sit upwind of openings from which vapors may escape. All engines should be:

Attended at all times and have a log of activity and performance.

Operated strictly within the manufacturer's specified engine speed and temperatures.

Shut down not less than once every twenty-four hours for removal and blow through of the exhaust system.

Protected from rain, snow, and extremely high and low temperatures.

It often makes sense to manifold over-the-top pump discharges for a more efficient transfer or to clean up the snake's nest that the tank deck of a casualty with hoses and power leads resembles. Manifolds are sized so the size of the manifold and the outlets have about the same cross-sectional area as the total cross-sectional areas of the inlets. Many salvors' stores have 8-inch manifolds with two 6-inch inlets or other combinations they have found useful. Any competent welder can make larger manifolds on site.

Manifolding is appropriate whenever several pumps transfer cargo to a lightering ship or to collecting tanks on the casualty. There is less risk of oil spillage with manifolding because the 8-inch and larger hose used with manifolds is more rugged than the 6-inch collapsible hose normally used as pump discharge hose.

Salvors strip pumps over the top in two ways that differ from one another and from the tankerman's stripping that removes all the cargo from a tank.

Tanks are *stripped back* when crude oil or product in the tank contacts seawater and emulsifies, losing value. Cargo is stripped back out of tanks with this condition and combined in sound tanks. In tanks open to the sea, water enters to maintain hydrostatic balance. The level in the tank remains constant and the pump can stay high in the cargo to reduce the head and increase pumping efficiency. In tanks with flooding too slow to maintain liquid level, adjusting the pump periodically keeps the suction in the layer of good oil above the emulsification.

As much oil as possible floating on a water bottom is *stripped out*. In operation, raising the pump suction periodically keeps it in the constantly thinning layer of oil. Frequent water cuts with an interface detector determine the depth of the layer. Very shallow layers call for small stripping pumps or a skimming system rather than large over-the-top pumps.

On some occasions safety demands that an over-the-top operation shut down temporarily. Shutting down does not mean just the pumping itself. It includes removing pumps from the tanks, wiping them down, and securing tank covers. Situations requiring mandatory shutdown include:

Any situation or emergency that requires shutdown of normal cargo transfer operations.

Electrical storms in the vicinity.

Ships mooring or unmooring alongside.

Securing pumping for long periods. The salvage master defines what is long.

Hesitancy in shutting down cargo operations is always wrong. Shutting down the operation and reducing the potential for an accident under questionable conditions is always good practice.

Combined Systems

That part of the casualty's cargo transfer system that can still operate should be combined with over-the-top pumping to transfer oil. Combining the installed system with over-the-top pumping is preferable to pumping totally over the top. One of the most common and effective ways of combining the casualty's system and an over-the-top system is to:

1. Pump tanks pumpable by the casualty's cargo system to the lightering vessel.
2. Pump over the top from damaged tanks to sound ship's tanks serving as collecting tanks through the tank drops.
3. Pump from the collecting tanks to the lightering vessel with the installed system.
4. Rig one or more hose strings to allow over-the-top pumping directly to the lightering vessel when the casualty's pumps do not have access to cargo.

Fig. 13-10. Several over-the-top pumps operating simultaneously from several tanks provide an adequate supply of oil to keep the operation flowing smoothly.

Discharging over the top from several tanks simultaneously (figure 13-10) and manifolding the over-the-top pumping helps keep an adequate supply of cargo in the collecting tanks for the high-capacity cargo pumps.

Whatever the situation on the casualty, using the cargo system wherever possible reduces dependence on the less desirable method of over-the-top pumping. Unless the salvage crew has little experience or the tanker crew is poor, cargo may be consolidated and transferred simultaneously.

Stress calculations must be made for the conditions—including transient conditions—that exist in these transfers. Some unusual loading patterns are likely to set up stress patterns quite different from those seen in intact ship operations.

Steam

The casualty's boiler can supply steam for operating pumps and cargo temperature control equipment. If the casualty has an unsafe boiler steam, the lightering vessels or a portable steam generator can supply steam. Portable steam generators provided by salvors are usually the easiest and most efficient to use. Any operation requires a minimum capacity of at least 1,000 pounds per hour at 200 psi; capacities in the order of 3,000 pounds per hour are better for sustained operations. Turbine-driven cargo pumps may require much greater amounts. Provision must be made for handling exhaust and condensate and for maintaining an adequate supply of water for the steam generator.

Cargo Temperature Control

Heating the cargo in heavy crudes, bunkers, and products carriers to a pumpable temperature is a major use for steam in a tanker casualty. When the casualty occurs in cold weather, the list of products lengthens. Steam to the installed heating coils heats cargo in its tanks. When these coils are inoperative or leaking badly, coils or hose loops into the tank through the Butterworth or tank hatches make a suitable replacement. Steam coils and loops must stay clear of hydraulic hoses and discharge hoses lest they overheat and weaken the hose.

Cargo pumped long distances in cold weather may need reheating along the way. Shell and tube or other types of heat exchangers placed on deck are suitable. Adequate heat exchangers made from various diameters of pipe can be put together on site. The total heat exchange area greatly affects the rate of heat exchange. This area should be as large as practical.

It is difficult to impossible to estimate the rate of cooling or the rate of heating of cargo in a tank. Mass of cargo, temperature differentials, surface areas, specific heats, and many other factors complicate the equation. In practice, it is seldom worthwhile to try to make such estimates. It is better to go ahead and heat tanks with equipment as it becomes available and to begin transferring as soon as the cargo is pumpable, regardless of the transfer rate.

Regulatory authorities may require removal of residues, clingage, and slops as a condition of port entry or as part of the final discharge program. To remove these nasties, a submersible salvage pump is combined with a heat exchanger on deck. The tank is partially filled with water that is pumped on deck through the heat exchanger and back into the tank. The hot water raises the temperature of the residues until they are pumpable.

Reciprocating Steam Pumps

Reciprocating steam pumps seem hopelessly old-fashioned alongside more modern salvage equipment, but their simplicity, reliability, and ability to handle high-viscosity liquids make them very useful aboard tankers. One of their best uses is pumping from the top of the cargo through the tank hatch to increase pumping rates when lowering the head in a breached tank. These pumps are still installed as stripping pumps on new buildings.

Eductors

Eductors have a significant place in tanker salvage. Although neither a common nor a favored practice, some companies have used large eductors to discharge cargo. Eductors large enough for the job and the equipment needed to operate and support them are bulky and complex. Smaller eductors, 6- and 8-inch eductors, are very useful for pumping slops, ballast, and oil-water mixtures from places where salvage pumps cannot operate or when salvage pumps are engaged fully on higher-priority work. Eductors are appropriate for pumping oil expected to leak into pump room bilges in poorly maintained tankers or during casualty operations on the best of ships.

Gauging

Oil has inherent value measured by the quantity of oil and its quality. During normal transfers, where custody of the cargo changes, independent cargo surveyors determine both. A ship's officer usually takes ullages for transfers within the same company. In salvage operations, it is good practice to have an independent surveyor present. When no independent surveyor is present and oil has spilled, the salvors and the crews of both ships must maintain careful records, particularly in countries like the United States where the question of quantity may be raised in connection with penalties for spillage.

Ships with inert gas systems have closed ullaging systems with floats, radar echoes, or submerged sensors that read out tank ullages at the control console. Ullages can be taken without leaking vapor in ships with vapor control systems by using specially designed devices that measure ullage and cargo temperature and determine the oil-water interface location. Despite these wonders of modern technology, salvors must be prepared to take ullages in the old way, hand-ullaging tapes through the ullage openings or vapor control valves. The MMC-type hand ullaging and interface system is much to be preferred to ullaging through ullage opening. The latter method is a last resort. In the event no other choice exists, salvors should carry several linen ullaging tapes with nonmetallic parts and fittings to prevent introducing metallic tapes into the tanks. Metallic tapes and tapes with metallic fittings are unsuitable when ullaging tanks containing static accumulator oils and any possibility of an explosive atmosphere exists. Hand ullaging through ullage openings has the disadvantage of requiring opening of tanks. Some tank atmosphere, inert gas, or vapor-laden air always escapes. Hands taking ullages should stand upwind or not more than 90 degrees from the direction of the wind while opening tanks, ullaging, and closing tanks.

Ullaging is the first step in determining the amount of oil transferred. Ship's trim and variations in oil temperature from the standard of 60 degrees F. (15.5 degrees C.) require adjustments to ullages. Salvors should not take the time to make these corrections during a transfer, but should make accurate and complete records at the outset and throughout the transfer so that exact amounts can be calculated after the operation. Specific initial information includes drafts, list, ullages, interfaces, quantity in gross barrels or cubic meters, and temperatures.

In addition to establishing the amount of oil transferred, frequent gauging of the cargo establishes the transfer rate and the location of the water bottom—important factors in the organization of the transfer operation. The information should be taken at half-hour intervals and logged in the cargo control room.

The quality of oil is determined by sampling, again, preferably by an independent cargo surveyor, but acceptable by ship's and salvage crew. Several different kinds of devices for sampling from cargo tanks are in service. All allow sampling at different levels and all consist of a weighted container with a device for opening the container so it can fill. Alternatively, samples can be drawn at the cargo pumps via the sampling bleeder on the discharge side. Pump room sampling is preferable because the tanks are not open to the atmosphere during sampling. Samples should come from each tank before commencing discharge of the casualty and following completion of loading of the lightering vessel. They must be marked clearly to show when and from where they were taken. Enough samples are taken that all interested parties can keep a set of samples. One set of samples is designated as a master set and a chain of custody maintained.

Pollution Prevention

Risk of spillage and pollution is always present during a cargo transfer. The ad hoc nature of the situation heightens the danger during a casualty transfer. Normal pollution prevention practices and the ship's spill prevention plan should be followed meticulously. Ullages are taken at short intervals on all tanks, not just those from which oil is being transferred. A log of all ullages is kept in the control room.

Sawdust, coagulants, dispersants, and sorbent pads for dealing with small spills on deck should be broken out on the tank deck ready for use. Salvors should carry a couple of small drums of an approved dispersant and two small eductors for applying it.

At many terminals, booming ships during transfers is a standard practice. In casualties booming may or may not be desirable, depending upon whether or not the boom can be effective in the sea and wind conditions at the site. Regulatory agencies with their fixation on pollution control may require booming in circumstances where booming cannot be effective. Booming should be decided case by case with the major factor in the decision being the potential effectiveness of the boom. Boom and skimmers standing by at the scene are an excellent public relations investment by the casualty management.

SALVAGE OF THE SHIP

Refloating the ship is the climax of the entire operation and is the event toward which all the preparation is directed. In a properly organized and structured operation, the final salvage should come almost as an anticlimax, just another planned event in a series of planned events with no surprises and no trauma. Achieving such a climax requires thorough planning and careful preparation.

In most strandings without breaching of the cargo containment, salvors can refloat the tanker by holding the ship with ground tackle or ballast, removing enough cargo to float the ship, and deballasting or hauling her away from shoal water. With breached cargo containment, the situation takes on a much higher degree of complexity.

Single-hull tankers and double-hull tankers with ruptured inner bottoms make such excellent candidates for refloating on air that experienced tanker salvage teams routinely carry compressors or blowers, manifolds, hoses, blowing fittings, and blank flanges to tanker casualties. Each tank has a large amount of recoverable buoyancy. Tanks in tankers are large and have few openings in the top. What openings exist are easily and quickly sealed. Inert gas or vapor control systems may be pressed into service for air distribution, or air-blowing fittings may be fitted to Butterworth hatches or other convenient locations. PV valves must be gagged or blanked. If the tank is blown completely, excess air vents through the damage.

Ballast tanks may be treated essentially the same way as cargo tanks. Ballast tanks have no PV valves or Butterworth opening, but they do have vents to be blanked and fittings suitable for blowing fittings.

In many ships, inert gas from the inert gas system or a portable inert gas system can blow cargo and ballast tanks. This very attractive option should be a first choice whenever even remotely possible. Blowing a tank with air necessarily raises the oxygen content in the tank and increases the chance of having an explosive atmosphere, while blowing with inert gas does not. Inert gas is preferred for blowing both cargo and ballast tanks. Cargo leakage into ballast tanks through either cracks existing before the casualty or casualty-related damage can cause explosive atmospheres in these tanks.

To blow a tank with inert gas, the discharge of the inert gas system is taken to a low-pressure blower or other compressor where its pressure is raised before admission to the tank through whatever storage and manifolding has been set up. Figure 13-11 shows a 900-cfm, diesel-driven, low-pressure blower rigged for tanker

Fig. 13-11. This 900-cfm, diesel-driven, low-pressure blower was built especially for tanker salvage. Photo courtesy of J.H. Leitz.

salvage. Two four-inch hoses bring gas from the inert gas generator to the blower inlet and the compressed gas discharges through two 3-inch hoses to fittings on the tank. Note that the hoses are made up with quick-connecting Cam-Lok fittings and that a check valve prevents back flow from the tank through the pump.

It is seldom necessary or desirable to blow tanks completely dry. Blowing tanks a few feet below the level of the sea surface with pressures so low they present no threat to the structure can restore large amounts of buoyancy. A pressure of 2 psig in a free-flooding tank drops the water level in the tank about 4.5 feet below the sea surface. With the additional buoyancy the draft decreases by:

$$\Delta T = \frac{\text{Buoyant volume}}{\text{TPI}}$$

where:

ΔT	=	change in draft in inches (centimeters)
Buoyant volume	=	the volume of the water displaced by the air in tons (tonnes)
TPI (TPC)	=	tons per inch (centimeter) immersion

Blowing just enough additional air into the tanks to maintain the pressure keeps the water level in the tank the same distance below the external water level as the ship rises. The ship continues to rise until it reaches equilibrium. Note that the decrease in draft does not equal the depth to which the water level falls unless the entire waterplane of the ship is blown down.

Blowing pressures should be chosen with care. The tanks can sustain a relatively low internal pressure; exceeding this level can damage the tank. The problem of determining the blowing pressure is another where sound engineering, an accurate appraisal of the situation, and evaluation of risk are major parts of the decision. To reach the desired water level in the tank, it may be necessary to exceed the pressure that the tank can sustain without lowering the factor of safety on yield or exceeding the yield point of the structure. Pressure should be based on a careful engineering analysis of the pressure the tank can hold without yielding and without failing catastrophically. When acceptable pressures and the accompanying water levels are known, the salvor must decide upon the adequacy of the results, if the risk of damage warrants blowing to the necessary pressure, and if damage to the structure is acceptable under the circumstances.

The combination of large tank volumes and carefully controlled blowing pressures allows buoyancy control within very narrow limits. By blowing various tanks with slightly different pressures, different liquid levels can be obtained, allowing control of trim and list. Salvors can put the ship into a variety of attitudes. Because very large volumes of air are needed to blow cargo tanks, high-capacity blowers or air compressors are most suitable for the jobs. Low-pressure centrifugal blowers make the most operationally satisfactory choice because they eliminate the need for high-pressure compressors and storage units while providing large volumes of air with enough pressure for the work.

With damage limited to the outer hull of double-hull tankers, air loses some advantage because double-bottom and wing tanks are smaller than cargo tanks. Most buoyancy must be regained by pumping cargo from intact tanks. Air can only blow the double-bottom tanks and provide the final lift needed. The condition of the ship must be analyzed carefully to determine if blowing the double-bottom tanks is necessary, or if discharging cargo can restore enough buoyancy. The best choice is the simplest operation that means the least work.

OTHER TANKERS

Tankships carry many products beside petroleum. Some products are dangerous, others very benign. Environmental authorities are unlikely to tolerate spillage or jettisoning of any products. Accordingly, any tanker casualty, regardless of the product, must be handled like a petroleum tanker casualty and the cargo treated and handled with great care.

Chemical tankers have a particularly severe problem. Some carry homogeneous cargoes or a limited number of products; drugstore ships carry a variety of products, some of which are dangerous and many of which are incompatible with one another. The difficulty in cargo handling in a chemical tanker casualty is complicated by the necessity for:

Strict segregation of the products.

Special attention to the products' sensitivity to static electricity.

Quick-release couplings or break-away spools on both manifolds.

Personal protective and fire-fighting equipment appropriate to the products.

Material Safety Data Sheets (MSDS) must be on scene for all the products handled and salvage crew members must be briefed in the cargoes' hazards and required safety measures. The three publications mentioned in conjunction with chemicals and hazardous materials—*The Chemical Data Guide for Bulk Shipment by Water*, the U.S. Department of Transportation's *Emergency Response Guidebook*, and the NIOSH *Pocket Guide to Chemical Hazards*—make valuable references and guides in chemical tanker casualties.

Liquefied gas carriers—LPG, LNG, or other products—have unique problems specific to their cargo and the structure of the ship. Help from the owner's emergency response team is absolutely mandatory. Salvors simply cannot undertake salvage of one of these complex and potentially dangerous ships without the specialized knowledge trained technicians bring to the situation. Earlier, this chapter advised against attempts to drag stranded tankers afloat. This advice becomes an absolute prohibition for liquefied gas carriers. The consequences of damaging or deforming the hull or containment system structure—outflow of cargo—are too great. In fully refrigerated ships, released cryogenic liquid contacting the hull can result in brittle fracture and massive structural failure. On the other side of the coin, seawater entering in contact with cryogenic liquid through containment system ruptures can cause cargo to boil off at a rate greater than relief valves can handle. A very big bang can result from boil-off if the containment vessel fails and the released cargo ignites.

SUMMARY

Tanker salvage is a specialized part of a specialized field. Emphasis on environmental protection brings much public, media, and regulatory attention to even the most minor tanker casualty and increases liability for all concerned with the casualty's actual or potential pollution and salvage. Salvors on their own can formulate and carry out salvage plans for any type of ship because that is what they do. With tankers, they now must deal with a plethora of parties, not all of whom have the same level of competence. This tremendous burden complicates tanker salvage without changing the technical aspects of the operation. Many parties to tanker salvage focus on cargoes rather than the ship and the overall circumstances of the casualty. In addition to going about their normal work with professionalism and care, salvors have the unofficial but very real task of bringing balance and common sense to the overall operation.

14

WRECKS

This book describes a "casualty" as a distressed ship that has sufficient value to warrant an effort to salvage her and return her to service. This chapter considers ships that have become "wrecks" and are no longer useful economic units. A casualty becomes a wreck with declaration of a constructive total loss when costs of salvage and repair exceed the insured value of the ship. With declaration of a constructive total loss the status of the ship changes as does the approach of the interested parties.

To salvors, the most significant change is that hull and machinery underwriters no longer have responsibility for the ship. Future action no longer solely depends upon the cost-benefit relationship, as in pure salvage. The vessel is now subject to the laws governing wrecks of the administration in whose waters she lies. These laws govern her fate without regard to the relative values of cost and benefit. The ship's P&I club indemnifies her owner for costs of removal or actions short of removal. The clubs undertake action on wrecks according to their rules that normally limit their liabilities to costs of actions required by law and chargeable to owners. The limitation on actions, the usually clear definition of the scope of the work, the similarity to a civil engineering or marine construction project, and the lack of time criticality militate against an open form type of salvage contract for wreck work. More conventional contracts, approaching construction contracts but sometimes incorporating a no cure–no pay provision, are common for wreck removals and associated work. Chapter 15 discusses wreck removal contracting in more detail.

Most nations, and some states or provinces within those nations, have laws requiring removal of wrecks from at least their navigable waterways and sometimes all their waters. Administrations without comprehensive wreck removal laws have used other, sometimes distantly related, legislation to force wreck removals. Some broadly interpret environmental laws and regulations to require removal of wrecks. Strictness of law enforcement varies from nation to nation and may vary within the nation. Wrecks are almost always removed when they block navigable waterways, create a hazard to navigation, block a berth, or otherwise disrupt a port or other facility. Laws requiring removal of wrecks may not be enforced when:

The wreck is in a remote location where it does not disrupt any activity.

The weather prevailing at the site makes wreck removal work impractical or outrageously expensive.

The owner has disappeared or gone bankrupt and is no longer indemnified, and the administration either cannot or does not choose to bear the cost of wreck removal.

The industrial effort required to remove the wreck can disrupt and damage the environment more than the presence of the wreck.

Wreck removals are very expensive major industrial operations. The cost increases greatly in a remote area with long lines of logistic support or with operational or environmental restraints. The decision to remove a wreck in an inhabited area or where it disrupts maritime or other commerce is easy and can be made quickly and without equivocation. Other cases, including borderline cases, justify careful consideration of measures less than total wreck removal.

ALTERNATIVES TO TOTAL WRECK REMOVAL

There are several alternatives to total wreck removal that may be appropriate and that may fulfill either the letter or the intent of the law. Eliminating materials that may cause a long-term hazard or be a source of pollution is a primary factor in choosing action less than total removal. The question to answer is: "What makes sense when all the factors are given proper weight?"

There is normally pressure from the administration to expedite the operation. When haste is likely to lead to wasteful lost motion, a high probability of failure, or pollution, the pressure should be resisted. Regulators may not see the forest of operational complexity and risk for the trees of their regulatory preoccupation. Nor may they have the technical expertise to evaluate the situation. Patient guidance from those with the technical expertise and responsibility for execution is appropriate.

Proper planning is a prerequisite of success. It is not sensible to undertake any operation without clearly defined goals and a plan for reaching them. An integral part of the planning is to get as much information about the wreck as possible. A thorough survey of the wreck by technically competent people, preferably by the people who will lead the working team aboard, is mandatory.

The crew is always gone from a wreck, but it is extremely useful for the owner to provide a licensed engineer who sailed in the vessel and who is familiar with the ship's tankage, systems, and storerooms. This person should be involved in the planning process. One of the goals of the survey is to determine which of the ship's systems and equipment can be made even marginally operable and what work is necessary to do this. The survey also should determine if any damage to the vessel has resulted in situations that make portions of any proposed work impractical, excessively dangerous, or impossible. Thorough documentation, including photographs and videotapes of conditions found, are extremely valuable as a guide to planning and for illustrations in discussions with regulators.

An environmental specialist knowledgeable in local environmental regulations and the types of materials found in ships is invaluable to the survey team. He should be equipped to take and carry away samples of questionable materials for identification.

Wrecks, no matter how inaccessible, are susceptible to pilferage and vandalism. Pilferable equipment and stores not removed before the wreck was abandoned may be removed during the survey and turned over to the P&I correspondent for disposition. It may not be practical to remove all pilferable items, but medical and bonded stores should receive priority attention. It is not necessary to inventory such stores unless time is available. They should be removed from the wreck and kept in the custody of the person in charge, preferably in locked stowage, until turned over to the P&I correspondent. Clinics serving the indigent often welcome donations of medical stores.

A complete listing of equipment necessary for the job is an important result of planning. If the wreck lies in an area remote from industrial support with long logistic lines, or if the operation is constrained by weather, a belt and suspenders approach to equipment duplication is far more economical than delays in the operation because of breakdowns. When a long period exists between the survey and execution, little reliance should be placed on shipboard equipment. The best rule is to take everything there is the slightest chance of needing.

Any operation to clean up a wreck generates large quantities of recyclable and nonrecyclable wastes. Recyclable wastes are identified at the outset, segregated, and recycled appropriately. Nonrecyclable wastes are disposed of at landfills or other facilities. Arrangements for disposal of wastes made before the operation help control potentially large costs for shipping and disposal of wastes. The costs for disposing of hazardous wastes can be horrendous. It may be necessary to ship hazardous wastes great distances to specialized disposal facilities.

Removal of Pollutants

There is no question but that oils and other obvious pollutants must be removed from wrecks to prevent their release into the environment as the hull breaks up. There are two primary differences between removing oils from a casualty under salvage and from a wreck:

Removals from a wreck are much more thorough. Oil removal from a casualty usually involves only petroleum products carried as bunkers and cargo. Removal from a wreck includes all oils—bunkers, cargo, lubricating, hydraulic, animal, and vegetable—from equipment or storage in tanks, drums, and other containers. It also includes greases and may include paints, thinners, and similar pollutants.

Operations on a casualty take advantage of the power and intact systems on the casualty. Operations on a wreck are more self-contained. All equipment—including tankage to receive the oil—must be supplied.

The procedures described and comments included in Chapter 5 for removing oil from ship's tanks apply to wrecks. Oils removed from wrecks should always be suspected of being contaminated but treated as clean oil. The value of oils that actually are clean may be recoverable after testing verifies cleanliness.

Oil should be drained from all machinery, drummed, and carried away for disposal. Oil drained from machinery is treated as waste oil and disposed of in compliance with local regulations. In cold climates, oil in machinery, both on deck and in the interior of the ship, may be very viscous and slow to drain. Heating the oil in the sump can speed up the process. Warming with a torch, or simply building a fire alongside, works.

Despite one's best efforts, the last drop of oil cannot be removed from the tanks and machinery sumps of a wreck. There is always residual oil in the tank when the operation is completed. Some tanks may be inaccessible by any means. Salvors have an obligation to remove as much oil as practical. They are not required to do the impossible. An on-site representative of the regulatory authorities can be extremely valuable to agree that as much oil as possible has been removed and that some tanks cannot be reached. This concurrence reduces argument and second-guessing upon completion of the work.

Where the geography and bathymetry permit, the barge or ship receiving the oil should lie alongside the wreck so the oil may be pumped directly to her tanks. Where she cannot lie alongside, the vessel furnishing the tankage may moor offshore for pumping via a floating hose. In this method, the pump should be on the wreck and the receiving vessel should lie as close as safety permits. Positive displacement pumps and floating hose—hose inherently buoyant both empty and when filled with fluid—are best for this work.

The hose is passed by first passing a messenger and hauling in the hose. Power is necessary to haul the hose, particularly where a longshore current acts. Portable winches can be set aboard dead wrecks for hauling hose ashore or the hauling line may be passed through a block and returned to the salvage ship for hauling. Small boats can help keep the hose in position and prevent a large bight from developing. Moorings placed along the length of long runs of hose help reduce stresses and keep the hose in position. Such moorings are particularly useful if the operation must continue for some time. Crossing beaches with a heavy dumping surf requires a great deal of power—not so much to haul the hose through the surf, but to prevent it from being carried seaward by the retreating surf.

Sometimes, the only hose available is negatively buoyant. It is better to go ahead with this type of hose than to delay the operation, especially with a sand or mud sea floor that is unlikely to tear the hose. Some procedural changes are in order. Capping and filling the hose with air well below its rated pressure and attaching floats provides buoyancy to float negatively buoyant hose ashore. Floating eliminates abrasion from dragging on the sea floor. Also, friction between the hose and sea floor makes hauling the hose along in contact with the sea floor practically impossible. The negatively buoyant hose lies on the sea floor during the transfer. This position protects it from wave and surface current action except where it emerges at both ends. Buoys with lines about 10 percent longer than the high water depth should mark the hose position. The long scope of the lines prevents them from placing any significant lift on the hose.

Before the operation completes, oil must be removed from the hose. The hose can be capped at the wreck end with a cap with an air fitting and then blown through until air vents at the receiving vessel. Alternatively, a pump on the receiving vessel may take suction on the hose until it becomes airbound.

Floating hose is retrieved by hauling from the receiving vessel. Negatively buoyant hose is retrieved by capping it and filling it with air and then taking the inshore end to the receiving vessel and hauling this end in.

Hazardous and Persistent Materials

In time, wrecks break up or deteriorate. As they do, hazardous or persistent materials contained in the ship are released to the environment and are dispersed in low concentrations. Releases from wrecks may occur over a long period, sometimes in small trickles, other times in large burps. Removal of the materials soon after the wreck occurs obviates any release.

Agencies responsible for the environment have sought to require the owner to remove all hazardous materials and potential pollutants. On some occasions, removals include persistent materials not listed in the IMDG Code. Materials that may be targeted for removal during these wreck-cleaning operations include not only lubricating, hydraulic, and cooling oils, greases, and other petroleum products, but also:

Paints, thinners, white lead, preservatives, and associated material.

Asbestos and other insulating materials, some of which are not hazardous but are persistent.

Refrigerants and bottled industrial and fire-fighting gases.

PCBs in electrical and electronic equipment.

Halides in halogen vapor lights.

Radioactive nuclides in cathode-ray tubes.

Foodstuffs.

Perishable cargoes or cargoes of organic material subject to decomposition.

Hazardous or obnoxious materials in cargoes, including materials that become hazardous or obnoxious in contact with seawater.

Furniture, joiner work, and other debris-forming material.

Vermin.

Any requirement to remove hazardous, obnoxious, or persistent materials from a wreck should be a reasoned decision based on realistic evaluation of the danger the material poses. The evaluation should consider at least:

The location of the wreck relative to assets and resources that may be damaged by release of the materials.

The type of material.

The concentration of material that could result from a discharge in the most likely case and in the worst case.

The dispersion that can be expected and the rate of dispersion.

A shipwreck is a catastrophic event that inevitably results in an insult to the environment. Preventing or limiting environmental insult should not be the result of an absolute uncompromising approach by any party.

In-place incineration is the quickest and most cost-effective means of removing oils and hazardous materials from wrecks. Not only is the material destroyed, but the heat effects on the hull speed deterioration of the hull. Many administrations prohibit or restrict incineration because the combustion products are released into the atmosphere. Thus, incineration may not be an option for a particular case. Hazardous and persistent materials can be removed manually by crews properly protected from exposure to the materials they are handling.

Note that most of the materials above are solid materials that can be containerized for removal from the site. Bulk cargo may be loaded into ships or barges by the means described in Chapter 11. Slurrying and pumping move bulk cargoes effectively to vessels moored offshore. The comments about pumping oils to offshore lightering vessels apply equally to slurrying.

The regulatory authorities and P&I club's representative negotiate the scope of the cleanup and the rules for the job. Negotiations can be difficult and time consuming. High-quality technical input to these negotiations covering materials, techniques, and scope of work is imperative to a realistic cost-effective agreement. An evaluation of all the risks associated with the work should be made. A determination of the relative risks of doing and not doing the work, including the results of credible accidents during the removal operations, is particularly important.

During the negotiations the conditions at the site are not stable. The wreck continues to deteriorate with results that may affect the scope and the nature of the work. If at all practical, a final joint survey should be made before signing anything to assure a realistic agreement for work that can actually be done. Cleanup of a wrecked ship differs significantly from cleanup of a hazardous waste site ashore, because of the ship's marine environment. Weather, for instance, can be a controlling factor when the wreck is exposed on a lee shore or when material from the ship must move across the beach and through the surf.

As the work becomes more complex, the risk of work-generated pollution grows. Salvors or environmental cleanup companies undertaking operations on a wreck should be expert in spill prevention and should take extraordinary spill prevention measures in keeping with their extraordinary workplace. Because of the nature and environment of the work, salvors and cleanup operators should be held liable only for spills and pollution that can be attributed to negligence.

The necessity for making field decisions and compromises to get the best attainable results also grows with operational complexity. As in all operations at sea, these decisions occur in real time. Delay for studying the situation or referring to a remote authority may increase the risk, reduce the options, or deprive the decision of practical significance. It is highly desirable that regulators participate in decision making on-site. Where regulators are not on-site, distance and communications may impede their effective participation in decision making. At these times, the salvors have no alternative but to go ahead and make decisions based on their best information, knowledge of operational goals, and knowledge of regulatory requirements. They should never allow themselves to be pushed into taking undue risks. They must bear in mind that the operationally sensible course may not be the best answer when all circumstances are considered. After making their decision, they must be prepared to defend it and to take their lumps.

Partial Removal

The conditions at the wreck site may be such that it is advantageous to remove only a portion of the wreck or simply to clear the wreck from an area where it interferes with marine activity. Partial wreck removals are most appropriate where:

Time is critical.

Assets, particularly the necessary floating industrial plant, are limited.

The remaining portions of the wreck do not interfere with maritime commerce or other activity.

No removable hazardous materials that can be released to the environment remain in the portions to be left.

Removal of the entire wreck would pose greater hazards to people and the environment than leaving portions in place.

The legal mandates for complete wreck removal can be modified by the particular circumstances of the case.

There are no legal mandates for complete wreck removal.

Partial removal leaves some portion of the wreck in place. The remaining portion of the wreck wastes away in time. The time may be quite long. The major disadvantage of partial removals is that the solution may work only in the short term. A portion of a wreck in a navigable waterway may lie in the way of future waterway deepening or channel maintenance dredging.

Examples of partial removal include:

Piecemealing a stranded or sunken wreck down to the mud or sand line and leaving the remainder.

Reducing the height of a wreck to get a minimum depth over the wreck that allows use of the waterway.

Burying the wreck.

Dispersing the wreck.

Removal to the sand or mud line employs piecemealing methods, described later in this chapter, to remove all wreckage above or to a short distance below the surface. In time, the remaining portions waste away. While the wreckage is wasting away beach erosion or shifting sands may uncover it or may require removal before the land is used. This type of partial removal is very attractive because of the high costs associated with removal of the portions below the sand or mud line.

The high costs derive from diver-intensive operations to remove mud and soil from the wreck, to keep it clear, and to tunnel or otherwise rig sections for removal.

In the past, many wrecks have been reduced in height to give a minimum clear depth of water over the wreck. The depth requirement can be met by piecemealing the upper portion of the wreck or by pounding the wreck down (flattening) with explosives. The techniques for flattening depend upon the attitude of the wreck. Ships lying on their side can be flattened by cutting away the very strong bow and stern sections and pounding the side down. Extra heavy pounding charges along bulkheads and decks and other structural hard points help break down the structure. Upright ships are flattened by removing top hamper and superstructure, cutting the decks at their junction with the side shell, and pounding the deck downward. Cutting charges along the deck edge detonate slightly (about one second) before pounding charges for maximum effect. Additional heavy pounding charges are placed along bulkheads, at stanchions, and in way of other structural hard points. Flattening compresses the wreck into a tight mass or produces a scattered, unpredictably connected pile of junk that is very difficult to remove later.

Burying is one of the most seldom used partial wreck removal techniques, normally chosen only when removal by other means is impractical or has been ruled out for other reasons. Wrecks can be buried by one of three methods:

1. Dredging a deep hole close to and under the wreck so the wreck capsizes into the hole.
2. Dredging a slope and skidding the wreck down the slope into the hole.
3. Alternatively dredging holes on each side of the wreck so the wreck "walks" down into the sea floor (figure 14-1).

Conventional hydraulic dredging or, when soil conditions are favorable, explosives can create the slopes and holes. Even more than other types of wreck removals, burying has the characteristics of civil engineering work and normally requires a major input from soils and dredging specialists. Some reduction of the wreck, such as removal of masts, deckhouses, and other top hamper, usually accompanies burying.

Wreck dispersal is a wartime expedient for removing an obstruction by placing heavy charges around the wreck and detonating them simultaneously. There is no finesse and no detailed planning in this type of work. The results are largely unpredictable and seldom very elegant.

Most of the methods described above include explosives, sometimes large charges, as a primary or optional tool. Rules governing explosives vary among administrations. Explosives regulations and questions of interest address the types of explosives available locally; explosives import, storage, transportation, licensing,

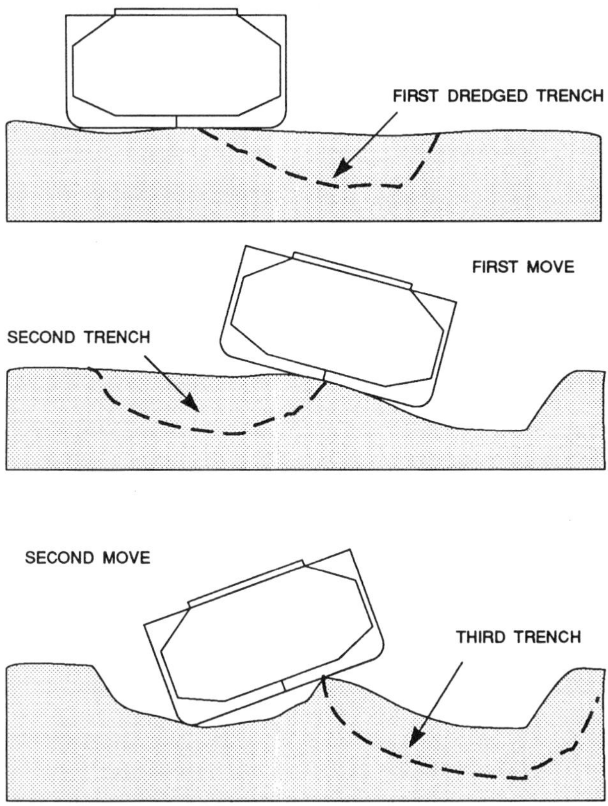

Fig. 14-1. Burying a wreck by trenching

and handling regulations; explosives workers' requirements; the sizes of charges that can be fired; and steps that must be taken for environmental protection. Technical considerations for their use also vary. These include the effects of air and water blast on other installations and potential environmental damage. While means, such as bubble curtains, exist for attenuating blast, side effects and their costs figure strongly into technique selection. Often restrictions on the use and handling of explosives, particularly in populated, environmentally sensitive, or politically unstable areas, may be so severe that explosives are uneconomical or impractical.

Wreck Removal Techniques

The following sections describe basic techniques for wreck removals. They do not, by any means, describe all the techniques that may be used. Only the salvors' imagination and engineering aptitude limit the techniques and combinations of techniques for removing a wreck and for coping with the environment in which the wreck lies. Each situation has unique qualities that challenge the imagination to develop the most effective way of dealing with it. Studying accounts of previous wreck removal operations can stimulate imagination. Fortunately, accounts abound in the maritime professional press and in journals directed to civil engineers. The edition of the *U.S. Navy Ship Salvage Manual*, Volume 3, published in 1973 contains a valuable collection of accounts of wreck-removal operations. The manual is long since out of print, but is found occasionally in used bookstores. The Bibliography at the back of this book has several accounts of wreck removals. The list is not comprehensive.

Wreck-removal techniques must be chosen carefully, because inappropriate ones can result in aggravating the situation both technically and economically. The location, condition of the wreck, schedule requirements, navigational restrictions, equipment availability, residual value, economics, environment, legal constraints, and the laws of physics all factor into the choice of wreck-removal techniques. Wreck removals defy cookbook solutions.

Floating Ships

Floating ships may become constructive total losses, especially when burned out. The line between disposal of a ship at the end of an unsuccessful salvage and a wreck is fuzzy. The same principles are apposite. Ships in ports or in protected waters present relatively simple problems. The greatest difficulties lie in pollution control, removal of cargo—perhaps turned into a soggy mess by fire fighting—and assuring that the vessel is watertight enough and stable enough for a tow to a ship breaker or to a shipyard for further securing and preparation for a voyage in tow.

Authorities generally cooperate with salvors working to rid their waters of an undesirable object. The same is not true when the salvor has control of a floating wreck at sea. Authorities often oppose entry of casualties and wrecks into their waters to avoid creating a situation that may evolve into a serious one for them. The salvor may be stuck with a marine leper for some time until a port entry can be negotiated.

In lieu of a port entry, it may be possible to take the vessel into a location in the nation's territorial waters for repairs. Casualties and floating wrecks should not go into waters that are poorly charted or those seldom used by large vessels. Casualties and wrecks are by definition not intact and are more susceptible to critical damage from such events as finding uncharted rocks. When a suitable location can be agreed upon, the logistics of repairs away from an industrial facility can make work on the vessel very expensive.

Sinking in deep water is a very satisfactory method of disposing of floating wrecks, providing the terms of any administration holding or claiming authority over the proposed dumping site can be met. Requirements for deep water sinking are very likely to include assurances of no release of pollutants.

A technically difficult problem arises when the ship is partially afloat. This condition usually occurs with tankers and bulk carriers that have sustained serious damage in the forward part of the ship but the engine room remains intact. The value of the engine room with its machinery and the accommodation is usually good enough to warrant salvage of this section. The basic technique for such an operation is to separate the stern from the remainder of the ship, then float the stern away and remove the remainder by one or a combination of the wreck removal methods described later. The difficulty comes in (1) assuring that the stern section is stable and secure when afloat and (2) separating the two sections. A detailed engineering analysis of the stern section is necessary to determine its stability and the need for supplying supplementary stability. The how and where of the separation depend very much on the remaining connection and how the sections lie. Explosives have been used with great success to separate ships. They are effective because the separation is almost instantaneous, so that transient conditions that could cause problems have no time to develop or act. The best-known case of separation with explosives was the *Igara*, sunk by the bow in the South China Sea about sixty miles east of Singapore. *Igara* was cut by 640 cutting charges in one shot to salvage the stern section. Restrictions on the use of explosives may force separation by other means or refloating intact and drydocking for separation.

Refloating Vessels Intact

Refloating the wreck intact is the cleanest and often the cheapest and most certain method of wreck removal. It is most effective for ships sunk upright or righted after capsizing. A thorough understanding of the differences in the stability of sunken ships is a prerequisite to understanding how to refloat them.

Stability of Sunken Ships

The laws of physics and the principles of naval architecture governing the stability of ships are the same whether the ship is afloat or sunken. The differences and the devil are in the details. The primary difference is that a completely submerged ship has no waterplane and thus no metacentric radius (BM). When the ship heels away from an upright position, righting moment and stability depend totally on the forces of weight and buoyancy acting through the centers of gravity and buoyancy. In a sunken ship, unlike a floating one, the forces of weight and buoyancy are not equal. Weight is likely to be much greater than buoyancy. As soon as the deck begins to emerge and waterplane develops, surface ship stability considerations apply. The emergence of the deck and the development of stability are critical periods during which the ship may capsize unless the stability is enhanced.

In any ship, the center of buoyancy lies at the geometric center of the submerged mass. When the ship is fully submerged, this may be quite high and significantly above the center of gravity. Submerged vessels are stable because the forces of buoyancy and weight, although unequal, form a righting moment. An appreciation of why submerged vessels are positively stable is necessary to a full understanding of stability, but of little practical significance in wreck removals.

As the ship breaks the surface and begins to develop a waterline, the metacentric radius develops in accordance with:

$$BM = \frac{I}{V}$$

where:

BM = metacentric radius
I = moment of inertia of the waterplane
V = underwater volume of the ship

As the ship rises out of the water, the waterplane and its moment of inertia increase and the underwater volume decreases. Metacentric radius increases. Simultaneously, the center of buoyancy moves downward toward its normal position below the center of gravity. During this process the metacentric height may be positive, negative, or zero. Free surface, almost invariably present, reduces the effective metacentric height.

Stability of sunken ships in general and of wrecks in particular can be difficult to predict because of the large number of unknowns. Some form of stability enhancement usually proves necessary as insurance against capsizing.

There are three ways in which the stability of a vessel can be enhanced during refloating:

1. She can be physically constrained from capsizing by holding one end on the bottom while floating the other.
2. The effective breadth of her waterline can be increased by rigging barges, pontoons, or lift craft alongside (figure 14-2).
3. Forces can be applied to counter the upsetting forces.

Leaving one end on the bottom while raising the other is most applicable to patch and pump jobs on small ships. This method provides an opportunity to reduce free surface and lower the center of gravity before starting to raise the other end. In a variation on this method, the vessel is made light and dragged into shallow water in contact with the sea floor. Lightening and dragging may be the first stage of a wreck removal in which the ship is dragged clear of a channel and then disposed of by other means.

To enhance stability, barges, pontoons, and lift craft must be rigged so tightly that they form a single entity with the ship. In this way they not only increase the effective beam and thus the waterplane area and metacentric radius, but also produce a righting force as the mass heels.

Stabilizing lift forces that act opposite to heeling forces is the most common method of stability enhancement. Cranes are the most common means of provid-

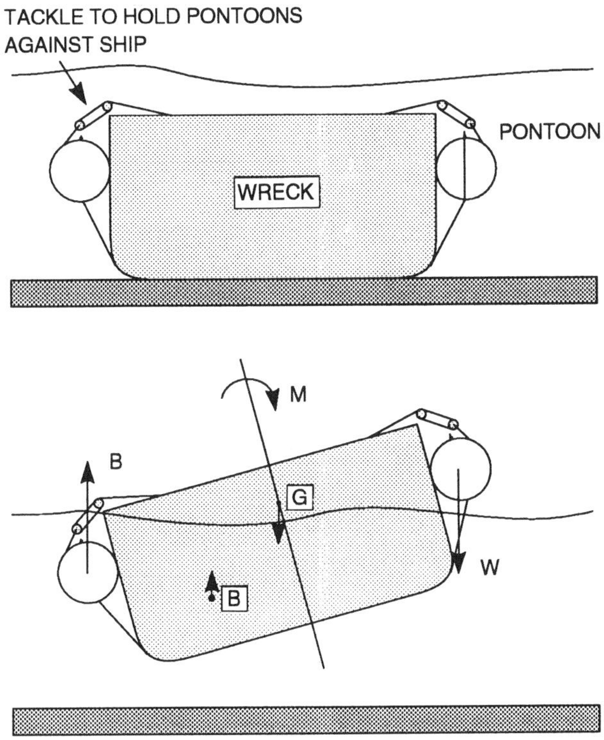

Fig. 14-2. Stabilizing with pontoons

ing such forces because the forces vary easily to meet the conditions of the moment. Horizontal pulling systems have been used with rigging, such as that shown in figure 14-3.

Strength

Many wrecks are so badly damaged that lack of strength is a very real problem. Structural failure in any ship to be floated and moved can make a bad situation worse. Three general conditions are possible:

1. Doubler plates or additional longitudinals can compensate for local strength reductions.
2. Changes in hull loading can compensate for failures or incipient failures that prevent the structure from carrying all types of its design loads and actual failures in tension, compression, or shear.
3. Massive failures preclude any measures other than piecemealing.

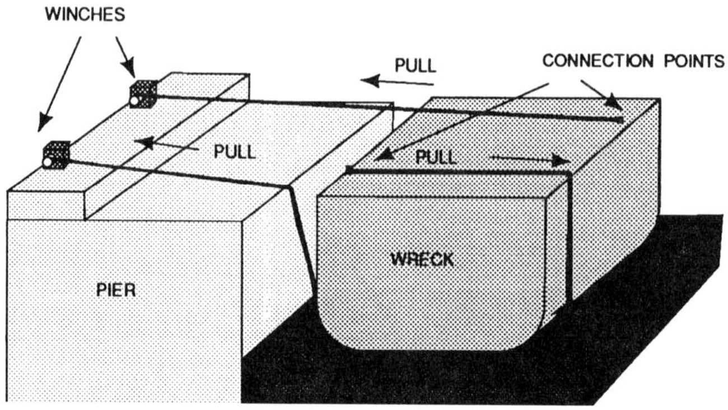

Fig. 14-3. Stabilizing with horizontal pull

Damaged structures can be analyzed by the same means described in Chapter 3 for intact structures. The safest assumptions in analyzing damaged structure are that any structural component with any damage is ineffective. Because any continuous structure has some residual strength, even when heavily damaged, an assumption of complete ineffectiveness may be too severe for wreck removal work. Unfortunately, there are no precise ways to define the residual strength of damaged structure. The best estimates of residual strength are made subjectively by experienced engineers. Repairs and strengthening of the hull in way of damage should comply strictly with the engineer's specifications. Failure to follow the specifications exactly can result in inadvertently setting up stress concentrations that are worse than the condition being cured. Temporary repairs made to wrecks are made to no higher standard than absolutely necessary. They are in every sense temporary repairs to be made in the cheapest and quickest manner.

It is often practical to work around failures or incipient failures that have left the hull intact and continuous. Loads on the ship can be adjusted to reduce the stresses or to keep stresses within acceptable limits. For instance, in the most common type of hull failure, compressive failure of the upper or lower flange of the hull girder, the plating loses its ability to carry compressive loads but retains most of its tensile strength. If weight and buoyancy can be distributed to keep the failed area in tension, the vessel can move intact. Similarly, weight and buoyancy can be distributed to keep shear stresses in areas that have failed in shear at no more than 25 percent of the design shear loads. Where damage is so severe that a hinge has developed or massive amounts of structure are missing, it may be desirable to load the hull so that there is zero bending stress and zero shear in way of the damage. This method is practical primarily in large vessels where the two sections can be treated individually and loading can be controlled in small increments to approach zero shear-zero stress.

Athwartships fractures amidships or in areas of high bending moment characterize tensile failures. Stiffened plate may bridge tensile fractures if the bridging structure is tied into the ship's structure properly. Proper tie-in includes:

1. Following the lines of existing stiffeners.
2. Carrying the bridging structure through to sound structure.
3. Tapering the longitudinal ends.

Structure not tied into the main structure properly is worse than useless because it sets up stress concentrations and may fail under low loads. Wise salvors do not trust bridged structure very much and combine bridging with load management to keep tensile loads on the bridge low.

There is a great temptation to tie structure that has failed in tension together with flexible tension members like chain and wire rope. This attractive idea has worked, but it is very difficult to execute. Much of the difficulty arises from uneven load distribution among the bridging members. A disproportionate portion of the load falls on a few members while others carry none. In keeping with the well-known truth about not being able to push on a rope, the tension member bridge is effective only in tension. When there is no choice other than this desperate method, loading always must keep the bridge in a low level of tension. The bridge does little to prevent growth of the existing failure.

A similar but more easily resisted temptation exists in way of shear failures. Doubler plates over the failed plating to restore the shear area of the structure may seem a good idea but are usually impractical because of the depth of the shear wrinkles and the absence of any means of tying the doublers to sound support structure.

Capsized Ships

As often as not, ships capsize as they sink and come to rest on the bottom in a position between inclined at 90 degrees and completely inverted. Capsizings complicate wreck removals. The only option for complete removal of severely damaged ships is likely to be piecemealing. However, ships with enough residual strength can be refloated upside down or on their side or righted, then refloated upright.

Floating a ship on her side or upside down can remove her from the initial wreck site reasonably quickly, a desirable action when the ship blocks a berth or waterway. Once cleared as an obstruction, the ship may be piecemealed, righted, or sunk in deep water. Floating need not be complete. Two sections of the Great Lakes bulk carrier *Sidney E. Smith* partially blocking the St. Clair River channel were lightened with polyurethane foam and dragged on their sides to the riverbank for disposal. Battleships of the German High Seas Fleet, scuttled at Scapa Flow, were refloated upside down and towed to ship breakers in that position. Numerous other wrecks have been removed in the same way.

Floating upside down or on her side puts a ship in a position that no one ever intended for her, but with careful attention to distribution of buoyancy and weight the ship can float secure and stable in those attitudes. A ship floated on her side (figure 14-4a) adjusts her attitude until the centers of gravity and buoyancy lie in the same vertical plane. The ship must float high enough to develop a waterplane that results in sufficient metacentric radius to give the ship positive stability. An inverted ship may, in fact, be more stable than the same ship floating upright, because the center of gravity normally lies far below the center of buoyancy (figure 14-4b). Usually, floating the ship to a draft that puts the waterplane at the level of the tank tops gives good stability. Ships that have no double bottoms should have a freeboard of about 3 feet (1 meter) when floating upside down. Ships floating at this level have enough waterplane to produce a large metacentric radius and enough freeboard not to lose much metacentric radius as the ship rolls. The same principles of naval architecture apply to the ship without regard to her floating attitude. Longitudinal loading and strength, like stability, follow basic naval architectural principles, regardless of attitude. Strength calculations should always be made so that salvors can adjust hull loading to keep stresses down and reduce the probability of hull failure. A naval architect should make calculations dealing with an unusual shape or attitude. The naval architect doing this work should be experienced in salvage operations that require a different type of thinking than is routine in a design office.

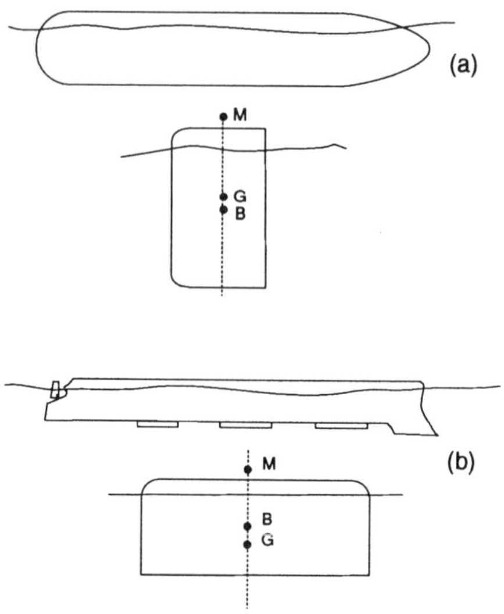

Fig. 14-4. Stability of a ship floating (a) on her side; (b) inverted

For several reasons, top hamper is removed before floating ships on their sides or upside down. One reason is to remove weight that must be countered by buoyancy put into the ship to raise the hull. Perhaps the most important reasons are to reduce weight that creates a moment that acts to upset a hull floating on a side and to remove material that greatly increases the navigational draft of an inverted ship.

Hulls selected for refloating must have sufficient buoyancy to float the ship at the desired waterline. If necessary, the hull may be patched or buoyancy introduced by one of the methods discussed in Chapter 11. Alternatively, external lift devices may add lift to the hull.

Good candidates for floating on a side are ships configured so that a great deal of buoyancy can be contained along the side of the ships. Such ships include small tankers, ships with wing tanks, and ships with long narrow hatches and broad underdeck spaces.

Any ship with an intact or patchable bottom and rolled more than 90 degrees is a good candidate for inverted refloating, provided that (1) the ship can be rolled to a completely inverted position by applying a small amount of internal or external buoyancy, and (2) the channel to the ultimate destination is deep enough for the ship to pass without grounding.

Air is the common means of raising ships, either on their side or inverted. The principles of the operation are simple:

All openings on the high side or bottom of the vessel are sealed airtight.

External lift is rigged; then air is introduced into the hull until the vessel rises in the desired attitude.

Such an operation includes all the devilish details of working with air in any kind of salvage, including air migration and leakage through small openings.

Thorough planning greatly increases the probability of success in any salvage operation. An inverted or on-the-side refloating is no exception. The planning process should specifically consider all the following:

1. Calculation of:

Transverse and longitudinal stability of the hull during and after refloating.

The hull's residual strength.

Weight to be rotated and lifted.

Amount and distribution of buoyancy to lift the ship in the desired attitude.

Determination of the composition of the air compression plant and where it is to be located.

2. Preparation of the wreck by:

Removal of top hamper and unnecessary material, including material that may fall from the wreck during transit. Particular care is called for during the removal of top hamper supporting the wreck, as the hull may rotate when the supporting material is cut away.

Removal of silt.

Rotation of the ship to the position desired for refloating.

Placement and rigging of additional lifting or pulling devices.

Placement and setup of air compressor plant.

3. Tug arrangements for moving the floating wreck, including:

The destination of the wreck and the mooring or securing arrangements there.

Provisions for supplying air to the wreck during movement to replace any that leaks out.

Arrangements with local authorities for Notices to Mariners and port closures or traffic restrictions during wreck movements.

Most important of all, planning must include a long, hard, thorough look at each thing that can go wrong at each stage of the operation and the action that can be taken to prevent or counter it.

Righting Capsized Ships

Righting a capsized ship is a major undertaking that is likely to be both very expensive and technically complex. Usually, righting is a wreck removal rather than a salvage action, as the costs of salvage, repair, and rebuilding capsized ships make salvage uneconomical.

Ships are righted by creating moments causing them to pivot about a point somewhere near the turn of the bilge. The moment of weight around this point holds the wreck in its capsized position (figure 14-5). The moments of buoyancy, applied force, or a combination of the two must overwhelm the moment of weight to rotate the ship.

Good candidates for righting rest on soil that is sufficiently firm, or that can be made firm enough by laying in rock, gravel, crushed coral, or shell to bear the loads put on it by the ship. The ship must have enough local strength to withstand the righting loads without failing both where it pivots on the sea floor and at attachments for applied forces. Old hulls deteriorated from long exposure are not good candidates. Developing the uprighting moment must be possible and very practical.

Obviously, if the moment of weight can be reduced, the moment necessary to overwhelm it is less, and less work and expense are necessary. A cost-benefit relationship applies. The cost and work of reducing the moment of weight may not justify the effort. For instance, increasing uprighting moment by 10 percent may be cheaper and easier than decreasing weight moment a similar amount. It all depends upon the particular ship and the conditions of the case. Both must be studied thoroughly before committing to a particular method.

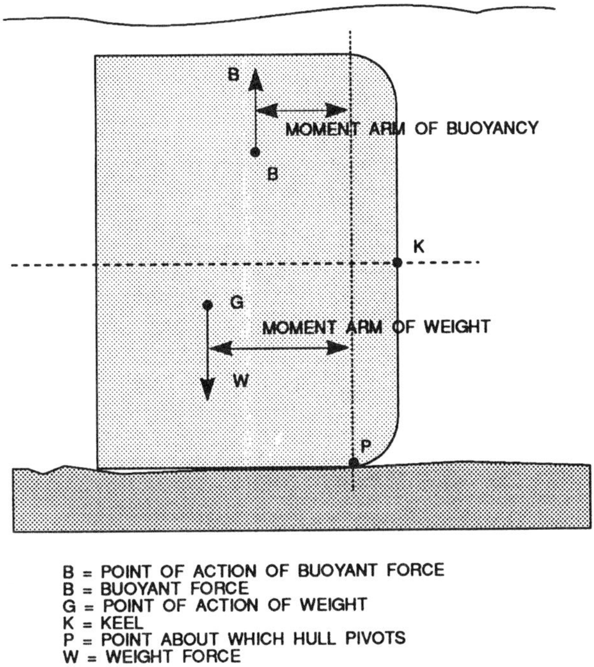

Fig. 14-5. Measurement points for a capsized ship

Weight moments can be reduced in two ways. The first reduces the amount of weight by removing cargo, top hamper, and unnecessary structure. Judicious choice of the weight for removal can move the center of gravity of the wreck toward the pivot point, further reducing the moment. Silt in the wreck is an excellent candidate as a weight to be removed. It may be necessary in some harbors to treat the removed silt as a pollutant or contaminated material and to remove it from the site. The second major way of reducing the moment moves the pivot point toward the center of gravity by dredging away the sea floor under the hull.

As illustrated in figure 14-6, as the hull rotates, the center of gravity moves from a position from which the weight moment opposes to one where it aids uprighting. Once the weight moment is aiding uprighting, the amount of applied uprighting moment needed decreases. The geometry of each case should be examined carefully in calculating moments to ensure the correct arms are used at each angle.

Many ways of creating uprighting moments exist; all involve buoyancy, applied forces, or a combination. Figure 14-7 illustrates several methods that have proven successful in various operations. The particular method chosen depends on the circumstances of the case. For instance, two almost contemporaneous opera-

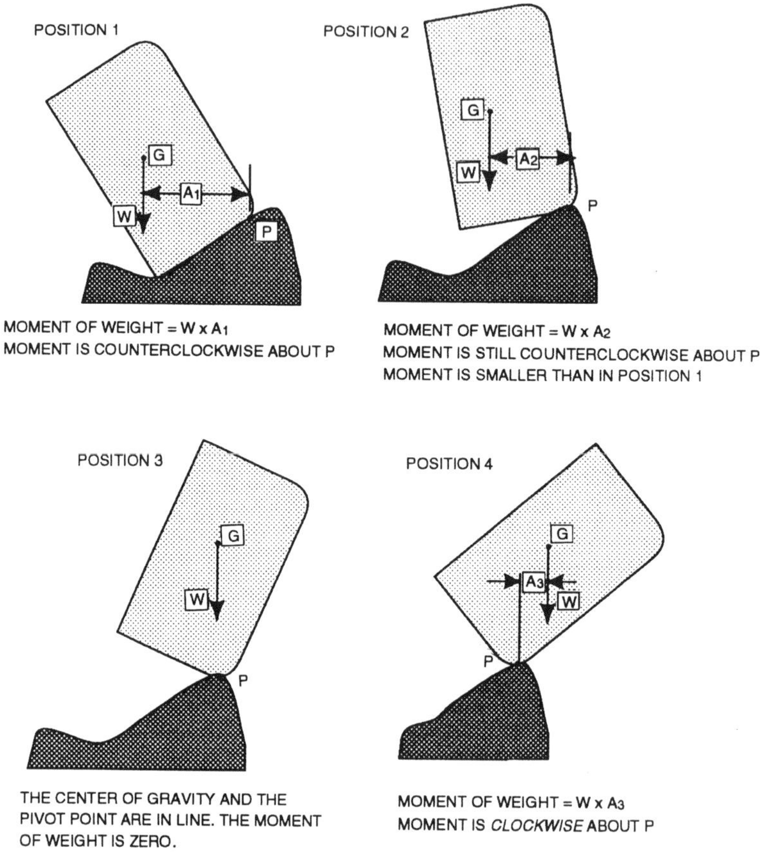

Fig. 14-6. Weight moment changes during uprighting

tions of comparable size and difficulty during World War II, the refloating of the liner *Lafayette* (ex-*Normandie*) in New York and the battleship *Oklahoma* in Pearl Harbor, were carried out by very different means. Salvors righted *Lafayette*, capsized to more than 80 degrees between two piers in New York Harbor, by sealing and pumping sections of the ship in a very diver-intensive, long operation. The battleship was parbuckled upright by building headframes and hauling purchases set up ashore and attached to the headframes. *Lafayette*'s position perpendicular to the shoreline and between two piled wooden piers in a busy harbor greatly influenced the method chosen. There was no space in which purchases could have been set up. *Oklahoma*, on the other hand, lay capsized to more than 150 degrees at a shallow angle to the shore of an island with both the space for purchases and soil conditions for anchorages. *Santhia*, lying alongside a wharf fronting the Hooghly River in India, was righted by purchases laid through warehouses ashore. The pur-

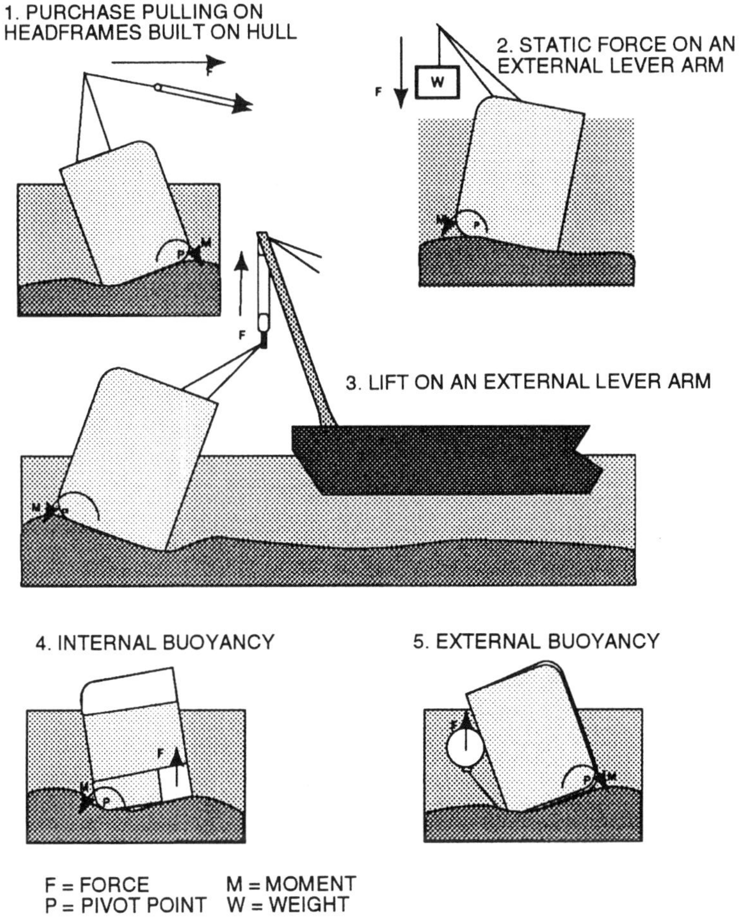

Fig. 14-7. Some methods of righting ships

chases were hauled by manually powered winches. *Malaysia Kita*, righted in Singapore in 1975, lay in a position suitable for parbuckling, but was nowhere near land suitable for purchases. That ship was uprighted with parbuckling purchases set on securely moored barges. *European Gateway* and *Leonardo da Vinci* were righted in similar operations. The technique selected depends entirely on the wreck being righted and its location; no possibility should be ignored or rejected without a sound reason.

Planning Righting Operations

The technical complexity and potential expense of righting operations demand careful planning to achieve success. The careful planning includes detailed engineering and operational analyses melded together to form a coherent, workable plan. Fortunately, righting operations are seldom very time critical and time is available for the orderly procurement of information, the development of a sound plan, and the examination of alternatives.

Site inspections that include the wreck itself, the sea floor under the wreck, and the surrounding area involved in the entire operation provide basic planning information. Surveys of wrecks have been discussed in other portions of this book and are not addressed further here, except to remark that siltation and rates of siltation of the wreck require careful noting. Extensive siltation can require either removal or an increase in the power needed to right the vessel.

Site surveys should pay particular attention to the soils under the wreck or in way of shore-based hauling systems or in sea floors planned as anchorage sites. Soil data come from cores taken by civil engineers specializing in soil mechanics. Analysis of these data provides a basis for action necessary to stabilize or strengthen the soils in critical areas. Soil conditions also determine the feasibility of dredging trenches alongside to facilitate righting or to move the pivot point farther up the hull. Consultation with local engineers can help determine soil strengthening methods. Often, materials (rubble, rock, coral, shell, sand, etc.) are chosen because of their local availability and with consideration of local requirements for restoring the sea floor on completion of the operation. Local experience and practice give a sure method of fixing quantities and methods of laying in the material.

Initial site investigations should consider the layout of the port and disruption to port activities by the righting operations. Discussions with port authorities and property users quickly reveal any disruptions that are unacceptable or extremely costly in fees for loss of use of properties and facilities.

While site investigations include as thorough a survey of the wreck as practical and measurement of all portions of the wreck and areas of interest, acquisition of all the needed data is never possible. Some assumptions are necessary for the calculations that provide the basic technical data for operational plans. Basic assumptions for calculations are laid out in detail with each assumption justified. Assumptions typically include:

The point about which the hull pivots during righting and any changes in the position of this point as the ship changes inclination.

The total weight of the ship including hull weights, stores, outfitting, and other material that may remain on board.

Allowances for changes to light ship weight and position of the center of gravity resulting from weight removal.

The position of the center of gravity and changes that occur in this position as the ship rotates.

The quantity of any buoyancy remaining in the hull.

The location of the center of buoyancy and the changes that occur as the hull rotates.

Where hull strength is indeterminate, assumptions about remaining hull strength and the ability of the hull to carry righting loads.

Both the engineering and the operational plans should begin to take form while the site investigations are in progress. The shoes-off discussions in the hotel room at the end of the day, with preliminary calculations and scratch pad, are an important part of the process of making a practical preliminary righting plan.

Refinement of the plan includes:

Design of the particular righting system.

Calculation of the movement of the center of gravity, buoyancy, moments, pull requirements, and ground pressures at various angles throughout the righting operations. Computers allow answering a great variety of "what if . . ?" questions easily and refining the righting system for efficiency and cost reductions.

Determination of the details of headframes, purchases, pulling power, anchorages, buoyancy, pumping sequences, attachment points, restraining systems, hull reinforcements, dredging, weight removal, etc.

Preparation of schedules.

Preparation of logistics, manning, project management, cost accounting and control, subcontractor, and other plans.

Identification of critical materials, critical paths, and alternatives.

Identification of potential problem areas and causes of delay.

Parbuckling with Headframes

Parbuckling systems use forces set remotely ashore or on a well-anchored barge to produce the righting moment. Winches acting through multifold purchases or continuous pull linear pullers produce the forces. Headframes set onto the side or bottom of a ship increase the moment arm of the pulling force and thereby decrease the amount of pulling force to rotate the ship. The total pull applied, the pulling power of individual pulling systems, the availability of the construction materials, and the ability of the hull to carry the loads transmitted through the headframes determine the number and strength of headframes.

Headframes are set along the parallel midbody of the ship or the heights are adjusted to conform with the curvature of the hull to keep the tops of the headframes in the same plane.

Headframes are usually one of four basic types:

1. *Braced girder* headframes (figure 14-8a) are similar to a bipod or tripod mast connected to the wreck's hull. The headframes land on decks or other structural hard point. Braced girder headframes are normally shop-fabricated for simplified field installation.
2. *Triangularly braced semicontinuous girder* headframes (figure 14-8b) are heavy tubular sections with the supporting legs welded to the hull. The headframes are shop-fabricated in sections for handling and installation at the site.
3. *Stayed leg* headframes (figure 14-8c) are most appropriate when little structural steel is available. In this design, wire rope backstays stay a simple triangular frame to the hull. Only the frame is shop-fabricated; field installation work includes installing and tensioning the backstay system. Uniform backstay tension is difficult to achieve.
4. *Cantilevered strut* headframes (figure 14-8d) are normally built of wood. The frame itself is a simple sheer leg stayed to a cantilevered strut stayed to the hull.

With any type of headframe, pulling wires are attached (1) directly to the frame or (2) led over the frame and attached to fittings on the hull. In the former case, the point of action of the pulling force is at the attachment point on the headframe and the moment arm is the distance between the attachment point on the

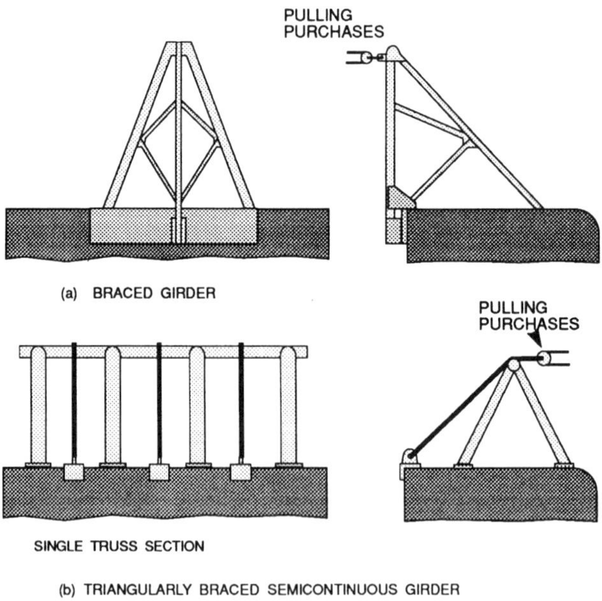

Fig. 14-8 (a) and (b). Parbuckling headframes

headframe and the pivot point. As the ship moves toward the upright position, the angle at which the force is applied changes, causing the magnitude of horizontal and vertical components of the pulling force to vary. The headframe itself must be attached heavily to the hull to carry the loads and moments transmitted through the landing points.

When wires attach directly to the hull, the headframes effectively act as fairleads that control the angle of application of pull. The moment arm is the distance between the attachment point on the hull and the pivot point. Attachment with the wire perpendicular to the hull throughout the operation gives the maximum moment at the maximum degree of inclination. Relative magnitudes of horizontal and vertical components vary as the ship rotates. Where pulling wires attach directly to the hull, a generous radius of the surface over which the hauling member leads reduces bending stresses and the accompanying strength reduction in the pulling wire.

Doubling sheaves attached at the head of the head frame (figure 14-9) multiplies the pulling force and the righting moment by a factor of 1.5 to 1.75. Friction and other losses in the sheave preclude actual doubling of the force. Headframe attachments, other structure, and anchorages must be strong enough to carry the additional load.

Headframes are best attached to the hull at structural hard points. Such landings may not always be possible or adequate and stiffening may be necessary. Exterior doubling and stiffening may be enough to carry and spread the load; when it is not, internal pillars, shores, or stiffening may be added.

Wires connect to the hull or headframes by fitting a double-cheeked fitting with a pin similar to that shown in figure 14-10, or by shackling or bolting to a

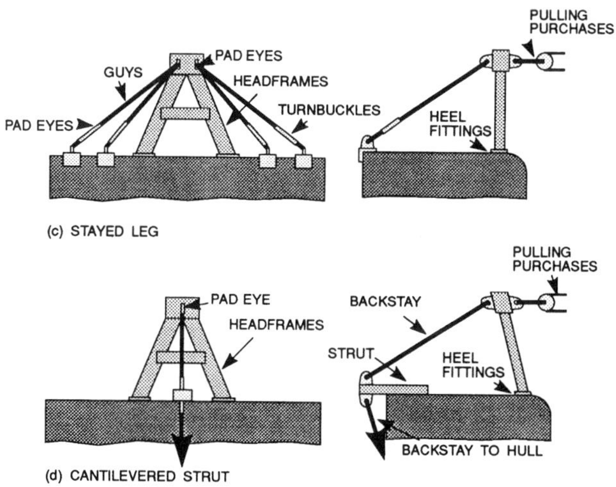

Fig. 14-8 (c) and (d). Parbuckling headframes

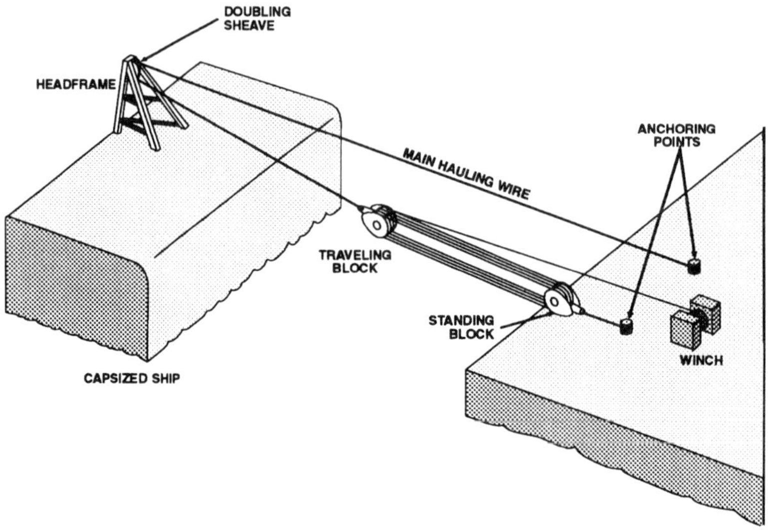

Fig. 14-9. Parbuckling with doubling sheaves. Courtesy of U.S. Navy.

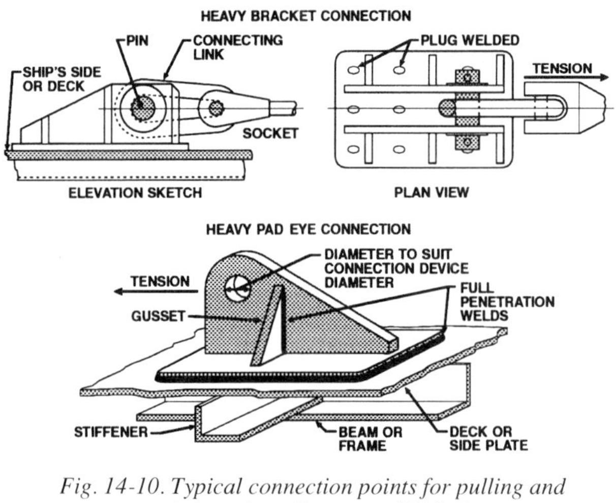

Fig. 14-10. Typical connection points for pulling and restraining wires. Courtesy of U.S. Navy.

heavy single plate pad eye. Connecting points on the headframe are an integral part of the headframe design. Connections to the hull should be made to hard points on the hull and the load spread over several structural members. Chain pigtails may be reeved through holes cut in the hull and attached to pulling wires. The holes through which the pigtails pass should be well separated so that the chain bight encompasses several frames or other heavy structural members. Even in the best-rigged chain system the possibility exists that the combination of load and cutting action can tear or fracture the shell.

Parbuckling systems should have load-measuring devices either integral to the winches or designed into each set of purchases or each puller. With such a system, the load in each wire can be measured and kept at its maximum. More importantly, the load can be divided evenly among the pulling systems so that no system either shirks the load or is overloaded.

Parbuckling systems produce not only a moment but also a horizontal force in the direction of the pull that tries to move the wreck. Horizontal movement during rotation of a wreck is very undesirable because energy is spent uselessly in moving the wreck. If the forces are not exactly perpendicular to the wreck—they never are in real life—the ship also may try to move fore and aft. To prevent undesirable movement, restraining tackle is added to the rigging. Figure 14-11 shows typical methods of rigging restraining tackle.

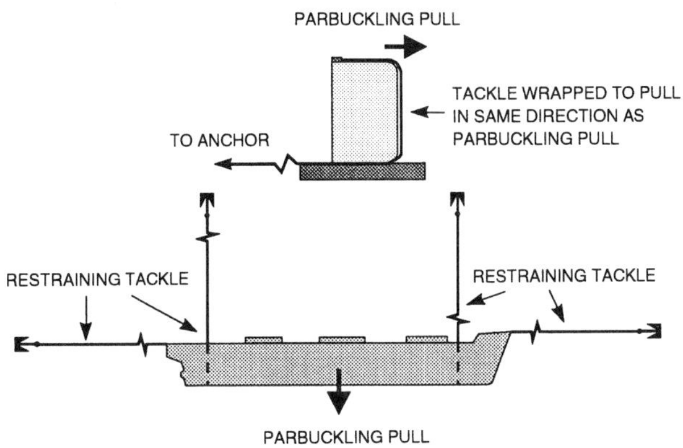

Fig. 14-11. Restraining tackle

Anchorages

Secure anchorages for the shore end of a parbuckling system are an absolute requirement for success. The primary factor in the design is the load that the anchorage must carry; accordingly, anchorages vary from simply buried anchors to elaborate structures containing hundreds of tons of reinforced concrete with drilled and grouted anchor points. Anchorages should be specifically designed and matched to each job. The temptation to use a particular design "because it worked fine last time" should be avoided. The minor differences this time can make last time's design completely inapplicable. A civil engineer should design any shore anchoring system; an ocean engineer with specific experience in heavy moorings should design a marine system.

Basic designs of anchorage systems include:

Buried anchors, often in tandem, in excavated pits packed with earth, gravel, or rock, or filled with concrete.

Deadman systems composed of a packed excavated pit with the pressure face (front) reinforced by vertical logs, heavy timbers, or heavy structural shapes and a chain wrapped around horizontal beams and led out through a trench.

Concrete-filled pits in which structural steel frames were built as winch foundations before being filled with concrete.

Multiple-unit foundation blocks consisting of piled, reinforced concrete blocks set in prismatic trenches.

Many variations in the above basic designs are practical, depending primarily on the forces involved and the shear strength and load-bearing characteristics of the soils. Cost of the construction and demolition of the anchorage and rehabilitation of the anchorage area is a major consideration. Any design analysis should consider cost savings from using locally available materials and equipment.

Underwater anchorages are similar to heavy moorings and may be designed by the methods for designing salvage moorings discussed in Chapter 10. The pulling load is the primary load on the mooring. The high loads on the moorings normally indicate large mooring anchors or piled anchors made of heavy-walled tubing driven into the sea floor.

Righting with Lift Devices

Righting with lift devices differs from parbuckling with head frames, mainly in that the forces are vertical rather than horizontal. Cranes, sheer legs, or pontoons can develop the vertical forces. Sheer legs are particularly good for this work because of their large lifts and the option of doubling the force by rigging deck tackles. Vertical forces have the additional advantage of not putting the entire parbuckling load on the mooring.

Attachments usually are made at the deck edge of the high side and chain or wire rope slings passed around and under the wreck so that a vertical lift is made from the deck side of the hull. Depending upon the way the wreck and other facilities lie, the wreck may be rolled either toward or away from the lifting equipment. If the wreck is rolled toward cranes or sheer legs, the lift vessels must be walked back in the mooring to keep them clear of the wreck as she rolls.

Lifting gear may attach to either heavy pad eyes or pinned connections similar to those used for parbuckling with headframes. Deck edges and bilges are supported with bolsters to prevent the slings from slicing the hull and to provide a suitable radius for the sling.

Combinations

There is no limit to the ways in which different methods of rotating a ship may be combined to use available equipment cost-effectively and to fit the situation. Any method that produces a moment about the pivot point is good. A method that produces a large moment cheaply with little labor is excellent. As the requirements for moment vary as the angle varies during righting, methods can be changed or added in mid-righting. For instance, when parbuckling frames are at such an angle that pulling on them is no longer effective, they may serve as hangers for counterweights. Pumping may be introduced when access to flooded compartments makes it practical.

Removal in Sections

Sometimes the most practical and economical way to remove a wreck is to cut it into two or more pieces and remove the sections individually. This situation occurs when the ship is so nearly broken that even zero-shear, zero-stress techniques are inadequate, or when explosion damage is so severe that large sections of the hull have been destroyed. Removal by sections is appropriate when the ship has broken without the salvor's assistance and thereby saved him the effort of making a decision. The choices to be made are:

How many sections to break the wreck into—the damage to the wreck, the way she lies, and the equipment available usually dictate the number of sections.

How to break the wreck—the wreck should be broken by the simplest and safest (not always the same thing) method. Ballasting large ships may develop bending moments large enough to break them. Locked-in stresses in the hull may cause the pieces to separate suddenly and violently, making mechanical, exothermic, or explosive cutting unpredictable and adding a degree of danger. There may be no option.

How to refloat the sections—any of the usual wreck removal methods as well as innovative ones may be used on the individual sections. Each should be treated separately and the most applicable techniques used; there are no extra points for using the same technique for all the sections. The design of ships is such that sections are inherently stable and may refloat individually, perhaps with a little help to enhance their stability or buoyancy.

Tankers, bulk carriers, and containerships large enough to sustain great damage in one part of the ship while retaining enough buoyancy to make some refloating practical are particularly good candidates for removal in sections. Tankers and OBO carriers with large tanks that can be isolated to provide buoyancy are very good candidates.

Piecemealing

Piecemealing, wrecking-in-place, and dismantling all mean the same thing—taking a wreck apart bit-by-bit. This technique can be used when the damage to the ship is so severe that no other technique is suitable or economical. The line between removal by sections and piecemealing is not clear, nor does it need to be. Piecemealing may be considered an extreme case of removal in sections. Any wreck can be piecemealed. The technique is particularly appropriate for old wrecks whose condition is suspect, as well as badly damaged newer wrecks. Because of the nature of the work, piecemealing is likely to be slow and expensive, but it works—always.

In a sort of backward relationship, the second stage of piecemealing, lifting, governs the first, cutting. The wreck must be cut into sections that can be handled by lifting equipment that is available, can get in close to the wreck to work, and has enough outreach. Once the allowable weight of sections is determined, a cutting plan that lays out the cut lines can be drawn up.

Section and lift size is determined by reference to the ship's weight curve (builder's weight distribution curve, construction weight curve) that can be obtained from the owner or builder and by as detailed a survey as possible. Without the curve, weights can be estimated from standard ship construction and classification society rules that determine scantlings. A generous margin for error must be allowed in any case. When estimating rather than working from weight curves, a greater margin for error and uncertainty must be allowed. Weight estimates must take into account cargo, debris, and silt in the wreck as well as the structure of the wreck, its outfit, and fittings. Where the wreck sees rough weather, an allowance in the weight estimates should be made for dynamic loads during lifting. It is impractical to size the loads and the dynamic lifting allowance for all conditions that may come up during the operation. The total lift estimates should permit lifting in any weather in which the lifting equipment can operate.

It may be more efficient and economical to remove cargo, pollutants, or hazardous or obnoxious materials in the wreck and handle them separately rather than to leave them in the wreck during the wreck removal. Leaving them in the wreck may result in classification of all the wreckage as hazardous waste, with tremendous escalation of disposal costs. Handling the cargo as part of the wreck removal lift may result in pollution, as cargo and other material may be dumped.

Before any cutting starts, as much oil as possible must be removed from the wreck. However, despite the best efforts of salvors, some residual oil always remains in tanks and there is some clingage to the tank structure. This oil inevitably is released to the environment when the tanks are cut and the structure lifted. There is no way to prevent this release. There are ways to mitigate its effects. Equipment for the spill and cleanup should be in place whenever tanks are cut, and any released oil should be cleaned up immediately. The measures for dealing with inevitable spills should be addressed in the spill prevention plan and brought to the attention of regulators before starting work. The regulator's position can vary on spills during wreck removal. Normally, salvors are not held liable for spills other than those caused by negligence during salvage operations. This practice may not prevail in wreck-removal operations. It is easy to envision enthusiastic and literal regulators levying penalties for inevitable spills about which they have been warned and which are a necessary part of the removal of the greater problem. There are extra costs in being well-prepared for spills and in cleaning them up as they happen, but these costs are likely to be much lower than the penalties, delays, and disruption resulting from lack of preparation. In countries where environmental regulation is pervasive, regulators are unlikely to allow the work to proceed without a spill prevention and cleanup plan and equipment in place.

Removal of oils and hazardous materials is not only for environmental protection but also for protection of the crew. Oils, their residues, and fumes are explosion hazards during cutting operations. Other materials in the cargo also may be explosion hazards or may be exposure hazards to the wrecking crew. Interior spaces, holds, and tanks that have contained oils and other polluting or hazardous material should be ventilated before cutting.

Costs may escalate sharply by lighterage and contaminated soil disposal costs if mud and silt in the wreck are contaminated and cannot simply be air lifted out and dispersed in the area. All the potential environmental problems, no matter how remote or illogical they may seem, must be discussed with the cognizant authorities and regulators and an approach agreed upon before signing the salvage contract.

Whenever possible, cuts should be clear of machinery spaces where structure is simpler and there is less interference. Interference on ships with large amounts of piping, wiring, joiner work, and insulation in cuts can slow the cutting and lifting process. In these ships, it is particularly important to be sure all interference is cut through and the cut is clear before attempting the lift. It may be simpler and quicker on ships like passenger ships, refrigerated ships, fish processors, and other industrial ships to cut smaller sections rather than to clear larger cuts. For simplicity and overall operational efficiency, cuts should be laid out as simply as possible, whatever method is used, and should be kept clear of heavy structural members like transverse frames, deep webs, and hatch coamings.

Piecemealing is a form of shipbreaking. It may be done without the industrial support and siting that professional shipbreakers enjoy, but it can take advantage of some of their techniques, particularly when much of the work is dry cutting. Hydraulic shears, semiautomatic cutting, and bulk cutting gas supplies have been successful in shipbreaking and in piecemealing of wrecks. Whatever might work should be given a shot.

Cutting

Wrecks may be cut either exothermically or mechanically. Exothermic cuts are made by topside crews with conventional oxyacetylene or oxypropane torches, oxy-arc cutting gear, semiautomatic cutting machines, and by divers with underwater cutting equipment. This type of cutting is labor-intensive, slow, and sure.

Explosives also cut. Mechanical cuts are heavy cuts made with chains and heavy lifting or heaving equipment or by wreck punches and grabs. These cuts are equipment-intensive, quick, and efficient. They are not elegant. Usually a variety of methods are used in cutting any wreck. Often the best combination is worked out in the field as the operation progresses with maximum efficiency and the most workable solution being reached as the last cut completes.

Exothermic Cutting

Manual exothermic cutting with conventional equipment often supplements heavy mechanical cutting. Manual cutting is particularly appropriate for removal of superstructures, top hamper, and wreckage obstructing main working areas or planned cut lines. Flame cutting may consist of single burners cutting in response to specific direction from the salvage master and salvage foremen or several gangs using bulk gas storage cutting all over the wreck under a clearly defined plan. Primary sites for gang-burning are large expanses of exposed side, bottom, or deck plating that make this type of cutting efficient. Manual exothermic cutting generates debris and heat, and with it terrific fire and traumatic injury hazards. The work area should be kept clear of debris and trash to keep the fire hazard down. Trash and debris receptacles, often improvised from wreckage and debris, should be kept near burning gangs and should be dumped before they reach the overflow point. The work area should be kept policed. Dedicating small cranes to handle debris may be necessary. In spite of the best efforts to reduce the fire hazard and keep the work areas cleaned up, fires can be expected. Shortcutting on the fire-fighting system on wrecks where gangs of burners are working is very poor salvage practice. The management discussion near the end of this chapter contains a more detailed discussion of fire-fighting provisions for exothermic wreck cutting.

Some underwater cutting by divers is a part of almost every piecemealing operation. Chapter 11 discusses the basic requirements for underwater cutting. Underwater cutting of wrecks is technically no different from any other kind of underwater cutting. The safety of the diving and underwater cutting operation requires some attention from the salvage master and senior supervisors.

The grade of oxygen is a major difference in underwater and surface oxy-arc cutting. Industrial grade oxygen is satisfactory for surface cutting while higher-grade, more expensive aviator's breathing oxygen is needed under water. Separate oxygen supplies should be maintained for surface and underwater crews and never mixed.

Diving operations should be separated from surface cutting operations and other diving operations, and should always be well clear of any lifts. Diving teams in wreck-removal operations work largely in near-total darkness. There is a learning curve to working in a particular area. The operation is much more efficient if a diving team works one cut from beginning to end rather than switching to other work sites.

Cuts for divers should be as straightforward as possible with a minimum of cuts made through very heavy structure or through interference. If convenient in the overall cutting plans, cut lines should lie close to transverse frames or deep webs that may serve as references. Overhead cuts should be minimized. Underwater cutting may generate hydrogen gas by dissociation of water molecules. Gases from underwater cutting must have a clear venting path to the surface so there is no chance of their pocketing in explosive mixtures.

Explosives

Explosives for cutting steel have been discussed in principle and general application in Chapter 11. Explosive cutting appears an attractive tool for piecemealing because it cuts quickly and large numbers of charges can be fired simultaneously. *Igara*, mentioned earlier in this chapter, is a classic case of explosive wreck cutting. The apparent ease and efficiency of explosive cutting is deceptive. In some cases, explosives have been effective tools, in others, they have been disasters. Careful planning, appropriate working conditions, and wise charge size selection are mandatory. The economics and practicalities of the job usually force the decision to use explosives. Seldom is a job done with explosives alone; normally, they are one of several methods combined on a particular job.

Surface explosive cutting is straightforward, following well-established principles. Underwater explosive cutting is another story. Done correctly, underwater cutting with explosives reduces diving time and expedites underwater cuts. Done incorrectly, without careful attention to detail, underwater explosive cutting can be messy, ineffective, and costly. Poor results usually come from:

- Incomplete planning.
- Poor preparation.
- Incorrect charges with too much or too little explosive, or incorrect design.
- Poor contact between the charge and the surface to be cut.

Chapter 11 discusses the basic considerations for cutting with both linear-shaped charges and hose charges. There are some lessons that have been learned (most of them the hard way) about cutting wrecks that warrant discussion here. Any wreck has its unique problems that can be solved only by trial and error. Time spent in setting up models and trying a technique is generally well spent.

The quantity of explosives is important. Like Baby Bear's porridge, the amount of explosives must be "just right." Too small a charge can result in a failed cut, while the secondary effects of too large a charge can result in so much damage that divers lose time attempting to orient themselves for the next task. Wreck cutting is one time when more is not better.

Wreck cutting with explosives is most effective for breaking structures along predetermined cut lines. Correct placement of explosives, often difficult in wreck removals because of near-zero underwater visibility, is vital in making effective cuts. Explosive cut lines should be parallel and close to heavy support structure because the cutting effect of the explosive is greater against the stiff plate. Scoring cut lines for hose charges with oxy-arc helps divers place the charges correctly and improves the cutting action. Several short cuts are often more effective and quicker in the long term than a few long cuts. Short cuts should be checked for completeness following each shot. There are times when there is no choice but to make one or a very few long cuts. In these critical cases, critical extreme redundancy is called for—not only belt and suspenders, but trousers a size too small. There should be no chance of a single fault or a single type of fault causing failure of the shot.

While lined cavity-shaped charges are most effective for cutting flat plate, they are not very effective in cutting the distorted and irregular plate of wrecks. More time can be spent trying to get the proper contact and a dry cavity than would be spent with nominally less efficient cutting methods. For irregular or distorted plate, hose charges are a better choice, despite the fact that they take larger amounts of explosive than shaped charges and therefore produce more secondary effects. It is extremely important that hose charges be secured tightly to the proposed cut line. The best methods of securing are positive mechanical means—well-anchored straps, wire, or bungee cord. Suction pads and magnetic clamps contribute to the salvage master's and explosive supervisor's premature graying.

Explosives are an effective tool for sectioning wrecks under the right conditions. Like any other salvage tool, they are not always the right tool. The variety of types of explosives with very different characteristics is great; explosives technology changes rapidly. Unless salvors have extensive, current personal or corporate experience in explosives technology and use, they should bring in consultants. Consultants who assist in selecting explosives and designing the applications are a major help in ensuring success.

Chain Cutting

Chain cutting or chain sawing is the most effective way of cutting wrecks mechanically. Chains cut wrecks by alternately hauling and veering chain with lifting or hauling equipment. The chain saws or rips its way through the wreck. The method is not precise, but works well where conditions in and around the wreck make cutting exothermically or with explosives difficult. Any hauling or lifting system that has two ways to pull can be rigged for chain cutting (figure 14-12). One hundred fifty to two hundred tons on each hook or deck tackle is about the minimum for cutting large steel ships. More is better, in that greater force means faster, more efficient cutting. Small steel ships with lighter scantlings and wooden ships may be cut with less.

High-quality chain is absolutely necessary for chain cutting. Chain is designed as a tension member; it was never intended for cutting heavy structures.

Only its ruggedness and strength make it possible to cut with chain; cutting with chain is chain abuse. Accordingly it makes sense to use the most rugged, toughest chain available. ORQ or higher-grade welded stud link chain or a similar grade of forged integral stud chain is required. The forged integral stud chain is preferred because it inherently can stand more abuse and misuse than welded stud link chain. Using lower-grade chain is a waste of time and money. The costs of clearing broken chain from cuts and of replacing or rerigging can easily exceed the costs of high-quality rather than junk chain. The chain should not have any loose and missing studs, obvious wear in the grip, or bent or elongated links. Chain diameters of 2¾ inches (70 mm) to 3½ inches (89 mm) have proven suitable for cutting large wrecks. Cutting chain should be as short as possible—just long enough to fit around the wreck at the section being cut with enough slack to allow hauling without the ends passing into the cut. Wire rope slings, sized to fail before the chain, attach the chains to the hook. Rerigging a broken sling is simpler, easier, and quicker than replacing a chain.

The cutting process proceeds as follows:

1. Divers gouge notches in the hull to provide a starting point for the cut and direct it along the cut line. The notches should be long enough and deep enough for three or four links of the chain to bury themselves in the notch when the chain is tensioned lightly.
2. A light strain snugs chain up into the cut.
3. The pull on one hook is increased to about 150 to 200 tons while the other hook holds about half this tension. The two tackles are alternately hauled and slacked until the chain begins to cut.
4. Cut progress is monitored by the hook load readouts and the travel of the purchases. Shortening successive hauls shows cutting progress.

Shorter slings replace the original slings as purchase fleet lengths shorten.

Figure 14-13 illustrates a typical chain-cutting process.

The method described is general. Chain cutting is marked more by practical improvisation than by scientific precision. Any system that works on the particular wreck is the right system.

Wire ropes, especially those designed for cutting, also may cut wrecks. Wire ropes are usually better suited for lightly built steel and wooden vessels. Chain is more efficient with heavily constructed steel vessels. Cuts should avoid machinery spaces and heavy structure. Where heavy structure cannot be avoided, exothermic or explosive cuts can help chain cuts to move along. Interference, piping, wiring, joiner work, and insulation seldom present an obstacle to cutting chains.

Cutting normally begins at the high end of the wreck and moves toward the deeper end. This method prevents the wreck from collapsing onto the section being removed and from sliding into its site after removal.

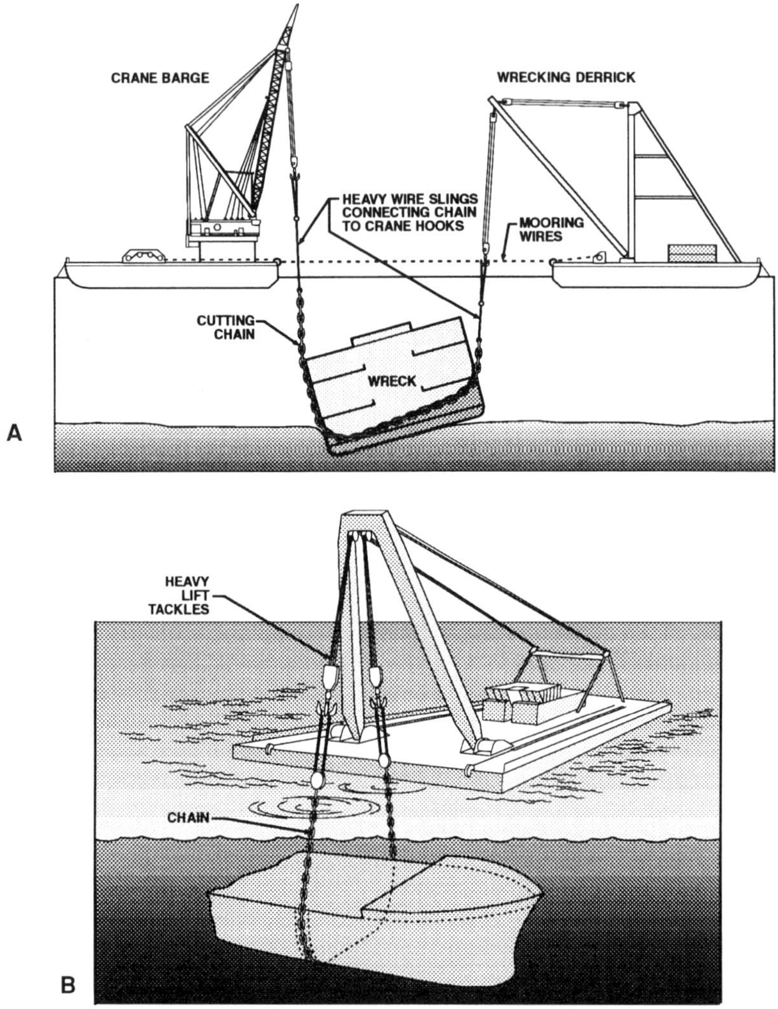

Fig. 14-12 (above and on facing page). *Chain cutting rigs: (a) two crane barges, (b) sheer leg with two hooks, (c) sheer leg with hook and deck tackle, (d) two deck tackles. Courtesy of U.S. Navy.*

Wreck Punches

Wreck punches (figure 14-14) are weighted steel weldments of 10 to 15 tons dropped onto wrecks by cranes to complete cuts started by other methods. Punches, normally built of stiffened heavy I or wide flange sections, may be as long as 40 feet. Weight and free-fall velocity give the punch enough energy to break structure on impact.

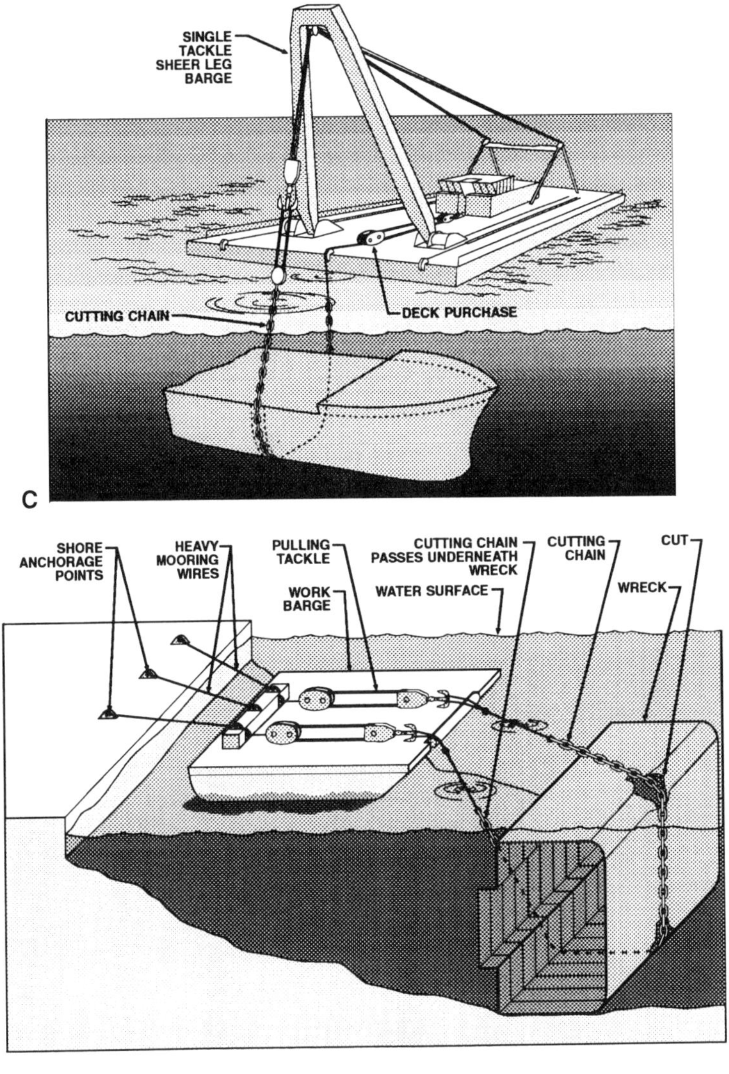

A crane operating a wreck punch must have a good free-fall capability and the ability to release the punch from a high boom elevation. Release from a high elevation allows the falling punch to strike with the highest possible velocity. Cranes for clamshell dredging and the auxiliary hook of offshore construction derricks make good candidates for wreck punch operations.

Wreck punches, once a very common tool, have largely been replaced by chain cutting or wreck grabs.

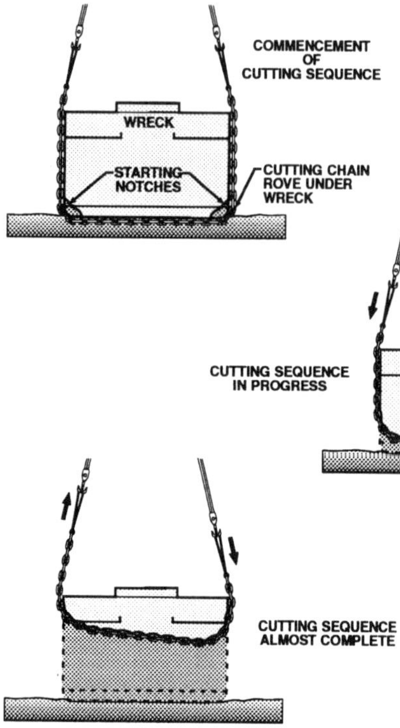

Fig. 14-13. Chain-cutting process. Courtesy of U.S. Navy.

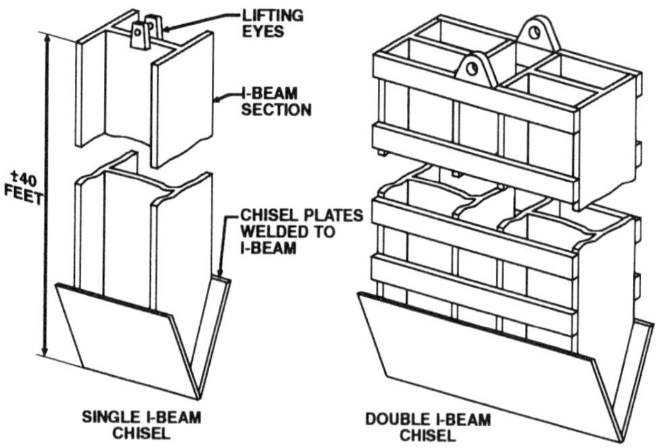

Fig. 14-14. Wreck punches. Courtesy of U.S. Navy.

Wreck Grabs

Very badly damaged, partially buried, and old wrecks are difficult to remove. The best way to remove these wrecks is usually unsophisticated brute force. In a typical process where a tool was adapted from another industry, rock dredging grabs were tried to tear away the structure of such wrecks. These cactus, or orange peel, grabs tear away plate weakened by explosives or age. A cactus grab (figure 14-15) is strong, but has a small opening. These grabs are very good for small wrecks and as rehandling grabs on large wreck demolitions.

Wreck grabs with an open jaw width of up to 30 feet (9 meters), breadth of 10 feet (3 meters), and capacities of several hundred tons have been built by European salvors. In practice, lifts of about half the rated capacity of the grab give a good production rate. The grabs close with a force of 300 to 500 tons. This much power behind hardened steel jaws is enough to crush steel structures. There is no standardization among grabs; the earliest grabs operated from sheer legs with two heavy-lifting systems. Later modified grabs work from whirly cranes. Only a small number of the grabs were ever built; a selection is shown in figure 14-16.

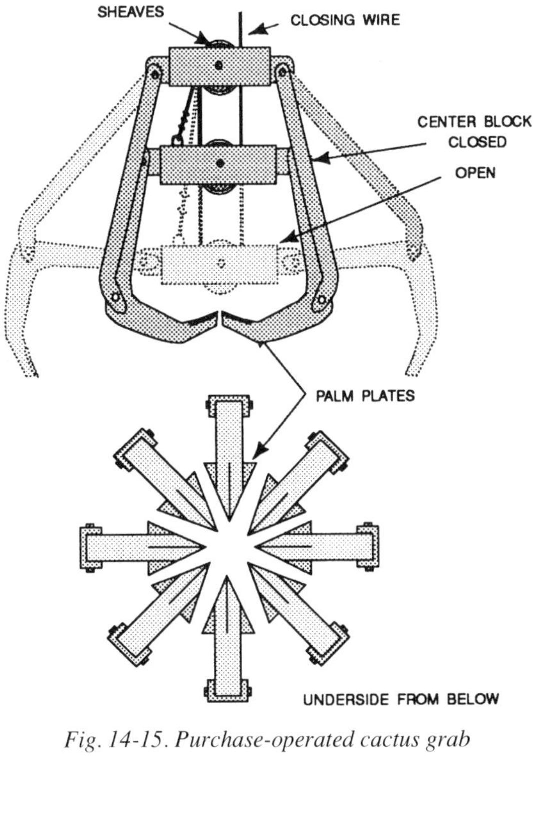

Fig. 14-15. Purchase-operated cactus grab

Fig. 14-16. A selection of relatively small wreck grabs

Grabs literally tear structure apart. Progressing work is difficult because the sea floor is disturbed, silt and the contents of the wreck may fall out, and the wreck is so badly distorted that identification and quantification become nearly pure guesswork. The principal advantage of grab operations is very large savings in diving time.

Wreckage accumulates quickly during grabbing operations. On large operations, scheduling wreckage barges and tugs in and out for wreckage removal often becomes the critical portion of the operation. Grabbing, like chain cutting, usually begins at the high end and works toward the deeper end.

Lifting

Salvage sheer legs, or offshore construction derricks, working singly or in gangs, normally lift wreck sections. Chapter 10 discusses these lift devices. Two points are critical in making the lift: insuring the cut is clear and complete and rigging the lifting slings.

By their nature and the fact that the chain bight passes completely through the cut, chain cuts are usually complete. Explosive and exothermic cuts may miss structure and interference that can be surprisingly tenacious and uncooperative about parting when the lift is made. Passing a wire rope or chain through the cut before lifting is a sure way to check the completeness of the cut. Doing so requires rigging the wire under the ship, a potentially time-consuming process.

Entire wrecks or large portions of them may be lifted with chain or wire rope passed around the hull. Chain is preferred for at least a portion of the sling, because it is much more rugged and less susceptible than wire rope to damage that can cause catastrophic failure. Cut wreck sections are always lifted with chain slings. The same comments made above about cutting chains apply to chain lifting slings. Lifting slings are no place for junk chain or some old pieces that have been lying about the yard. Forged integral stud chain is much preferred to welded stud link chain. Welded stud link chain should be ORQ grade chain, not for strength, but because the seal-welded stud is less likely than a pressed-in stud to be jarred out. Lifting slings should be 2¼-inch (62 mm)-diameter or larger.

There is a high probability that chain can tear unsupported shell plating. Chain should be rigged in one opening cut in the shell around one—preferably more—transverse frame or other stiffeners and out a second opening. Figure 14-17 illustrates some correct ways of rigging chain lifting slings in wreck sections. Padding the openings with timbers prevents high local stresses where the chain bends through the opening.

Multiple Wrecks

Natural disasters—typhoons, hurricanes, etc.—and military action have left ports with a number of wrecks to be removed to restore the harbor to operation. The normal spectrum of wreck removal techniques is used for these operations. Size and scope make the operations unique. Some clearances have been large enough to require that a consortium of salvage companies be formed for the work, and the

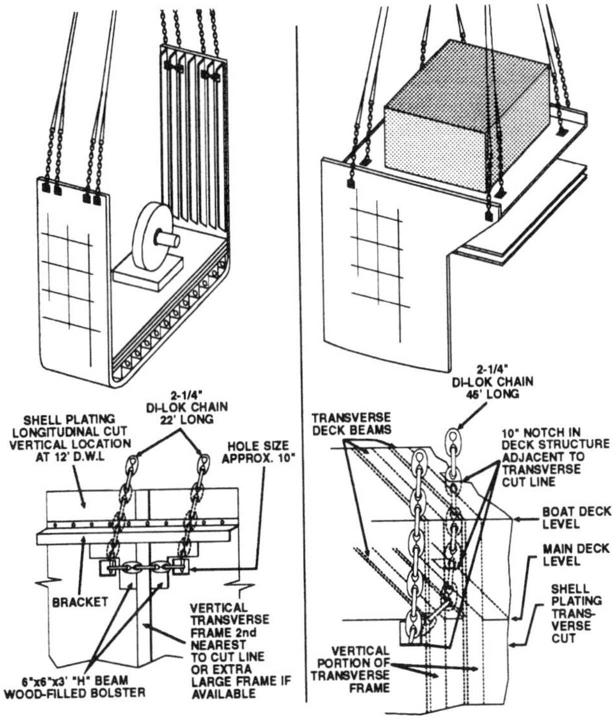

Fig. 14-17. Chains directly rove through cut holes.
Courtesy of U.S. Navy.

work sponsored by governments or international organizations such as the United Nations. Other operations involving several wrecks can be handled by one salvage operator. Normally, the primary concern is restoration of services in the port; salvage and preservation of value in individual ships is less important. No cure–no pay contracts or awards based on salved value are not appropriate for large-scale clearances. "Cure" may be almost impossible to define completely, and much of the material removed may have little value—certainly not value that approaches the cost of removal. Lump-sum or daily hire contracts are fair to all parties for large-scale clearance operations.

The first step in dealing with multiple wrecks is establishing priorities for the work. The process is in some ways similar to, but more complicated than, the medical process of triage. Similar to, because it involves evaluation of each casualty, its status, and the work necessary to remove or salvage it. More complicated, because the process considers not only the wrecks but also the relative importance of facilities—berths, piers, moorings, channels, etc.—and the ability to use salvaged vessels as tools in future work. The port authorities can help define the facilities of the port, the importance of various facilities, and the urgency of removing blocking wrecks.

In addition to those wrecks whose removal frees needed facilities, other candidates for high-priority removals include:

- Vessels whose condition is likely to deteriorate and complicate the operation if they remain in place.
- Work vessels—tugs, barges, cranes, etc.—that can be placed in service to increase the salvage plant and expedite the operation or make it unnecessary to bring in additional salvage plant.
- Vessels that are serious potential pollution problems or have large quantities of hazardous or obnoxious materials aboard.
- Vessels that have high value or high-value cargo.
- Vessels that can be removed quickly with relative ease.

Equipment selected for major clearance operations should be the best available and should represent the most modern salvage thinking. An excellent comparison of current and dated salvage equipment occurred in the 1974 clearance of the Suez Canal. During this operation both the lift crafts *Crilley* and *Crandall* (ex-*Energie* and *Ausdauer*), built in the late 1930s, and the sheer legs *Thor* and *Roland*, built by the same company in the early 1970s, worked on similar tasks. The original plan called for the vessels to work at the same rate; however, while the total lift capacity of the older craft exceeded that of the sheer legs, the latter could work faster and more efficiently. The difference was enough to cause major changes in the work plan and scheduling.

Any salvage operation requires flexibility in the approach, scheduling, and use of equipment. A large clearance operation with many wrecks requires a degree of flexibility that is a great multiple of that required for a single wreck. Despite the best planning and scheduling, things can be counted on not to follow the plan. Failure to be flexible can bring the operation to an extremely expensive halt. The project manager or senior salvage officer should go over the "what ifs..." constantly and lay out his options so that emerging events do not catch him unprepared.

In large operations, particularly where several wrecks are removed by the same general method, two teams, one to do the preliminary preparation and the second to do the removals, is very efficient. For instance, such an approach is particularly useful when expensive equipment is brought in for the second phase. Where several wrecks are piecemealed:

A cut and rig team can section the wrecks and rig them for lifting.

The cut and rig team is followed by a lifting team with cranes and sheer legs that clear the wrecks.

Meanwhile, the cut and rig team has moved on and is cutting and rigging the next wreck.

Like the need for flexibility, the problem of what to do with a wreck removed from its original location is multiplied in a major clearance operation. A solution that has worked well in past operations is to take the wrecks and wreckage to a dump site or storage location where they can be held for later disposal or cut up. Dump sites may be specified by local authorities or negotiated between the salvor and the authority responsible for the clearance. Salvors should be prepared to lay out their requirements for a dump site. Among the usual requirements are:

Enough space.

Protected waters where the wrecks and wreckage can be secure.

Dry stowage with work space for cutting up wreckage.

Good beaching ground.

Beach slopes that allow sheer legs and cranes to approach dry dump sites closely.

Road access.

It may be necessary to have different dump and holding sites for wreckage dumped in the dry and vessels in wet storage.

Just as sunken vessels may be raised and placed in service, wrecks awaiting removal or removed and taken to a dump or holding area are a source of structural steel and rigging materials for the operation.

An overall operational plan that balances and schedules resources and equipment with the work is necessary for orderly operational management. The overall plan must pay particular attention to logistics. Logistics and a self-contained operation are particularly important in operations in remote areas or in ports devastated by natural disasters or military action. Under such conditions even the best organized and run self-contained operation can be grim for the participants. The crews must be motivated to remain on the job and to work efficiently. Good pay, decent living conditions, good food, safe practices, and fair treatment go a long way in providing motivation. In very long operations in particularly bad conditions it may be necessary to give crews out-of-area breaks or to rotate crews to maintain operational effectiveness or safety.

Oil Rig Removals

Offshore oil exploration and production have put many pieces of floating and sea floor–supported equipment at sea. Some of this equipment has come to grief as a result of maritime or industrial accidents. Additionally, equipment abandoned in depleted fields is dismantled and removed as a matter of course. Salvage companies, independent salvage consultants in the employ of the oil company, offshore construction companies, or consortiums assembled for the specific operation may undertake "special wreck removals" of oil field equipment following marine or industrial accidents and removals after abandonment.

The responsibility for wreck removal of oil field equipment, particularly mobile offshore drilling units (MODUs) is not as straightforward as that for ships. While the rig owner—a drilling contractor—may carry the normal P&I coverage, it may exclude coverage for wreck removal arising from a blowout or drilling operations. The drilling contract may specify that the operator is responsible for wreck-removal costs or may indemnify the drilling contractor in cases exempted by his usual P&I. Before signing any wreck-removal contract for oil rigs or equipment, the salvor should be sure where his money is coming from.

The techniques used in both types of operation generally parallel those for ship wreck removal operations. The specific techniques for any job, as always, depend upon the characteristics of the equipment being removed and how it lies. They also depend upon the experience and practices of the wreck-removal contractor. The surest methods are normally employed by professional salvors who are more likely to apply a positive belt and suspenders approach than ad hoc wreck-removal contractors with less specific experience.

The most interesting casualties are normally the MODUs. Several things make these operations interesting and challenging:

MODUs are built for drilling for oil. Where compromises with normal marine design are necessary, the options taken are those that give a more efficient drilling platform. The vessels are not designed ever to be more than a few degrees from the upright. Severely inclined or damaged rigs and parts of rigs do not have the stability and buoyancy expected of ships or portions of ships in the same situation.

Bottom-supported rigs normally keep most support following a casualty. One or more legs or the mat are likely to be jammed into the sea floor, or the legs may be distorted and damaged, or the jacking system damaged.

The rigs are complex mechanisms that have inherent potential for innovations useful in the salvage operation.

Because they are mechanically complex and different from ships, a salvor approaching an oil rig salvage does well to study the plans and operating manual for the rig to understand as much as possible about the rig and its normal operation. If he contemplates such work, he is advised to read as many accounts of previous rig removals as he can. Because organizations other than professional salvors often undertake rig removals, accounts can be found in magazines and journals directed toward the offshore industry and in journals of civil and general engineering societies.

Follow-up Surveys

Many contracting authorities require the salvor to show that the site is clear of debris and that no debris lies on the sea floor between the wreck site and the disposal area. These requirements should be spelled out in the contract and understood by both parties before operations begin. In areas that have been high-traffic areas for hundreds of years, a survey before the operation may be necessary to establish the "as found" condition and to avoid any conflicts about materials found.

Any of the common techniques are satisfactory for the kind of coarse grain survey appropriate for a wreck site and wreck passage. A simple wire drag produces adequate results quickly and is very inexpensive. In these high technology days, side-scan sonar, magnetometer, and sub-bottom profiler surveys are not prohibitively expensive. The electronic surveys are more reliable than the wire drag and inherently produce a permanent survey record. A simple ROV fitted as an inspection vehicle can provide video documentation of any obstruction.

Cleanup of the shore storage site following the operation may be required. The requirements for cleaning up the disposal site must be worked out before starting the operation and included in the wreck-removal contract.

Management of Wreck Operations

The management of wreck operations bears little resemblance to time-critical salvage operations like strandings. In wreck operations, time exists for comprehensive surveys, planning, task analysis, and scheduling. Progress in the job is more a matter of schedule adherence and cost control than in stranding salvage. In this regard wreck operations closely resemble construction projects. As in construction projects, close, hard-nosed management increases profits.

The guidelines of occupational health and safety authorities are likely to apply. With these standards come the requirements for site safety plans and working practices that often appear incompatible with wreck operations.

Wreck operations are intensely commercial. Safety is an important aspect of the work. Compliance with safety regulations and good safety practices may seem onerous and costly. They are not nearly so costly as noncompliance and the accidents that follow. Accidents are expensive in lost time, damaged equipment costs, and worker efficiency. The lost time and direct costs of accidents can easily far exceed the cost of good safety practices and equipment. The human factor aside, no wreck operations manager can afford to slight safety.

In a construction project, the workplace becomes more complete as the work progresses and, thus, becomes inherently safer. The opposite situation occurs in wreck removals, especially in piecemealing and jobs with much manual cutting. In these operations the workplace diminishes and becomes inherently more dangerous as the job goes on. Additionally, workers who are not regular salvage crew may be hired for wreck operations. Experienced salvage crews develop a safety consciousness and a sense of self-preservation as a matter of necessity. Other crews may not have these senses as well developed. In repetitious and boring work like cutting, safety consciousness declines as familiarity grows. Crews must be kept aware of safety, and safety practices must be so simple they that are second nature. Serious, potentially fatal accidents happen when safety standards slip. There is no margin for laxity in any kind of salvage.

Work on wrecks generates large amounts of trash and debris, creating both a safety hazard and a potential pollutant. Good housekeeping forms an integral part of the safety program. Cleaning up regularly as well as not allowing trash and debris to build up removes fire hazards and sources of traumatic injury to people. Clean people working in an environment that, if not actually clean, is no dirtier than necessary, work more carefully and efficiently.

Fire can break out and sweep through a wreck in short order, not only exposing all hands working on the wreck to extreme hazard, but also wiping out any chance of commercial success. The greatest fire hazards are burning and temporary electrical systems. In large-scale burning operations, some fires are inevitable. At the same time, the combustion products and by-products in the air seriously degrade one of the best human detection systems, the sense of smell. Good housekeeping, work area inspections before burning, a combination of fire watches on the opposite side of the plate from the burner, and roving fire patrols reduce fire danger.

Explosions can occur when gases build up in closed spaces. The explosion may be disastrous in itself and may result in serious fire. Inspection, atmospheric monitoring, ventilation, and constant vigilance prevent explosions.

The size and nature of the fire-fighting plant on board the wreck is directly proportional to the fire threat. With little fire danger, a few carbon dioxide extinguishers may suffice. With high fire danger, complete fire-fighting plants with an alarm system, dedicated main and backup pumps, hoses and nozzles, a steel piped fire-fighting water distribution system, ventilation blowers, hydrants, tools, personal protective equipment, and main and backup fire-fighting control stations may be barely enough. In every case the fire-fighting plant should be planned for all classes of fire likely to occur and the most severe probable fire.

A fire-fighting team of experienced salvors specifically trained in marine fire fighting should be designated and activated whenever a fire occurs. These fire fighters are the first response team, whose job is to contain and control the fire. Local shore or port fire fighters augment the salvage fire team. The participation of local fire fighters, fire-fighting agents employed, and command and control should be spelled out in arrangements made before the operations start. Local fire fighters, trained primarily to fight fires ashore, may lack training for ship fires and may try to use inappropriate methods. Salvors should discourage fire fighters from fighting shipboard fires with huge quantities of water, as the ship may sink or capsize if fire-fighting water is not removed quickly. Workers aboard the wreck should leave the vessel as soon as practical after fire breaks out. Evacuation should not be delayed pending the results of initial fire-fighting efforts. It is better to lose time getting people out of the way and back on the job than to have them underfoot in a serious fire.

Having experienced salvage personnel is one of the best and most effective safety measures. As mentioned earlier, experienced salvors develop an unconscious sense of self-preservation which not only keeps them out of trouble but allows them to anticipate potentially unsafe conditions. At least one experienced salvor should supervise each group of inexperienced workers on wrecks.

To a salvor working there, the wreck may be the most important place in the world. Port authorities, regulators, and others have a very different view. They see the wreck as an object that makes their life more difficult and has the potential for making it monumentally difficult. Both viewpoints are valid and important; cooperation of the authorities can make the salvor's life easier; their enmity can make it hell. It behooves salvage managers to establish good relations with authorities early and to make extraordinary efforts to maintain these relationships. Mutual respect is the best way.

Sometimes, salvors find xenophobic or greedy and dishonest local authorities. In the first case, there is seldom a solution other than living with it. The author offers no solution to the second problem. Local cultures, the salvor's home nation's laws, and personalities affect the solution. Fine judgment and experience are called for.

The safety and unimpeded flow of traffic in the harbor are primary interests of the port and other authorities. Salvors should be prepared to recommend measures to control or restrict traffic near wreck operations. When the wreck is moved, the port should be closed or a generous moving safety zone set up around the wreck.

Much has been said throughout this chapter about the prevention of pollution during the operation. Little more needs to be said here other than to emphasize that the high cost of inattention and spillage justifies attention to the problem by salvage management. The headache of preparing and following a spill control plan cannot approach the pain of not doing so.

Wreck operations, more than other salvage operations, lend themselves to conventional project management practices. It is easy to identify tasks and critical paths, determine manning levels, and prepare schedules. Schedules and schedule adherence, along with man-hour expenditures, are excellent tools for monitoring progress and controlling costs. Wise managers do not rely on seat-of-the-pants techniques; rather, they take advantage of management tools that computerized systems can provide. These systems should fit the job and should contain the specific information the manager wants. Computerized management information systems can generate much more information than the manager can use. His time is not well spent wading through information of little use to him when he could be aboard the wreck applying his technical knowledge and solving emergent problems.

SUMMARY

This chapter has skimmed the surface of wrecks, wreck removal operations, and their management. It has discussed some of the methods of wreck removal that have proven successful. Improvisation and innovation mark all of salvage, nowhere more than wreck removal. Good wreck removals—those that are technically successful and profitable—are a result of good engineering, good management, and—hardest of all—thinking, thinking, and thinking some more.

15

THE BUSINESS OF SALVAGE AND CASUALTY MANAGEMENT

While the greater part of this book addresses the technical and operational part of salvage, salvage as a commercial venture that must produce a profit has received emphasis at every opportunity. Through salvage, the provider of a needed service can earn a reward and make a profit. Part I of this chapter addresses a few business features that, if not truly unique in salvage, have more importance than in other businesses.

Part II moves to the specific casualty-management factors from the viewpoints of the owner (and his insurers) interested in reducing their cost and of the salvor interested in increasing his return. They are virtually the same, but are approached from opposite directions.

PART I—THE BUSINESS OF SALVAGE

The traditional motivation for salvage operations is simple. The law of ancient Rhodes established the principle of salvage awards based on the value of salved property. In a continuum since, right through the Industrial Revolution, salvors have practiced their trade to gain awards for saving property.

Compensation based on the value of property saved is unique to the maritime world. Persons acting as Good Samaritans ashore neither expect nor receive part of the value of the salvaged property as their reward. In the maritime world, a person who furnishes a salvage service, with or without a contract, gains a reward based on property value. Awards by courts and arbitrators traditionally have followed this principle. The owner and the salvor were principal parties to salvage contracts, with the salvor's payment coming primarily from hull and machinery and cargo underwriters. Of importance is that marine salvors are working for a reward, not performing a public service. Anything within the law and within the bounds of ethics and responsibility that they can do to increase their award is proper.

In the late 1960s, a major new factor—concern about the environment and the prevention of pollution—appeared in the delicately balanced casualty response equation. This concern, focused by the March 1967 loss of *Torrey Canyon*, grew as other polluting casualties occurred. It became very apparent that the transportation of oil and dangerous goods at sea carried with it the potential for very large, damaging releases and that the new and growing worldwide environmental concern made such releases unacceptable.

Governments entered the game with legislation that gave them broad powers to intervene in marine casualties where pollution was actual or threatened. Governments assumed the right and responsibility to take control of casualty-response operations to reduce pollution. Permitted action included destruction of casualties. Owners and salvors no longer were concerned solely with the saving of property in casualties; now they had to consider how to deal with oils—both cargo and bunker—and a growing list of hazardous materials. P&I clubs with their pollution cover began playing a bigger role in casualty response.

The specter of government intervention, particularly in tanker casualties, loomed large. Salvors became rightly concerned with risking great losses and greater liabilities from responding to potentially polluting casualties. P&I clubs became concerned with heavy pollution claims and the potential for payment to salvors.

Following discussions between the International Salvage Union and the major P&I clubs, additional cover was arranged in the early 1970s through a protective clause known as the "Piopic Clause." This clause was operative until the 1980 revision to Lloyd's Standard Salvage Agreement (Lloyd's Open Form), the most widely used open form agreement, departed from the strict principle of no cure–no pay in tanker casualties. The new contract permitted the salvor of a laden or partially laden tanker to collect his expenses plus a bonus of up to 15 percent of expenses when only partially successful or prevented from completing an operation. The 1990 revision of this contract extended the provisions from laden tankers to all ships that threaten damage to the environment in coastal waters and increased the amount of special compensation available. The 1995 version continues the same provisions. Other open form contracts contain similar provisions. Article 14 of the International Convention on Salvage, 1989 (incorporated into LOF90 and 95), formalizes the principle of rewards for preventing pollution without regard to the type of contract. The potential for awards under Article 14 means that P&I clubs have a serious interest in almost every casualty and are specifically interested in the actions of salvors. It is not at all unusual for the clubs to hire a knowledgeable salvage person to attend the casualty on their behalf to liaise with the salvor, to observe, assist and expedite the salvage operations, and, especially, to monitor the salvor's efforts in environmental matters.

The motivation for salvors is now twofold: saving property and preventing pollution. Both may earn him an award and both influence the structure and nature of his response to a casualty. In the United States environmental legislation is so strong that it is widely recognized that the primary motivation for salvage in U.S. waters is environmental protection rather than protection of property.

Business Climate

The maritime business climate exerts a strong influence on how the salvage business is conducted. Business climate includes the opportunity for doing business and the specific market conditions, such as regulatory attitudes, that influence how business is done and the potential for profit.

Casualty type and frequency in an area are basic to structuring response posture. As in any business, the strength of the services offered is directly proportional to the need for the services. Good business practice would not condone establishing a strong salvage presence in an area where very few casualties occurred or where casualties were either so simple that they could easily be handled without professional salvors or so complex that no salvage was practical. The salvage capability in any area must match the expected casualties.

Demand for services depends upon both the frequency and the type of casualties. The Salvage Working Group, in a study undertaken by Bureau Veritas for the International Salvage Union (ISU), reported a long-term decline in worldwide casualty incidence despite an increase in the numbers of ships at sea. This apparent anomaly results from significant improvements in marine safety. Continuation of the trend can only increase the difficulty of maintaining purely commercial salvage capability. Future demand may not produce enough income for salvors to keep their doors open.

One of the great difficulties of salvage as a business is that salvage work is neither regular nor predictable. Salvors can neither foresee their future workload nor control their sales volume. Despite legends and folklore to the contrary, they cannot generate work; they are at the mercy of accident. Salvors' business skills come into play only after a casualty occurs. Cash flow from salvage is as unpredictable as the work. Payment is often a long time coming and there may be long dry periods between lucrative casualties. In practice, the irregular cash flow has led to most salvage companies being part of multifaceted organizations. In these organizations, the core business puts the meat and potatoes on the table and carries the salvage company through the dry spells; salvage adds the gravy by providing windfall profits to the organization.

Operation of a salvage company is expensive. Experienced salvage crews are expensive to keep available. Ships are expensive; salvage equipment is expensive.

The expense comes not only from initial capital expenditure to buy ships and equipment, but in maintenance costs to keep the equipment working and ready for immediate deployment, and in costs to replace ships and equipment that have reached the end of their service life or been lost or destroyed. High expenditure for purchase and maintenance is justified when equipment use is high and rental income offsets equipment costs. Salvage ships and equipment are used irregularly and sometimes infrequently for salvage work. The salvor's options are to accept the expense as a cost of being in the business, or use his ships and equipment for other purposes to generate income, accepting the risk that they may not be available when needed for salvage.

For most salvors, only the latter is practical. Neither salvors nor salvage vessels can be put on the shelf between operations. They must be kept ready and worked up to respond effectively when needed.

The same factors apply to personnel. The salvor must decide whether he should keep his crews on the payroll or keep only a cadre of key people, calling in the balance when he needs them. For most salvors only the latter is possible. Personnel problems are complicated by the graying of experienced salvors and hesitancy of younger people to enter and stay with the business long enough to gain the experience that makes them effective.

The regulatory atmosphere in a particular area is an important factor in the casualty response business climate. As is to be seen a bit farther along in this chapter, regulatory attitudes affect such basics as the type and structure of salvage contracts. They greatly affect day-to-day operations.

Major marine casualties are traumatic for all directly concerned with them. They become traumatic for a wide spectrum of the population and awaken regulatory interest when they damage or threaten to damage the environment and when emotions, heightened by environmental insult, become involved. As traumatic events, casualties do not lead to normal industrial operations. No matter how much contingency planning is done, casualty responses cannot be completely programmed; conditions requiring changes emerge constantly. Changes are often time critical; they are expensive in expertise, equipment, and labor. Effective casualty response requires complete professionalism and attention to detail in high-stress environments.

Because casualties are unusual events in any geographic area, local government experience is often very limited. It is counterproductive for local authorities to treat people responding to the casualty as hostiles who have caused the problem; but, when people act out of inexperience, it happens. It is equally counterproductive for those who have expert knowledge of casualty operations to treat well-intentioned, inexperienced local authorities shabbily. Local people have legitimate concerns and should have a voice. Regulators have legally assigned responsibilities; they should pursue them aggressively and competently. Regulators normally exert pressure to expedite the operation. When haste is likely to lead to wasted time, a high probability of failure, or pollution, the pressure should be resisted, but not to the point of stubborn intransigence. Regulators may not see the forest of operational complexity and risk for the trees of their regulatory preoccupation. Nor may they have the technical expertise to evaluate the situation as a whole. Patient guidance from those with the technical expertise and responsibility for execution is appropriate.

With serious and potentially lucrative casualties becoming fewer, salvors find a highly competitive business becoming more so. Competition for the same work is on three levels:

1. Professional salvors.
2. Yellow pages salvors.
3. Alternative arrangements.

In addition to cutthroat competition, salvors must contend with de facto competition from subsidized or quasi-government operators, sometimes acting with the full force of local governments behind them. Local cabotage laws or regulations may favor subsidized salvors or national flag salvors.

A strongly competitive market benefits both salvors and their potential customers. When acceptance of services from a subsidized or quasi-governmental salvor or a national flag salvor is not directed, the shipowner may have his choice of several salvors offering competitive services on similar contract arrangements. When the situation permits, he may be able to save some money by hiring a yellow pages salvor or making alternative arrangements to a professional salvor on more favorable terms than conventional salvage contracts. The advantage to the salvage operation is not so clear-cut. In many cases the advantages of alternative arrangements may be a fiction. For owners or underwriters with valuable property at risk, eschewing professional salvors for alternative arrangements is much like shopping for a cheap brain surgeon. Unless the alternative arrangement—individual or company—is highly qualified technically in salvage and related environmental matters, financially sound, and thoroughly familiar with local resources, operating conditions, and restrictions, employing him may turn out to be a costly choice.

Professional salvors must meet the competition as they find it. Competitiveness means technical and commercial sharpness—never complacency.

Commercial Instruments

A commercial instrument (contract) that is fair to all the parties and gives adequate rewards to the provider of services must cover any salvage operation not undertaken by casual salvors. A salvage contract, like any equitable contract, must serve the interests of all parties while protecting them—hardly a unique concept, but one that bears repeating periodically.

In this century, the no cure–no pay open form contract has been most common in the international salvage industry, especially for time-critical salvage. An open form contract provides a set of terms without addressing specific compensation. The terms are well known and standard, reducing any need to haggle over contract terms and delay the start of work. The contracts generally adhere to the principle of no cure–no pay: the salvor earns an award only through success. Compensation is determined after successful salvage by arbitration under terms and conditions spelled out in the contract. The advantage of this type of arrangement for time-critical casualty response is obvious. An open form contract is not suitable for all time-critical salvage cases. For instance, no salvor can afford to take an open form contract in a region where he may deploy assets long distances and find on arrival the casualty so deteriorated that no cure is possible. Alaska is such a place.

A number of these contracts exist; Lloyd's Standard Salvage Agreement or Lloyd's Open Form (LOF) is the most common and best known. Appendix B gives the text of the LOF80, 90, and 95 (1980, 1990, and 1995 revisions) and two other common open form no cure–no pay contracts. The standard contracts are revised periodically to keep them consistent with modern salvage practice. Inclusion and expansion of a "safety net" provision deviating from strict no cure–no pay for casualties that threaten pollution is the most significant recent revision in major open form contracts.

The safety net, formalized in Article 14 of the 1989 Convention as well as in the contracts, violates strict no cure–no pay in some cases by assuring salvors receive at least their costs when regulatory authorities intervene. The safety net, introduced in LOF80 and subsequently included in other open form contracts, was broadened in LOF90. Even with these changes, a perception exists that the existing open form contracts, with rewards based on salved value, are inappropriate where the measure of success has changed from the saving of property to environmental protection.

Many variations of the standard form—recognized national forms or homegrown versions—may be offered by national salvors working in or near their own waters. The wise shipowner, where he is in a position to do so (not in national waters of a nation where salvage is restricted by cabotage regulations), should insist on one of the better-known contracts, as he may inadvertently put himself at a serious disadvantage with a little-known form in a foreign procedure. As an illustration of the pitfalls of such contracts, one national form provides that the fee for the arbitrators who determine the award is a percentage of the salvage award. Good for the salvors; not so good for the shipowners. Another requires that shipowners provide security for all cargo interests—a situation that becomes onerous where the casualty carries numerous owners' cargoes.

Shipowners often feel open form contracts favor salvors to the point of being a license to steal. Salvors offering an open form contract are seen as one step (or less) away from piracy. This is not correct—at least insofar as the major forms are concerned. Under an open form or other no cure–no pay contract the salvor may invest quite a large sum and lose it all if there is no success. Open form contracts are high-risk contracts for salvors, especially with regulators playing an increasing role in salvage operations. Salvors who face an impossible or unprofitable job cannot simply declare no cure and walk away from a job. They must follow established procedures to get relief from their contracted responsibilities. While the procedures progress, costs and losses continue. Few businessmen outside the salvage business would agree to such terms for operations in which success is far from assured. The salvor's advantage lies in the contract being more familiar to him because he deals with it regularly than it is to the shipowner who has casualties infrequently.

The decision to offer an open form contract is not one a salvor should take lightly. Factors to be considered include:

Technical feasibility of the work.
Probability of success.
The regulatory climate.
Salved value and potential award.
Relative values of the work and award.
Potential for an Article 14 award.

Because it is seldom practical to assess these factors from afar, practice allows salvors to offer open form contracts *subject to inspection*. Following a physical inspection of the casualty the salvor may withdraw the "subject to" and offer the contract in the normal manner, may offer on other terms, or may walk away. The "subject to" allows the salvor to determine if the prospect of salvage is such that the chance of technical and commercial success is high enough for him to take the risk of an open form contract.

Under the LOF and other open form contracts, arbitration determines the salvor's award. Arbitrators consider the factors delineated in Article 13 of the International Convention on Salvage, 1989, in determining the award. The entire convention is reprinted in Appendix B. The portion of Article 13 dealing with criteria for fixing the award reads as follows:

> (1) The reward shall be fixed with a view to encouraging salvage operations, taking into account the following criteria without regard to the order in which they are presented below:
> (a) the salved value of the vessel and other property;
> (b) the skill and efforts of the salvors in preventing or minimizing damage to the environment;
> (c) the measure of success obtained by the salvor;

(d) the nature and degree of the danger;
(e) the skill and efforts of the salvors in salving the vessel, other property and life;
(f) the time used and expenses and losses incurred by the salvors;
(g) the risk of liability and other risks run by the salvors or their equipment;
(h) the promptness of the services rendered;
(i) the availability and use of vessels or other equipment intended for salvage operations;
(j) the state of readiness and efficiency of the salvor's equipment and the value thereof.

Although arbitrators are experienced and knowledgeable in salvage, the award is unpredictable. The amount of the award depends on the completeness and accuracy of the information given to the arbitrator and the skill in its presentation, as well as upon the skill in salvage. The international salvage industry feels that awards in recent years have been inadequate. The arbitration process has not always been prompt. Steps coincident with the introduction of LOF90 cut the delays in LOF arbitrations. Arbitrations procedures under the JSE (Japanese Shipping Exchange) salvage agreement are deliberately short so that the salvor receives his money promptly.

Increasing emphasis on environmental protection and a parallel increase in environmental legislation gives greater uncertainty in the business aspects of salvage. Regulatory intervention is unpredictable and adds a factor that the salvor must consider in protecting his income. A salvor taking an open form no cure–no pay contract in an environment where regulators are likely to prescribe or proscribe salvage actions takes an undefined risk—one few can afford. A salvor operating under a no cure–no pay arrangement must be in control of the salvage actions he takes to ensure that costs are kept under control and the actions most likely to lead to success are taken. When the salvor loses control of the salvage actions to regulators, his risk increases beyond acceptability.

Space does not permit a complete discussion of open form salvage contracts. *LOF90 and the New Salvage Convention* by Darling and Smith[1] provides a detailed discussion of not only those important subjects but several other types of open form salvage contracts.

In an environment where environmental protection overrides consideration of property loss, no cure–no pay loses viability. In U.S. waters and other highly sensitive regions salvors may prefer to work on a daily rate contract, often with an incentive bonus of a percentage of salved value. These contracts protect salvors' income and eliminate many of the problems associated with open form contracts and arbitration under foreign law. They are safe contracts in an environmentally sensitive region because the salvor is paid for the services he provides despite intervention by regulatory authorities. Shipowners are not always familiar with these contracts or may feel obligated to negotiate quoted rates, so some negotiation with accompanying delay is inevitable. Appendix B gives a typical daily rate plus bonus salvage contract such as is often used in the United States. Many other contract forms may be used for salvage operations; they include daily rate, lump sum, and time and materials contracts with and without various forms of bonuses and performance awards. Appendix B contains an example of a daily rate with bonus contract.

Salvors determining the form of contract to offer must consider the job, probability of success, physical and financial risk, environmental climate, and regulatory atmosphere, and offer the contract form and terms that provide them reasonable expectation of return for acceptable risk. Owners and insurers in evaluating salvors' offers must protect themselves while recognizing the salvors' right to earn a reasonable reward for their services.

Calculation of Salved Value and Security

Calculation of salved value upon which security and the award are ultimately based is a relatively straightforward process of:

1. Determining the value of the intact ship and deducting from it the costs of repairs and other services and costs necessary to restore it to serviceable condition.
2. Determining the shipped value of the cargo and deducting from it any diminution of value that occurs because of the casualty. The process may be very complicated for ships carrying many separate consignments, for each must be valued individually.

Rough estimates should be made at the outset and refined as the operation continues. The point may come when the salved value decreases to below what is necessary to give the salvor commercial success on an open form contract. He must then be prepared to ask for relief from his responsibilities under the contract or to revise the type of contract.

The security required from the ship and cargo owners is a percentage of the salved value based on the probable award and the delays expected in bringing a case to arbitration. Too much security is better than too little, but demands for excessive security can count against the salvor at arbitration.

Security may be provided in a number of ways depending upon the contract requirements and the jurisdiction. Means of providing security under the LOF, the longest established and most frequently used contract, are well established. "Security may be provided to the Committee of Lloyd's in cash or by insured guarantees or in another form approved by the Committee and shall be given by persons, firms, or corporations resident in the United Kingdom. Security may also be given directly to the salvor in the form of letters of undertaking or guarantees."

In any particular case, the security may be given to either the Committee or the salvor in a variety of forms.

Other open form contracts have similar provisions for security. A salvor needs to know how security is handled before entering into a specific contract form.

Redelivery

With the ship safely afloat and secure, the job is not over, for the salvor must redeliver the ship to her owner to bring the operation to definite closure. Most open form contracts designate a place of redelivery and contain a provision for changing the place to fit circumstances. Lloyd's Open Form (LOF80, 90, or 95) goes considerably farther by requiring the owner to assist in getting authority to enter the appropriate port and to accept redelivery when reasonably offered. In LOF90 and 95 the requirement to accept redelivery is incorporated by including Article 8 of the International Convention on Salvage, 1989, as a part of the contract. Nonstandard contracts should include similar provisions.

Despite the contract provisions, disputes at redelivery time are likely. Some are legitimate. The casualty must truly be safely afloat without heavy leakage, instability, or other conditions that may lead to the loss of the ship. It is in the salvors' interest to provide a ship that is in as good condition as possible and to document the conditions on board the casualty. Even when the ship is secure and the port is suitable for delivery, owners may have reasons unrelated to the salvage to attempt refusal of redelivery. Owners have been reluctant to accept redelivery, sometimes going so far as to fail to put up port guarantees, abandoning the ship and crew, selling the ship from one shell company to another, and doing other dastardly deeds to reduce the value of the ship or the worth of the salvage award. If an owner refuses delivery the salvor is left with the ship and the expenses it accrues—potentially a very expensive business. A salvor working under an LOF has the recourse of applying to the Salvage Arbitration Branch of Lloyd's for an order stating the services are completed and requiring the owner to accept the casualty. Because of the widespread use of the LOF, procedures for forcing redelivery are not as clearcut in other forms of salvage agreements.

Perhaps the most onerous act of a shipowner is to abandon physical interest in a casualty before the vessel is brought into port and before the salvor has obtained any securities. The salvor is likely to face a long and expensive process in entering a port and enforcing his lien.

Although the owner may accept responsibility for the casualty, local authorities may require continued attendance by the salvor. Such attendance can become costly and can tie up assets that could be better employed elsewhere. Alternatively—or additionally—authorities may call upon the salvor for a substantial financial guarantee for the casualty. Providing a financial guarantee for a third party who is vacillating on contractual agreements is hardly a sound business practice.

Wreck Removal Contracts

Wreck removals fall into two general categories:

1. Those in which some urgency is attached to the removal because of the location of the wreck or some hazard it presents.
2. Those in which timely removal is not so urgent.

In the past, both types have been done on lump sum no cure–no pay contracts where the cure depends upon removal to a certain point—complete, to the mud line, etc.—and verification that the removal is complete. Rarely, urgent wreck removals have been done on open form contracts, but using open form contracts for this type of work is much like driving a nail with a screwdriver—it's the wrong tool for the job.

Major wreck removals are multimillion dollar operations, so that the salvor operating on a no cure–no pay contract is heavily exposed during the entire operation and any wrangling or litigation that may follow. In this era of environmental awareness the salvor is also exposed if the wreck contains oils, other pollutants, or hazardous materials, or lies in an environmentally sensitive area. The salvor must write a very large contingency into his bid to cover the unrevealed—indeed, unknown—risks he may encounter. This commercial necessity produces a catch-22 situation: because all bidders must cover themselves in the same way, no bidder can bid with a truly sharp pencil. The result is that all bids are higher than the value of the work, particularly when the wreck is removed solely for aesthetic or environmental purposes.

Two standard wreck removal contracts developed by the International Salvage Union and the Baltic and International Maritime Council were introduced in 1993. These are two-part contracts, the first part being a box layout format containing information relative to the particular case while the second part contains the standard clauses. The contracts are:

A daily hire contract intended for situations where time is an important factor or the contractor may not consider it feasible to offer on a lump sum basis.

A lump sum contract with progress payments for use when complete surveys may be carried out, the work quantified in detail, and a price developed.

These contracts are reproduced in Appendix B.

While these contracts are very sound and fair to all parties, some companies and some insurers may prefer to use their own contract forms and bidding procedures. Government agencies at all levels can be counted on to use their own procedures and contracts. In wreck-removal contracting as in operations, salvors must be flexible and shrewd.

Business Operations

One of the unusual aspects of the business of salvage is that conventional marketing practices cannot be followed. Potential customers, shipowners, and insurers do not want to have to do business with salvors because they do business with salvors only when they are in trouble and see themselves in a vulnerable situation. Salvors cannot very well court their potential customers beyond advertising in *Lloyd's List* or trade journals. The salvor's opportunity to provide services is completely beyond his control. Salvors must be ready to respond immediately when opportunities present themselves. Relations between salvors and the remainder of the maritime industry have been marked by mistrust and suspicion. The International Salvage Union, recognizing that these conditions are good for neither group, has supported the establishment of The Salvage Liaison Group to improve relations.

Maritime operations by their nature cover very large geographical areas and many casualties occur in remote areas. The first thing a salvor must do is to learn of a casualty. Doing so requires intelligence that may range from simply subscribing to Lloyd's Intelligence Services for the salvor's operating area, to monitoring marine communications, to paying bonuses to employees or agents who report casualties that result in salvage operations.

Upon learning of a casualty the salvor must aggressively contact owners and underwriters to offer his services as specifically as possible. Dispatching some senior salvage crew to the site or sailing salvage ships on speculation is often sound practice. Even the most tenuous report should be followed up, especially wreck removals, when expressions of interest and requests for bids may not appear for a long time after the casualty.

Positioning of resources—vessels, equipment, and people—is basic in the business of salvage. The days are past when salvors could afford to have fully found salvage tugs crammed to the gunwales with salvage crew and equipment waiting on station at major traffic choke points for casualties. Ships are too expensive to operate and the steady stream of casualties at these points no longer occurs. There are two exceptions to this change:

1. Ex-Soviet Union tugs available for charter at very low prices have been chartered and put on salvage station by some western salvors.
2. Governments have subsidized salvage stations at some points directed primarily at tanker casualties and preventing environmental damage from them.

The way that a salvor elects to operate influences his choice of equipment and how he uses his resources. If the salvor is part of a multifaceted marine operation, he may be able to call upon other divisions of the company for ships and personnel. Personnel from other parts of the company augment a cadre of full-time salvors when casualties occur. Equipment and ships may be modified to work together so that equipment may be brought aboard and put into service quickly. This method of operation takes constantly reaffirmed dedication to salvage by the parent corporation to assure that petty grievances stemming from individual or departmental self-interest do not impede the salvor's ability to operate.

Salvors may choose not to operate ships but rather to have their equipment packaged for air transportation to a port near the salvage site for loading aboard vessels chartered there or nearby or brought in for the purpose. This method of operation requires attention to packing of equipment, arrangements with cargo airlines, special attention to supporting the equipment at the remote site, and skilled crews to accompany and install equipment. The feasibility of it depends to some degree on the availability of suitable vessels and the charter market in the operating area. The fly-away method of operation may be much more difficult and requires more attention to logistics detail than salvage with company-operated ships. A well-set-up and supported fly-away system gives the salvor the ability to respond more quickly over a larger geographical area than he can with ships that may not be able to reach the casualty promptly.

The Salvor's Management Technique

The salvor's overall management technique affects much of his approach to the job. Two basic techniques are practiced:

1. Management at the site where the salvage master and the supporting staff at the site conduct the operation with only necessary support coming from the salvor's home office. This technique puts decision making with the people who have the best facilities for gathering and analyzing information in real time. It requires a larger staff on-site to do the engineering and logistics support work. On-site does not necessarily mean aboard the casualty. Some staff, particularly logistics and similar types, may be located nearby ashore or in ports where an industrial capacity exists.
2. Centralized management where technical and logistics support comes from the salvor's home office. Under this system, senior staff in the home office approve salvage plans and make major tactical decisions and transmit them to the salvage site. This system is suitable when the salvor has a small staff of highly experienced people and field people who are less experienced. Communications between the casualty and home office must be excellent for this system to work.

Both systems can work. The choice depends upon the salvor's preferences. I prefer as many management decisions as possible to be made on-site. My experience is that something is lost in long-distance communication, and the man on-site has a better feel for the validity of the information that forms the basis of decisions.

Documentation of Salvage Work

The nature and quantity of salvage documentation depends to a large extent upon the type of contract under which the work is undertaken and the purpose for which the documentation is to be used. Documentation for preparing a case for arbitration under an open form contract is at the upper end of the spectrum. Not far below it is the documentation for a day rate and fixed price contract. In an arbitrated case, the documentation forms the evidence upon which the arbitrator makes the award. In a more conventional contract, documentation provides evidence for any dispute that must be settled by arbitration or litigation. The lowest level of documentation, but probably the most expensive to produce, is that which the salvor may use in the future to develop or include in promotional material.

The purpose of salvage documentation is to present factual information as clearly as possible to the judge or arbitrator. It must be not only clear and complete within itself, but be organized in such a way that a person familiar with salvage, but completely unfamiliar with the specific operation, can understand it quickly. Salvage documentation also allows in-house study of an operation by the salvage company to note areas of weakness.

The discussion that follows centers about documentation for an arbitrated case on the basis that, being the most complex, it necessarily includes the less complex cases and that the salvor can make an informed decision of what to include based upon his evaluation of documentation requirements.

Whatever its end use, salvage documentation must be accurate, legible, correct, and consistent with both the work and other documentation. Documentation is not a worrisome evil that can be sloughed off as a bunch of damned paperwork; it is an integral part of the operation upon which commercial success may depend. Salvage documentation requires the attention of senior salvage personnel on a daily basis. The salvage master who does not assure good documentation is not doing his job.

Documentation for any job may consist of most of the following:

Deck logs of salvage ships, tugs, and other craft under the control of the salvor.

Salvage logs and notebooks.

Rough logs and notebooks.

Personal logs, notes, and tape recordings.

Daily reports.

Diving logs.

Lists of equipment and equipment-operating logs.

Calculations and computer printouts.

Survey reports.

Checklists.

Sketches.

Faxes, telexes, radio messages, and any other correspondence between parties to the operation.

Weather information, including weather forecasts, faxes, advisories, and storm plots.

Photographs and videotapes.

Sounding records.

Draft surveys.

Time sheets.

Cargo plans.

Cargo condition reports.

Tally sheets.

Ullage sheets.

Working charts.

Salvage plans.

Casualty plans.

Technical reports.

Subcontractor records.

Invoices from service providers, subcontractors, and suppliers.

Consultants' reports.

Flight logs of hired aircraft.

Correspondence between the home office and parties to the salvage.

Tape recording of voice radio transmissions and telephone conversations with any party connected with the salvage.

The salvage master should be responsible for the collection and safekeeping of all documentation. He may and should delegate some of the record keeping, but should stay on top of it to be sure it is current and correct. A system developed either by the salvage master or in the office as a company standard should be followed for organizing and keeping track of the documentation.

The necessity for neatness in record keeping cannot be overemphasized. Smooth logs should be just that: smooth and professional in appearance. Rough logs and notebooks in which events are recorded as they happen for later transfer may look like what they are, but should not be filled with erasures and scribbled-through entries. Changes should be made by lining through the material with a single line and initialing it or x-ing through and initialing large deletions. Times should be recorded meticulously.

All senior salvors should keep notes. They should be amply supplied with whatever type of notebooks they like. I personally prefer notebooks of waterproof paper made for civil engineers. These books are expensive, but are rugged and take full immersion without blurring the writing or later falling apart. They are available in sizes that fit easily into jeans, jacket, or coverall pockets. How personal notes are kept is very much a matter of individual choice. However they are kept, all notes kept by the salvage crew should be collected at the end of the operation to form part of the total record of the job.

A single working chart or charts should be used throughout the operation and should not be erased or altered during or afterwards. The working chart should be taken out of service immediately after the operation and preserved "as-is."

All calculations and sketches, including those made on scrap paper, on deck, or in chalk on the side of a house or a container should be kept. Photographs of the chalked sketches or calculations are easier to carry about and preserve than portions of the ship or containers. Where either the salvor's notebook computer or the ship's PC is used, it is generally not practical to keep all the calculations. In these calculations there is generally a great deal of what-iffing that produces voluminous calculations of little or no ultimate importance. Additionally, paper for the printer may be at a premium aboard the casualty. The salvor should use his best judgment in deciding what material to print, what material to save, and what to let disappear. The salvor's notebook computer is very convenient for keeping records on disk and for keeping track of records as well as for making calculations.

Photographs and videotapes are compelling evidence of conditions and operations. The salvor's bag of gear should include video cameras for surface and underwater use and several cameras with various types of film. There are a variety of weatherproof point-and-shoot cameras on the market that fit nicely into shirt, jacket, or coverall pockets and are well within the capability of a salvor to operate. These cameras are excellent tools for salvage. All cameras on site should be supported by a more-than-adequate supply of batteries, film, tapes, and other necessary accessories. Adequacy and redundancy are as important in the means of documenting a job as they are in equipment for the job.

On some operations a professional filmmaker may be brought to the site to record the operation for development into promotional material and for arbitration or litigation. Professional filmmakers are likely to be artistic in their temperament and try to be artistic in their work. Their artistic flair may be detrimental in work produced for arbitration or litigation. They should be supervised to prevent their artistic flair from leading them astray. Local television reporters may take videotape footage of operations close to a port. This footage may be useful in documenting the operation or developing promotional material. Negotiations with television stations should be straightforward and open with suitable payment being made for the footage.

The foregoing discussion is equally applicable to shipowners as to salvors. Shipowners and underwriters must require meticulous collection and preservation of documentation for the presentation of their case and should select the documentation they should keep from the shopping list given above.

Following the operation, the documentation is assembled and bundled for presentation in an arbitration or litigation by an attorney. The attorney needs complete cooperation from the working salvors or the ship or shipowners in preparing their case. An attorney preparing a case has a difficult job because he does not have firsthand knowledge of the information he must present. He must rely on the salvors to provide him with all the significant details. The attorney may not understand salvage, but he understands the law and presentation of a case better than the salvor. The salvor should be patient and tactful in explaining technical detail and procedures that are second nature to him but foreign to the attorney.

Operations conducted on contracts other than open form contracts should be as carefully documented as contracts to be arbitrated. The type of contract is no guarantee that the case may not be settled in court where full records, particularly contemporaneous records, are a great advantage.

In summary, preparing, collecting, and preserving paperwork and other documentation for salvage is an onerous task for both salvors and shipowners. There is no way around it. It is a very important part of salvage work because proper documentation, nearly as much as technical excellence, determines commercial success.

Lessons Learned—or Unlearned

The preceding section mentioned briefly that salvage documentation allows in-house study to determine areas of weakness. At the end of a job there is a tendency for the crew to head off to a local watering hole for a few and to rehash the job—usually in more agonizing (but blurry) detail as the session goes along. Similarly, when the money is in the bank there is a tendency to put the file away and move on to something else.

Seldom, if ever, is an operation conducted perfectly—although successful operations are often treated as though they were. There are always lessons to be learned and applied to future operations. A great opportunity for improving both the technical and commercial aspects of the company's operations is lost if the operation is not gone over in detail in a formal review following the operation.

The review of the operation should be led by the salvage master with the close cooperation of the salvage manager. The results of the review should be circulated for comment among the senior salvage staff. Following the review and comment session the senior salvage master and salvage master should see to the implementation of the lessons learned. Reviews, comments, and results are at all times treated as company confidential and held closely.

Such a review may seem to be a bunch of bureaucratic nonsense to practical salvors who know their job. It is not; it is a sound management practice, particularly in a business where work is not repetitious. It is a means of assuring valuable lessons are not lost or remain the property of only a few and that the company benefits from the knowledge and experience of its employees. There is a vast difference between twenty years' experience and one year's experience twenty times. Much of that difference is learning from what has gone before.

PART 2—CASUALTY MANAGEMENT

Choice of Salvor

Owners do not choose salvors frequently, and except for those companies required under U.S. law to have a designated salvor, may not have given selection of salvors any serious thought. It is both trite and erroneous to say all salvors are equal. One salvor may specialize in a particular type of salvage, another in a region with special problems and difficulties. Owners may come to regret signing with the first salvor who dangles an LOF under their noses or makes claims that in a less stressful situation would be carefully evaluated. In many cases, particularly serious casualties with high values at risk and a potential for large liabilities, a large international salvor may be the best choice. A regional salvor who is a specialist in local conditions may be a better choice if the same casualty is in a remote region or one with an extreme environment. Unfortunately, the owner, his manager, or other agent is seldom in a position to make a reasoned, deliberate choice. He must choose quickly, often from competing offers, all of which sound good. Things to be considered in choosing a salvor include:

Reputation—reputation is important, but insufficient reason for choosing a particular salvor. The best references are former customers for salvage services. If a salvor pleads confidentiality as a reason for not revealing customers' names and contacts, throw his telephone number away. There is some reason he does not want you to talk to his customers. Self-aggrandizing and chest-thumping by salvors creates wariness, not confidence.

Capability—capability claimed by salvors should be demonstrable. As difficult as it may be to believe, salvors have been known to inflate things like tug speeds, horsepower, and bollard pulls ever so slightly in an effort to lock up a job. Take time to ask the hard questions; it can save time and grief in the long term.

Response time—how quickly can the salvor be on site and with what resources? A very rapid response with limited resources may gain nothing but more mouths to feed on the casualty. A salvor who can deliver more useful resources a little more slowly may be the best choice.

Regional experience—a salvor should have specific experience in the region in which the casualty lies. Such experience leads to knowledge of the geography and bathymetry of the salvage site, specialized techniques for the area, logistics requirements and methods, industrial support availability, local cabotage laws, local environmental regulations, and the quirks of working effectively with local authorities.

Pollution consciousness—the threat of environmental damage is so pervasive in casualty operations that salvors must take it into account with a responsible attitude. A salvor who implies in any way that environmental matters may be given lip service can cause an owner more headaches than he needs. All casualties are environmentally sensitive. Salvors and shipowners must be also. Environmental sensitivity and preventive measures—absolutely necessary or not—are cheaper than environmental damage.

Financial stability—this is a consideration, particularly with smaller regional salvors. The salvor must be in a position to carry the jobs on the contract terms. A salvage contractor who goes belly-up in the midst of an operation may leave the owners and insurers in serious trouble.

Several sources of information and assistance are available to assist owners in the selection of salvors. These include salvage consultants, along with lawyers, insurers, and others in the usual maritime network. The owners, lawyers, and insurers may know a consultant who can assist in salvor selection. Usually, an owner is in a position to play hardball with a salvor when that salvor is not the only game in town. Owners have the problem, but they are the ones spending money the salvors are hungry for.

In what may seem to be contrary advice, the owner should not delay the initiation of action by haggling and putting off a decision to initiate salvage services. Salvors can be fired when they do not perform. The conditions of the casualty may make a quick contract with the first available salvage contractor the best choice. Choice of salvage contractor, like most decisions in salvage, is driven by the conditions of the moment and the information on hand.

The owner may also choose a salvor who is not a professional salvor, and make what is euphemistically known as "alternative arrangements" by hiring another type of marine company (a yellow pages salvor or a consultant) to act as general contractor and salvage master for the operation. In some parts of the world this may offer the only workable solution to a time-critical problem. In others it may offer an opportunity, real or illusory, to save money. Such alternative arrangements and the hazards they represent have been discussed earlier in this chapter where an analogy is drawn with bargain brain surgery.

Consultants and Surveyors

Consultants and surveyors are part of the casualty management team. These people should have a high level of experience in casualties, understand salvage business and contracting, and be conversant with the proper roles of all the parties, especially the party they represent. Appreciation by all consultants and surveyors that they can serve their principals without those interests always being overriding is very helpful to a smooth operation.

There are many consultants and surveyors representing a broad range of expertise scattered about the world. Outfits dealing with many casualties—hull underwriters, P&I clubs, etc.—often have individuals they normally employ. Consultants and surveyors who have been on the dirty end of the salvage stick, that is, have actually been salvage officers concerned with both the technical and commercial ends of salvage, are most effective as salvage consultants. Geographical experience is important, because methods vary with geography. For instance, salvage in Northern Europe is very different from salvage in the Pacific, and consultants in North America need a working knowledge of national and regional pollution laws and regulations.

Most surveyors deal infrequently with major casualties and have little qualification to take a major role. Casualty management in any capacity, like any knowledge-based skill, requires practice. Most surveyors recognize their limitations and act accordingly. They are very useful in providing initial inputs, assisting with local knowledge, and providing specialized information. Unfortunately, a small minority of surveyors fails to recognize that their talent and experience do not lie in salvage and develop a bad habit of standing up when they should shut up.

Initial Response

A problem in any complex casualty is choosing the aspect of the casualty to attack first. The answer seems obvious and simple: attack the part of the casualty that presents the greatest danger first. However, the greatest danger is not always clear-cut. Is the greatest danger one that can cause loss of property or one likely to cause environmental damage? In modern salvage it is almost always environmental damage. Can the danger of environmental damage be attacked indirectly? For example, can environmental damage be minimized by leaving potential pollutants in place in the ship and salvaging the ship? Is some level of environmental damage permissible to forestall greater damage? Can a portion of polluting cargo be jettisoned to allow the ship to be salvaged without spilling the remainder of the cargo?

Skillful management of casualties requires that conflicting requirements be balanced carefully and that clear priorities be set. At all phases of the casualty, real or perceived environmental concerns require attention. Special attention to these concerns, *even at the cost of delaying noncritical salvage actions*, may be necessary at the outset to establish that casualty managers are concerned with the environment. Establishing this perception with authorities and regulators can pay big dividends in cooperation as the salvage operation proceeds.

There are no cookbook solutions for setting priorities and choosing initial response. The correct action is different for every casualty and requires immediate realization on the part of the casualty managers of the scope of the entire problem. A major and most difficult requirement is a rapid recognition of the governing factors in a particular casualty. The entire tone of the work can be set and the foundation for technical and commercial success or failure laid by the initial response.

Navigation of the Casualty and in the Casualty Area

Casualty management necessarily includes the practical business of navigation in and around the casualty area and navigation of the casualty to a port. Waters in which casualties occur seldom have been charted recently enough or with sufficient accuracy or detail for total dependence on published charts and sailing directions. Putting a tug or salvage ship aground because of insufficient attention to detail in navigating in the salvage area is not only expensive and likely to delay the operation—it quite correctly makes the salvor look like an incompetent fool.

A casualty is not a normal ship; its inherent ability to maneuver and stay afloat and upright is compromised. Good seamen, wise salvors, owners, and regulators treat a casualty like an invalid, with consideration and respect for its limitations. They do not put a casualty in a position that would be hazardous for intact ships navigated to a high standard. GPS and other electronic navigation systems should be checked by comparing the positions obtained from them with positions plotted by conventional navigational methods. Charted positions of reefs, islands, etc., are not always consistent with positions obtained by electronic means. The differences can be the difference between one casualty and two or more in restricted waters.

Salvors should survey waters around and approaches to a casualty as soon as practical to assure that ships expected to maneuver in these waters can do so safely. The surveys should mark depths; check bottom contours and clearances from shoal waters; and mark danger bearings and shoals, rocks, and obstructions on approaches in areas where ground tackle can be laid, or where tugs, salvage vessels, lightering vessels, or the casualty are likely to maneuver during or after the operation. Approach routes and routes away from the site should be laid out with as much care and in at least as much detail as goes into any voyage plan preparation. Extraordinary caution is justified. The price of an error—a salvage or supporting ship becoming a casualty, or the casualty becoming a casualty for the second time—is just too high to risk when the precautions are both very simple and good seamanship.

Masters of vessels entering the area should be given a chart and visual tour of the area before taking their ships into it. When it is impossible to make these tours, they should maneuver with extreme care until they are fully familiar with the operating area. After they have gained this familiarity, extra caution is still called for.

Night operations with ships close to one another or in restricted or shoal waters should be avoided unless immediate danger to the casualty requires immediate action and warrants the risk. Darkness adds another seriously limiting factor to operations in restricted shoal waters. It is particularly unwise to take the first salvage vessel or tug into the area at night if delaying the operation until there is light is not a hazard to the casualty.

Local knowledge of the area can be extremely helpful but should be evaluated carefully to assure that the conditions are safe for the vessels to be brought in and that the salvors and local people are "singing from the same sheet."

The salvage site may contain environmentally sensitive areas. These areas may be identified early in the operation by environmental authorities. Salvors should work with both environmental authorities and the representative of the casualty's pollution insurance carrier to identify and protect these areas and thereby to reduce potential claims for environmental damage. Most important of all, whenever possible, operations should be kept clear of sensitive areas. Close cooperation with environmental interests is in the salvor's interest, for it opens the possibility of an Article 14 award as well as avoiding liability.

Good casualty management requires a plan for handling the casualty after refloating. The first step is a complete set of soundings of all tanks, bilges, and other spaces to define the internal of the ship, to locate any flooding or unexpected conditions, and to decide which of the selected options is most appropriate. Deflection readings of motorships should be taken on the main engine and the rudder operated while the casualty is either under tow or controlled by tugs or ground tackle.

An underwater survey of a refloated ship normally is called for, but an underwater survey in open water is of little value and can be a waste of precious time if the ship is secure and able to make a voyage or voyage-in-tow to sheltered waters. In the open sea, divers have great difficulty in making accurate surveys, even with underwater video. They have even more difficulty making underwater repairs. Whenever it is practical to do so, the casualty should be taken to sheltered waters for the survey.

The route to sheltered waters should be selected, plotted, and cleared with local authorities before the ship refloats. Local authorities have been known to pressure salvors to take the casualty into some convenient dog hole (protected cove or inlet) for the survey. The difficulties and dangers of taking the casualty into waters that only smaller ships normally navigate should be carefully balanced against the advantages of doing so. It is very easy to wind up with the casualty aground or with the bottom ripped out. Remote dog holes on occasion may be suited for underwater surveys but are not necessarily good locations for emergency repairs. It is normally much more convenient to take the ship to a port where there is some degree of industrial and transportation support.

Any route the casualty follows should be selected to reduce the danger from navigational accident. It may be necessary to choose between a route that is environmentally safe but dangerous, and one that passes environmentally sensitive areas. Choices must be made individually, but protecting the sensitive areas during the casualty's passage may be cheap compared to the risk of a second casualty.

Decision Making

Clear, positive decision making is vital throughout any salvage operation. No room exists for error, equivocation, or delay. Poor decisions can result in catastrophic consequences. Salvage work demands logical, methodical, and effective decisions—the kind that can be reached only through a logical, methodical, effective decision-making process.

In a casualty three influences work against good decisions:

1. The situation is dynamic. Many of the dynamic influences, especially weather, are completely beyond the control of the people on the scene.
2. A clear and complete picture of the situation is not available in the beginning and may never be. Accordingly, salvage plans and decisions are made with limited information and must be continuously modified and updated as better information becomes available. Opportunities for error are legion.
3. Casualties always deteriorate with time. It is not possible to delay decisions without increasing the risk to property and the risk of environmental damage.

Salvage and military decision making are identical. A well-qualified professional capable of evaluating and extrapolating information and recommendations of advisers makes timely, effective decisions. Only such authoritarian decisions by a single professional are effective throughout salvage operations. Unlike oil spills, forest fires, floods, or other prolonged disasters, salvage operations never move beyond the immediate emergency phase. Salvage operations never reach the point where many organizations are involved and democratic decisions are appropriate. Attempts at democratic or committee decisions in salvage serve only to delay the operation and divert effort from effective salvage, usually with catastrophic results.

Analysis of and response to casualties require expert knowledge applied expertly. Salvage decisions are time-critical, on-the-feet judgments, requiring practical seamanship, seat-of-the-pants engineering, and the ability to analyze, extrapolate, and decide. Where the buck stopped has been clear in the past under no cure–no pay open form contracts. The salvage master was in charge; the decisions were his. Now the situation is not always so clear.

At each step of a salvage operation the decision maker may have several options, none of which is an optimum, or even a particularly good, solution. The decision maker must have the expert knowledge to choose the best of poor choices. A committee can skew the decision away from a hard, operationally sound decision toward a compromise that may not only be unsatisfactory to everyone but may make the situation worse.

Knowledge and experience with marine casualties are not widespread in the marine industry. Most mariners go through their entire careers without becoming involved with a major casualty. Regulators, even seamen, may have a smattering of knowledge in a wide variety of maritime matters without deep experience and true expertise in any. Representatives of interested environmental agencies may be on very unfamiliar territory aboard a casualty. Only those who deal with casualties regularly have the expertise necessary to make soundly based decisions.

An unproductive situation arises when a regulatory body directs or forbids specific salvage actions. Often, these directions are given against the advice and over the objections of the experienced salvage people technically and financially responsible for the salvage operation. Regulatory authorities may have so much power that the only choices are to follow the direction or appeal to higher authority. At best, time is wasted during the appeal and energy is diverted from solving the problem. At worst, inappropriate directed action may remove viable options and degrade overall operational effectiveness. It is particularly troubling to those bearing operational responsibility when the regulators give direction without assuming liability for the results.

The proliferation of environmental regulations and the variation among jurisdictions complicate salvage decision making. It is virtually impossible for a salvor to be expert in all the environmental regulations in a reasonably sized operations area. Without that expertise, a salvor may make an operationally sound decision that inadvertently violates one or more environmental regulations and incur criminal or civil penalties. More insidious and potentially dangerous, threat of environmental penalties may force the choice of an operationally and technically poor option. In marine casualty operations, the risk of penalties from inadvertent and unintentional violation of the ever-increasing volumes of environmental regulations is very real. An operator must protect himself by pricing his services higher or avoiding operations in which the risk is present. A wise operator also retains competent legal counsel specifically experienced in environmental law in the jurisdiction where he operates.

Attorneys—even one's own attorney—and the media can inhibit effective salvage decision making. Attorneys properly act as advocates for their clients and represent only their interests. Strong advocacy of a particular position during a dynamic emergency can delay the decision-making process and lead away from the soundest decision. Media reports, developed without adequate technical knowledge, may alter public perception of the operation away from the true situation and raise public pressure for a specific action. Regulators are sensitive and responsive to public pressure.

Professional management and supervision of salvage operations is mandatory. Every marine casualty operation, by its nature, involves unknowns and decisions that must be made on the spot and without equivocation by professional decision makers. People get hurt when decision makers equivocate or are directed away from sound decisions during casualty operations.

On-Site

The front lines of casualty management are on the site aboard the casualty. As has been emphasized often throughout this book, there are many parties with different interests in any salvage operation. Surveyors or consultants with different levels of expertise in the particular type of salvage in progress represent most interests at the site. It is not essential that these people cooperate. They may each represent their principal's interest alone and take no interest in the work as a whole. If they do, the job—and the work of the lawyers that follows the actual salvage work—is likely to be drawn out and very expensive.

While elements that could lead to adversarial relationships are present, there is neither room for nor purpose to these kinds of relations at the salvage site. The salvage operation is not a competition; the goal of everyone at the salvage site is to salvage the casualty with a minimum of environmental damage and maximum retention of value. Operations go much better and are more likely to reach these goals when each person with responsibilities in casualty management functions as a team member.

Good communication among the parties at the site is essential to an efficient operation. Good communication means sharing of knowledge among all the parties. There is no question that the salvage master is in charge, but a wise salvage master has the confidence to listen to, evaluate, absorb, and act upon or reject the knowledge other experienced people bring to the operation.

Frequent, regular meetings of all concerned are essential to good communication. Meetings should take place daily and whenever significant events are planned, results of action are available, or plans change. These meetings provide a forum for the exchange and discussion of ideas and concerns by all parties. These meetings should never be omitted and should never be replaced by informal exchanges on deck. Someone always fails to get—or misunderstands—the information, and the first links of error chains are forged.

Meetings in which persons taking part in specific evolutions discuss all plans fully are particularly important. All persons must come away from these meetings with a clear idea of the purposes and procedures and, especially, of their role. During an evolution, senior people must be alert to loss of situational awareness or other evidence of error chain development. This alertness must apply to all hands—not just to those being supervised directly.

Frequent, written reports from the salvage master to the master and from the salvage master or the salvor's home office to the owner are useful. The Japanese Shipping Exchange, Inc., Salvage Agreement requires written daily reports from the salvor to the master and owner. The master and owner should be given access to and, whenever possible, copies of all surveys, calculations, plans, and other documents that affect the operation and the safety of the ship.

The salvage master, being in charge of the salvage operation, does not alter the master's authority. The master remains in command of the ship and has a responsibility to ensure that he is fully aware of any salvage actions, particularly those that affect the safety of the ship and the crew. When the salvor does not provide complete information on the operation, the master and the owner have the right and duty to request the salvor to stop his services; the salvor must comply.

The master and all consultants and surveyors should cooperate fully with the salvors unless the salvors' proposed actions threaten the ship or the environment. The salvors at the same time should cooperate fully with the master and surveyors or consultants, particularly in matters concerning the cargo and handling and other idiosyncrasies of the ship. Mutual respect on the part of all parties goes a long way toward making a cohesive ad hoc organization for the duration of the operation.

Teamwork is the key word, not only teamwork among the salvage crew but teamwork on the part of all hands connected with the salvage operation. The aim of everyone is to save the value of the ship and the cargo and to prevent environmental damage. Each casualty has unique features so that no action at a casualty site should become casual or routine. The principles of the concept of bridge team management that have become widely accepted in the maritime industry are equally applicable to casualty management.

Health, Safety, and Comfort

Health, safety, and comfort belong in a single grouping and are a major casualty management factor that concerns the salvor and the master and owner.

Housekeeping on a casualty is difficult. The ship is out of its normal routine and normal services may be reduced and salvage crew and surveyors may crowd accommodations. Work and living generates extra trash, garbage, and debris. Under these conditions, ships often become progressively dirtier as the salvage operation goes along. There is no excuse for allowing the ship to become dirty. The master and the salvage master should reach agreement on the measures necessary to keep the casualty sanitary and free from unnecessary risks arising from dirt and debris.

Salvage crew, like beasts of burden, must be fed, watered, and allowed to rest. Under the best of circumstances, the former are treated considerably better than the latter; under the worst of circumstances, the situation reverses. When no specialized salvage craft with accommodation for salvage crew is at the site, salvage crew must be accommodated aboard the casualty. Casualties offer a broad range of accommodation to crew, from staterooms with toilets and showers and separate mess rooms to coils of line in the forecastle and "Don't ask me for a drink of water, Mate, get your own." Whenever it is at all possible, salvors should have at least a warm, dry place to sleep, food, water, and facilities for washing to keep minimum cleanliness standards. These minimum facilities are necessary to keep salvors in a mental and physical state to do their work effectively and safely. Salvors should be offered—or find, when it is not offered—a place where they can shelter from the weather, eat meals in their working clothes, rest, and gather to discuss the job or take a blow. Under some circumstances, establishing a rough camp ashore may be the most practical way to accommodate salvors decently.

Feeding salvors can present a special problem. Salvors need a reasonably high caloric intake in a form they recognize and are comfortable with to permit them to work without excessive fatigue. When working from a salvage ship, selection of meal hours and the food served are completely within the control of the salvors. Money spent by the salvage company on feeding salvage crew is well spent. When necessary, a good salvage crew can work a long time on cold corned beef, but a well-fed crew that gets regular hot meals does its job faster and better. Salvage crews accommodated aboard casualties may find food from a very different culture unpalatable. In such cases it may become necessary for salvors to bring aboard and prepare their own food.

Cleanliness helps maintain crew morale and efficiency. When salvage crew is accommodated on the casualty and water rationing is in effect, the hours when water is available should be juggled to assure that both salvors and ship's company coming off watch or shift have water for basic ablutions. Whenever conditions permit, salvors should be offered an opportunity to wash their coveralls, both for the boost in morale a clean set of coveralls brings and for prevention of diseases associated with being dirty.

Salvors are used to make-do accommodations and may sleep where they drop in the engine room or on deck. Salvors normally work hard for long hours; they need their sleep and should be allowed to get it wherever they fall. Waking people unnecessarily is stupid, can be dangerous, and is not in anyone's interest.

FINALE

The preceding several hundred pages have discussed some aspects of the fascinating business of marine salvage. Not every aspect has been covered. The problems and solutions faced in the most routine salvage operation are so diverse that there may be no way to do so. Only two things are constant in salvage: the need to think and the need to use common sense. Most of all to think.

APPENDIX

A

SALVAGE CALCULATIONS

Some calculations are required on all salvage operations. Simple jobs may need nothing more than a few simple calculations that can be jotted down in the salvage master's pocket notebook. Most operations require the presence of a naval architect with portable computational tools (calculators, programmable calculators, or notebook computers on-site). The most complex require off-site analysis with mainframe computer. The very large majority of salvage calculations are straightforward and repetitious. Some are tedious.

Common calculations in salvage include:

Basic naval architectural calculations.

Stability calculations.

Grounding calculations.

Weight management, displacement, and trim calculations.

Strength calculations.

Cargo calculations.

General nautical calculations.

Plant's *Formulae for the Mariner* is an excellent companion for this Appendix.[1]

Everyone in the management of a casualty needs to be able to make and understand basic salvage calculations. Most calculations are made by computer or at least with an engineering calculator. Salvors must be prepared for dead batteries—that is, those situations where they cannot foist the work off onto chips and must do it the hard way. Doing it the hard way demands that the salvor knows precisely what he is doing with the calculation and does not just plug in a formula.

Ships' on-board load computers can be used within the limits of their programming for stability and strength calculations. With a little imagination, ground reaction can be simulated by varying loading. Flooding can be accounted for by ballasting or loading the affected space.

Notebook computers are invaluable to engineers aboard casualties, particularly when there are repetitious calculations or examination of a number of similar conditions. A number of excellent salvage engineering programs exist. Most are designed for and should be operated by engineers or naval architects who understand the limits of the program, particularly how it applies—or does not apply—to the problem at hand.

Ships are for the most part irregularly shaped, thus the geometric characteristics are difficult to calculate. A working knowledge of an old standby of naval architects, approximation of geometric characteristics by numerical integration, is invaluable for salvors. These techniques can be used equally for calculations made by hand, by calculator, or by computer. They are especially useful when computers without specialized programs are used and the calculation is developed on a spreadsheet.

Throughout this book equations have been presented for many of the calculations common in salvage. No examples have accompanied these equations. Instead, the examples have been collected in this Appendix. This Appendix presents a sample calculation for each equation presented in the text in the sequence in which the equations appear. In normal salvage calculations one or more of the quantities for the equation must be estimated from the salvor's store of knowledge and experience. This Appendix spares the user that agony by presenting all needed information for the examples.

The organization of this Appendix bears some explanation. The examples are divided into five groups:

1. Numerical Integration
2. Naval Architecture, Stability, and Strength
3. Oil-Water Hydrostatics
4. Rigging
5. General Salvage Calculations

Group 1 describes a technique that is general and is not specifically addressed in the text. Groups 2, 3, and 4 address equations presented in Chapters 2, 5, and 7, respectively, and Group 5 addresses equations from Chapters 4, 8, 9, 11, and 12. The equations are numbered sequentially.

To help the user locate a specific example quickly, table A-1 gives the example number, title, and page references in this Appendix and in the text.

TABLE A-1. EXAMPLE LISTING.

Example Number	*Example Title*	*Example Page*	*Text Reference Page*
Group 1: Numerical Integration			
1	Area of Waterplane	568	None
2	Displacement	570	None
3	Center of Gravity	571	None
4	Moment of Inertia	572	None
Group 2: Naval Architecture, Stability, and Strength			
5	Block Coefficient	573	50, 51
6	Midships Section Coefficient	574	51
7	Waterplane Coefficient	574	51, 53
8	Estimated Block Coefficient	575	51, 53
9	Estimated Waterplane Coefficient	575	53
10	Tons per Inch (TPI) (Tonnes per Centimeter [TPC]) Immersion	576	53, 54
11	Height of the Center of Buoyancy (KB)	577	55
12	Longitudinal Position of the Center of Buoyancy (LCB)	578	55
13	Position of the Center of Flotation (LCF)	578	56
14	Metacentric Radius (BM)	579	59
15	Height of the Center of Gravity (KG)	579	54
16	Metacentric Height (GM)	580	60
17	Movement of the Center of Gravity	581	61, 62
18	List from Weight Movement	582	62
19	Free Surface	582	63–64
20	Free Communication	583	64
21	Longitudinal Metacentric Radius (BM_L)	583	70
22	Longitudinal Metacentric Height (GM_L)	584	70
23	Moment to Trim One Inch (MT1) (Centimeter [MTC])	584	54, 70–71
24	Trim Calculation	585	72
25	Lightship Weight Distribution	587	75–76
26	Buoyancy Curve	589	77–78
27	Bending Strength	590	79–80

Example Number	*Example Title*	*Example Page*	*Text Reference Page*
28	Minimum Section Modulus	600	81
	Group 3: Oil-Water Hydrostatics		
29	Conversion between Specific and API Gravities	601	133
30	Hydrostatic Pressure inside and outside a Tank	601	134
31	Water Bottom Depth	603	138–39
	Group 4: Rigging		
32	Estimated Breaking Strength of Wire Rope	604	175
33	Estimated Breaking Strength of Fiber Rope	604	185
34	Snapback Energy	604	187
35	Storage Volume for Faked Rope	605	188–89
36	Length of Rope That Can Be Stored on a Drum	605	188–89
37	Weight of Chain	605	192
38	Approximate Breaking Strength and Proof Loads of Chain	606	192–93
39	Safe Working Load of Shackles	608	196
40	Safe Working Load of Hooks	608	197
41	Actual Mechanical Advantage	608	201, 246
42	Sling Leg Tension	609	207
	Group 5: General Salvage Calculations		
43	Height of Tide at Any Time	609	98
44	Ground Reaction	610	101
45	Neutral Loading Point	612	102–3
46	Change in Ground Reaction Caused by Tide	613	103
47	Virtual Rise in Center of Gravity from Grounding	613	105
48	Tractive Force to Free a Ship	613	223
49	Effective Force	614	235
50	Bollard Pull	614	236
51	Holding Power of an Anchor	615	242

GROUP 1—NUMERICAL INTEGRATION

All numerical integration works by approximating the shape with a standard type curve, dividing a curvilinear figure into a number of segments, and calculating the area under the curve. There are a number of rules; each has its advantages. The two most common rules are the Trapezoidal Rule and Simpson's First Rule. Both are explained with examples below.

Detailed naval architectural calculations by hand are seldom necessary in modern salvage. Detailed hydrostatic information is available from the owners or builders of most ships. With older ships, the situation is often such that detailed calculations are unnecessary or not permitted by the time available. The techniques, like celestial navigation in the age of GPS, are still valuable and a basic skill for professionals, who must understand not only how to use them but when it is appropriate to do so.

In practice, since ships are symmetrical about the centerline waterplanes, midships sections and the like are usually cut along the centerline and the half area calculated. *The result must be multiplied by 2 to get the full area.* Failing to multiply by 2 is a common mistake that induces a feeling of total stupidity upon discovery.

The Trapezoidal Rule

The Trapezoidal Rule divides a curvilinear figure into a number of trapezoids with bases of equal length, as shown in figure A–1 on page 594. The area of each trapezoid is:

$$A = h \times \frac{(y_1 + y_2)}{2}$$

where:

A = area under the curve in appropriate square units

h = interval between ordinates, the length of the base of the trapezoid in linear units

y = height of the ordinates in linear units

For adjacent trapezoids the expression becomes:

$$A = \frac{h}{2} \times ((y_1 + y_2) + (y_2 + y_3))$$

which is:

$$A = \frac{h}{2} \times (y_1 + 2y_2 + y_3)$$

then generalized as:

$$A = \frac{h}{2} \times (y_1 + 2y_2 + 2y_3 \ldots\ldots + 2y_{(n-1)} + y_n)$$

also expressed as:

$$A = h \times (\frac{y_1}{2} + y_2 + y_3 \ldots\ldots + y_{(n-1)} + \frac{y_n}{2})$$

The Trapezoidal Rule is best suited for long radius, rather flat curves, such as ship's waterlines. The calculated area is smaller than the actual area of convex curves and larger than the actual area of concave curves. Accuracy decreases with increasing curvature and increases as the base is shortened and the ordinates move closer together.

On very shapely curves, ordinates at half the standard base length improve accuracy. With this method the multipliers for the ordinates change. It is better to calculate the multipliers following the basic principles of the rule rather than attempting to memorize them or use them as reproduced in a text.

Simpson's First Rule

Simpson's First Rule, the most common numerical approximation for ship calculations and the one that all grey-haired naval architects learned in school, approaches the problem the same way as the Trapezoidal Rule with the important exception that the boundary (curve) is replaced by a second order parabola rather than a series of trapezoids. The base is divided into an even number of equal-length segments giving an odd number of ordinates.

The resulting equation is:

$$A = \frac{h}{3} \times (y_1 + 4y_2 + 2y_3 + 4y_4 + 2y_5 + \ldots\ldots + 2y_{n-2} + 4y_{n-1} + y_n)$$

For the special case of three ordinates, the multipliers are 1-4-1.

Other rules for numerical integration exist, but are not used as frequently as Simpson's First and the Trapezoidal Rules. Simpson's First Rule is so common and so useful that naval architectural students have been heard mumbling 1-4-2-4-2-4-1 in their sleep. The other rules offer no advantage in salvage calculations and will not be discussed further.

Applications of Numerical Integration

Tabular formats are best for most numerical integrations.

Example 1—Area of a Waterplane

The half waterplane of a ship has been divided into stations spaced 52 feet apart. Ordinates are as shown in the following tables. Calculate the area of the waterplane by the Trapezoidal Rule and Simpson's First Rule.

TABLE A-2. AREA BY TRAPEZOIDAL RULE AND BY SIMPSON'S FIRST RULE.

Area by Trapezoidal Rule			
Station	*Ordinate*	*Multiplier*	*f(A)*
0	0.00	0.50	0.00
1	9.25	1.00	9.25
2	21.85	1.00	21.85
3	32.70	1.00	32.70
4	37.65	1.00	37.65
5	38.00	1.00	38.00

Table A-2 continued on next page

Table A-2 continued

Area by Trapezoidal Rule			
Station	*Ordinate*	*Multiplier*	*f(A)*
6	38.00	1.00	38.00
7	37.45	1.00	37.45
8	31.75	1.00	31.75
9	18.10	1.00	18.10
10	8.70	0.50	4.35
		SUM f(A)	269.10
		S	52.00
		HALF AREA	13,993.20
		AREA	27,986.40
Area by Simpson's First Rule			
Station	*Ordinate*	*Multiplier*	*f(A)*
0	0.00	1.00	0.00
1	9.25	4.00	37.00
2	21.85	2.00	43.70
3	32.70	4.00	130.80
4	37.65	2.00	75.30
5	38.00	4.00	152.00
6	38.00	2.00	76.00
7	37.45	4.00	149.80
8	31.75	2.00	63.50
9	18.10	4.00	72.40
10	8.70	1.00	8.70
		SUM f(A)	809.20
		S	52.00
		HALF AREA	14,026.13
		AREA	28,052.27

The same rules may be used to find the volume of irregular three-dimensional figures by considering the area of evenly spaced slices as the ordinates. Typically, displacement volume and displacement can be calculated from the areas of waterplanes or from areas of transverse sections.

Example 2—Displacement

The underwater portion of a vessel is divided into transverse sections 10 feet apart. The whole section areas are as given in the table below. What is the displacement volume?

TABLE A-3. VOLUME BY TRAPEZOIDAL RULE AND BY SIMPSON'S FIRST RULE.

Volume by Trapezoidal Rule			
Station	*Ordinate*	*Multiplier*	*f(A)*
1	0.30	0.50	0.15
2	22.70	1.00	22.70
3	48.80	1.00	48.80
4	73.30	1.00	73.30
5	88.40	1.00	88.40
6	82.80	1.00	82.80
7	58.70	1.00	58.70
8	26.20	1.00	26.20
9	3.90	0.50	1.95
		SUM f(A)	403.00
		S	10.00
		VOLUME	4,030.00 CU FT
Volume by Simpson's First Rule			
Station	*Area*	*Multiplier*	*f(A)*
1	0.30	1.00	0.30
2	22.70	4.00	90.80
3	48.80	2.00	97.60
4	73.20	4.00	292.80
5	88.40	2.00	176.80
6	82.80	4.00	331.20
7	58.70	2.00	117.40
8	26.20	4.00	104.80
9	3.90	1.00	3.90
		SUM f(A)	1,215.60
		S	10.00
		VOLUME	4,052.00 CU FT

Two other uses for numerical integration, calculation of centers of gravity and of moments of inertia, are described below. In these and other applications the Trapezoidal Rule, Simpson's First Rule, and the numerical integration methods can be used. In the interest of simplicity, only examples for Simpson's First Rule are presented.

The procedure is:

1. Set the table up with ordinates and multipliers for calculating f(A) in the same manner as with a normal area calculation.
2. Calculate the values for f(A), then sum as in an area calculation.
3. Assign lever arms to each station. Lever arms are usually assigned from the midships station and position of the center of gravity expressed relative to this station. Assignment of the lever arm to the midships station rather than an end or other station is purely a matter of convenience.
4. Calculate f(M) at each station by multiplying the lever arm.
5. Sum f(M) separately for the forward and after sections.
6. Take the difference of the two sums.
7. Now:

$$\mathrm{CG} = \frac{\mathrm{diff\ f\,(M)} \times \frac{1}{3} \times \mathrm{S} \times \mathrm{S} \times 2}{\mathrm{f\,(A)} \times \frac{1}{3} \times \mathrm{S} \times 2}$$

which with cancellations:

$$\mathrm{CG} = \frac{\mathrm{diff\ f\,(M)}}{\mathrm{f\,(A)}} \times \mathrm{S}$$

Example 3—Center of Gravity

Find the center of gravity of the waterplane whose half ordinates are given in example 1.

TABLE A-4. CENTER OF GRAVITY BY SIMPSON'S FIRST RULE.

Station	*Ord*	*Mult*	*f(A)*	*Lever from*	*f(M)*	
				Amidships		
0	0.00	1.00	0.00	5	0	
1	9.25	4.00	37.00	4	148.0	
2	21.85	2.00	43.70	3	131.1	
3	32.70	4.00	130.80	2	261.6	

Table A-4 continued on next page

Table A-4 continued

Station	*Ord*	*Mult*	*f(A)*	*Lever from*	*f(M)*	
				Amidships		
4	37.65	2.00	75.30	1	75.3	
5	38.00	4.00	152.00	0	SUM f(M) f	616
6	38.00	2.00	76.00	1	76.0	
7	37.45	4.00	149.80	2	299.6	
8	31.75	2.00	63.50	3	190.5	
9	18.10	4.00	72.40	4	289.6	
10	8.70	1.00	8.70	5	43.5	
		SUM f(A)	809.20		SUM f(M) a =	899.2
					DIFF =	283.2
					DIFF/SUM f(A)	0.349975
					S	52
					CG	18.19871
					CG is abaft station 5	

Example 4—Moment of Inertia about the Centerline of a Plane Curvilinear Figure by Simpson's Rule

Calculation of the moment of inertia (second moment of area) about the centerline employs the equation:

$$I = \int \frac{1}{3} ydxy^2 \text{ or } I = \frac{1}{3} \int y^3 dx$$

It may be approximated with Simpson's First Rule by:

1. Using the half ordinates of a plane curvilinear figure such as a waterplane;
2. Substituting the common interval (CI) for dx; and
3. Multipying by 2 to account for both sides of the figure.

The equation then becomes:

$$I = \frac{2}{3} CI \times \sum f(I)$$

where f(I) is the half ordinate cubed times the appropriate Simpson's Multiplier

To find the moment of inertia about its centerline for the waterplane given in Example 1, a table of the usual sort is set up:

TABLE A-5. MOMENT OF INERTIA BY SIMPSON'S RULE.

Station	*Ordinate (y)*	y^3	*SM*	*f(I)*
0	0.00	0	1	0
1	9.25	791.45	4	3165.80
2	21.85	10,431.68	2	20,863.13
3	32.70	34,965.78	4	139,863.13
4	37.65	53,369.72	2	106,739.44
5	38.00	54,872.00	4	219,488.00
6	38.00	54,872.00	2	109,744.00
7	37.45	52,523.72	4	210,094.87
8	31.75	32,005.98	2	64,011.97
9	19.10	6,967.87	4	27,871.48
10	8.70	658.50	4	658.50
			Sum	902,500.58
		Interval	52	
			I (ft^4)	31,286,668.85

GROUP 2—NAVAL ARCHITECTURE, STABILITY, AND STRENGTH

Example 5—Block Coefficient

A containership is 581 feet (177.1 meters) between perpendiculars, has a beam of 78 feet (23.78 meters), and draws 31.5 feet (9.60 meters) with a displacement of 24,848 tons (25,300 tonnes). What is the block coefficient?

Displacement volume must be used in lieu of displacement tonnage:

$$V = 35 \times \Delta$$

where:

V = displacement volume in cubic feet (cubic meters)

Δ = displacement in tons (tonnes)

In this case:

$$V = 35 \times 24{,}848$$

and:

$$C_B = \frac{V}{L \times B \times T}$$

$$C_B = \frac{35 \times 24{,}848}{581 \times 78 \times 31.5}$$

$$C_B = 0.609$$

in SI units:

$$C_B = \frac{25{,}300 \times 0.975}{177.1 \times 23.78 \times 9.60}$$

$$C_B = 0.610$$

Example 6—Midships Section Coefficient

The area of the midships section, A_M, in the same ship is 2,396 square feet (222.7 square meters). What is the midships section coefficient?

$$C_M = \frac{A_M}{B \times T}$$

$$C_M = \frac{2{,}396}{78 \times 31.5}$$

$$C_M = 0.975$$

in SI units:

$$A_M = \frac{222.7}{23.78 \times 9.6}$$

$$A_M = 0.975$$

Example 7—Waterplane Coefficient

The area of the waterplane in the same ship is 33,535 square feet (3,117 square meters). What is the waterplane coefficient?

$$C_{WP} = \frac{A_{WP}}{L \times B}$$

$$A_{WP} = \frac{33{,}535}{581 \times 78}$$

$$A_{WP} = 0.740$$

in SI units:

$$A_{WP} = \frac{3{,}117}{177.1 \times 23.78}$$

$$A_{WP} = 0.740$$

Example 8—Estimated Block Coefficient

A 581-foot containership has a service speed of 20 knots. Estimate the block coefficient.

$$C_B = k \times (1.10736 - 0.550401 \times \frac{v}{\sqrt{L}})$$

where:

C_B = block coefficient
v = the service speed of the ship in knots
L = length between perpendiculars in feet
k = a constant that depends upon ship type

TABLE A-6. BLOCK COEFFICIENT CONSTANT.

Ship Type	*k*
Bulk Carrier	1.08
LPG Carrier	1.06
LNG Carrier	1.04
OBO or Lumber Carrier	1.03
Product or Chemical Carrier	1.025
Crude Carrier	1.01
General Cargo Ship	1.00
Containership	0.97
RO/RO	0.95

$$C_B = 1.08 \times (1.10736 - 0.550401 \times \frac{20}{\sqrt{581}})$$

$$C_B = 0.601$$

Example 9—Estimated Waterplane Coefficient

Estimate the waterplane coefficient of a containership with a block coefficient of 0.601.

$$C_{WP} = k + 0.702 \times C_B$$

where k is a constant that varies with ship type:

k = 0.325 for containerships
0.336 for RO/ROs
0.306 for all other types

$$C_{WP} = 0.325 + 0.702 \times C_B$$

$$C_{WP} = 0.325 + 0.702 \times 0.601$$

$$C_{WP} = 0.325 + 0.422$$

$$C_{WP} = 0.747$$

Example 10—Tons per Inch (Tonnes per Centimeter) Immersion

What are the tons per inch and tonnes per centimeter immersion for a containership with the following characteristics:

LBP = 581 feet (177.1 meters)
B = 78 feet (23.78 meters)
C_{WP} = 0.740

1. Tons per inch:

$$TPI = \frac{A_{WP}}{420}$$

$$TPI = \frac{0.74 \times 581 \times 78}{420}$$

$$TPI = 79.85 \text{ tons}$$

2. Tonnes per centimeter:

$$TPC = 0.01025 \times A_{WP}$$

$$TPC = 0.01025 \times 0.74 \times 177.1 \times 23.78$$

$$TPC = 31.94 \text{ tonnes}$$

3. Change in TPI with decrease in draft:

What is the TPI if the ship's mean draft decreases by 4 feet?

$$TPI_2 = TPI_1 \times (1.0 - 0.0075 \times (T_1 - T_2))$$

$$TPI_2 = 79.85 \times (1.0 - 0.0075 \times 4)$$

$$TPI_2 = 77.45 \text{ tons}$$

Example 11—Height of the Center of Buoyancy (KB)

1. What is the height of the center of buoyancy (KB) in a containership drawing 31.5 feet if the ship has a block coefficient of 0.61 and a waterplane coefficient of 0.74?

$$KB = \frac{C_{WP}}{(C_B + C_{WP})} \times T_M$$

$$KB = \frac{0.74}{(0.61 + 0.74)} \times 31.5$$

$$KB = 17.27 \text{ feet}$$

Note that this height is 0.548 of the mean draft. This figure is consistent with the method of making initial estimates (0.55 of mean draft, or a range of 0.53 to 0.58 of mean draft) given in Chapter 3.

2. What is the height of the center of buoyancy by Morrish's formula if:

LBP = 581 feet
B = 78 feet
T_M = 31.5 feet
C_B = 0.61
C_{WP} = 0.74

$$KB = T_M - \left(\frac{1}{3} \times \left(\frac{T_M}{2} + \frac{V}{A_{WP}}\right)\right)$$

$$KB = T_M - \left(\frac{1}{3} \times \left(\frac{T_M}{2} + \frac{(C_B \times L \times B \times T_M)}{(C_{WP} \times L \times B)}\right)\right)$$

$$KB = T_M - \left(\frac{1}{3} \times \left(\frac{T_M}{2} + \frac{C_B \times T_M}{C_{WP}}\right)\right)$$

$$KB = T_M - \left(\frac{T_M}{3} \times \left(\frac{1}{2} + \frac{C_B}{C_{WP}}\right)\right)$$

$$KB = 31.5 - \left(\frac{31.5}{3} \times \left(\frac{1}{2} + \frac{0.61}{0.74}\right)\right)$$

$$KB = 17.59 \text{ feet}$$

Example 12—Longitudinal Position of the Center of Buoyancy (LCB)

What is the longitudinal position of the center of buoyancy in a ship 581 feet long with a block coefficient of 0.61?

$$LCB = L \times (0.5 - (0.160 \times C_B - 0.112))$$

$$LCB = 581 \times (0.5 - (0.160 \times .61 - 0.112))$$

$$LCB = 298.86 \text{ feet abaft the forward perpendicular}$$

Example 13—Position of the Center of Flotation (LCF)

What is the longitudinal position of the center of flotation in a bulk carrier that is 700 feet long and has a service speed of 14 knots?

TABLE A-7. FORMULA FOR LOCATION OF LCF.

Ship Type	*Location of LCF*
Tankers	$LCF = 0.5 \times L \times (\frac{V}{160} + 0.914)$
Bulk carriers	$LCF = 0.485 \times L \times (\frac{V}{100} + 0.90)$
Single-screw cargo	$LCF = 0.50 \times L \times (\frac{V}{135} + 0.924)$
Twin-screw cargo transom sterns	$LCF = 0.50 \times L \times (\frac{0.95}{V} + 1.03)$
Twin-screw cargo cruiser sterns	$LCF = (0.50 \times L \times (\frac{V}{135} + 0.23)) \times L$

$$LCF = 0.485 \times L \times (\frac{V}{100} + 0.90)$$

where:

LCF = longitudinal position of the center of flotation in feet from the forward perpendicular

L = length between perpendiculars in feet

V = speed in knots

$$LCF = 0.485 \times 700 \times (\frac{14}{100} + 0.90)$$

$$LCF = 353 \text{ feet}$$

Example 14—Metacentric Radius (BM)

What is the approximate metacentric radius of a ship whose length is 670 feet, beam is 85 feet, draft is 31.5 feet, and that has a block coefficient of 0.71 and a waterplane coefficient of 0.74?

$$BM_T = \frac{C_{IT} \times B^2}{C_B \times T}$$

where:

BM_T = approximate transverse metacentric radius in feet

C_{IT} = transverse inertia coefficient

$$C_{IT} = \frac{C_{wp}^2}{11.7}$$

B = beam in feet

T = draft in feet

C_{wp} = waterplane coefficient

$$C_{IT} = \frac{0.74^2}{11.7}$$

$$C_{IT} = 0.0468$$

$$BM_T = \frac{0.0468 \times 85^2}{0.71 \times 31.5}$$

$$BM_T = 15.21 \text{ feet}$$

Example 15—Height of the Center of Gravity (KG)

1. Salvage estimate:

What is the estimated height of the center of gravity (KG) of a ship with amidships depth of 53 feet?

For an initial "salvage" estimate:

$$KG = 0.60 \times D$$

where:

KG = height of the center of gravity above the keel

D = depth of the hull

$$KG = 0.60 \times 51$$

$$KG = 30.6 \text{ feet}$$

2. Full calculation:

A barge has the following weights aboard with their individual centers of gravity the distance shown above the keel. What is the height of the center of gravity?

TABLE A-8. WEIGHTS AND HEIGHTS OF CENTER OF GRAVITY.

Item	*Weight (w) tons*	*kg (feet)*
Structure	2,715	17
Dry cargo	15,472	19
Liquid cargo	4,200	3.5
Crane	35	37

$$KG = \frac{\Sigma (w \times kg)}{\Sigma w}$$

where:

$\Sigma(w \times kg)$ = the sum of the products of the individual weights and the height of its center of gravity above the keel

Σw = the sum of the individual weights (total weight of the vessel)

TABLE A-9. PRODUCT OF WEIGHTS AND kg.

Item	*Weight (w) tons*	*kg (feet)*	*w x kg*
Structure	2,715	17	46,155
Dry cargo	15,472	19	293,968
Liquid cargo	4,200	3.5	14,700
Crane	35	37	1,295
Σ	22,422		356,118

$$KG = \frac{356{,}118}{22{,}422}$$

$$KG = 15.88 \text{ feet}$$

Example 16—Metacentric Height (GM)

What is the metacentric height in a ship with the following characteristics: KB = 17.59 feet, BM = 15.21 feet, KG = 30.6 feet? Is the ship initially stable?

$$GM = KB + BM - KG$$

where:
GM = metacentric height in feet
KB = height of the center of buoyancy above the keel in feet
BM = metacentric radius in feet
KG = height of the center of gravity above the keel in feet

$$GM = 17.59 + 15.21 - 30.6$$

$$GM = 2.20 \text{ feet}$$

GM is positive. Therefore, the ship is initially stable.

Example 17—Movement of the Center of Gravity

1. New position of the center of gravity:

The original position of the center of gravity of a 35,000-ton (displacement) ship is 11 feet abaft amidships. What is the position of the center of gravity in a 35,000-ton ship if 500 tons is added on the centerline 125 feet forward of midships?

$$D_1 = \frac{(D \times W) + (d \times w)}{(W + w)}$$

where:
D_1 = new distance of the center of gravity from the reference plane
D = original distance of the center of gravity from the reference plane
W = displacement before weight addition or removal
d = distance of the center of gravity of the weight added or removed from the reference plane
w = weight added or removed

$$D_1 = \frac{(-11 \times 35{,}000) + (125 \times 500)}{35{,}000 + 500}$$

$$D_1 = \frac{(-385{,}000 + 62{,}500)}{35{,}500}$$

$$D_1 = 9.085 \text{ feet abaft amidships}$$

2. Distance the center of gravity moves:

How far does the center of gravity move in the previous case?

$$D_1 = \frac{d_G \times w}{W + w}$$

where:

D_1 = the distance between the old and new centers of gravity

d_G = the distance between the center of gravity of the ship and that of the weight being added or removed

w = the weight added

W = the displacement of the ship

$$D_1 = \frac{(11 + 125) \times 500}{35{,}000 + 500}$$

$$D_1 = 1.915 \text{ feet}$$

Not surprising, although it would have been if the result had been anything else!

Example 18—List from Weight Movement

How much list occurs when 500 tons is removed 25 feet from the centerline of a 35,000-ton upright ship with a GM of 3 feet?

$$\Phi = \arctan \frac{w \times d_G}{W \times GM}$$

where all quantities have been defined.

$$\Phi = \arctan \frac{500 \times 25}{34{,}500 \times 3}$$

$$\Phi = 6.89 \text{ degrees}$$

Example 19—Free Surface

What is the virtual rise in the center of gravity (without pocketing) caused by a free surface in a hold 73 feet long and 85 feet wide in a 35,000-ton (displacement) ship?

$$GG_1 = \frac{i}{V}$$

where:

GG_1 = the virtual rise in the center of gravity

i = the moment of inertia of the free surface about the proper axis

$$i = \frac{b^3 \times l}{12}$$

where:

b = the transverse dimension of the free surface

l = the longitudinal dimension of the free surface

V = the underwater volume of the ship, in cubic feet 35 times displacement

$$GG_1 = \frac{\frac{(85_3 \times 73)}{12}}{(35{,}000 \times 35)}$$

$$GG_1 = 3.05 \text{ feet}$$

Example 20—Free Communication

In a tanker displacing 135,436 tons, a tank 125 feet long and 33.5 feet wide is in free communication with the sea following a collision. The center of gravity of the tank is 49.25 feet off the centerline. What is the virtual rise in gravity caused by free surface effect?

$$GG_1 = \frac{a \times y^2}{V}$$

where:

GG_1 = the virtual rise in the center of gravity from free communication effect

a = the surface area of the affected space

y = the distance from the ship's centerline to the center of gravity of the affected space

$$GG_1 = \frac{(135 \times 33.5) \times 49.5^2}{(135{,}436 \times 35)}$$

$$GG_1 = 2.16 \text{ feet}$$

Example 21—Longitudinal Metacentric Radius (BM_L)

What is the approximate metacentric radius of a ship whose length is 670 feet, beam is 85 feet, draft is 31.5 feet, and that has a block coefficient of 0.71 and a waterplane coefficient of 0.74?

$$I_L = C_{IL} \times B \times L^3$$

where:

$$C_{IL} = 0.143 \times C_{WP} - 0.0659$$

$$C_{IL} = \text{a dimensionless coefficient}$$

The longitudinal metacentric radius (BM_L) may be calculated by:

$$BM_L = \frac{C_{IL} \times L^2}{C_B \times T}$$

$$C_{IL} = (0.143 \times 0.74) - 0.659$$

$$C_{IL} = 0.03992$$

$$BM_L = \frac{0.03992 \times 670^2}{0.71 \times 31.5}$$

$$BM_L = 801.3 \text{ feet}$$

Example 22—Longitudinal Metacentric Height (GM_L)

What is the longitudinal metacentric height of the ship in the foregoing example if KB = 17.59 feet and KG = 30.6 feet?

$$GM_L = KB + BM - KG$$

$$GM_L = 17.9 + 801.3 - 30.6$$

$$GM_L = 788.6 \text{ feet}$$

Example 23—Moment to Trim One Inch (Centimeter) MT1, (MTC)

What is the moment to trim one inch for the ship in the foregoing examples if the displacement is 36,391 tons?

1. Exact method:

$$MT1 = \frac{GM_L \times W}{12 \times L}$$

$$MT1 = \frac{788.6 \times 36{,}391}{12 \times 670}$$

$$MT1 = 3{,}567.5 \text{ foot-tons}$$

2. Approximations:

a. Method 1:

$$MT1 = \frac{BM_L \times W}{12 \times L}$$

$$MT1 = \frac{801.3 \times 36{,}391}{12 \times 670}$$

$$MT1 = 3{,}626.9 \text{ foot-tons}$$

b. Method 2:

$$MT1 = \frac{k \times TPI^2}{B}$$

TABLE A-10. BLOCK COEFFICIENT CONSTANTS.

Block Coefficient – C_B	*k*
0.65	28
0.70	29
0.75	30
0.80	31
0.85	32

$$TPI = \frac{C_{wp} \times L \times B}{420}$$

$$TPI = \frac{0.74 \times 670 \times 85}{420}$$

$$TPI = 100.3$$

$$MT1 = \frac{29 \times 100.3^2}{85}$$

$$MT1 = 3{,}435 \text{ foot-tons}$$

c. Method 3:

$$MT1 = \frac{L^2 \times B}{10{,}000}$$

$$MT1 = \frac{670^2 \times 85}{10{,}000}$$

$$MT1 = 3{,}815.6 \text{ foot-tons}$$

Example 24—Trim Calculation

A ship is 700 feet long and draws 33.5 feet forward and 35 feet aft. The LCF is 14 feet abaft amidships, TPI = 112.2 tons, and MT1 = 4,326 foot-tons. 4,176 tons of cargo with its center of gravity 125 feet forward of amidships is removed. What are the drafts?

TABLE A-11. TRIM CALCULATION.

ITEM	*VALUE*	*UNITS*
Length (LBP)	700	feet
LCF from bow (Df)	364	feet
LCF from stern (Da)	336	feet
Weight (W): added removed	4,176	tons
Distance of weight from LCF (Dw): forward aft	139	feet
TPI	112.5	tons
MT1	4,326	feet/tons
Parallel sinkage or rise: sinkage (rise) $= +(-)\dfrac{W}{TPI}$	–2.96	feet
Total change of trim: Δ trim $= \dfrac{W \times Df}{MT1}$	11.19	feet
DRAFT CHANGES		
Draft Forward (Tf)		
Original draft forward	33.5	feet
Parallel sinkage or rise	–2.96	feet
Change of trim forward $\delta\,Tf = \pm\ \Delta\,trim \times (\dfrac{Df}{L})$	–5.82	feet
New Draft Forward (Tf)	24.72	feet
Draft Aft (Ta)		
Original draft aft	35	feet
Parallel sinkage or rise *(Same sign as draft forward)*	–2.96	feet
Change of trim aft *(Opposite sign from forward)* $\delta\,Ta = \mp\ \Delta\,trim \times (\dfrac{Df}{L})$	5.37+	feet
New Draft Aft	37.77	feet

Example 25—Lightship Weight Distribution

Calculate the lightship weight distribution in a tanker 843 feet long with a lightship weight of 19,700 tons.

$$w_S = \frac{K_{LS}}{\Sigma K_{LS}} \times \frac{W_{LS}}{\frac{LBP}{40}}$$

where:

w_S = weight per unit length (tons per foot) over one specified station
K_S = weight distribution constant for the station
ΣK_{LS} = the sum of the weight distribution constants for the ship, for tankers 26.381
W_S = lightship displacement
LBP = length between perpendiculars

$$w_S = \frac{K_S \times 19{,}700}{26.381 \times \frac{843}{40}}$$

$$w_S = 35.43 \times K_S$$

TABLE A-12. WEIGHT DISTRIBUTION COEFFICIENTS.

Station	K_S	w_S
–0.55-0	–	–
0-0.5	0.431	15.27
0.5-1	0.459	16.26
1-1.5	0.473	16.76
1.5-2	0.501	17.75
2-2.5	0.515	18.25
2.5-3	0.529	18.74
3-3.5	0.557	19.74
3.5-4	0.570	20.20
4-4.5	0.598	21.19
4.5-5	0.612	21.68
5-5.5	0.658	23.31
5.5-6	0.658	23.31
6-6.5	0.658	23.31

Table A-12 continued on next page

Table A-12 continued

Station	K_S	w_S
6.5-7	0.658	23.31
7-7.5	0.658	23.31
7.5-8	0.658	23.31
8-8.5	0.658	23.31
8.5-9	0.658	23.31
9-9.5	0.658	23.31
9.5-10	0.658	23.31
10–10.5	0.658	23.31
10.5-11	0.658	23.31
11-11.5	0.658	23.31
11.5-12	0.658	23.31
12-12.5	0.658	23.31
12.5-13	0.658	23.31
13-13.5	0.658	23.31
13.5-14	0.658	23.31
14-14.5	0.658	23.31
14.5-15	0.658	23.31
15-15.5	0.658	23.31
15.5-16	0.668	23.67
16-16.5	0.668	23.67
16.5-17	0.668	23.67
17-17.5	0.904	32.03
17.5-18	1.043	36.96
18-18.5	1.016	36.00
18.5-19	0.904	32.03
19-19.5	0.557	19.74
19.5–20	0.473	16.76
20-20.5	0.417	14.76
20.5-21	–	–

Example 26—Buoyancy Curve

Calculate the approximate buoyancy curve for a tanker 843 feet long with a beam of 134 feet, draft of 52 feet, block coefficient of 0.81, and midships coefficient of 0.98 by the five trapezoid method.

$$L_{pmb} = (1.74 \times C_B - 1.002) \times L$$

$$L_{fb} = (1.186 - 1.17 \times C_B) \times L$$

$$L_{ab} = L - L_{pmb} - L_{fb}$$

where:
L_{pmb} = length of the parallel midbody
C_B = block coefficient
L = length between perpendiculars
L_{fb} = length of the forebody
L_{ab} = length of the afterbody

$$L_{pmb} = (1.174 \times 0.81 - 1.002) \times 843$$

$$L_{pmb} = 343.4 \text{ feet}$$

$$L_{fb} = (1.186 - 1.17 \times C_B) \times L$$

$$L_{fb} = 200.88 \text{ feet}$$

$$L_{ab} = 843 - 343.4 - 200.88$$

$$L_{ab} = 298.71 \text{ feet}$$

The total buoyancy of the parallel midbody is:

$$B_{pmb} = \frac{(L_{pmb} \times B \times T_M \times C_M)}{35}$$

where:
B_{pmb} = total buoyancy of the parallel midbody
B = beam
T_M = mean draft
C_M = midships coefficient

$$B_{pmb} = \frac{(343.4 \times 134 \times 52 \times 0.98)}{35}$$

$$B_{pmb} = 66{,}999 \text{ tons}$$

The weight per foot of the parallel midbody (b_{pmd}) is:

$$b_{pmb} = \frac{B_{pmb}}{l_{pmb}}$$

$$b_{pmb} = \frac{66{,}999}{343.4}$$

$$b_{pmb} = 195.33 \text{ tons per foot}$$

TABLE A-13. BUOYANCY CURVE.

	l	*b*
1	$l_1 = (0.61 - 0.615 \times C_B) \times L$ $l_1 = (0.61 - 0.615 \times 0.81) \times 843$ $l_1 = 94.29$ feet	$b_1 = 0.04 \times b_{pmb}$ $b_1 = 0.04 \times 195.33$ $b_1 = 7.81$ tons per foot
2	$l_2 = L_{fb} - l_1$ $l_2 = 200.88 - 94.29$ $l_2 = 106.59$	$b_2 = C_B \times b_{pmb}$ $b_2 = 0.81 \times 195.33$ $b_2 = 158.22$ tons per foot
4	$l_4 = L_{ab} - l_5$ $l_4 = 298.7 - 168.6$ $l_4 = 130.11$ feet	$b_4 = C_B \times b_{pmb}$ $B_4 = 0.81 \times 195.33$ $l_4 = 158.22$ tons per foot
5	$l_5 = 0.2 \times L$ $l_5 = 0.2 \times 843$ $l_5 = 168.6$ feet	$l_5 = 0.08 \times b_{pmb}$ $l_5 = 0.08 \times 195.44$ $l_5 = 14.82$ tons per foot

Example 27—Bending Strength

The bending strength calculation is a seven-step operation consisting of:

1. Calculating the weight distribution along the length of the vessel and producing a weight distribution curve.

2. Calculating the buoyancy distribution down the length of the vessel and producing a buoyancy curve.
3. Adding the weight distribution and buoyancy curves to obtain a load curve.
4. Integrating the load curve to obtain a shear force curve.
5. Integrating the shear force curve to obtain a bending moment curve.
6. Calculating the section modulus of the ship.
7. Dividing bending moment by section modulus to obtain stress.

For the bending strength calculation, a type of vessel familiar to all naval architectural students, but seldom if ever seen at sea, is the example vessel. This vessel is the box-shaped lighter, a type that allows illustration of the principles and methods of making the calculation without the obfuscation and tediousness of ship-shaped calculations.

Our box-shaped lighter is 200 feet long, 40 feet wide, and 25 feet deep. She is divided into five equal-length (40-foot) holds numbered in the usual way (1 through 5, forward to aft). The holds are divided by bulkheads designated A through D, forward to aft. The lightship weight of the barge is 914 tons divided evenly along her length, or 4.57 tons per foot. The barge is loaded with 4,000 tons of cargo distributed as shown in the table below, so that she floats on an even keel at a draft of 21.5 feet.

TABLE A-14. CARGO DISTRIBUTION IN BOX-SHAPED LIGHTER.

Hold	*Cargo (tons)*
1	900
2	500
3	1,200
4	500
5	900

1. The weight curve

The abscissa (horizontal axis) of the weight curve is the length of the vessel. In this case, the division into five equal holds makes a convenient division for preparation of all the curves leading to and including the bending moment curve.

The weight curve is prepared by summing all the weight per unit length in the areas in which the weights act. The weights acting in way of Hold 1 are the lightship weight at 4.57 tons per foot and the cargo at 15 tons per foot (600 tons of cargo divided by 40 feet, the length of hold). Thus for the entire vessel:

TABLE A-15. THE WEIGHT CURVE.

Hold	*Cargo*	*Cargo tons per foot*	*Lightship tons per foot*	*Weight tons per foot*
1	900	22.5	4.57	27.07
2	500	12.5	4.57	17.07
3	1,200	30	4.57	34.57
4	500	12.5	4.57	17.07
5	600	22.5	4.57	27.07

2. The buoyancy curve

Buoyancy is evenly distributed down the length of this conveniently box-shaped lighter. Buoyancy per unit length is the displacement of the lighter (4,914 tons) divided by the length of the vessel (200 feet), or 24.57 tons per foot.

3. The load curve

The load curve is the sum of the weight and buoyancy curves. Since the two forces act in opposite directions, one is taken as negative, the other positive. Weight, acting downward, is usually taken as negative.

TABLE A-16. THE LOAD CURVE.

Hold	*Weight tons per foot (negative)*	*Buoyancy tons per foot (positive)*	*Load tons per foot*
1	27.07	24.57	–2.5
2	17.07	24.57	+7.5
3	34.57	24.57	–10.00
4	24.57	24.57	+7.5
5	27.07	24.57	–2.5

4. The shear force curve

The shear force at any point along the barge is the sum of all the forces to the left of the point. The shear force at any point is also equal to the area under the load curve to that point. For convenience, the shear force is summed at the bulkheads. Thus, if the load throughout Hold 1 is –2.5 tons per foot and the hold is 40 feet long, the force at Bulkhead A is –100 tons.

TABLE A-17. THE SHEAR FORCE CURVE .

Hold	*Bulkhead*	*Force*	*Shear Force* Σ *Forces*
	FP		0
1		40(–2.5) = –100	
	A		–100
2		40(7.5) = 300	
	B		200
3		40(–10) = –400	
	C		–200
4		40(7.5) = 300	
	D		100
5		40(2.5) = –100	
	AP		0

The shear force curve has three important features:

a. The curve closes or goes to zero on each end.
b. Each point where the shear force is zero is a maximum or minimum on the bending moment curve.
c. Each place where the shear force curve changes direction is a point of inflection on the bending moment curve.

5. The bending moment

The bending moment at any point is the sum of the shear forces to the left of that point. Because the shear force is zero at points not on the bulkheads, the bending moments at these points, as well as the bending moments at the bulkheads, must be calculated.

TABLE A-18. THE BENDING MOMENT.

Hold	*Point*	*Moment*	*Bending Moment*
	FP		0
1		½ (40)(–100) = –2,000	
	A		–2,000
2	⅓ Hold 2	½ (13.3)(–100) = –665	–2,665
2		½ (26.7)(200) = 2,670	
	B		5

Hold	*Point*	*Moment*	*Bending Moment*
3	½ Hold 3	½ (20)(200) = 2,000	2,005
	C	½ (20)(–200) = –2,000	5
4	⅔ Hold 4	½ (26.7)(–200) = –2,670	–2,665
4		½ (13.3)(100) = 665	
	D		–2,000
5		½ (40)(100) = 2,000	
	E		0

Figure A-1 shows the weight, buoyancy, load, shear force, and bending moment curves.

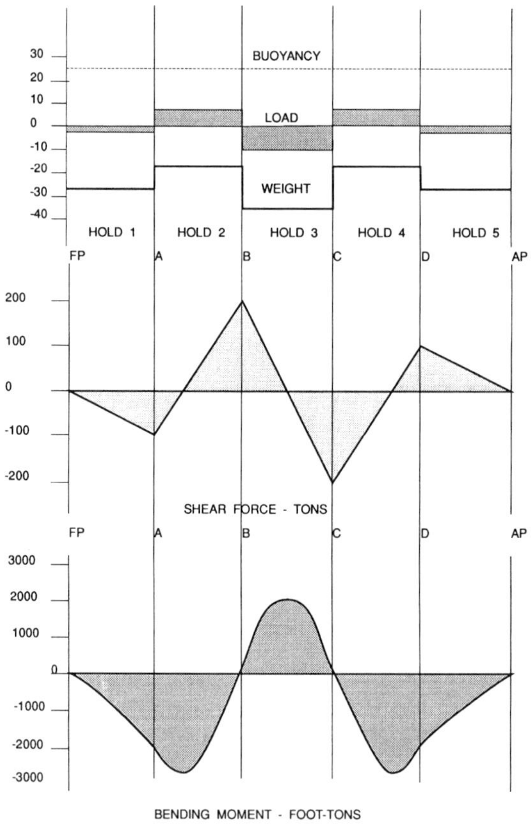

Figure A-1. Weight, buoyancy, load, shear force, and bending moment curves for example 27 (1-5).

6. The section modulus

Chapter 3 describes the section modulus calculation as tedious and difficult, and so it is. Chapter 3 goes on to suggest that computer calculation with pre-entered numbers is the most feasible way to make a salvage calculation of section modulus and gives no detailed discussion. This example calculates a section modulus for the box-shaped lighter using a simplified section that, like the lighter itself, illustrates the steps and principles of the procedure with all of the tedium of a complex structure. The section is as shown in figure A-2.

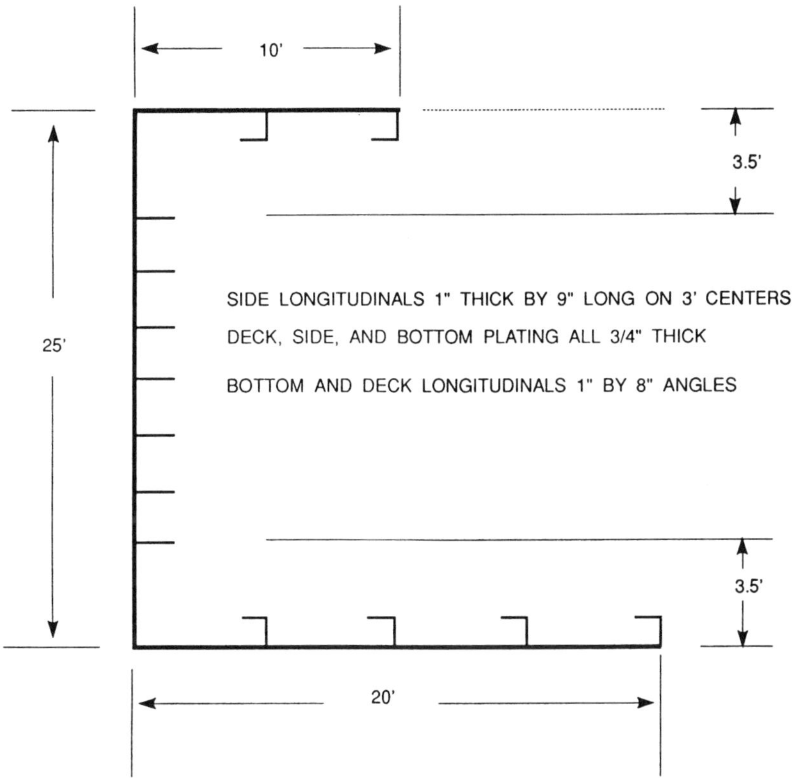

Figure A-2. Half section of barge for strength calculation for example 27

But, first, a little explanation and a few definitions. The bending stress at any section depends upon the bending moment at the section and the amount of material in the section and its distribution.

$$\sigma = \frac{M \times y}{I}$$

where:
σ = stress in pounds (or tons) per square inch
M = bending moment
y = distance from the neutral axis in feet
I = moment of inertia of the structure about the neutral axis

The neutral axis is the plane at which the stress is zero. It also passes through the center of mass of the section. The distance from the neutral axis to any axis is found by dividing the sum of the moments of areas about that axis by the sum of the areas. A baseline is established, normally at the keel, and the height of the neutral axis is calculated in a tabular format such as the one shown below:

TABLE A-19. CALCULATING THE NEUTRAL AXIS.

Section	*a (sq in)*	*y (in)*	*ay* (in^3)
Section 1			
Section 2			
Total	A		AY

$$\text{height of neutral axis} = \frac{AY}{A}$$

Only elements that are continuous for at least half the length of the vessel contribute to the longitudinal strength of the ship and are included in strength calculations.

For the half section shown in the sketch:

TABLE A-20. CALCULATING THE NEUTRAL AXIS FOR THE HALF SECTION.

Section	*b*	*h*	*n*	*a*	*y*	*ay*
Bottom plating	240	0.75	1	180	0.5	90
Bottom long (vert.)	1	8	4	32	4	128
Bottom long (hor.)	8	1	4	32	8.5	272
Side plating	0.75	300	1	225	150	33,750
Side long 1	9	1	1	9	42.5	382.5
Side long 2	9	1	1	9	45.5	409.5
Side long 3	9	1	1	9	48.5	436.5

Table A-20 continued on next page

Table A-20 continued

Section	*b*	*h*	*n*	*a*	*y*	*ay*
Side long 4	9	1	1	9	51.5	463.5
Side long 5	9	1	1	9	54.5	490.5
Side long 6	9	1	1	9	57.5	517.5
Side long 7	9	1	1	9	60.5	544.5
Deck plating	120	0.75	1	90	300	27,000
Deck long (vert.)	1	8	2	16	296	4,736
Deck long (hor.)	8	1	2	16	292	4,672
TOTALS				654		73,892

$$H_{NA} = \frac{73{,}892}{654}$$

$$H_{NA} = 112.99 \text{ inches}$$

$$H_{NA} = 9.42 \text{ feet}$$

The neutral axis is 9.42 above the keel, skewed toward the bottom because the lower part has more structure than the upper.

The preceding calculation is seldom done alone. Instead, it is part of a calculation that determines the moment of inertia and section modulus in a single tabular calculation.

The moment of inertia of any section about an axis is equal to:

$$I = I_c + a \times d^2$$

where:

I = moment of inertia about any axis

I_c = moment of inertia about an axis through the center

a = area of the section

d = distance between the axes

For the section shown in figure A-2, the tabular calculation above can be expanded:

TABLE A-21. CALCULATING THE NEUTRAL AXIS FOR THE HALF SECTION

Section	b	h	n	a	y	ay	ay^2	i_c	i
Bottom plating	240	0.75	1	180	0.5	90	45	8.44	53.44
Bottom long (vert)	1	8	4	32	4	128	512	170.67	682.67
Bottom long (hor)	8	1	4	32	8.5	272	2312	2.67	2314.67
Side plating	0.75	300	1	225	150	33750	5062500	1687500	6750000
Side long 1	9	1	1	9	42.5	382.5	16256	0.75	16257
Side long 2	9	1	1	9	45.5	409.5	18632	0.75	18633
Side long 3	9	1	1	9	48.5	436.5	21170	0.75	21171
Side long 4	9	1	1	9	51.5	463.5	23870	0.75	23871
Side long 5	9	1	1	9	54.5	490.5	26732	0.75	26733
Side long 6	9	1	1	9	57.5	517.5	29756	0.75	29757
Side long 7	9	1	1	9	60.5	544.5	32942	0.75	32943
Deck plating	120	0.75	1	90	300	27000	8100000	4.22	8100004
Deck long (vert)	1	8	2	16	296	4736	1401856	85.33	1401941
Deck long (hor)	8	1	2	16	292	4672	1364224	1.33	1364225
TOTALS				654		73893			17788587

TABLE A-22. SYMBOLS AND DEFINITIONS FOR SECTION MODULUS CALCULATION.

Symbol	*Definition*
d	Distance of the neutral axis above the keel. $d = \frac{\Sigma ay}{\Sigma a}$
I_K	Moment of inertia of the hull section about an axis at the keel. The value of the whole section is twice the value of the half section. $I_K = 2 \times (\Sigma i_C + \Sigma ay^2)$
I_{NA}	Moment of inertia about the neutral axis. $I_{NA} = I_K - \Sigma a \times d^2$
y_t	Distance of the uppermost part of the structure from the neutral axis. yt = Depth – d
Z_t	Section modulus for the upper part of the structure. $Z_t = \frac{I_{NA}}{Y_t}$
y_b	Distance of the bottommost part of the structure from the neutral axis. d
Z_b	Section modulus for the lower part of the structure. $Z_b = \frac{I_{NA}}{Y_t}$

For the barge:

TABLE A-23. QUANTITIES FOR SECTION MODULUS CALCULATION.

d	9.42 feet
I_K	35,577,173 inches4
I_{NA}	18,879,615 inches4
y_t	11.42 feet
Z_t	137,767 inches3
Y_b	9.42 feet
Z_b	167,017 inches3

Note two points:

a. The moment of inertia of structural components with very small vertical dimensions makes little difference in the moment of inertial calculation and can usually be ignored.

b. Units must be tracked and accounted for very carefully. The use of inches throughout results in very large numbers. These numbers can be kept to figures that do not resemble a national debt by measuring cross-sectional dimensions in inches and distances in feet. This results in moments of inertia measured in $in^2 - ft^2$ and section modulus measured in $in^2 - ft$. These units and a few calculations with them will make you a strong believer in metric units.

7. Bending stress

Bending stress at any point can be determined by dividing the bending moment at that point by the section modulus at that point.

What is the bending stress at the midships section (i) in the deck? (ii) In the bottom plating?

(i)

$$\sigma_t = \frac{M}{Z_t}$$

$$\sigma_t = \frac{2{,}005 \times 12 \times 2{,}240}{137{,}767}$$

$$\sigma_t = 391 \text{ lbs per sq. in.}$$

(ii)

$$\sigma_b = \frac{M}{Z_b}$$

$$\sigma_b = \frac{2{,}005 \times 12 \times 2{,}240}{167{,}017}$$

$$\sigma_b = 322 \text{ lbs per sq. in.}$$

All that work and practically no stress in the barge!

Example 28—Minimum Section Modulus

A ship is 581 feet between perpendiculars with a beam of 78 feet and a block coefficient of 0.74. What is the minimum section modulus the ship can be expected to have?

For a ship of this length:

$$SM_{min} = 0.01 \times k \times L^2 \times B \times (C_B + 0.70)$$

where:

$$k = 0.01441 \times (10.75 - (\frac{984 - L}{328})^{1.5})$$

$$k = 0.01441 \times (10.75 - (\frac{984 - 581}{328})^{1.5})$$

$$k = 0.135$$

$$SM_{min} = 0.10 \times 0.135 \times 581^2 \times 78 \times (0.74 + 0.70)$$

$$SM_{min} = 356{,}925 \text{ inches}^2 - \text{feet}$$

Note that the formulas for the minimum section modulus and the associated constants found in Chapter 3 vary with the length of the ship.

GROUP 3—OIL-WATER HYDROSTATICS

Chapter Five—Oil and Hazardous Substances

Example 29—Conversion between Specific and API Gravities

1. A product has a specific gravity (SG) of 0.90 at 60° F. What is its API gravity?

Degrees API = (141.5/SG at 60° F.) – 131.5
Degrees API = (141.5/0.90) – 131.
Degrees API = 154.2 – 131.5
Degrees API = 25.75

2. A product has an API gravity of 20 at 60° F. What is its specific gravity?

SG at 60° F. = 141.5/(degrees API + 131.5)
SG = 141.5/(20 + 131.5)
SG = 141.5/151.5
SG = 0.934

Example 30—Hydrostatic Pressure inside and outside a Tank

1. A tank 50 feet deep in a tanker floating in seawater at a draft of 35 feet contains oil with a specific gravity (SG) of 0.90. If the tank ruptures at the bottom, is flow into or out of the tank?

The hydrostatic pressure of each fluid is equivalent to the product of the depth of the fluid and its specific gravity:

$$P = SG \times D$$

for oil:

$$P_O = SG_O \times D_O$$

$$P_O = 0.90 \times 50$$

$$P_O = 45$$

for water:

$$P_W = SG_W \times D_W$$

$$P_W = 1.024 \times 35$$

$$P_W = 35.875$$

Since: $P_O > P_W$, oil flows out of the tank

2. What will the depth of oil in the tank be when the pressure balances?

When the pressure balances:

$$P_O = P_W$$

$$0.90 \times D_O = 1.025 \times 35$$

$$D_O = \frac{1.025 \times 35}{0.90}$$

$$D_O = 39.86$$

When the depth of oil in the tank drops to 39.86 feet, spillage will stop. This calculation gives a rough first estimate, for the ship will rise as the cargo spills. Iterative calculations including the rise are necessary to determine the precise depth. The calculation should be very close with three iterations. In the field, the rough calculation is usually adequate.

3. A double-bottom tank has a depth of 5 feet. The tank is filled with diesel oil with a specific gravity of 0.85. The ship draws 30 feet. If the tank ruptures, is flow in or out of the tank?

$$P = SG \times D$$

$$P_O = 0.85 \times 5$$

$$P_O = 4.25$$

$$P_W = 1.025 \times 30$$

$$P_W = 30.75$$

$P_W > P_O$, water flows into the tank

4. How far will the oil rise in the sounding tubes and vents?

Oil will rise into the sounding tubes and vents until:

$$P_O = P_W$$

$$SG_O \times D_O = SG_W \times D_W$$

$$0.85 \times D_O = 1.025 \times 30$$

$$D_O = \frac{1.025 \times 30}{0.85}$$

D_O = 36.17 feet above the keel – 31.17 feet above the tanktop

Example 31—Water Bottom Depth

A deep tank in a ship drawing 32 feet of seawater is holed in the bottom. The tank contains 15 feet of oil with a specific gravity of 0.80. What is the depth of the water bottom that forms?

Water will flow into the ship until the hydrostatic pressures inside (P_I) and outside the hull (P_o) are equal. Internal pressure is the sum of the hydrostatic pressures of the oil and the water in the water bottom. External pressure is the hydrostatic pressure at the depth of the hole.

$$P_I = P_O$$

$$(SG_O \times D_O) + (SG_{WB} \times D_{WB}) = SG_W \times T$$

$$D_{WB} = \frac{(SG_W \times T) - (SG_O \times D_O)}{SG_{WB}}$$

$$D_{WB} = \frac{(1.025 \times 32) - (0.80 \times 15)}{1.025}$$

$$D_{WB} = 21.2 \text{ feet}$$

$$\text{Total liquid depth} = 36.03 \text{ feet}$$

GROUP 4—RIGGING

Example 32—Estimated Breaking Strength of Wire Rope

What is the estimated nominal breaking strength of 2-inch diameter 6 × 37 EIPS IWRC bright wire rope?

$$BS = C \times (\pi \times d)^2$$

where:

C is a constant from the table in Chapter 7. For the wire rope specified:

C = 5.14

d = diameter of the wire rope in inches

$$BS = 5.14 \times (\pi \times 2)^2$$

$$BS = 202.92 \text{ tons}$$

The catalog nominal breaking strength of this wire rope is 198 tons. The result of the calculation is 2.1 percent greater than the catalog strength. This degree of inaccuracy is consistent with data given in the table in Chapter 7.

Example 33—Estimated Breaking Strength of Fiber Rope

What is the estimated breaking strength of a 7-inch, 3-strand polyester rope?

$$BS = kC^2$$

where:

BS = minimum breaking strength of new, dry rope in pounds

k = a constant from the table in Chapter 7 that varies with rope material and construction. For 3-strand polyester k = 1840.

C = circumference of the rope in inches

$$BS = 1{,}840 \times 7^2$$

$$BS = 90{,}160 \text{ pounds}$$

Example 34—Snapback Energy

What is the snapback energy in foot-pounds of a 200-foot length of the 7-inch, 3-strand polyester rope when it is elongated 5 percent?

$$S = \frac{1}{3}(BS \times L \times E)$$

where:

S = snapback energy in foot-pounds

BS = minimum breaking strength in pounds

L = length of the line in feet

E = percentage elongation

$$S = \frac{1}{3}(90{,}169 \times 200 \times 5)$$

$$S = 30{,}056{,}333 \text{ foot-pounds}$$

Example 35—Storage Volume for Faked Rope

How much volume is required to stow 600 feet of 7-inch (circumference) rope?

$$V = \frac{C^2 \times L}{1{,}090}$$

where:

V = required storage volume in cubic feet
C = rope circumference in inches
L = rope length in feet

$$V = \frac{7^2 \times 600}{1{,}090}$$

$$V = 26.97, \text{ say 27 cubic feet}$$

Example 36—Length of Rope That Can Be Stored on a Drum

What length of 2-inch diameter rope can be stowed on a 6-foot-long drum with a drum diameter of 30 inches and a flange diameter of 72 inches?

$$L = \frac{l\,(d_f^{\,2} - d_b^{\,2})}{15.3 \times d_r^{\,2}}$$

where:

L = length of the rope to be stored in feet
l = length of the barrel of the spool or drum in feet
d_f = diameter of the drum flange in inches
d_b = diameter of the drum barrel in inches
d_r = rope diameter in inches

$$L = \frac{6 \times (72^2 - 30^2)}{15.3 \times 2^2}$$

$$L = 420 \text{ feet}$$

Example 37—Weight of Chain

What is the weight of a shot (15 fathoms) of 3-inch chain?

$$w = C_W d^2$$

where:

w = chain weight per foot in lbs/ft
C_W = weight coefficient, 9.92 for Imperial units
d = chain bar (wire) diameter in inches

Weight of 1 foot of chain is:

$$w = 9.92 \times 9^2$$

$$w = 89.28 \text{ pounds per foot}$$

Weight of 90 feet is:

$$W = 90 \times 89.28$$

$$W = 8{,}035.2 \text{ pounds}$$

What is the weight of a shot (27.5 meters) of 76-mm chain?

In SI units:
w = chain weight per foot in kg/m
C_W = weight coefficient, 0.0228 for SI units
d = chain bar (wire) diameter in millimeters

$$w = 0.0228 \times 76^2$$

$$w = 131.6 \text{ kg per meter}$$

Weight of 27.5 meters is:

$$W = 27.5 \times 131.6$$

$$W = 3{,}621.5 \text{ kg}$$

Example 38—Approximate Breaking Strength and Proof Loads of Chain

1. What is the approximate proof load and breaking strength of 3-inch Grade 3 chain?

$$PL = C_{PL} \times d^2 \times (44 - 2.032d)$$

where:
PL = proof load of the chain in pounds
C_{PL} = proof load coefficient from following table
d = bar (wire) diameter of chain in inches

and

$$BS = C_{BS} \times d^2 \times (44 - 2.032 \times d)$$

where:
BS = breaking strength of the chain in pounds
C_{BS} = breaking strength load coefficient from following table
d = bar (wire) diameter of chain in inches

TABLE A-24. APPROXIMATE BREAKING STRENGTH AND PROOF LOADS OF CHAIN.

Chain Grade	C_{PL}	C_{BS}
1	995	1,422
2	1,422	1,991
3	1,991	2,844
Di–Lok	2,020	3,058
ORQ	2,031	3,060
4	3,125	3,978

The Classification Society proof load and breaking strength for 3-inch Grade 3 chain is: 679,000 and 970,000 pounds. All grades and sizes may not be as close as this one was.

2. What is the breaking strength in tonnes of 76-mm Grade 3 chain?

$$BS = \frac{K \times d^2}{600}$$

where:

BS = chain breaking strength in tonnes

K = a constant for the chain grade

Grade	K
1	20
2	30
3	43

d = bar diameter in millimeters

$$PL = 1{,}991 \times 3^2 \times (44 - 2.032 \times 3)$$

$$PL = 679{,}202 \text{ pounds}$$

since the equations are the same except for the coefficients:

$$\frac{BS}{PL} = \frac{C_{BS}}{C_{PL}}$$

then:

$$BS = PL \times \frac{C_{BS}}{C_{PL}}$$

$$BS = 679{,}202 \times \frac{2{,}844}{1{,}991}$$

$$BS = 970{,}191 \text{ pounds}$$

$$BS = \frac{43 \times 76^2}{600}$$

$$BS = 413.9 \text{ tonnes}$$

Example 39—Safe Working Load of Shackles

What is a conservative safe working load for an unmarked shackle with a bow diameter of 1¼ inches?

$$SWL = 3.6d^2$$

where:

SWL = safe working load in tons

d = diameter of the bow of the shackle in inches

$$SWL = 3.6 \times 1.25^2$$

$$SWL = 5.625 \text{ tons}$$

Example 40—Safe Working Load of Hooks

What is the safe working load in tons for an unmarked hook with a diameter (back of hook below the eye) of 1¼ inches?

$$SWL = \frac{2}{3} \times d^2$$

where:

SWL = safe working load in tons

d = diameter of the hook at the back of the hook below the eye in inches

$$SWL = \frac{2}{3} \times 1.25^2$$

$$SWL = 1.04 \text{ tons}$$

Example 41—Actual Mechanical Advantage

What is the actual mechanical advantage of a purchase system with two five-sheave blocks rigged with the becket on the hauling block if the blocks are well lubricated and have bronze bushings in good condition?

$$AMA = \frac{TMA}{1 + (k \times N)}$$

where:

AMA = actual mechanical advantage

TMA = theoretical mechanical advantage (number of rope parts at the moving block)

k = friction factor: 0.10 for wires bending not more than 180 degrees on the sheave and bronze bushings in good condition

N = *total* number of *sheaves* in the system

For two five-sheave blocks with the becket rigged to the moving block the TMA is 11.

$$\text{AMA} = \frac{11}{1 + (0.10 \times 10)}$$

$$\text{AMA} = 5.5$$

Example 42—Sling Leg Tension

What is the tension in each leg of a four part sling lifting 3,500 pounds if the angle at the top is 30 degrees?

$$T = \frac{w}{n \times \cos \Theta}$$

where:

T = tension in each sling leg
w = weight being lifted
n = number of legs in the sling
Θ = angle at the top of the plan

$$T = \frac{3{,}500}{4 \times 0.866}$$

$$T = 1{,}010.4 \text{ pounds}$$

GROUP 5—GENERAL SALVAGE CALCULATIONS

Chapter Four—Types of Casualties

Example 43—Height of Tide at Any Time

What is the height of the tide two hours after high water if the tide range is 6.5 feet, the interval between high and low water 5.8 hours, and the height of low water relative to datum is 1.5 feet?

$$H_n = \frac{R}{2} \times \cos N\,\Theta + \left(\frac{R}{2} + H_{lw}\right)$$

where:

H_n = height of tide at n hours before or after high water (feet or meters)
N = hours before or after high water (decimal hours) = 2.0
Θ = tidal phase angle for one hour (180/T degrees or π/T radians where T is the duration of the ebb or flood tide) = π/5.8
R = tide range (feet or meters) = 6.5
H_{lw} = height of low water relative to datum (feet or meters) = 1.5

$$H_n = \frac{6.5}{2} \times \cos\left(2 \times \frac{\pi}{5.8}\right) + \left(\frac{6.5}{2} + 1.5\right)$$

$$H_n = 6.27 \text{ feet above datum}$$

Example 44—Ground Reaction

1. Difference of displacements

A small ship is aground. Drafts have been taken and the displacement aground taken from the Capacity Plan is 4,375 tons. From pre-sailing drafts and consumption of fuel and stores before grounding the pre-grounding displacement is calculated as 4,846 tons. What is the ground reaction?

$$R = W_{afloat} - W_{aground}$$

where:

R = ground reaction in tons (tonnes)
W_{afloat} = displacement immediately before grounding in tons (tonnes)
$W_{aground}$ = displacement as the ship lies aground in tons (tonnes)

$$R = 4{,}846 - 4{,}375$$

$$R = 471 \text{ tons}$$

2. Tons per inch immersion

A somewhat larger ship has run aground. The difference between her pre-grounding mean draft (calculated by adjusting her sailing drafts for consumption of bunkers and stores) and her grounded mean draft (by the mean-of-quarter-means method) is 71". Her TPI (the mean of grounded and pre-grounded conditions) from the Capacity Plan is 127 tons. What is her ground reaction?

$$R = \delta T_M \times TPI$$

where:

R = ground reaction in tons (tonnes)
δT_M = difference in grounded and pre-grounded mean draft in inches (centimeters)
TPI(C) = tons (tonnes) per inch (centimeter) immersion

$$R = 71 \times 127$$

$$R = 9{,}017 \text{ tons}$$

3. Change of trim

A ship whose LBP is 700 feet is aground. The center of flotation is 0.02L abaft the midships section. The center of ground reaction is estimated to lie at 0.25L from the forward perpendicular. MT1 from the Capacity Plan is estimated at 4,880 foot-tons. The total trim is 17.5 feet. What is the ground reaction?

$$R = \frac{MT1 \times t}{d_r}$$

where:

t = total trim in inches

d_r = distance between the center of ground reaction and the center of flotation in feet

$$d_r = 0.52L - .25L$$

$$d_r = 0.27 \times 700$$

$$d_r = 189 \text{ feet}$$

then:

$$R = \frac{4{,}880 \times (17.5 \times 12)}{189}$$

$$R = 5{,}422 \text{ tons}$$

4. Change of draft forward

The same 700-foot ship, now under a different master, is aground again. TPI and MT1 are 127 tons and 4,880 foot-tons respectively. The difference in draft forward before and after grounding is 12 feet, the distance from the forward perpendicular to the center of flotation is 364 feet, the distance from the center of flotation to the center of ground reaction is 75 feet. What is the ground reaction?

$$R = \frac{TPI \times MT1 \times L \times (T_{fb} - T_{fa})}{(MT1 \times L) + (d_r \times d_f \times TPI)}$$

where:

T_{fb} = draft forward before stranding in inches

T_{fa} = draft forward after stranding in inches

d_f = distance between the forward perpendicular and center of flotation in feet

d_r = distance between the center of ground reaction and the center of flotation in feet

$$R = \frac{127 \times 4{,}880 \times 700 \times (15 \times 12)}{(4{,}880 \times 700) + (364 \times 75 \times 127)}$$

$$R = 11{,}345 \text{ tons}$$

It should be obvious from the calculations, but it bears repeating that:

1. The tons per inch immersion method depends primarily upon parallel rise and in its simplest form does not take into account trim. Accuracy of the

calculation can be improved by applying trim corrections from the casualty's Trim and Stability Booklet.

2. Both the change in trim and the change in draft forward method are very sensitive to accurate estimates of the location of the center of ground reaction. This quantity is very difficult to estimate except in those rare (usually hypothetical) cases where the ship is grounded on a pinnacle. Whenever an estimated position of the center of gravity is used, suspect the results. Always check the suspect results by the change in displacement or tons per inch immersion method. The results are unlikely to be exact, but should be reasonably close. If they are not, recheck the calculation with the estimated position of the ground reaction first.

Ground reaction calculations are at the very best estimates and should always be treated as such.

Example 45—Neutral Loading Point

1. Find the neutral loading point of our 700-foot friend if the center of ground reaction lies 125 feet ahead of the center of flotation.

$$d_n = \frac{MT1 \times L}{TPI \times d_r}$$

where:

d_n = distance from the center of flotation to the neutral loading point

$$d_n = \frac{4{,}880 \times 700}{127 \times 125}$$

$$d_n = 215 \text{ abaft the center of flotation}$$

$$d_n = 215 + 364 = 579 \text{ feet abaft the FP}$$

2. If the center of ground reaction is 70 feet from the center of flotation, where is the neutral loading point?

$$\frac{L}{d_n} = \frac{70}{700} = \frac{1}{10}$$

$$\text{since } \frac{1}{10} < \frac{1}{9}$$

d_n lies off the vessel

3. Just down the beach from our 700-foot ship, a 350-foot barge ($C_{WP} = 1$) lies aground with her center of ground reaction 100 feet forward of the center of flotation (midships). Where is the neutral loading point?

For a full-bodied vessel:

$$d_n = \frac{C_{WP} \times L^2}{14 \times d_r}$$

$$d_n = \frac{1.00 \times 350^2}{14 \times 100}$$

$$d_n = 87.5 \text{ feet abaft midships}$$

Example 46—Change in Ground Reaction Caused by Tide

The 700-foot ship grounded so she trims freely where the tide range is 6 feet. The center of ground reaction is 125 feet from the center of flotation. The ship grounded at high water. What is the change in ground reaction at low water?

$$\delta R = \frac{R_t \times TPI \times MT1 \times L}{(TPI \times d_r^2) + (MT1 \times L)}$$

where:

R_t = tide range in feet

All other quantities are as defined previously

$$\delta R = \frac{6 \times 127 \times 4{,}880 \times 700}{(127 \times 125) + (4{,}880 \times 700)}$$

$$\delta R = 758.5 \text{ tons}$$

Example 47—Virtual Rise in Center of Gravity from Grounding

The before-grounding displacement and KG of a ship 8,300 tons aground are 62,000 tons and 33 feet. What is the effective position of the center of gravity?

$$KG_1 = \frac{KG \times W}{W - R}$$

where:

KG_1 = the effective position of the center of gravity

KG = the pre-grounding height of the center of gravity

W = the pre-grounding displacement of the casualty

R = ground reaction

$$KG_1 = \frac{33 \times 62{,}000}{62{,}000 - 8{,}300}$$

$$KG_1 = 38.1 \text{ feet}$$

Chapter Eight—Strandings

Example 48—Tractive Force to Free a Ship

A ship is 3,000 tons aground on sand. What tractive force is required to free the ship?

$$F = \mu \times R$$

where:

F = the tractive force required to free the ship in long tons (tonnes)
μ = the coefficient of friction between the ship and sea floor (dimensionless)
R = ground reaction in long tons (tonnes)

From Chapter 8:

TABLE A-25. SHIP–SEA FLOOR COEFFICIENT OF FRICTION.

Type of Sea Floor	*Coefficient of Friction*
Mud or silty soil	0.2 to 0.3
Sand	0.3 to 0.4
Coral	0.5 to 0.8
Rock	0.8 to 1.5

$$F = 0.40 \times 3{,}000$$

$$F = 1{,}200 \text{ tons}$$

Example 49—Effective Force

What is the effective force of a leg of ground tackle tensioned to 75 tons pulling at an angle of 30 degrees to the direction of retraction?

$$F_{effective} = F \times \cos\Theta$$

where:

$F_{effective}$ = the force in the direction of retraction
F = the magnitude of the applied force
Θ = the angle between the desired direction of retraction and the direction in which the force is applied

$$F_{effective} = 75 \times \cos\Theta$$

$$F_{effective} = 69.5 \text{ tons}$$

Example 50—Bollard Pull

What is the bollard pull of a 7,200 brake horsepower tug with a shrouded fixed pitch propeller?

$$BP = K \times bhp$$

where:
BP = static bollard pull
K = a factor that considers the propeller type and shrouding
bhp = the total brake horsepower of the tug's propulsion engines

Propulsion System Type	*K Factor*
Open, fixed pitch propeller	0.011
Open, controllable pitch propeller	0.012
Shrouded, fixed pitch propeller	0.013
Shrouded, controllable pitch propeller	0.016

$$BP = 0.13 \times 7{,}200$$

$$BP = 93.6 \text{ tons}$$

Example 51—Holding Power of an Anchor

What is the estimated holding power of a 12,000-pound Danforth anchor in mud?

$$H_M = k_R \times \left(\frac{W_A}{10{,}000}\right)^b$$

where:
H_M = the holding power of the anchor in kips (thousands of pounds)
k_R = a coefficient from the following table
W_A = anchor weight in thousands of pounds
b = an exponent from the following table

TABLE A-26. HOLDING POWER FOR VARIOUS ANCHOR TYPES.

Anchor Type	*Soft Soils (Soft Clays and Muds)*		*Hard Soils (Sands and Stiff Clays)*	
	k_R	*b*	k_R	*b*
Boss	210	0.94	270	0.94
Bruce Cast	32	0.92	250	0.80
Danforth	87	0.92	126	0.80
Flipper Delta	139	0.92	–	–
AC14	87	0.92	126	0.80

Table A-26 continued on next page

Table A-26 continued

Anchor Type	*Soft Soils (Soft Clays and Muds)*		*Hard Soils (Sands and Stiff Clays)*	
LWT	87	0.92	126	0.80
Moorfast	87	0.92	100[1]	0.80
Stato	210	0.94	250[2]	0.94
Stevin	139	0.92	165	0.80
Stockless (fixed fluke)	46	0.92	70	0.80
Stockless (movable fluke)	24	0.92	70	0.80

[1] For 28-degree fluke angle.
[2] For 30-degree fluke angle.

$$H_M = 87 \times \left(\frac{12{,}000}{10{,}000}\right)^{0.92}$$

$$H_M = 102.9 \text{ tons}$$

Example 52—Ground Leg Scope

What is the desirable scope of the wire rope in the ground leg of a leg of ground tackle laid where the height of the deck edge above the sea floor is 150 feet, the tension is 160,000 pounds, and the wire rope weighs 9.15 pounds per foot?

$$s = \sqrt{2 \times h \times \frac{T}{w} + h^2}$$

where:

s = scope of wire rope in the ground leg (feet)
h = height from the sea floor to the deck edge (feet)
T = tension in the ground leg (pounds)
w = weight per foot of the wire rope (pounds per foot)

$$s = \sqrt{2 \times 150 \times \frac{160{,}000}{9.15} + 150^2}$$

$$s = 2{,}295 \text{ feet}$$

Example 53—Wind Force on a Ship

A barge with a ship-shaped hull lies in a two-point moor. A 25-knot wind is blowing. The principal dimensions of the barge are:

LBP = 400 feet
B = 50 feet

Freeboard = 15 feet
T = 25 feet

The barge has the structures listed in the table below on deck:

TABLE A-27. BARGE STRUCTURES.

Structure	*Shape*	*l*	*w*	*h*
House	Box	50	40	20
Kingpost	Cylinder	4 (dia.)		35
Kingpost	Cylinder	3.5 (dia.)		30
Crane cab	Box	12	8	10

1. What is the wind force on the vessel if:
a. The wind is from dead ahead?
b. The wind is directly on the beam?
c. The wind is 30 degrees off the bow?

2. What is the direction of the wind force when the wind is 30 degrees off the bow?

1. Wind force directly on the bow or side of a vessel

$$F_w = C_w \Sigma (C_s C_h A) v^2$$

where:
F_w = wind force in pounds (Newtons)
C_w = 0.0034 lb/(ft^2 × kt^2), (0.612 Nsec^2/m^2)
C_s = shape coefficient
C_h = height coefficient
A = projected area of each surface exposed to the wind, ft^2 (m^2)
v = wind speed, knots, (m/sec)

TABLE A-28. WIND FORCE SHAPE COEFFICIENTS.

Exposed Area	*Ch*
Cylindrical shapes	0.50
Hull surface above the waterline	1.00
Deck houses	1.00
Isolated structures (cranes, etc.)	1.50

TABLE A-29. WIND FORCE HEIGHT COEFFICIENTS.

Height of Centroid above Water Line		
Between (feet)	*Between (meters)*	*Height Coefficient*
0–50	0–15.3	1.00
50–100	15.3–30.5	1.10
100–150	30.5–46.0	1.20

TABLE A-30. WIND FROM DEAD AHEAD.

Structure	*Centroid Height*	*A (w × h)*	C_s	C_h	AC_sC_h
Hull	7.5	50 x 15	1.0	1.0	750
House	25	40 x 20	1.0	1.0	800
Kingpost	32.5	4 x 35	0.5	1.0	70
Kingpost	30	3.5 x 30	0.5	1.0	52.5
Crane cab	20	8 x 10	1.5	1.0	120

$$\Sigma AC_S C_h = 1{,}724.5$$

$$F_{W1} = 0.0034 \times 1{,}724.5 \times 25^2$$

$$F_{W1} = 3{,}702.8 \text{ pounds}$$

TABLE A-31. WIND FROM ABEAM.

Structure	*Centroid Height*	*A (l × h)*	C_s	C_h	AC_sC_h
Hull	7.5	400 x 15	1.0	1.0	6,000
House	25	50 x 20	1.0	1.0	1,000
Kingpost	32.5	4 x 35	0.5	1.0	70
Kingpost	30	3.5 x 30	0.5	1.0	52.5
Crane cab	20	12 x 10	1.5	1.0	180

$$\Sigma AC_S C_h = 7{,}302.5$$

$$F_{W2} = 0.0034 \times 7{,}302.5 \times 25^2$$

$$F_{W2} = 15{,}517.81 \text{ pounds}$$

Wind 30 degrees off the bow:

$$F_{w\,fa} = F_{W1}\left(\frac{2\cos^2\Theta}{1 + \cos^2\Theta}\right)$$

$$F_{w\,beam} = F_{W2}\left(\frac{2\sin^2\Theta}{1 + \sin^2\Theta}\right)$$

$$F_R = \sqrt{F_{w\,fa\,2} + F^2_{wbeam}}$$

where:

$F_{w\,fa}$ = wind force component fore and aft (parallel to the centerline) in pounds (Newtons)

$F_{w\,beam}$ = wind force component on the beam (perpendicular to the centerline) in pounds (Newtons)

F_{W1} = wind force calculated as though the wind were dead fore and aft in pounds (Newtons)

F_{W2} = wind force calculated as though the wind were dead abeam

Θ = the angle between the wind direction and the centerline in degrees

F_R = the resultant wind force acting on the ship in pounds (Newtons)

$$F_{w\,fa} = 3{,}708.2\left(\frac{2\cos^2 30}{1 + \cos^2 30}\right)$$

$$F_{w\,fa} = 3{,}708.2\left(\frac{2\,(.866)^2}{1 + .866^2}\right)$$

$$F_{w\,fa} = 3{,}178.4 \text{ pounds}$$

$$F_{w\,beam} = 15{,}571.8\left(\frac{2\sin^2 30}{1 + \sin^2 30}\right)$$

$$F_{w\,beam} = 15{,}571.8\left(\frac{2\,(0.5)^2}{1 + 0.5^2}\right)$$

$$F_{w\,beam} = 6{,}228.7 \text{ pounds}$$

$$F_R = \sqrt{3{,}178.4^2 + 6{,}228.7^2}$$

$$F_R = 6{,}992.8 \text{ pounds}$$

2. Direction of the resultant force:

$$\alpha = \tan^{-1}\frac{F_{w\,fa}}{F_{w\,beam}}$$

where:

α = angle of action between the resultant force and the centerline in degrees

$$\alpha = \tan^{-1}\left(\frac{3{,}178.4}{6{,}228.7}\right)$$

$$\alpha = 27 \text{ degrees}$$

Example 54—Current Force on a Ship

The ship-shaped barge in the previous example is exposed to a 2-knot current. The block coefficient of the barge is 0.81.

1. What is the force of the current on the ship if:
a. The current is from dead ahead?
b. The current is directly on the beam?
c. The current is 30 degrees off the bow?

What is the direction of the resultant current force when the current is 30 degrees off the bow?

$$F_{cbow} = C_{cbow}\, S v_c^2$$

and

$$F_{cbeam} = C_{cbeam}\, S v_c^2$$

where:

F_{cbow} = current force on the bow or stern (parallel to the centerline), lbs (N)

F_{cbeam} = current force on the beam (perpendicular to the centerline), lbs (N)

C_{cbow} = current force coefficient on the bow 0.016 lb/ft^2-kt^2, (2.89 Nsec^2/m^4)

C_{cbeam} = current force coefficient on the beam 0.40 lb/ft^2-kt^2, (72.37 Nsec^2/m^4)

S = wetted surface of the hull, ft^2 (m^2). May be approximated by:

$$S = C_B\, LB + 1.7\, LT$$

v_c = current speed, knots (m/sec)

$$S = 0.81 \times 400 \times 50 + 1.7 \times 400 \times 25$$

$$S = 33{,}200 \text{ square feet}$$

a. Current dead ahead:

$$F_{cbow} = 0.016 \times 33{,}200 \times 2^2$$

$$F_{cbow} = 17{,}262 \text{ pounds}$$

b. Current on beam:

$$F_{cbeam} = 0.40 \times 33{,}200 \times 2^2$$

$$F_{cbeam} = 53{,}120 \text{ pounds}$$

c. Current 30 degrees to centerline:

$$F_{cbow} = (C_{cbow} \times S \times v^2) \times \left(\frac{2 \cos^2 \Theta}{1 + \cos^2 \Theta}\right)$$

$$F_{cbeam} = (C_{cbeam} \times S \times v^2) \left(\frac{2 \sin^2 \Theta}{1 + \sin^2 \Theta}\right)$$

$$F_c = \sqrt{F_{cbow}^2 + F_{cbeam}^2}$$

where:

F_{cbow} = current force component fore and aft parallel to the centerline in pounds (Newtons)

F_{cbeam} = current force component athwartships perpendicular to the centerline in pounds (Newtons)

F_c = the resultant current force acting on the ship in pounds (Newtons)

$$F_{cbow} = 17{,}262 \times \left(\frac{2 \cos^2 30}{1 + \cos^2 30}\right)$$

$$F_{cbow} = 14{,}796 \text{ pounds}$$

$$F_{cbeam} = 53{,}120 \times \left(\frac{2 \sin^2 30}{1 + \sin^2 30}\right)$$

$$F_{cbeam} = 17{,}530 \text{ pounds}$$

$$F_R = \sqrt{14{,}796^2 + 17{,}530^2}$$

$$F_R = 22{,}939 \text{ pounds}$$

2. Direction of the resultant current force:

$$\beta = \tan^{-1}\left(\frac{F_{cbow}}{F_{cbeam}}\right)$$

where:

β = the angle between the resultant force and the centerline

$$\beta = \tan^{-1}\left(\frac{14{,}796}{17{,}530}\right)$$

$$\beta = 40.2 \text{ degrees}$$

Example 55—Flow through a Hole

What is the flow of seawater in tons per hour through a 2-square-foot hole located 17 feet below the surface?

$$Q = K_1 \times K_c \times A \times \sqrt{D}$$

where:

Q = flow rate in various units

K_1 = a constant depending upon the units of Q. The table below gives values of K_1.

K_c = contraction coefficient, discussed below

A = area of the hole in square feet or meters

D = depth of the center of area of the hole below the surface

TABLE A-32. VALUES OF K_1.

A in Square Feet D in Feet			
Time units → *Volume units ↓*	*Second*	*Minute*	*Hour*
Cubic feet	8.02	481	28,890
Tons (seawater)	0.229	13.74	825
Gallons	60	3,600	216,000
A in Square Meters D in Meters			
Time units → *Volume units ↓*	*Second*	*Minute*	*Hour*
Cubic meters	4.43	266	15.960
Tonnes (seawater)	4.32	259	25,570

K_c = 1.00 in salvage calculations to give maximum flow for worst case conditions

$$Q = 825 \times 1.00 \times 2 \times \sqrt{17}$$

$$Q = 6{,}803 \text{ tons per hour}$$

Example 56—Stiffeners Spacing for Patches

1. Steel patches

What is the maximum spacing for stiffeners on a mild steel patch one-quarter-inch thick installed at a depth of 28 feet?

$$d = 289 \times \sqrt{\frac{t^2}{D}}$$

where:

d = stiffener spacing in inches
t = patch thickness in inches
D = water depth in feet

$$d = 289 \times \sqrt{\frac{0.25^2}{28}}$$

$$d = 13.65 \text{ inches}$$

2. Wooden patches

What is the maximum spacing if the same patch is to be built of 2-inch-thick American standard mill lumber?

The thickness of American standard mill lumber in this size is ⅜-inch less than the nominal thickness, or 1.625 inches for a 2-inch board.

$$d = 67 \times \sqrt{\frac{t^2}{D}}$$

$$d = 67 \times \sqrt{\frac{1.625^2}{28}}$$

$$d = 20.5 \text{ inches}$$

Example 57—Pump Capacity

What is the estimated capacity in tons per hour of a 6-inch salvage pump?

$$Q = 5 \times D^2$$

where:

Q = discharge in tons per hour at a 25-foot suction head
D = pump suction diameter in inches

$$Q = 5 \times 6^2$$

$$Q = 180 \text{ tons per hour}$$

Example 58—Pumping Calculations

1. Size of the pumping battery.

How many 6-inch pumps are required to pump a hold 70 feet long, 50 feet wide, and flooded to a depth of 33 feet in three hours if 98 percent of the volume is flooded?

$$v_s = \frac{\mu \times l \times w \times t}{35}$$

where:

v_s = volume of the space to be pumped in tons of seawater or tons of water to be removed

μ = permeability (floodable volume) of the space in percent

l = length of the space in feet

w = width of the space in feet

t = flooded depth of the space in feet

$$v_s = \frac{.98 \times 70 \times 50 \times 33}{35}$$

$$v_s = 3{,}234 \text{ tons}$$

Volume to be pumped in one hour:

$$v_1 = \frac{v_s}{3}$$

$$v_1 = \frac{3{,}234}{3}$$

$$v_1 = 1{,}078 \text{ tons}$$

From example 57, one 6-inch pump can pump 180 tons per hour, then:

$$n = \frac{v_1}{Q}$$

where:

n = number of pumps required

v_1 = volume to be pumped in one hour in tons

Q = capacity of each pump in tons per hour

$$n = \frac{1{,}078}{180}$$

$$n = 5.98 \text{ pumps}$$

Since pumps usually come in whole numbers, say six pumps, add at least one pump for reserve capacity if time is critical.

2. Time to pump with a given pumping battery.

To pump the same space the salvor has four 4-inch pumps, two 6-inch pumps, and two 8-inch pumps. How long will it take to pump the space?

$$t = \frac{v_S}{Q}$$

where:

t = pumping time in hours
v_S = volume of the space in tons
Q = total capacity of the pumping battery
q = capacity of each pump

TABLE A-33. PUMPING BATTERY CAPACITY.

Pump Size	D_2	*q*	*n*	*nq*
4	16	80	4	320
6	36	180	2	360
8	64	320	2	640
TOTAL (Q)				1,320

$$t = \frac{3{,}234}{1{,}320}$$

$$t = 2.45 \text{ hours}$$

Example 59—Standard Cubic Feet per Minute

How many standard cubic feet of air will it take to blow a space 70 feet long, 50 feet wide, and 40 feet deep dry if the space has a permeability (floodable volume) of 97 percent, a depth of 62 feet, the air temperature is 27 degrees F., and the water temperature is 34 degrees F.?

$$scf = acf \times \frac{D + 33}{33} \times \frac{T_A + 460}{T_W + 460}$$

where:

scf = standard cubic feet required to fill the space
acf = volume of the space in cubic feet
D = depth of water in feet
T_A = air temperature in degrees Fahrenheit
T_W = water temperature in degrees Fahrenheit

$$scf = (70 \times 50 \times 40 \times 0.97) \times \left(\frac{62 + 33}{33}\right) \times \left(\frac{27 + 460}{34 + 460}\right)$$

$$scf = 135{,}800 \times 2.88 \times 0.986$$

$$scf = 385{,}628 \text{ standard cubic feet of air}$$

Note that omission of the temperature correction factor would cause less than a 2 percent error in the result.

Example 60—Blowing Pressure

How much pressure is required to blow the above space if line pressure loss is 2 psi?

$$P_B = 0.445 \times D \times P_L$$

where:

P_B = blowing pressure
D = depth of vent holes or standpipe inlet in feet
P_L = pressure loss allowance

$$P_B = (0.445 \times 62) + 2$$

$$P_B = 29.59\text{, say 30 psig}$$

Chapter Ten—Lifting

Example 61—Volume of Air for Collapsible Pontoons

How many cubic feet of air are required to lift two 4-foot diameter, 8-foot-long collapsible pontoons from a depth of 52 feet?

$$V = 1.3 \times (\Sigma W \times p_a)$$

where:

V = total air requirements in cubic feet
1.3 = a constant multiplier to allow for air loss
ΣW = the total displacement volume of the collapsible pontoons in cubic feet
p_a = pressure at depth in atmospheres

$$\Sigma W = 2 \times \left(\frac{4^2 \times \pi}{4} \times 8\right)$$

$$\Sigma W = 201.1 \text{ cubic feet}$$

$$p_a = \frac{52 + 33}{33}$$

$$p_a = 2.58 \text{ atmospheres}$$

$$V = 1.3 \times 201.1 \times 2.58$$

$$V = 673.38 \text{ cubic feet}$$

Example 62—Time to Fill Collapsible Pontoons

The pontoons in example 61 are to be filled with a compressor that supplies 100 scfm. How long will it take to fill the pontoons?

$$V \times t = V$$

$$t = \frac{V}{v}$$

where:

v = total compressor capacity in cubic feet

t = time in minutes

$$t = \frac{673.38}{100}$$

$$t = 6.73 \text{ minutes}$$

Example 63—Hull Cutting by Lift Wires

A barge with a total dead lift of 1,250 tons is to be lifted by a pair of tidal lifting craft with six pairs of lift wires rigged conventionally. The beam of the lift craft is 30 feet and the depth of the lift is 27 feet.

1. What is the tension in the lift wires, assuming the load is balanced equitably among the wires?

$$T = \frac{W}{n} \times \left(\frac{1}{2 \times (1 + \sin \varphi)}\right)$$

where:

W = weight to be lifted in pounds

n = number of pairs of lift wires

$$\varphi = \tan^{-1}\left(\frac{\text{depth}}{\text{beam}}\right)$$

$$T = \frac{1{,}250 \times 2{,}240}{6} \times \left(\frac{1}{2 \times (1 + \sin 42)}\right)$$

$$T = 139{,}793 \text{ pounds}$$

2. If the bilge radius of the barge is 15 inches and the plating thickness is ⅜ inch (0.375 inch), will the lift wires cut the hull?

The probability of cutting depends upon the stress levels in the hull.

$$\sigma = T \times S$$

where:
σ = the hull stress in psi
S = the stress factor

The stress factor is defined by the expression:

$$S = \sqrt{\frac{9.470}{r^3 \times t} + \frac{0.203}{r^2 \times t^2} + \sqrt{\frac{22.42}{r^6 \times t^2} + \frac{0.959}{r^5 \times t^3}}}$$

where:
r = the bilge radius in inches
t = the plating thickness in inches

$$S = \sqrt{\frac{9.470}{15^3 \times 0.375} + \frac{0.203}{15^2 \times 0.375^2} + \sqrt{\frac{22.42}{15^6 \times 0.375^2} + \frac{0.959}{15^5 \times 0.375^3}}}$$

$$S = \sqrt{\frac{9.470}{1{,}265.6} + \frac{0.203}{31.64} + \sqrt{\frac{22.42}{1{,}601{,}807} + \frac{0.959}{40{,}045}}}$$

$$S = \sqrt{0.0075 + 0.0064 + \sqrt{0.00014 + 0.00002}}$$

$$S = 0.163$$

$$\sigma = T \times S$$

$$\sigma = 139{,}793 \times 0.163$$

$$\sigma = 22{,}786 \text{ pounds per square inch}$$

With a stress level of over 22,000 psi, cutting failure is possible. A wise salvor would take action to prevent cutting. Since the level is just over 22,000 psi, he would take into consideration the age and condition of the structure and the potential results of failure, including job delay and pollution probability.

Example 64—Air Volume for Air Lifts

1. How many cubic feet per minute of air is required to drive a 4-inch air lift? Estimate flow in gallons at twelve to fifteen times the air lift area. Choose 13.5.

$$q = 13.5 \times \frac{\pi \times 4^2}{4}$$

$$q = 169.6\text{, say 170 gallons per minute}$$

Divide by 2.5 to 4 (say 3.25) to obtain cubic feet per minutes of air required.

2. What is the lift that can be driven by a 100-cfm compressor if the desired flow is 250 gpm?

$$Q = \frac{q}{3.25}$$

$$Q = \frac{170}{3.25}$$

$$Q = 52 \text{ cfm}$$

$$s = 3 \times \frac{q}{c}$$

where:

s = size of the air lift in inches
q = water flow in gallons per minute
c = compressor capacity

$$s = 3 \times \frac{250}{100}$$

$$s = 7.5 \text{ inches}$$

3. What is the air flow per gallon of water flow if the overall air lift length is 60 feet, the water depth is 52 feet, and the air lift entrance is 2 feet clear of the sea floor?

$$Q = 0.1337 \times \frac{L}{(D + 33) \times \log\left(1 + \frac{(D - d_1)}{(D + 33)}\right)}$$

where:

Q = air flow in cubic feet per minute
L = total lift in feet
D = water depth at the sea floor in feet
d_1 = distance from the sea floor to the air entrance in feet

$$Q = 0.1337 \times \frac{60}{(52 + 33) \times \log\left(1 + \frac{(52 - 2)}{(52 + 33)}\right)}$$

$$Q = 0.1337 \times \frac{60}{85 \times \log 1.588}$$

$$Q = 0.47 \times \frac{\text{cubic feet}}{\text{gallon}}$$

Example 65—Potential Fish Kill Radius of Explosives

An explosive charge of 10 pounds is to be detonated at a depth of 50 feet. What is the range at which 90 percent of fish 1 pound and above survive?

$$R = Kw^k$$

where:

R = range in feet at which 90 percent of marine life survives
K = coefficient from the table that follows
w = weight of the charge in pounds
k = exponent from the table that follows

TABLE A-34. FISH KILL RADIUS OF EXPLOSIVES.

Fish Weight	*Depth of Blast (feet)*	*K*	*k*
1 oz	10	328	0.220
1 oz	50	385	0.256
1 oz	200	475	0.262
1 lb	10	174	0.264
1 lb	50	235	0.275
1 lb	200	272	0.299
30 lb	10	86	0.284
30 lb	50	131	0.314
30 lb	200	139	0.342

$$R = 235 \times 10^{0.275}$$

$$R = 443 \text{ feet}$$

Example 66—Safe Distance from an Explosion

What is the minimum safe distance for people from a surface detonation of 50 pounds of explosives?

$$d = 300 \times \sqrt[3]{w}$$

where:

d = minimum safe distance from the explosion in feet
w = weight of the explosive charge in pounds

$$d = 300 \times \sqrt[3]{50}$$

$$d = 1{,}103 \text{ feet}$$

Example 67—Explosive Cutting

How much untamped explosive (C-4) is needed to cut a ½-inch plate 4 feet wide: (1) on the surface? (2) under water?

$$P = \frac{3}{8} \times A$$

for surface cutting, and

$$P = \frac{3}{4} \times A$$

for underwater cutting, where:

P = weight (quantity) of explosives in pounds
A = cross-sectional area of section being cut in square inches

1. On the surface:

$$P = \frac{3}{8} \times (\frac{1}{2} \times 48)$$

$$P = 9 \text{ pounds}$$

2. Under water:

$$P = \frac{3}{4} \times (\frac{1}{2} \times 48)$$

$$P = 18 \text{ pounds}$$

Example 68—Flat Width of Fenders

What is the flat width of a 5-foot-diameter cylindrical fender compressed 30 percent?

$$\text{flat width} = 0.0157 \times \% \text{ compression} \times \text{fender diameter}$$

$$\text{flat width} = 0.0157 \times 40 \times 5$$

$$\text{flat width} = 3.14 \text{ feet}$$

Example 69—Equivalent Ship Size for Fendering

A 43,000-ton deadweight ship is to berth alongside a 125,000-ton deadweight ship for cargo transfer. What is the equivalent size for determining fendering?

$$C = \frac{2AB}{(A + B)}$$

where:

C = equivalent size (tons)
A and B = deadweight tonnage of the two ships (tons)

$$C = \frac{2 \times 43{,}000 \times 125{,}000}{43{,}000 + 125{,}000}$$

$$C = 63{,}988 \text{ tons}$$

APPENDIX

B

SALVAGE CONTRACTS

This book emphasizes the symbiotic relationship between the commercial and technical portions of salvage. While the majority of the information is technical in nature, the commercial portions warrant particular attention. This Appendix contains the commercial instruments—the contracts—that are the heart and soul of the commercial endeavor. Contracts for both time-critical salvage and wreck removal are given along with the International Convention on Salvage, 1989, and the International Salvage Union Sub-Contract (Award Sharing). Prospective salvors are warned that their commercial success in salvage is based on both knowing their contract well and knowing the nuances of working with the particular contract. The same warning applies to the owners of salved property whom it behooves to know salvage contracts and to understand how salvors work. Anyone entering a salvage contract without fully understanding the contract is a fool undeserving of commercial success.

The specific contents of this Appendix are:

INTERNATIONAL CONVENTION ON SALVAGE, 1989

The States parties to the present Convention,

Recognizing the desirability of determining by agreement uniform international rules regarding salvage operations,

Noting that substantial developments, in particular the increased concern for the protection of the environment, have demonstrated the need to review the international rules presently contained in the Convention for the Unification of Certain Rules of Law relating to Assistance and Salvage at Sea, done at Brussels, 23 September 1910,

Conscious of the major contribution which efficient and timely salvage operations can make to the safety of vessels and other property in danger and to the protection of the environment,

Convinced of the need to ensure that adequate incentives are available to persons who undertake salvage operations in respect of vessels and other property in danger,

Have agreed as follows:

CHAPTER 1—GENERAL PROVISIONS

Article 1. Definitions

For the purpose of this Convention:

(a) *Salvage operation* means any act or activity undertaken to assist a vessel or any other property in danger in navigable waters or in any other waters whatsoever.

(b) *Vessel* means any ship or craft, or any structure capable of navigation.

(c) *Property* means any property not permanently and internationally attached to the shoreline and includes freight at risk.

(d) *Damage* to the environment means substantial physical damage to human health or to marine life or resources in coastal or inland waters or areas adjacent thereto, caused by pollution, contamination, fire, explosion or similar major incidents.

(e) *Payment* means any reward, remuneration or compensation due under this Convention.

(f) *Organization* means the International Maritime Organization.

(g) *Secretary-General* means the Secretary–General of the Organization.

Article 2. Application of the Convention

This Convention shall apply whenever judicial or arbitral proceedings relating to matters dealt with in this Convention are brought in a State Party.

Article 3. Platforms and drilling units
This Convention shall not apply to fixed or floating platforms or to mobile offshore drilling units when such platforms or units are on location engaged in the exploration, exploitation or production of seabed mineral resources.

Article 4. State-owned vessels
(1) Without prejudice to article 5, this Convention shall not apply to warships or other non-commercial vessels owned or operated by a State and entitled, at the time of salvage operations, to sovereign immunity under generally recognized principles of international law unless that State decides otherwise.
(2) Where a State Party decides to apply the Convention to its warships or other vessels described in paragraph 1, it shall notify the Secretary-General thereof specifying the terms and conditions of such application.

Article 5. Salvage operations controlled by public authorities
(1) This Convention shall not affect any provisions of national law or any international convention relating to salvage operations by or under the control of public authorities.
(2) Nevertheless, salvors carrying out such salvage operations shall be entitled to avail themselves of the rights and remedies provided for in this Convention in respect of salvage operations.
(3) The extent to which a public authority under a duty to perform salvage operations may avail itself of the rights and remedies provided for in this Convention shall be determined by the law of the State where such authority is situated.

Article 6. Salvage contracts
(1) This Convention shall apply to any salvage operations save to the extent that a contract otherwise provides expressly or by implication.
(2) The master shall have the authority to conclude contracts for salvage operations on behalf of the owner of the vessel. The master or the owner of the vessel shall have the authority to conclude such contracts on behalf of the owner of the property on board the vessel.
(3) Nothing in this article shall affect the application of article 7 nor duties to prevent or minimize damage to the environment.

Article 7. Annulment and modification of contracts
A contract or any terms thereof may be annulled or modified if:
(a) the contract has been entered into under undue influence or the influence of danger and its terms are inequitable; or
(b) the payment under the contract is in an excessive degree too large or too small for the services actually rendered.

CHAPTER II—PERFORMANCE OF SALVAGE OPERATIONS

Article 8. Duties of the salvor and of the owner and master
(1) The salvor shall owe a duty to the owner of the vessel or other property in danger:
(a) to carry out the salvage operations with due care;

(b) in performing the duty specified in subparagraph (a), to exercise due care to prevent or minimize damage to the environment;
(c) whenever circumstances reasonably require, to seek assistance from other salvors; and
(d) to accept the intervention of other salvors when reasonably requested to do so by the owner or master of the vessel or other property in danger; provided however that the amount of his reward shall not be prejudiced should it be found that such a request was unreasonable.

(2) The owner and master of the vessel or the owner of other property in danger shall owe a duty to the salvor:
(a) to co-operate fully with him during the course of the salvage operations;
(b) in so doing, to exercise due care to prevent or minimize damage to the environment; and
(c) when the vessel or other property has been brought to a place of safety, to accept redelivery when reasonably requested by the salvor to do so.

Article 9. Rights of coastal States

Nothing in this Convention shall affect the right of the coastal State concerned to take measures in accordance with generally recognized principles of international law to protect its coastline or related interests from pollution or the threat of pollution following upon a maritime casualty or acts relating to such a casualty which may reasonably be expected to result in major harmful consequences, including the right of a coastal State to give directions in relation to salvage operations.

Article 10. Duty to render assistance

(1) Every master is bound, so far as he can do so without serious danger to his vessel and persons thereon, to render assistance to any person in danger of being lost at sea.
(2) The States Parties shall adopt the measures necessary to enforce the duty set out in paragraph 1.
(3) The owner of the vessel shall incur no liability for a breach of the duty of the master under paragraph 1.

Article 11. Co-operation

A State Party shall, whenever regulating or deciding upon matters relating to salvage operations such as admittance to ports of vessels in distress or the provision of facilities to salvors, take into account the need for co-operation between salvors, other interested parties and public authorities in order to ensure the efficient and successful performance of salvage operations for the purpose of saving life or property in danger as well as preventing damage to the environment in general.

CHAPTER III—RIGHTS OF SALVORS

Article 12. Conditions for reward

(1) Salvage operations which have had a useful result give right to reward.
(2) Except as otherwise provided, no payment is due under this Convention if the salvage operations have had no useful result.

(3) This chapter shall apply, notwithstanding that the salved vessel and the vessel undertaking the salvage operations belong to the same owner.

Article 13. Criteria for fixing the reward

(1) The reward shall be fixed with a view to encouraging salvage operations, taking into account the following criteria without regard to the order in which they are presented below:
  (a) the salved value of the vessel and other property;
  (b) the skill and efforts of the salvors in preventing or minimizing damage to the environment;
  (c) the measure of success obtained by the salvor;
  (d) the nature and degree of the danger;
  (e) the skill and efforts of the salvors in salving the vessel, other property and life;
  (f) the time used and expenses and losses incurred by the salvors;
  (g) the risk of liability and other risks run by the salvors or their equipment;
  (h) the promptness of the services rendered;
  (i) the availability and use of vessels or other equipment intended for salvage operations;
  (j) the state of readiness and efficiency of the salvor's equipment and the value thereof.

(2) Payment of a reward fixed according to paragraph 1 shall be made by all of the vessel and other property interests in proportion to their respective salved values. However, a State Party may in its national law provide that the payment of a reward has to be made by one of these interests for their respective shares. Nothing in this article shall prevent any right of defense.

(3) The rewards, exclusive of any interest and recoverable legal costs that may be payable thereon, shall not exceed the salved value of the vessel and other property.

Article 14. Special compensation

(1) If the salvor has carried out salvage operations in respect of a vessel which by itself or its cargo threatened damage to the environment and has failed to earn a reward under article 13 at least equivalent to the special compensation assessable in accordance with this article, he shall be entitled to special compensation from the owner of that vessel equivalent to his expenses as herein defined.

(2) If, in the circumstances set out in paragraph 1, the salvor by his salvage operations has prevented or minimized damage to the environment, the special compensation payable by the owner to the salvor under paragraph 1 may be increased up to a maximum of 30% of the expenses incurred by the salvor. However, the tribunal, if it deems is fair and just to do so and bearing in mind the relevant criteria set out in article 13, paragraph 1, may increase such special compensation further, but in no event shall the total increase be more than 100% of the expenses incurred by the salvor.

(3) Salvor's expenses for the purpose of paragraphs 1 and 2 means the out-of-pocket expenses reasonably incurred by the salvor in the salvage operation and a fair rate for equipment and personnel actually and reasonably used in the salvage opera-

tion, taking into consideration the criteria set out in article 13, paragraph 1 (h), (i) and (j).

(4) The total special compensation under this article shall be paid only if and to the extent that such compensation is greater than any reward recoverable by the salvor under article 13.

(5) If the salvor has been negligent and has thereby failed to prevent or minimize damage to the environment, he may be deprived of the whole or part of any special compensation due under this article.

(6) Nothing in this article shall affect any right of recourse on the part of the owner of the vessel.

Article 15. Apportionment between salvors

(1) The apportionment of a reward under article 13 between salvors shall be made on the basis of the criteria contained in that article.

(2) The apportionment between the owner, master and other persons in the service of each salving vessel shall be determined by the law of the flag of that vessel. If the salvage has not been carried out from a vessel, the apportionment shall be determined by the law governing the contract between the salvor and his servants.

Article 16. Salvage of persons

(1) No remuneration is due from persons whose lives are saved, but nothing in this article shall affect the provisions of national law on this subject.

(2) A salvor of human life, who has taken part in the services rendered on the occasion of the accident giving rise to salvage, is entitled to a fair share of the payment awarded to the salvor for salving the vessel or other property or preventing or minimizing damage to the environment.

Article 17. Services rendered under existing contracts

No payment is due under the provisions of this Convention unless the services rendered exceed what can be reasonably considered as due performance of a contract entered into before the danger arose.

Article 18. The effect of salvor's misconduct

A salvor may be deprived of the whole or part of the payment due under this Convention to the extent that the salvage operations have become necessary or more difficult because of fault or neglect on his part or if salvor has been guilty of fraud or other dishonest conduct.

Article 19. Prohibition of salvage operations

Services rendered notwithstanding the express and reasonable prohibition of the owner or master of the vessel or the owner of any other property in danger which is not and has not been on board the vessel shall not give rise to payment under this Convention.

CHAPTER IV—CLAIMS AND ACTIONS

Article 20. Maritime lien

(1) Nothing in this Convention shall affect the salvor's maritime lien under any international convention or national law.

(2) The salvor may not enforce his maritime lien when satisfactory security for his claim, including interest and costs, has been duly tendered or provided.

Article 21. Duty to provide security

(1) Upon the request of the salvor a person liable for a payment due under this Convention shall provide satisfactory security for the claim, including interest and costs of the salvor.

(2) Without prejudice to paragraph 1, the owner of the salved vessel shall use his best endeavours to ensure that the owners of the cargo provide satisfactory security for the claims against them including interest and costs before the cargo is released.

(3) The salved vessel and other property shall not, without the consent of the salvor, be removed from the port or place at which they first arrive after the completion of the salvage operations until satisfactory security has been put up for the salvor's claim against the relevant vessel or property.

Article 22. Interim payment

(1) The tribunal having jurisdiction over the claim of the salvor may, by interim decision, order that the salvor shall be paid on account such amount as seems fair and just, and on such terms including terms as to security where appropriate, as may be fair and just according to the circumstances of the case.

(2) In the event of an interim payment under this article the security provided under article 21 shall be reduced accordingly.

Article 23. Limitation of actions

(1) Any action relating to payment under this Convention shall be time-barred if judicial or arbitral proceedings have not been instituted within a period of two years. The limitation period commences on the day on which the salvage operations are terminated.

(2) The person against whom a claim is made may at any time during the running of the limitation period extend that period by a declaration to the claimant. This period may in the like manner be further extended.

(3) An action for indemnity by a person liable may be instituted even after the expiration of the limitation period provided for in the preceding paragraphs, if brought within the time allowed by the law of the State where proceedings are instituted.

Article 24. Interest

The right of the salvor to interest on any payment due under this Convention shall be determined according to the law of the State in which the tribunal seized of the case is situated.

Article 25. State-owned cargoes

Unless the State owner consents, no provision of this Convention shall be used as a basis for the seizure, arrest or detention by any legal process of, nor for any proceedings *in rem* against, non-commercial cargoes owned by a State and entitled, at the time of the salvage operations, to sovereign immunity under generally recognized principles of international law.

Article 26. Humanitarian cargoes
No provision of this Convention shall be used as a basis for the seizure, arrest or detention of humanitarian cargoes donated by a State, if such State has agreed to pay for salvage services rendered in respect of such humanitarian cargoes.

Article 27. Publication of arbitral awards
States Parties shall encourage, as far as possible and with the consent of the parties, the publication of arbitral awards made in salvage cases.

CHAPTER V—FINAL CLAUSES

Article 28. Signature, ratification, acceptance, approval and accession

(1) This Convention shall be open for signature at the Headquarters of the Organization from 1 July 1989 to 30 June 1990 and shall thereafter remain open for accession.

(2) States may express their consent to be bound by this Convention by:
  - (a) signature without reservation as to ratification, acceptance or approval; or
  - (b) signature subject to ratification, acceptance or approval, followed by ratification, acceptance or approval; or
  - (c) accession.

(3) Ratification, acceptance, approval or accession shall be effected by the deposit of an instrument to that effect with the Secretary-General.

Article 29. Entry into force

(1) This Convention shall enter into force one year after the date on which 15 States have expressed their consent to be bound by it.

(2) For a State which expresses its consent to be bound by this Convention after the conditions for entry into force thereof have been met, such consent shall take effect one year after the date of expression of such consent.

Article 30. Reservations

(1) Any State may, at the time of signature, ratification, acceptance, approval or accession, reserve the right not to apply the provision of this Convention:
  - (a) when the salvage operation takes place in inland waters and all vessels involved are of inland navigation;
  - (b) when the salvage operations take place in inland waters and no vessel is involved;
  - (c) when all interested parties are nationals of that State;
  - (d) when the property involved is maritime cultural property of prehistoric archaeological or historic interest and is situated on the sea-bed.

(2) Reservations made at the time of signature are subject to confirmation upon ratification, acceptance or approval.

(3) Any State which has made a reservation to this Convention may withdraw it at any time by means of a notification addressed to the Secretary-General. Such withdrawal shall take effect on the date the notification is received. If the notification states that the withdrawal of a reservation is to take effect on a date specified

therein, and such date is later than the date the notification is received by the Secretary-General, the withdrawal shall take effect on such later date.

Article 31. Denunciation

(1) This Convention may be denounced by any State Party at any time after the expiry of one year from the date on which this Convention enters into force for that State.

(2) Denunciation shall be effected by the deposit of an instrument of denunciation with the Secretary-General.

(3) A denunciation shall take effect one year, or such longer period as may be specified in the instrument of denunciation, after the receipt of the instrument of denunciation by the Secretary-General.

Article 32. Revision and amendment

(1) A conference for the purpose of revising or amending this Convention may be convened by the Organization.

(2) The Secretary-General shall convene a conference of the States Parties to this Convention for revising or amending the Convention, at the request of eight States Parties, or one fourth of the States Parties, whichever is the higher figure.

(3) Any consent to be bound by this Convention expressed after the date of entry into force of an amendment to this Convention shall be deemed to apply to the Convention as amended.

Article 33. Depositary

(1) This Convention shall be deposited with the Secretary-General.

(2) The Secretary-General shall:

(a) inform all States which have signed this Convention or acceded thereto, and all Members of the Organization, of:

(i) each new signature or deposit of an instrument of ratification, acceptance, approval or accession together with the date thereof;

(ii) the date of the entry into force of this Convention;

(iii) the deposit of any instrument of denunciation of this Convention together with the date on which it is received and the date on which the denunciation takes;

(iv) any amendment adopted in conformity with article 32;

(v) the receipt of any reservation, declaration or notification made under this Convention;

(b) transmit certified true copies of this Convention to all States which have signed this Convention or acceded thereto.

(3) As soon as this Convention enters into force, a certified true copy thereof shall be transmitted by the Depositary to the Secretary-General of the United Nations for registration and publication in accordance with Article 102 of the Charter of the United Nations.

Article 34. Languages

This Convention is established in a single original in the Arabic, Chinese, English, French, Russian and Spanish languages, each text being equally authentic.

In witness whereof the undersigned being duly authorized by their respective Governments for that purpose have signed this Convention.

Done at London this twenty-eighth day of April one thousand nine hundred and eighty-nine.

ATTACHMENT 1

Common Understanding Concerning Articles 13 and 14 of the International Convention on Salvage, 1989

It is the common understanding of the Conference that, in fixing a reward under article 13 and assessing special compensation under article 14 of the International Convention on Salvage, 1989 the tribunal is under no duty to fix a reward under article 13 up to the maximum salved value of the vessel and other property before assessing the special compensation to be paid under article 14.

ATTACHMENT 2

Resolution Requesting the Amendment of the York-Antwerp Rules, 1974

The International Conference on Salvage, 1989,

Having Adopted the International Convention on Salvage, 1989,

Considering the payments made pursuant to article 14 are not intended to be allowed in general average,

Requests the Secretary-General of the International Maritime Organization to take the appropriate steps in order to ensure speedy amendment of the York-Antwerp Rules, 1974, to ensure that special compensation paid under article 14 is not subject to general average.

LOF 1995

LLOYD'S

STANDARD FORM OF

SALVAGE AGREEMENT

> NOTES
>
> *1. Insert name of person signing on behalf of Owners of property to be salved. The Master should sign wherever possible.*
>
> *2. The Contractor's name should always be inserted in line 4 and whenever the Agreement is signed by the Master of the Salving vessel or other person on behalf of the Contractor the name of the Master or other person must also be inserted in line 4 before the words "for and on behalf of." The words "for and on behalf of" should be deleted where a Contractor signs personally.*
>
> *3. Insert place if agreed in clause 1(a)(i) and currency if agreed in clause 1(e).*

(APPROVED AND PUBLISHED BY THE COUNCIL OF LLOYD'S)

NO CURE – NO PAY

On board the____________________

Dated___________

IT IS HEREBY AGREED between Captain[1]___________________________________
for and on behalf of the Owners of the "___________________________________" her cargo freight bunkers stores and any other property thereon (hereinafter collectively called "the Owners") and___________________________for and on behalf of _______________ (hereinafter called "the Contractor"[2]) that:–

1. (a) The Contractor shall use his best endeavors:–

(i) to salve the " ___________________________________ " and/or her cargo freight bunkers stores and any other property thereon and take them to[3] _________ ____________________________or to such other place as may hereafter be agreed either place to be deemed a place of safety or if no such place is named or agreed to a place of safety and
(ii) while performing the salvage services to prevent or minimize damage to the environment.

(b) Subject to the statutory provisions relating to special compensation the services shall be rendered and accepted as salvage services upon the principle of "no cure–no pay."

(c) The Contractor's remuneration shall be fixed by Arbitration in London in the manner hereinafter prescribed and any other difference arising out of this Agreement or the operations thereunder shall be referred to Arbitration in the same way.

(d) In the event of the services referred to in this Agreement or any part of such services having been already rendered at the date of this Agreement by the Contractor to the said vessel and/or her cargo freight bunkers stores and any other property thereon the provisions of this Agreement shall apply to such services.

(e) The security to be provided to the Council of Lloyd's (hereinafter called "the Council") the Salved Value(s) the Award and/or any Interim Award(s) and/or any Award on Appeal shall be in[3] ________________________________currency.

(f) If clause 1(e) is not completed then the security to be provided and the Salved Values(s) the Award and/or Interim Award(s) and/or Award on Appeal shall be in Pounds Sterling.

(g) This Agreement and Arbitration thereunder shall except as otherwise expressly provided be governed by the law of England, including the English law of salvage.

PROVISIONS AS TO THE SERVICES

2. *Definitions:* in this Agreement any reference to "Convention" is a reference to the International Convention on Salvage, 1989, as incorporated in the Merchant Shipping (Salvage and Pollution) Act 1994 (and any amendment thereto). The terms "Contractor" and "services"/ "salvage services" in this Agreement shall have the same meanings as the terms "salvor(s)" and "salvage operation(s)" in the Convention.

3. *Owners Cooperation*: The Owners their Servants and Agents shall co-operate fully with the Contractor in and about the salvage including obtaining entry to the place named or the place of safety as defined in clause (1). The Contractor may make reasonable use of the vessel's machinery gear equipment anchors chains stores and other appurtenances during and for the purpose of the salvage services free of expense but shall not unnecessarily damage abandon or sacrifice the same or any property the subject of this Agreement.

4. *Vessel Owners Right to Terminate*: When there is no loner any reasonable prospect of a useful result leading to a salvage reward in accordance with Convention Article 13 the owners of the vessel shall be entitled to terminate the services of the Contractor by giving reasonable notice to the Contractor in writing.

PROVISIONS AS TO SECURITY

5. (a) The Contractor shall immediately after the termination of the services or sooner notify the Council and where practicable the Owners of the amount for which he demands salvage security (inclusive of the costs expenses and interest) from each of the respective Owners.

(b) Where a claim is made or may be made for special compensation, the owners of a vessel shall on the demand of the Contractor whenever made provide security for the Contractor's claim for special compensation provided always that such demand is made within two years of the date of termination of the services.

(c) The amount of any such security shall be reasonable in the light of the knowledge available to the Contractor at the time when the demand is made. Unless otherwise agreed such security shall be provided (i) to the Council (ii) in a form approved by the Council and (iii) by persons firms or corporations either acceptable to the Contractor or resident in the United Kingdom and acceptable to the Council. The Council shall not be responsible for the sufficiency (whether in amount or otherwise) of any security which shall be provided nor for the default or insolvency of any person firm or corporation providing the same.

(d) The owners of the vessel their Servants and Agents shall use their best endeavors to ensure that the cargo owners provide their proportion of salvage security before the cargo is released.

6. (a) Until security has been provided as aforesaid the Contractor shall have a maritime lien on the property salved for his remuneration.

(b) The property salved shall not without the consent in writing of the Contractor (which shall not be unreasonably withheld) be removed from the place to which it has been taken by the contractor under clause 1(a). Where such consent is given by the Contractor on condition that the Contractor is provided with temporary security pending completion of the voyage the Contractor's maritime lien on the property salved shall remain in force to the extent necessary to enable the Contractor to compel the provision of security in accordance with clause 5(c).

(c) The Contractor shall not arrest or detain the property salved unless:-

(i) security is not provided within 14 days (exclusive of Saturdays or Sundays or other days observed as general holidays at Lloyd's) after the date of the termination of the services or
(ii) he has reason to believe that the removal of the property salved is contemplated contrary to clause 6(b) or
(iii) any attempt is made to remove the property salved contrary to clause 6(b).

(d) The Arbitrator appointed under clause 7 or the Appeal Arbitrator(s) appointed under clause 13(d) shall have power in their absolute discretion to include in the amount awarded to the Contractor the whole or part of any expenses reasonably incurred by the Contractor in:-

(i) ascertaining demanding and obtaining the amount of security reasonably required in accordance with clause 5.
(ii) enforcing and/or protecting by insurance or otherwise or taking reasonable steps to enforce and/or protect his lien.

PROVISIONS AS TO ARBITRATION

7. (a) Whether security has been provided or not the Council shall appoint an Arbitrator upon receipt of a written request made by letter telex facsimile or in any other permanent form provided that any party requesting such appointment shall if required by the Council undertake to pay the reasonable fees and expenses of the Council and/or any Arbitrator or Appeal Arbitrator(s).

(b) Where an Arbitrator has been appointed and the parties do not proceed to arbitration the Council may recover any fees costs and/or expenses which are outstanding.

8. The Contractor's remuneration and/or special compensation shall be fixed by the Arbitrator appointed under clause 7. Such remuneration shall not be diminished by reason of the exception to the principle of "no cure–no pay" in the form of special compensation.

REPRESENTATION

9. Any party to this Agreement who wishes to be heard or to adduce evidence shall nominate a person in the United Kingdom to represent him failing which the Arbitrator or Appeal Arbitrator(s) may proceed as if such party had renounced his right to be heard or adduce evidence.

CONDUCT OF THE ARBITRATION

10. (a) The Arbitrator shall have power to:-

- (i) admit such oral or documentary evidence or information as he may think fit
- (ii) conduct the Arbitration in such manner in all respects as he may think fit subject to such procedural rules as the Council may approve
- (iii) order the Contractor in his absolute discretion to pay the whole or part of the expense of providing excessive security or security which has been unreasonably demanded under clause 5(b) and to deduct such sum from the remuneration and/or special compensation
- (iv) make Interim Award(s) including payment(s) on account on such terms as may be fair and just
- (v) make such orders as to costs fees and expenses including those of the Council charged under clauses 10(b) and 14(b) as may be fair and just.

(b) The Arbitrator and the Council may charge reasonable fees and expenses for their services whether the Arbitration proceeds to a hearing or not and all such fees and expenses shall be treated as part of the costs of the Arbitration.

(c) Any Award shall (subject to Appeal as provided in this Agreement) be final and binding on all the parties concerned whether they were represented at the Arbitration or not.

INTEREST & RATES OF EXCHANGE

11. *Interest*: Interest at rates per annum to be fixed by the Arbitrator shall (subject to Appeal as provided in this Agreement) be payable on any sum awarded taking into account any sums already paid:-

- (i) from the date of termination of the services unless the Arbitrator shall in his absolute discretion otherwise decide until the date of publication by the Council of the Award and/or Interim Award(s) and
- (ii) from the expiration of 21 days (exclusive of Saturdays and Sundays or other days observed as general holidays at Lloyd's) after the date of publication by the Council of the Award and/or Interim Award(s) until the date payment is received by the Contractor or the Council, both dates inclusive.

For the purpose of sub-clause (ii) the expression "sum awarded" shall include the fees and expenses referred to in clause 10(b).

12. *Currency Correction*: In considering what sums of money have been expended by the Contractor in rendering the services and/or in fixing the amount of the Award and/or Interim Award(s) and/or Award on Appeal the Arbitrator or Appeal Arbitrator(s) shall to such an extent and in so far as it may be fair and just in all the circumstances give effect to the consequences of any change or changes in the relevant rates of exchange which may have occurred between the date of termination of the services and the date on which the Award and/or Interim Award(s) and/or Award on Appeal is made.

PROVISIONS AS TO APPEAL

13. (a) Notice of Appeal if any shall be given to the Council within 14 days (exclusive of Saturdays and Sundays or other days observed as general holidays at Lloyd's) after the date of the publication by the Council of the Award and/or Interim Award(s).

(b) Notice of Cross-Appeal if any shall be given to the Council within 14 days (exclusive of Saturdays and Sundays or other days observed as general holidays at Lloyd's) after notification by the Council to the parties of any Notice of Appeal. Such notification if sent by post shall be deemed received on the working day following the day of posting.

(c) Notice of Appeal or Cross-Appeal shall be given to the Council by letter telex facsimile or in any other permanent form.

(d) Upon receipt of Notice of Appeal the Council shall refer the Appeal to the hearing and determination of the Appeal Arbitrator(s) selected by it.

(e) If any Notice of Appeal or Cross-Appeal is withdrawn the Appeal hearing shall nevertheless proceed in respect of such Notice of Appeal or Cross-Appeal as may remain.

(f) Any Award on Appeal shall be final and binding on all the parties to that Appeal Arbitration whether they were represented either at the Arbitration or at the Appeal Arbitration or not.

CONDUCT OF THE APPEAL

14. (a) The Appeal Arbitrator(s) in addition to the powers of the Arbitrator under clauses 10(a) and 11 shall have power to:-

(i) admit the evidence which was before the Arbitrator together with the Arbitrator's notes and reasons for his Award and/or Interim Award(s) and any transcript of evidence and such additional evidence as he or they may think fit.
(ii) confirm increase or reduce the sum awarded by the Arbitrator and to make such order as to the payment of interest on such sum as he or they may think fit.
(iii) confirm revoke or vary any order and/or Declaratory Award made by the Arbitrator.

(iv) award interest on any fees and expenses charged under paragraph (b) of this clause from the expiration of 21 days (exclusive of Saturdays and Sundays or other days observed as general holidays at Lloyd's) after the date of publication by the Council of the Award on Appeal and/or Interim Award(s) on Appeal until the date payment is received by the Council both dates inclusive.

(b) The Appeal Arbitrator(s) and the Council may charge reasonable fees and expenses for their services in connection with the Appeal Arbitration whether it proceeds to a hearing or not and all such fees and expenses shall be treated as part of the costs of the Appeal Arbitration.

PROVISIONS AS TO PAYMENT

15. (a) In case of Arbitration if no Notice of Appeal be received by the Council in accordance with clause 13(a) the Council shall call upon the party or parties concerned to pay the amount awarded and in the event of non-payment shall subject to the Contractor first providing to the Council a satisfactory Undertaking to pay all the costs thereof realize or enforce the security and pay therefrom to the Contractor (whose receipt shall be a good discharge to it) the amount awarded to him together with interest if any. The Contractor shall reimburse the parties concerned to such extent as the Award is less than any sums paid on account or in respect of Interim Award(s).

(b) If Notice of Appeal be received by the Council in accordance with clause 13 it shall as soon as the Award on Appeal has been published by it call upon the party or parties concerned to pay the amount awarded and in the event of non-payment shall subject to the Contractor first providing to the Council a satisfactory Undertaking to pay all the costs thereof realize or enforce the security and pay therefrom to the Contractor (whose receipt shall be a good discharge to it) the amount awarded to him together with interest if any. The Contractor shall reimburse the parties concerned to such an extent as the Award on Appeal is less than any sums paid on account or in respect of the Award or Interim Award(s).

(c) If any sum shall become payable to the Contractor as remuneration for his services and/or interest and/or costs as the result of an agreement made between the Contractor and the Owners or any of them the Council in the event of non-payment shall subject to the Contractor first providing to the Council a satisfactory Undertaking to pay all the costs thereof realize or enforce the security and pay therefrom to the Contractor (whose receipt shall be a good discharge to it) the said sum.

(d) If the Award and/or Interim Award(s) and/or Award on Appeal provides or provide that the costs of the Arbitration and/or of the Appeal Arbitration or any part of such costs shall be borne by the Contractor such costs may be deducted from the amount awarded or agreed before payment is made to the Contractor unless satisfactory security is provided by the Contractor for the payment of such costs.

(e) Without prejudice to the provisions of clause 5(c) the liability of the Council shall be limited in any event to the amount of security provided to it.

GENERAL PROVISIONS

16. *Scope of Authority*: The Master or other person signing this Agreement on behalf of the property to be salved enters into this Agreement as agent for the vessel her cargo freight bunkers stores and any other property thereon and the respective Owners thereof and binds each (but not the one for the other or himself personally) to the due performance thereof.

17. *Notices*: Any Award notice authority order or other document signed by the Chairman of Lloyd's or any person authorized by the Council for the purpose shall be deemed to have been duly made or given by the Council and shall have the same force and effect in all respects as if it had been signed by every member of the Council.

18. *Sub-Contractor(s)*: The Contractor may claim salvage and enforce any Award or agreement made between the Contractor and the Owners against security provided under clause 5 if any on behalf of any Sub-Contractors his or their Servants or Agents including Masters and members of the crews of vessels employed by him or by any Sub-Contractors in the services provided that he first provides a reasonably satisfactory indemnity to the Owners against all claims by or liabilities to the said persons.

19. *Inducements prohibited*: No person signing this Agreement or any party on whose behalf it is signed shall at any time or in any manner whatsoever offer provide make give or promise to provide demand or take any form of inducement for entering into this Agreement.

For and on behalf of the Contractor	**For and on behalf of the Owners of property to be salved.**
______________________	______________________
(To be signed either by the Contractor personally or by the master of the salving vessel or other person whose name is inserted in line 4 of this Agreement.)	(To be signed by the Master or other person whose name is inserted in line 1 of this Agreement.)

INTERNATIONAL CONVENTION ON SALVAGE, 1989

The following provisions of the Convention are set out for information only.

Article 1

Definitions

(a) *Salvage Operation* means any act or activity undertaken to assist a vessel or any other property in danger in navigable waters or in any other waters whatsoever

(b) *Vessel* means any ship or craft, or any structure capable of navigation

(c) *Property* means any property not permanently and intentionally attached to the shoreline and includes freight at risk

(d) *Damage to the environment* means substantial physical damage to human health or to marine life or resources in coastal or inland waters or areas adjacent thereto, caused by pollution, contamination, fire, explosion or similar major incidents

(e) *Payment* means any reward, remuneration or compensation due under this Convention

Article 6

Salvage Contracts

1. This Convention shall apply to any salvage operations save to the extent that a contract otherwise provides expressly or by implication.

2. The master shall have the authority to conclude contracts for salvage operations on behalf of the owner of the vessel. The master or owner of the vessel shall have the authority to conclude such contracts on behalf of the owner of the property on board the vessel.

Article 8

Duties of the Salvor and of the Owner and Master

1. The salvor shall owe a duty to the owner of the vessel or other property in danger:

(a) to carry out the salvage operations with due care;

(b) in performing the duty specified in subparagraph (a), to exercise due care to prevent or minimize damage to the environment;

(c) whenever circumstances reasonably require, to seek assistance from other salvors; and

(d) to accept the intervention of other salvors when reasonably requested to do so by the owner or master of the vessel or other property in danger; provided however that the amount of his reward shall not be prejudiced should it be found that such a request was unreasonable.

2. The owner and master of the vessel or the owner of other property in danger shall owe a duty to the salvor:

(a) to co-operate fully with him during the course of the salvage operations;

(b) in so doing, to exercise due care to prevent or minimize damage to the environment; and

(c) when the vessel or other property has been brought to a place of safety, to accept redelivery when reasonably requested by the salvor to do so.

Article 13

Criteria for Fixing the Reward

1. The reward shall be fixed with a view to encouraging salvage operations, taking into account the following criteria without regard to the order in which they are presented below:

(a) the salved value of the vessel and other property;

(b) the skill and efforts of the salvors in preventing or minimizing damage to the environment;

(c) the measure of success obtained by the salvor;
(d) the nature and degree of the danger;
(e) the skill and efforts of the salvors in salving the vessel, other property and life;
(f) the time used and expenses and losses incurred by the salvors;
(g) the risk of liability and other risks run by the salvors or their equipment;
(h) the promptness and use of vessels or other equipment intended for salvage operations;
(i) the availability and use of vessels or other equipment intended for salvage operations;
(j) the state of readiness and efficiency of the salvor's equipment and the value thereof.

2. Payment of a reward fixed according to paragraph 1 shall be made by all of the vessel and other property interests in proportion to their respective salved values.

3. The rewards, exclusive of any interest and recoverable legal costs that may be payable thereon, shall not exceed the salved value of the vessel and other property.

Article 14

Special Compensation

1. If the salvor has carried out salvage operations in respect of a vessel which by itself or its cargo threatened damage to the environment and has failed to earn a reward under Article 13 at least equivalent to the special compensation assessable in accordance with this Article, he shall be entitled to special compensation from the owner of that vessel equivalent to his expenses as herein defined.

2. If, in the circumstances set out in paragraph 1, the salvor by his salvage operations has prevented or minimized damage to the environment, the special compensation payable by the owner to the salvor under paragraph 1 may be increased up to a maximum of 30% of the expenses incurred by the salvor. However, the Tribunal, if it deems it fair and just to do so and bearing in mind the relevant criteria set out in Article 13, paragraph 1, may increase such special compensation further, but in no event shall the total increase be more than 100% of the expenses incurred by the salvor.

3. Salvor's expenses for the purpose of paragraphs 1 and 2 means the out-of-pocket expenses reasonably incurred by the salvor in the salvage operation and a fair rate for equipment and personnel actually and reasonably used in the salvage operation, taking into consideration the criteria set out in Article 13, paragraph 1(h), (i) and (j).

4. The total special compensation under this article shall be paid only if and to the extent that such compensation is greater than any reward recoverable by the salvor under article 13.

5. If the salvor has been negligent and has thereby failed to prevent or minimize damage to the environment, he may be deprived of the whole or part of any compensation due under this article.

6. Nothing in this article shall affect any right of recourse on the part of the owner of the vessel.

LOF 1990

LLOYD'S

STANDARD FORM OF

NOTES

1. Insert name of person signing on behalf of Owners of property to be salved. The Master should sign wherever possible.

2. The Contractor's name should always be inserted in line 3 and whenever the Agreement is signed by the Master of the Salving vessel or other person on behalf of the Contractor the name of the Master or other person must also be inserted in line 3 before the words "for and on behalf of." The words "for and on behalf of" should be deleted where a Contractor signs personally.

3. Insert place if agreed in clause 1(a) and currency if agreed in clause 1(c).

SALVAGE AGREEMENT

(APPROVED AND PUBLISHED BY THE COUNCIL OF LLOYD'S)

NO CURE–NO PAY

On board the ____________________

Dated ___________

IT IS HEREBY AGREED between Captain[1] ____________________________________
and on behalf of the Owners of the "____"
her cargo freight bunkers stores and any other property thereon (hereinafter collectively called "the Owners") and ___________________ for and on behalf of _________________ (hereinafter called "the Contractor"[2]) that:-

1. (a) The Contractor shall use his best endeavors:-

(i) to salve the "____________________________________" and/or her cargo freight bunkers stores and any other property thereon and take them to[3] ______ ____ or to such other place as may hereafter be agreed either place to be deemed a place of safety or if no such place is named or agreed to a place of safety and

(ii) while performing the salvage services to prevent or minimize damage to the environment.

(b) Subject to clause 2 incorporating Convention Article 14 the services shall be rendered and accepted as salvage services upon the principle of "no cure–no pay."

(c) The Contractor's remuneration shall be fixed by Arbitration in London in the manner hereinafter prescribed and any other difference arising out of this Agreement or the operations thereunder shall be referred to Arbitration in the same way.

(d) In the event of the services referred to in this Agreement or any part of such services having been already rendered at the date of this agreement by the Contractor to the said vessel and/or her cargo freight bunkers stores and any other property thereon the provisions of this Agreement shall apply to such services.

(e) The security to be provided to the Council of Lloyd's (hereinafter called "the Council") the Salved Value(s) the Award and/or any Interim Award(s) and/or any Award on Appeal shall be in[3] ______________________ currency.

(f) If clause 1(e) is not completed then the security to be provided and the Salved Values(s) the Award and/or Interim Award(s) and/or Award on Appeal shall be in Pounds Sterling.

(g) This Agreement and Arbitration thereunder shall except as otherwise expressly provided be governed by the law of England, including the English law of salvage.

PROVISIONS AS TO THE SERVICES

2. Articles 1(a) to (e), 8, 13.1, 13.2 first sentence, 13.3 and 14 of the International Convention on Salvage 1989 ("the Convention Articles") set out hereafter are hereby incorporated into this Agreement. The terms "Contractor" and "services"/"salvage services" in this Agreement shall have the same meaning as the terms "salvor(s)" and "salvage operations(s)" in the Convention Articles.

3. The Owners their Servants and Agents shall co-operate fully with the Contractor in and about the salvage including obtaining entry to the place named or the place of safety as defined in clause 1. The Contractor may make reasonable use of the vessel's machinery gear equipment anchors chains stores and other appurtenances during and for the purpose of the salvage services free of expense but shall not unnecessarily damage abandon or sacrifice the same or any property the subject of this Agreement.

PROVISIONS AS TO THE SECURITY

4. (a) The Contractor shall immediately after the termination of the services or sooner notify the Council and where practicable the Owners of the amount for which he demands security (inclusive of the costs expenses and interest) from each of the respective owners.

(b) Where the exception to the principle of "no cure–no pay" under Convention Article 14 becomes likely to be applicable the owners of the vessel shall on the demand of the Contractor provide security for the Contractor's special compensation.

(c) The amount of any such security shall be reasonable in the light of the knowledge available to the Contractor at the time when the demand is made. Unless otherwise agreed such security shall be provided (i) to the Council (ii) in a form approved by the Council and (iii) by persons firms or corporations either acceptable to the Contractor or resident in the United Kingdom and acceptable to the Council. The Council shall not be responsible for the sufficiency (whether in amount or otherwise) of any security which shall be provided nor for the default or insolvency of any person firm or corporation providing the same.

(d) The owners of the vessel their Servants and Agents shall use their best endeavors to ensure that the cargo owners provide their proportion of security before the cargo is released.

5. (a) Until security has been provided as aforesaid the Contractor shall have a maritime lien on the property salved for his remuneration. The property salved shall not without the consent in writing of the Contractor (which shall not be unreasonably withheld) be removed from the place to which it has been taken by the contractor under clause 1(a).

(b) The Contractor shall not arrest or detain the property salved unless:

(i) security is not provided within 14 days (exclusive of Saturdays or Sundays or other days observed as general holidays at Lloyd's) after the date of the termination of the services or
(ii) the has reason to believe that the removal of the property salved is contemplated contrary to clause 5(a) or
(iii) any attempt is made to remove the property salved contrary to clause 5(a).

(c) The Arbitrator appointed under clause 6 or the Appeal Arbitrator(s) appointed under clause 11(d) shall have power in their absolute discretion to include in the amount awarded to the Contractor the whole or part of any expenses reasonably incurred by the Contractor in:-

(i) ascertaining demanding and obtaining the amount of security reasonably required in accordance with clause 4
(ii) enforcing and/or protecting by insurance or otherwise or taking reasonable steps to enforce and/or protect his lien.

PROVISIONS AS TO ARBITRATION

6. (a) Where security is provided to the Council in whole or in part the Council shall appoint an Arbitrator in respect of the property covered by such security.

(b) Whether security is provided or not the Council shall appoint an Arbitrator upon receipt of a written request made by letter telex facsimile or in any other permanent form provided that any party requesting such appointment shall if required by the Council undertake to pay the reasonable fees and expenses of the Council and/or any Arbitrator or Appeal Arbitrator(s).

(c) Where an Arbitrator has been appointed and the parties do not proceed to arbitration the Council may recover any fees costs and/or expenses which are outstanding and thereupon terminate the appointment of such Arbitrator.

7. The Contractor's remuneration shall be fixed by the Arbitrator appointed under clause 6. Such remuneration shall not be diminished by reason of the exception to the principle of "no cure-no pay" under Convention Article 14.

REPRESENTATION

8. Any party to this agreement who wishes to be heard or to adduce evidence shall nominate a person in the United Kingdom to represent him failing which the Arbitrator or Appeal Arbitrator(s) may proceed as if such party had renounced his right to be heard or adduce evidence.

CONDUCT OF THE ARBITRATION

9. (a) The Arbitrator shall have power to:-

(i) admit such oral or documentary evidence or information as he may think fit
(ii) conduct the Arbitration in such manner in all respects as he may think fit subject to such procedural rules as the Council may approve
(iii) condemn the Contractor in his absolute discretion in the whole or part of the expense of providing excessive security and deduct the amount in which the Contractor is so condemned from the salvage remuneration and/or special compensation
(iv) make Interim Award(s) on such terms as may be fair and just
(v) make such orders as to cost fees and expenses including those of the Council charged under clauses 9(b) and 12(b) as may be fair and just.

(b) The Arbitrator and the Council may charge reasonable fees and expenses for their services whether the Arbitration proceeds to a hearing or not and all such fees and expenses shall be treated as part of the cost of the Arbitration.

(c) Any Award shall (subject to Appeal as provided in this Agreement) be final and binding on all the parties concerned whether they were represented at the Arbitration or not.

INTEREST

10. Interest at rates per annum to be fixed by the Arbitrator shall (subject to Appeal as provided in this Agreement) be payable on any sum awarded taking into account any sums already paid:-

(i) from the date of termination of the services unless the Arbitrator shall in his absolute discretion otherwise decide until the date of publication by the Council of the Award and/or Interim Award(s) and
(ii) from the expiration of 21 days (exclusive of Saturdays and Sundays or other days observed as general holidays at Lloyd's) after the date of publication by the Council of the Award and/or Interim Award(s) until the date payment is received by the Contractor or the Council both dates inclusive.

PROVISIONS AS TO APPEAL

11. (a) Notice of Appeal if any shall be given to the Council within 14 days (exclusive of Saturdays and Sundays or other days observed as general holidays at Lloyd's) after the date of the publication by the Council of the Award and/or Interim Award(s).

(b) Notice of Cross-Appeal if any shall be given to the Council within 14 days (exclusive of Saturdays and Sundays or other days observed as general holidays at Lloyd's) after notification by the Council to the parties of any Notice of Appeal. Such notification if sent by post shall be deemed received on the working day following the day of posting.

(c) Notice of Appeal or Cross-Appeal shall be given to the Council by letter telex facsimile or in any other permanent form.

(d) Upon receipt of Notice of Appeal the Council shall refer the Appeal to the hearing and determination of the Appeal Arbitrator(s) selected by it.

(e) If any Notice of Appeal or Cross-Appeal is withdrawn the Appeal hearing shall nevertheless proceed in respect of such Notice of Appeal or Cross-Appeal as may remain.

(f) Any Award on Appeal shall be final and binding on all the parties to that Appeal Arbitration whether they were represented either at the Arbitration or at the Appeal Arbitration or not.

CONDUCT OF THE APPEAL

12. (a) The Appeal Arbitrator(s) in addition to the powers of the Arbitrator under clauses 9(a) and 10 shall have power to:-

- (i) admit the evidence which was before the Arbitrator together with the Arbitrator's notes and reasons for his Award and/or Interim Award(s) and any transcript of evidence and such additional evidence as he or they may think fit.
- (ii) confirm increase or reduce the sum awarded by the Arbitrator and to make such order as to the payment of interest on such sum as he or they may think fit.
- (iii) confirm revoke or vary any order and/or Declaratory Award made by the Arbitrator.

(b) The Appeal Arbitrator(s) and the Council may charge reasonable fees and expenses for their services in connection with the Appeal Arbitration whether it proceeds to a hearing or not and all such fees and expenses shall be treated as part of the costs of the Appeal Arbitration.

PROVISIONS AS TO PAYMENT

13. (a) In case of Arbitration if no Notice of Appeal be received by the Council in accordance with clause 11(a) the Council shall call upon the party or parties concerned to pay the amount awarded and in the event of non-payment shall subject to the Contractor first providing to the Council a satisfactory Undertaking to pay all the costs thereof realize or enforce the security and pay therefrom to the Contractor (whose receipt shall be a good discharge to it) the amount awarded to him together with interest if any. The contractor shall reimburse the parties concerned to such extent as the Award is less than any sums paid on account or in respect of Interim Award(s).

(b) If Notice of Appeal be received by the Council in accordance with clause 11 it shall as soon as the Award on Appeal has been published by it call upon the party or parties concerned to pay the amount awarded and in the event of non-payment shall subject to the Contractor first providing to the Council a satisfactory Undertaking to pay all the costs thereof realize or enforce the security and pay therefrom to the Contractor (whose receipt shall be a good discharge to it) the amount awarded to him together with interest if any. The Contractor shall reimburse the parties concerned to such an extent as the Award on Appeal is less than any sums paid on account or in respect of the Award or Interim Award(s).

(c) If any sum shall be payable to the Contractor as remuneration for his services and/or interest and/or costs as the result of an agreement made between the Contractor and the Owners or any of them the Council in the event of non-payment shall subject to the Contractor first providing to the Council a satisfactory Undertaking to pay all the costs thereof realize or enforce the security and pay therefrom to the Contractor (whose receipt shall be a good discharge to it) the said sum.

(d) If the Award and/or Interim Award(s) and/or Award on Appeal provides or provide that the costs of the Arbitration and/or of the Appeal Arbitration or any part of such costs shall be borne by the Contractor such costs may be deducted from the amount awarded or agreed before payment is made to the Contractor unless satisfactory security is provided by the Contractor for the payment of such costs.

(e) Without prejudice to the provisions of clause 4(c) the liability of the Council shall be limited in any event to the amount of security provided to it.

GENERAL PROVISIONS

14. The Master or other person signing this Agreement on behalf of the property to be salved enters into this Agreement as agent for the vessel her cargo freight bunkers stores and any other property thereon and the respective Owners thereof and binds each (but not the one for the other or himself personally) to the due performance thereof.

15. In considering what sums of money have been expended by the Contractor in rendering the services and/or in fixing the amount of the Award and/or Interim Award(s) and/or Award on Appeal the Arbitrator or Appeal Arbitrator(s) shall to such an extent and in so far as it may be fair and just in all the circumstances give effect to the consequences of any change or changes in the relevant rates of exchange which may have occurred between the date of termination of the services and the date on which the Award and/or Interim Award(s) and/or Award on Appeal is made.

16. Any Award notice authority order or other document signed by the chairman of Lloyd's or any person authorized by the Council for the purpose shall be deemed to have been duly made or given by the Council and shall have the same force and effect in all respects as if it had been signed by every member of the Council.

17. The Contractor may claim salvage and enforce any Award or agreement made between the Contractor and the Owners against security provided under clause 4 if any in the name and on behalf of any Sub-Contractors Servants or Agents including Masters and members of the crews of vessels employed by him or by any Sub-Contractors in the services provided that he first provides a reasonably satisfactory indemnity to the Owners against all claims by or liabilities to the said persons.

18. When there is no longer any reasonable prospect of a useful result leading to a salvage reward in accordance with Convention Article 13 the owners of the vessel shall be entitled to terminate the services of the Contractor by giving notice to the Contractor in writing.

19. No person signing this Agreement or any party on whose behalf it is signed shall at any time or in any manner whatsoever offer provide make give or promise to provide demand or take any form of inducement for entering into this Agreement.

THE CONVENTION ARTICLES

Article 1

Definitions

(a) *Salvage Operation* means any act or activity undertaken to assist a vessel or any other property in danger in navigable waters or in any other waters whatsoever

(b) *Vessel* means any ship or craft, or any structure capable of navigation

(c) *Property* means any property not permanently and intentionally attached to the shoreline and includes freight at risk

(d) *Damage to the environment* means substantial physical damage to human health or to marine life or resources in coastal or inland waters or areas adjacent thereto, caused by pollution, contamination, fire, explosion or similar major incidents

(e) *Payment* means any reward, remuneration or compensation due under this Convention

Article 8

Duties of the Salvor and of the Owner and Master

1. The salvor shall owe a duty to the owner of the vessel or other property in danger:

(a) to carry out the salvage operations with due care;

(b) in performing the duty specified in subparagraph (a), to exercise due care to prevent or minimize damage to the environment;

(c) whenever circumstances reasonably require, to seek assistance from other salvors; and

(d) to accept the intervention of other salvors when reasonably requested to do so by the owner or master of the vessel or other property in danger; provided however that the amount of his reward shall not be prejudiced should it be found that such a request was unreasonable.

2. The owner and master of the vessel or the owner of other property in danger shall owe a duty to the salvor:

(a) to co-operate fully with him during the course of the salvage operations;
(b) in so doing, to exercise due care to prevent or minimize damage to the environment; and
(c) when the vessel or other property has been brought to a place of safety, to accept redelivery when reasonably requested by the salvor to do so.

Article 13

Criteria for Fixing the Reward

1. The reward shall be fixed with a view to encouraging salvage operations, taking into account the following criteria without regard to the order in which they are presented below:

(a) the salved value of the vessel and other property;
(b) the skill and efforts of the salvors in preventing or minimizing damage to the environment;
(c) the measure of success obtained by the salvor;
(d) the nature and degree of the danger;
(e) the skill and efforts of the salvors in salving the vessel, other property and life;
(f) the time used and expenses and losses incurred by the salvors;
(g) the risk of liability and other risks run by the salvors or their equipment;
(h) the promptness and use of vessels or other equipment intended for salvage operations;
(i) the availability and use of vessels or other equipment intended for salvage operations;
(j) the state of readiness and efficiency of the salvor's equipment and the value thereof.

2. Payment of a reward fixed according to paragraph 1 shall be made by all of the vessel and other property interests in proportion to their respective salved values.

3. The rewards, exclusive of any interest and recoverable legal costs that may be payable thereon, shall not exceed the salved value of the vessel and other property.

Article 14

Special Compensation

1. If the salvor has carried out salvage operations in respect of a vessel which by itself or its cargo threatened damage to the environment and has failed to earn a reward under Article 13 at least equivalent to the special compensation assessable in accordance with this Article, he shall be entitled to special compensation from the owner of that vessel equivalent to his expenses as herein defined.

2. If, in the circumstances set out in paragraph 1, the salvor by his salvage operations has prevented or minimized damage to the environment, the special compensation payable by the owner to the salvor under paragraph 1 may be increased up to a maximum of 30% of the expenses incurred by the salvor. However, the Tribunal, if it deems it fair and just to do so and bearing in mind the relevant criteria set out in Article 13, paragraph 1, may increase such special compensation further, but in no event shall the total increase be more than 100% of the expenses incurred by the salvor.

3. Salvor's expenses for the purpose of paragraphs 1 and 2 means the out-of-pocket expenses reasonably incurred by the salvor in the salvage operation and a fair rate for equipment and personnel actually and reasonably used in the salvage operation, taking into consideration the criteria set out in Article 13, paragraph 1(h), (i) and (j).

4. The total special compensation under this article shall be paid only if and to the extent that such compensation is greater than any reward recoverable by the salvor under article 13.

5. If the salvor has been negligent and has thereby failed to prevent or minimize damage to the environment, he may be deprived of the whole or part of any compensation due under this article.

6. Nothing in this article shall affect any right of recourse on the part of the owner of the vessel.

For and on behalf of the Contractor	**For and on behalf of the Owners of property to be salved.**
____________________	____________________
(To be signed either by the Contractor personally or by the Master of the salving vessel or other person whose name is inserted in line 4 of this Agreement.)	(To be signed by the Master or other person whose name is inserted in line 1 of this Agreement.)

LOF 1980

LLOYD'S

STANDARD FORM OF

NOTES

1. Insert name of person signing on behalf of Owners of property to be salved. The Master should sign wherever possible.

2. The Contractor's name should always be inserted in line 3 and whenever the Agreement is signed by the Master of the Salving vessel or other person on behalf of the Contractor the name of the Master or other person must also be inserted in line 3 before the words "for and on behalf of." The words "for and on behalf of" should be deleted where a Contractor signs personally.

3. Insert place if agreed in clause 1(a) and currency if agreed in clause 1(c).

SALVAGE AGREEMENT

(APPROVED AND PUBLISHED BY THE COMMITTEE OF LLOYD'S)

NO CURE – NO PAY

On board the __________________
Dated __________________ 19___

IT IS HEREBY AGREED between Captain[1] ________________________________ for and on behalf of the Owners of the " ________________________________ " her cargo freight bunkers and stores and ________________ for and on behalf of __________ ________ (hereinafter called "the Contractor"[2]):–

1. (a) The Contractor agrees to use his best endeavors to salve the " __________________ " and/or her cargo bunkers and stores and take them to[3] ____________________ or other place to be hereafter agreed or if no place is named or agreed to a place of safety. The Contractor further agrees to use his best endeavors to prevent the escape of oil from the vessel while performing the services of salving the subject vessel and/or her cargo bunkers and stores. The services shall be rendered and accepted as salvage services upon the principle of "no cure–no pay" except that where the property being salved is a tanker laden or partly laden with a cargo of oil and without negligence on the part of the Contractor and/or his Servants and/or Agents (1) the services are not successful or (2) are only partially successful or (3) the Contractor is prevented from completing the services the Contractor shall nevertheless be awarded solely against the Owners of such tanker his reasonably incurred expenses and an increment not exceeding 15 per cent of such expenses but only if and to the extent that such expenses together with the increment are greater than any amount otherwise recoverable under this Agreement. Within the meaning of the said exception to the principle of "no cure–no pay" expenses shall in addition to actual out of pocket expenses include a fair rate for all tugs craft personnel and other equipment used by the Contractor in the services and oil shall mean crude oil fuel oil heavy diesel oil and lubricating oil.

(b) The Contractor's remuneration shall be fixed by arbitration in London in the manner herein prescribed and any other difference arising out of this Agreement or the operations thereunder shall be referred to arbitration in the same way. In the event of the services referred to in this Agreement or any part of such services having been already rendered at the date of this Agreement by the Contractor to the said vessel and/or her cargo bunkers and stores the provisions of this Agreement shall apply to such services.

(c) It is hereby further agreed that the security to be provided to the Committee of Lloyd's the Salved Values the Award and/or Interim Award and/or Award on Appeal of the Arbitrator and/or Arbitrator(s) on Appeal shall be in[3] ______________________________ currency. If this Clause is not completed then the security to be provided and the Salved Values the Award and/or Interim Award and/or Award on Appeal of the Arbitrator and/or Arbitrator(s) on Appeal shall be in Pounds Sterling.

(d) This Agreement shall be governed by and arbitration thereunder shall be in accordance with English law.

2. The Owners their Servants and Agents shall co-operate fully with the Contractor in and about the salvage including obtaining entry to the place named in Clause 1 of this Agreement or such other place as may be agreed or if applicable the place of safety to which the salved property is taken. The Owners shall promptly accept redelivery of the salved property at such place. The Contractor may make reasonable use of the vessel's machinery gear equipment anchors chains stores and other appurtenances during and for the purpose of the operations free of expense but shall not unnecessarily damage abandon or sacrifice the same or any property the subject of this Agreement.

3. The Master or other person signing this Agreement on behalf of the property to be salved is not authorized to make or give and the Contractor shall not demand or take any payment draft or order as inducement to or remuneration for entering into this Agreement.

PROVISIONS AS TO SECURITY

4. The Contractor shall immediately after the termination of the services or sooner in appropriate cases notify the Committee of Lloyd's and where practicable the Owners of the amount for which he requires security (inclusive of costs expenses and interest). Unless otherwise agreed by the parties such security shall be given to the Committee of Lloyd's and security so given shall be in a form approved by the Committee and shall be given by persons firms or corporations resident in the United Kingdom either satisfactory to the Committee of Lloyd's or agreed by the Contractor. The Committee of Lloyd's shall not be responsible for the sufficiency (whether in amount or otherwise) of any security which shall be given nor for the default or insolvency of any person firm or corporation giving the same.

5. Pending the completion of the security as aforesaid the Contractor shall have a maritime lien on the property salved for his remuneration. Where the aforementioned exception to the principle of "no cure–no pay" becomes likely to be applicable the Owners of the vessel shall on demand of the Contractor provide security for the Contractor's remuneration under the aforementioned exception in accordance with Clause 4 hereof. The salved property shall not without the consent in writing of the Contractor be removed from the place (within the terms of Clause 1) to which the property is taken by the Contractor on the completion of the salvage services until security has been given as aforesaid. The Owners of the vessel their Servants and Agents shall use their best endeavors to ensure that the Cargo Owners provide security in accordance with the provision of Clause 4 of this Agreement before the cargo is released. The Contractor agrees not to arrest or detain the property salved unless (a) the security be not given within 14 days (exclusive of Saturdays and Sundays or other days observed as general holidays at Lloyd's) after the date of the termination of the services (the Committee of Lloyd's not being responsible for the failure of the parties concerned to provide the required security within the said 14 days) or (b) the Contractor has reason to believe that the removal of the property is contemplated contrary to the above agreement. In the event of security not being provided or in the event of (1) any attempt being made to remove the property salved contrary to this agreement or (2) the Contractor having reasonable grounds to suppose that such an attempt will be made the Contractor may take steps to enforce his aforesaid lien. The Arbitrator appointed under Clause 6 or the person(s) appointed under Clause 13 hereof shall have power in their absolute discretion to include in the amount awarded to the Contractor the whole or such part of the expense incurred by the Contractor in enforcing or protecting by insurance or otherwise or in taking reasonable steps to enforce or protect his lien as they shall think fit.

PROVISIONS AS TO ARBITRATION

6. (a) Where security within the provisions of this Agreement is given to the Committee of Lloyd's in whole or in part the said Committee shall appoint an Arbitrator in respect of the interests covered by such security.

(b) Whether security has been given or not the Committee of Lloyd's shall appoint an Arbitrator upon receipt of a written or telex or telegraphic notice of a claim for arbitration from any of the parties entitled or authorized to make such a claim.

7. Where an Arbitrator has been appointed by the Committee of Lloyd's and the parties do not wish to proceed to arbitration the parties shall jointly notify the said Committee in writing or by telex or by telegram and the said Committee may thereupon terminate the appointment of such Arbitrator as they may have appointed in accordance with Clause 6 of this Agreement.

8. Any of the following parties may make a claim for arbitration viz.:– (1) The Owners of the ship. (2) The Owners of the cargo or any part thereof. (3) The Owners of any freight separately at risk or any part thereof. (4) The Contractor. (5) The Owners of the bunkers and/or stores. (6) Any other person who is a party to this Agreement.

9. If the parties to any such Arbitration or any of them desire to be heard or to adduce evidence at the Arbitration they shall give notice to that effect to the Committee of Lloyd's and shall respectively nominate a person in the United Kingdom to represent them for all the purposes of the Arbitration and failing such notice and nomination being given the Arbitrator or Arbitrator(s) on Appeal may proceed as if the parties failing to give the same had renounced their right to be heard or adduce evidence.

10. The remuneration for the services within the meaning of this Agreement shall be fixed by an Arbitrator to be appointed by the Committee of Lloyd's and he shall have power to make an Interim Award ordering such payment on account as may seem fair and just and on such terms as may be fair and just.

CONDUCT OF THE ARBITRATION

11. The Arbitrator shall have power to obtain call for receive and act upon any such oral or documentary evidence or information (whether the same be strictly admissible as evidence or not) as he may think fit and to conduct the Arbitration in such manner in all respects as he may think fit and shall if in his opinion the amount of the security demanded is excessive have power in his absolute discretion to condemn the Contractor in the whole or part of the expense of providing such security and to deduct the amount in which the Contractor is so condemned from the salvage remuneration. Unless the Arbitrator shall otherwise direct the parties shall be at liberty to adduce expert evidence at the Arbitration. Any Award of the Arbitrator shall (subject to appeal as provided in this Agreement) be final and binding on all parties concerned. The Arbitrator and the Committee of Lloyd's may charge reasonable fees and expenses for the services in connection with the Arbitration whether it proceeds to a hearing or not and all such fees and expenses shall be treated as part of the costs of the Arbitration. Save as aforesaid the statutory provisions as to Arbitration for the time being in force in England shall apply.

12. Interest at a rate per annum to be fixed by the Arbitrator from the expiration of 21 days (exclusive of Saturdays and Sundays or other days observed as general holidays at Lloyd's) after the date of publication of the Award and/or Interim Award by the Committee of Lloyd's until the date payment is received by the Committee of Lloyd's both dates inclusive shall (subject to appeal as provided in this Agreement) be payable upon any sum awarded after deduction of any sums paid on account.

PROVISIONS AS TO APPEAL

13. Any of the persons named under Clause 8 may appeal from the Award but not without leave of the Arbitrator(s) on Appeal from an Interim Award made pursuant to the provision of Clause 10 hereof by giving written or telegraphic or telex Notice of Appeal to the Committee of Lloyd's within 14 days (exclusive of Saturdays and Sundays or other days observed as general holidays at Lloyd's) after the date of the publication by the Committee of Lloyd's of the Award and may (without prejudice to their right of appeal under the first part of this Clause) within 14 days (exclusive of Saturdays and Sundays or other days observed as general holidays at Lloyd's) after receipt by them from the Committee of Lloyd's of notice of such appeal (such notice if sent by post to be deemed to be received on the day following that on which the said notice was posted) give written or telegraphic or telex Notice of Cross–Appeal to the Committee of Lloyd's. As soon as practicable after receipt of such notice or notices the Committee of Lloyd's shall refer the Appeal to the hearing and determination of a person or persons selected by it. In the event of an Appellant or Cross-Appellant withdrawing his Notice of Appeal or Cross-Appeal the hearing shall nevertheless proceed in respect of such Notice of Appeal or Cross-Appeal as may remain. Any Award on Appeal shall be final and binding on all the parties concerned whether such parties were represented or not at either the Arbitration or at the Arbitration on Appeal.

CONDUCT OF THE APPEAL

14. No evidence other than the documents put in on the Arbitration and the Arbitrator's notes of the proceedings and oral evidence if any at the Arbitration and the Arbitrator's Reasons for his Award and Interim Award if any and the transcript if any of any evidence given at the Arbitration shall be used on the Appeal unless the Arbitrator(s) on the Appeal shall in his or their discretion call for or allow other evidence. The Arbitrator(s) on Appeal may conduct the Arbitration on Appeal in such manner in all respects as he or they may think fit and may act upon any such evidence or information (whether the same be strictly admissible as evidence or not) as he or they may think fit and may maintain increase or reduce the sum awarded by the Arbitrator with the like power as is conferred by Clause 11 on the Arbitrator to condemn the Contractor in the whole or part of the expense of providing security and to deduct the amount disallowed from the salvage remuneration. And he or they shall also make such order as he or they shall think fit as to the payment of interest on the sum awarded to the Contractor. The Arbitrator(s) on the Appeal may direct in what manner the costs of the Arbitration and of the Arbitration on Appeal shall be borne and paid and he or they and the Committee of Lloyd's may charge reasonable fees and expenses for their services in connection with the Arbitration on Appeal whether it proceeds to a hearing or not and all such fees and expenses shall be treated as part of the costs of the Arbitration on Appeal. Save as aforesaid the statutory provisions as to Arbitration for the time being in force in England shall apply.

PROVISIONS AS TO PAYMENT

15. (a) In case of Arbitration if no Notice of Appeal be received by the Committee of Lloyd's within 14 days (exclusive of Saturdays and Sundays or other days observed as general holidays at Lloyd's) after the date of the publication by the Committee of the Award and/or Interim Award the Committee shall call upon the party or parties concerned to pay the amount awarded and in the event of non-payment shall realize or enforce the security and pay therefrom to the Contractor (whose receipt shall be a good discharge to it) the amount awarded to him together with interest as hereinbefore provided but the Contractor shall reimburse the parties concerned to such extent as the final Award is less than the Interim Award.

(b) If Notice of Appeal be received by the Committee of Lloyd's in accordance with the provisions of Clause 13 hereof it shall as soon as but not until the Award on Appeal has been published by it call upon the party or parties concerned to pay the amount awarded in the event of non-payment shall realize or enforce the security and pay therefrom the Contractor (whose receipt shall be a good discharge to it) the amount awarded to him together with interest if any in such manner as shall comply with the provisions of the Award on Appeal.

(c) If the Award and/or Interim Award and/or Award on Appeal provides or provide that the costs of the Arbitration and/or of the Arbitration on Appeal or any part of such costs shall be borne by the Contractor such costs may be deducted from the amount awarded before payment is made to the Contractor by the Committee of Lloyd's unless satisfactory security is provided by the Contractor for the payment of such costs.

(d) If any sum shall become payable to the Contractor as remuneration for his services and/or interest and/or costs as the result of an agreement made between the Contractor and the parties interested in the property salved or any of them the Committee of Lloyd's in the event of non-payment shall realize or enforce the security and pay therefrom to the Contractor (whose receipt shall be a good discharge to it) the amount agreed upon between the parties.

(e) Without prejudice to the provisions of Clause 4 hereof the liability of the Committee of Lloyd's shall be limited in any event to the amount of security held by it.

GENERAL PROVISIONS

16. Notwithstanding anything hereinbefore contained should the operations be only partially successful without any negligence or want of ordinary skill and care on the part of the Contractor his Servants or Agents and any portion of the vessel her appurtenances bunkers stores and cargo be salved by the Contractor he shall be entitled to reasonable remuneration and such reasonable remuneration shall be fixed in case of differencc by Arbitration in the manner hereinbefore prescribed.

17. The Master of other person signing this Agreement on behalf of the property to be salved enters into this Agreement as Agent for the vessel her cargo freight bunkers and stores and the respective owners thereof and binds each (but not the one for the other or himself personally) to the due performance thereof.

18. In considering what sums of money have been expended by the Contractor in rendering the services and/or in fixing the amount of the Award and/or Interim Award and/or Award on Appeal the Arbitrator or Arbitrator(s) on Appeal shall to such an extent and in so far as it may be fair and just in all the circumstances give effect to the consequences of any change or changes in the value of money or rates of exchange which may have occurred between the completion of the services and the date on which the Award and/or Interim Award and/or Award on Appeal is made.

19. Any Award notice authority order or other document signed by the Chairman of Lloyd's or any person authorized by the Committee of Lloyd's for the purpose shall be deemed to have been duly made or given by the Committee of Lloyd's and shall have the same force and effect in all respects as if it had been signed by every member of the Committee of Lloyd's.

20. The Contractor may claim salvage and enforce any Award or agreement made between the Contractor and the parties interested in the property salved against security provided under this Agreement if any in the name and on behalf of any Sub-Contractors Servants or Agents including Masters and members of the Crews of vessels employed by him in the services rendered hereunder provided that he first indemnifies and holds harmless the Owners of the property salved against all claims by or liabilities incurred to the said persons. Any such indemnity shall be provided in a form satisfactory to such Owners.

21. The Contractor shall be entitled to limit any liability to the Owners of the subject vessel and/or her cargo bunkers and stores which he and/or his Servants and/or Agents may incur in and about the services in the manner and to the extent provided by English law and as if the provisions of the Convention on Limitation of Liability for Maritime Claims 1976 were part of the law of England.

For and on behalf of the Contractor	**For and on behalf of the Owners of property to be salved.**
(To be signed either by the Contractor personally or by the Master of the salving vessel or other person whose name is inserted in line 3 of this Agreement.)	(To be signed by the Master or other person whose name is inserted in line 1 of this Agreement.)

The Documentary Committee of The Japan Shipping Exchange, Inc.

SALVAGE AGREEMENT

(No Cure–No Pay)

Issued 18/12/1980
Amended 5/6/1985
Amended 3/10/1991

Copyright.
Published by
The Japan Shipping
Exchange, Inc.

Place and date:____________________________

This SALVAGE AGREEMENT (hereinafter called "the Agreement") is made and entered into by and between the Master ____ for and on behalf of the Owners of the "________________________________" (hereinafter called "the Vessel"), her cargo and other properties (Owners of the Vessel, her cargo and other properties are hereinafter to be called "the Salved Parties"), and__________ for and on behalf of ____________________________(hereinafter called "the Salvor"):

Clause 1 (Salvage Services)

The Salvor agrees to use his best endeavours and render all necessary services to salve the Vessel and/or her cargo and other properties, and to take them to the nearest place of safety or other place to be hereafter agreed for delivery to the Salved Parties. The Salvor further agrees while performing the salvage services to use his best endeavours to prevent or minimize damage to the environment (which means substantial physical damage to human health and to marine life or resources in coastal or inland waters or areas adjacent thereto, caused by pollution, contamination, fire, explosion or similar major incidents).

Clause 2 (Assistance from Other Salvors)

Whenever circumstances reasonably require, the Salvor shall seek assistance from other salvors. The Salvor shall further accept the intervention of other salvors when reasonably requested to do so by the Salved Parties or the Master of the Vessel; provided however that the amount of his award shall not be prejudiced should it be found that such a request was unreasonable.

Clause 3 (Co-operation of Salved Parties)

The Salved Parties and their employees shall co-operate fully with the Salvor in and about the salvage services including obtaining entry to the place stipulated in Clause 1, and in so doing, shall exercise due care to prevent or minimize damage to the environment. The Salved Parties shall promptly accept redelivery of the salved properties at the place stipulated in Clause 1.

Clause 4 (Termination of Salvage Services)

Even if the Salvor has commenced salvage services under the Agreement, the Owners of the Vessel shall be entitled to terminate the services when there is no longer any reasonable prospect of success in salvaging the Vessel and/or her cargo and other properties after consideration of every relevant factor by giving notice to the Salvor in writing.

Clause 5 (Salvage Services Rendered Prior to the Date of the Agreement)

In the event of the services referred to in the Agreement or any part of such services having been already rendered at the date of the Agreement by the Salvor to the Vessel and/or cargo and other properties, it is agreed that the provision of the Agreement shall retroactively apply to such services.

Clause 6 (Use and Disposal of Hull, etc.)

With consent of the Master, obtained in advance, the Salvor and/or his employees may, without being held liable for any costs and expenses, or without being attached any responsibility or obligation in respect of restitution, loss and/or damage which may arise during the period of the salvage services, use the hull, engines, machineries, appurtenances of the Vessel and the whole or part of her cargo, and also may dismantle, sever and work upon any part of the Vessel and/or jettison the whole or any part of her cargo, which may be reasonably required for the purpose of the salvage services. However, in the event of urgent and inevitable emergency, the Salvor may, at his own discretion and without obtaining prior consent of the Master, resort to the aforementioned measures in such manner and to such extent as would be within the scope of reasonable necessity for the purpose of the salvage services.

Clause 7 (Daily Report of Salvage Services)

The Salvor shall report daily to the Master and the Owner of the Vessel concerning the condition of the Vessel and the situation regarding the salvage services.

Clause 8 (Salvage Remuneration)

(1) In the event that the Salvor succeeds in salving the Vessel, her cargo or other properties whether entirely or partially, the Salvor is entitled to claim salvage remuneration against the Salved Parties.

(2) The amount of salvage remuneration shall be decided taking into account the costs and expenses reasonably incurred by the Salvor as a main factor, and further taking into account the value of the salved properties and other factors collectively; these are the nature and degree of the danger to which they were exposed, the degree of difficulty and dangers encountered by the Salvor, the skill of the Salvor in performing the services, the measure of success obtained by the Salvor, the promptness of the services rendered, the state of readiness and efficiency of the Salvor's equipment and the value thereof and the skill and efforts of the Salvor in preventing or minimizing damage to the environment.

The amount of salvage remuneration shall not exceed the total value of salved properties at the time of termination of the salvage services, exclusive of any interest and legal costs (including costs of mediation and/or arbitration; should the same be applied as hereinafter provided).

(3) The Salved Parties shall each bear the salvage remuneration in proportion to the respective values of their property salved.

Clause 9 (Special Compensation)

(1) Notwithstanding paragraphs 1 and 2 of Clause 8, if the Salvor has carried out salvage services in respect of a vessel which by itself or its cargo threatened damage to the environment and has failed to earn an award under Clause 8 at least equivalent to the special

compensation assessable in accordance with this Clause, he shall be entitled to claim special compensation against the Owners of the Vessel equivalent to the expenses incurred by him as herein defined.

(2) If, in the circumstances set out in paragraph 1, the Salvor by his salvage services has prevented or minimized damage to the environment, he shall be entitled to claim special compensation against the Owners of the Vessel equivalent to the expenses incurred by him plus an increment of up to a maximum of 30% of such expenses. However in exceptional circumstances if it should be fair and just to do so bearing in mind the relevant criteria set out in paragraph 2 of Clause 8, he shall be entitled to claim special compensation equivalent to the expenses incurred by him plus an increment of up to a maximum of 100% of such expenses.

(3) Expenses incurred by the Salvor for the purposes of paragraphs 1 and 2 means out-of-pocket expenses reasonable incurred by the Salvor in the salvage services and a fair rate for the equipment and personnel actually and reasonably used in the salvage services.

(4) The special compensation under this Clause shall be paid only if and to the extent that such compensation is greater than the award recoverable by the Salvor under Clause 8.

(5) If the Salvor has been negligent and has thereby failed to prevent or minimize damage to the environment, he may be deprived of the whole or part of any special compensation due under this clause.

(6) Nothing in this Clause shall affect the right of recourse on the part of the Owners of the Vessel.

Clause 10 (Security)

(1) The Salved Parties upon the successful termination of the salvage services, shall on demand on the Salvor provide security of a reasonable amount to ensure payment of the salvage remuneration (inclusive of interest and costs). In the event of failure to lodge the aforesaid security, the Salvor may exercise a maritime lien on the salved properties. The Owners of the Vessel shall use their best endeavors to ensure that the cargo owners provide security before the cargo is released.

(2) The Salved Parties shall each bear security in proportion to the respective values of their property salved.

(3) Where Clause 9 becomes likely to be applicable, the Owners of the Vessel shall on demand of the Salvor provide security of a reasonable amount for the Salvor's special compensation payable under Clause 9.

(4) In case the amount of security demanded by the Salvor under preceding paragraph (1) or (3) is excessive, the Salvor shall bear the whole or part of the expense incurred in lodging such excessive security.

(5) The aforesaid security means cash money and/or a written guarantee issued by bank, insurance company, P & I Association and/or surety company, or any other form of guarantee, acceptable to the Salvor.

In case the security is in the form of a written guarantee issued by bank, insurance company, P & I Association and/or surety company, the amount of such security shall be specified in Japanese currency unless otherwise agreed by the parties to the Agreement. In case the security is in cash and/or in any other forms equivalent thereto, such security shall be specified in Japanese currency.

(6) The aforesaid security shall be lodged with the Japan Shipping Exchange, Inc. (hereafter called "the Shipping Exchange"). The Shipping Exchange shall keep the security until such time as payment of the salvage remuneration or the special compensation is effected in accordance with the decision made either by amicable settlement, mediation or otherwise.

If expenses should be incurred in keeping the security, such expenses shall be borne by the party who has lodged the said security.

No interest shall accrue upon the security. In case interest accrues upon the cash security lodged, the said interest shall be credited to the account of the depositor.

(7) The Shipping Exchange shall not be responsible for any insufficiency arising from the difference between the amount of the security lodged and the salvage remuneration or the special compensation finally decided. Nor shall the Shipping Exchange be liable for any loss caused by any fluctuation in value of stocks, bonds or any other investment securities which are deposited with the Shipping Exchange.

Clause 11 (Payment of Salvage Remuneration or Special Compensation)

When the parties to the Agreement agree on the amount of salvage remuneration prescribed in Clause 8 and/or of the special compensation in Clause 9, the Salved Parties shall pay the said salvage remuneration and/or special compensation and interest due under Clause 14 to the salvor without delay in exchange for the security prescribed in Clause 10.

Clause 12 (Mediation for Settlement of Dispute)

(1) In case the parties to the Agreement fail to agree on the amount of the salvage remuneration and/or of the special compensation within 90 (ninety) days after the date of termination of the salvage services, the parties shall file a claim with the Mediation Commission of the Shipping Exchange (hereinafter called "the Commission") for mediation of the said dispute.

(2) The parties may also by mutual consent file a claim with the Commission for mediation on any matters arising out of the Agreement other than those stipulated in the preceding paragraph.

(3) Where both parties in dispute so desire, the period stipulated in paragraph (1) of this clause may be shortened and a claim may be filed for mediation before 90 (ninety) days.

(4) Mediation of the Commission shall be held in accordance with the Rules of Mediation Procedures Pertaining to Salvage Remuneration, etc. instituted by the Shipping Exchange.

(5) When the Commission, in accordance with the Rules referred to in the preceding paragraph, instructs the parties in dispute to continue their negotiations, the parties in dispute must continue the negotiations using their best endeavors to settle the case amicably.

(6) During the period of negotiation or mediation under this clause, neither of the parties may foreclose or otherwise enforce his interest in the security by any available judicial procedure or reduce his claim to judgement or take any other legal action, except taking judicial prodedure for preserving his claim when there is a danger of facing difficulties in its enforcement.

Clause 13 (Arbitration)

(1) In case the mediation provided in Clause 12 ends in failure, the parties in dispute shall submit the case to arbitration by the Shipping Exchange, whose judgement or award shall be final and binding.

(2) The Arbitration shall be held in accordance with the Rules of Maritime Arbitration of the Shipping Exchange.

Clause 14 (Interest)

Interest shall be payable on the amount of the salvage remuneration prescribed in Clause 8 and/or of the special compensation in Clause 9 from a date three months after of the termination of the salvage services until the date of payment (or the date of payment on account in case there is any payment on account). Interest shall be at 6% per annum unless otherwise agreed.

Clause 15 (Changes in the Rates of Exchange)

In deciding the amount of salvage remuneration prescribed in Clause 8 and/or of the special compensation in Clause 9, the consequences of any changes in the relevant rates of exchange which may have occurred between the date of termination of the salvage services and the date on which such amount is fixed shall be taken into account.

Clause 16 (Currency in Mediation or Arbitration)

Where the dispute in respect of the amount of the salvage remuneration and/or of the special compensation has been submitted to Mediation provided in Clause 12 or to Arbitration provided in Clause 13, the amount fixed by Mediation or Arbitration shall be specified in Japanese currency unless otherwise agreed by the parties to the Agreement.

Clause 17 (Jurisdiction)

Any action under the Agreement shall be brought before the Tokyo District Court in Japan.

Clause 18 (Governing Law)

This Agreement shall be governed by and construed in accordance with Japanese law.

IN WITNESS WHEREOF, the Parties hereto have signed and executed TWO (2) ORIGINAL COPIES of this Agreement at the place and on the date above written and each party shall hold one (1) original copy.

For and on behalf of the Salved Parties	For and on behalf of the Salvor
______________________________	______________________________
Master	

The Rules of Mediation Procedures Pertaining to Salvage Remuneration, etc. of The Japan Shipping Exchange, Inc.

Made 18th December, 1980
In force 18th December, 1980
Amended 5th June, 1985
Amended 3rd October, 1991

Article 1. (Items for Mediation and Acceptance for Mediation)

The Mediation Commission of the Japan Shipping Exchange, Inc. (hereinafter called "the Mediation Commission") shall accept the application for mediation as provided in Clause 12 of the Salvage Agreement instituted by the Documentary Committee of the Japan Shipping Exchange, Inc. (hereinafter called "Salvage Agreement") in accordance with the procedures provided in Articles 2 and 3 of these Rules when any party to the Salvage Agreement submits such application as a result of failure amongst the parties concerned to agree on the amount of the salvage remuneration (including special compensation, hereinafter called "salvage remuneration") and/or on other issues under dispute. The parties entitled to apply for mediation shall be the Salvor, the Owner of the salved vessel, the Owner(s) of her cargo and other properties.

Article 2. (Filing of Application for Mediation)

Any party who wishes to apply for mediation to the Mediation Commission under the prescribed Article shall submit to the Mediation Commission the Application for Mediation (hereinafter called "the Application") in triplicate (one original, one duplicate and one copy) with the following particulars:

(i) the names and addresses of the parties in dispute or their agencies (in case of a corporation, the trade name, and the names and capacities of its representatives),

(ii) the amount of salvage remuneration which the Applicant considers reasonable and/or other items to be settled by mediation.

The above Application shall be accompanied by the documents and papers hereafter provided:

(a) In case the Applicant is the Salvor:– Particulars of Costs and Expenses of the Salvage Services, Estimate of Values of the Salved Properties, Daily Report of the Salvage Services, etc.

(b) In case the Applicant is the Owner of the salved vessel:- Sea Protest, Log Book, etc.

(c) In case the Applicant is a person other than those prescribed heretofore:– Statements and/or Papers describing the facts in dispute.

Article 3. (Deposit Covering Costs and Expenses of Mediation)

The Applicant shall deposit in advance with the Japan Shipping Exchange, Inc. (hereinafter called "the Shipping Exchange") an amount covering the costs and expenses which will be incurred in the mediation, in accordance with the rates as specified by the Shipping Exchange.

Article 4. (Representative of Non-Resident Applicant of Japan)

In case the Applicant is a non-resident of Japan, the Applicant shall nominate and appoint his representative who resides in Japan.

Article 5. (Filing of Counter-Statement)

(1) The Mediation Commission shall forward without delay to the other party the duplicate of the Application accompanied by the attached documents and papers, and request the other party to file with the Mediation Commission a Counter–Statement within a limited period of time.

The other party shall, upon the aforesaid request by the Mediation Commission, submit the Counter-Statement in triplicate (one original, one duplicate and one copy) within the specified period, and shall cooperate in accordance with Clause 12, paragraph 1, of the Salvage Agreement with the Mediation Commission so that the mediation may proceed without delay.

(2) The Mediation Commission may apply the aforesaid measures upon any other person(s) concerned whose participation in the mediation is deemed to be appropriate or advisable.

(3) When the Counter-Statements are filed with the Mediation Commission by the other party to the Application and/or the other person(s) concerned, the Mediation Commission shall forward without delay the duplicate of the Counter-Statements to the Applicant.

Article 6. (Item to be Described on Counter-Statement)

The Counter-Statement shall have the following particulars:

(i) the name and address of the party who lodges the Counter-Statement (in case of a corporation, the trade name, and the names and capacities of its representatives),

(ii) the amount of salvage remuneration which the party lodging the Counter-Statement considers reasonable and/or the desirable terms of mediation.

The above Counter-Statement shall be accompanied by the documents hereinafter provided:

(a) In case the other party to the Application is the Owner of the salved vessel: – Sea Protest, Log Book, etc.

(b) In case the other party to the Application is the Salvor: – Particulars of Costs and Expenses of the Salvage Services, Estimate of Values of the Salved Properties, Daily Report of the Salvage Services, etc.

(c) In case the other party to the Application is any person other than either of the aforesaid parties: – Statements and/or Papers verifying the values of properties salved in the salvage services, etc.

Article 7. (Nomination of Mediator(s) by Parties)

The parties to the Application may each nominate one or two Mediators from among the persons listed in the Panel of the Mediators of the Mediation Commission. In case the parties unanimously agree, they may jointly nominate one Mediator instead of the above.

The Mediators nominated as aforesaid may nominate another Mediator by unanimous agreement.

Article 8. (Hearing)

The Mediator(s), upon and after deliberate examination of all the documents and papers filed with the Mediation Commission, shall hold hearings from the parties to the Application and, when necessary, from person(s) concerned and/or those whose cooperation is useful in mediation.

Article 9. (Mediation Commission and Mediator(s))

The Mediator(s) shall report, prior to presenting his (their) recommendation for settlement of the case in dispute (hereinafter called "the recommendation"), the details of the case of the circumstances involved to the Mediation Commission, who may give advice(s), if necessary, to the Mediator(s), provided however that the Mediator(s) shall not be bound by any opinions and/or comments made by the Mediation Commission.

Article 10. (Mediation)

When the Mediator(s) is (are) ready to present the recommendation, the Mediator(s) shall fix the date to summon the parties concerned or their representatives, and shall present to them the recommendation which the Mediator(s) consider(s) to be fair and reasonable regarding the amount of salvage remuneration and/or other items required for mediation.

Article 11. (Production of Mediation Agreement)

(1) When the settlement is reached by mediation as aforesaid, a Mediation Agreement shall be produced, which shall contain the outline of the Application and the recommendation accepted by the parties concerned, with seals and signatures of the parties concerned affixed thereto, and counter-signed by the Mediator(s) with the date.

In addition to the original copy, duplicate copies of the Mediation Agreement may be produced in any number as required by the parties concerned.

(2) The Mediator(s) shall produce the Statement of the Reasons which clarifies the grounds for the recommendation and shall report to the Mediation Commission by presenting the said Statement of the Reasons together with the original of the Mediation Agreement. Duplicate copies of the Statement of the Reasons shall be attached to the duplicate copies of the Mediation Agreement when so desired by the parties concerned.

(3) The Mediation Agreement and the Statement of the Reasons shall be produced in English, if required, provided however that any discrepancy arising in interpretation between the Japanese and the English texts, the Japanese text shall prevail.

Article 12. (Additional Deposit)

(1) In case the costs and expenses for the mediation prove likely to exceed the amount deposited under Article 3, the Mediation Commission may request an additional deposit from the parties concerned.

(2) The aforesaid additional deposit shall be borne equally by the Salvor and the Owners of the salved properties.

(3) In the event the parties concerned fail to deposit the additional amount requested as provided for in the aforesaid paragraph (1), the Mediation Commission may suspend further proceedings of the mediation thereafter and close the mediation.

Article 13. (Mediation Fee)

(1) The Salvor and the Owners of the salved properties shall equally bear the Mediation Fee fixed by the Mediation Commission.

(2) In case both the Salvor and the Owners of the salved properties or either of them are several in number, the respective parties shall each bear half of the Mediation Fee as prescribed in the above paragraph in proportion to:-

(a) the amount of salvage remuneration received and/or paid by the respective parties, in case an agreement is reached by the mediation.

(b) the amount of salvage remuneration claimed by each Salvor, or the respective values of the salved properties, in case the mediation fails.

(3) The deposit and the additional deposit set forth under Articles 3 and 12 of the Rules shall be allotted for advance payment of the Mediation Fee and shall be adjusted according to the aforesaid provisions by the Shipping Exchange at the time of settlement of the Mediation Fee.

Article 14. (Payment of Salvage Remuneration and Release of Security)

(1) The Owners of the salved properties shall pay to the Salvor the salvage remuneration without delay after the Mediation Agreement is produced under Article 11.

(2) Upon confirmation of the payment of the salvage remuneration under the aforesaid paragraph, the Shipping Exchange shall release the Security under Clause 10, paragraph 6, of the Salvage Agreement, and refund and/or return the said Security directly to the respective Owners of the salved properties.

Article 15. (Mediation Commission and its Secretariat)

(1) The Mediation Commission shall be managed in accordance with the Rules of the Mediation Commission.

(2) The Documentary and Arbitration Department of the Shipping Exchange shall be assigned as Secretariat of the Mediation Commission in order to render its service smoothly.

(3) Details with regard to the Mediation Commission and its Secretariat shall be set forth in the Rules of the Mediation Commission.

Any question regarding the above Rules shall be referred to:

The Japan Shipping Exchange, Inc.
The Documentary and Arbitration Dept.
Mitsui Rokugokan Bldg., 3-16, Nihonbashi-Muromachi 2-chome, Chuo-ku,
Tokyo, Japan 103.
Phone: 03–3279–1651
Telex: 0222–2140–SHIPEX

SCANDINAVIAN SALVAGE CONTRACT

"No Cure–No Pay"

Standard Form of Salvage Agreement 1994, approved by

Sweden
Sjossuradorernas Forening
Sveriges Rederiforbund
Scandinavian Tugowners Association

Norway
Gjensidige Skibassuranceforeningers Komite
Norge Rederifobund
SjoassurandorernesCentralforening
Scandinavian Tugowners Association

Denmark
Foreningen af danske Soassurandoerer
Danmarks Rederiforening
Scandinavian Tugowners Association

1. Place and date	2. Name and home port of distressed vessel
3. Cargo	4. Nature of distress
5. Salvor	6. Port of refuge
Signature (for the Salvor)	Signature (for the owners of the Vessel)

It is hereby agreed between the Captain of the Vessel named in Box 2, hereinafter called "the Vessel", (or other representative of the owners of the Vessel) which with a cargo of the composition stated in Box 3 is in distress for the reason(s) mentioned in Box 4, and the Salvor mentioned in Box 5, hereinafter called "the Salvor" that

1. The Salvor agrees to use his best endeavors to salve the Vessel and its cargo and in connection therewith to use his best endeavors to prevent or minimize damage to the environment, cf. the International Salvage Convention 1989 ("the Salvage Convention") art. 1, d and in accordance with separate agreement—or in the absence of such agreement, at the discretion of the Salvor—to take the Vessel to the port named in Box 6 or to the nearest port or place of repairs.

2. The services are rendered on the basis "No Cure–No Pay" except where the Vessel itself or its cargo constitutes a threat of damage to the environment, cf the Salvage Convention art. 1, d. When the salvage services have been concluded in accordance with art. 1 the remuneration is assessed by agreement or, when that is not possible, by arbitration in accordance with art. 6.

3. It is agreed that articles 1(a) through (e), 8, 13.1, 13.2, first sentence, 13.3, and 14 of the Salvage Convention are deemed to be incorporated in this contract for which reason the remuneration to the Salvor shall be assessed in accordance with the conditions and principles which are provided for in Lloyd's Standard Form of Salvage Agreement 1990.

4. When carrying out the salvage services the Salvor has a right to use without remuneration to a reasonable extent the equipment, stores and provisions of the Vessel. The owner of the Vessel shall fully cooperate with the Salvor and immediately after the conclusion of the services accept redelivery of the Vessel. Should it not be possible to salve the Vessel and its cargo the Salvor is reserved the rights to salve parts thereof.

5. The Vessel must not be removed from the port or place where it has been brought after the completion of the salvage services until an acceptable security for the salvage award for the Vessel has been provided. Nor must salved cargo be removed until an acceptable security for the salvage award has been provided.

6. Disputes in respect of the award to the Salvor including payments in accordance with art. 3 as well as any other dispute which has arisen out of this contract shall be resolved by final arbitration in accordance with the rules of the Scandinavian Court of Arbitration in Salvage Cases.

7. A party is obliged to meet such obligations which are put upon him in an arbitral award against which appeal has not been made within the given time limit or in the case of appeal when a final award has been rendered.

ARBITRATION RULES

of the Scandinavian Court of Arbitration in Salvage Cases

1. Request for arbitration shall be submitted to The Baltic and International Maritime Council (BIMCO) 161 Bagsvaerdvej DK– 2880 Bagsvaerdvej, Denmark-2880, telephone 44 44 45 00, fax 44 44 44 50, telex 19086, which out of a panel of permanent arbitrators (vide article 2) appoints one sole arbitrator, which shall decide the case in first instance.

2. The panel of permanent arbitrators are for the time being (1994):
Lagdommer Gunnar Vefling, Oslo
Hoyesterettsadvokat Erling C. Hjort, Oslo
Advokat Jan–Fredrik Rafen, Oslo
Advokat Jan Erlund, Copenhagen
Advokat Bent Nielsen, Copenhagen
Advokat Lars Rahmn, Gothenburg
Advokat Robert Romlov, Gothenburg, and
Advokat Jan Melander, Stockholm.
These permanent arbitrators have been appointed jointly by Sjoassuradorernas Forening, Sweden, Gjensidige Skibsassuranceforeningers Komite, Norway, Sjoassurandorernes Centralforening, Norway, Foreningen af danske Soassurandorer, Sveriges Redareforening, Nor-

ges Rederiforbund, Danmarks Rederiforening and Scandinavian Tugowners' Association, which organizations also may jointly alter such appointment or appointments.

3. Prior to the appointment of an arbitrator BIMCO shall get in touch with the prospective arbitrator to make sure that such person is not disqualified. Before BIMCO makes a final appointment BIMCO shall request a written declaration from the prospective arbitrator confirming that he is not disqualified. An arbitrator is deemed to be disqualified i.a., if he within the last three years has assisted one of the parties as a lawyer. If possible each one of the permanent arbitrators shall be used in deciding cases to the same extent irrespective of that having the result that the arbitrator in question does not have the same nationality as the Salvor. In all event an arbitrator of the same nationality as the parties shall be appointed should the parties jointly so request. In case of dispute between the parties as to disqualification of an arbitrator such a dispute may be referred to the Courts of the country where the arbitration shall be held (vide article 4) in accordance with the laws of that country.

4. The arbitration proceedings shall be held in Sweden, Norway or Denmark respectively depending on the nationality of the Salvor, and at the place decided by the arbitrator.
The arbitrator shall apply Swedish, Norwegian or Danish substantive law and procedural law according to the nationality of the Salvor.
Should the Salvor not be Swedish, Norwegian or Danish the arbitration proceeds shall be held in Denmark according to Danish substantive law and procedural law.
When applying Swedish law the Swedish Arbitration Act of 1929 (1929:145) shall apply to the extent these rules do not provide otherwise.
When assessing the salvage award to the salvor the arbitrator is entitled to take into consideration for him known practice in settling salvage awards in addition to court cases and arbitral cases.

5. The court of arbitration gives directions at the commencement of the case and if necessary after consultation with the parties as to times for the submission of written pleadings and other documentation and also as to the time for the trial.
The parties exchange and submit apart from points of claim and defence also each one set of pleadings.
The proceedings at the trial shall be oral unless the parties at the suggestion of the arbitrator agree upon written proceedings, which in particular should be the case in minor and uncomplicated disputes.
Pleadings may be written in Swedish, Norwegian, Danish or English.
During the oral proceedings and in the award the Swedish, Norwegian or Danish language may be used or, provided the parties so agree, the English language.
Statements or other written declarations by witnesses may be used unless a party objects.
During the trial witnesses and parties may be examined.
In the default of a party the case shall be decided on the material before the court of arbitration.

6. Normally the arbitration proceedings shall be conducted in such an expeditious manner that no longer than six months elapse from the time at which the arbitrator was appointed until the time the award is given.

7. The award shall be in writing and contain reasons.
The arbitrator has the power to make an intermediate award by which the Salvor is given an amount on account against putting up of a security if so deemed fit.

8. The arbitrators are obliged to keep the case and their award secret. The award may not be published unless the parties so agree.

9. Such costs which may arise in connection with the appointment of an arbitrator according to article 1 shall be paid by the claimant. BIMCO has under no circumstances any liability for the costs of the court of arbitration.
The parties are liable in solidum for the costs of the court of arbitration.
The court of arbitration apportions the costs between the parties and normally awards the winning party its full costs. However, under the circumstances the court of arbitration can at its discretion reduce the costs to be awarded. In disputes in respect of the amount of a salvage award a party has the right to give the arbitrator in a sealed envelope particulars as to the amount of award he has offered. Such an envelope is opened by the arbitrator when he has given his award as to the amount of the salvage award and the particulars of the offer will form part of the arbitrator's basis for assessing the question of costs.

10. By the award interest should be given on the salvage award from 30 days after the claim for salvage was made but at the earliest 90 days from the time when the salvage was completed. Interest is the rate of interest in court proceedings which is provided by the law of the country which the court of arbitration shall use in accordance with article 4 although in respect of Norwegian law less 2%, and the salvage award shall be given in the currency of the country whose law is applicable.

11. An appeal can be made against an award to an appeal court of arbitration. This is made by a written submission to BIMCO. Should an appeal not be entered against an award within 14 days from the time it was made, such an award is final and a party is obliged to meet such obligations which are put upon him by such an award. Should that not be done the award can be enforced in accordance with the applicable rules or if necessary be used as a basis for a claim against that party before the ordinary courts. The appeal court of arbitration consists of three of the permanent arbitrators which are appointed case by case by BIMCO, which also appointments the chairman of the tribunal.
In case of disagreement between the three arbitrators in the appeal court of arbitration the case is decided by majority. Otherwise the rules in respect of arbitration cases in first instance are applicable to the extent possible. The period of time in article 6 of six months shall be counted from the time the request for appeal was transmitted to the chairman of the appeal court of arbitration.

PER DIEM PLUS BONUS SALVAGE SERVICES AGREEMENT

Re: Salvage of the____, her equipment, cargo, freight, bunkers, stores, and other property thereon.

I
Services

It is hereby agreed between the _______________ (hereinafter Salvor) and____________, acting for and on behalf of the owners of (hereinafter Owners) that Salvor use their best efforts:

(1) To salvage the ____ , her equipment, cargo, freight, bunkers, stores, and other property therein and take them from the present location at ________________________________ to _____________________________________ or such other place as may be agreed upon or directed by competent Government authority as a place of safety.

(2) To prevent or minimize damage to the environment while performing the salvage services.

II
Terms and Conditions

The services described above shall be provided under the following terms and conditions:

(1) Salvor shall perform the salvage services as promptly as prudently possible under the conditions and circumstances prevailing.

(2) Owners and his employees, agents, and persons acting under his direction and control shall:

(a) Cooperate fully with Salvor in and about the salvage.

(b) Exercise due care to prevent damage to the environment.

(c) Use his best efforts to obtain entry into the place of safety mentioned above.

(d) Accept redelivery of the vessel when reasonably requested by Salvor to do so.

(3) Salvor and its employees may without being held liable for any costs and expenses or for any responsibility or obligation in respect to restitution, loss and/or damage that may arise during the period of the salvage operation use the hull, engines, machinery, appurtenances, fittings, and outfit of the vessel and the whole or part of her cargo and may dismantle sever and work upon any part of the vessel and/or jettison the whole or any part of her cargo as required by salvage services. Salvor shall not unnecessarily damage, abandon, or sacrifice any property covered by this agreement.

(4) The Master of the vessel retains sole authority and responsibility for the vessel's crew and the safety of the vessel. Requests for assistance from the crew will be directed through the master of a ship's officer designated by him.

(5) Salvor will not be responsible for any type of pollution having its source in the vessel or its cargo or for any damage to the vessel or property of any third party providing such pollution or damage does not arise from its own negligence. Owners will hold harmless and indemnify Salvor in any lawsuit or action resulting from pollution or third party damages whatsoever. Such defense shall be provided without cost to Salvor, its officers, and employees.

(6) Both Salvor and Owners recognize that Salvor is under the regulatory authority of the United States whose agencies have the right to direct or proscribe salvage actions that Salvor may not believe to be technically correct and which may result in delay or failure of the operation. If Salvor is prevented by Regulatory authorities from carrying out salvage action he deems unnecessary or required to take salvage actions he considers unnecessary or correct and failure of the operation results or if Salvor is prevented from completing the operation, Salvor shall be entitled to full time and materials compensation including demobilization as described in paragraph III below and delineated in Attachment A.

(7) Owners may at any time and in their sole discretion request the intervention of other salvors. Salvor will accept such intervention and shall cooperate with Owners and other salvors. Salvor's compensation shall be unaffected by the intervention of other salvors.

(8) Owners may at any time at their sole discretion direct Salvor to terminate operations. If the owner exercises this option, Salvor will receive its entire compensation on a time and materials basis and described in paragraph III including reasonable demobilization costs.

III
Compensation

Salvor will be compensated on a time and materials basis based upon the rates delineated in Attachment A to this contract which is made a part of this Agreement.

In the event the salvage is successful in addition to compensation on a time and materials basis, Salvor shall receive a bonus of _______ percent of the salved value of the vessel, her cargo, bunkers, and equipment. Salved value is defined as the insured value of the vessel and cargo less the cost of the salvage operation, repairs to the vessel, and loss of value of cargo and bunkers.

Full payment shall be due thirty (30) days after submission of an invoice. Invoices paid within ten days of submission of an invoice may be discounted by two (2) percent. Invoices not paid within thirty days of the invoice shall be liable for interest at the rate of 18 percent per annum compounded monthly. Owners agree to pay reasonable attorney's fees in the event Salvor finds it necessary to retain an attorney for collection.

The compensation herein above provided for is the full and complete compensation for all services, efforts, expenditures, materials and all other things done or furnished by Salvor its employees and agents or anyone in its direction or control in conjunction with salvage of the vessel its equipment and cargo. No other payments or awards shall be due to Salvor its employees or agents or anyone acting under its direction and control for services in connection with the salvage.

This Agreement made this ______________ day of ______________________ 19 ___

For Salvor:

____
(Signed)

____
(Printed Name)

____
(Title)

For Owners:

____
(Signed)

____
(Printed Name)

____
(Title)

INTERNATIONAL SALVAGE UNION
SUB-CONTRACT (AWARD SHARING) 1994

BETWEEN

The Contractor

– and –

The Sub-Contractor

THIS AGREEMENT is made the day of 19

Between:

for and on behalf of ("the Contractor") and

for and on behalf of ("the Sub-Contractor").

WHEREAS:

(1) The Contractor is presently or is about to become engaged in rendering salvage services to the " ___________", her cargo, freight, bunkers and stores, under a Lloyd's Standard Form of Salvage Agreement "No Cure–No Pay" dated ____________ ("the L.O.F.") and the Contractor wishes to engage the services of the Sub-Contractor on "No Cure-No Pay" terms to assist him in the performance of his obligations under the L.O.F.

(2) The Sub-Contractor is willing to assist the Contractor and will provide the personnel, equipment and services set out in the schedule, together with any further personnel, equipment or services which may reasonably be requested by the Contractor from time to time during the performance of the services.

NOW in consideration of the mutual promises and undertakings contained herein it is agreed as follows:–

Definitions

1. In this Agreement the following expressions shall have the following meanings:–

(a) "ISU Terms" means award sharing terms which are the same (mutatis mutandis) or substantially the same as the terms of this Agreement;

(b) "Non-Award Sharing Terms" means terms which provide for the remuneration of a sub-contractor otherwise than by way of a share of the Salvage Remuneration payable under the L.O.F;

(c) "Relevant Sub-Contract" means a sub-contract whereby the Contractor engages the service of a sub-contractor on ISU Terms to assist him in the performance of his obligations under the L.O.F.;

(d) "Salvage Remuneration" means any and all remuneration plus interest thereon paid or payable whether awarded, agreed or received in respect of services rendered under the L.O.F., including out of pocket expenses, interim payments and costs;

OBLIGATIONS OF CONTRACTOR

2. The Contractor agrees:-

(a) To engage the Sub-Contractor on "No Cure–No Pay" terms to assist him in the performance of his obligations under the L.O.F.;

(b) To share with the Sub-Contractor the Salvage Remuneration as finally awarded under the L.O.F. or as agreed by the parties thereto and received by the Contractors;

(c) To use his best endeavors to recover, as part of those legal costs as finally awarded to him under the L.O.F., or as agreed between the parties thereto, such legal costs (calculated on the standard basis) incurred by the Sub-Contractor in and about the provision and presentation of evidence by him for use in the L.O.F. proceedings, and thereafter to account to the Sub-Contractor for his legal costs recovered as aforesaid;

(d) As soon as is reasonably practical to instruct solicitors in London to open an identified interest bearing client deposit account established in accordance with the Solicitors Act 1974 (as amended) (the "Trust Account") and to hold in the Trust Account any and all such remuneration as may be received pursuant to the L.O.F. as stakeholder on trust for the Contractor and the Sub-Contractor with authority, upon final agreement or determination of the share due to each party, to release such share on being requested in writing by such party so to do;

(e) As soon as reasonably practicable to inform the Committee of Lloyd's and the owners of the salved property and the Guarantors of the existence of this Agreement, the identity of the Sub-Contractor and to give them irrevocable instructions to pay any and all monies due under the L.O.F. to the Trust Account.

OBLIGATIONS OF SUB-CONTRACTOR

3. The Sub-Contractor agrees:–

(a) To use his best endeavors to assist the Contractor in the performance of his obligations under the L.O.F., including the provision of such personnel, equipment and services as are set out in the attached schedule or as are reasonably requested by the Contractor during the performance of the service;

(b) To assist the Contractor in the presentation of the salvage claim by the provision and retention of evidence relating to the salvage services and to the Sub-Contractor's contribution to the same;

(c) Not to claim salvage against the Owner(s) of the property salved or any part thereof, nor to make any claim for remuneration in respect of the services rendered pursuant to this Agreement, save insofar as this Agreement provides; and

(d) To provide a satisfactory indemnity to the Contractor against any successful claim for salvage made by the Sub-Contractor's servants and/or agents and/or sub-contractors (and/or the servants and/or agents of the same) against the Owner(s) of such property.

TRUST

4. (a) From the time when this Agreement is concluded all sums paid or payable by way of Salvage Remuneration due under the L.O.F. or this Agreement shall be owned in law by the Contractor and the Sub-Contractor jointly and shall be subject to a trust in favor of the Contractor and Sub-Contractor as beneficiaries. Save as is expressly provided in this Agreement, neither party shall have the right to assign or otherwise dispose of or deal with such sums or any part thereof or any interest therein.

(b) In the event of either party receiving any sum howsoever on account of or in payment of Salvage Remuneration in respect of any of the services rendered under the L.O.F. or this Agreement, such sum shall be held on trust as aforesaid for the Contractor and the Sub-Contractor and shall forthwith be paid into the Trust Account.

CONDUCT OF L.O.F. ARBITRATION

5. (a) The Arbitration under the L.O.F. and/or any negotiations for an amicable settlement shall be conducted solely by the Contractor but the Sub-Contractor agrees to provide all necessary evidence and assistance in connection therewith.

(b) The Contractor shall keep the Sub-Contractor fully advised as to the amount of the security demanded from the owners of the salved property and as to the nature and form of the guarantees received and the identity of all guarantors.

(c) The Contractor, so far as the circumstances reasonably permit, shall consult with the Sub-Contractor and keep the Sub-Contractor informed at all significant stages of the Arbitration or of any settlement negotiations, but failing agreement by the Sub-Contractor the Contractor shall be entitled at his discretion to proceed with the Arbitration or to conclude a bona fide settlement;

(d) The Sub-Contractor shall be entitled to attend the arbitration as an observer but at his own cost.

ASSIGNMENT

6. (a) The Contractor shall not without the consent in writing of the Sub-Contractor (such consent not to be unreasonably withheld) make or purport to make any assignment of the benefit of the L.O.F. or of the whole or any part of the Salvage Remuneration.

(b) Neither the Contractor nor the Sub-Contractor shall without the consent in writing of the other (such consent not to be unreasonably withheld) make or purport to make any assignment of the benefit of this Agreement or of the share of the Salvage Remuneration to which it is entitled under the joint operation of the L.O.F. and this Agreement or of its interest under the trust hereinbefore contained.

INDEMNITIES

7. (a) The Contractor agrees to indemnify fully and hold harmless the Sub-Contractor, his servants or agents against any claim by the Owners of the property to be salved or by any other person (other than the Sub-Contractor's own servants or agents) for loss or damage caused by the negligence in the salvage operations of the Contractor, his servants or agents and/or by any defects (other than latent defects) in any equipment of the Contractor used in the salvage operation.

(b) The Sub-Contractor agrees to indemnify fully and hold harmless the Contractor, his servants or agents against any claim by the Owners of the property to be salved or by any other person (other than the Contractor's own servants or agents) for loss or damage caused by the negligence in the salvage operation of the Sub-Contractor, his servants or agents and/or by any defects (other than latent defects) in any equipment of the Sub-Contractor used in the salvage operation.

(c) The Contractor will make no claim against the Sub-Contractor, his servants and/or agents for loss or damage sustained by the Contractor's equipment or by any servant or agent of the Contractor caused by the negligence of the Sub-Contractor, his servants and/or agents and/or by defects in the Sub-Contractor's equipment and hereby agrees to indemnify fully and hold harmless the

Sub-Contractor in respect of any such claim made by the Contractor's servants and/or agents.

(d) The Sub-Contractor will make no claim against the Contractor, his servants and/or agents for loss or damage sustained by the Sub-Contractor's equipment or by any servant or agent of the Sub-Contractor caused by the negligence of the Contractor, his servants and/or agents and/or by defects in the Contractor's equipment and hereby agrees to indemnify fully and hold harmless the Contractor in respect of any such claim made by the Sub-Contractor's servants and/or agents.

LIMITATION OF LIABILITY

8. Notwithstanding anything contained herein, and in particular Clause 7, either party to this Agreement shall be entitled to limit any liability to the other party which he and/or his servants and/or agents may incur in and about the services under this Agreement in the manner and to the extent provided by English law, save that this Clause shall not apply to any liability under Clause 3(d) above.

TRUSTEE EXONERATION

9. Neither the Contractor nor any other trustee of the trust hereinbefore contained shall be liable for or for the consequences of any error or mistake (whether by way of commission or omission and whether on the part of the Contractor or other trustee himself, or on the part of any agent or adviser employed or instructed by the Contractor or other trustee) made or committed in or about the agreement or ascertainment or recovery of the salvage remuneration receivable under the L.O.F. or the obtaining enforcement or release of any security therefor or otherwise in or about the execution of the trust hereinbefore contained unless such error or mistake shall be proved to have occurred or been committed in personal conscious bad faith of the party sought to be made liable.

RELATIONSHIP TO OTHER SUB-CONTRACTS

10. (a) Save as may be specifically advised, the Contractor hereby warrants that he has not hitherto engaged the services of any other party to assist him in the performance of his obligations under L.O.F. except upon ISU Terms or Non–Award Sharing Terms.

(b) The Contractor may at any time hereafter engage the services of such other parties as he may think fit to assist him in the performance of his obligations under the L.O.F. but the terms upon which every such party is engaged shall either be ISU Terms or Non–Award Sharing Terms.

(c) Where in relation to the performance of his obligations under the L.O.F., the Contractor has entered or hereafter enters into any engagement with another party on ISU Terms he will, at the request of the Sub-Contractor, furnish to the Sub-Contractor all information in his possession concerning the identity and address of every such other party.

(d) In case this Agreement is not the only Relevant Sub-Contract, the following provisions shall apply:–

(i) Clause 2(d) (release of money from the Trust Account pursuant to written direction), Clause 4 (declaration of trust by this Agreement) and Clause 11 (quantification of the shares of the Contractor and the Sub-Contractor in the Salvage Remuneration) shall have effect as if references to every sub-contractor under all Relevant Sub-Contracts were substituted for references to the Sub-Contractor;

(ii) The Contractor will so instruct Solicitors in London that a single account becomes the Trust account in relation to every Relevant Sub-Contract;

(iii) Whenever a matter or dispute has to be determined or resolved by arbitration pursuant to this Agreement and an Arbitrator has already been appointed to determine or resolve the same, or an equivalent matter or dispute under another Relevant Sub-Contract, then notwithstanding anything to the contrary in Clause 11(a) of this Agreement, that matter or dispute shall be referred to the same Arbitrator (if he so consents) and so far as possible he will determine or resolve that matter in relation to every Relevant Sub-Contract in a single arbitration.

ARBITRATION

11. (a) Any dispute arising hereunder, including any dispute as to the shares of the Salvage Remuneration due to the Contractor and Sub-Contractor, shall be referred to the arbitrament of an Arbitrator, to be selected by the first party claiming arbitration from the persons currently on the panel of Lloyd's Salvage Arbitrators with a right of Appeal from an award made by the Arbitrator to either party by notice in writing to the other within 28 days of the date of publication of the original Arbitrator's Award.

(b) The Arbitrator on appeal shall be the person currently acting as Lloyd's Appeal Arbitrator.

(c) Both the Arbitrator and the Appeal Arbitrator shall have the same powers as an Arbitrator and Appeal Arbitrator respectively would have under L.O.F. 1980 or any standard revision thereof, including a power to order a payment on account of a share due to a party pending final determination of any dispute between the parties hereto.

(d) For the purposes of any apportionment between the parties the term "Salvage Remuneration" shall include all expenses, unrecovered costs and brokers' commissions. The Arbitrator or Arbitrator on Appeal, unless he/she considers it unfair or unjust to do so, in determining the shares of the aforesaid Salvage Remuneration, shall first apportion to the Contractor and/or Sub-Contractor(s) all sums specifically awarded other than the sums for remuneration and interest under L.O.F. and all reasonably incurred out of pocket expenses, unrecovered but customary costs and brokers' commissions. Where interest has been awarded or earned in respect to any of the foregoing by reason of the L.O.F. Award or Award on Appeal, and/or by reason of being held in the Trust Account, the said interest shall be included in the initial apportionment.

RELEVANT LAW

12. This Agreement shall be governed and construed in accordance with English Law.

AS WITNESS the hands of the duly authorized representatives of the parties hereto.

For and on behalf of the Contractor	For and on behalf of the Sub-Contractor
________________________	________________________

SCHEDULE OF PERSONNEL, EQUIPMENT, AND SERVICES

INTERNATIONAL SALVAGE UNION—
BALTIC AND INTERNATIONAL MARITIME COUNCIL

Recommended International Wreck Removal and
Marine Services Agreement
(Daily Hire)
Code Name: "Wreckhire"

Enclosure VI
D.C. 1993-05
Item 10)

1. Date and Place of Agreement	PART 1
2. Contractor/place of business	3. Company/place of business
4. Vessel Specifications (Cl. 1, 2, 4.1) (a) Name (b) Flag (c) Place of Registry	5. Condition of Vessel (Cl. 2, 4.1)
(d) Length (e) Beam (f) Max. Draft (g) Displacement (h) Details and Nature of Cargo	6. Position of Vessel and Condition of Worksite (Cl. 2,4.1)
(i) Any other Vessel's details relevant	7. Nature of Services (Cl. 2, 4.1, 4.3)
8. Place of Delivery/Disposal of Vessel (Cl. 2., 9.1)	

9. Payment and Rates of Hire (Cl. 1, 4.2, 7, 8.1, 10.1)

(a) Daily Working Rate for Craft and Equipment

(b) Daily Working Rate for Personnel

(c) Daily Standby Rate for Craft and Equipment

(d) Daily Standby Rate for Personnel

(e) Payment of the appropriate Working Rate of Hire is to be made in advance every (state number of days)

(i) commencing from

(ii) and continuing until

(iii) in any event with a minimum payment of hire (state number of days hire)

. Payment Details (Cl. 10.5)

(a) Currency

(b) Bank

(c) Address

(d) Account Number

(e) Account Name

11. Time of Payment and Interest (state period within which sums must be received by the Contractor and rate of interest per month) (Cl. 11)	12. Extra Costs (Cl. 12) (a) Handling Charge to be applied (state percentage)

13. Security Requirements (Cl. 10.6, 13)

14. Law and Arbitration (State 18.1 or 18.2 of Cl. 18 as agreed: if 18.2 agreed, also state place of arbitration) (Cl. 18)

15. Number of Additional Clauses covering special provisions, if agreed

It is agreed that this Agreement shall be performed subject to the Terms and Conditions which consist of PART I, including additional clauses, and PART II, as well as Annex I, PERSONNEL, CRAFT AND EQUIPMENT, and Annex II, METHOD OF WORK or any other Annexes attached to this Agreement.

The undersigned warrant that they have full power and authority to sign this Agreement on behalf of the parties represented by them.

Signature (for and on behalf of the Contractor)	Signature (for and on behalf of the Company)

INTERNATIONAL WRECK REMOVAL AND MARINE SERVICES AGREEMENT

CODE NAME: W R E C K H I R E DAILY RATE PART II

1. DEFINITIONS

The term "Vessel" shall include any vessel, craft, property, or part thereof, of whatsoever nature, including anything contained therein or thereon, such as but not limited to cargo and bunkers, as described in Box 4, Part I.

2. THE SERVICES

The Contractor agrees to exercise due care in rendering the services indicated in Box 7, Part I, and, if applicable, will endeavor to deliver and/or dispose of the Vessel at the place indicated in Box 8, Part I. Insofar as it is not inconsistent with the nature of the services to be rendered under this Agreement, the Contractor will also exercise due care to minimize damage to the environment.

The Contractor shall provide the Personnel, Craft and Equipment set out in Annex I of this Agreement which the Contractor deems necessary for the services based upon the Specifications, Condition and Position of the Vessel and Worksite set out in Boxes 4, 5 and 6, Part I.

The Contractor's Method of Work shall be described in Annex II, utilizing the Personnel, Craft and Equipment described in Annex I.

The Contractor shall consult with the Company if there is any need for substantial change in the Method of Work and/or Personnel, Craft or Equipment.

3. COMPANY REPRESENTATIVE

The methods and procedures to be employed in the services shall at all times be discussed and agreed between the Company and the Contractor.

A representative of the Company will be available during the operations with the full authority to act on behalf of the Company. The Company will use its best endeavors to provide all information required by the Contractor.

In addition, the Company will provide at its sole risk and expense sufficient officers or their equivalents, who are fully conversant with the cargo system and/or layout of the Vessel, and who shall be in attendance when reasonably required during the operations in order to give assistance to the Contractor.

4. CHANGE OF METHOD OF WORK and/or PERSONNEL, CRAFT AND EQUIPMENT

4.1 The Rates of Hire are based upon the Nature of the Services, Box 7, Part I, Method of Work, and Personnel, Craft and Equipment set out in Annexes I and II and the

Description, Specifications, Position, Condition of the Vessel and the Worksite as set out in Boxes 4, 5 and 6, Part I.

If before or during the operation, and without fault on the part of the Contractor, there is a substantial change in the work to be done under this Agreement, or in the Personnel, Craft and Equipment required to undertake the services due to:–

(1) any misdescription by the Company or error in the specification provided by the Company, upon which the Contractor has relied, or,

(2) a material change in the position and/or condition of the Vessel or the worksite,

the Contractor shall forthwith give notice in writing thereof to the Company and of the estimated additional costs to effect the services.

4.2 The parties shall, without delay, consult each other to reach agreement on the amount of the additional costs to be added to the Rates of Hire.

5. MISCELLANEOUS

5.1 The Company shall arrange and pay for any marking of the Vessel and cautioning required. The Contractor shall arrange and pay for any marking or cautioning required in respect of its own equipment during the services under this Agreement.

5.2 The Contractor may make reasonable use of Vessel's machinery, gear, equipment, anchors, chains, stores and other appurtenances during and for the purposes of these services free of expense but shall not unnecessarily damage, abandon or sacrifice the same or any property the subject of this Agreement.

5.3 Subject to approval of the Company which shall not be unreasonably withheld, and subject to it being permitted by the competent authorities, the Contractor shall be entitled to remove, dispose or jettison cargo, or parts of the Vessel, or equipment from the Vessel if such action is considered by the Contractor to be reasonably necessary to perform the services under this Agreement.

5.4 The Company will indemnify the Contractor and hold him harmless from any claims by the owners or insurers of property which is removed, disposed or jettisoned following approval by the Company.

5.5 The Company will provide the Contractor with such plans and drawings of the Vessel, cargo manifests, stowage plans, etc. as the Contractor may require.

6. PERMITS

The Company shall obtain and maintain at its own costs all necessary licenses, approvals, authorizations or permits required to undertake and complete the services without let or hinderance. The Contractor shall provide the Company with all reasonable assistance in connection with the obtaining of such licenses, approvals, authorizations or permits.

7. DELAYS

If the Contractor is prevented from performing any meaningful work in and about the services under this Agreement due to any reason outside its control, then during all such delays the Contractor shall be remunerated by the Company at the appropriate Standby Rate set out in Box 9, Part I, which shall apply on a pro rata basis for parts of a working day.

The Company shall promptly advise the Contractor of all periods when it considers the Standby Rate should apply, and shall confirm same in writing without delay.

8. DISCONTINUANCE OF TERMINATION

8.1 The Company has the right to discontinue or terminate the services to be carried out under this Agreement at any time, provided always that notice of such discontinuance or termination is given to the Contractor in writing. In such event the Contractor is entitled to be paid all sums due at the time of discontinuance or termination in accordance with the provisions of Box 9, Part 1.

8.2 Such discontinuation or termination of the services will be carried out with all reasonable dispatch by the Contractor, subject always to the safety of Personnel, Craft and Equipment involved in the services. Any additional direct expenses arising as a consequence of the instructions to discontinue or terminate the services shall be for the account of the Company.

9. DELIVERY

9.1 The Vessel shall be accepted forthwith and taken over by the Company or its duly authorized representative at the place of delivery indicated in Box 8, Part I. References to delivery or the place of delivery shall include disposal or the place of disposal, if applicable.

The place of delivery shall always be safe and accessible for the Contractor's own or hired-in craft and the Vessel to enter and operate in and shall be a place where the Contractor is permitted by governmental or other authorities to deliver or dispose of the Vessel.

In the event the Vessel is not accepted forthwith by the Company or delivery is prevented or delayed by action of governmental or other authorities outside the control of the Contractor all costs necessarily incurred by the Contractor from the moment of the tender for delivery shall be for account of the Company, and the Daily Rate of Hire shall continue to be payable to the Contractor.

9.2 If the Company fails, on completion of the services, to take delivery of the Vessel within five (5) days of the Contractor tendering written notice of delivery, or if in the opinion of the Contractor the Vessel is likely to deteriorate, decay, become worthless or incur charges whether for storage or otherwise in excess of its value, the Contractor may, without prejudice to any other rights the Contractor may have against the Company, without notice and without any responsibility whatsoever attaching to the Contractor, sell or dispose of the Vessel and apply the proceeds of sale in reduction of the sums due to the Contractor from the Company under this Agreement. Any remaining proceeds will be refunded to the Company.

In the event that such sale or other disposal of the Vessel fails to raise sufficient net funds to pay the monies due to the Contractor under the terms of this Agreement then the Company shall remain liable to the Contractor for any such shortfall.

9.3 Reference to delivery of the Vessel shall include parts of the Vessel and/or cargo and/or any other thing emanating from the Vessel and such delivery may take place at different times and different places.

10. PRICE AND CONDITIONS OF PAYMENT

10.1 The Company shall pay the Contractor the Daily Working and Standby Rates of Hire for Personnel, Craft and Equipment set out in Box 9, Part I.

10.2 Such hire shall be fully and irrevocably earned on a daily basis and shall be non-returnable.

10.3 Within 14 days of termination or completion of the Services set out in Box 7, Part I the Contractor shall return any overpayments to the Company.

10.4 All monies due and payable to the Contractor under this Agreement shall be paid without any discount, deduction, set-off, lien, claim or counterclaim.

10.5 All payments to the Contractor shall be made in the currency and to the bank account stipulated in Box 10, Part I.

10.6 If any amount payable under this Agreement has not been paid within seven, (7), days of the due date, or if the security required in accordance with Box 13, Part I and Clause 13, Part II, is not provided within five, (5), banking days of the request by the Contractor, then at any time thereafter the Contractor shall be entitled to terminate this Agreement without prejudice to the sums already due to the Contractor and to any further rights or remedies which the Contractor may have against the Company. Provided always that the Contractor shall give the Company at least three, (3), working days notice of its intention to exercise this right.

11. TIME OF PAYMENT AND INTEREST

The Contractor shall promptly invoice the Company for all sums payable under this Agreement. If any sums which become due and payable are not actually received by the Contractor within the period specified in Box 11, Part I, they shall attract interest in accordance with the rate set out in Box 11, Part I.

12. EXTRA COSTS

The following expenses/costs shall be paid by the Company as and when they fall due:

12.1 all port expenses, pilotage charges, harbor and canal dues and all other expenses of a similar nature levied upon or payable in respect of the Vessel and the Contractor's own or hired-in craft.

12.2 the costs of the services of any assisting tugs when reasonably deemed necessary by the Contractor or prescribed by port or other authorities.

12.3 all costs in connection with clearance, agency fees, visas, guarantees and all other expenses of such kind.

12.4 all taxes and social security charges (other than those normally payable by the Contractor in the country where it has its principal place of business), stamp duties, or other levies payable in respect of or in connection with this Agreement, any import-export dues and any customs or excise duties.

12.5 all costs incurred due to requirements of governmental or other authorities or unions over and above those costs which would otherwise be reasonably incurred by the Contractor in the execution of the Agreement.

12.6 all reasonable costs of transportation of equipment and the travel and accommodation costs of personnel identified in Annex I, (other than the crews of craft utilized in the services).

12.7 all costs incurred by the Contractor in respect of equipment, materials, or stores which are lost, damaged or consumed during the services.

If any such expenses/costs are in fact paid by or on behalf of the Contractor, (notwithstanding that the Contractor shall under no circumstances be under any obligation to make such payments on behalf of the Company), the Company shall reimburse the Contractor on the basis of the actual cost to the Contractor plus a handling charge of the percentage amount indicated in Box 12, Part I, upon presentations of invoice.

13. SECURITY

The Company shall provide on signing of this Agreement, an irrevocable and unconditional bank guarantee in the sum and at the place indicated in Box 13, Part I, or other security to the satisfaction of the Contractor.

If required by the Contractor and also in the event that initially no security is requested, the Company shall provide security or further security to the satisfaction of the Contractor for all or part of any amount which may be or become due under this Agreement. Such security shall be given on one or more occasions as and when required by the Contractor.

14. LIABILITIES

14.1.1 The Contractor will indemnify and hold the Company harmless in respect of any liability adjudged due or claim reasonably compromised arising out of injury or death occurring during the services hereunder to any of the following persons:

- any servant or agent of the Contractor

- any other person at or near the site of the operations for whatever purpose on behalf or at the request of the Contractor.

14.1.2 The Company will indemnify and hold the Contractor harmless in respect of any liability adjudged due or claim reasonably comprised arising from injury or death occurring during the services hereunder to any of the following persons:

- any servant or agent of the Company
- any other person at or near the site of the operations for whatever purpose on behalf or at the request of the Company.

14.2.1 The following shall be for the sole account of the Contractor without any recourse to the Company, its servants, or agents, whether or not the same is due to breach of contract, negligence or any other fault on the part of the Company, its servants or agents:

(i) Loss or damage of whatsoever nature, howsoever sustained by the Contractor's own or hired-in craft or equipment.

(ii) Any liability in respect of wreck removal or in respect of the expense of moving or lighting or buoying the Contractor's own or hired-in craft or equipment.

The Contractor will indemnify and hold the Company harmless in respect of any liability adjudged due to a third party or any claim by a third party reasonably comprised arising out of any such loss or damage in this sub-paragraph.

14.2.2 The following shall be for the sole account of the Company without any recourse to the Contractor, its servants or agents, whether or not the same is due to breach of contract, negligence or any fault on the part of the Contractor, its servants or agents:

(i) Loss or damage of whatsoever nature, howsoever caused to or sustained by the Vessel.

(ii) Any liability in respect of wreck removal or in respect of the expense of moving or lighting or buoying the Vessel.

The Company will indemnify and hold the Contractor harmless in respect of any liability adjudged due to a third party or any claim by a third party reasonably compromised arising out of any such loss or damage in this sub paragraph.

14.3 Save as otherwise expressly stipulated in this Agreement neither the Contractor nor the Company shall be liable to the other party for loss of profit, loss of use, loss of production or any other indirect or consequential damage for any reason whatsoever.

14.4 Notwithstanding any provisions of this Agreement to the contrary the Contractor shall have the benefit of all limitations of, and exemptions from liability, accorded to the owners, charterers, managers or operators of vessels by an applicable statute or rule of law for the time being in force and the same benefits are to apply regardless of the form of signatures given to this Agreement.

15. HIMALAYA CLAUSE

All exceptions, exemptions, defences, immunities, limitations of liability, indemnities, privileges and conditions granted or provided by this Agreement for the benefit of the Contractor or the Company shall also apply to and be for the benefit of their respective subcontractors, operators, masters, officers and crews and to and be for the benefit of all bodies corporate parent of, subsidiary to, affiliated with or under the same management as either of them, as well as all directors, officers, servants and agents of the same and to and be for the benefit of all parties performing services within the scope of this Agreement for or on behalf of the Contractor or the Company as servants, agents and subcontractors of such parties. The Contractor or the Company shall be deemed to be acting as agent or trustee of and for the benefit of all such persons, entities and vessels set forth above but only for the limited purpose of contracting for the extension of such benefits to such persons, bodies and vessels.

16. LIEN

Without prejudice to any other rights which the Contractor may have, whether in rem or in personam, the Contractor shall be entitled to exercise a possessory lien upon the Vessel in respect of any amount howsoever or whatsoever due to the Contractor under this Agreement and shall for the purpose of exercising such possessory lien be entitled to take and/or keep possession of the Vessel, provided always that the Company shall pay to the Contractor all costs and expenses howsoever or whatsoever incurred by or on behalf of the Contractor in exercising or attempting or preparing to exercise such lien.

17. TIME FOR SUIT

Save for the indemnity provisions under Clause 14 of this Agreement any claim which may arise out of or in connection with this Agreement or any of the services performed under shall be notified by telex, facsimile, cable or otherwise in writing to the party against whom such claim is made, within 12 months of completion or termination of the services hereunder, and any suit shall be brought within two years of the time when the cause of action first arose. If either of these conditions is not complied with the claim and all rights whatsoever and howsoever shall be absolutely barred and extinguished.

18. GOVERNING LAW AND ARBITRATION

18.1 This Agreement shall be governed by and construed in accordance with English law and any dispute arising out of this Agreement shall be referred to Arbitration in London in accordance with the Arbitration Acts 1950 and 1979 or any statutory modification or re-enactment thereof for the time being in force.

Any dispute arising hereunder shall be referred to the arbitrament of a sole Arbitrator, to be selected by the first party claiming arbitration from the persons currently on the panel of Lloyd's Salvage Arbitrators with a right of appeal from an award made by the Arbitrator to either party by notice in writing to the other within 28 days of the date of publication of the original Arbitrator's Award.

The Arbitrator on appeal shall be the person currently acting as Lloyd's Appeal Arbitrator.

No suit shall be brought before another Tribunal, or in another jurisdiction, except that either party shall have the option to bring proceedings to obtain conservative seizure or other similar remedy against any assets owned by the other party in any state or jurisdiction where such assets may be found.

Both the Arbitrator and Appeal Arbitrator shall have the same powers as an Arbitrator and an Appeal Arbitrator under LOF 1990 or any standard revision thereof, including a power to order a payment on account of any monies due to the Contractor pending final determination of any dispute between the parties hereto.

18.2 Any dispute arising out of this Agreement shall be referred to Arbitration at the place indicated in Box 14, Part I, subject to the procedures applicable there. The laws of the place indicated in Box 14, Part I, shall govern this Agreement.

18.3 If Box 14, Part I, is not filled in, clause 18.1 shall apply.

19. WARRANTY OF AUTHORITY

If at the time of making this Agreement or providing any services under this agreement at the request, express or implied, of the Company, the Company is not the Owner of the Vessel, the Company warrants that it is authorized to make this Agreement.

INTERNATIONAL WRECK REMOVAL AND MARINE SERVICES AGREEMENT

CODE NAME: **WRECKHIRE** DAILY HIRE ANNEX I

DATE:

VESSEL:

SCHEDULE OF PERSONNEL, CRAFT AND EQUIPMENT:
[CL. 2 and 4.1 Part II]:

INTERNATIONAL WRECK REMOVAL AND MARINE SERVICES AGREEMENT

CODE NAME: **W R E C K H I R E** DAILY HIRE ANNEX II

DATE:

VESSEL:

METHOD OF WORK AND ESTIMATED TIME SCHEDULE:
[CL. 2 and 4.1 Part II]:

INTERNATIONAL SALVAGE UNION—
BALTIC AND INTERNATIONAL MARITIME COUNCIL

Recommended International Wreck Removal and Marine Services Agreement (Lump Sum) Code Name: "Wreckcon"

Enclosure VII
D.C. 1993-05-8
Item 10)

1. Date and Place of Agreement	PART 1
2. Contractor/place of business	3. Company/place of business
4. Vessel Specifications (Cl. 1, 2, 4.1) (a) Name (b) Flag (c) Place of Registry	5. Condition of Vessel (Cl. 2, 4.1)
(d) Length (e) Beam (f) Max. Draft (g) Displacement (h) Details and Nature of Cargo	6. Position of Vessel and Condition of Worksite Cl. 2,4.1)
(i) Any other Vessel's details relevant to this Agreement	7. Nature of Services (Cl. 2, 4.1, 4.3)
8. Place of Delivery/Disposal of Vessel (Cl. 2., 9.1, 9.2)	9. Payment and Rates of Hire (Cl. 1, 4.2, 8.2, 10.1, 10.2)

10. Payment Details (Cl. 10.4)	9. Continued (a) Lump Sum Price (in figures and letters)
(a) Currency	(b) Amount due and Payable on Signing this Agreement
(b) Bank	(c) Mobilization Costs (Amount Due and Payable on)
(c) Address	(d) Amount Due and Payable on
	(e) Amount Due and Payable on
(d) Account Number	(f) Amount Due and Payable on
(e) Account Name	(g) Amount Due and Payable on

11. Time of Payment and Interest (state period within which sums must be received by the Contractor and rate of interest per month) (Cl. 11)
12. Extra Costs (Cl. 4.2, 8.2, 12)
(a) Contractor shall be responsible for and pay for the following extra costs
(b) Company shall be responsible for and pay for the following extra costs
(c) Handling Charge to be applied, where applicable (state percentage)

13. Delay Payment Rate (Cl. 4.2, 7, 8.2, 8.3, 9.1, 9.2)	14. Security Requirements (Cl. 10.5, 13)
15. Cancellation Fee (Cl. 4.2, 8.1)	

16. Number of Unworkable Days due to Adverse Weather or Sea Conditions (Cl. 7)
17. Law and Arbitration (state 18.1 or 18.2 of Cl. 18 as agreed; if 18.2 agreed, also state place of arbitration) (Cl. 18)
18. Number of Additional Clauses covering special provisions, if agreed

It is agreed that this Agreement shall be performed subject to the Terms and Conditions which consist of PART I, including additional clauses, and PART II, as well as Annex I, PERSONNEL, CRAFT AND EQUIPMENT, and Annex II, METHOD OF WORK or any other Annexes attached to this Agreement.

The undersigned warrant that they have full power and authority to sign this Agreement on behalf of the parties represented by them.

Signature (for and on behalf of the Contractor)	Signature (for and on behalf of the Company)

INTERNATIONAL WRECK REMOVAL AND MARINE SERVICES AGREEMENT

CODE NAME: W R E C K C O N LUMP SUM PART II

1. DEFINITIONS

The term "Vessel" shall include any vessel, craft, property, or part thereof, of whatsoever nature, including anything contained therein or thereon, such as but not limited to cargo and bunkers, as described in Box 4, Part I.

The term "mobilization costs" in Box 9, Part I, shall mean the costs of mobilization and demobilization of the Personnel, Craft and Equipment set out in Annex I.

2. THE SERVICES

The Contractor agrees to exercise due care in rendering the services indicated in Box 7, Part I, and, if applicable, will endeavor to deliver and/or dispose of the Vessel at the place indicated in Box 8, Part I. Insofar as it is not inconsistent with the nature of the services to be rendered under this Agreement, the Contractor will also exercise due care to minimize damage to the environment.

The Contractor shall provide the Personnel, Craft and Equipment set out in Annex I of this Agreement which the Contractor deems necessary for the services based upon the Specifications, Condition and Position of the Vessel and Worksite set out in Boxes 4, 5 and 6, Part I.

The Contractor's Method of Work shall be described in Annex II, utilizing the Personnel, Craft and Equipment described in Annex I.

The Contractor shall consult with the Company if there is any need for substantial change in the Method of Work and/or Personnel, Craft or Equipment. In the event that time does not permit such consultation, or agreement to the proposed change(s) is unreasonably withheld, then the Contractor may proceed with such change(s). (See Clause 4 hereof.)

3. COMPANY REPRESENTATIVE

If reasonably required by the Contractor a representative of the Company will be available during the operations with the full authority to act on behalf of the Company. The Company will use its best endeavors to provide all information required by the Contractor.

In addition, the Company will provide at its sole risk and expense sufficient officers or their equivalents, who are fully conversant with the cargo system and/or layout of the Vessel, and who shall be in attendance when reasonably required during the operations in order to give assistance to the Contractor.

4. <u>CHANGE OF METHOD OF WORK and/or PERSONNEL, CRAFT AND EQUIPMENT</u>

4.1 The lump sum is based upon the Nature of the Services, Box 7, Part I, Method of Work and Personnel, Craft and Equipment set out in Annexes I and II, and the Description, Specifications, Position, Condition of the Vessel and the Worksite set out in Boxes 4, 5 and 6, Part I.

If before or during the operation, and without fault on the part of the Contractor, there is a substantial change in the work to be done under this Agreement, or in the Personnel, Craft and Equipment required to undertake the services due to:–

(1) any misdescription by the Company or error in the specification provided by the Company, upon which the Contractor has relied, or,

(2) a material change in the position and/or condition of the Vessel or the worksite,

the Contractor shall forthwith give notice in writing thereof to the Company and of the estimated additional costs to effect the services.

4.2 The parties shall, without delay, consult each other to reach agreement on the amount of the additional costs to be added to the lump sum. In the event that the parties are unable to reach agreement on the additional costs within 5 days of the Contractor providing details of the extra costs, either party may terminate the services under this Agreement, provided always that such termination is permitted by the competent authorities. In such event the Contractor is entitled to be paid all sums due at the time of termination in accordance with the provision of Boxes 9, 12, 13 and 15, Part 1.

If permission to terminate is not given by the competent authorities the Contractor shall be paid by the Company at the Delay Payment Rate set out in Box 13, Part I, during any standby period, and Company shall be liable for the Contractor's reasonable and necessary costs of continuing with the services.

4.3 Alternatively the parties may by agreement refer the matter to Arbitration in accordance with the provisions of this Agreement for a decision by the Arbitrator on the reasonableness and quantum of such extra costs.

In the event the matter is referred to Arbitration the Contractor will continue to provide the services set out in Box 7, Part I, without prejudice to his claim for additional remuneration.

5. <u>MISCELLANEOUS</u>

5.1 The Company shall arrange and pay for any marking of the Vessel and cautioning required. The Contractor shall arrange and pay for any marking or cautioning required in respect of its own equipment during the services under this Agreement.

5.2 The Contractor may make reasonable use of Vessel's machinery, gear, equipment, anchors, chains, stores and other appurtenances during and for the purposes of these services free of expense but shall not unnecessarily damage, abandon or sacrifice the same or any property the subject of this Agreement.

5.3 Subject to approval of the Company which shall not be unreasonably withheld, and subject to it being permitted by the competent authorities, the Contractor shall be entitled to remove, **dispose** or jettison cargo, or parts of the Vessel, or equipment from the Vessel if such action is considered by the Contractor to be **reasonably** necessary to perform the services under this Agreement.

5.4 The Company will indemnify the Contractor and hold him harmless from any claims by the owners or insurers of property which is removed, **disposed** or jettisoned following approval by the Company.

5.5 The Company will provide the Contractor with such plans and drawings of the Vessel, cargo manifests, stowage plans, etc. as the Contractor may require.

6. PERMITS

The Company shall obtain and maintain at its own costs all necessary licenses, approvals authorizations **or** permits required to undertake and complete the services without let or hinderance. The Contractor shall provide the Company with all reasonable assistance in connection with the obtaining of such licenses, approvals, authorizations **or** permits.

7. DELAYS

If the Contractor is delayed in performing its obligations under this Agreement due to adverse weather or sea conditions, in excess of the number of days set out in Box 16, Part I, or due to any other reason outside the control of the Contractor, the Contractor shall receive from the Company an additional compensation – per working day or pro rata – at the rate set out in Box 13, Part 1 for the time the Contractor is delayed in commencing or continuing the services with the customary progress. The Company shall be promptly advised by the Contractor about all delays, which shall be confirmed in writing as soon as possible.

8. TERMINATION

8.1 The Company may terminate this Agreement at any time prior to commencement of mobilization of **either** the Personnel **or** the Craft **or** the Equipment identified in Annex I, **whichever may be the first**, upon payment of the Cancellation Fee set out in Box 15, Part I.

8.2 The Contractor, with the agreement of the Company, which shall not be unreasonably withheld, may terminate this Agreement without any further liability if completion of the services or any agreed change of work under Clause 4 hereof, utilizing the Personnel, Craft and Equipment set out in Annex I, or any amendment thereto, becomes technically or physically impossible. In the event of such termination, the Contractor shall be entitled to payment of all monies due in accordance with the provision of Boxes 9, 12, and 13, Part I.

8.3 If permission to discontinue or terminate is not given by the competent authorities the Contractor shall be paid by the Company at the Delay Payment Rate set out in Box 13, Part I, for Personnel, Craft and Equipment during any standby period, and the Company shall be liable for the Contractor's reasonable and necessary costs of continuing with the services.

9. DELIVERY

9.1 The Vessel shall be accepted forthwith and taken over by the Company or its duly authorized representative at the place of delivery indicated in Box 8, Part I. References to delivery or the place of delivery shall include disposal or the place of disposal, if applicable.

The place of delivery shall always be safe and accessible for the Contractor's own or hired-in craft and the Vessel to enter and operate in and shall be a place where the Contractor is permitted by governmental or other authorities to deliver or dispose of the Vessel.

In the event the Vessel is not accepted forthwith by the Company or delivery is prevented or delayed by action of governmental or other authorities outside the control of the Contractor all costs necessarily incurred by the Contractor from the moment of the tender for delivery shall be for account of the Company. These costs shall be in addition to the delay payment as set out in Box 13, Part I.

9.2 If it is considered by the Contractor to be impossible or unsafe for the Vessel to be delivered or disposed of at the place indicated in Box 8, Part I and the Company is unable to nominate an acceptable alternative place the Contractor is at liberty to deliver or dispose of the Vessel at the nearest place it can reach safely and without unreasonable delay and such delivery or disposal shall be deemed a due fulfillment by the Contractor of this Agreement.

The Company shall reimburse the Contractor for any additional time used pursuant to this sub-clause at the Delay Payment Rate, Box 13, Part I, and shall be liable to the Contractor for any additional expenses arising under this sub-clause.

9.3 In the event the Vessel is delivered under the control of pumps and/or compressors or other equipment the Company shall with all due dispatch arrange for their own equipment and operators to replace the Contractor's equipment and their operators.

Until such replacement the Company shall pay the Contractor for the use of its equipment and operators at reasonable rates as from the day of delivery, until and including the day of arrival of the equipment and personnel at the Contractor's base, plus any additional costs relating thereto and incurred by the Contractor.

9.4 If the Company fails, on completion of the services, to take delivery of the Vessel within five (5) days of the Contractor tendering written notice of delivery, or if in the opinion of the Contractor the Vessel is likely to deteriorate, decay, become worthless or incur charges whether for storage or otherwise in excess of its value, the Contractor may, without prejudice to any other rights the Contractor may have against the Company, without notice and without any responsibility whatsoever attaching to the Contractor, sell or dispose of the Vessel and apply the proceeds of sale in reduction of the sums due to the Contractor from the Company under this Agreement. Any remaining proceeds will be refunded to the Company.

In the event that such sale or other disposal of the Vessel fails to raise sufficient net funds to pay the monies due to the Contractor under the terms of this Agreement then the Company shall remain liable to the Contractor for any such shortfall.

9.5 Reference to delivery of the Vessel shall include parts of the Vessel and/or cargo and/or any other thing emanating from the Vessel and such delivery may take place at different times and difference places.

10. PRICE AND CONDITIONS OF PAYMENT

10.1 The Company shall pay the Contractor for the services the sum set out in Box 9, Part I (hereinafter called "the lump sum"), which amount shall be due and payable as set out in Box 9, Part I.

10.2 Each installment of the lump sum shall be fully and irrevocably earned at the moment it is due as set out in Box 9, Part I. Any other monies due under this Agreement shall be fully and irrevocably earned on a daily basis or pro rata.

10.3 All monies due and payable to the Contractor under this Agreement shall be paid without any discount, deduction, set-off, lien, claim or counterclaim.

10.4 All payments to the Contractor shall be made in the currency and to the bank account stipulated in Box 10, Part I.

10.5 If any amount payable under this Agreement has not been paid within seven, (7), days of the due date, or if the security required in accordance with Box 14, Part I and Clause 13, Part II, is not provided within five, (5), banking days of the request by the Contractor, then at any time thereafter the Contractor shall be entitled to terminate this Agreement without prejudice to the sums already due to the Contractor and to any further rights or remedies which the Contractor may have against the Company. Provided always that the Contractor shall give the Company at least three, (3), working days notice of its intention to exercise this right.

11. TIME OF PAYMENT AND INTEREST

The Contractor shall promptly invoice the Company for all sums payable under this Agreement. If any sums which become due and payable are not actually received by the Contractor within the period specified in Box 11, Part I, they shall attract interest in accordance with the rate set out in Box 11, Part I.

12. EXTRA COSTS

The following expenses/costs shall be paid as and when they fall due by the party designated in Box 12, Part I:

12.1 all port expenses, pilotage charges, harbor and canal dues and all other expenses of a similar nature levied upon or payable in respect of the Vessel and the Contractor's own or hired-in craft.

12.2 the costs of the services of any assisting tugs when reasonably deemed necessary by the Contractor or prescribed by port or other authorities.

12.3 all costs in connection with clearance, agency fees, visas, guarantees and all other expenses of such kind.

12.4 all taxes and social security charges (other than those normally payable by the Contractor in the country where it has its principal place of business), stamp duties, or other levies payable in respect of or in connection with this Agreement, any import-export dues and any customs or excise duties.

12.5 all costs incurred due to requirements of governmental or other authorities or unions over and above those costs which would otherwise be reasonably incurred by the Contractor in the execution of the Agreement.

12.6 all costs incurred by the Contractor in respect of equipment, materials, or stores which are reasonably sacrificed during the disposal of, or other operations on the Vessel.

If any or all of the above expenses/costs identified in Box 12, Part I, are payable by the Company, they shall be paid by the Company direct to those entitled to them. If, however, any such expenses/costs are in fact paid by or on behalf of the Contractor (notwithstanding that the Contractor shall under no circumstances be under any obligation to make such payments on behalf of the Company) the Company shall reimburse the Contractor on the basis of the actual cost to the Contractor plus a handling charge of the percentage amount indicated in Box 12, Part I, upon presentation of invoice.

13. SECURITY

The Company shall provide on signing of this Agreement an irrevocable and unconditional bank guarantee in the sum and at the place indicated in Box 14, Part I, or other security to the satisfaction of the Contractor.

If required by the Contractor and also in the event that initially no security is requested, the Company shall provide security or further security to the satisfaction of the Contractor for all or part of any amount which may be or become due under this Agreement. Such security shall be given on one or more occasions as and when required by the Contractor.

14. LIABILITIES

14.1.1 The Contractor will indemnify and hold the Company harmless in respect of any liability adjudged due or claim reasonably compromised arising out of injury or death occurring during the services hereunder to any of the following persons:

- any servant or agent of the Contractor

- any other persons at or near the site of the operations for whatever purpose on behalf or at the request of the Contractor.

14.1.2 The Company will indemnify and hold the Contractor harmless in respect of any liability adjudged due or claim reasonably comprised arising from injury or death occurring during the services hereunder to any of the following persons:

- any servant or agent of the Company
- any other person at or near the site of the operations for whatever purpose on behalf or at the request of the Company.

14.2.1 The following shall be for the sole account of the Contractor without any recourse to the Company, its servants, or agents, whether or not the same is due to breach of contract, negligence or any other fault on the part of the Company, its servants or agents:

(i) Loss or damage of whatsoever nature, howsoever sustained by the Contractor's own or hired-in craft or equipment.

(ii) Any liability in respect of wreck removal or in respect of the expense of moving or lighting or buoying the Contractor's own or hired-in craft or equipment.

The Contractor will indemnify and hold the Company harmless in respect of any liability adjudged due to a third party or any claim by a third party reasonably compromised arising out of any such loss or damage in this sub-paragraph.

14.2.2 The following shall be for the sole account of the Company without any recourse to the Contractor, its servants or agents, whether or not the same is due to breach of contract, negligence or any fault on the part of the Contractor, its servants or agents:

(i) Loss or damage of whatsoever nature, howsoever caused to or sustained by the Vessel.

(ii) Any liability in respect of wreck removal or in respect of the expense of moving or lighting or buoying the Vessel.

The Company will indemnify and hold the Contractor harmless in respect of any liability adjudged due to a third party or any claim by a third party reasonably compromised arising out of any such loss or damage in this sub paragraph.

14.3 Save as otherwise expressly stipulated in this Agreement neither the Contractor nor the Company shall be liable to the other party for loss of profit, loss of use, loss of production or any other indirect or consequential damage for any reason whatsoever.

14.4 Notwithstanding any provisions of this Agreement to the contrary the Contractor shall have the benefit of all limitations of, and exemptions from liability, accorded to the owners, charterers, managers or operations of vessels by an applicable statute or rule of law for the time being in force and the same benefits are to apply regardless of the form of signatures given to this Agreement.

15. HIMALAYA CLAUSE

All exceptions, exemptions, defences, immunities, limitations of liability, indemnities, privileges and conditions granted or provided by this Agreement for the benefit of the Contractor or the Company shall also apply to and be for the benefit of their respective sub-contractors, operations, masters, officers and crews and to and be for the benefit of all bodies corporate parent of, subsidiary to, affiliated with or under the same management as either of them, as well as all directors, officers, servants and agents of the same and to and be for the benefit of all parties performing services within the scope of this Agreement for or on behalf of the Contractor or the Company as servants, agents and subcontractors of such parties. The Contractor or the Company shall be deemed to be acting as agent or trustee of and for the benefit of all such persons, entities and vessels set forth above but only for the limited purpose of contracting for the extension of such benefits to such persons, bodies and vessels.

16. LIEN

Without prejudice to any other rights which the Contractor may have, whether in rem or in personam, the Contractor shall be entitled to exercise a possessory lien upon the Vessel in respect of any amount howsoever or whatsoever due to the Contractor under this Agreement and shall for the purpose of exercising such possessory lien be entitled to take and/or keep possession of the Vessel, provided always that the Company shall pay to the Contractor all costs and expenses howsoever or whatsoever incurred by or on behalf of the Contractor in exercising or attempting or preparing to exercise such lien.

17. TIME FOR SUIT

Save for the indemnity provisions under Clause 14 of this Agreement any claim which may arise out of or in connection with this Agreement or any of the services performed under shall be notified by telex, facsimile, cable or otherwise in writing to the party against whom such claim is made, within 12 months of completion or termination of the services hereunder, and any suit shall be brought within two years of the time when the cause of action first arose. If either of these conditions is not complied with the claim and all rights whatsoever and howsoever shall be absolutely barred and extinguished.

18. GOVERNING LAW AND ARBITRATION

18.1 This Agreement shall be governed by and construed in accordance with English law and any dispute arising out of this Agreement shall be referred to Arbitration in London in accordance with the Arbitration Acts 1950 and 1979 or any statutory modification or re-enactment thereof for the time being in force.

Any dispute arising hereunder shall be referred to the arbitrament of a sole Arbitrator, to be selected by the first party claiming arbitration from the persons currently on the panel of Lloyd's Salvage Arbitrators with a right of appeal from an award made by the Arbitrator to either party by notice in writing to the other within 28 days of the date of publication of the original Arbitrator's Award.

The Arbitrator on appeal shall be the person currently acting as Lloyd's Appeal Arbitrator.

No suit shall be brought before another Tribunal, or in another jurisdiction, except that either party shall have the option to bring proceedings to obtain conservative seizure or the similar remedy against any assets owned by the other party in any state or jurisdiction where such assets may be found.

Both the Arbitrator and Appeal Arbitrator shall have the same powers as an Arbitrator and Appeal Arbitrator under LOF 1990 or any standard revision thereof, including a power to order a payment on account of any monies due to the Contractor pending final determination of any dispute between the parties hereto.

18.2 Any dispute arising out of this Agreement shall be referred to Arbitration at the place indicated in Box 17, Part I, subject to the procedures applicable there. The laws of the place indicated in Box 17, Part I, shall govern this Agreement.

18.3 If Box 17, Part I, is not filled in, clause 18.1 shall apply.

19. WARRANTY OF AUTHORITY

If at the time of making this Agreement or providing any services under this agreement at the request, express or implied, of the Company, the Company is not the Owner of the Vessel, the Company warrants that it is authorized to make this Agreement.

INTERNATIONAL WRECK REMOVAL AND MARINE SERVICES AGREEMENT

CODE NAME: **W R E C K C O N** LUMP SUM ANNEX I

DATE:

VESSEL:

PERSONNEL, CRAFT AND EQUIPMENT:
[CL. 1, 2, 4.1, 8.1, 8.2 and 12.6, Part II]:

INTERNATIONAL WRECK REMOVAL AND MARINE SERVICES AGREEMENT

CODE NAME: **W R E C K C O N** LUMP SUM ANNEX II

DATE:

VESSEL:

METHOD OF WORK AND ESTIMATED TIME SCHEDULE:
[CL. 2 and 4.1, Part II]:

APPENDIX C

SURVEYS, FORMS, AND CHECKLISTS

Survey reports, forms, and checklists are important tools for collecting and recording information during salvage operations. For the salvor, checklists are an important memory aid to insure no detail is forgotten or overlooked in collecting information or preparing for an operation. They are not a guarantee of success or of correct information. They should never be a crutch for the inexperienced. They have absolutely no value used without care, accuracy, and common sense. The last is the most important.

The forms and checklists presented in this Appendix have been collected from many sources. Most have grown through experience. Some contain much more information than is necessary for a particular operation; some may not contain enough. They are not dogma; they are guidance and suggestions. Wise users adapt and modify them to fit the circumstances of the geography and the casualty they are working with. Other types of checklists produced ad hoc in the field are very useful. Making, using, and continually updating checklists are excellent habits for salvors to cultivate. All checklists should be preserved in their original form as part of the documentation of the salvage operation.

Equipment checklists are not included. Such lists are tailored to specific equipment and include shipping (mobilization and demobilization), and operational checklists and logs. Shipping lists should contain inventories of all operating accessories and spare parts shipped with the equipment. Accessories and spares should be double-checked on both the shipping and receiving end. There is nothing more frustrating than being unable to operate equipment because a fitting or filter was not shipped. Support requirements (power voltage, type, frequency, fuels, etc.) should also be checked to assure the equipment's requirements can be met at the operations site.

This Appendix includes the following forms and checklists:

1. General Survey Form
2. Stranding Survey Form
3. Sinking Survey Form
4. Wreck Removal Survey Form
5. Beach Survey Form
6. Petroleum Cargo Transfer Checklist
7. Draft Survey Form
8. Trim Calculation Form
9. Mean-of-Quarter-Means Draft Calculation
10. Contract Information

The forms and checklists are presented in terms of the information needed and in a logical sequence rather than as finished lists that can be photocopied and taken to the field. Every user has the option to make up checklists that are most useful and that best fit a particular method of operation.

1. GENERAL SURVEY FORM

This survey form contains general information that is applicable to all types of casualties.

Casualty's name:

Type of ship:

No. of holds or tanks:

Cargo:

Bound from:

Bound for:

Date and time of casualty:

General location:

Lat.: Long.:

Nearest port:

National administration:

Chart no. (large scale):

Type of casualty:

Ship's particulars:

- LOA
- LBP
- B
- T (design)
- Depth
- GRT
- NRT
- Deadweight
- Lightship displacement
- Propulsion

Built in:
Built by:
Principal construction material:
Registry:
Flag:
Official number:
Call sign:
INMARSAT number:
Master's name:
Nationality:
Officers' nationality:
Crew nationality:
Language on board:
Language difficulty:

Name and address of owners:
Name and address of managers:
Name and address of agents:
Hull insurance on the ________________ market.

Name of underwriter:
P&I club:
Cargo shippers:
Cargo receivers:
Local authorities:

Time and date salvage party arrived on board:

Time and date survey commences:

Heading:

Lively?

Vessel secured? How?

List:

Trim:

Assist vessels on site:

Is there pollution from the casualty?

What is the extent of the pollution?

Is spillage continuing?

Is pollution response action in progress?

By whom?

Is oil or hazardous material leaking internally?

DRAFTS

BEFORE CASUALTY			AFTER CASUALTY Time Date	
Port	Starboard		Port	Starboard
		Forward		
		Midships		
		Aft		

Hog/sag?

Cargo description hold by hold or tank by tank:

Total weight of cargo:

Damage to cargo:

Is there dangerous or potentially polluting cargo aboard?

Applicable IMDG codes or UN numbers:

Has manifest been checked?

Is expert on cargo hazards needed?

Describe how cargo can be handled:

Is material and equipment for handling cargo available locally?

If cargo handling gear is not available locally, where can it be obtained?

Are stevedores or extra labor required?

Are stevedores or extra labor available locally?

Will water damage protection be required for the cargo? Machinery?

LIQUID LOAD

MARINE DIESEL OIL	QUANTITY	LOCATION
Heavy fuel oil		
Lubricating oils		
Miscellaneous oils		
Fresh water		
Gray water		
Ballast water		
Permanent ballast		
Sewage		
Other		
Total		

Pre-casualty stability information:

GM:

GZ:

KG:

KM:

TPI or TPC:

MT1 or MTC:

Do minimum GM or GZ criteria apply?

Is the following documentation on board?

Trim and Stability Booklet:

Capacity plan:

Hydrostatic data or curves of form:

General arrangement plan:

Sounding or ullage tables:

Midships section:

Shell expansion:

Cargo plan:

Does the ship have a load computer?

Is it operable?

Does it have a grounded condition option?

Describe known damage to casualty:

Tide tables in use:

Reference station:

Tidal range:

Tide calculations being made by:

Tide gauge in place:

Tide gauge monitored by:

Tidal currents:

Tidal current calculations by:

Weather forecasts available from:

Schedule:

Weather faxes available from:

Schedule:

Site is exposed to:

- Swell (height and direction):
- Seas (height and direction):
- Wind (speed and direction):
- Current (speed and direction):
- Water temperature:

Sea floor:

- Material:
- Slope:

Does ship have its own power available?

Type?

Serviceable machinery (with identifying data):

- Main engine(s):
- Main generators:
- Boilers:

Deck machinery:

Fire pumps:

Watermakers:

Steering gear:

Other:

Fire-fighting equipment:

Fire pumps:

Pump room:

Accommodation:

Deck:

Firemen's outfits:

General condition:

Life-saving equipment:

Boats:

Breathing apparatus:

Immersion suits:

Life jackets:

General condition:

2. STRANDING SURVEY FORM

This survey form contains information specific to strandings. It should augment the information in the general survey form.

Soundings all around the vessel:

Soundings by: Time and date:

Previous highwater (time and height above datum):

Tide height at time of soundings:

Have soundings been corrected to datum?

Soundings away from casualty:

Distance from casualty that soundings have been made:

Ahead:

Starboard:

Port:

Astern:

Soundings made by (person and method):

Sounding chart made up?

Spots for diver investigation marked?

Divers' report:

Time and date:

Divers:

Depth:

Current:

Visibility:

Extent of grounding:

Length of sea floor contact:

Contact general or local?

Sea suctions clear:

Running gear clear:

Damage to hull:

Suggested repair methods:

Damage to running gear:

Position of rudder:

Photographs or videos made?

Are tanks containing oils or other pollutants clear of the grounded area?

Can the ship be defueled with its own defueling system?

If not, how can tanks be accessed for defueling?

Estimated ground reaction:

Estimated center of ground reaction:

Shear forces and bending moments in current condition acceptable?

Internal survey:

Tank soundings:

Flooding:

Continuing?

Rate?

Source identified?

Fire damage:

Structural damage:

3. SINKING SURVEY FORM

This survey form contains information specific to sinkings. It can be used to supplement the information in the general survey form.

Is vessel capsized?

To what angle?

Is the main deck submerged?

Water depth over main deck:

HIGH TIDE		LOW TIDE
	Forward	
	Aft	

Soundings all around the vessel:

Soundings by:

Time and date:

Previous highwater (time and height above datum):

Tide height at time of soundings:

Have soundings been corrected to datum?

Soundings away from casualty:

Distance from casualty that soundings have been made:

Ahead:

Starboard:

Port:

Astern:

Soundings made by (person and method):

Sounding chart made up?

Spots for diver investigation marked?

Divers' report:

Time and date:

Divers:

Depth:

Current:

Visibility:

Damage to hull:

Has damage been videotaped or photographed?

Suggested repair methods:

Internal survey:

Is diving necessary for internal survey?

Can internal damage be reached?

If no, can material be moved to reach internal damage?

Damage to hull and internal structure:

Has damage been videotaped or photographed?

Suggested repair methods:

Is internal floodwater polluted?

Is pollution from the casualty occurring?

What is the type and source?

Can pollution be contained?

Suggested action:

What tanks contain oil or other pollutants?

How can oil or pollutants be removed from each?

Can tanks be sealed?

What hazardous materials are in the cargo?

How can they be removed?

What weights can be removed?

Can the casualty be refloated in one piece?

4. WRECK REMOVAL SURVEY FORM

This contract contains information specific to vessels that have been declared constructive total losses and whose removal is being carried out under their P&I cover.

Wreck's name:

Type of ship:

No. of holds or tanks:

Deadweight:

Cargo:

Is any cargo munitions or dangerous goods?

What are IMDG codes or UN numbers for dangerous goods?

What is nation of origin of munitions?

How was cargo verified?

Does any cargo retain value?

Is there any cargo with special value?

Does the vessel contain any solid or liquid fuel, lubricants, or other petroleum products?

Loss of this vessel was caused by:

Wreck is entered with the _______________ P&I club for the risk that caused her loss.

P&I club managers have confirmed the above.

P&I club contacts:

Head office:

Local correspondent:

Technical consultant:

If wreck is not entered with P&I club, who covers wreck removal liability?

Contacts:

Head office:

Local representative:

Technical consultant:

Government body coordinating wreck removal or requiring removal:

Officer-in-charge:

Project officer:

Project engineer:

Date and time of loss:

Specific location:

Lat: Long:

Port:

National administration:

Chart no. (large scale):

Sailing directions:

Is the wreck currently blocking a berth, impeding navigation or port development, or a hazard to navigation?

Ship's particulars:

LOA
LBP
B
T (design)
Depth
GRT
NRT
Deadweight
Lightship displacement
Propulsion

Built:
Built by:
Registry:
Flag:
Owner:
Official number:
Call sign:
Name and address of owners:
Who holds title to the wreck?

Survey and bid requested or authorized by:
Is the cost of the survey being paid?
By whom:
Time and date of survey:
Comment on quality of data:
Was a diving survey made?
By whom?
Have local attempts been made to salvage or remove the wreck?

Tide range is:
Prevailing swell height is:
Prevailing winds are:
Local weather:
Best working months:
Underwater visibility:
Current:

Estimated daily diving time:

Sea floor is:

Have sea floor cores been taken?

Analyzed by:

What were the results of core analysis?

Has wreck silted up?

Is the wreck dug into the sea floor?

To what depth?

Is wreck impaled or entangled with other wreckage or structures?

Heading:

List:

Fore and aft attitude:

Note local regulations and business requirements that will affect the operation:

Can explosives be used?

Have local authorities conducted surveys?

Are they available?

Are any crew available for interview?

What local contractors are available?

5. BEACH SURVEY FORM

This checklist is to document beach and surf conditions for operations where men and materials must move across the beach or through the surf.

Beach material is (sand, gravel, rock, turf):

Beach width from high-water mark to vegetation line:

Beach slope:

Is beach usable by wheeled vehicles?

Is beach useable by tracked vehicles?

Is there road access to beach?

Can helicopters land on the beach?

Is there a sheltered helicopter landing area?

Distance to first breaker line from high-water mark:

Sea condition between first breaker line and beach:

Average breaker height:

Maximum breaker height:

Number of breaker lines:

Distance between breaker lines:

Time interval between breakers:

Breakers are: spilling? plunging? dumping? mixed?

Breaker angle to the beach:

Tide range (vertical):

Tide range (horizontal):

Tidal period:

Reference station:

Is there an offshore reef?

Is there a channel through the reef?

Is the channel marked?

Can the boats on hand work through the surf?

Can local boats work through the surf?

6. PETROLEUM CARGO TRANSFER CHECKLIST

This checklist is intended for use with a ship-to-ship (STS) transfer of a liquid petroleum cargo from a casualty to a receiving vessel under casualty conditions. Those parts of the list dealing with mooring and fendering are applicable to all STS transfers. When cargoes are other than liquid petroleum products, checklists for the specific cargoes and for the receiving ship should be drawn up and used.

Date:

Location:

PART 1—CASUALTY INFORMATION

Casualty name:

Registry:

Is crew aboard?

Master:

Nationality of officers:

Nationality of crew:

Common language:

English spoken?

Ambient temperature range _______to ________(F/C):

Sea temperature:

Casualty condition (stranded / sunk / collision damage / fire damage, etc.):

Cargo:

Type:

Quantity:

Specific gravity:

Pumpable at ambient temperature:

Special characteristics:

Tank information:

The following information can often be provided most conveniently by marking up a tank arrangement plan and attaching it to the checklist:

Tank arrangement and capacities:

Quantity of cargo in each tank:

Tank damage—known and suspected:

Water bottom depth:

Is tank inerted?

If so, note pressure and oxygen percentage:

Is automatic gauging system operable?

If not, how can tanks be gauged?

Can tank be pumped through installed piping?

Is ship's load computer operable?

Does the load computer have a grounded ship option?

Is there a salvage program aboard?

Is there a qualified operator for the salvage program?

Pumprooms:

How many pumprooms are there?

Where are they?

General condition of pumprooms:

List the following information for each cargo pump:

Location:

Type:

Capacity:

Operable? If no, repairable?

Is pumproom ventilation operable? Adequate? If no, how can ventilation be provided?

Are pumproom bilges free of large accumulations of oil?

Can they be cleaned and kept oil free?

Is pumproom lighting adequate?

Size of piping mains?

Locate known or suspected piping damage on piping diagrams.

Note inoperable or leaking valves and pumproom cross connections.

Are valves mechanically/hydraulically/pneumatically operated?

Are all power-operated valves operable by power?

Can inoperable valves be hand operated?

Cargo manifold:

Distance from bow to center of manifold?

Distance from stern to center of manifold?

Number of valves on manifold?

Are all valves operable?

Vent systems:

Is vent system open or closed?

Are open vents clear and protected with proper safety devices?

Are all PV valves set and operable?

Is the installed inert gas system operable?

If not, can it be made operable?

Mooring:

On a plan view of the deck note the:

Type:

Location:

Type, amount, and general condition of line:

Brake holding power:

General condition of all mooring winches:

Location, type, and condition of all bitts, chocks, Panama leads, and other mooring fittings:

PART 2—RECEIVING SHIP INSPECTION

Name:
Previous names:
Registry:
Built at:
Year:
Particulars:
- LOA:
- LBP:
- Beam:
- Light draft:
- Full summer draft:
- Deadweight:
- Available deadweight:

Call sign:
INMARSAT:
FAX:
Classification society:
In class?
P&I club:

Master's name:
Nationality:
Nationality of officers:
Nationality of crew:
Common language:
English spoken?
Are the master and crew experienced in STS transfers?
Owner/manager:

Does crew meet Flag State requirements?
What exceptions are there?
Is the vessel acceptable to Port State authorities?
What exceptions are there?

Are the following certificates on board and valid?

Loadline Certificate:

SOLAS Safety Equipment Certificate:

SOLAS Safety Construction Certificate:

Radio Safety Certificate:

International Oil Pollution Prevention Certificate (IOPP):

TOLAVOP Certificate:

Does the vessel carry all other certificates required by the Flag State and the Port State? If not, list exceptions:

Does the vessel comply with current SOLAS regulations? If not, list exceptions:

If operation is in U.S. waters or if ship is U.S.-flagged:

Does the vessel have a COFER on file?

Does the vessel comply with all current USCG requirements?

Does the vessel carry the OCIMF/ICS publications:

International Safety Guide for Oil Tankers and Terminals?

Ship-to-Ship Transfer Guide?

Cargo:

Provide drawing or sketch of cargo tank arrangement:

What was last cargo?

Have tanks been cleaned since the last cargo?

By what method?

What is the nature and quantity of residues in the tanks?

Are the tanks suited to receive the cargo from the casualty? If not, why not?

Is the automatic gauging system operable?

If not, what system of gauging is proposed for the transfer?

Is the inert gas system fully operational?

Pumprooms:

How many pumprooms are there?

Where are they?

General condition of pumprooms:

List the following information for each cargo pump:

Location:

Type:

Capacity:

Operable? If no, repairable?

Is pumproom ventilation operable? Adequate? If no, how can ventilation be provided?

Are pumproom bilges free of large accumulations of oil?

Can they be cleaned and kept oil free?

Is pumproom lighting adequate?

Size of piping mains?

Locate known or suspected piping damage on piping diagrams.

Note inoperable or leaking valves and pumproom cross connections.

Are valves mechanically/hydraulically/pneumatically operated?

Are all power-operated valves operable by power?

Can inoperable valves be hand operated?

Cargo manifold:

Distance from bow to center of manifold:

Distance from stern to center of manifold:

Number of valves on manifold:

Are all valves operable?

Vent systems:

Is vent system open or closed?

Are open vents clear and protected with proper safety devices?

Are all PV valves set and operable?

Fendering system:

Does the vessel carry her own fendering system? If yes, what are the types, sizes, and location of fenders?

Is the fendering system suitable for the proposed operation? If no, what changes must be made?

Are the fenders properly rigged? If no, what changes must be made?

Mooring:

On a plan view of the deck note the:

Type:

Location:

Type, amount, and general condition of line:

Brake holding power, and general condition of all mooring winches:

Location, type, and condition of all bitts, chocks, Panama leads, and other mooring fittings.

Overall:

Comment on the overall impression given by the ship and crew.

Is the ship suitable for the proposed operation? If not why not?

Can the ship be made ready in the time available?

PART 3—TRANSFER OPERATIONS

A. *General*

Salvage master (person in overall charge of the operation):

PRINCIPAL PERSONNEL	
On the casualty	On the receiving ship
Salvors:	Salvors:
Master:	Master:
Chief officer:	Chief officer:
Chief engineer:	Chief engineer:

The amount to be transferred is:

The capacity of the receiving vessel is:

The limiting draft of the receiving vessel is:

The maximum pumping rate of the casualty is:

The maximum receiving rate of the receiving vessel is:

The estimated time of the transfer is:

Transfer is to be conducted ______ hours per day.

Have all hands in each ship's crew and the salvage crew been briefed on the purpose and overall plan of the operation?

Has provision been made for watches with supervision and crew rest?

Have all hands on the salvage crew, casualty, and receiving ship been briefed that the salvage master, either master or other responsible person, may stop the operation in the event of:

Pollution or spillage:

Thunderstorms:

Still air:

Fire:

Tank overflow:

Burst hose:

Man overcome by fumes:

Unexpected refloating:

Have all hands on the salvage crew, casualty, and receiving ship been briefed that the signal for stopping operations is: *Continuous blast on the whistle or siren* combined with *Ringing of the general alarm*?

Have radio communications been established between the ships? On what frequencies or channels?

Have hand-held radios been distributed and tested?

Has the cathodic protection system operation been checked?

Have local authorities been advised of the operation?

Have local authorities approved the operational plan?

Have appropriate navigational warnings been broadcast or issued?

Are navigational signals for the transfer ready?

Have weather forecasts and updates for the operation been arranged?

B. *Fendering*

Are fenders to be rigged from the casualty or receiving vessel?

FENDERS			
	Type	Size	Location
Primary			
Secondary			
Tertiary			

Are hand-held fenders available forward and aft on both vessels?

C. *Mooring*

Mooring operations should be conducted only during daylight hours unless there are overriding reasons for accepting the risks of night mooring operations.

The mooring operation is to begin at _(time)_ on _(date)_. The expected state of the tide is _____. Tidal current is expected to be _____, slack water is scheduled at _(time)_, minimum acceptable weather conditions are:

Attach a sketch showing ships lying alongside each other with positions of manifolds and reference points for positioning vessels.

Attach a sketch showing the type, size, and location of each mooring line. Note whether fiber rope tails are to be used on wire rope mooring lines.

Note tugs to be used in mooring and how they are to be placed.

Have the masters of both vessels agreed to the method of approach, mooring methods, emergency procedures, and unmooring procedures?

Have the chief engineers of both vessels been briefed on and agreed to engine requirements?

What assistance in the mooring is to be given by salvors on the casualty?

On the receiving ship?

Freeboards at mooring:

Casualty:

Receiving ship:

Are the ships as nearly upright as possible?

Are all constant tensioning winches in manual?

Are all mooring lines ready for use?

Are messengers, stoppers, and heaving lines in place on both ships?

Have line-throwing guns been broken out and put in place?

Are axes available at each mooring station?

Salvage crew to provide ____________________ hand mooring party aboard the casualty; ____ is in charge.

Salvage crew to provide ____________________ hand mooring party aboard the receiving ship; ____ is in charge.

Line handling boat is to be provided by: Line handling boat is to be manned by:

Continuous mooring watch on casualty is to be provided by:

Continuous mooring watch on receiving ship is to be provided by:

	CASUALTY	RECEIVING SHIP
Are all scuppers plugged and sealed?		
Has everything extending past the side of the ship been rigged in?		
Are accommodation doors and ports closed?		
Is the off-side anchor ready for letting go?		

Access between the ships is to be provided by:

Is access laid out and ready to rig?

D. *Fire*

	CASUALTY	RECEIVING SHIP
Are all pump room fans working?		
If all pump room fans are not working, has emergency ventilation been: Rigged? Tested? Is it operable?		
Are fire pumps running and mains pressurized?		
Emergency fire pump locations are:		
Are fire pump suctions clear?		
Are at least 4 fire hoses with at least 2 spray/jet and 2 foam nozzles rigged on each vessel?		
Number and type of portable extinguishers available near the manifold on each ship:		
Location of breathing equipment with spare charged cylinders on deck:		
Inert gas system operable?		
Tanks *not* inerted below 8% oxygen?		
Tanks ballasted?		
Can attending tugs' and salvage ships' fire mains be cross-connected with the tug or salvage ship that attends in case of fire?		

The international fire connection is located on the casualty at:

Is a portable inert gas generator on board?

Location:

Capacity:

List fire-fighting equipment on tugs or salvage ships standing by:

Foam:

Monitors:

Monitors with foam capability:

Hoses (number and size):

Foam lines:

Carbon dioxide connections:

E. *Pollution prevention and response*

Local agency with spill control responsibility:

Responsible officer:

Is there a local area spill contingency plan?

Person responsible for its implementation:

Copy located:

Spill response equipment on scene:

Aboard casualty:

Aboard receiving vessel:

Aboard attending vessels (by vessel):

Who is the oil pollution response contractor?

Who is in charge for the oil pollution response contractor?

What additional equipment is standing by?

Is site boomed or to be boomed during transfer?

Vessel handling boom?

Who is tasked to deal with spills:

Between the ships?

Escaping?

F. *Machinery and electrical systems*

	CASUALTY	RECEIVING VESSEL
Is all electronic equipment except VHF radios turned off and grounded?		
Is all portable electrical equipment including radios and flashlights intrinsically safe?		
Are all fixed central air-conditioning units set on *recirculate*?		
Are all window-type air-conditioners disconnected?		
Is the galley an air-conditioned electric galley?		
If the galley is not an air-conditioned electric galley, is it shut down?		

	CASUALTY	RECEIVING VESSEL
Are all pantry and other cooking appliances isolated?		
Are all unsafe electrical circuits isolated at the main switchboard?		
Have engine room watches for the transfer been designated and procedures established?		
What machinery is inoperable?		
Have chief engineers been briefed that tubes are not to be blown and that spark control and smoke emission are to be enforced while the ships are alongside?		

G. *Cargo manifolding and hoses*

	CASUALTY	RECEIVING SHIP
Is the cargo manifold 10 feet (3 meters) or less from amidships?		
Is the center of the cargo manifold at least 3 feet (1 meter) and not more than 6' 10" (2.1 m) above the deck or working platform?		
Does the ship have 8-inch (400mm) manifold connections? If not, what sizes are available?		
Are all manifold connections marked?		
Are drip pans in place?		
Are sawdust and sorbents available near the manifolds?		
Are all the tools required for connecting, standing by, draining, and disconnecting available?		
Are manifold connections that are not to be used closed and blanked?		
Cargo hoses are provided by?		
Derricks required: Side SWL		
Is the hose properly supported?		

Have hoses offered been inspected and found satisfactory?

Hose information:

Number:

Diameter:

Length:

Minimum bend radius (6 × nominal hose bore):

Have all hoses been tested?

Date of test:

	SHIP'S CREW	SALVAGE CREW
Hoses on the casualty are to be connected and disconnected by:		
Hoses on the receiving ship are to be connected and disconnected by:		
Hoses are to be tended by:		

Are hoses bonded or insulated?

If bonded, how?

Are all hoses made up with new gaskets?

Are all hose couplings locked, pinned, or lashed? Specify which:

Are all hose saddle support lines off winches and stopped off properly?

H. *Cargo operations*

Is the gangway in position and secured?

Are the proper navigation signals being shown? Is the red loading light on?

Have all communications been checked and found satisfactory?

Is the safety equipment listed below on board?

EQUIPMENT	YES/NO	LOCATION
Explosiometer		
Oxygen analyzer		
Multi-gas detector		
Anemometer		
Interface detector		

Linen ullage tapes		
Dispersant		
Loud hailer		
Protective clothing		
Resuscitator		
Rescue stretcher		

Have the proper watches been set?

	CASUALTY	RECEIVING SHIP	SALVAGE CREW
Bridge			
Engineroom			
Pumproom			
Deck			

	CASUALTY	RECEIVING SHIP
Is smoking restricted or banned completely?		
Are cargo gas lines on bypass or set at an inert gas pressure of:		
Are PV valves in the operating position or locked open?		
Is the inert gas system operating?		
The inert gas system is feeding which tanks at what capacity and pressure?		
Is the inert gas capacity adequate?		
Are ullage ports free and shut?		
Are all sea valves closed and lashed?		
Are cargo calculations and shear and bending force calculations complete and satisfactory to the salvage master?		

	CASUALTY	RECEIVING SHIP
Are the casualty's discharge plan and receiving ship's loading plan complete and attached?		

	SHIP'S CREW	SALVAGE CREW
Tanks on the casualty are to be gauged by: automatic gauging system/innages/ ullages at intervals of ______ minutes by:		
Tanks on the receiving ship are to be gauged by: automatic gauging system/innages/ullages at intervals of ______ minutes by:		

I. *Over-the-top pumping*

HYDRAULIC/ELECTRIC salvage pumps are to transfer cargo over the top from tanks ________________________ in the casualty to tanks ___________________in the CASUALTY/RECEIVING VESSEL or to the manifold located at ________________ .

Pumps to be used:

Number:

Type:

Size:

Location:

The following accessories are on board:

ACCESSORY	NUMBER
Power supply and return lines	
Discharge hose	
Hose guides and rubber mats	
Tripod and handling gear	
Static ground strap	
Gas prevention escape collar	

Are all discharge and hose fittings made up properly and checked tight?

Power for the pumps is supplied by _(number)_ _(hydraulic power supplies or generator)_ located at ____.

Are the power supplies located in an area that should remain free of fume accumulation?

The power supplies are fueled for _(number)_ hours of operation.

Additional fuel for _(number)_ hours of operation is located at ______________________.

Electric pumps only:

Is the power supply intrinsically safe?

Are all connectors a sealed type?

The fuse/ circuit breaker is set at _(number)_ and located at:_______________.

Are all pumps grounded or bonded?

Location of the pump control panel:

Does the control panel have voltmeters and ammeters for each pump?

Have all pumps been tested satisfactorily?

At what time and date?

Pump watches are (name and time):

Power supply watches are (name and time):

J. *Unmooring*

Do both masters and the salvage master agree on the methods of letting go and disengaging?

	CASUALTY	RECEIVING VESSEL
Have all cargo hoses been unrigged and secured?		
Are hoses and manifolds blanked?		
Are gangways clear?		
Is the transfer side clear of obstructions and projections?		
Have fenders, towing lines, and securing lines been checked?		
Is power on to winches and windlasses?		
Are messengers and stoppers in place?		
Has the quantity of cargo transferred been agreed?		

	CASUALTY	RECEIVING VESSEL
Salvage crew is to provide how many hand mooring party to:		
Pilots required?		
Pilot on board?		
All stations manned and ready?		
Have communications with all stations been established?		

Tugs available:

Tug stations:

Are all tugs on station and ready?

Upon unmooring the receiving ship is to:

Has traffic been checked?

Have appropriate local authorities been informed?

Have navigational warnings been cancelled?

7. DRAFT SURVEY FORM

This form is used to calculate the quantity of cargo transferred to a relief vessel on the basis of draft surveys.

Date:

Location:

Receiving vessel:

Casualty:

Cargo:

Density:

	FIRST SURVEY	SECOND SURVEY
Date and time		
Water specific gravity		
Drafts		
1. Forward–port		
Forward–starboard		
2. Aft–port		
Aft–starboard		
3. Midships–port		

	FIRST SURVEY		SECOND SURVEY	
Midships–starboard				
4. Mean of midships				
5. Mean of forward and aft				
6. Mean of means (4+5)/2				
7. Mean of quarter means (4+6)/2				
Displacement for 7.		TONS		TONS
SG correction	(+/-)		(+/-)	
Trim correction	(+/-)		(+/-)	
8. Corrected displacement	A	TONS	B	TONS
Deductions				
Diesel fuel				
Heavy fuel				
Lube oils				
Fresh water				
Ballast				
Miscellaneous:				
(1)				
(2)				
(3)				
Total deductions	a.	TONS	b.	TONS
8. Corrected displacement	A	TONS	B	TONS
Final	C=A-a	TONS	D=B-b	TONS
Cargo loaded	D-C			TONS
Cargo discharged	C-D			TONS
Cargo on board				TONS
Scale deadweight				TONS
Difference				TONS
For salvors	(Signed)			
For casualty	(Signed)			
For receiving vessel	(Signed)			

8. TRIM CALCULATION FORM

TRIM CALCULATION		
ITEM	VALUE	UNITS
Length (LBP)		feet
LCF from bow (Df)		feet
LCF from stern (Df)		feet
Weight (W): Added Removed		tons
Distance of weight from LCF (Dw): Forward Aft		feet
TPI		tons
MT1		ft/tons
Parallel sinkage or rise: Sinkage (Rise) = + (–) $\frac{W}{TPI}$		feet
Total change of trim: Δ trim = W × $\frac{Df}{MT1}$		feet
DRAFT CHANGES		
Draft Forward (Tf)		
Original draft forward		feet
Parallel sinkage or rise	±	feet
Change of trim forward $\delta Tf = \pm\delta trim \times (\frac{Df}{L})$	±	feet
New draft forward (Tf)		feet
DRAFT AFT (Ta)		
Original draft aft		feet
Parallel sinkage or rise. *Same sign as draft forward*	±	feet
Change of trim aft. *Opposite sign from forward* $\delta Tf = \pm\delta trim \times (\frac{Df}{L})$	±	feet
New draft aft		

9. MEAN-OF-QUARTER-MEANS DRAFT CALCULATION

1. Draft forward (port)	feet/meters
2. Draft forward (starboard)	feet/meters
3. Draft forward (mean) $3. = \frac{(1. + 2.)}{2}$	feet/meters
4. Draft aft (port)	feet/meters
5. Draft aft (starboard)	feet/meters
6. Draft aft (mean) $6. = \frac{(4. + 5.)}{2}$	feet/meters
3. Draft forward (mean)	feet/meters
6. Draft aft (mean)	feet/meters
7. Calculated mean draft $7. = \frac{(3. + 6.)}{2}$	feet/meters
8. Mean draft port (observed)	feet/meters
9. Mean draft starboard (observed)	feet/meters
10. Observed mean draft $10. = \frac{(8. + 9.)}{2}$	feet/meters
7. Calculated mean draft	feet/meters
10. Observed mean draft	feet/meters
11. Working mean draft $11. = \frac{(7. + 10.)}{2}$	feet/meters

10. CONTRACT INFORMATION

No cure–no pay contract feasible?

Services offered on ______________________________ basis.

Time: __________ Date: __________

Salvage contract signed:

Type:

Time:

Date:

By:

For salvors:

For owners:

Contract currency:

Are other salvors involved?

On what basis?

Who is principal salvage contractor?

Who are other salvors' principal parties?

Date and time of first situation report:

Date and time of completion of services or redelivery of casualty:

NOTES

CHAPTER 1

1. 10 USC 7361.
2. 46 USC 316(d).

CHAPTER 3

1. A highly recommended text on this subject is by G.W. White, *Elementary Beam Theory and the Ship Girder* (London: Stanford Maritime Ltd, 1979).

CHAPTER 4

1. The Oil Companies International Marine Forum and the International Chamber of Shipping, *Peril at Sea and Salvage, A Guide for Masters*, 4th ed. (London: Witherby and Co. Ltd., 1992).

CHAPTER 5

1. IMO Code for Construction and Equipment of Ships Carrying Dangerous Chemicals in Bulk and the IMO Code for Construction and Equipment of Ships Carrying Liquefied Gases in Bulk.
2. Cleopatra Elmira Henry, *The Carriage of Dangerous Goods by Sea* (New York: St. Martin's Press, 1985).
3. U.S. Coast Guard, *Chemical Data Guide for Bulk Shipment by Water*, CIM 16616.6A (Washington, D.C.: U.S. Department of Transportation, 1990); *Emergency Response Guidebook,* DOT P 5800.5, Research and Special Programs Administration (Washington, D.C.: U.S. Department of Transportation, 1990); *Pocket Guide to Chemical Hazards,* National Institute for Occupational Safety and Health (NIOSH) (Washington, D.C.: U.S. Department of Health and Human Services, June 1990).
4. 46 CFR 140-155.

5. *Ship-to-Ship Transfer Guide (Liquefied Gases)* (London: The International Chamber of Shipping, The Oil Companies International Marine Forum, 1980).

CHAPTER 7

1. *Wire Rope Users Manual*, Committee of Wire Rope Producers, American Iron and Steel Institute, 1000 16th Street, NW, Washington, DC 20036.
2. Irving L. Stern and Michael F. Wheatcroft, *Toward Improving the Reliability of Anchor Chain and Accessories,* OTC 3206, Offshore Technology Conference, Houston, May 1978.

CHAPTER 8

1. Captain Richard A. Cahill, *Strandings and Their Causes* (London: Fairplay Publications, 1985).
2. *General Principles for Ship Reporting Systems and Ship Reporting Requirements, Including Guidelines for Reporting Incidents Involving Dangerous Goods, Harmful Substances, and/or Marine Pollutants*, International Maritime Organization Resolution A.648(16).
3. The Oil Companies International Marine Forum and the International Chamber of Shipping, *Peril at Sea and Salvage, A Guide for Masters*, 4th ed. (London: Witherby and Co. Ltd., 1992).
4. William E. George, ed. *Stability and Trim for the Ship's Officer*, based on the original editions by John La Dage and Lee Van Gemert (Centreville, Md.: Cornell Maritime Press, 1983).

CHAPTER 10

1. Lieutenant Commander John L. Ulrich, U.S.N., George D. Mott, and David R. Keyser, "How to Minimize Barge Damage during Salvage," *Ocean Industry* (July 1968).

CHAPTER 11

1. Captain David Hancox, *Commercial Salvage Practice* (Sunderland, England: Thomas Reed Publications Ltd., 1987), chap. 38, part 1;_________, "The Development of the Modern Salvage Vessel," *Jane's Merchant Shipping Review*, A.J. Ambrose, ed. (London: McDonald and Janes Ltd., 1984); Dr. John Hoogenbosch, "The Development and Decline of the Oceangoing Tug," in Proceedings of the Eighth International Tug Convention, Singapore, 1984.
2. Salvatore J. Guarino, "The Offshore Supply Vessel as a Naval Auxiliary," Gulf Section Paper (Biloxi, Miss.: The Society of Naval Architects and Marine Engineers, September 27, 1974); R.D. Jaeschke, "Proposed New American Flag Salvage Tug," unpublished memorandum to R.E. Gross, President, United States Salvage Association, Inc., December 17, 1976; Commander William I. Milwee, Jr., U.S.N., "Considerations in the Naval Architecture of Salvage Ships," *Naval Engineers Journal*, vol. 90, no. 5 (October 1978); __________, "Design Considerations in the Design Architecture of Salvage Ships," *Naval Engineers Journal* (March 1984); Commander J. Michael Ringelberg, U.S.N., "Salvage Ships," unpublished memorandum to Supervisor of Salvage, undated, circa 1976.

3. Captain Charles A. Bartholomew, U.S.N., Commander Bert Marsh, U.S.N., and Lieutenant Commander Richard Hooper, U.S.N., *Salvage Engineering* (Washington, D.C.: Commander Naval Sea Systems Command (U.S. Navy), 1992).
4. *Guide to Helicopter/Ship Operations,* 3d ed. (London: International Chamber of Shipping, 1989).

CHAPTER 12

1. Captain O.O. Thomas, Captain John Agnew, and K.L. Cole, *Thomas' Stowage—The Properties and Stowage of Cargoes*, 2d ed. (Glasgow: Brown, Son & Ferguson, 1985).
2. *The Storage and Segregation Guide to IMDG Code*, 12th ed. (Hamburg: K.O. Storck Vertag).
3. *Ship-to-Ship Transfer Guide (Liquefied Gases)* (London: The International Chamber of Shipping, The Oil Companies International Marine Forum, 1980).
4. *Tanker Safety Guide (Liquefied Gas)* (London: International Chamber of Shipping, 1978).
5. *Tanker Safety Guide* (*Chemicals*) (London: International Chamber of Shipping, 1974).

CHAPTER 13

1. The Oil Pollution Act of 1990 (OPA-90), Public Law 101-381; 104 Statutes at Large 484.
2. The Oil Companies International Marine Forum and the International Chamber of Shipping, *Peril at Sea and Salvage, A Guide for Masters*, 4th ed. (London: Witherby and Co. Ltd., 1992).
3. Captain G.S. Marton, *Tanker Operations—A Handbook for the Ship's Officer*, 3d ed. (Centreville, Md.: Cornell Maritime Press, 1992).
4. Captain Colin Baptist, *Tanker Handbook for Deck Officers*, 7th ed. (Glasgow: Brown, Son & Ferguson Ltd., 1991).
5. The Oil Companies International Marine Forum and the International Chamber of Shipping, International Association of Ports and Harbors, *International Safety Guide for Oil Tankers and Terminals*, 3d rev. ed. (London: 1991).
6. *IMO Recommendations Concerning Emergency Towing Requirements for Tankers*, Merchant Shipping Notice M1406 (London: Department of Transportation, Marine Directorate, October 1984).
7. *Ship-to-Ship-Transfer Guide* (*Petroleum*), 2d ed. (London: International Chamber of Shipping, The Oil Companies International Marine Forum, 1988).

CHAPTER 15

1. Gerald Darling, Q.C., and Christopher Smith, *LOF90 and the New Salvage Convention* (London: Lloyd's of London Press Ltd., 1991).

APPENDIX A

1. Richard M. Plant, *Formulae for the Mariner*, 2d ed. (Centreville, Md.: Cornell Maritime Press, 1986).

SELECTED BIBLIOGRAPHY

A very large amount of written material pertaining to salvage exists, but it is not easy to find and not always easily identified. Many maritime publications published with no or only incidental reference to salvage can be important to salvors and others concerned with salvage operations. These include material on naval architecture and ship design, cargo characteristics and handling, pollution prevention and response, law, seamanship, firemanship, underwater work systems, tugs and towing, rigging, and myriad other subjects. Product catalogs, engineering handbooks, technical papers, and even advertising materials provide useful information on salvage.

Generalized books on salvage are often autobiographical or other accounts of operations. These and technical papers describing specific operations are of great value to salvors for reviewing techniques that have worked—or have not worked. Reading between the lines is often necessary in these books to discern what actually happened. Salvage companies and government agencies undertaking salvage are understandably more enthusiastic about presenting their successes rather than their failures and mistakes. Films and videos produced by salvors are excellent sources of information.

Books discussing a spectrum of salvage techniques and the salvage business in English are few. A few exist in other languages, specifically German, Russian, and Japanese. Some of the books are dated, particularly in their discussions of techniques, but are valuable for the principles and sound basic information they contain. The U. S. Navy has published its six-volume salvage manual group, a text on salvage engineering, and a handbook for field use, among others. These books are designed primarily for Navy use; the information in them has to be filtered and adapted to commercial salvage operations. U.S. Navy–conducted salvage and wreck removal operations are documented in some very comprehensive reports. The Royal Navy's seamanship manual contains an excellent section on salvage.

The listing that follows cannot in any way be considered a comprehensive list of salvage references. It is representative of the material available and the types of materials that should be in the salvor's library and make up his normal professional reading.

Admiralty Manual of Seamanship. Vol. 1, 1967. Vol. 2, 1972, and Vol. 3, 1983. London: Her Majesty's Stationery Office.

Allen, Mike. *International Convention on Salvage 1989 and LOF 90*. Halifax: The Eleventh International Tug Convention and Marine Salvage Symposium, 1990.

Allieve, Captain A. "Chemical Carriers: Sophisticated Ships," *Proceedings of the Marine Safety Council*, U.S. Coast Guard, vol. 40, no. 5, October/November 1983.

A. Mackenzie Salvage Operation NAVSHIPS 0994-016-7010. Washington, D.C.: Supervisor of Salvage, U.S. Navy, Naval Ship Systems Command, 1970.

Analysis of Spread Mooring Systems for Floating Drilling Units. 2d ed. Washington, D.C.: API Recommended Practice 2P (RP 2P), American Petroleum Institute, May 1, 1987.

Anderson, Captain M.J. "Removal of the Wreck of *Seawise University* from Hong Kong Harbor." *Journal of the Marine Technology Society*, vol. 3, no. 4, Aug./Sept. 1979.

Arrow—Report on Recovery of Fuel Cargo NAVSHIPS 0994-008-1010. Washington, D.C.: Supervisor of Salvage, U.S. Navy, Naval Ship Systems Command, 1970.

Attwood, Edward L. and Herbert S. Pengelly. *Theoretical Naval Architecture*. London: Longmans, Green and Co. Ltd., 1953.

Baptist, Captain C. *Salvage Operations*. London: Stanford Maritime Limited, 1979.

____________. *Tanker Handbook for Deck Officers*, 7th ed. Glasgow: Brown, Son & Ferguson, 1991.

Barracca, Peter S. and Warren D. Thomas. "Suez Canal Clearance—1974." *Ocean Industry*, March 1975.

Bartholomew, Captain C.A., U.S.N. *Mud, Muscle, and Miracles*. Washington, D.C.: Naval Historical Center and Naval Sea Systems Command, 1990.

Bartholomew, Captain Charles A., U.S.N., Commander Bert Marsh, U.S.N., and Lieutenant Commander Richard Hooper, U.S.N. *Salvage Engineering*. Washington, D.C.: Commander Naval Sea Systems Command (U.S. Navy), 1992.

Bes, J. *Bulk Carriers*. 2d ed. New York: W.S. Heinman, 1972.

Bishop, Archie. *Current Development in Lloyd's Form—Article 14, Special Compensations*. Southampton, England: International Tug and Salvage Conference, 1994.

Blank, Captain John S. III. *Modern Towing*. Centreville, Md.: Cornell Maritime Press, 1989.

Borwick, J.R. and G. Elliott. *Dynamic Properties of Marine Fiber Ropes*. Second International Tug Conference.

Boyd, Captain J.H. and J.H. Madeo. "Suez Canal Wreck Clearance—1974." Columbus, Oh.: Proceedings of *The Working Diver, 1976* Symposium, Battelle Memorial Institute, 1976.

Brady, Edward M. *Marine Salvage Operations*. Centreville, Md.: Cornell Maritime Press, 1960.

___________. *Tugs, Towboats and Towing*. Centreville, Md.: Cornell Maritime Press, 1967.

Buckle, A.K. "Anchoring and Mooring Equipment on Ships." London: Royal Institute of Naval Architects, 1974.

___________. "Ten Year Review of Defects and Failures in Large Ships' Anchoring and Mooring Equipment." *Proceedings of the Conference on Mooring Large Ships over 150,000 Tons Deadweight*. London: The Institute of Marine Engineers, December 1979.

Butt, J.A., S.T. Lawrie, and Captain L. Westdijk. "Fundamental Considerations in Rescue Towing." *Proceedings of the International Symposium on Marine Salvage, New York, October 1–3, 1979*. Washington, D.C.: Marine Technology Society, 1980.

Cahill, Captain Richard A. *Strandings and Their Causes*. London: Fairplay Publications, 1985.

Chemical Data Guide for Bulk Shipment by Water. CIM 16616.6A, United States Coast Guard, U.S. Department of Transportation, 1990.

Clay, John S. "Salvage of Stranded Tankers with the Aid of Computers." *Marine Technology*, vol. 22, no. 4, October 1985.

Clement, Cris. "Vapor Recovery on Tankers from Design to Operation." *Marine Technology*, vol. 30, no. 3, July 1993.

Code for the Construction and Equipment of Ships Carrying Dangerous Materials in Bulk. London: IMO Resolution A 212, 1971.

Colquhoun, Allan. *Raising from the Depths (In the Antipodes)*. Southampton, England: International Tug and Salvage Conference, 1994.

___________. "Refloating from a Strand—Practical Naval Architectural Aspects." *Proceedings of the Eleventh International Tug Convention/Marine Salvage Symposium*. East Molesey, England: Thomas Reed Publications Limited, 1991.

Cordage Directory and Catalog. Hingham, Mass.: The Cordage Institute, 1989.

Danton, Captain Graham. *The Theory and Practice of Seamanship*. 9th ed. London: Routledge & Kegan Paul, 1985.

Darling, Gerald, Q.C., and Christopher Smith. *LOF 90 and the New Salvage Convention*. London: Lloyd's of London Press Ltd., 1991.

Departmental Investigation into the Loss of the Bow Section of the Greek Registered Motor Tanker Kirki, *the Subsequent Fire, Evacuation of the Crew and Salvage Operation from 20 July 1991 to 23 August 1991*. Australian Department of Transport and Communications, Report No. 33.

Derrett, D.R. *Ship Stability for Masters and Mates*. London: Stanford Maritime, Limited, 1979.

Diving Manual BR 2806. London: Ministry of Defence (Navy), Her Majesty's Stationery Office, 1972.

Driver, Captain Dara E. *P & I Clubs*. Bombay: Rumar Publications.

Effective Mooring. London: The Oil Companies International Marine Forum, 1989.

Emergency Response Guidebook. Washington D.C.: U.S. Department of Transportation, DOT P 5800.5 Research and Special Programs Administration, 1990.

Fiske, Captain R., U.S.N. "Jettison of Petroleum During Ship Salvage." Genoa: The Twelfth International Tug and Salvage Convention, 1992.

Flory, John F. and Steve P. Woehleke. "Strength of Chain Tensioned over a Curved Surface." Houston: Offshore Technology Conference Paper OT 3855, 1980.

Fosberg, Captain Gerald. *Brown's Pocket-Book for Seamen*. Glasgow: Brown, Son & Ferguson, 1981.

Freitag, Mark and Anthony Woods. *Commercial Diving, Reference and Operations Handbook*. Chichester: John Wiley and Sons, 1983.

Forsberg, Captain Gerald. *Salvage from the Sea*. London: Routledge & Kegan Paul, 1977.

Gaston, M.J. *Tugs and Towing*. Sparkford, England: Patrick Stephens Limited, 1991.

General Principles for Ship Reporting Systems and Ship Reporting Requirements, including Guidelines for Reporting Incidents Involving Dangerous Goods, Harmful Substances and/or Marine Pollutants. International Maritime Organization Resolution A.648(16).

George, William E., ed. *Stability and Trim for the Ship's Officer*. Centreville, Md.: Cornell Maritime Press, 1983.

Gibbs, Captain William B., William I. Milwee, and Captain Heinrich Detlev. *Double Hull Tankers—A Salvor's Perspective*. Halifax: The Eleventh International Tug Convention and Marine Salvage Symposium, 1990.

Gillmer, Thomas C. and Bruce Johnson. *Introduction to Naval Architecture*. Annapolis, Md.: U.S. Naval Institute Press, 1982.

Gores, Joseph N. *Marine Salvage*. Garden City, N.Y.: Doubleday & Company, Inc., 1971.

Guarino, Salvatore J. "The Offshore Supply Vessel as a Naval Auxiliary." Gulf Section Paper. Biloxi, Miss.: The Society of Naval Architects and Marine Engineers, September 27, 1974.

Hackman, Donald J., P.E., and Don W. Caudy, P.E. *Underwater Tools*. Columbus, Oh.: Battelle Press, 1981.

Halfweeg, Nan. "State of the Art of Offloading Cargo from Stricken Vessels." *Proceedings of the International Symposium on Marine Salvage, New York, October 1–3, 1979*. Washington, D.C.: Marine Technology Society, 1980.

Hancox, Captain David. *Commercial Salvage Practice*. Sunderland, England: Thomas Reed Publications Limited, 1987.

_______________. "The Development of the Modern Salvage Vessel." *Jane's Merchant Shipping Review*, A.J. Ambrose, ed. London: McDonald and Janes Ltd., 1984.

_______________. *Salvage Staff Training*.Genoa: The Twelfth International Tug and Salvage Convention, 1992.

_______________. "Some Personal Thoughts on Tanker Salvage Operations." Address to Workshop for On-Scene Coordinators. Canberra: Department of Transport, 1987.

Hancox, Captain Michael. *Oilfield Seamanship*. Vol. 1 of *Rescue Towing*. Ledbury, England: Oilfield Publications, Ltd., 1993.

Harbor Clearance Operations in Guam Following Typhoons Karen and Olive. Washington, D.C.: Supervisor of Salvage, U.S. Navy, Bureau of Ships, 1964.

Hayler, Captain William B., ed. *Merchant Marine Officer's Handbook*. 5th ed. Centreville, Md.: Cornell Maritime Press, 1989.

Hebden, David. *Maximization of the Salvage Award*. Southampton, England: International Tug and Salvage Conference, 1994.

Henry, Cleopatra Elmira. *The Carriage of Dangerous Goods by Sea*. New York: St. Martin's Press, 1985.

Hoogenbosch, Dr. John. "The Development and Decline of the Oceangoing Tug." *Singapore: Proceedings of the Eighth International Tug Convention*, 1984.

Huber, Professor Mark. "Vapor Control Operations and Vessel Safety." *Seaways*, March 1993.

International Safety Guide for Oil Tankers and Terminals. 3d rev. ed. London: The International Chamber of Shipping, The Oil Companies International Marine Forum, The International Association of Ports and Harbors, 1991.

Jaeschke, R.D. "Proposed New American Flag Salvage Tug." Unpublished memorandum to R.E. Gross, President, United States Salvage Association, Inc., December 17, 1976.

Kemp & Young. *Ship Stability Notes and Examples.* 2d ed. London: Stanford Maritime, 1971.

Kerr, Donald, Q.C. *The Philosophy of No Cure–No Pay.* Halifax: The Eleventh International Tug Convention and Marine Salvage Symposium, 1990.

Knott, Captain John R. *Lashing and Securing of Deck Cargoes.* 2d ed. London: The Nautical Institute, co-sponsored by Brookes, Bell, & Company, 1994.

Lambeth, R.J. *Templeman on Marine Insurance, Its Principles and Practice.* 5th ed. Plymouth: Macdonald and Evans, Ltd., 1981.

Larn, Richard, and Rex Whistler. *Commercial Diving Manual.* London: David & Charles, 1985.

Lewis, Edward V., ed. *Stability and Strength.* Vol. 1 of *Principles of Naval Architecture.* New York: Society of Naval Architects and Marine Engineers, 1988.

Liang, San and Gin Liang Yang. "The Refloating of the MV *American Sioux.*" *Journal of the Marine Technology Society,* vol. 18, no. 2, 1984.

McKenna, Henry A. *High Performance Polyester Rope.* Washington, D.C.: Marine Technology Society Conference, 1990.

Malatich, John M. and Wayne C. Tucker. *Tricks of the Trade for Divers.* Centreville, Md.: Cornell Maritime Press, 1986.

Marshall, Commander W.L. "Raising and/or Removal of Wrecks/Refloating of Stranded Vessels." Baltimore: *Report of Proceedings of Twentieth International Navigation Congress,* 1961.

Marshall, Captain W.L. "A Unique Use of a Floating Drydock." *U.S. Naval Institute Proceedings,* October 1965.

Marton, G.S. *Tanker Operations.* 3d ed. Centreville, Md.: Cornell Maritime Press, 1992.

The Master's Role in Collecting Evidence. London: The Nautical Institute, 1989.

Miller, Tony. *Amoco Cadiz—A Salvor's Perspective.* Southampton, England: International Tug and Salvage Conference, 1994.

Milwee, Commander William I., Jr., U.S.N. "A Ship Aground: The Do's and Dont's." *U.S. Naval Institute Proceedings,* March 1984.

______________. "Clearing Harbors Imaginatively." *The Military Engineer,* no. 469, September-October 1980.

______________. "Considerations in the Naval Architecture of Salvage Ships." *Naval Engineers Journal,* vol. 90, no. 5, American Society of Naval Engineers, October 1978.

Milwee, William I., Jr. "A Draft Standard for Towing Tank Barges Carrying Oil or Hazardous Substances in Bulk in the Northwestern United States." Santa Margherita, Italy: The Twelfth International Tug and Salvage Convention, 1992.

______________. "Design Considerations in the Design Architecture of Salvage Ships." *Naval Engineers Journal,* American Society of Naval Engineers, March 1984.

______________. "Living with OPA-90, Salvage Contracting in a Highly Regulated Environment." Southampton, England: International Tug and Salvage Conference, 1994.

MODU Towing Manual. Houston: Exxon Production Research Co., 1986.

Muckle, W. *Naval Architecture for Marine Engineers.* London: Butterworths, 1975.

Mullen, Craig T. "Salvage of the *Sidney E. Smith, Jr.*" Columbus, Oh.: Proceedings of *The Working Diver, 1974* Symposium, Battelle Memorial Institute, 1974.

Munro-Smith, R. *Elements of Ship Design.* London: Marine Media Management, 1975.

_______________. *Ships and Naval Architecture.* London: The Institute of Marine Engineers, 1988.

MV Oriental Warrier *Salvage, Jacksonville, Florida.* Washington, D.C.: Supervisor of Salvage, U.S. Navy, Naval Sea Systems Command, 1973.

Niemann, Captain G.A. "Salvage of the *Malaysia Kita," Journal of the Marine Technology Society*, vol. 3, no. 4, Aug./Sept. 1979.

Noble, Peter G. "Safer Transport of Oil at Sea: A Social Responsibility for Naval Architects and Marine Engineers," *Marine Technology,* vol. 30, no. 2, April 1993.

Noel, Captain John V., U.S.N. (ret.), ed. *Knight's Modern Seamanship.* 18th ed. New York: Van Nostrand Reinhold, 1989.

Olsen, Richard. "The Enhancement of Salvage Awards." Halifax: The Eleventh International Tug Convention and Marine Salvage Symposium, 1990.

Olsen, Richard F. "LOF 90 and Environmental Protection." Genoa: The Twelfth International Tug and Salvage Convention, 1992.

_______________. "Sacking a Salvor." Southampton, England: International Tug and Salvage Convention, 1994.

Parodi, Giorgio. "The Haven Disaster." Genoa: The Twelfth International Tug and Salvage Convention, 1992.

Pazos, Hector. "Heavy Salvage Operations and the Use of Tug Boats." Halifax: The Eleventh International Tug Convention and Marine Salvage Symposium, 1990.

Peril at Sea and Salvage, A Guide for Masters. 4th ed. London: The International Chamber of Shipping, The Oil Companies International Marine Forum, 1992.

Pocket Guide to Chemical Hazards. Washington, D.C.: National Institute for Occupational Safety and Health (NIOSH), U.S. Department of Health and Human Services, June 1990.

Porricelli, Joseph D., J.H. Boyd, and Keith E. Schleiffer. "Modern Analytical Techniques in Salvage Engineering Using Portable Computers." New York: *Transactions of the Society of Naval Architects and Marine Engineers,* vol. 91, 1983.

Pursey, J.J. *Merchant Ship Construction.* 6th rev. ed. Glasgow: Brown, Son & Ferguson, 1983.

Ratcliffe, A.T. and M.R. Parsey. "Man-Made-Fibre Ropes for Marine Use." North East Coast Institution of Engineers and Shipbuilders, April 1985.

Rawson, K.J. and E.C. Tupper. *Basic Ship Theory.* 3d ed. Harlow, Essex, England: Longman Scientific and Technical, 1983.

Refloating of the USS Missouri *(BB-63) NAVSHIPS 250-694-3.* Washington, D.C.: Supervisor of Salvage, U.S. Navy, Naval Ship Systems Command, 1950.

Reid, George H. *Primer of Towing.* 2d ed. Centreville, Md.: Cornell Maritime Press, 1992.

Reinigert, Klaas J. "The Future of the Professional Salvage Industry." Genoa: The Twelfth International Tug and Salvage Convention, 1992.

_______________. "Marine Emergency Services—Toward a New Understanding." Halifax: The Eleventh International Tug Convention and Marine Salvage Symposium, 1990.

Rigger's Handbook. 11th ed. Sedalia, Mo.: Broderick & Bascomb Rope Company, 1991.

Ringelberg, Commander J. Michael, U.S.N. "Salvage Ships." Unpublished memorandum to Supervisor of Salvage, undated, circa 1976.

Rope Specifications and Standards. Hingham, Mass.: The Cordage Institute, 1986.

Ross, Captain Ken. "The Role of the Helicopter in Marine Salvage Operations." Gold Coast, Queensland, Australia: International Maritime Pilots Association Satellite Congress, 13–16 February, 1988.

Rynecki, Alex. "Salvage Operations on *T.V. Igara*." Columbus, Oh.: Proceedings of *The Working Diver, 1976 Symposium*, Battelle Memorial Institute, 1974.

_______________. "Salvage of the Tankers *Elias* and *Corinthos*." Columbus, Ohio: Proceedings of *The Working Diver, 1976* Symposium, Battelle Memorial Institute, 1976.

Safety in Chemical Tankers. London: The International Chamber of Shipping, 1977.

Safety in Liquified Gas Tankers. London: The International Chamber of Shipping, 1980.

Safety in Oil Tankers. London: The International Chamber of Shipping, 1978.

Safe Use of Rope. Hingham, Mass.: The Cordage Institute, 1986.

Salvage of the Dredge Jamaica Bay, *January to March 1967, at My Tho, Vietnam, NAVSHIPS 0994-002-0810*. Washington, D.C.: Naval Ship Research and Development Center, January 1968.

Salvage of the USS Lafayette, *NAVSHIPS 0994-001-3010*. Washington, D.C.: Supervisor of Salvage, U.S. Navy, Naval Ship Systems Command, 1946.

SALVOPS-69 through 74, NAVSHIPS 0994-012-6010 through 0994-012-6010. (Series published annually) Washington, D.C.: Supervisor of Salvage, U.S. Navy, Naval Sea Systems Command.

Sampson Rope Manual. Boston: Sampson Ocean Systems, Inc., 1982.

Saunders, R.E. *The Practice of Ocean Rescue*. Glasgow: Brown, Son & Ferguson, Ltd., 1977.

Searle, Captain W.F., Jr., and Alex Rynecki. "Salvage of the USS *Frank Knox*." *The Military Engineer*, March/April 1968.

Sharp, D.M. *Rope in the Marine Environment*. London: The Institution of Mechanical Engineers, 1976.

Ship Salvage. Washington, D.C.: Supervisor of Salvage, U.S. Navy, Bureau of Ships, 1944.

Ship Salvage Operations, Miscellaneous Techniques, BUSHIPS 0283-261-0000. Washington, D.C.: Supervisor of Salvage, U.S. Navy, Bureau of Ships, February 1946.

Ship-to-Ship Transfer Guide (Petroleum). 2d ed. London: The International Chamber of Shipping, The Oil Companies International Marine Forum, 1988.

Shirley, James, Jr. "Liability Salvage." Genoa: The Twelfth International Tug and Salvage Convention, 1992.

Specification for Underwater Welding. ANSI/AWS D3.6-89. Miami: American Welding Society, 1989.

SS Sidney E. Smith, Jr., *Salvage Operations NAVSHIPS 0994-LP-017-4010*. Washington, D.C.: Supervisor of Salvage, U.S. Navy, Naval Ship Systems Command, 1972.

Stern, Irving L. and Michael F. Wheatcroft. "Toward Improving the Reliability of Anchor Chain and Accessories." OTC 3206. Houston: Offshore Technology Conference, May 1978.

Storage and Segregation Guide to IMDG Code. 12th ed. Hamburg: K.O. Storck Vertag.

Suez Canal Salvage Operations in 1974. Washington, D.C.: Supervisor of Salvage, Naval Sea Systems Command, 1975.

Sullivan, Rear Admiral William A. "Marine Salvage." *Transactions of the Society of Naval Architects and Marine Engineers*, vol. 56, New York, 1948.

Swift, Captain A.J. *Bridge Team Management—A Practical Guide.* London: The Nautical Institute, 1993.

Taggert, Robert, ed. *Ship Design and Construction.* New York: The Society of Naval Architects and Marine Engineers, 1980.

Tatham, Simon. "International Wreck Removal & Marine Services Agreements 'WRECKCON' and 'WRECKHIRE.'" Southampton, England: International Tug and Salvage Conference, 1994.

Technical Manual for Use of Explosives in Underwater Salvage, NAVSEA SW061-AA-MMA-010. Washington, D.C.: Naval Sea Systems Command, 1 March 1987.

Technical Report on Salvaging AFDM-2, NAVSHIPS 0997-001-4010. Washington, D.C.: Supervisor of Salvage, U.S. Navy, Naval Ship Systems Command, 1967.

Terrell, Mark. *The Principles of Diving.* London: Stanley Paul & Co., 1965.

Thomas, Captain O.O., Captain John Agnew, and K.L. Cole. *Thomas' Stowage—The Properties and Stowage of Cargoes.* 2d ed. Glasgow: Brown, Son & Ferguson, 1985.

Thomas, Warren D. and Peter S. Barracca. "The Salvor and the Prevention of water Pollution by Marine Transportation." *Fairplay International Shipping Journal,* March 29, 1973.

Turner, Harold A., ed. *The Principles of Marine Insurance.* 7th ed. London: Stone & Cox (Publications) Limited, 1986.

Underwater Cutting and Welding, NAVSEA 0929-LP-000-8010. Washington, D.C.: Supervisor of Salvage, U.S. Navy, 1979.

U.S. Navy Diving Manual Volume 1, (Air Diving), NAVSHIPS 0994-LP-001-9010. Revisions 2. Washington, D.C.: Naval Ship Systems Command, 1988.

U.S. Navy Salvage Safety Manual SO400-AA-SAF-010. Washington, D.C.: Naval Sea Systems Command, 1988.

U.S. Navy Salvor's Handbook, SO300-A7-HBK-010. Washington, D.C.: Naval Sea Systems Command, 1990.

U.S. Navy Ship Salvage Manual Volume 1 (Strandings) SO300-A6-MAN-010. Washington, D.C.: Naval Sea Systems Command, 1989.

U.S. Navy Ship Salvage Manual Volume 2 (Harbor Clearance) SO300-A6-MAN-020. Washington, D.C.: Naval Sea Systems Command, 1990.

U.S. Navy Ship Salvage Manual Volume 3, Harbor Clearance Operations, NAVSHIPS 0994-000-3030. Washington, D.C.: Naval Ship Systems Command, 1973.

U.S. Navy Ship Salvage Manual Volume 5 (POL Offloading) SO300-A6-MAN-050. Washington, D.C.: Naval Sea Systems Command, 1991.

U.S. Navy Towing Manual SL740-AA-MAN-010. Washington, D.C.: Naval Sea Systems Command, 1988.

U.S. Navy Underwater Cutting and Welding Manual SO300-BB-MAN-010. Washington, D.C.: Naval Sea Systems Command, 1 April 1989.

USNS Chauvenet *(T-AGS 29) Stranding Salvage Operations.* 82-01 SUPSALV Report. Washington, D.C.: Naval Sea Systems Command, 1982.

USS Frank Knox *(DDR-742) Stranding Salvage, NAVSHIPS 0994-002-6010.* Washington, D.C.: Supervisor of Salvage, U.S. Navy, Naval Ship Systems Command, 1968.

Wire Rope Users Manual. Washington, D.C.: American Iron and Steel Institute, 1979.

van den Haak, R. "Design of Anchors, Cables and Mooring Wires." London: *Proceedings of the Conference on Mooring Large Ships over 150,000 tons Deadweight,* The Institute of Marine Engineers, December 1979.

Wallin, Vice Admiral Homer N., U.S.N. (ret.) *Pearl Harbor, Why, How, Fleet Salvage and Final Appraisal.* Washington, D.C.: U.S. Naval History Division, 1968.

Wheeler, Captain G.J. *Ship Salvage.* London: George Phillip and Son Limited, 1958.

Whitaker, Captain F.H., U.S.N. "The Salvage of USS *Oklahoma.*" New York: *Transactions of the Society of Naval Architects and Marine Engineers,* vol. 52, 1944.

White, G.W. *Elementary Beam Theory and the Ship Girder.* London: Stanford Maritime Limited, 1979.

Wierzbicki, T., D.B. Peer, and E. Rady. "The Anatomy of Tanker Grounding." *Marine Technology,* vol. 30, no. 2, April 1993.

Witte, J. Arnold. "Salvage, Pollution & Liability, Interface and Cooperation amongst the Salvor, Owner & Underwriter." Genoa: The Twelfth International Tug and Salvage Convention 1992.

Woolcott, Captain T.V.W. *Liquified Petroleum Gas Tanker Practice.* 2d ed. Glasgow: Brown, Son & Ferguson, Ltd., 1987.

Yang, Gin Liang. "The Theory and Practice of the Refloating Project of the MV *Damodar Ganga.*" *Journal of the Marine Technology Society,* vol. 18, no. 2, 1984.

INDEX

INDEX TO FORMULAS

ABOUT THE AUTHOR

William I. Milwee, Jr., received a Bachelor of Science from the United States Naval Academy and a Bachelor of Science in Marine Engineering and Master of Science in Naval Architecture from the Webb Institute of Naval Architecture. He served as a naval officer (Commander, U.S. Navy, Ret) and currently is a consultant in salvage and related disciplines.

Mr. Milwee has attended casualties as a U.S. Navy salvage officer and commercially as salvage master, salvage engineer, and consultant to owners, hull insurers, P&I Clubs, and other interests. He has worked on all seven continents and in many remote locations in conjunction with salvage work.

Author of numerous technical papers and articles published in the United States and Great Britain, he is a frequent contributor to *Naval Engineers Journal*, *Naval Institute Proceedings*, *Seaways*, the Journal of the Nautical Institute, and several technical publications on marine salvage, diving, ocean engineering, and marine operations. He was guest editor, *Marine Technology Society Journal* Special Issue on Diving, and technical editor for *U.S. Navy Ship Salvage Manual*.

ISBN 0-87033-471-9
56500
9 780870 334719